HOMETOWN HEROES:

The Single Franchise Baseball Stars of the 20th Century

by

CLAY SIGG

Foreword by

DUSTY BAKER

N|T NEW**TYPE**

Published in the United States by NEWTYPE PUBLISHING.

N|T NEWTYPE

www.HometownBaseballHeroes.com

ISBN 978-1-942306-21-4

Printed and bound in China

Library of Congress Catalogue # 2015911337

First Edition

Book design by Mystic Design.
www.mysticdesign.net

DEDICATION

*To my grandfather, William Frederick Julius Sigg, whose love
of the game has been handed down through three generations.*

*To my father, Robert William Sigg, who introduced me to the
game and enjoyed the game with me and through me.*

*And to my son, Anthony Martin Sigg, who has shared
the love of the game with his father.*

FOREWORD BY
Dusty Baker

Washington Nationals Manager

National League Manager of the Year • 1993, 1997, 2000

As a major leaguer for 19 years and as a major-league manager for another 20, I have had the fortunate experience of playing, coaching or managing with and against a number of the single-franchise stars featured in *Hometown Heroes*.

I played for four organizations and appreciate how extraordinary it is for a baseball player to stay with one team for his entire career. Certainly there must be some luck attached to the outcome, but the players that ultimately qualify are a rare breed indeed.

These ballplayers achieved their position by not only performing on the baseball field, but also by showing character traits that made them invaluable to their teams, their fans and their cities. They are the kind of individuals fans root for because they have built positive relationships with their adopted home-towns over long careers.

While I played with the Dodgers, Jim Gilliam was one of our coaches up until his untimely death in 1979. Jim personified a great one-franchise player. He taught me how to be a big leaguer- how to dress, how to honor the uniform, how to meet the press- all the little things that together add up to a quality professional approach. The Dodgers retired his uniform number 19, the only Dodger to be recognized in that way who has not been elected into the National Baseball Hall of Fame.

Bill Russell and Mike Scioscia were both fantastic teammates on the 1981 World Series Champion Los Angeles Dodgers. Billy and I played together from 1976 to 1983. He was a great person who honored the game by the way he played as a bedrock contributor on some historic Dodger teams. Mike and I played together from 1980 to 1983 and later managed against each other in the 2002 World Series. Mike is another fine example of a single-franchise player who elevated his teammates, the game, and himself by his character and approach on and off the field. Our teammate Orel Hershiser called him "indispensable."

Scott Garrelts was my Giants teammate in 1984 before he became a National League All-Star pitcher but he is another model of why the single franchise player is a rare breed. He was always about the team.

In my 17 years in the National League, I also played against such Hall of Famers as Johnny Bench, Roberto Clemente, Bob Gibson, Mike Schmidt and Willie Stargell. In my two American League seasons, I competed against stars George Brett, Ron Guidry, Don Mattingly, Alan Trammell, Lou Whitaker, Frank White and Robin Yount, among others.

During my time as the manager of the Giants, Rob-by Thompson was a heads up competitor and leader who I admired for his grit and determination to win. I was sincerely impressed by his return to help us try to win the 1993 pennant on the last day despite the beaning that shattered his cheekbone less than two weeks before.

I also came to respect and admire other single franchise players as a National League manager with my teams competing against men like Jeff Bagwell, Craig Biggio, Tony Gwynn, Todd Helton, Chipper Jones and Barry Larkin.

I saw something special in all of these players. The hallmark of this group is their shared history as outstanding ambassadors of the game. Besides being popular with their hometown fans, they have been great teammates and high-impact, high class, first-rate ballplayers and people.

Clay Sigg's tribute to these influential players is a read that also touches on most of the history of Major League Baseball in the 20th century. Enjoy!

Dusty Baker

National League Championship Series MVP • 1977

Louisville Slugger Silver Slugger Award 1980 & 1981

National League All-Star • 1981 & 1982

World Series Champion • 1981

Rawlings Gold Glove Award • 1981

TABLE OF CONTENTS

PREFACE

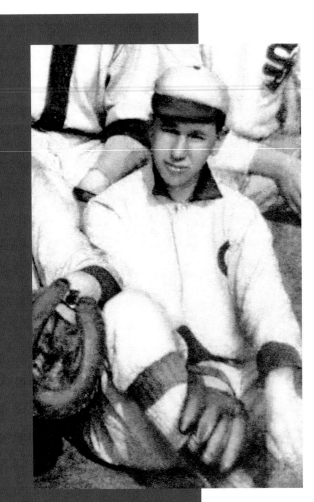

Will Sigg
Dexter Park, 1917
Queens, New York

My father held my hand as we slowly worked our way through the parking lot of the Los Angeles Memorial Coliseum and up through the turnstiles. I was seven years old. He had already sized up my interest in the game of baseball and was taking me to my first live major league game. The Brooklyn Dodgers had become the Los Angeles Dodgers that year in 1958 for their first season in Southern California.

As my father walked me through the Coliseum portals, the marvelous expanse of a baseball field suddenly opened up in front of me. The Los Angeles Coliseum would not be rated particularly high as a ballpark today. Its short left field, only 251 feet from home plate, required two 40-foot-high curtains, an awkward retrofit from its primary role as a football venue. But that day all my young eyes could see was the emerald green grass, the crushed brick infield, the white bases, and the grace of the players on the field. I was spellbound.

There below us were the hometown Dodgers in their royal blue caps and uniform lettering, set off by the small red numbers on their ivory home whites. Those Dodgers became my early baseball heroes. That day they were playing the St. Louis Cardinals. The legendary Stan "The Man" Musial trotted by in his gray road uniform with the iconic redbirds-on-a-bat logo. All that summer we watched the likes of Pee Wee Reese, Carl Furillo, Junior Gilliam, Carl Erskine, Don Drysdale and Sandy Koufax in my first introduction to Major League Baseball. Those players might as well have been baseball gods to me at that early age. My father later told me that when he looked down at me on my first day attending a Dodger game at the Coliseum, "he knew he had me."

Former Baseball Commissioner Fay Vincent put it this way: "The game is absolutely magical. A spiritual event that people cannot get a hold of. It defies all of us. It's historic, ageless, beautiful, and, by and large, it's outdoors in the summertime. It's luxurious."

My father was born in Jersey City and raised in Hollis, Queens in New York City. As a youngster growing up in the late 1920s and early 1930s, he and his "Pop" rode the subway to the Polo Grounds to watch his favorite team, the New York Giants. He had engaged me with stories of his own childhood hometown heroes. The great Giants championship teams of his youth featured such stars as "King" Carl Hubbell, "Prince" Hal Schumacher, Travis

"Stonewall" Jackson, Harry "The Horse" Danning, Jo-Jo Moore and Bill Terry.

My father also told me how he would ride the subway trains to old Yankee Stadium to see the first of the Bronx Bombers dynasty teams. The Yankees that he regularly talked about included Lou Gehrig, Bill Dickey, Joe DiMaggio, Frankie Crosetti, Earle Combs and Babe Ruth.

His father was a 119-pound left-handed shortstop who played in the semi-professional leagues around New York City during the first years of the 20th century. Before my grandfather volunteered at age 31 to fight in the infantry in World War I, he played baseball on the same fields opposite such famous New York City area semi-pro teams as the Brooklyn Bushwicks of Queens' Dexter Park and New Jersey's Paterson Silk Sox. Much later in the early 1960s, my grandfather pointed out to me several of the big-league players on my early T206 tobacco baseball cards he had played against during the Deadball Era.

Another baseball relative of that period was my mother's favorite uncle, Horace "Spitz" Davies. He was the captain and cleanup hitter for the 1922 Cornell University Big Red baseball nine that played in the Ivy League and met some of the best East Coast intercollegiate competition during the Roaring 20s.

And so it goes. The game of baseball has been passed down from grandfather to father to son, generation upon generation. Fathers and sons have enjoyed essentially the same American game throughout the entire 20th century.

Growing up in the Southern California town of Downey in the 1950s and early '60s, my friends and I often played baseball all afternoon in the summers and many times didn't even come home for dinner. When we couldn't get enough boys together for a game, we played catch or went to the school yard to play "over-the-line." Or absent a group of boys, we played "lemon ball" with a pitcher, a hitter and the hollow plastic lemon curving and darting against the garage door. Every boy in the neighborhood dreamed of becoming a major league ballplayer.

I pedaled my stingray bike down to Dan's Liquors to give him my $1.04 for a full box of *Topps* baseball card packs each time a new series came out. Some of my less particular friends put their cards in their bicycle spokes to make a motoring noise. I divided them by team and studied them while listening on the transistor radio to the Dodger broadcasts of the great Vin Scully, still the Voice of the Dodgers today.

At age 11 in the Northwest Downey Little League I wore my first full length baseball uniform. Anticipating the games at Furman Park, I arrived hours before the first pitch just waiting to play before my father, the rest of the coaches, and the other players came.

As I entered high school, our family moved to the Mojave Desert town of Trona. I played center field for three years on a home diamond that had no grass. During those years the Los Angeles Angels hosted the Helms Athletic Foundation All-Southern California high school awards at Angel Stadium. It was a thrill to be down on the Angel Stadium infield with the major leaguers to accept my award.

By then my family had moved to Sacramento, a baseball hotbed in the late '60s. It gave me the opportunity to compete in the local semi-pro circuits and allowed me to develop and play with and against dozens of future major leaguers. We played some of our games at William Land Park's Doc Oliver Field where a young semi-pro Stan Hack played in 1930 before the Sacramento Solons picked him up for the Pacific Coast League. "Smiling Stan" went on to become the Chicago Cubs All-Star third baseman for a generation.

In college, I was a part of UC Davis baseball squads that played Division I schedules, facing some of the best intercollegiate competition on the West Coast. I had the privilege to be a senior leader on the first UC Davis Baseball Hall of Fame team.

Until I was 45, I played hardball in the senior baseball leagues, two of those years with national champion clubs. I have loved every part of the game... playing it, watching it, collecting cards and memorabilia, reading about it, or just talking about it.

And I have passed the baseball experience on to my son. Coaching him from age four, the two of us played catch by the hour and worked out together. Later we took two ballpark odyssey tours together to see games at many of the big-league parks across the country, both old and new.

The game of baseball has been a family heirloom and part of the daily soundtrack of our lives now for four generations- not unlike in millions of other American homes over the past century. Baseball has been an invisible bond between our family's generations, linking my son to my grandfather, a gentleman my son never met but whose person he has come to know through this greatest of games.

The lifetime players featured in this book have enhanced

Spitz Davies,
Cornell University, 1922
Ithaca, New York

our joy and fascination with baseball. Capturing our imagination, these influential stars have become hometown treasures in regions all across America.

Growing up, much of what I learned about my own hometown baseball heroes I gleaned from the short blurbs on the back of their baseball cards. Much more informative than that, the in-depth player features invite the reader to explore more fully the impact of these wonderful players' careers and lives. And as it turns out, embedded within the stories of these cornerstone ballplayers is the essential history of Major League Baseball in the 20th century.

It is my hope that this book will add to your appreciation of our national pastime. Every town has its baseball heroes. Many of yours are given tribute in this book.

Clay Sigg
Granite Bay, California
April, 2016

The Uncommon Phenomenon of the Single Franchise Baseball Star

Ernie Banks – "Mr. Cub"

Playing an entire career with one major league franchise is an extraordinary achievement. It is a triumph that takes athletic skill, good character, integrity, perseverance and good luck. These qualities appear so frequently in these foundational ballplayers, it is no surprise that as a group they have captured the imagination of their hometown fans.

Hometown fans have strong emotional ties to players who maintain longstanding connections with their towns and their teams. The hometown fans have enjoyed an unbroken relationship with these men who possess the qualities that make a one-team professional career possible.

The fans reserve their strongest identification and affection for players who have competed for their hometown team for many years. Hometown fans not only treasure a loyal player, but also an organization that is loyal to its players. Loyalty goes both ways... or perhaps three ways: player-to-team; team-to-player; and fan-to-team-to-player.

How special can these relationships become that develop over the course of many summers? Such ties can mature to such a strong bond they may even eclipse the ephemeral satisfaction of a World Series title. The late "Mr. Cub" Ernie Banks once spoke about his relationship with the city of Chicago, "You don't get a ring for it. You don't get a trophy for it. When I started playing, the grandparents of the children that are coming to Wrigley Field now were coming to Wrigley Field then. It's family. It's really family. That's what my relationship is with the city of Chicago."

These players as a group have honored baseball, honored their teammates, and honored themselves by the respect that they have shown for the game. As Derek Jeter's last season of his unblemished 20 years as a Yankee wound down, the word *respect* kept coming up in the encomiums for his historic career. Jeter embodies the great single franchise player who is respected by everyone associated with the game, including the umpires. He was never ejected from a major league game. Jeter has stated, "I've always tried to meet people with respect, the way I wanted to be treated. I've always had the mentality that I never wanted to embarrass my parents. That fear is still in there."

Performing for a single team for an entire career is a badge synonymous with high personal and professional standards. Almost to a man, these players are modest, humble, self-effacing, team-oriented men of high character who are great teammates and outstanding influences in the clubhouse. Nearly all have held their emotions close and avoided controversial words and provocative actions. It is significant that not one of these ballplayers has ever been accused of cheating the game by using steroids, or any other performance enhancing drug, to artificially enhance his performance.

The single franchise star epitomizes the valuable traits that define the best in a professional ballplayer. However, due to a variety of factors, the number of men who finish long major league tenures with one team is decreasing. Performing for only one team for an entire career has become a fragile balancing act that can disintegrate with the first public controversy or private misfortune.

The one-franchise hometown hero has become something of an anomaly. In modern-day professional baseball, it often seems that a player's loyalty to one team for the duration of his career is a bygone reminiscence. Then again, when we notice the rare player who stays with one organization for his entire major league career, it strikes us as remarkable. The teams that have employed these distinctive players have also shown a loyalty that is uncommon in professional sports.

The one-franchise player not only has to be exceptional enough on the field to be valued long term by management, but he also must fit in well with his teammates, possess qualities that inspire fan loyalty, and manage the press well.

The Kansas City Royals' great star George Brett, often referred to as "The Franchise," has remarked, "To have a player play his entire career for one team is good, and it ought to be more common. It means something to me, and hopefully the fans, to flip my baseball card over and see only one team and one city. That doesn't happen a lot anymore, but it should." Brett is simply recognizing the underlying dynamics that make a single-team career significant.

So why should it be more common? One of the key reasons baseball fans root for their home team is the personal connection they feel with its players. For much of the 20th century, it was assumed that every red-blooded American 11-year-old dreamed of growing up to be a Major League Baseball star. For decades young Americans have idolized the baseball professionals who have starred for their hometown teams.

Until the advent of free agency in 1976, this often meant that from a youngster's early elementary school years through high school, most of his favorite players would return each spring for another season performing in front of the hometown fans. Young fans could bond with their hometown players and identify with their baseball heroics throughout their impressionable years.

Then free agency changed the game in profound ways. Gone were the days when players, constrained by the yoke of the reserve clause, were bound to their team as virtual chattel property with no real chance of ever playing for another team. Curt Flood's principled and courageous stand against that unfair feudal system led eventually to these athletes having more freedom to choose the team they wanted to play with and share more equitably in the dollar they created.

On the surface the great American pastime today has reached new levels of financial health and stature. In the middle of the second decade of the 21st century, fan attendance for Major League Baseball has set new records almost every year. In 2014, fans surged through the turnstiles 73,739,622 times during the 162-game schedule. Twenty-four of baseball's 30 teams drew at least two million fans and five teams drew over three million. As a whole, Major League Baseball averaged over 30,000 fans per game.

By contrast, in the middle of the game's "Golden Era" in 1956, Mickey Mantle's memorable Triple Crown season, 16 major league clubs played to 16,543,250 fans in a 154-

George Brett of the Kansas City Royals – "The Franchise"

game season. Even considering the average attendance per game, the 2014 numbers overwhelm the 1956 totals. Moreover, increased attendance doesn't even begin to tell the story of the income streams produced by television and other media today. Major League Baseball generated

PNC Park, Home of the Pittsburgh Pirates

over $9 billion in gross revenues for the first time in 2014.

Equally important, starting with the New York Yankees' third consecutive World Series title in 2000, ten different clubs, including four wild card entries, have lifted the World Series championship trophy in triumph, a sign of competitive balance not seen since the advent of World War II.

Much of baseball's appeal is wrapped up in its history and tradition. The fan connection and feel of the game is retro. Baseball's timeless rhythms and ambiance has changed little from grandfather to grandson. This appreciation of the past has fueled the return to baseball-only ballparks, enhancing the fan experience across the country. Newer parks that provide amenities and atmosphere

unheard of only a few short years ago have been built in Arlington (Texas), Atlanta, Baltimore, the Bronx, Chicago (Southside), Cincinnati, Cleveland, Denver, Detroit, Houston, Miami, Milwaukee, Minneapolis, Philadelphia, Phoenix, Pittsburgh, Queens (New York), St. Louis, San Diego, San Francisco, Seattle, Toronto and Washington, D.C.

Wrigley Field and Fenway Park are the only historic ballparks left from the early 20th century. Not coincidentally, Boston and Chicago fans are among the most ardent and knowledgeable as they celebrate in their ancient shrines. Cub fans at Wrigley Field's "Friendly Confines" enjoy virtually the same atmosphere today as when the Great Bambino called his shot in the 1932 World Series. Red Sox Nation roots in the same Fenway Park where fans agonized for 86 years before their Sox's curse-dispelling, cathartic victory of 2004.

Both new and historic ballpark experiences are being embraced as never before as fans marvel at the strength and grace they see on the field. Could it be that the American Game has even increased its hold on the imagination of the American public? Outward appearances seem to say so.

The ballplayers themselves are also prospering more than ever before. In a time long ago, a major league journeyman lived in a middle class neighborhood and rode the subway to work with the very fans who would watch him perform later that day at the ballpark. Gone are the days when a big-league star was so underpaid during the regular season that it was financially important for his team to reach the postseason. If his team qualified for the postseason, it meant he would receive extra compensation totaling a good percentage of his regular season paycheck.

Many ballplayers in the early part of the 20th century had to work during the winter months to make ends meet for their young families. Professional athletes have always had small windows of opportunity to maximize their incomes before their skills eroded through injury or advancing age. But that window now opens wider for today's professional baseball player. He can devote his winter months to rehabilitation, strength training and conditioning. The 21st century ballplayer can concentrate year-round on improving himself in countless ways.

Advances in nutrition, conditioning knowledge, surgical breakthroughs and rehab protocols have already made it possible for many athletes to compete at the highest level well into their early forties. With personal trainers, dedicated money managers and specialized sports agents, players today take better care of themselves than ever before in order to extend their careers. The general performance on the field is simply the best that the baseball fan has ever witnessed.

In spite of this progress and professionalization, not all of the changes in Major League Baseball have been in the best interest of the fan. Some would say that greed has corrupted the National Pastime. The modern game can leave the fan feeling a little neglected. Beneath the surface, the foundation of goodwill the sport has enjoyed may be eroding. Fewer ballplayers start and finish their major league careers with one team, especially the smaller market organizations that don't have the resources or the winning tradition to retain their superstar free agent players.

"Mr. Brewer" Robin Yount once lamented, "You're still going to have hometown heroes. Just look at Derek Jeter in New York. But [with free agency] I don't think the city gets to know the individuals, or develop the same love affair with the team, because the faces are so different year in and year out. In a way, I don't think that's in the best interest of the game."

Today's superstar can earn upwards of $25 million per year. A young Alex Rodriquez signed his first ten-year contract for a quarter of a billion dollars and his second contract for more than that. Twenty-four major league stars earned at least $20 million for the 2015 season. With the average major league salary in 2015 at over $4 million and the major league minimum increasing to $505,500 per year, the professional ballplayer appears to the regular fan to inhabit an untouchable, inaccessible financial league more akin to other rich, removed entertainers.

On the other hand, when a likeable 25-year-old slugger like Giancarlo Stanton of the Miami Marlins signed a 13-year contract for $325 million in 2014, it may portend a future in which superstars complete their entire careers with one team. Stanton's contract will pay him an average of $25 million per year until he is 38 years old. In this instance, the money might be so substantial that it may encourage megastars to stay in one place by purchasing their long term loyalty.

Free agency has been the entrée for players to sign one or two big multi-year contracts to assure their family's fi-

nancial independence for generations. In many instances, the fans' perspective doesn't even enter into the decision-making. The cynical business approach is to be indifferent to the fans and simply go where the money is.

This has caused many a disillusioned fan to conclude that his one-time devotion to the game was misplaced. Some players have demonstrated their contempt for the fans and the game itself by perceiving it exclusively as a money-making vehicle. Certainly the 1994 baseball strike appeared that way to fans across the country. When the players' union and owners summarily dispensed with the World Series, they disregarded a century of historical context and tradition and opened wounds that may not yet have healed for some fans.

Incomes of such magnitude, when coupled with a player's immature mindset, can open a divide between the multi-millionaire ballplayer and his once idolizing fan. Even putting nostalgia aside, the game was much better scripted for hero worship in days gone by. There was a time when a big-league ballplayer's behavior on and off the field reflected a sense of societal responsibility. Or if it didn't, he could expect an enabling press corps to muffle anything that might smack of a scandal that happened off the field.

By contrast, today it is not unusual for a star to discount his role as an ambassador for the game. In extreme examples, a player's arrogant demeanor demonstrates his indifference to what the fans think and feel. This modern star doesn't grasp that the fan is directly responsible for his high salary. He may flippantly refuse to sign an autograph or even acknowledge his young admirers. Boorish player behavior has had a detrimental effect on the appeal of the sport for some, stripping it of its romance and charm.

An increasing number of ballplayers who are marvelously gifted on the playing field don't see the value of balancing their own interests with those of owners, managers, teammates, media and fans. Media scrutiny has continued to increase. A ubiquitous social media allows for more access to the players but the attendant pitfalls are well documented. Many players lack the wisdom to grasp that a wide variety of people do indeed matter to them and their careers.

Unfortunately in this atmosphere the superbly gifted, itinerant athlete has become commonplace. As a result,

Robin Yount –
"Mr. Brewer"

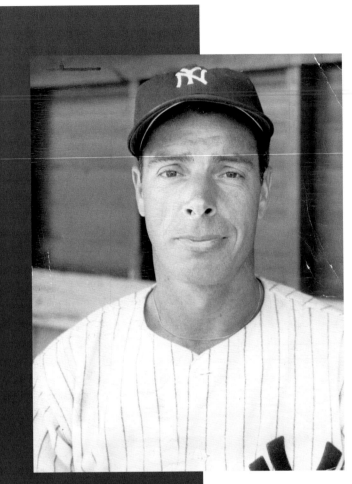

Joe DiMaggio –
"The Yankee Clipper"

many a fan has branded his childhood team as an ungrateful band of mercenaries, renting the cherished major league uniform of his youth and then taking the next money deal when the short-term lease expires. This adds up to a decreasing number of players who have the values and outlook to complete their entire major league careers with one team.

It is also true that even if the contemporary ballplayer has all of the requisite intangibles, he might not have the crucial athletic skills required for a long-running performance in one town. Examples are legion where a ballplayer is the face of the franchise for several years, but when his skills decline or he is injured, he is traded to another city or simply released.

Within this big money environment, new dynamics have emerged that might keep a player from performing for only one team for his entire career. The financial markets, state tax laws, team performance, injuries, and bad luck all have become factors that have increased player mobility.

And woe to the loyal, high-character ballplayer that started his major league career with a general manager with the philosophy of a Branch Rickey, a Frank "Trader" Lane or a Billy Beane. Rickey's dictum of "trade a player one year early instead of one year late" and Beane's annual rearrangement of his rosters have given only the rarest of players a chance to play their whole career with one organization.

If Lane was your general manager during his tenure with the White Sox, Cardinals, Indians, Athletics or Brewers, your chances of staying with your hometown team for your entire career were marginal. In seven years with the White Sox, he made 241 trades.

When Lane took over the Cardinals for two years, even the legendary Stan Musial was purported to have been on the trading block for future Hall of Famer Robin Roberts. When rumors of the proposed deal were revealed to the radio media, Cardinals owner Gussie Busch stopped it dead. But Lane successfully traded off such marvelous stars as Norm Cash, Rocky Colavito, Harvey Kuenn, Roger Maris, Red Schoendienst, Enos Slaughter and Early Wynn.

The story goes that a straight up trade between the Red Sox and the Yankees for two of baseball's greatest players, Joe DiMaggio and Ted Williams, was actually agreed upon. Over an alcohol-laced dinner between owners Dan Topping and Tom Yawkey at Toots Shor's restaurant in late April of 1947, the two men decided to swap Teddy Ballgame for The Yankee Clipper straight up. Nothing was to be put in writing until they could both sleep on it.

The idea was that the left-handed hitting Splendid Splinter would be playing his home games at old Yankee Stadium (originally built for Babe Ruth) which measured only 296 feet down the right field foul line. And the right-handed hitting Joltin' Joe would have a field day hammering line drives off and over Fenway Park's Green Monster. Fenway's left field line measured only 310 feet from home plate. DiMaggio's drives to deepest center field at 390 feet would be home runs, as compared to the cavernous 461-foot distance to dead center in old Yankee Stadium.

The next morning Yawkey decided he would not make the trade unless a little known rookie leftfielder was thrown in on the deal. That player was future Hall of Fame catcher Yogi Berra. The transaction that would have altered baseball history was never consummated.

For every DiMaggio, Jeter, Koufax or Williams who leaves the game with grace at the proper time, there are dozens who miss that golden moment by a year or two. It is regrettable to see a great player identified with only one team decide not to retire near his peak and as a result forfeit the achievement of being a single-franchise player.

This once-magnificent player desires to extend his career, but his longstanding team no longer recognizes his value. Examples of distinguished stars whose careers might have ended on a well-deserved, more climactic note with their original team are Henry Aaron, Richie Ashburn, Mark Belanger, Phil Cavarretta, Dwight Evans, Lefty Gomez, Hank Greenberg, Buddy Harrelson, Gabby Hartnett, Gil Hodges, Harmon Killebrew, Eddie Mathews, Juan Marichal, Willie Mays, Dave McNally, Sam Rice, Jimmy Rollins, Ron Santo, Ray Schalk, Mike Shannon, John Smoltz, Duke Snider, Warren Spahn and Zack Wheat.

National Baseball Hall of Famers Mathewson and Berra are perhaps the two most conspicuous examples of a player who narrowly missed the rigid touchstone of being a single franchise player. Berra was a Yankee through and through, playing on 14 American League pennant-winners and ten World Series champions, but he lost his single-franchise standing by coming to the plate a mere nine times as a pinch hitter while coaching for the Mets in 1965. Mathewson pitched for the New York Giants for 17 years before hurling one single game while field manager of the Cincinnati Reds during the last 68 games of the 1916 season.

Through no fault of their own, other brilliant stars have played their entire careers with one team except for their initial major league campaign. The Cardinals' Lou Brock, the Cubs' Ryne Sandberg and the Padres' closer Trevor Hoffman were traded early in their careers and are notable cases in point.

On the other hand when the planets align in some circumstances, a single franchise player becomes a city's favorite son because his qualities resonate with the town's cultural identity. During the Depression 30s, Joe DiMaggio became a hero to New York City's vigorous Italian American community. In the Golden Era of the 50s, Al Kaline's hard-working, self-effacing approach to the game melded perfectly with Detroit's blue-collar lifestyle.

During the Free Agency Era, Robin Yount felt that Milwaukee's small-market charm provided a perfect home for him, acknowledging that "I was a pretty shy kid at that stage and certainly didn't need the attention. We were pretty much under the radar in Milwaukee for a long time, and that kind of fit my personality just fine." When he had the chance to leave for more money, his loyalty to the Brewers franchise took precedence over other considerations, "When I put everything on the scale, it weighted a lot heavier on the Milwaukee side."

To underscore this town connection to player, San Diego's Tony Gwynn and Baltimore's Cal Ripken, Jr. were inducted into the National Baseball Hall of Fame together in 2007. The more than 75,000 fans in attendance during Cooperstown induction weekend broke the previous record by 25,000. The pilgrimage from each player's home city was astounding, with San Diegans crossing the continent to show their homage and gratitude. The previous record for attendance was 1999 when two other single-franchise players, Kansas City's Brett and Milwaukee's Yount, were inducted together. Brett, Gwynn, Ripken and Yount all validate the notion that being a class act tends to come with being a one-team performer.

Yes, there are some exceptions. The great Ted Williams might not have fit that model perfectly. He could be hostile to Boston's fourth estate and sometimes to his own fans, but The Splendid Splinter was such a brilliant hitting vir-

tuoso that his petulance was tolerated within his bigger-than-life persona. And Williams eventually evolved into one of baseball's most enduring and beloved icons.

The outpouring of affection for him before the 1999 All-Star Game at Fenway Park proved it. Before the first pitch, after he had been chauffeured in from right field, Hall of Famers and future Hall of Famers in uniform surrounded him on the pitchers' mound in a profound show of tribute in his last hurrah before his hometown fans. The love fest had to be broken up so the game could begin.

Despite all the ballplayers that have come through major league clubhouses in almost a century and a half, only a small percentage of them have played exclusively for one franchise for a minimum of ten years. From the inception of the game in the 19th century, about 18,500 ballplayers have put on a major league uniform. During the 20th century, of all the men who have worn the uniform, only 177 have played their entire major league careers with the same team for at least ten years.

There are currently 50 members of this remarkable group that already have been enshrined in the National Baseball Hall of Fame. As of 2015, there are 215 National Baseball Hall of Fame inductees, not including the 35 Negro League stars denied the opportunity to play Major League Baseball during the first half of the 20th century. Even at that, one-team lifetime ballplayers represent over one-fifth of the baseball immortals in Cooperstown.

Of the remaining 127 single-franchise stars, as many as a dozen more may eventually be delivering their induction speeches at Cooperstown. Certainly Jeff Bagwell, Bill Freehan, Ron Guidry, Todd Helton, Derek Jeter, Chipper Jones, Don Mattingly, Edgar Martinez, Thurman Munson, Tony Oliva, Mariano Rivera and Alan Trammell all deserve the ultimate recognition at Cooperstown. As a result, almost one-third of this select one-team fraternity may eventually achieve baseball immortality.

The men in this select brotherhood of single-team ballplayers are among the most influential and beloved players in the American Game. Lou Gehrig delivered baseball's "Gettysburg Address" as he was dying of ALS after a magnificent career. Jackie Robinson became an American historical figure, transcending the game by breaking the color line in professional sports. Roberto Clemente has meant every bit as much to his Latino community. Joe DiMaggio became such a cultural icon that

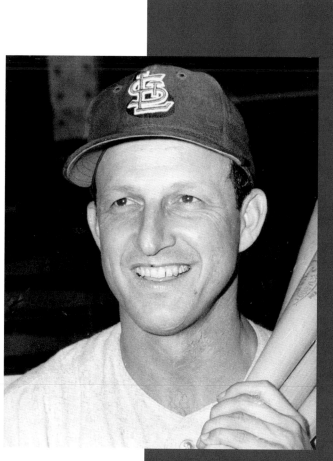

Stan "The Man" Musial of the St. Louis Cardinals

AMERICAN LEAGUE
TEAMS 1 2 3 4 5 6 7 8 9 10 11 12 R. H. E.
ST. LOU
PHILA
CHGO
WASH
DETRT 0
BOST 0
CLEVE 0 0 0 0
YANKS 0 0 0
AT BAT   STRIKES   BALLS   OUTS
UMPIRES · PLATE   BASES   TOMORROW   2:10 PM   N.Y. VS CLEVE

NATIONAL LEAGUE
TEAMS 1 2 3 4 5 6 7 8 9 10 11 12 R. H. E.
PHILA
PITTS
BOST
CINTI   RAIN
BROOK 0 0 0 0
CHGO 0 0 0 0
GIANTS
ST. LOU   RAIN
407 FT.

Bob Feller tossing April 30, 1946 no-hitter at Yankee Stadium. Joe DiMaggio at the plate. The umpire is Eddie Rommel.

Ernest Hemingway alluded to him in his novella *The Old Man and the Sea* and Simon & Garfunkel sang about Joltin' Joe as a symbol of American lost innocence. Ted Williams is a true American hero, perhaps more John Wayne than "The Duke" himself. Mickey Mantle is the embodiment in the flesh of the fictional athletic champion Jack Armstrong.

Even their nicknames are mostly signs of respect or endearment... The Big Train and the Flying Dutchman; The Iron Horse and the Yankee Clipper; The Iron Man and The Vacuum Cleaner; King Carl and Prince Hal; The Mechanical Man and Old Reliable; The Great One and The Little General; Campy and Pee Wee; Captain Clutch and Super Mariano; The Chairman of the Board and The Commerce Comet; Skeeter and Scooter; Big D and Special K; The Deacon and Maz; Teddy Ballgame and Yaz; Donnie Ballgame and Louisiana Lighting; Mr. Perfection and Stan the Man; Smiling Stan and Old Aches &

Pains... Mr. Cub, Mr. Padre, Mr. Royal, Mr. Brewer, Mr. Cardinal, Mr. Tiger, Mr. Mariner, Mr. Oriole, Mr. Pirate, Mr. Angel, Mr. Indian, Mr. Phillie, Mr. Red, Mr. Red Sox and Mr. White Sox.

A single-franchise player sticks with his team, which also sticks with him. Certain franchises have the tradition of signing young players, training them up to be established stars, and then retaining them throughout their careers. The teams that have succeeded most in this kind of player loyalty and long term stability through history are the New York Yankees with 27 players; the Detroit Tigers with 15 players; the Pittsburgh Pirates with 14 players; the New York/San Francisco Giants with 13; the Brooklyn/Los Angeles Dodgers, Boston Red Sox and Washington Senators/Minnesota Twins with 12 each; the Cleveland Indians with eight; the St. Louis Cardinals and Chicago White Sox with seven; the Baltimore Orioles and Philadelphia/Kansas City/Oakland Athletics with six; and the Cincinnati Reds and Kansas City Royals with five each.

Playing in Yankee pinstripes apparently offers an experience that many stars have decided they could not replicate elsewhere. The combination of playing on winning teams before zealous Big Apple crowds in the largest media market is difficult to replace. After they proved that they could make it there, many preferred not to play anywhere else. Notable Yankees who retired early rather than play for any other big-league club include Jerry Coleman, Joe Collins, Earle Combs, Ron Guidry, Tommy Henrich, Don Mattingly, Gil McDougald, Jorge Posada, Bobby Richardson, Phil Rizzuto, Red Rolfe, Roy White and Bernie Williams. To these men it was an honor to retire exclusively as a Yankee.

Conversely, since expansion began in 1961 with the Los Angeles Angels and the Washington Senators, the 14 newly formed franchises have had only a grand total of 13 single-team players in almost four decades of competition. The Angels have boasted Tim Salmon and Gary DiSarcina, but the expansion Senators, which morphed into the Texas Rangers, have never had a single player make the grade.

Four other expansion teams have never had a player who has played exclusively with that franchise for his entire career- the Arizona Diamondbacks, Miami Marlins, Tampa Bay Rays and Toronto Blue Jays. The Montreal Expos, before becoming the third incarnation in the nation's capital, had only one representative in pitcher Steve Rogers. The Seattle Mariners can claim only Edgar Martinez, their designated hitter extraordinaire. The San Diego Padres with Tim Flannery and Tony Gwynn and the New York Mets with Ron Hodges and Ed Kranepool each have nurtured two lifetime players. The grand prize for expansion teams goes to the Kansas City Royals. Formed in 1969, the Royals have five one-franchise stars in George Brett, Dennis Leonard, Paul Splittorff, Johnny Wathan and Frank White.

Major League teams have found a number of ways to salute their revered hometown heroes. Statues have been erected in and around ballparks in many cities: Roberto Clemente, Bill Mazeroski, Willie Stargell and Honus Wagner (Pittsburgh); Ted Williams, Bobby Doerr, Dominic DiMaggio and Carl Yastrzemski (Boston); Jim Palmer, Cal Ripken, Jr., and Brooks Robinson (Baltimore); Tony Oliva, Kirby Puckett and Kent Hrbek (Minneapolis); Stan Musial and Bob Gibson (St. Louis); George Brett and Frank White (Kansas City); Charlie Gehringer and Al Kaline (Detroit); Jeff Bagwell and Craig Biggio (Houston); Jackie Robinson and Pee Wee Reese (Brooklyn); Ernie Banks (Chicago); Johnny Bench (Cincinnati), Bob Feller (Cleveland); Tony Gwynn (San Diego); Walter Johnson (Washington, D.C.); Mike Schmidt (Philadelphia); and Robin Yount (Milwaukee).

Monuments have been erected at Yankee Stadium for Bronx Bomber legends Lou Gehrig, Mickey Mantle and Joe DiMaggio. Plaques have also been erected there for Earle Combs, Bill Dickey, Whitey Ford, Ron Guidry, Derek Jeter, Don Mattingly, Thurman Munson, Jorge Posada, Phil Rizzuto, Mariano Rivera and Bernie Williams.

Other hometown heroes who have been honored with plaques at their home ballparks include Ray Chapman (Progressive Field), Scott Garrelts and Robby Thompson (AT & T Park), Jerry Augustine and Bill Wegman (Miller Park), and Don Wilson (Minute Made Park). In another demonstration of lasting respect, almost half of the 177 players in this exclusive fraternity have either had their

uniform numbers retired by their own organizations or have been inducted into their franchise's Hall of Fame in their home city.

Many of these hometown heroes have also served their teams as field captains. Yankee captains include Lou Gehrig, Thurman Munson, Ron Guidry, Don Mattingly and Derek Jeter. The Red Sox have honored captains Carl Yastrzemski, Jim Rice and Jason Varitek. Other

Kauffman Stadium – Kansas City, Missouri

team captains include Bill Mazeroski and Willie Stargell (Pirates); Dave Concepción and Barry Larkin (Reds); Pepper Martin and Terry Moore (Cardinals); George Brett and Frank White (Royals); Travis Jackson and Mel Ott (Giants); Luke Appling (White Sox); Pee Wee Reese (Dodgers); Mike Schmidt (Phillies); Clyde Milan (Nationals); and Al Rosen (Indians).

Within this rare assemblage of major league stars, there are 55 pitchers – almost one-third of the group.

These hurlers have not only succeeded on the mound, but they have done it for only one team despite the ever-present specter of overuse arm injury. Many a pitcher has been sidelined prematurely from the enormous stress the unnatural bio-mechanical motion puts on the pitching elbow and shoulder. Walter Johnson leads the one-franchise hurlers with 21 seasons, but Red Faber (White Sox), Mel Harder (Indians) and Jim Palmer (Orioles) are right behind him at 20 years of service.

Certain defensive positions on the field have tended to lend themselves to long-running hometown performances. An astonishing number of high caliber third basemen qualify, including George Brett, Stan Hack, Chipper Jones, Pepper Martin, Red Rolfe, Brooks Robinson, Al Rosen, Mike Schmidt and Pie Traynor.

From 1939 to 1988, left field at Fenway Park was manned continuously by single-franchise Red Sox. Ted Williams, Carl Yastrzemski, Jim Rice and Mike Greenwell have been back-to-back-to-back-to-back guardians of the Green Monster.

The marquee position of center field at Yankee Stadium was occupied continuously from 1924 to 1966 by Earle Combs, Joe DiMaggio and Mickey Mantle – all three of whom played for the Yankees exclusively. The position of shortstop for the Cincinnati Reds was manned nonstop by Dave Concepción and then Barry Larkin from 1970 through to 2004.

The single-franchise player fraternity includes 24 catchers. A number of organizations have chosen to hold on securely to receivers who work hard and often take on the role of another coach on the field. The array of single-franchise catchers runs the gamut from All-Stars such as Johnny Bench, Harry Danning, Bill Dickey, Roy Campanella, Bill Freehan, Thurman Munson, Jorge Posada and Jason Varitek to outstanding defensive backstops like Bruce Benedict, Ron Karkovice, Tom Pagnozzi and Mike Scioscia.

The Brooklyn Dodgers long enjoyed one of the most intimate relationships with their Flatbush community fans. Many of the fabled *Boys of Summer* highlighted in Roger Kahn's famous book played only for "Dem Bums" including Roy Campanella, Don Drysdale, Carl Erskine, Carl Furillo, Junior Gilliam, Sandy Koufax, Pee Wee Reese and Jackie Robinson. Later in Southern California, aces Koufax and Drysdale combined to comprise one of the greatest lefty-righty starting tandems in the history of the game.

Sadly, a number of highly respected single-team stars had their careers cut short by death or injury while in their prime. ALS felled Lou Gehrig; Roberto Clemente and Thurman Munson died in airplane crashes; Hall of Famer Addie Joss passed away of meningitis; Ray Chapman was beaned by a Carl Mays pitch and died the next day; Don Wilson succumbed to accidental carbon monoxide poisoning; and Bob Moose was killed in an automobile accident. Roy Campanella's paralyzing auto accident; Kirby Puckett's glaucoma; and Sandy Koufax's arm damage all ended their careers prematurely. J. R. Richard's stroke made it impossible for him to return. Joss, Chapman and Wilson each played nine years and were gone too soon, but are included in this extraordinary brotherhood because of the circumstances of their death.

Military service to their country also significantly shortened several major league careers. Perhaps the most well-chronicled of these have been Ted Williams, Bob Feller and Joe Coleman, but there have been many more.

Arguably the most affected was Nationals shortstop Cecil Travis, a career .327 hitter after completing his marvelous 1941 season. He batted .359 behind only Ted Williams' .406 in the American League batting race and ahead of Joe DiMaggio in his 56-game hit streak year. After serving in combat and having his feet frozen during the Battle of the Bulge as one of the "Battered Bastards of Bastogne," Travis was not the same future Hall of Fame player. George Selkirk, who

The great Roberto Clemente strokes out his 3,000th and last hit

replaced Babe Ruth in right field for the Yankees, also had his career shortened by service to his country in World War II and is justly included.

The two stalwarts forever linked together with consecutive game streaks are Lou Gehrig and the man who broke his record, Cal Ripken, Jr. "The Iron Horse" Gehrig and "The Iron Man" Ripken are inextricably joined together by their incredible streaks, and both are remembered and honored for their endurance, dedication, humility and character.

The threesome of Derek Jeter, Jorge Posada and Mariano Rivera, all lifetime Yankees, played as teammates together for an unprecedented 17 years as leaders of the last great Yankee dynasty of the 20th century.

Sometimes single-franchise players run in pairs as longtime teammates. George Brett and Frank White played together for the Royals for 17 years. Walter Johnson and Clyde Milan were both signed on the same scouting trip and not only played on the Nationals for 15 years together, but also were roommates and hunting buddies. Jeff Bagwell and Craig Biggio, the two most famous of the Astros' "Killer Bees," played together for 15 years, the longest stretch of any two Astros teammates in history.

Tigers' shortstop Alan Trammell and second baseman Lou Whitaker teamed up for 17 years as one of the finest keystone combinations the game has ever known. There were other outstanding double play combinations made up of one-team stars. Yankees Phil Rizzuto and Jerry Coleman were one of the best combos of their era. Pee Wee Reese and Jackie Robinson were the heart of the Brooklyn infield during the Dodgers' glory years. Gene Alley and Bill Mazeroski were spectacular during the 1960s for the Pirates. Ron Oester teamed with Davey Concepción and then with Barry Larkin during the 1970s and 1980s.

From the earliest baseball history, National Baseball Hall of Famers Adrian "Cap" Anson of the Chicago Cubs and Bid McPhee of the Cincinnati Red Stockings were the most high-profile 19th century players exclusive to one club. Mike Tiernan of the New York Giants also enjoyed a single franchise 19th century career from 1887 to 1899.

In the contemporary game, ballplayers still competing for their respective clubs in the 21st century with a chance to complete their entire careers with one team include the Giants' Buster Posey; the Phillies' Ryan Howard; the Twins' Joe Mauer; the Mets' David Wright; the Cardinals' Yadier Molina; the Dodgers' Andre Ethier; and the Red Sox's Dustin Pedroia. Scot Shields (2001-2010) of the Anaheim Angels/Los Angeles Angels of Anaheim is the only exclusively 21st century ballplayer to have finished his career in the bigs with one team to date.

Stars that have competed for over 20 years for a single team are the most uncommon. Brooks Robinson of the Baltimore Orioles, generally considered the best defensive third baseman of all time, shares top billing in this category with Boston Red Sox icon Carl Yastrzemski. Brooksie and Yaz each played 23 seasons and are both considered community treasures in their respective cities.

At 22 years of service are the Tigers' Al Kaline, the Cardinals' Stan Musial, and the Giants' Mel Ott. Eight players competed 21 summers for their teams exclusively – Pirates Fred Clarke, Willie Stargell and Honus Wagner; White Sox Luke Appling and Ted Lyons; the Royals' George Brett; the Nationals' Walter Johnson; and the Orioles' Cal Ripken, Jr.

The one-franchise major league warrior is not extinct, but he is assuredly an endangered species. That is even more reason to celebrate the triumph and symmetry of a long career begun and finished with a single team. The talent, character and dedication necessary to earn inclusion into this remarkable pantheon is worthy of special tribute indeed.

Unforgettable Hall of Fame teammates Jackie Robinson and Pee Wee Reese in the Brooklyn dugout

CHAPTER ONE

THE DEADBALL ERA

1901-1919

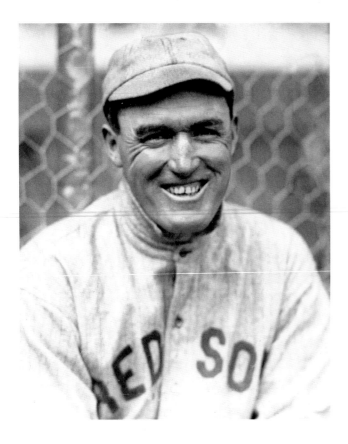

BILLY CARRIGAN

BOSTON AMERICANS & RED SOX
CATCHER

1906-1916

*"Billy Carrigan
was the best manager
I ever played for."*

~ George Herman Ruth

One of the most successful skippers of the Deadball Era, "Rough" Billy Carrigan led Boston to World Series titles in 1915 and 1916 as their player-manager. He was the only Red Sox manager with two titles until Terry Francona got his second one in 2007.

The 5'9" 175-pound Carrigan was ultra scrappy, compensating for his relatively small stature with authentic toughness. Predictably confrontational on the field, Carrigan never backed down from a fight and was soon labeled "Rough" by his teammates.

The right-handed hitting Carrigan provided Boston with serviceable offense at his position with his high water mark being .290 in 1909, good for eighth in the American League. He was not a power hitter, connecting for only six career round trippers.

Carrigan earned his reputation as a quality defensive catcher, leading all AL receivers in fielding twice. He was a master at handling his pitching staffs, but it was the resolute way that he blocked home plate that was noticed throughout the Junior Circuit.

★ ★ ★ ★ ★

William Francis Carrigan was born to Annie and John Carrigan on October 22, 1883 in Lewiston, Maine- the youngest of three children. His parents were Irish Catholic. He worked on local farms while excelling in two sports for Lewiston High School.

He matriculated to Holy Cross College in 1904 and quickly gained notoriety as a halfback for legendary Coach Frank Cavanaugh. On the baseball diamond, Carrigan also starred for future Hall-of-Famer Tommy McCarthy, who converted him into a catcher.

At the end of his sophomore year in 1906, he signed a professional contract with the Boston Americans of the new American League. He joined the undermanned Bosto-

nians directly in the middle of the season, making his major league debut on July 7.

Although Carrigan impressed during the short audition defensively, he did not hit well and spent the 1907 year with the Toronto (ON) Maple Leafs in the Eastern League. He hit .320 and rejoined the newly christened Red Sox in 1908, assuming a backup role.

Rough took over as the starting Boston catcher in 1909. In May, both dugouts watched as he and Detroit's George Moriarty brawled at home plate after Moriarty steamrolled him in a violent collision. He also clashed with the Tigers' Sam Crawford two years later.

Carrigan was enjoying a great 1911 season, averaging .289 in 72 games, before he suffered a leg fracture sliding into second in early September. He was a major factor for the 1912 World Series Champions, leading all American League receivers in fielding.

In July 1913 the Red Sox were injury riddled and squabbling in the clubhouse, stumbling along in fifth place. Red Sox president Jimmy McAleer took action, dismissing manager Jake Stahl, and convinced the 29-year-old Carrigan to replace him.

Split along religious lines, the club's Protestants (Tris Speaker, Joe Wood and Harry Hooper) often bickered with the Catholics. Despite the antipathy pervading the team, the pugnacious Carrigan commanded respect through his distinct brand of toughness.

In 1914, Carrigan engineered the purchase of a young pitcher named Babe Ruth from the minor league Baltimore Orioles. Carrigan saw his protégé needed discipline and was there to supply it. He was Ruth's catcher in his debut on July 11, and soon Ruth developed into one of baseball's top pitchers. Carrigan could see that he was a hitter, but decided not to tinker with baseball's best out-

G	AB	R	H	2B	3B	HR	RBI	SB	BB	SO	BA	OBP	SLG	TB
709	1970	194	506	67	14	6	235	37	206	109	.257	.334	.314	619

field of Duffy Lewis, Speaker and Hooper.

After a strong runner up finish to the Athletics in 1914, Carrigan guided the Red Sox to consecutive World Series titles in 1915 and 1916. Fenway Park was only four years old, but with the exception of 1918, Sox fans would have to wait until the 21st century for the World Series championship to return to Boston.

In early September of 1916, Old Rough announced that he would be retiring at the end of the campaign and made his last appearance as a player on September 30. The team was sold after the 1916 World Series and Carrigan abruptly left the game.

Only 32 years old, he went home to Lewiston to go into banking and spend more time with his new wife, Beulah Bartlett, and an infant daughter. They would raise two daughters and a son. Carrigan also became co-owner of a number of movie theatres in New England, eventually selling them for a significant profit, and became well-to-do.

Red Sox owner Harry Frazee convinced him to come back to manage the team in 1927 after it had finished in the AL cellar nine of the previous 11 years. After three more last-place showings, Carrigan retired again with an overall career record of 489-500.

Repairing back to his beloved Lewiston for good, he returned to banking, joined the town's Board of Finance in 1938, and became president of Peoples Savings Bank in 1953. The now mild-mannered Carrigan remained a regular guest for reunions at Fenway Park.

He was named to the Honor Roll in the Major League Baseball Hall of Fame in 1946 and was inducted into the Holy Cross College Hall of Fame in 1968. Carrigan passed away in a local hospital on July 8, 1969 and was interred in Lewiston's Riverside Cemetery. He was honored as a member of the Boston Red Sox Hall of Fame in 2004.

RAY CHAPMAN

*"Chapman was the greatest
shortstop, that is, considering
all-around ability, batting,
throwing, base-running, bunting,
fielding and ground covering
ability, to mention nothing of his
fight, spirit and conscientiousness,
ever to wear a Cleveland uniform."*

~ *The Cleveland News*

Ray Chapman is the only major leaguer ever to die as a result of a thrown pitch. A star shortstop with would-be Hall of Fame credentials, his loss was devastating. Chapman was one of the most popular players in Cleveland history, a raconteur and enthusiastic personality beloved by teammates and fans alike. His tragic demise prompted the requirement that umpires remove soiled baseballs from play, as well as the outlawing of the spitball after the 1920 season.

Bunting artistry and explosive speed made the 5'10" 170-pound Chapman the ideal #2 hitter in the lineup. He could round the bases in 14 seconds and sprint 100 yards in ten seconds flat. He paced the AL in sacrifice bunts three times and his 67 sacrifices in 1917 are still the big-league standard. Flashy in the field, he led the league in putouts three times and assists once.

★   ★   ★   ★   ★

Raymond Johnson Chapman was born to Barbara and Everette Chapman on January 15, 1891 on a farm near Beaver Dam, Kentucky, about 80 miles southwest of Louisville. The family settled in Herrin in southern Illinois in 1905. He played his first organized semi-pro ball in 1909.

Chapman began his professional career in the Class-B Illinois-Indiana-Iowa League with the Davenport (IA) Prodigals in 1910. In June of 1911, Cleveland bought his contract. With the Toledo (OH) Mud Hens in 1912, he hit .310 with 101 runs scored and 49 steals to earn his debut on August 30. The Naps won 22 of 31 games while he was auditioning at shortstop.

In his first full season, he topped the AL in 1913 with 45 sacrifices and teamed with the club's namesake, Napoleon Lajoie, to form a stellar middle infield in Lajoie's last Cleveland year. He sparkled in 1917, hitting .302 with an AL-high 691 plate appearances and a franchise-best 52 steals. During a ten-game September stretch, he hit .517 and stole home four times.

Chapman led the AL in 1918 with 84 runs and 84 walks while posting a personal-best .390 on-base percentage. He batted an even .300 to help the Indians finish runner up in 1919 with 84 wins. After the season, he married Kathleen Daly, the daughter of a well-to-do businessman.

Before the 1920 season began, Chapman thought about retiring from baseball, as he had already mapped out his business future with his father-in-law. However, his best friend, new manager Tris Speaker, persuaded him to come back to help secure the team's first AL title.

During this era, it was common to dirty up the new *Spalding* baseball as soon as it was put into play. Players smeared it with mud or tobacco juice and scuffed it, cut it, or spit on it. It would routinely soften in later innings and take erratic turns.

Chapman was enjoying a first-rate year going into the fateful August 16 game, hitting .304, with 97 runs scored, 52 walks and 27 doubles. Before 20,000 fans at the Polo Grounds in the top of the fifth, he dug in- hunched over and crowding the plate as usual. It was late afternoon, almost twilight- rainy and dark. The ball was even more difficult to pick up because of the right-handed Mays' unorthodox windup and his near underhanded submariner release point.

With the count 1-and-1, Mays slung a high fastball aimed for the inside corner. Chapman usually jumped back, but this time he never moved. The darkened ball barely missed the strike zone and crashed into Chapman's left temple with a sound so loud that Mays assumed it had hit the end of his *Louisville Slugger* bat. Fielding the ball on the first base side, he tossed it to first.

First baseman Wally Pipp stopped when he saw Chapman drop to his knees with blood flowing from his left ear. Umpire Tommy Connolly ran toward the stands pleading for a doctor. Speaker rushed over from the on-deck circle. Finally, a Yankees team physician came to his aid.

G	AB	R	H	2B	3B	HR	RBI	SB	BB	SO	BA	OBP	SLG	TB
1051	3785	671	1053	162	81	17	364	238	452	414	.278	.358	.377	1428

C

Though mortally wounded and unable to speak, Chapman stood up and bravely tried to walk across the infield toward the clubhouse in center. His knees gave way again near second base. Two teammates put his arms around their shoulders and carried him the rest of the way.

Chapman was taken to nearby Saint Lawrence Hospital where surgeons cut a three-inch incision at the base of his skull, revealing a ruptured lateral sinus. Mrs. Chapman was summoned from Cleveland, but he expired early the next morning before she could say farewell. He was 29.

Chapman's death produced one of the largest outpourings of grief in Cleveland history. His funeral at St. John's Cathedral was attended by thousands with 34 priests involved in the service. Speaker and Jack Graney were so overcome that they could not even attend the service.

When play resumed, the heartbroken team lost seven of nine games. Speaker suggested the players wear black arm bands to honor its fallen comrade and the Indians began to rally. Adding pitcher Duster Mails and shortstop Joe Sewell, the inspired team finished 24-8 to secure the pennant and then defeated the Brooklyn Dodgers for the franchise's first World Series title.

Ray Chapman was buried in East Cleveland's Lakeview Cemetery not far from Alvason Road, where he and his wife had been building their new home. The team awarded Mrs. Chapman a full Series share of $3,986.34. Once an avid fan, she never attended another game.

A bronze memorial plaque was soon dedicated and hung at League Field featuring his bust framed by a baseball diamond and flanked by two bats, one of them cradling a baseball glove. The plaque was inscribed with the words, *"He lives in the hearts of all who knew him."* In 2007, the plaque was re-discovered in a storage room at Cleveland's beautiful Progressive Field. The surface had oxidized a dark brown making the text unreadable. The plaque has been restored and now hangs in Heritage Park, a history exhibit at Progressive Field.

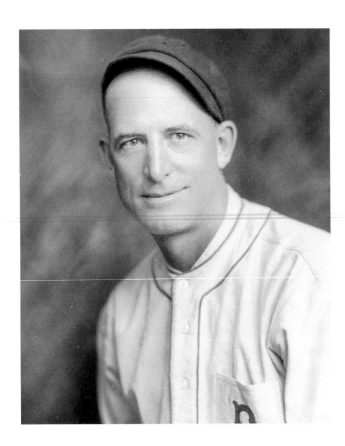

FRED CLARKE

LOUISVILLE COLONELS & PITTSBURGH PIRATES
LEFT FIELD

1894-1915

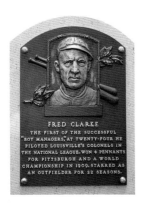

Fred Clarke earned distinction as a fierce competitor and successful player-manager. He was a 19th century National League version of the all-out, combative style of Ty Cobb and skippered four of the nine pennant-winners in Pirates franchise history.

Clarke averaged over .300 in 11 seasons, swiped 30+ bases in seven seasons, and was the Senior Circuit's triples leader 11 seasons. His hitting streak of 35 consecutive games in 1895 was the second-longest in major league history at that time.

He was a marauding base runner, leaving no doubt that he owned the base paths. Any infielder in Clarke's way paid the price, as he used his arms and legs to jar balls loose and broke up double plays with bruising slides. He never backed down from a fight.

Clarke was the winningest player-manager in history. In his 16 managerial campaigns, his teams won four NL pennants with an incredible 14 straight first-division finishes, 1,422 victories and a .595 won-loss percentage- all franchise records.

★　★　★　★　★

Fred Clifford Clarke was born on October 3, 1872, to Lucy Cutler and William D. Clarke on a farm near Winterset, Iowa. He grew up with seven sisters and four brothers. His father, a blacksmith and farmer, moved his family north of Winfield, Kansas in 1875.

The family relocated again five years later to Des Moines. In his youth, Clarke idolized the stars of the town team, the Des Moines Mascots. He later played for them in 1889 and 1890 before moving up a rung to play semi-pro ball in Carroll, Iowa in 1891.

His first three forays into pro ball each ended in abbreviated seasons. His 1892 Hastings Brickmakers saw the Nebraska State League fold. His 1893 St. Joseph (MO) Saints

saw the Western Association dissolved. And his 1893 Montgomery (AL) Colts ceased play when the Southern League was cancelled due to an outbreak of yellow fever.

Clarke tried to stake a claim on a section of land in the last great Oklahoma Cherokee Outlet Land Opening on September 16, 1893. He failed, however, and re-signed with the Savannah (GA) Modocs in 1894. When the Southern League club disbanded on June 27, his manager John McCloskey sold him to the Louisville Colonels of the National League.

Finally catching his break, Clarke put together one of the most auspicious starts in major league history. On June 30, wielding a small, light *Louisville Slugger*, he laced out four singles and a triple in five at-bats for a big-league debut hit record that still stands.

Colonels' treasurer Barney Dreyfuss saw stardom in his young charge and championed him. Clarke emerged in 1897 to hit .390, slug .530, score 122 runs and swipe 59 bases. In midyear, Dreyfuss tapped the 24-year-old rising star as his field manager.

When the NL contracted from 12 teams to eight in 1900, Dreyfuss consolidated his franchise to Pittsburgh, bringing Clarke. He would lead the NL in eight offensive categories from 1900 to 1911, managing from left field and hitting at the top of the order.

The Pirates won titles in 1901, 1902 and 1903, a year Clarke led the majors with a .532 slugging average and .946 OPS. His 32 doubles topped the NL and his .351 average was second. In the first "World's Series," the Pirates fell to the Boston Americans in eight games.

Clarke's clutch hitting in each win of the 1909 Series helped the Bucs to outlast Cobb's Tigers in seven games. After the triumph he considered retiring to his 1,320-acre Little Pirate Ranch near Winfield to spend more

G	AB	R	H	2B	3B	HR	RBI	SB	BB	SO	BA	OBP	SLG	TB
2246	8584	1622	2678	361	220	67	1051	509	875	509	.312	.386	.429	3680

P

time with his family. He had married the vivacious Annette Gray of Chicago in 1898, by whom he had two daughters.

Dreyfuss convinced him to stay, but after two straight second division finishes, Clarke decided to retire in September, 1915. "Fred Clarke Day" was proclaimed on September 23 with Clarke going one-for-two against the Braves' Dick Rudolph.

By 1917, oil had been discovered on his ranch and Clarke's personal wealth was in excess of $1,000,000- an enormous sum then. In addition, he created and held several patents including flip down sunglasses. Clarke was an avid fisherman and hunter, a Kansas state champion amateur trap shooter, and a horseman who could do riding tricks.

In 1925, Dreyfuss needed an extra spark to get a good Pirates team past rival John McGraw's Giants. The Bucs were 5½ games back of the Giants on June 12 when he coaxed Clarke back as his personal assistant, scouting director and assistant manager.

With Clarke sitting on the bench with manager Bill McKechnie, the Pirates went into overdrive, finishing 8½ games ahead of the Giants. Down three games to one against the Nationals in the Fall Classic, the Bucs rallied valiantly to win three in a row.

The famous "ABC Affair" boiled up in 1926 when three players — Babe Adams, Carson Bigbee and Max Carey — questioned Clarke's role in the dugout and asked McKechnie to call a players' meeting. After the players voted 18-6 to affirm Clarke, the three veterans lost their jobs, the Bucs lost the pennant, and Clarke re-retired in October.

Clarke was inducted into the National Baseball Hall of Fame (1945), Iowa Sports Hall of Fame (1951), and Kansas Sports Hall of Fame (1963). He died in Winfield at age 87 of pneumonia on August 14, 1960, and is buried in Winfield's St. Mary's Cemetery.

HOOKS DAUSS

DETROIT TIGERS
RIGHT-HANDED PITCHER

1912-1926

"My first flash thought was that Hooks Dauss must be considered the greatest of all Tigers pitchers. After all, Dauss won 223 games for the Tigers in Ty Cobb's era. And Dauss' name still is in blue type in the Tigers record book as the pitcher with the most victories since the ballclub was founded 110 years ago."

~ *Detroit News sportswriter Jerry Green*

Hooks Dauss won more games and lost more games than any other pitcher in Motor City history. A workhorse, he toiled for mostly mediocre teams in the later part of the Deadball Era, yet had ten winning seasons. He is among the top 100 winningest hurlers of all-time.

The slender 5'10½" 168-pound Dauss was surprisingly durable and versatile. He pitched over 200 innings 11 years in a row and made 150 career relief appearances, closing out 121 games with 40 saves. He is second in Tigers history in both games and innings pitched. "Hooks" Dauss was named for his curveball which he spun off with precision control to compensate for a pedestrian fastball. Although known for his easygoing personality, he didn't hesitate to back hitters off the plate. He led the American League in hit batsmen three times.

The agile Dauss was a great fielding pitcher with a career .968 fielding average and a notable 1,128 assists. In 1923 and 1924 combined, he committed only a single error in 95 games. He would have been a perennial *Rawlings* Gold Glove winner if the award had existed.

★　★　★　★　★

George August Daus (He later added an extra "s") was born of German stock in Indianapolis, Marion County, Indiana to Anna E. Magel and Edward H. Daus on September 22, 1889. He was the youngest of three brothers who saw their parents divorce before he was ten.

After pitching for Manual Training High in Indianapolis, he made his first pro roster at age 19 with the South Bend (IN) Greens in the Class-B Central League. Manager Aggie Green released him for being too small but allowed him throw in an exhibition against the Duluth (MN) White Sox. He tossed a complete game shutout and Duluth nabbed him for the 1909 season.

Dauss went 19-10 for Duluth in 37 games that year

and returned there to pitch in 1910. He was assigned to the Winona (MN) Pirates of the Minnesota-Wisconsin League in 1911 and won 22 games with a 2.13 ERA. Pittsburgh bought his rights and sent him to the St. Paul Apostles (American Association) where he posted a sparkling 2.22 ERA in 271 innings in 1912.

Detroit scout Jim "Deacon" McGuire was impressed and the Tigers purchased his rights. Dauss was given his major league debut on September 28. In his first full season in 1913, he won 13 games with a 2.48 ERA and 22 complete games.

After Dauss was courted briefly by the new outlaw Federal League's Indianapolis Hoosiers, Tigers owner Frank Navin quickly signed him. His 1914 campaign made Navin look clairvoyant. Dauss put up an 18-15 mark with 22 complete games in 302 innings pitched, 150 Ks, 87 walks and a 2.86 ERA. He also paced both leagues with a career-high 18 hit batters.

The Tigers' high water mark during his era was 1915. Harry Coveleski, Jean Dubuc and Dauss made up an imposing hurler trio, winning 63 games between them. The Tigers won 100 games and finished only 2½ games behind the World Champion Red Sox. Dauss went a team-leading 24-13 with a 2.50 ERA in 309⅔ innings pitched including some clutch relief outings. It was also a key year for him personally as he married Olie M. Speake on May 19. When the team arrived in St. Louis, Dauss was part of a double ceremony where Olie and her sister Jessie were both married. Later that day, he bested the Browns at Sportsman's Park, 7-1.

The Tigers came up four games short to the Red Sox in 1916. Coveleski won 21 and Dauss 19, but Detroit's pitching depth was already starting to fray. In 1917, Dauss won 17 and put up a career-best 2.43 ERA, but

G	IP	W	L	PCT	SHO	GS	CG	H	ER	SO	BB	ERA
538	3390.2	223	182	.551	22	388	245	3407	1245	1201	1067	3.30

the team slid back into the second division.

World War I shortened the 1918 season and Dauss had a losing record for the first time as the team finished seventh. He rebounded with a 21-9 mark in 1919, as the Tigers earned an 80-60 record. But in 1920, the team reverted to seventh again and Dauss lost 21 games.

Like many other Deadball Era pitchers, Dauss saw his ERA rise with the unveiling of the hotter *Spalding* ball in 1920. Indeed, his ERA after 1920 was almost a full run per game higher, yet he still remained one of the most consistent and successful hurlers in the game. Ty Cobb replaced Hughie Jennings as Tigers manager in 1921 and continued to utilize Dauss irregularly as both a starter and reliever. By 1923, Cobb was relying on him more and more. Dauss responded with 21 wins and pitched 316 innings in a career-high 50 games.

It would be Dauss' last big year as the miles on his arm were beginning to show. He had toiled for over 3,500 professional innings by the time he was age 33. In 1924, Cobb went to him mostly in relief, but then suddenly reinstated him as a starter in 1925.

By early 1926, Dauss' sturdy right arm was all but used up. He pitched his final season mainly in relief, registering a gutsy career-high nine saves that year and an AL-best 11 wins in relief. But when a heart condition was detected after the season, Dauss hung up his spikes.

He retreated to his 320-acre farm outside of St. Louis and eventually took a job in St. Louis at Pinkerton's National Detective Agency office. The self-effacing Dauss told area ballplayers he was never a great pitcher and that he had never pitched any important games. Eventually, his heart condition caught up to him. Hooks Dauss passed away at Firmin Desloge Hospital in St. Louis on July 27, 1963 of a ruptured aorta after an extended period of poor health. He is buried at Sunset Memorial Park & Mausoleum in the St. Louis suburb of Affton, Missouri.

PATSY GHARRITY

WASHINGTON NATIONALS
CATCHER · FIRST BASE · LEFT FIELD
1916-1923 · 1929-1930

Versatile Patsy Gharrity was the roommate and preferred battery mate of Walter "Big Train" Johnson. Primarily a receiver, the 5'10" 170-pound right-handed hitting Gharrity also filled in as a respectable first baseman, and even patrolled the outfield for 35 games in his career.

★   ★   ★   ★   ★

Edward Patrick Gharrity was born of Irish Catholic stock on March 13, 1892 to Sarah and Thomas Henry Gharrity in Parnell, Fillmore Township, Iowa. Gharrity grew up in the 200-resident rural hamlet, attending the Locust Grove schools with his four brothers and four sisters.

He signed his first professional contract in 1914 at 22 with the Class-B Dayton (OH) Veterans of the Central League. After a 300 at-bat baptism in 91 games, he was promoted to the Double-A Minneapolis (MN) Millers of the American Association. He remained with the Millers in 1915 and was a key to the club winning the AA title. He caught 86 games and hit a solid .308.

The Nationals held their 1916 spring training at the University of Virginia in Charlottesville. Gharrity earned his major league debut on May 16, but manager Clark Griffith utilized him sparingly as a backup to starting catcher John "Bull" Henry. In 1917, his playing time increased as a catcher, first baseman and pinch hitter, batting .284 in 76 games.

On May 23, 1918, Secretary of War Newton Baker handed down a "work or fight" order and directed Judge Advocate General Enoch Crowder to implement it pursuant to the Selective Service Act of 1917. The order led some major leaguers to defect to jobs at designated "vital industries."

As a result, the shipbuilders and steelmakers leagues in 1918 had the highest level of baseball ever played outside of the majors. Gharrity only played four games for the Nats in 1918 before hiring on with Harlan and Hollingsworth, a major shipbuilder in Wilmington, Delaware.

The Wilmington Shipbuilders team won all of the east coast league titles that year with stars like Shoeless Joe Jackson, Lefty Williams and Patsy Gharrity. Due to the wholesale attrition from players avoiding conscription, baseball had to shut down prematurely on Labor Day.

After World War I, Gharrity returned to the Nationals in 1919 and became the starting catcher when Eddie Ainsmith was traded to the Tigers. He played in 111 games, hitting .271 with 19 doubles. On June 23, he went 5-for-5 versus the Boston Red Sox with an inside-the-park home run, an outside-the-park homer, two doubles and a single for an unheard of 13 total bases.

Gharrity played in 131 games in 1920, caught 121 games and fielded .965. At Comiskey Park on September 12, the Nats' Frank Ellerbe was on first with two outs. Gharrity hammered a pitch into the left field stands for a two-run homer. Ellerbe heard the fans cheering and assumed the White Sox superb leftfielder Shoeless Joe Jackson had caught the ball to end the inning.

After rounding third base, Ellerbe had turned and jogged out to his shortstop position. Meanwhile, Gharrity trotted toward third and was called out for passing Ellerbe. The Nats argued that since the ball was out of play, it didn't matter. The *New York Times* headline the next morning read: GHARRITY'S HOMER RETIRES HIS SIDE. The Nationals still beat the White Sox, 5-0.

The year 1921 would be Gharitty's high water mark as a major leaguer. He hit a stellar .310 in 121 games including 120 hits, 62 runs scored, 19 doubles, eight triples, seven home runs and 57 runs batted in. He also had a .386 on-base percentage, slugged .455 and fielded .977.

> *"The American League does not desire to impugn the motives of players who have gone into this [industrial] work. Some of them are patriotic. But if there are any of them who are Class 1A, I hope Provost General Crowder yanks them from the shipyards and steel works by the coat collar and places them in cantonment to prepare for future events on the western front ... The American League does not approve of players trying to evade military service."*
>
> ~ AL President Ban Johnson, 1918

G	AB	R	H	2B	3B	HR	RBI	SB	BB	SO	BA	OBP	SLG	TB
676	1961	237	513	92	96	20	249	32	188	231	.262	.331	.366	717

W

Gharitty played in 96 games in 1922, hitting .256, but slumped to .207 in 1923, appearing in 93 games. The highlight of his year came on July 1. Batting cleanup behind Hall of Famer Goose Goslin in the Nationals' order, he hit a rare inside-the-park grand slam home run.

The Sporting News published an article in 1924 quoting Baseball Commissioner Judge Kenesaw Mountain Landis as expressing doubts that Major League Baseball would survive competing against industrial giants for the services of ballplayers. Salaries had shot up overnight.

Gharrity decided to play for the Beloit (WS) Fairies, a factory squad owned by the Fairbanks Morse Engine in the outlaw Midwest League. It offered a good salary, an easy four games a week, and the possibility of an occupation afterward. He played for Beloit through 1928.

His decision to leave the Nationals meant that he missed playing in two straight World Series in 1924 and 1925 and some substantial bonuses. When Johnson was appointed Washington manager in 1929, he immediately asked his old roommate and battery mate to be his bullpen catcher. Before Gharrity could take the job, he had to be officially reinstated by Commissioner Kenesaw Mountain Landis.

By now in his late thirties, Gharrity got into five more games as an active player in 1929 and 1930. His last major league game was on July 31, 1930. Gharrity remained a non-playing coach with the Nats until the end of the 1932 season and then followed The Big Train over to the Indians when Johnson was appointed skipper in Cleveland. The position lasted until 1935.

Gharrity served as field manager for the 1938 Class-D Eau Claire (WS) Bears of the Northern League. Afterward, he took employment back in Beloit with Fairbanks Morse Engine and made his permanent home there. He passed away at age 74 in Beloit on October 10, 1966 and is buried in Beloit's Calvary Cemetery.

JACK GRANEY

CLEVELAND NAPS & INDIANS
LEFT FIELD

1908 • 1910-1922

> "He had a distinctive voice, high-pitched and raspy, but quite clear. You always knew, listening to him, that he knew what was going on and he told it to you simply and accurately."
>
> ~ broadcaster Jack Buck

Fun-loving Jack Graney will be forever linked with the Indians, not only because of his 14-year playing career, but also for his brilliant 21 years as a radio broadcaster, a ubiquitous icon to generations of Cleveland baseball fans.

The durable 5'9" 180-pounder was a disciplined, patient leadoff hitter, getting on base by any means, taking until he had two strikes. He led the AL in walks twice and doubles once while setting the record for games played by a Canadian-born player.

Graney became a first-rate leftfielder, accomplished at navigating the demanding sun field at Cleveland's spacious League Park, which went out as far as 505 feet to deepest left-center. League Park highlighted his good range and strong throwing arm.

★ ★ ★ ★ ★

John Gladstone Graney was born on June 10, 1886 in St. Thomas, Ontario, Canada, the sixth of nine children to Mary Ann McFeely and James S. Graney. His Irish Catholic father was chief train dispatcher on the Canadian Southern Railway.

St. Thomas local and NL umpire Bob Emslie discovered the young southpaw pitching for the town team in early 1907. The Cubs signed him. He won 24 games for the Rochester (NY) Bronchos and Wilkes-Barre (PA) Barons before being sold to the Naps.

Still unpolished, he was invited to 1908 spring training with the big club in Macon, Georgia. Throwing batting practice and trying to impress player-manager Napoleon Lajoie with his velocity, he let a fastball slip up-and-in and knocked him out.

Despite the incident, Graney debuted in the bigs on April 30, giving up two runs in 3⅓ innings before breaking a finger on a line shot through the box. He

was sent to the Columbus (OH) Senators, brought back briefly to Cleveland, and then exiled to the Portland (OR) Beavers. Lajoie was overheard saying, "All wild men belong in the West."

Although Graney was an impressive 17-9 the next year in 31 games in Oregon, the Cleveland brass abruptly decided to make him a leftfielder. He hit .252 in 385 at-bats the rest of the summer and made the leap to the big time for good the next year.

The first hitter rookie Red Sox pitcher Babe Ruth faced was Jack Graney in 1914. He singled and scored. And Graney was the first big-leaguer to wear a number on his uniform. In 1916, he pinned the #1 to his sleeve leading off versus the White Sox.

The high-spirited Graney's bull terrier named "Larry" began traveling as the team's official mascot. Larry regaled fans by leapfrogging over players' backs before games and scampering after foul balls. During a game in Washington in 1914, Larry refused to give up a foul ball to umpire "Big Bill" Dinneen (required of humans at the time) and was banned from National Park by order of AL president Ban Johnson.

Graney's best friend and travel roommate was shortstop Ray Chapman who was beaned by Yankee submariner Carl Mays on August 16, 1920 at the Polo Grounds. Tragically, Chapman died the next day and Graney was inconsolable. Despite the profound loss, the Indians, led by Tris Speaker, went on to win their first World Series title, a 5-2 victory over the Brooklyn Robins. Graney went hitless in three at-bats.

He retired on June 28, 1922 at age 36 and managed the Des Moines (IA) Boosters for the rest of the season for Indians owner Jim Dunn. From 1923 to 1927, Graney operated a successful Cleveland Ford dealer-

G	AB	R	H	2B	3B	HR	RBI	SB	BB	SO	BA	OBP	SLG	TB
1402	4705	706	1178	219	79	18	420	148	712	345	.250	.354	.342	1609

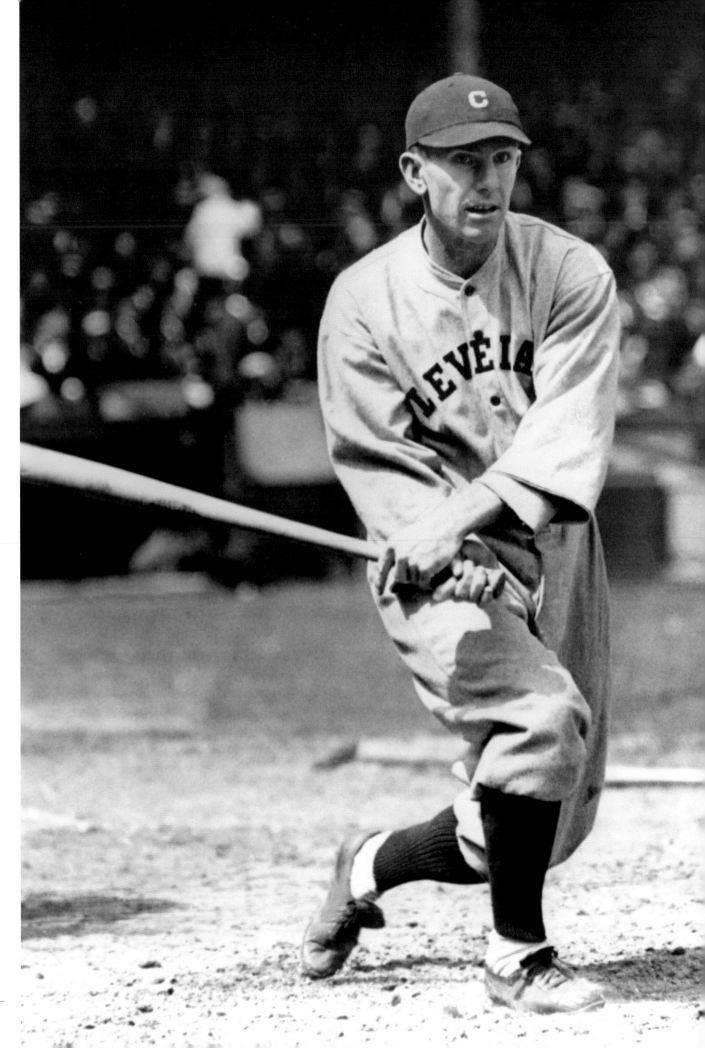

ship. When the Ford plant closed for a year to convert to the new Model A, it put him out of business. Graney hit bottom, reduced to selling used cars.

In 1932, Radio WHK won the Indians broadcast rights, but sponsors were unhappy with the Indians' previous announcers. Indians General Manager Billy Evans quickly made Graney the first former major league player to become a professional broadcaster. His clear, smooth delivery and knowledge made him instantly popular in the booth. Except for 1945, he was the voice of Indian Baseball through 1953. Graney called the All-Star Game in Cleveland on CBS Radio and was the first former player to announce a World Series in 1935.

Until later, he did not travel to away games and re-created them by telegraph wire reports. Calling on his familiarity with AL ballparks and his dramatic flair, Graney became a master of the art, using canned crowd noise and a simulated crack of the bat.

He broadcast thousands of games and went through six partners before retiring after more than two decades. His final play-by-play was the 1954 World Series sweep by the New York Giants over his beloved Indians.

In 1984, Graney was inducted into the Canadian Baseball Hall of Fame which later instituted an award in his name presented periodically to journalists who had made significant contributions to promoting base-ball in the Dominion of Canada.

He and his wife Pauline retired comfortably to Bowl-ing Green, Missouri to be near their daughter and her family. Jack Graney died of natural causes in a nursing home on April 20, 1978 at 91. He is buried in Memorial Gardens Cemetery in Bowling Green.

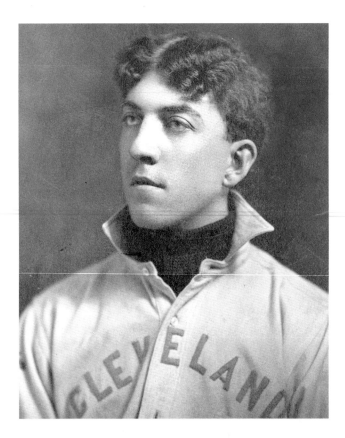

ADDIE JOSS

CLEVELAND BLUEBIRDS & NAPS
RIGHT-HANDED PITCHER

1902-1910

"He would turn his back toward the batter as he wound up, hiding the ball all the while, and then whip around and fire it in."

~ Roger Peckinpaugh

ADRIAN (ADDIE) JOSS
CLEVELAND A.L. 1902-1910
ONE OF PREMIER PITCHERS OF AMERICAN
LEAGUE'S FIRST DECADE. SPEED, SHARP
CONTROL HELPED HIM TO WIN 20 OR MORE
GAMES FOUR SEASONS IN A ROW. POSTED
LEAGUE-LEADING 27 VICTORIES AND THREE
ONE-HITTERS IN 1907. HURLED PERFECT
GAME IN 1908. HAD ANOTHER NO-HITTER
IN 1910. CREDITED WITH 45 SHUTOUTS
AMONG HIS 160 CAREER VICTORIES.

Addie Joss was the first great pitcher in Cleveland franchise history. His dazzling 1.89 career ERA ranks him second only to Big Ed Walsh's 1.82 for pitchers with 1,000+ innings. Joss completed a remarkable 234 of his 260 big-league starts and remains the only hurler in baseball annals to no-hit the same team twice-the Chicago White Sox. He also tossed seven one-hitters.

Joss corkscrewed his body away from home plate and then kicked his leg high before delivering with a deceptive sidearm motion. He never considered doctoring a spitball, utilizing a live fastball, a late breaking curve and a changeup to post ERAs of less than 2.00 six times.

The 6'3" 185-pound Joss won 20+ games four straight seasons. His 160 wins included a staggering 45 shutouts. His WHIP (Walks + Hits/Innings Pitched) is the best ever at 0.968. No pitcher has allowed fewer runners to reach base per nine innings in baseball history.

* * * * *

Adrian Joss was born April 12, 1880 in Woodland, Dodge County, Wisconsin, the only child of Theresa Staudenmeyer and Jacob Joss. His father emigrated from Switzerland to learn cheese-making and in time owned his own cheese factory. His father died when he was ten.

The tall, lanky Joss grew up a leading athlete at Wayland Academy in Beaver Dam, Wisconsin. With long arms, big hands and long fingers, he possessed the ideal physique for a pitcher. Joss was so razor thin, he was labeled the "Human Hairpin" and the "Human Slat."

He taught school in 1896 in Horicon and was the winning pitcher in the state town ball title game. Joss played for the Sacred Heart Military Academy team in Watertown in 1899 and in the summer starred for Manitowoc in the Wisconsin State League, posting a 4-1 mark. Toledo (OH) Mud Hens player-manager Bob Gilks recognized his talent and signed him to a professional contract.

On April 28, 1900, Joss pitched the Mud Hens' opener and won. His future wife, Lillian Shinavar, happened to be in the stands that day (they would marry on October 11, 1902). He went 19-16 and followed with a 25-18 season, hurling 351⅓ innings with 216 strikeouts.

Joss was invited to the 1902 spring camp of the newly formed Cleveland Bluebirds of the American League. He pitched his debut on April 26, shutting out the St. Louis Browns, 3-0, on one infield hit. He finished at 17-13, a 2.77 ERA, and an AL-best five shutouts.

The ballplayers themselves found the name "Bluebirds" objectionable. When star second baseman Napoleon Lajoie joined the club on June 4, Cleveland drew 10,000 fans to League Park in his first game. The team took on the name "Naps" at the end of the season in his honor.

Joss followed with an 18-13 mark in 1903 and a 2.19 ERA. In 1904, his 1.59 ERA paced the AL although he got only 24 starts because of a bout with malaria. In 1905, a healthy Joss went 20-12 with a 2.01 ERA. He improved to 21-9 in 1906 with a 1.72 ERA and nine shutouts.

Joss began working as a Sunday sports columnist for the *Toledo News-Bee* after the 1906 season and became quite popular writing about a wide variety of baseball topics. He also went on to write for the *Cleveland Press*, covering the World Series from 1907 to 1909.

Settled with a new $4,000 contract, Joss began the 1907 season with ten straight wins in his first ten starts and won a career-high 27 games, tying him for the most pitching victories in the American League alongside Doc White of the White Sox.

His best year was 1908. He won an AL-high 24 games with a career-best 1.16 ERA. In his 325 innings pitched, he walked only 30. On October 2, Joss and the White Sox's Ed Walsh tangled in a pitching duel for the ages as the Naps, Sox and Tigers battled in a taut pennant race.

G	IP	W	L	PCT	SHO	GS	CG	H	ER	SO	BB	ERA
286	2327	160	97	.623	45	260	234	1888	488	920	364	1.89

Walsh, going for his 41st win, threw a four-hitter with 15 strikeouts, allowing only a run. Joss trumped him by hurling a perfect game, completing his masterpiece with just 74 pitches. Only four balls were hit out of the infield. The Naps finished AL runner up (90-64) only a half game behind Detroit (90-63). It would be the closest Joss ever got to being on a pennant winner.

In 1909, he slipped to 14-13 despite a 1.71 ERA, but complained of an ill-defined fatigue. Although limited to 13 appearances in 1910, Joss tossed another no-hitter early against the Pale Hose on April 20, winning 1-0 while aiding his own cause with ten assists. On July 25, he left in the fifth inning because of a torn elbow ligament, never to throw another big-league pitch.

Before the 1911 season on April 3, Joss collapsed on the field before an exhibition game in Chattanooga, Tennessee. He initially brushed it off, but returned home to Toledo where he was soon hospitalized and died suddenly of bacterial meningitis on April 14. He was just 31.

Evangelist-ballplayer Billy Sunday delivered the eulogy at his April 17 funeral, one of the largest in Toledo history. The Naps were scheduled to play that day, but the game was cancelled by AL president Ban Johnson when his teammates all insisted on attending the funeral.

His tragic death stunned baseball. Joss was so respected by his contemporaries they formed an AL all-star team to play the Naps on July 24 for his wife's benefit. The game brought almost $13,000 to defray medical costs. He was buried at Toledo's Woodlawn Cemetery.

Although he was undeniably a brilliant pitcher, Addie Joss was kept out of Cooperstown because of the requirement that a player had to play ten years in the major leagues to qualify. The Veterans Committee finally voted him into the National Baseball Hall of Fame posthumously 67 years later in 1978.

SAM LEEVER

PITTSBURGH PIRATES
RIGHT-HANDED PITCHER

1898-1910

Though struggling with arm injuries off and on throughout his career, Sam Leever won 194 games and earned a .660 winning percentage that still ranks ninth highest in baseball history. He allowed only 29 home runs in 2,660²/₃ major league innings.

The 5'10½" 175-pound Leever was the Senior Circuit's "Leading Pitcher" in 1901, 1903 and 1905 in an era when the best hurler had the highest winning percentage. A four-time 20-game winner, he showed precision control and was a master at exploiting hitters' weaknesses.

Leever was known as "The Goshen Schoolmaster" as much for his serious countenance and taciturn disposition as for his tenure in the classroom. With intense, piercing blue eyes and brown hair that was thinning even early in his baseball career, he fit the part perfectly.

★   ★   ★   ★   ★

Samuel William Leever was born on December 23, 1871 to Amerideth Ardelia Watson and Edward Clark Leever on a farm in Goshen Township, Clermont County, Ohio, about 20 miles northeast of Cincinnati. He was the fourth of eight children in a large German household.

After graduating from Goshen High, Leever taught school during the week and pitched on Sundays. He was a teammate of future major leaguer Norman "Kid" Elberfield with the local Norwood Maroons and starred for several years on club teams in southwestern Ohio.

Leever signed his first professional contract at the advanced age of 25 because he did not throw particularly hard, relying on changes of speed, movement and location. His initial pro summer was 1897 with the Richmond (VA) Giants in the Class-B Atlantic League. Leever went 20-18 with a 1.05 ERA in 316 innings pitched and led the circuit with 179 strikeouts.

Pittsburgh purchased his contract in 1898 and gave him his big-league debut on May 26. When he developed a sore arm, the Pirates returned him to Richmond, where he won 14 games and helped the team to the Atlantic League title. It won him a late season recall by the Bucs.

As a true rookie in 1899, the 27-year old Leever pitched in a NL-high 51 games and threw 379 innings, going 21-23 with 35 complete games and a 3.18 ERA. He also completed 11 games for other pitchers- three of them equivalent to what we now call a "save."

Pirates' manager Fred Clarke employed a five-pitcher rotation from 1900 to 1902 because he had a deep, talented staff. This limited Leever's innings, although he won 44 games with a 2.62 ERA and paced the Senior Circuit in winning percentage in 1901 at .737.

Two of those Pirates starters, Jack Chesbro and Jesse Tannehill, were wooed away by the New York Highlanders of the upstart American League in early 1903. Leever and his good friend Deacon Phillippe were then called upon to share a heavier load. Leever responded by producing his best season, a 25-7 mark with a league-best 2.06 ERA and seven shutouts.

In July, Pittsburgh pitchers ran off a record six straight shutouts, with Leever hurling the second and sixth games in the consecutive game streak. Late in the year, he injured his pitching shoulder in a trapshooting contest. It would prove costly in the 1903 World Series.

Leever started Game 2 but after only one inning he couldn't continue. Six days later he was asked to start Game 6, but couldn't finish and took the loss. The Boston Americans defeated the Pirates, 5-3. The difference was Leever's inability to contribute because of the injury.

In February of 1904, Leever married the former Margaret Molloy. In his first regular season game that April, he argued a balk call so vociferously that he was ejected and suspended for a week. His new bride was present at the game and witnessed her normally reserved husband's outburst. She was asked for her reaction: "It sure looked like a balk to me."

G	IP	W	L	PCT	SHO	GS	CG	H	ER	SO	BB	ERA
388	2660.2	194	100	.600	39	299	241	2449	731	847	587	2.47

P

After winning 18 in 1904, Leever went 20-5 and 22-7 his next two years, topping the NL in winning percentage again in 1905. He fought arm trouble in 1907, winning only 14 games despite a career-low 1.66 ERA. Leever posted a 15-7 mark with a 2.10 ERA in 1908, but by then half his work was in relief. He threw mainly in relief his last two seasons- each year going 14-6.

Prior to the 1911 season, the Pirates sent him a contract that was not commensurate with what he had meant to the franchise. The 38-year-old veteran refused to report to spring training in protest. Owner Barney Dreyfuss offered to send Leever to a minor league team and give him a share of the proceeds, which only insulted him more. He requested and was granted his release.

Leever signed on with the Minneapolis (MN) Millers, joining prior teammate Rube Waddell, and won seven games to help win the American Association title. After a year off, he managed the Covington (KY) Blue Sox in the outlaw Federal League in 1913, an independent third major league that only lasted two years. After the season, he retired permanently.

Leever was an avid outdoorsman, and went on many long hunting trips during and after his baseball career, often with his good friends Deacon Phillippe and Honus Wagner. He also maintained his passion for trap shooting, scoring 99 out of 100 as late as age 71.

Leever and his wife retired to their 70-acre farm in Goshen, acquired with money saved from his baseball earnings. He continued to teach school for many years, was the postmaster of Goshen for two terms and became one of its leading citizens.

Leever eventually retired from farming and he and his wife moved into her family's home closer to town. He often attended ballgames in town, but would seldom offer advice or talk much about his own career. The Goshen Schoolmaster died at age 81 in Goshen on May 19, 1953.

CLYDE MILAN

WASHINGTON NATIONALS
CENTER FIELD

1907-1922

*"Milan the Marvel, the
Flying Mercury of the
diamond, the man who
shattered the American
League record, and the
greatest base runner
of the decade."*

~ writer F. C. Lane

AMERICAN LEAGUE

Clyde Milan became renowned as one of the premier base stealers of his generation. Only Ty Cobb (765) and Eddie Collins (564) stole more bases that Milan's 481 during the Deadball Era. He set the major league record of 88 stolen bases in a season in 1912 before Cobb surpassed it with his 96 thefts in 1915.

Nationals owner Clark Griffith regarded Milan as the greatest overall centerfielder in franchise history. He played perhaps the shallowest center field in baseball annals, using his brilliant speed to dash back quickly for balls hit over his head. For all his consistent excellent play, Milan never played for a pennant winner, although he hit over .300 four times and scored over a thousand runs.

The compact 5' 9" 168-pound Milan was a left-handed hitting artist who rarely struck out and was a master at getting on base. Nicknamed "Deerfoot", he hit leadoff and was an accomplished bunter who could outrun the ball to first base. If opposing infielders played him in on the grass, Milan would simply slash the ball by them.

★ ★ ★ ★ ★

Jesse Clyde Milan was born to Mary Anna Anderson and William Milan on March 25, 1887, in Linden, Perry County, Tennessee. Linden was a hamlet of about 700 townspeople tucked into the wooded hills above the Buffalo River. A blacksmith's son of Scotch-Irish and Native American stock, he was one of eight children. Baseball was not Milan's focus growing up in middle Tennessee. His main outdoor activity up until he was 18 was hunting wild turkey and quail with his two Irish setters.

In 1905, Milan joined up with a semi-pro team in Clarksville, Texas in the North Texas League. It was there that he met his future wife, Margaret Bowers. Milan visited her each winter there for eight years before they were married after the 1913 season. The couple eventually settled in Clarksville where they raised their two daughters.

He began the 1906 season by hitting .356 for the Shawnee Blues (then in Indian Territory), but the team disbanded. He was immediately picked up by the Wichita (KS) Jobbers of the Class-C Western Association, but adapted slowly to the better competition. Milan came back and atoned in 1907 by hitting .304 and pilfering 38 bases in 114 games.

Washington Nationals Manager "Pongo Joe" Cantillon sent a scout to Wichita with orders to purchase Milan's contract and then go to Idaho to sign a young pitcher named Walter Johnson. As a result, the Nats' two franchise players for a generation were signed on the same scouting trip. Both were from rural upbringings, quiet and modest. They would become roommates, hunting companions and inseparable lifelong friends.

Milan made his big-league debut on August 19, 1907 then struggled with no home runs and nine RBI in 48 games. He continued to regress in 1908 and stole only ten bases in 130 games in 1909. A frustrated Cantillon wanted to banish Milan to the minors.

But Jimmy McAleer took the manager's reins in 1910 and instantly recognized Milan's upside. With McAleer's support, his confidence was renewed. He hit .279 with 44 steals and began showing progress in every facet of his game. Milan began to read pitchers' pickoff moves better and started getting much better jumps. He began to steal on random pitch counts and perfected a sensational hook slide.

In 1911, Milan became a bona fide star, hitting .315 with 58 steals. It would be the first of three peak years where he missed only one game, hit over .300 each sea-

G	AB	R	H	2B	3B	HR	RBI	SB	BB	SO	BA	OBP	SLG	TB
1982	7359	1004	2100	240	105	17	617	495	685	197	.285	.353	.353	2601

W

was 1912, when he batted .306 with 79 RBI and stole 88 bases. The total would have been 91 had not a St. Louis game been rained out. He finished fourth in the AL Chalmers Award Most Valuable Player voting.

Milan again led the AL in 1913 with 75 stolen bases. He missed six weeks with a broken jaw sustained in an outfield collision in 1914, but returned to start 150 games each year through 1917. He hit a career-high .322 in 1920 and played regularly through 1921.

In late July in 1921, Nationals manager George Mc-Bride was severely injured by a thrown ball before a game. Now the Nats popular captain, Milan was asked to take over as interim manager while continuing to be an active player. He would only last as manager that one year of 1922 as Washington finished sixth at 69-85. He suffered from ulcers and was not brought back the next year for being too laissez faire with his players.

It would be Milan's final year as a big-league player or manager, but he played afterward with the Minneapolis (MN) Millers and served the New Haven (CT) Profs and Memphis (TN) Chickasaws as a player/manager. He also skippered the Birmingham (AL) Barons and Chattanooga (TN) Lookouts to Southern Association titles, but came home to be a coach for the Nationals for his final 17 seasons.

Milan spent his last day alive in the March sunshine in the Orlando, Florida doing what he loved. He insisted on hitting infield fungoes during both morning and afternoon session workouts, despite the debilitating heat. Feeling faint, he retreated to the clubhouse locker room at Tinker Field and collapsed of a heart attack. Milan succumbed at the Orlando hospital hours later on March 3, 1953 and was buried in the Clarksville Cemetery, in his adopted hometown.

OTTO MILLER

Otto Miller was the stalwart catcher for the 1916 and 1920 Brooklyn National League Champion teams. He spent his entire career playing under only two managers – the volcanic "Bad Bill" Dahlen and Wilbert Robinson – while catching almost half of Brooklyn's games.

The burly 6' 196-pound Miller was a Gold Glove-quality receiver, the best throwing catcher in the Senior Circuit. He had an instinctive rapport with his pitchers and was a master at calling for the right pitch. Ironman pitcher Jack Coombs once said that he only had to shake off Miller three times in his career. Miller was known for his sense of humor to calm pitchers, and was especially adept at catching pop flies. He reputedly never dropped a foul fly at Ebbets Field.

Called "Mooney" because of his distinctly round face, Miller amassed 3,870 putouts and 1,053 assists and was charged with only 135 errors in 5,058 chances for a .973 fielding average. His work with the lumber was less notable. He was steady, but showed only occasional power.

★ ★ ★ ★ ★

Lowell Otto Mueller was born on June 1, 1889 to Mary K. and Ephraim Mueller on a farm near Minden, Nebraska. His father, a Union veteran of the War Between the States, moved the family to Indianapolis, Indiana when he was a small boy where he was raised.

Miller starred in football and baseball for Manual High before beginning his pro career with the Class-C Sharon (PA) Giants (Ohio-Penn League) in 1908. He caught 107 games for the Class-D Duluth (MN) White Sox (Minnesota-Wisconsin League) in 1909, batting only .193. Yet, Brooklyn saw his promising defensive capability and took him in the Rule 5 Draft in September.

Miller got his major league debut on July 16, 1910 with the Superbas, breaking into the big time at the age of 21 as one of the ten youngest players in the National League. A

backup for regular catcher Bill Bergen in his rookie year, Miller hit .278 in 316 at-bats. After a short stint for seasoning at Louisville in 1911, he was promoted back up to the newly-named Dodgers, so designated because of the difficulty fans and players had in getting to the ballpark dodging the borough's many trolley lines. By 1912, Miller was enjoying his first season as a regular.

Club owner Charles Ebbets bought up an entire block in Brooklyn's Flatbush section, starting in 1908. By early 1913, a beautiful new Ebbets Field was completed. Miller was the catcher when it formally opened on April 9 against the Phillies. When Wilbert Robinson took over as manager with his outsized personality in 1914, Brooklyn became the "Robins."

The Robins won the 1916 NL pennant by 2½ games over the Phillies as Mooney Miller shared receiving duties with Chief Meyers and hit .255. Brooklyn featured leading hitters Jake Daubert (.316) and Zack Wheat (.312) and top pitcher Jeff Pfeffer (25-11).

It was the franchise's first appearance in a World Series. The Robins were beaten in five games by the Red Sox, led by a 21-year-old pitcher named Babe Ruth. Miller caught in two games including Ruth's 14-inning victory in Game 2, the longest game in Series history.

Miller's signature campaign was 1920, when he posted a career-high .289 average and led all NL catchers in fielding with a .986 percentage. The Robins were seven games ahead of the Giants at the end, despite being the oldest team in history to go to the Fall Classic.

Miller competed in six games in the 1920 World Series and found himself a part of baseball lore in Game 5. Deadlocked at two games each with Cleveland, the Robins trailed in the fifth inning, 7-0. Pete Kilduff led off with a single and Miller followed with his own. With a 3-2 count and the base runners going, Brooklyn pitcher Clarence Mitchell smashed a line drive to the right side

> *"Well, Otto Miller, from first base, was just standing there, with his mouth open, not more than a few feet away from me. I simply took a step or two over and touched him lightly on the right shoulder, and that was it. Three out."*
>
> *~ Bill Wambsganss on his unassisted triple play in the 1920 World Series*

G	AB	R	H	2B	3B	HR	RBI	SB	BB	SO	BA	OBP	SLG	TB
927	2836	229	695	97	33	5	231	40	104	301	.245	.275	.308	873

for what looked to be a sure hit. Indians second baseman Bill Wambsganss dashed a few steps to his right and made a leaping grab of the liner. He quickly stepped on second, doubling up Kilduff, and then was surprised to see Miller standing a bit shocked just a few feet from the bag. Wambsganss tagged Miller to finish off the only unassisted triple play in World Series history. Brooklyn never recovered, losing the next two games without scoring a run.

Miller caught in his final big-league game on September 24, 1922 at the relatively young age of 33. In 1923, the Dodgers appointed Miller player-manager of the Double-A Atlanta (GA) Crackers of the Southern Association. While managing a colorful young Babe Herman, he also hit .267 in 326 at-bats. In 1924, he coached under Donie Bush and played in 43 games for the Class Double-A Indianapolis (IN) Indians of the American Association, hitting .377.

After a season playing for the independent, semi-pro Brooklyn Bushwicks at Dexter Park, Miller served as a Dodgers coach from 1926 to 1936. His coaching longevity was due to his acumen in pitching and catching, as well as his tolerant nature. He was good at soothing over the ruffled feelings of young players who had just been upbraided by the manager. After 24 years of cumulative Dodgers service, he was released after the 1936 season, at the same time as manager Casey Stengel. His final baseball work was as a scout for Brooklyn and then the Red Sox.

Starting in 1938, he ran the Eastern Baseball School for many years at Dexter Park. He also spent time on Wall Street, worked at the World's Fair and managed a bar and grille in Brooklyn. He and his wife, the former Madeline Dowe, raised two sons and a daughter.

Mooney Miller died on March 29, 1962 at age 72 when he fell from the fourth story window of the Brooklyn Eye & Ear Hospital where he had just had cataract surgery. He was laid to rest at St. John's Cemetery in the village of Goshen, New York in upstate Orange County.

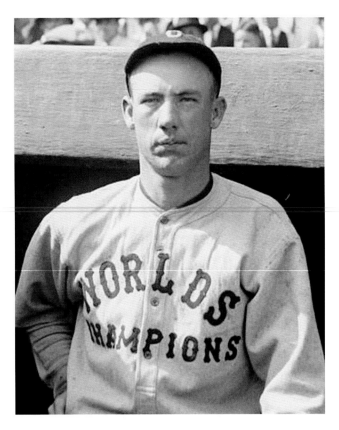

GUY MORTON

CLEVELAND NAPS & INDIANS
RIGHT-HANDED PITCHER

1914-1924

Guy Morton was the first native Alabamian to win 100 games as a professional pitcher. Called the "Alabama Blossom," he still rates among the all-time top ten Cleveland moundsmen in ERA, shutouts and strikeouts. Morton's best work was from 1915 to 1919 when his ERA was below 3.00 each year. Only Hall of Famer Bob Feller has tossed more one-hitters for the Indians.

★ ★ ★ ★ ★

Guy Morton was born on June 1, 1893 to Mary E. Nelson and Martin Morton in Vernon, Lamar County, Alabama. The youngest of nine siblings, he developed his pitching accuracy by hunting squirrels with rocks in rural west Alabama close by the Mississippi border.

The 6'1" 175-pound Morton broke in with the Class-D Columbus (GA) Joy Riders of the Cotton States League in 1913. The next spring he was sent to the Waterbury (CT) Contenders of the Class-B Eastern Association. Backed by a team that boasted seven future major leaguers, he went 8-1 with a 1.49 ERA in 103 innings pitched, allowing only 17 runs. When Morton threw a no-hitter on June 16, the Cleveland Naps promptly bought up his contract.

He began his major league career on June 20, 1914, but got off to an inauspicious start. Morton was defeated in his first 13 decisions, setting a record for most consecutive losses to begin a career. He pitched well with a 3.02 ERA, finally winning his last game, but got no run support. The Naps scored just 538 runs and earned the worst record in franchise history (51-102).

Napoleon Lajoie was sold to the Athletics in 1915 and the club was renamed the "Indians." Morton had his best year, ranking second in the AL with six shutouts. He won 16 games and paced the Tribe with 240 innings pitched, 15 complete games and a 2.14 ERA. His showcase was an August 24 one-hit, 6-0, whitewash of the Yankees at Cleveland's League Park.

On June 11, 1916, Morton became only the second hurler in AL history (Walter Johnson was the first) to strike out four hitters in one inning. His 13 Ks that day were the most in Major League Baseball that year. Morton pitched another one-hitter on June 1, 1917, versus the Red Sox at Fenway Park. A single by Boston's pitcher, Babe Ruth, was the only safe hit in a 3-0 gem.

Although used in relief as much as he started in 1916 and 1917, he was returned to the regular starting rotation in 1918, going 14-8 with a 2.64 ERA. Morton was fourth best in the AL with 123 strikeouts and led the Junior Circuit with 5.2 strikeouts per nine innings.

He tossed another one-hitter on May 23 at Fenway Park, beating Sad Sam Jones, 1-0. The Indians had been closing in on Boston, but settled for second place, 2½ games out. The campaign was cut short by a month, due to the escalating American involvement in World War I.

The 1920 Indians nipped the White Sox for the American League pennant. Morton pitched well through the first half and hurled his fourth career one-hitter on July 31, besting Sad Sam Jones again, 2-1. However, he was not himself in his next four starts. After teammate Ray Chapman was beaned by the Yankees' Carl Mays on August 16, he and Jack Graney carried the mortally stricken shortstop off the field to the Polo Grounds visitors' clubhouse.

Perhaps still shaken by the sudden demise of his comrade, Morton allowed 12 runs on August 21 to the same Boston lineup he had one-hit three weeks earlier and was yanked from the rotation. He saw no action in the Indians' first ever World Series win over the Brooklyn Robins.

The Deadball Era was effectively over by 1921 with whiter, fresher, more tightly wound baseballs being brought into play to prevent a repeat of the Chapman tragedy. Morton remained in the bullpen for most of 1921, but posted a low 2.76 ERA and led the AL with five relief wins.

"They [The Indians] weren't much better in 1915, but Morton was. It remains one of the best pitching seasons in franchise history, comparable with CC Sabathia (2007) and Cliff Lee's (2008) recent Cy Young winning campaigns."

~ writer Jason Lukehart

G	IP	W	L	PCT	SHO	GS	CG	H	ER	SO	BB	ERA
317	1629.2	98	86	.533	19	185	82	1520	567	830	583	3.13

His strong showings helped him work his way back into the rotation for 1922, when he once again led the American League in strikeouts per nine innings. Morton worked exclusively in relief in 1924 and had difficulty with his command, walking 13 hitters in $12^1/_3$ innings.

On June 6, he mopped up in an 11-7 loss, pitching a scoreless ninth inning in his final big-league game at 31. Five days later Morton was released to the Double-A Kansas City (MO) Blues and later pitched for the Indianapolis (IN) Indians of the American Association.

His professional career was far from over. From 1925 to 1927, he was a workhorse for the Memphis (TN) Chickasaws in the Class-A Southern Association, posting an aggregate 39-39 record with a 3.17 ERA in 126 games pitched and toiling 692 innings. Morton returned to the Southern Association in 1928 and part of 1929, throwing for the Mobile (AL) Bears and finishing with the Birmingham (AL) Barons. He wrapped up his career with the Class-C High Point (NC) Pointers of the Piedmont League in 1930 and 1931.

By the summer of 1933 Morton was living back in his native Alabama, working for the Tennessee Valley Authority (TVA), a company established as part of President Franklin Delano Roosevelt's New Deal and charged with modernizing the largely impoverished region.

On March 24, 2001, an expert panel selected the "Top 100 Greatest Indians" to celebrate the franchise's 100th anniversary. Morton was named as one of the top 36 pitchers and ranked #68 overall. He was inducted posthumously into the Alabama Sports Hall of Fame in 2003.

Morton passed away at his home in Sheffield, Alabama from a heart attack at 41 on October 18, 1934, leaving behind his wife Edna and a young son. Guy "Moose" Morton, Jr. would go on to play football and basketball for the Alabama Crimson Tide and have a one at-bat cup of coffee with the 1954 Red Sox. Guy Morton was laid to rest in the Vernon City Cemetery.

DEACON PHILLIPPE

LOUISVILLE COLONELS & PITTSBURGH PIRATES
RIGHT-HANDED PITCHER

1899-1911

"Deacon Phillippe wanted to hurl against the other team's best pitcher and often worked out of turn to do it."

~ teammate Honus Wagner

Deacon Phillippe is the preeminent control pitcher in modern baseball history. His 1¼ walks per nine innings is the lowest ratio ever of any hurler after the distance of 60'6" was established in 1893. A workhorse, he toiled over 2,600 innings while issuing a mere 363 walks.

Phillippe never had a losing season, won 20 games six times and owned a microscopic 2.59 ERA. He will always be recalled as the winner of the first World Series game. During Baseball's 1969 Centennial, fans voted him the Greatest Right-Handed Pitcher in Pirates History.

Though not a clergyman, he came by the name "Deacon" early because of his reserved temperament, humble manner and moderate lifestyle. His mound success was due to impeccable command of his fastball and curveball and an uncanny knack of keeping hitters off balance.

★ ★ ★ ★ ★

Charles Louis Phillippe was born on May 23, 1872 to Margaret Hackler and Andrew Jackson Phillippe in Rural Retreat, Virginia, a hamlet in Wythe County where his ancestors had lived for generations. He was one of eight children with five sisters and two brothers.

When he was just three, his family relocated to the Dakota Territory. He learned baseball on the prairies and toiled semi-professionally there for years. The 6' 180-pound Phillippe pitched for the 1896 Mankato (MN) Merchants, and then signed with Minneapolis of the Western League. After going 21-19 in 1898 for the Millers, he was drafted by the Louisville Colonels.

Phillippe did not get his National League debut until he was almost 27 on April 21, 1899. A month later on May 25, he pitched a 7-0 no-hitter facing the Giants in his seventh start. He would go on to register a 21-17 mark in 321 innings pitched for the eighth place Colonels.

When the NL contracted to eight teams in 1900, Colonels owner Barney Dreyfus purchased the Pirates and merged his best Louisville players. With the aid of Phillippe's 20 wins, the Pirates met the Brooklyn Superbas in the first *Pittsburgh Chronicle-Telegraph* Cup. He pitched the Bucs' only victory in Game 3, a 10-0 shutout.

The Pirates took the 1902 National League pennant with a 103-38 record, featuring a talented pitching staff including Jack Chesbro, Jesse Tannehill, Sam Leever, Ed Doheny and Phillippe. The Deacon notched 20 victories for the fourth consecutive year.

Yet, his signature campaign was 1903 when he and Leever had to step into the breach after Tannehill and Chesbro bolted to the new American League. Phillippe pitched a two-hitter in the opener against Cincinnati. When the staff notched a record six straight shutouts during June, Phillippe pitched two of the games. He finished a stellar 25-9 for the NL Champions.

After a bitter two-year turf war, the upstart American League and the National League made peace and agreed to play the first "World's Series" in a best five-of-nine showdown. The Pirate pitching was thin as 25-game winner Leever had injured his arm in a trapshooting accident, and eccentric lefty Ed Doheny, a 16-game-winner, had suffered a nervous breakdown.

Phillippe responded by winning the inaugural World Series game against the Boston Americans on October 1, 1903. He outdueled 28-game winner Cy Young, 7-3, while striking out a season-high ten hitters and issuing no walks. He followed up with a four-hitter to win Game 3 at Boston's Huntington Avenue Grounds. After a long train trip home and a postponement, he pitched a rain-soaked Game 4 and won a cliff-hanger, 5-4, surviving a ninth inning Boston rally.

With the Series knotted at three each, Phillippe pitched valiantly before an expectant home throng in Game 7, but lost to Young, 7-3. Three days later, exhausted but tenacious, he was nipped in the Game 8 finale, 3-0. His fielders let him

G	IP	W	L	PCT	SHO	GS	CG	H	ER	SO	BB	ERA
372	2607	189	109	.634	27	289	242	2518	749	929	363	2.59

P

down with seven errors in the final two games. He pitched 44 innings, five complete games and three victories in 13 days, walking only three batters with a 2.86 ERA. Dreyfus rewarded him with ten shares of stock in the club.

The Deacon parlayed his fame by playing basketball that winter for Honus Wagner's famous "Pittsburg Five" hard-court team. However, he fell ill in 1904 with a virus that settled in his eyes and was hospitalized in late May. It resulted in his worst year- 10-10 with a 3.24 ERA.

Phillippe came back the next year to win 20 games with a 2.19 ERA. But by 1906, he started experiencing the recurring arm ailments that would afflict him for the rest of his career. He started 50 games and relieved in 18 more over two years, going an aggregate 29-21.

The veteran pitcher performed as a spot-starter and reliever for the 1909 World Series Champion Pirates in their first year at Forbes Field. He was 8-3 with a 2.32 ERA, and pitched six scoreless innings in the Fall Classic as the Bucs overcame Ty Cobb's Detroit Tigers in seven.

The next season Phillippe was mostly a reliever, using guile and deception, and finished 14-2 with a 2.29 ERA. He won his last 13 decisions, which turned out to be the final victories of his career when the 40-year old left the Pirates after a several ineffective appearances in 1911.

He returned to organized baseball the next year as the player-manager of the Pittsburgh Filipinos (a takeoff on his surname) of the United States League. In 1913 he skippered the short-lived outlaw Federal League Pittsburgh entry, also called the Filipinos.

Deacon Phillippe lived the remainder of his days in the greater Pittsburgh area, scouting for the Pirates and working in the ticket office. He also owned a cigar store, acted as a court bailiff, and worked with the Allegheny County Parks Department. Phillippe died while watching TV in his Avalon home at age 79. He is buried in Pittsburgh's Allegheny County Memorial Park.

NAP RUCKER

BROOKLYN SUPERBAS & DODGERS & ROBINS
LEFT-HANDED PITCHER

1907-1916

Fireballing Nap Rucker was one of the Deadball Era's best left-handed pitchers. He burst suddenly on the National League scene directly from Class-C, gaining baseball's attention with his electrifying fastball. Just as unexpectedly, he flamed out in an all too short career.

Baseball Magazine selected the 5'11" 190-pound Rucker for its National League All-Star team four times and its Major League All-Star squad three times. The legendary sportswriter Ring Lardner picked him for his all-time All-Star lineup.

The Brooklyn franchise was mostly dreadful during his tenure. The team won exactly half of its games when Rucker got the decision. Without him, it lost 175 more games than it won. Yet the gentlemanly Rucker appreciated hurling for the vocal, blue-collar Flatbush fans.

Rucker's 38 shutouts (11 ended 1-0) represented 28 percent of his wins, the second highest ever, behind only Big Ed Walsh. His 2.42 career ERA was 16 percent below the NL average of 2.87. He was a Giant Killer, always pitching stoutly against the NL rival Giants.

Despite hurling for a second-rate club, Rucker earned a first-rate reputation as a hard thrower with near-perfect command and an unflappable, steady disposition. His delivery was so smooth that his "sneaky fast" heat surprised hitters as it exploded through the strike zone.

$\star$ $\star$ $\star$ $\star$ $\star$

George Napoleon Rucker was born on September 30, 1884 to Sarah Hembree and Confederate veteran John Rucker in Crabapple, Fulton County, Georgia. Red-headed and freckle-faced, he worked as a printer's apprentice after quitting school. One day he typeset: *$10,000 FOR PITCHING A BASEBALL* and decided right there to become a pitcher.

Bill Nye, well-known as the bodyguard to presidents Teddy Roosevelt, Taft and Wilson, observed him throwing for a local semi-pro team and recommended Rucker to the Atlanta (GA) Crackers of the Class-A Southern League. His first professional game was September 2, 1904.

He was farmed out to the Class-C Augusta (GA) Tourists of the South Atlantic League in 1905 and roomed with teammate Ty Cobb. The two Georgians often went to the ballpark early so the left-handed hitting "Georgia Peach" could practice against a left-handed thrower.

After posting a 13-11 record in 1905, he started off his 1906 Augusta campaign red hot and finished the year at an eye-popping 27-6. That off-season, Brooklyn Superbas owner Charles Ebbets drafted Rucker for $500 and gave him his debut on April 15, 1907.

The 22-year-old rookie suddenly established himself as the ace of the staff. He went 15-13 and led the club with 275 1/3 innings pitched, 131 strikeouts and a 2.06 ERA. He was even better in 1908, miraculously winning 17 games for a 53-101 Brooklyn edition. At Washington Park on September 5, Rucker pitched a no-hitter, striking out 14 Boston Doves without walking a single batsman. Only Brooklyn's porous defense denied him a perfect game.

On July 24, 1909, Rucker struck out 16 Cardinals in a 1-0 victory, tying the modern mark for a nine-inning game held by Rube Waddell and Noodles Hahn. He was the best pitcher on an inferior team, going 13-19 with a 2.24 ERA, while ringing up a career-high 201 NL hitters.

After NL-highs in 1910 of 320 1/3 innings pitched, 27 complete games, and six shutouts, Rucker began 1911 0-6 on ten runs of support. He finished 22-18 for 34+ percent of the Dodgers' 64 wins. He was one out away from a no-hitter on July 22 before the Reds' Bob Bescher singled.

Rucker had lost his dominant stuff by 1913. He adapted and relied on a knuckleball and slow curveball to fashion another workhorse 260-inning year. A poll of sportswriters identified him as the best southpaw pitcher in baseball that year.

"Rucker is the finest pitcher I have ever seen. Yes, even greater than Mathewson. Rucker is the best that ever stepped on the pitcher's mound."

~ Giants manager John J. McGraw

G	IP	W	L	PCT	SHO	GS	CG	H	ER	SO	BB	ERA
336	2375.1	134	134	.500	38	274	186	2089	639	1217	701	2.42

By 1914, Rucker's arm was shredded. For his last three years, he pitched well only with two full weeks rest. He was also a mentor to many Brooklyn players, including Casey Stengel, spending many a pre-game morning helping Stengel to learn to hit his nemesis low pitch.

Rucker was a favorite of Mr. Ebbets, who always waved off probes about his trade availability. He was loyal to the franchise and vocal about a player's moral obligation to his home city fans, even as eight of his teammates jumped to the outlaw Federal League in 1914.

To earn his 134th and final career victory, Rucker pitched $5\frac{2}{3}$ innings of scoreless relief on August 1, 1916 against Cincinnati. The club held a "Nap Rucker Day" at Ebbets Field on October 2 to honor him as the franchise's best pitcher of the Deadball Era.

Knowing the veteran warhorse was retiring after the World Series, manager Wilbert Robinson gave him two innings in relief in Game 4 of the 1916 Fall Classic. He pitched scoreless ball, striking out three Red Sox in his satisfying last appearance as a big-league pitcher.

Rucker and his wife of almost 60 years Edith retired to their mansion called "Great Oaks" in Roswell, Georgia. He owned the local wheat mill, oversaw two small cotton plantations, and also scouted the South for the Dodgers, signing stars Dazzy Vance, Al Lopez and Hugh Casey.

Rucker ran as a Democrat for mayor of Roswell unopposed in 1934, serving two years. During the Depression years, he was influential in bringing running water to the town and later served as its water commissioner for several decades.

In 1967, Rucker became the third professional baseball player behind Ty Cobb and Luke Appling to be inducted into the Georgia Sports Hall of Fame. He passed away at age 86 in Alpharetta, Georgia on December 19, 1970 and is buried in the Roswell Presbyterian Church Cemetery.

LEE TANNEHILL

CHICAGO WHITE STOCKINGS & WHITE SOX
SHORTSTOP - THIRD BASE

1903-1912

Lee Tannehill was considered one of the great middle infielders of the Deadball Era. A Gold Glove-quality infielder long before the award was established, he was an absolute virtuoso at the hot corner and the only shortstop to record two unassisted double plays in the same game.

The human vacuum of his time, Tannehill had the best arm of any third baseman of that early period. He was quick, smooth and sure-handed with great natural instincts, leading AL third basemen in assists four years and range factor three years. Four different Chicago skippers penciled him in the starting lineup, although he was only an ordinary hitter.

★ ★ ★ ★ ★

Lee Ford Tannehill was born on October 26, 1880 to Julia and William Tannehill in Dayton, Campbell County, Kentucky. He grew up as the youngest of three children in a baseball family. Tannehill's ship carpenter father played for the historic Dayton Eagles of the 1860s, one of the founding baseball clubs in Cincinnati, just across the Ohio River from Dayton.

His older brother by six years was Jesse Tannehill, later a left-handed pitcher with five big-league clubs. Tannehill was first scouted on the Queen City sandlots and then excelled for the famous semi-pro Cincinnati Shamrocks in 1899. At age 19 in 1900, he signed on with the independent Richmond Blue Birds of the Class-D Virginia League and played 37 games.

In 1901, Tannehill performed first for the Minneapolis (MN) Millers and then the Colorado Springs (CO) Millionaires in the Class-A Western League. After playing for George Tebeau's Kansas City (MO) Blues and Louisville (KY) Colonels in the American Association in 1902, White Stockings skipper Jimmy Callahan gave him his debut at age 22 on April 22, 1903.

His rookie year did not start out well. On May 6, Chicago committed 12 errors and the Detroit Tigers commit-

ted six. The 18 total established a modern major league mark by two teams in one game. Thirteen of the errors were by infielders- an AL record. Tannehill led the way with four miscues, but the White Stockings rallied in the ninth to squeeze out a 10-9 win.

On August 17, 1904 against the Boston Americans, Tannehill went 0-for-3 hitting against his brother Jesse, who went on to stifle the White Stockings' lineup with the third no-hitter in American League history, a 6-0 complete-game gem on Boston's way to the AL pennant.

The angular 6'1/2" 174-pound Tannehill was the regular third baseman for the 1906 "Hitless Wonders" White Sox. In the middle of a torrid pennant race on September 3, the White Sox were bumped out of first place with a doubleheader sweep by the Cleveland Naps.

In the second game in front of 13,000 Cleveland fans, Tannehill was injured in a collision at third on an attempted double steal and presumed lost for the year. Chicago used speed, pitching and defense to outlast the New York Highlanders by three games to win the AL pennant. The club hit .230 with only seven home runs. Tannehill batted .183 in 116 games.

"Tannie" beat the medical odds and did come back to play in three games in the 1906 World Series. The White Sox overcame the cross-town Cubs in the one and only All-Windy City matchup. The White Sox were victorious despite hitting just .198 in the six game series.

By 1910, Tannehill was a valuable utility man, playing third, shortstop and even first. At the new White Sox Park on July 31, he stroked a windblown fly that bounced under an outfield gate for a grand slam- the first homer in the new park and Tannehill's first four-bagger since 1903. The White Sox hit only two more home runs at home in 1910, both bouncing under outfield gates.

On August 4, 1910 in a 3-2 win over the Nats in Washington, Tannehill became the first and only shortstop to

"Tannehill is a good old war horse. Any youngster who can keep him on the bench will have to look pretty sweet to me. I expect to see him loosen up down in Texas and come back as he has always done in the past."

~ White Sox manager Jimmy Callahan, January 1912

G	AB	R	H	2B	3B	HR	RBI	SB	BB	SO	BA	OBP	SLG	TB
1090	3778	331	833	135	27	3	346	63	229	375	.220	.269	.273	1031

execute two unassisted double plays in the same game. The game was so action-packed the record was not even mentioned in the *Chicago Tribune* write up the next day.

On the Sox's first Opening Day April 24, 1911 before 33,000 fans at the new Southside ballpark, Big Ed Walsh threw a 3-0 three-hitter versus the Browns. Tannehill provided the only run support he needed when he hit a high chopper to shortstop to drive in Shano Collins from third in the fifth. He batted a career-high .254 in 1911 and led all AL shortstops in fielding.

His last year in the majors was an abbreviated one. On May 8, 1912, the White Sox beat Walter Johnson and the Nationals, 7-6, to stop The Big Train's five-game win streak. Although unintentional, a Johnson fastball fractured Tannehill's right forearm. The Washington crowd booed when he rubbed his arm trotting down to first, as the pitch seemed to have struck his bat.

Tannehill gamely went out to his shortstop position the next inning, but his only practice throw to first base proved he was in such pain that he could not continue. The White Sox released him unceremoniously that day, ending his ten-year major league career.

After his arm healed, Tannehill caught on with the Double-A Kansas City (MO) Blues of the American Association that year and part of 1913. He played with the Minneapolis (MN) Millers (1913-14) and the Omaha (NE) Rourkes (1915). Tannehill finished up as the player-manager of the Class-B South Bend (IN) Benders of the Central League (1916) and the player-manager of the Class-C Jacksonville (FL) Roses of the South Atlantic League (1917).

Tannehill lived in South Bend, Indiana during his playing days, but moved to Florida later with his wife Thelma. He passed away on February 16, 1938 at the age of 57 and is buried in the Antioch Baptist Church Cemetery in Live Oak, Suwannee County, Florida.

HONUS WAGNER

LOUISVILLE COLONELS & PITTSBURGH PIRATES SHORTSTOP

1897-1917

> "He was a gentle, kind man, a storyteller, supportive of rookies, patient with the fans, cheerful in hard times, careful of the example he set for youth, a hard worker, a man who had no enemies and who never forgot his friends. He was the most beloved man in baseball before Ruth."
>
> ~ historian Bill James

Honus Wagner was baseball's greatest all-around player during the Deadball Era. His National League standard of 3,420 hits stood for over four decades until finally eclipsed by Stan Musial in 1961. Wagner still is on Major League Baseball's all-time career lists for hits, runs, doubles, triples, total bases, and runs batted in.

Wagner's barrel-chest, broad shoulders, bowlegs, immensely long arms and huge hands belied his athleticism. He led all NL shortstops in fielding 11 times and still was a regular shortstop at the age of 42. Wagner once was timed running to first base in 3.4 seconds from a standing start from the right side and ran 100 yards in ten seconds flat. He led his league in stolen bases five times, stealing home 14 times. His fleetness and his lineage marked him the "Flying Dutchman"–the German *Deutsch* becoming *Dutch*.

In sharp contrast to the "good field-no hit" shortstops of his day, the burly 5'11" 200-pound Wagner averaged over .300 for his first 17 seasons and knocked in 100 runs nine times. He earned the batting title a National League-high eight times, while pacing the Senior Circuit seven times in doubles and six times in slugging percentage.

Wagner's style was to set up in the extreme back corner of the batter's box and step into the pitch, keeping his hands apart on his 50-ounce *Louisville Slugger* so he could shorten up to place the pitch to all fields. Or he would bring his hands together and take a full swing to power one of his record 252 triples.

* * * * *

Johannes Peter Wagner was born in Mansfield, Pennsylvania (now Carnegie) outside of Pittsburgh on February 24, 1874 to Katheryn and Peter Wagner, both im-

migrants from Bavaria. Wagner left school at 12 to go to work in the coal mines with his father. He escaped to play professional baseball at 21 and made his major league debut with the National League's Louisville Colonels on July 19, 1897.

The National League was contracted to eight teams after the 1899 season with Louisville owner Barney Dreyfuss purchasing a 50 percent interest in the Pittsburgh franchise, shifting the Louisville charter to Pittsburgh, and transferring Wagner, manager Fred Clarke and 13 other ballplayers. Wagner was returning home and told Clarke, "I aim to stay a Pirate all my life."

For the next 18 years, Wagner personified loyalty, even to his financial detriment. A representative of the new American League tempted him to bolt to New York in 1901, laying down $20,000 in cash. He immediately refused. It mattered more to Wagner where he played and who his teammates were.

Wagner competed in his first World Series in 1903 against Cy Young's Boston Americans in a losing cause, and his performance was subpar. He got his redemption in Forbes Field's inaugural year when the Pirates beat the Detroit Tigers and Ty Cobb in the 1909 Series, winning their first World Series Championship. Wagner batted .333 (8-for-24) including two doubles, a triple, six RBI and six stolen bases.

In his last season in 1917, Dreyfuss convinced him to be the player-manager, but Wagner lasted less than a week and retired at the end of the year at 43. He coached for Carnegie Tech (now Carnegie Mellon University), and then started a sporting goods store with Pie Traynor. When it went under in 1929, Wagner served briefly as the sergeant-at-arms for the Pennsylvania leg-

G	AB	R	H	2B	3B	HR	RBI	SB	BB	SO	BA	OBP	SLG	TB
2794	10439	1739	3420	643	252	101	1732	735	963	327	.328	.391	.467	4870

P

islature while hiding his bankrupt-
cy from Dreyfuss.

The Pirates discovered his plight
in 1933, offering him a coaching position which he filled with good humor and grace for the next 18 years,
tutoring many Pirate greats early
in their careers. Later he became
a popular raconteur, telling some-
what embellished stories to the de-
light of local audiences.

The Baseball Hall of Fame
opened in 1939, honoring its first
five immortals. Behind only Cobb,
he was second in the voting, tied
with Babe Ruth, ahead of Walter
Johnson and Christy Mathewson.
His Pirates uniform #33 was retired
forever in 1956.

When professional baseball observed its 100th anniversary in
1969, Wagner was selected as the
best shortstop of all-time. Over a
century after Wagner debuted, he
was one of 30 superstars honored
on Major League Baseball's prestigious All-Century Team.

Only about 60 originals exist of
Wagner's 1910 T206 tobacco baseball card with the "Mona Lisa" card
selling in 2007 for $2.8 million. He
was responsible for its scarcity as
he raised objections to his image being used to sell tobacco and the card was recalled. In 1955, a huge statue
of Wagner was unveiled outside the left field gates of

Forbes Field. An elderly Wagner attended the tribute before passing away in his sleep at his home in Carnegie on
December 6. When the Pirates moved to Three Rivers
Stadium in 1970, the statue was relocated there. It now
resides at the main gate entrance of the new PNC Park, a
site near Exposition Park, Wagner's first home field with
the Pirates. It could be said that The Flying Dutchman
had finally come home.

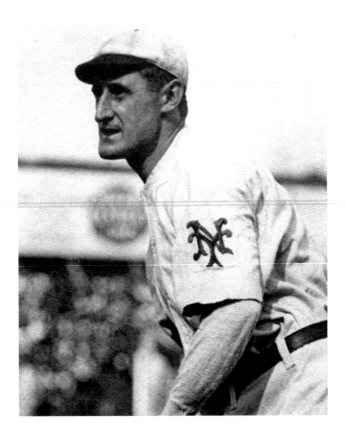

HOOKS WILTSE

NEW YORK GIANTS
LEFT-HANDED PITCHER

1904-1914

"Some pitchers have a peculiar hook delivery, a species of curve which owes its chief baffling influence to the fact that it comes from an unexpected angle while the eye is deceived by a complicated wind-up motion. Wiltse of the Giants is generally known as Hooks on account of his delivery."

~ writer F.C. Lane

Hooks Wiltse teamed up with the great Christy Mathewson to form one of the most successful lefty-righty tandems in history with 435 combined wins. Winning in double figures his first eight seasons, he pitched for five pennant-winners and one World Series champion.

The lean 6' 185-pound Wiltse was the only left-handed starter to pitch consistently for manager John J. McGraw until Rube Marquard joined the rotation in 1909. The tall side-wheeler was dubbed "Hooks" as one of the first hurlers to throw his curve as effectively as his fastball.

With deep-set eyes and a wad of tobacco in his mouth, he compiled a .615 winning percentage on 139 victories. However, his tobacco habit cost him at least one win. In a game against the Reds on June 19, 1905, he swallowed his chaw, suffering major stomach distress.

★　★　★　★　★

George LeRoy Wiltse was born on September 7, 1879 to Jane and Henry Wiltse on the family farm in tiny Pecksport, Madison County, New York. The youngest of nine, he was introduced to baseball by his brother Lewis (eight years older), a future big-league pitcher. His father moved the family to Syracuse when he was 16 and entered the carpet business.

Wiltse began professional baseball in 1902 with the independent Scranton (PA) club. After the league dissolved in June, he signed a contract with the visiting Troy Trojans of the Class-B New York State League. He went 20-8 in 1903 and the Giants purchased his contract.

Wiltse had the best start of any pitcher in major league history. He made his debut on Opening Day 1904, beat the Brooklyn Superbas in his first start on May 29, and kept reeling off victories until he was defeated at the hands of the Cincinnati Reds on September 22.

Wiltse won 12 straight games to open his career. It is a record that has never been eclipsed, although it was equaled by Giants and Padres hurler Butch Metzger from 1974 to 1976. Wiltse finished at 13-3 with a 2.84 ERA and hit .340. He married Della Schaffer that November.

As McGraw's #5 starting pitcher in 1905, Wiltse went 15-6 with a 2.47 ERA, helping the Giants to the pennant. From there he just observed from the dugout as his roommate Mathewson pitched the Giants to a World Series title with three complete-game shutouts in six days.

Over the next two years Wiltse won a combined 29 games and set a mark that may never be broken. On May 15, 1906, he punched out seven hitters in successive innings. After fanning three Reds in the fourth, he whiffed four more in the fifth. Catcher Roger Bresnahan could not handle the third strike on leadoff hitter Jim Delahanty, who reached first.

Wiltse's high water mark was 1908 when he supplanted Joe "Iron Man" McGinnity as the Giants' #2 starter and went 23-14 with a 2.24 ERA. He labored 330 innings and established career-bests with 44 games pitched, 38 starts, 30 complete games and seven shutouts.

On July 4, 1908, Wiltse pitched the front end of a twin bill in Philadelphia. He retired the first 26 Phillies batters in a row before the opposing pitcher George McQuillan came to the plate. On a 1-2 pitch, he threw strike three, but umpire Cy Rigler inexplicably called it a ball.

Wiltse then nicked McQuillan with his next offering. When his teammates pushed across a run in the top of the tenth, he settled for a major league record ten-inning no-hitter. Rigler later admitted that he missed the call and spent years giving Wiltse cigars as a form of apology.

Wiltse also had a part in one of the most famous incidents in history on September 23, 1908. He was coaching first base when Fred Merkle failed to touch second base on a would-be game-winning hit that ultimately cost the team a win over Chicago. The Cubs reached the World Series after beating the Giants in the makeup

G	IP	W	L	PCT	SHO	GS	CG	S	H	ER	SO	BB	ERA
339	2053	136	85	.615	27	222	151	28	1843	565	948	491	2.48

game for the tie that the Merkle boner had created.

For the second straight season, Wiltse won 20 games in 1909. He went 20-11 with a 2.00 ERA but only pitched 269$^1/_3$ innings, unable to maintain the same workload he had carried in 1908. He still pitched well in the cold weather, but was wearing down in the heat of the summer.

Wiltse turned age 30 in 1910, the last year he pitched over 200 innings. He finished with a 14-12 record and a 2.72 ERA. McGraw was aware that Wiltse was beginning to decline and used him judiciously so he could contribute to the 1911 and 1912 pennant-winning seasons.

By that time, Wiltse's skills were eroding noticeably and McGraw limited his pitching opportunities during the 1912 season. After throwing just 57$^2/_3$ innings with no decisions despite a 1.56 ERA, he did not toss a single pitch in the 1912 World Series loss to the Boston Red Sox.

Beset with injuries entering the 1913 Fall Classic, McGraw placed Wiltse at first base in Game 2 at Shibe Park. With Mathewson pitching in the ninth inning with a 0-0 tie, no out and A's on second and third, the next two batters hit sharp grounders to him. Wiltse gunned down the winning run at the plate twice with the game on the line. The Giants won in the tenth, 3-0.

In 1914, the Giants used Wiltse in only 20 games and then released him on August 29. He started the 1915 season with the Jersey City (NJ) Skeeters in the Double-A International League and then moved to the Brooklyn

Tip-Tops of the short-lived outlaw Federal League.

Wiltse was a player-manager through 1924, mainly with the International League's Buffalo Bisons. He was the Yankees pitching coach under manager Miller Huggins in 1925. Wiltse retired after spending 1926 back in the IL with the Reading (PA) Keystones at age 46.

He was elected to the International League Hall of Fame (1952) and the Greater Syracuse Sports Hall of Fame (1990). Wiltse passed away from emphysema at age 79 on January 21, 1959, in Long Beach, New York and is interred in Syracuse's Oakwood-Morningside Cemetery.

THE ROARING 20s
1920-1930

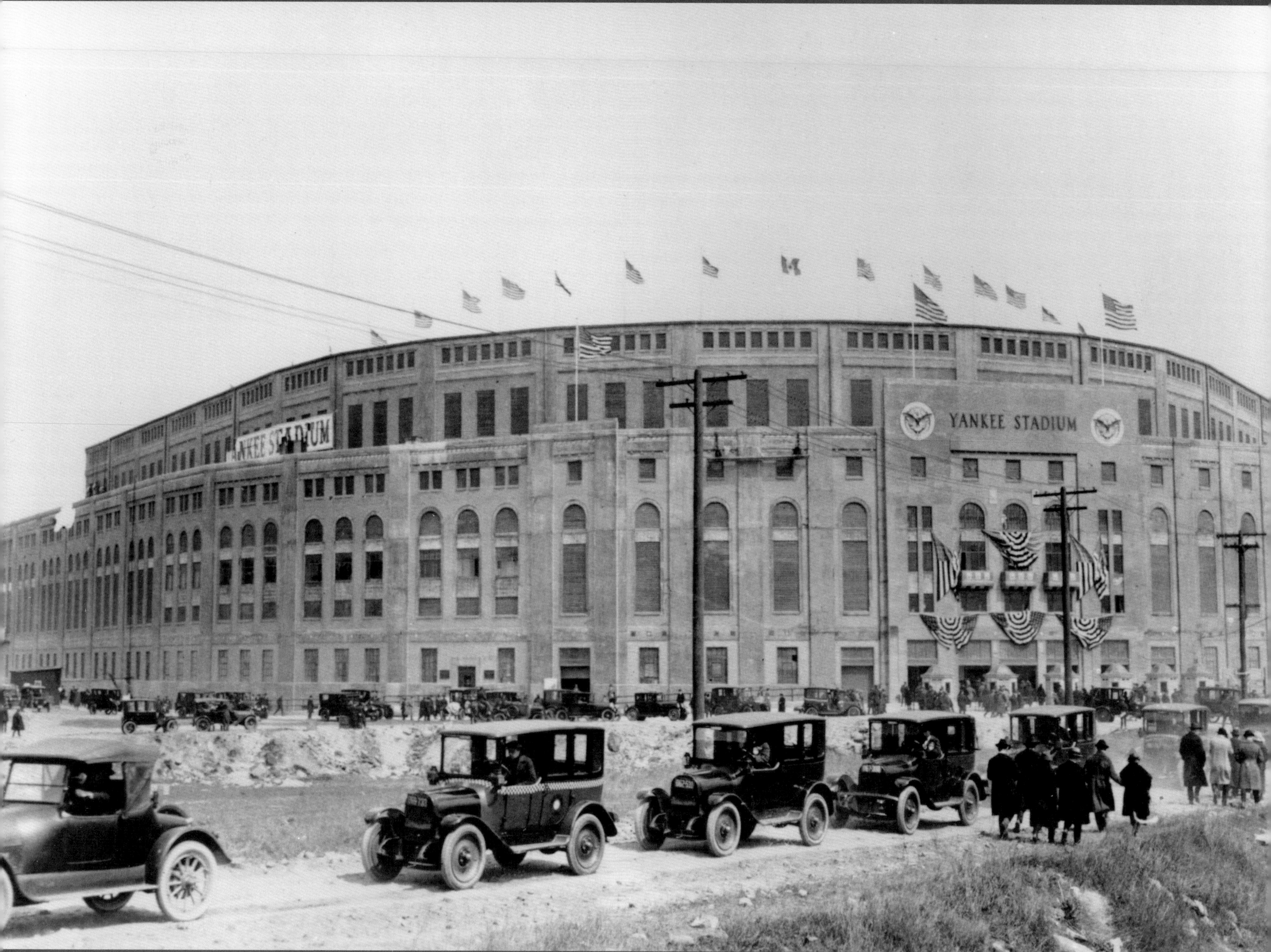

Old Yankee Stadium Opening Day 1923 –
Bronx, New York

CARSON BIGBEE

PITTSBURGH PIRATES
LEFT FIELD

1916-1926

*"There's no crying
in baseball!!"*

~ *actor Tom Hanks in*
A League of Their Own

Carson Bigbee began his career in baseball's Deadball Era as a teammate of Honus Wagner and finished out in the Roaring 20s as a teammate of Pie Traynor. A .287 lifetime hitter, he was a member of the 1925 World Series Champion Pittsburgh Pirates.

A reliable left-handed contact hitter, Bigbee was the consummate leadoff man. He put the ball in play, striking out an infinitesimal 161 times in 4,192 career at-bats. His ratio of at-bats to strikeouts of .0384 even topped the great Joe DiMaggio's .0541.

The 5'9" 157-pound Bigbee came to be known as "Skeeter" because of his slight build, his quickness and his exceptional agility. He swiped a career-high 31 bases for two consecutive years and ranked in the top five in the National League in stolen bases three times. Bigbee still remains on the Pirates all-time stolen bases list. He also ranked in the top five in the NL in triples three times and led the Senior Circuit in singles twice.

Bigbee played all but 42 games of his career as an outfielder. As a leftfielder, he appeared in 892 games, accepted 2,006 chances, grabbed 1,819 putouts, had 118 assists (including 27 double plays), committed only 69 errors, and posted a fine .966 fielding average. His relatively weak throwing arm was the only skill that kept him from playing center field, as he was blessed with extraordinary running speed and great hands.

★ ★ ★ ★ ★

Carson Lee Bigbee was born in Waterloo, Linn County, Oregon on March 31, 1895 to Callie Morris and Claiborne Fox Bigbee. He was the youngest of three brothers. His older brother Lyle pitched for the Pirates and was a teammate in 1920 and 1921.

He starred for the University of Oregon Ducks from 1913 to 1915 and started his professional career with the Class-B Tacoma (WA) Tigers in the Northwestern League in 1916. Bigbee hit .340 in 111 games before earning his major league debut on August 24.

At Ebbets Field on August 22, 1917, the Pirates played the Brooklyn Robins in a third straight extra-inning game. The Robins won in 22 innings, 6-5, with the 22-year-old Bigbee coming to the plate 11 times. He equaled the big-league record with six hits.

With the beginning of the Liveball Era in 1920, Bigbee's offensive output began to progress to a higher plateau. He started to drive the ball into the outfield gaps for extra bases, and continued to steal bases at a fast clip, hitting .280 in 137 games.

Bigbee reached his high water mark during the 1921 and 1922 seasons, pacing the NL in singles and registering over 600 at-bats each year. Bigbee hit .323 in 1921 with 100 runs scored, 23 doubles and 17 triples, including a 23-game hitting streak. In 1922, he finished fourth in the NL batting race at .350 and fifth in RBI with 99. He accumulated 113 runs, 215 hits, 29 doubles, 15 triples, 24 steals and an on-base percentage of .405.

His subsequent downward spiral could not have been more precipitous. Although Bigbee hit .299 in 123 games in 1923, his production eroded significantly thereafter. He was relegated to a backup role in his last three major league campaigns. He contended with weakened vision and irregular health for the balance of his career.

As a reserve with the 1925 National League Champion Pirates, he went 1-for-3 with a pinch-hit RBI double in the eighth inning of Game 7 of the World Series versus the Nationals and pitcher Walter "Big Train" Johnson. Pittsburgh overcame a 3-1 game deficit, and he received the winning share of $5,332.72 and a ring for his efforts.

In Boston on September 25, 1926, the Pirates released

G	AB	R	H	2B	3B	HR	RBI	SB	BB	SO	BA	OBP	SLG	TB
1147	4192	629	1205	139	75	17	324	182	344	161	.287	.345	.369	1545

veteran Stuffy McInnis near his home in Gloucester, Massachusetts. He told the Boston writers about a team vote that had been taken as to whether current stockholder and former Pirate manager Fred Clarke should be asked to remove himself from the Pirates dugout during games.

Manager Bill McKechnie and Clarke were philosophical opposites and the clash came to a head after a twin bill loss to the Boston Braves in August. Pirate captain Max Carey called a team meeting in order to pass a resolution banning Clarke from the field.

Carey became the sacrificial lamb in what would become known as the "Great Pirate Mutiny." The owner's son, Sam Dreyfuss (his father Barney in Europe) suppressed the uprising by suspending Carey and then shipped him off to the Dodgers. The fading Bigbee also became collateral damage when he and 44-year-old Babe Adams were both given their release. The three protested to NL president John Heydler, but to no avail.

During his 11 years in the Steel City, Bigbee played with 11 National Baseball Hall of Fame teammates- Carey, Joe Cronin, Frankie Frisch, Burleigh Grimes, George Kelly, Kiki Kuyler, Rabbit Maranville, Casey Stengel, Traynor, Paul Waner and Wagner. His career ended at a regrettably early age (31) like many other players of his time.

Bigbee married Grace Ellen early in his career. The couple raised two daughters, Jean and Maryilyn. After World War II, he became a manager in the All-American Girls Professional Baseball League. The AAGPBL also hired Hall of Fame slugger Jimmie Foxx as a manager. Foxx was the Tom Hanks character in the film *A League of Their Own*. Bigbee skippered the 1948 Springfield (IL) Sallies and 1949 Muskegon (MI) Lassies. Skeeter Bigbee passed away on October 17, 1964 in Portland, Multnomah County, Oregon at age 69 and was buried in Portland's Willamette National Cemetery.

RAY BLADES

"A great baseball man is Ray Blades. A fighter: yes. With a terrible temper: yes. But a great leader: yes. The baseball writers at Columbus and Rochester tell me Ray has lost some of his temperament, but he hasn't lost any of his baseball cunning."

~ *Cardinals General Manager Branch Rickey*

Ray Blades was a smart, hard-nosed player with excellent speed and baseball instincts who hit over .300 in six of his ten major league campaigns. He competed in three Fall Classics with the Cardinals (1928, 1930 & 1931), helping to win the World Series trophy in 1931.

The compact 5'7½" 170-pound Blades was known as an intense competitor with a hair-trigger temper. An outstanding defensive leftfielder with great range, he paced the National League in fielding twice; and putouts, assists, double plays and range factor once each.

★   ★   ★   ★   ★

Francis Raymond Blades was born on August 6, 1896 to Mary Magdalena Donaldson and Francis Marion Blades in Mount Vernon, Hamilton County, Illinois. When he was two years old, his family moved to McLeansboro, Illinois. In 1909, they relocated west to St. Louis Ward 15.

Blades pitched for the Franz Siegel Grammar School nine in the 1913 St. Louis City Championships at Sportsman's Park. The umpire was Branch Rickey, who was then the St. Louis Browns business manager. It was there that Blades and Rickey struck up a friendship. Blades attended McKinley High in St. Louis before his family moved back to McLeansboro in 1915.

In May of 1918, Blades quit his job with St. Louis' Emerson Electric Company and enlisted in the U.S. Army. He soon was in LeHavre, France as a member of the 119th Field Artillery, 32nd Division and fought in the Argonne Offensive until the Armistice was signed.

Blades was back in St. Louis on May 15, 1919. He was playing semi-professional baseball in 1920 with the Fairfield (IL) team when the Cardinals, managed by Branch Rickey, came out to play Fairfield in an exhibition game. Rickey inked him to a contract on the spot.

Blades started with the 1920 Memphis (TN) Chickasaws of the Class-A Southern Association. Promoted to the 1921 Houston Buffaloes in the Class-A Texas League, he got 515 at-bats, and then broke out with the 1922 Buf-

faloes, hitting .330 and slugging .540. At 26, he earned his major league debut on August 19, 1922, playing left field in an 8-7 loss to the Phillies.

The peak of Blades' big-league career was from 1924 through 1926. As the Cardinals' regular leftfielder, he hit a three-year aggregate .320 (427-for-1,334) and played superb defense as St. Louis' fastest ballhawk. While chasing a fly ball at Sportsman's Park late in the 1926 season, however, Blades crashed heavily into the hard right field wall, shattering his kneecap.

Surgery was performed by the Cardinals' team physician Dr. Robert Hyland, but Blades never regained his former running speed. He had batted .305 in almost 500 plate appearances in 1926, but was unable to contribute to the Cardinals' World Series triumph over the Yankees.

He still hit .317 in 1927, but got into only 61 games and probably would have proved ideal as a designated hitter. Unfortunately, the AL DH rule was not instituted until 1973. When the Cardinals sent him to the minors in early 1930, Blades stormed into Rickey's office, kicked the furniture around and told Rickey off in a grand tirade. He begrudgingly spent the entire 1929 season with Houston and the Rochester (NY) Red Wings of the Double-A International League.

Blades came back to St. Louis as a player-coach in 1930. On September 28, the last day of the 1930 season, 20-year old Cardinals rookie Dizzy Dean pitched his 3-1 debut victory over the Pirates. Blades needed a single hit to finish at .400, but went 0-for-2 to drop to .396 (40-for-101) for the year. His final line was impressive with a .504 OBA and a .614 slugging percentage.

The Cardinals hoisted the NL pennant flag in 1931, winning 101 games and upending the favored Athletics in the World Series. By that time, however, Blades' mastery with his *Louisville Slugger* had begun to ebb. He played his last big-league game on September 25, 1932 at age 36.

Blades played a duel role as player-manager in 1933

G	AB	R	H	2B	3B	HR	RBI	SB	BB	SO	BA	OBP	SLG	TB
767	2415	467	726	133	51	50	340	33	331	310	.301	.395	.460	1111

and 1934 for St. Louis' Double-A affiliate, the Columbus (OH) Redbirds. The team took the American Association title both years. After managing Columbus again in 1935, Blades skippered the Rochester Red Wings for three seasons in the International League. His minor league managerial record was 909-755 (.546).

Branch Rickey hired Blades to manage the Cardinals on November 6, 1938. From the inception, he forbade his players to drink alcohol. The 1939 team responded to his tough regimen, winning 92 games to finish in second place in the NL. His lineup included Ducky Medwick, Johnny Mize and Enos Slaughter. In spite of this, when the 1940 squad sputtered to a 14-24 start, owner Sam Breadon gave Blades his walking papers and hired Billy Southworth.

Blades managed the 1941 New Orleans (LA) Pelicans of the Southern Association and did so again in 1943. He led the St. Paul (MN) Saints of the American Association from 1944 to 1946 and then coached for the Reds, Dodgers, Cubs and Cardinals.

Blades never had full-time managerial work again in the major leagues. During his time with Brooklyn, he and fellow coach Clyde Sukeforth both declined the job as the Dodgers' interim manager in 1947 after Leo Durocher's suspension during Jackie Robinson's rookie year.

Dodgers president Branch Rickey ultimately chose scout Burt Shotton and Brooklyn won the 1947 pennant. When the reinstated Durocher bolted the Dodgers for the New York Giants in July of 1948, Blades served as interim Dodgers skipper for a single game before Shotton succeeded him. Blades' final record as a big-league manager was 107–85.

Blades and his first wife, Golda Marie Bennett, were married on October 29, 1924. She passed away in 1968. He and his second wife, Ruth Daily, lived out their years in Lincoln, Illinois. He died there on May 18, 1979 and is buried in the I.O.O.F. Cemetery in McLeansboro.

OSSIE BLUEGE

WASHINGTON NATIONALS
THIRD BASE

1922-1939

*"I've been in the majors
for thirty years but never
have I seen a glove man
like Bluege. Never mind
what he hit... he was
wonderful in that infield."*

~ teammate Luke Sewell

Ossie Bluege spent five decades with his team as a player, coach, field manager and comptroller. From the Roaring 20s to the Depression 30s, he was one of the finest fielding third basemen in baseball. Nationals Owner Clark Griffith proclaimed him the greatest at the hot corner he'd ever seen, and he was chosen on the All-Time Washington Team by C. Norman Willis in his 2003 book *Washington Senators' All-Time Greats.*

The mild-mannered Bluege didn't partake of tobacco or alcohol and was always a team player and a steadying influence. He joins Goose Goslin and Sam Rice as the only three men to play on all the Washington pennant-winners (1924, 1925 and 1933).

Bluege appeared in 1,487 games at the hot corner, leading the American League in assists four seasons and double plays three times. He had sure hands and great reflexes and could play shallower than anyone else, making bunts easier to cover. Bluege enhanced all of the shortstops that played next to him with his range. He was also the first to guard the foul line in late innings. He preferred taking grounders to batting practice.

At 5'11" and 162 pounds, Bluege never hit for great power, but was a reliable right-handed clutch hitter with a career high 98 RBI in 1931. He beat out many an infield hit on sheer foot speed, could work a pitcher for a walk, and was hit by pitches 71 times.

* * * * *

Oswald Louis Bluege was born of German descent on October 24, 1900 in Chicago, Illinois to Olga Gothe and Adam Bluege. He roamed the south side sandlots with his two brothers. One of whom, Otto, later played with the Cincinnati Reds.

Bluege was the shortstop for the Peoria (IL) Tractors (Three-I League) in 1920 and 1921, batting .293 in 140 games the last year. Griffith sent legendary scout Joe Engel to confirm that Bluege's knee injury had healed. Engel signed him for a $3,500 bonus.

The 21-year-old Bluege debuted in the major leagues on April 24, 1922, but was shortly sent down to the Minneapolis (MN) Millers. After hitting .315 in 44 games, he was recalled and installed as the regular third baseman on April 23, 1923.

Experts called the 1924 Nationals infield of Joe Judge, Bucky Harris, Bluege and Roger Peckinpaugh the finest fielding infield of all time. Bluege hit .281 and batted sixth in a "Murderers' Row" order that featured Earl McNeely, Harris, Rice, Goslin, Judge, Peckinpaugh and Muddy Ruel. Washington finished strong, winning 16 of 21.

In World Series Game 1, Bluege scored the tying run in the ninth before his team prevailed in extra innings. In Game 2, he laid down a key ninth inning sacrifice which led to the winning run and drove in two in the eighth inning of Game 4 to ensure a 7-4 win.

Ace Walter Johnson lost his first two Series starts, but the Nats battled back to set the stage in Game 7 at Griffith Stadium. It proved to be one of the most dramatic Series games ever. President Calvin Coolidge and 31,677 fans saw the "Big Train" come on in relief in the ninth and lead Washington to its only world title in a 12-inning cliffhanger.

In 1925, Bluege was among the top ten MVP vote-getters with his .287 average on 150 hits. In Game 1 of the Fall Classic, he rapped out two hits and drove in a run, but was beaned in Game 2 and was ineffective the rest of the Series. The Bucs won in seven.

Bluege moonlighted as an accountant in the off-season, working for some of the best hotels in the nation's capital. Griffith ordered him to stop because he feared

G	AB	R	H	2B	3B	HR	RBI	SB	BB	SO	BA	OBP	SLG	TB
1867	6440	883	1751	276	67	43	848	140	723	515	.272	.352	.356	2290

W

his eyes might be affected, but Bluege needed the money. His salary never reached over $10,000.

By the time the Nationals had won the 1933 pennant, he was a 32-year-old veteran of a dozen major league campaigns. On September 9, he was honored on "Ossie Bluege Day" at Griffith Stadium and received an automobile, a silver service and other gifts.

Starting in 1934, Bluege transitioned into one of the game's most versatile middle infielders. His only All-Star selection came in 1935, when playing mostly second base. He set an American League record in 1936 by accepting 205 chances flawlessly at second base in 37 consecutive games.

Bluege finished his active playing career on July 13, 1939, coached the Nationals for three years, and skippered Washington from 1943 to 1947. He was *The Sporting News* 1945 Major League Manager of the Year. Bluege's 379-394 record included two over-achieving runner-up finishes.

Bluege was appointed farm director in 1948 and became the scout that signed future Hall of Famer Harmon Killebrew in 1954. A U.S. Senator from Idaho, Herman Welker, had tipped off Griffith about a slugger in the Idaho-Oregon League. Bluege flew out to see Killebrew bomb a 435-foot homer and go an eye-popping 12-for-12.

In 1957, he became the team's comptroller shortly before the franchise relocated to Minnesota and served until 1971. Ossie Bluege passed away from cardiac arrest on October 14, 1985 in Edina, Minnesota. He had just returned from a trip to Washington where he had been inducted into the "Washington Hall of Stars" at Robert F. Kennedy Stadium. He left his wife, Wilor Marie Maxwell Bluege, three daughters and three grandsons and is buried in the Lakewood Cemetery in Minneapolis.

EARLE COMBS

*"...if young DiMaggio
turns out to be as
good a ball player as
you were, everybody
will be satisfied."*

~ Yankees General Manager
Ed Barrow

EARLE BRYAN COMBS
NEW YORK YANKEES 1924-1935

LEAD-OFF HITTER AND CENTER FIELDER OF
YANKEE CHAMPIONS OF 1926-'27-'28-'32.
LIFETIME BATTING AVERAGE .325, 200 OR
MORE HITS THREE SEASONS. LED LEAGUE
WITH 231 HITS IN 1927 WHILE BATTING .356,
PACED A.L.IN TRIPLES THREE TIMES AND
TWICE LED OUTFIELDERS IN PUTOUTS.
BATTED .350 IN FOUR WORLD SERIES

Earle Combs was the first of a great triumvirate of Yankee centerfielders who played their entire careers in pinstripes in succession over half a century. He was the catalyst for the devastating lineups of the Roaring 20s and early 30s, peppering line-drives all over the field and setting the table for the feared sluggers of "Murderers' Row."

Combs earned nine Yankee World Series title rings as a player and coach. In 16 Fall Classic games, he hit .350 with a .443 on-base average and had 43 putouts without an error. A skillful bunter who drew long pitch counts, he averaged 75 walks and only 31 strikeouts a season. Combs batted over .300 ten times, rapped out at least 190 hits five seasons and once had a 29-game hitting streak. He was a run-scoring juggernaut, averaging 132 runs scored per year for his career.

At a muscular 6' 185 pounds, the popular "Kentucky Greyhound" used speed and sure hands to pace AL outfielders in putouts three times in route to hauling in an amazing 3,449 in his career. Combs was blessed with incredible running ability. To highlight his speed, he made the three-base hit his calling card. He legged out a Yankee record 23 triples in 1927, averaged 17 triples per season, and topped the AL in triples three times.

Combs was popular with his teammates, the fans and beat writers. Some of his high-spirited teammates couldn't fathom how a Kentuckian didn't drink. A dignified Christian gentleman both on and off the field, he used neither alcohol nor tobacco.

*   *   *   *   *

Earle Bryan Combs was born on May 14, 1899 in rural Pebworth, Owsley County, Kentucky to Nannie Brandenburg and James Jesse Combs, the fifth of seven children. Combs' father supplied his brood with homemade bats from thick poplar tree branches and made baseballs from old shoe leather. The young Combs organized pickup games in the rolling eastern Kentucky farm countryside whenever possible.

Despite his affection for baseball, he aspired to be a teacher first and enrolled at Eastern State Normal School (now Eastern Kentucky University) in Richmond. He soon was starring for the Eastern State team and finished his senior year in 1921 hitting .591. Combs played semi-professionally that summer and gained notice outside the region.

He married his high school sweetheart Ruth McCollum in 1922 (they would raise three sons) and switched his career focus to baseball. Combs signed a contract with the Louisville Colonels that dwarfed his $37 per month teacher's salary and right away began to dismantle American Association pitching. He hit .344 in 1922 and .380 in 1923, becoming notorious for shooting line drives through the infield and into the outfield alleys. With the support of Colonels manager Joe McCarthy (later his Yankees skipper), he quickly developed into a relentless outfield ball hawk, earning the sobriquet "The Mail Carrier" for his fleet outfield play and his clever base running.

The New York Yankees outbid all comers for the young prodigy in early 1924, paying the then extravagant sum of $30,000. Combs enjoyed immediate success in Gotham that summer hitting .400 in his first 40 games, but broke his ankle in a home plate collision in mid-June. The following year manager Miller Huggins installed him as his leadoff hitter. Combs responded by hitting .342 with 203 hits and scored 117 times.

G	AB	R	H	2B	3B	HR	RBI	SB	BB	SO	BA	OBP	SLG	TB
1455	5746	1186	1866	309	154	58	632	96	670	278	.325	.397	.462	2657

The 1927 Yankees are still hailed as one of the best teams in history. The Bronx Bombers ran roughshod over the league with a 110-44 record, spending all 154 games in first place, and winning by 19 games. It would be Combs' finest campaign as he hit a career-high .356 and led the American League with 648 at-bats, 231 hits, 23 triples and 411 putouts.

On July 24, 1934, his career would be altered forever on a 100-degree St. Louis afternoon. In pursuit of a towering drive, Combs barreled into Sportsman's Park's cement outfield wall at full speed, sustaining a fractured skull, a broken shoulder and a damaged knee. He was near death for several days and was hospitalized for over two months.

Combs returned in 1935 only to suffer a broken collarbone in an outfield collision which persuaded him to retire after playing in only 89 games. He was also aware young Joe DiMaggio was coming up the next spring. Combs opted to be a Yankee coach, teaching his young protégé the nuances of the Yankee Stadium outfield.

He remained a coach for almost two decades after his playing days. His Yankee coaching tenure ended after the 1944 season, but ever the teacher, Combs returned to mentor the Browns (1947), Red Sox (1948-1952) and Phillies (1954).

Thereafter, "The Silver Fox" retreated to his farm in Madison County, Kentucky, but stayed active as the Kentucky State Banking Commissioner (1955-1959) and as an Eastern Kentucky University Regent (1959-1975). EKU also honored him as a charter member of its Athletics Hall of Fame. Combs was voted into the National Baseball Hall of Fame by the Veterans Committee in 1970. He passed away in Richmond, Kentucky on July 21, 1976 and was buried in the Richmond Cemetery.

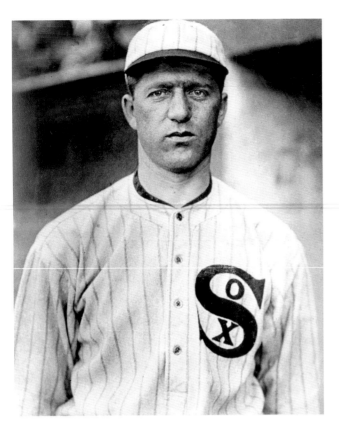

RED FABER

CHICAGO WHITE SOX
RIGHT-HANDED PITCHER

1914-1933

"Red wouldn't throw more than four or five spitters in some games. In fact, his best pitch was his fastball. He'd just keep the batters guessing."

~ battery mate Ray Schalk

Red Faber appeared in more games than any White Sox pitcher in history and was one of only six hurlers to win 100 games in both the Deadball and Liveball eras. A four-time 20-game winner, he was the last legal American League spitball pitcher.

A workhorse, Faber established franchise records for victories, innings pitched, games started and complete games while laboring for second division teams in 15 of his 20 years. Mediocre run support kept him from qualifying for the exclusive 300-win club.

The 6'2" 185-pound Faber had regular success against great hitters such as Babe Ruth and Ty Cobb. Poised and cagey, his approach was to pitch to contact early in the count, forcing hitters to drive his heavy fastball and drop curveball into the ground.

★ ★ ★ ★ ★

Urban Clarence Faber was born on September 6, 1888 to Margaret A. Greif and Nicholas Faber on the family farm near Cascade, Iowa. He was raised with three sisters and a younger brother by Catholic parents born in Germany of Luxembourger descent.

Nicknamed "Red" for his ginger-colored hair, Faber signed with the Dubuque (IA) Dubs of the Class-B Three-I League in 1909. He won 18 games in 1910 and pitched a perfect game over the Davenport (IA) Prodigals. Only one ball reached the outfield.

The Pirates purchased his contract right after the game and he made the 1911 Pittsburgh Opening Day roster. Before pitching an NL inning, he was sent to the Minneapolis (MN) Millers with a sore arm. After discovering the spitball from Millers teammate Harry Peaster, he was sold to the Pueblo (CO) Indians of the Western League.

In the 1912 and 1913 seasons with the Des Moines (IA) Boosters in the same Class-A league, Faber refined his spitball and won 41 games while pitching a remarkable 677⅓ innings. As the 1913 season came to a close, the White Sox bought up his contract.

Faber was part of an around-the-world tour with the Giants that fall. He was loaned to the Giants only to win four exhibition games against his future teammates. It earned him his major league debut on April 17, 1914. He came within three outs of no-hitting the A's on June 17. A slow ground ball was the only hit in the top of the ninth.

In 1915, Faber went 24-14 with a 2.55 ERA while his 50 appearances led the AL. On May 12, he tossed a three-hit shutout, throwing a record-low 67 pitches in defeating the Washington Nationals. Three times he retired the side on just three pitches.

Fighting off an arm injury in 1916, Faber still went 17-9 with a 2.02 ERA for a team that finished runner up, only two games behind the Red Sox. In 1917, he posted a career-low 1.92 ERA with three of his 16 wins coming in starts over a two-day stretch.

Faber was the pitching stalwart of the 1917 World Series. Working 27 innings, he won three games and lost one, including the complete game clincher in Game 6. He still holds the all-time Junior Circuit mark of four pitching decisions in a single Fall Classic.

After serving most of the 1918 season in the Navy, he returned to help the White Sox win the 1919 pennant. He earned 11 victories, but struggled all year with influenza, arm trouble and an ankle injury. He saw action only once during September.

Faber did not appear in the tainted 1919 World Series against the Reds because of his weakened state. The Black Sox Scandal may not have happened had he been healthy. Some of his regular turns went to hurlers on the take- Lefty Williams and Eddie Cicotte.

The Liveball Era dawned in 1920 and Faber came back strong, pitching 319 innings, pacing the league

G	IP	W	L	PCT	SHO	GS	CG	H	ER	SO	BB	ERA
669	4086.2	254	213	.544	29	483	273	4106	1430	1471	1213	3.15

with 39 starts, and compiling a 23-13 record. The spit-ball was barred after 1920, but he was one of 17 hurlers allowed to continue to ply the pitch.

When the eight Black Sox stars were banned after 1920, the team tumbled to seventh place in 1921. His 25 wins accounted for 40+ percent of the Sox's 62 victories that year. He topped the AL with a 2.48 ERA and 32 complete games in 39 starts.

The durable right-hander followed with his third consecutive 20-victory season in 1922 (21-17), leading the AL with 352 innings pitched, 31 complete games and a 2.81 ERA. By 1924, he had dropped down a level. Wear-and-tear had begun to take its toll.

Yet Faber remained effective long past his prime. At age 40 he tossed a one-hitter against Detroit on May 29, 1929, walking none and striking out only two. Faber pitched his last major league game on September 20, 1933 as the league's oldest player at 45.

In the years after retirement, Faber was an auto sales-man, real estate agent and bowling alley owner outside of Chicago. Early in 1946, his old teammate, manager Ted Lyons, hired him as the White Sox pitching coach, a position he held through 1948.

Faber married Irene Walsh in 1920, but she died of a stroke in 1943. He wed Frances Knudtzon in 1947 and had one son, Urban Clarence Faber, Jr. Providing for his family, he worked on a Cook County Highway Department survey crew until he was 79.

Fifty years after his rookie season, Faber was induct-ed into the National Baseball Hall of Fame in 1964. He suffered heart and respiratory illness in his later years and died at his Chicago home on September 25, 1976. Faber's grave marker in Chicago's Acacia Park Cemetery refers to his navy service but does not mention his base-ball renown.

TRAVIS JACKSON

NEW YORK GIANTS
SHORTSTOP

1922-1936

"You'd like him. He's skinny with not much power at the plate just now, but he'll get better as he goes along. But he can hound the ball, and you never saw a shortstop with a better arm. Have somebody look at him. He should be ready for you after one more year in this league."

~ Kid Elberfeld to
John J. McGraw, early 1922

Travis Jackson was a foundational player on four pennant-winning teams and one World Series titlist. The Giants' defensive anchor, he was an elite glove man honored as *The Sporting News* Major League All-Star shortstop for 1927, 1928 and 1929.

Jackson let nothing penetrate his side of the infield. His rock-solid play earned him the nickname "Stonewall" after Confederate chieftain Thomas "Stonewall" Jackson. He had range, sure hands, a quick release and the most powerful infield arm in the game.

Jackson paced NL shortstops in assists four times, total chances three times, and fielding average and double plays twice. Even today, almost 80 years after his retirement, Jackson still tops the Giants shortstop lists with 2,877 putouts and 4,635 assists.

The 5'10" 160-pound Jackson hit over .300 six times and drove in over 70 runs eight times. Showing surprising power for his size, he ranked among the NL's home run leaders four times. He was a master of the sacrifice and one of the best drag bunters ever.

★   ★   ★   ★   ★

Travis Calvin Jackson was born on November 2, 1903 in Waldo, Columbia County, Arkansas, near the Louisiana border, the only child of Etta and William Jackson. He was named for Colonel William Barrett Travis, the commander hero of the Alamo.

When he was 14, his uncle took him to meet Kid Elberfeld, manager of the Little Rock Travelers of the Southern Association. Thereafter, several times each summer, Jackson visited Little Rock and Elberfeld would fungo him ground balls by the hour.

The 17-year old upstart signed with the Travelers and played in 39 games in 1921. He also starred on his college team at Ouachita Baptist College in Arkadelphia. There he first damaged his right knee, an injury that would plague him throughout his career.

In early 1922, Elberfeld tipped off former teammate and Giants manager John J. McGraw about Jackson. After sending scout Dick Kinsella to verify, McGraw purchased Jackson's contract from Little Rock on June 30 to take effect when the season ended.

Chasing a Texas leaguer in midseason, he collided violently with centerfielder Elmer Leifer and sustained such a concussion that he didn't awaken until after the wide gash that connected his eyebrows had been stitched up in the hospital. Jackson didn't stop to heal, playing 147 games. It compromised his immune system for the rest of his life.

He debuted with the Giants on September 27, but unseating veteran shortstop Dave Bancroft seemed remote in early 1923. Yet Bancroft started to experience leg pains, fell ill with pneumonia in late June, and was down for six weeks. Filling in, Jackson impressed by driving in eight runs in one game at Crosley Field on August 8.

McGraw decided to trade Bancroft to the Boston Braves after the season, but the experts questioned the 19-year-old Jackson's readiness. After a slow start and despite committing a National League-high 58 errors, he batted a solid .302 in 151 games.

The Giants earned their fourth straight pennant and met Washington in the World Series. In the ninth inning of Game 7, Walter Johnson came on in relief to shut the team down for three innings. Jackson's error in the last of the twelfth was costly in the loss.

Fully in his prime by 1927, he hit .318 with 14 homers and 98 RBI. His career-high .339 in 1930 added to

G	AB	R	H	2B	3B	HR	RBI	SB	BB	SO	BA	OBP	SLG	TB
1656	6086	833	1768	291	86	135	929	71	412	565	.291	.337	.433	2636

the best hitting infield ever. With Bill Terry at .401, Hughie Critz at .265 and Fred Lindstrom at .379, the foursome sported a combined .349 average.

He served as the Giants captain his last five years. Affected in 1932 by bone chips in his knees, Jackson had surgery. He played just 53 games in 1933. Fully healed, he was the 1934 NL starting All-Star shortstop and finished with a career-high 101 RBI.

Slowing down, Jackson finished out his last two years at third base. The 1936 Game 6 World Series loss to the Yankees was Jackson's last big-league game. He soon signed to skipper the Double-A Jersey City (NJ) Giants and did so until July of 1938.

A Giants coach for the rest of 1938 through 1940, Jackson contracted tuberculosis in 1941. After five long years of recovery in a sanitarium, he returned in 1946 to manage the Class-B Jackson (MS) Senators (Southeastern League) in the Braves farm system.

Manager Mel Ott hired Jackson to his Giants coaching staff in 1947. When Leo Durocher replaced Ott in July of 1948, the Giants and Jackson parted after the season. He managed a total of nine different Braves farm clubs from 1949 through 1960. Finally weary of the long bus treks in the low minors, Jackson retired after the 1960 season.

Jackson was inducted into the National Baseball Hall of Fame in 1982 by a vote of the Veterans Committee. He joined the rest of his 1927 Giant infield (Rogers Hornsby, Lindstrom and Terry), finally given his due as a vital factor in the Giants' Glory Years.

Jackson enjoyed a long, happy marriage of almost 60 years to Mary Blackman, his childhood sweetheart from Waldo. The couple raised a daughter and a son at their home in Waldo. Jackson passed away from Alzheimer's disease on July 27, 1987.

WALTER JOHNSON

WASHINGTON NATIONALS
RIGHT-HANDED PITCHER

1907-1927

"Walter Johnson, more than any other ballplayer, probably more than any other athlete, professional or amateur, became the symbol of gentlemanly conduct in the heat of battle."

~ *writer Shirley Povich*

With the most victories, shutouts and complete games of any 20th century hurler, Walter Johnson has claim to the title of baseball's greatest pitcher. His American League-best 417 wins and 521 complete games were earned mostly with second division teams.

The AL Strikeout King 12 times, wins leader six times and ERA titlist five times, the 6'1" 200-pound Johnson enjoyed 11 seasons with an ERA less than 2.00. He held the career strikeout record until Nolan Ryan surpassed him over a half century later in 1983.

Johnson won at least 20 games a season 12 times and ten years straight (1910-19), averaging over 26 wins a year over that stretch. He lost 65 games when the Nats didn't score at all and holds the standard for number of 1-0 wins (38) as well as 1-0 losses (27).

His fastball came at the hitter like a freight train and arrived in the catcher's mitt sounding like a rifle shot. Called "The Big Train," Johnson started his delivery in the three-quarters slot, and then dropped down to release with a sweeping sidearm motion.

He was admired not only for his pitching virtuosity, but also for his modesty, humility, kindness and dignity. He didn't argue with umpires … didn't doctor the baseball… and didn't brush back hitters, even though he plunked a record 206 batsmen.

Additionally, Johnson could hit and field. He slammed 24 career four-baggers and set an all-time high batting average for pitchers in 1925, batting .433 (42-for-97). In an era of undersized gloves, Johnson fielded at a *Rawlings* Gold Glove-quality .968.

⭐ ⭐ ⭐ ⭐ ⭐

Walter Perry Johnson was born to Minnie Olive Perry and Frank Edwin Johnson near Humboldt, Allen County, Kansas on November 6, 1887. The second of six, he attended Crescent Valley School and worked long hours on his family's 160-acre farm.

After years of drought, his father gave up the farm and moved the family to Olinda, California in 1902 to work as a teamster. Johnson enrolled at Fullerton Union High and began pitching in strong Southern California semi-pro leagues year round.

In 1906, he traveled to throw for the Weiser Kids of the Idaho State League. In his second year, Washington manager Joe Cantillon was reading news about a "Weiser Wonder" and his 86 straight scoreless innings, two no-hitters, and 21-strikeout game.

Cantillon sent a makeshift scout west. Johnson signed and debuted at National Park on August 2, 1907 in front of 500 diehard fans. He had joined a club that was the butt of a vaudeville joke, "First in war, first in peace, and last in the American League."

Over Labor Day 1908, Johnson completed one of the greatest ironman feats ever. With the pitching staff in shambles in New York, he started three games in four days and shut out the Highlanders on a 3-0 five-hitter, a 6-0 three-hitter and a 4-0 two-hitter.

In the first Presidential Opener, Johnson won with William Howard Taft on hand in 1910. Taft inadvertently created the seventh inning stretch ritual when he stood up. Out of respect, the crowd arose, assuming he was leaving, only to see him take his seat again.

In 1912, The Big Train was 32-12 with a 1.39 ERA and 303 strikeouts, taking only 51 days to claim a record sixteenth straight win on August 23. He was even better as the 1913 AL MVP … 36-7, a 1.09 ERA, 12 shutouts, only 38 walks and five one-hitters.

The 1924 Nationals won the pennant. Johnson was the AL Most Valuable Player again with a 23-7 line and

G	IP	W	L	PCT	SHO	GS	CG	H	ER	SO	BB	ERA
802	5914.1	417	279	.599	110	666	531	4913	1424	3509	1363	2.17

Wled the AL in shutouts, ERA and strikeouts. He pitched masterfully in World Series Game 1 versus the Giants but lost 4-3 in 12 innings, throwing 165 pitches. Still fatigued, he turned in a subpar Game 5, losing 6-2.

In Game 7, Johnson was called in to save the day in the eighth with the score tied, 3-3. He worked out of jams repeatedly, shutting down the Giants for four innings. In the twelfth, Earl McNeely's grounder to third hit a stone and bounced over Fred Lindstrom, scoring Muddy Ruel, for Washington's lone 20th century World Series title.

Johnson won 20 games to lead the Nats to the 1925 pennant. After he tossed 4-1 and 4-0 gems in the Fall Classic against the Pirates, he threw Game 7 in a pouring rain at Forbes Field with the fielders barely visible. He took the loss in a crushing 9-7 defeat.

Johnson's last major league action was on September 30, 1927 as a pinch hitter in the same game Babe Ruth launched his legendary 60th home run. He went on to manage the Newark Bears (1928), the Nationals (1929-32), and the Cleveland Indians (1933-35).

After baseball, he busied himself working his Maryland Mountain View Farm, served several terms as a Montgomery County Commissioner, announced the Nationals' play-by-play on WJSV radio for 1939, and ran for Congress unsuccessfully in 1940.

Johnson was one of five charter inductees chosen on June 12, 1936 for the new National Baseball Hall of Fame. The highest-ranking pitcher on *The Sporting News'* 1999 list of the "100 Greatest Baseball Players," he was also chosen for Major League Baseball's prestigious All-Century Team.

Johnson died of a brain tumor at 59 in Washington on December 10, 1946. He is interred next to his wife at Union Cemetery in Rockville, Maryland. The great pitcher is venerated with a white bronze statue on the center field plaza of the new Nationals Park.

RAY KREMER

"There is nothing mysterious about [Kremer's] delivery but the velocity of the ball at different angles makes it difficult for the batsman."

~ Pirates beat reporter
Lee Wollen

Ray Kremer spent a decade throwing more than 2,100 minor league innings before emerging as a Steel City World Series hero. He was the best pitcher in history to get his major league debut after the age of 30 and still holds the big-league record of 22 straight home wins.

Remarkably durable and consistent, Kremer ranks seventh all-time for the Pirates with 143 wins and a .627 winning percentage. He won at least 15 games for seven consecutive seasons (1924-1930) and averaged 235 innings pitched per season from 1924 through 1931.

Kremer had nasty stuff, delivering the ball overhand, sidearm or submarine. He pitched to contact, spotting his fastball to set up his other pitches, and only threw as hard as he needed to according to the situation. A great fielder, he also had one of the league's best pickoff moves.

★　　★　　★　　★　　★

Remy Peter Kremer was born on March 23, 1893 in Oakland, Alameda County, California to Mary Gargaden and Nicholas Kremer, the third of five children. Both of his parents emigrated from France in the early 1870s and eventually settled in Northern California.

Kremer grew up near Freeman's Park, the home of the Pacific Coast League's Oakland Oaks. Attending Oakland's Polytechnic High and then San Francisco's St. Ignatius College Preparatory High, the young Kremer also pitched the semi-pro Sebastopol Warriors to a title.

Kremer signed with the Pacific Coast League's Sacramento Wolves in 1914, but was overmatched against Double-A hitters with a PCL-high 5.20 ERA in 136⅔ innings. For the Class-B Vancouver (BC) Beavers (Northwestern League) in 1915, he went 7-5 with a 3.14 ERA.

New York Giants manager John J. McGraw signed him in 1916, but he didn't perform well in spring training because of a bout of rheumatism. Still suffering severe joint pain, he was sent down to the International League's Roch-

ester Hustlers, pitched poorly and was released.

In 1917, Kremer married Beulah Vera Miller, who helped him recuperate fully from the rheumatism at home in Oakland. Soon he signed on with manager Del Howard of his hometown Oaks and would pitch for the local franchise for the next seven seasons through 1923.

The PCL was regarded as a pitchers' circuit at that time because of the mild weather. His weak performance in 1916 with the Giants and Rochester pigeonholed him as a warm weather pitcher. Yet for five seasons, starting in 1919, Kremer averaged 325 innings and almost 18 wins.

Dubbed "Bush Wiz" (for bush league), which was then shortened to "Wiz," the 6'1" 190-pound Kremer grew from dependable workhorse into dominant ace. Winning 20 games in 1922 with a 2.78 ERA, he drew interest from the Yankees, but negotiations with the Oaks broke down.

Kremer was clearly the PCL's best right-hander by 1923, winning a league-high 25 games. Scout Joe Devine pushed Pirates owner Barney Dreyfuss to obtain the major league-ready veteran. In December, the Bucs traded three players plus $20,000 to the Oaks to get him.

Referred to as "The Frenchman" by writers, the ruggedly handsome 31-year-old Kremer pitched his major league debut on April 18 at Cincinnati's Redland Field, losing 3-2 in the bottom of the ninth. He then proceeded to win four in a row, including a two-hit, 2-0 gem over the Cubs that took less than 1½ hours. He tired down the stretch, but set a Pirate rookie record 18 wins in 259⅓ innings pitched, tying for the NL lead in shutouts (4) and games pitched (41).

Kremer finished at 17-8 for the 1925 pennant-winning Pirates. In the Fall Classic against the Washington Nationals, his complete-game effort in Game 3 ended in a loss, 4-3. However, he rallied with a clutch complete-game six-hitter in the Game 6 elimination game, winning 3-2.

In a steady downpour making conditions horrendous in Game 7, Kremer came on in the sixth inning with the

G	IP	W	L	PCT	SHO	GS	CG	H	ER	SO	BB	ERA
308	1954.2	143	85	.627	14	247	134	2108	816	516	483	3.76

Pirates trailing 6-2 to Walter Johnson. He was almost perfect, retiring 12 of 13 batters, while Pitt surged back to win, 9-7. He was hailed as the "Hero of the World Series."

Although the Bucs underachieved in 1926, Kremer was masterful. Starting on July 10, he won 14 times, completed 13 starts and posted a 2.18 ERA. He placed third in the MVP balloting in his best year, going 20-6 to lead the NL in victories, ERA (2.61) and winning percentage.

Over the last nine weeks of 1927, Kremer went 11-4 with a 2.03 ERA, tossing eight complete-game victories in 23 days and closing with his major league record 22nd straight home win over the Giants. At 19-8, he was the NL ERA titlist again at 2.47 for the pennant-winners.

The Big Frenchman started World Series Game 1 against the Yankees' powerful Murderers' Row. He lasted just five frames after his defense betrayed him with two infield errors and three unearned runs. When the Yankees swept, he never got the chance to redeem himself.

The "Wiz" paced the Bucs with 18 wins in 1929, even without a victory in the first five weeks. In 1930, despite the loss of several feet off his fastball, he survived on guile, leading the NL with 20 wins in 276$\frac{1}{3}$ innings pitched. He was the first 20-game winner to post a 5.00+ ERA.

His final career shutout was a three-hitter versus the Braves on July 15, 1932, but he was pulled after only an inning in his last start against the same Braves just three weeks later. Though signed for 1933 by a grateful Dreyfuss, Kremer never regained his form. With a 10.35 ERA in seven games, he was waived on July 1. After pitching for the Oaks in 1933 and 1934, he retired.

Afterward, Kremer worked as a Bay Area postal carrier for more than 20 years. In the late 1950s, he and his wife retired to nearby Pinole. Suffering from heart problems, Kremer died at age 71 on February 8, 1965, and was laid to rest at Sunset View Cemetery in El Cerrito.

TED LYONS

CHICAGO WHITE SOX
RIGHT-HANDED PITCHER

1923-1942 • 1946

"If he'd pitched for the Yankees, he would have won over 400 games."

~ Yankees manager
Joe McCarthy

Ted Lyons never threw a single pitch in the minors, but he also never threw in a single World Series. He was extremely popular on Chicago's South Side and is still the White Sox leader in pitching victories. His staggering 356 complete games place him second only to the inimitable Warren Spahn among modern pitchers in the 20th century.

Despite hurling for mediocre White Sox teams, Lyons won 20 games three times. When he did not pitch, the club had an anemic .447 winning percentage. Though powerfully built, the 5'11" 200-pound Lyons was a control artist, not a strikeout pitcher.

For every nine innings he worked in his career, he averaged only 2.4 walks. Early on, his repertoire consisted of a cut fastball, curveball, knuckler and change. He was also a good hitting pitcher, a switch-hitter that was used often in pinch-hit situations.

* * * * *

Theodore Amar Lyons was born on December 28, 1900 in Lake Charles, Calcasieu Parish, Louisiana to Sudie E. Fancher and Asa Foreman Lyons. He grew up with two brothers and a sister on a ranch in Vinton, Louisiana close to the Texas border.

He played basketball and baseball at Vinton High and in the fall of 1919 enrolled at Baylor University in Waco, Texas. As a freshman, he went 10-2, which led to professional offers, but he elected to stay in school, studied to be an attorney, and graduated in 1923 after pitching Baylor to the Southwest Conference title.

The Chicago White Sox were training in Waco and owner Charles Comiskey was trying to reconstruct a new starting rotation after the 1919 Black Sox Scandal. Comiskey outbid all Lyons' suitors with a pledge to retain him on the big club for at least a year.

He joined up with the team on the road against the Browns and retired the three hitters he faced on July 2, 1923. It was the first big-league game he ever saw. His first two wins came in relief on both ends of a twin bill versus the Indians on October 6.

Lyons worked his way into the starting rotation the following year, posting a 12–11 record. In 1925, he paced the AL with 21 victories and five shutouts for a fifth place team. Late in the year, Lyons pitched a perfect game against the Nationals at Griffith Stadium until Bobby Veach singled with two out in the bottom of the ninth inning.

Lyons threw his lone no-hitter against the Red Sox on August 21, 1926, taking only 67 minutes and 81 pitches. He hurled an AL-best 22 wins in 1927 with 30 complete games and 307$^2/_3$ innings for a fifth place squad. He won 22 more games in 1930, leading the American League with 29 complete games and 297$^2/_3$ innings for a seventh place club.

In a 1931 spring training exhibition game against the Giants on a cold damp Houston evening, he felt something tear in his right shoulder. To save his arm, he pitched in only 21 games while experimenting with a new version of his knuckleball.

From 1934 forward, the Sox metered his appearances to no more than 30 games a year. Lyon reinvented himself with his improved knuckleball and complemented it with a slow curveball and an even slower curve which served as his changeup.

Manager Jimmy Dykes began using him exclusively in Sunday afternoon games in 1939. Lyons was billed as "Sunday Teddy" and the White Sox marketed "Sundays with Lyons" as one of the team's few gate attractions of that era. Often he was matched up with the opposing team's ace, including a young Bob Feller, in many a classic duel.

It helped him revitalize his career. Lyons went 52-30 in

G	IP	W	L	PCT	SHO	GS	CG	H	ER	SO	BB	ERA
594	4161	260	230	.531	27	484	356	4489	1696	1073	1121	3.67

his last four full campaigns for the best winning percentage (.634) stretch of his career. An All-Star in 1939, at one point he threw 42 straight innings without issuing a single base on balls.

Lyons led the AL with four shutouts in 1940 and had a 12-8 record with a 3.24 ERA. That year Windy City fans showered him with thousands of dollars in gifts, much of it in small denominations by youngsters, among whom he was quite popular.

In his last full season at 41 in 1942, Lyons was the AL ERA champion at 2.10, finishing all 20 of his starts. While far past draft age, he freely enlisted as a Marine Corps private in late 1942. Lyons spent part of his three-year tour in combat in the Pacific.

After World War II, he returned to the South Side in 1946 as the oldest player in the major leagues at 45. The old man put on a pitching clinic, tossing five consecutive complete games with a nifty 2.32 ERA, and notched his 260th and final career victory.

When Dykes abruptly quit only 30 games into the season, he was recruited to replace him. Lyons' managerial record through 1948 was an ordinary 185-245. He received some criticism for being too easy on his players and was glad to step away.

Lyons served as the Tiger pitching coach from 1949 to 1953 and for the Dodgers in 1954. After scouting for his White Sox from 1955 to 1966, he retired to help manage a Louisiana rice plantation with his older sister Pearl. He remained a bachelor all his life.

Ted Lyons was inducted into the National Baseball Hall of Fame in 1955. The White Sox retired his uniform #16 in 1987. Lyons passed away in Sulphur, Louisiana on July 25, 1986 and was laid to rest at Big Woods Cemetery in Edgerly, Calcasieu Parish.

JOHNNY MOSTIL

CHICAGO WHITE SOX
CENTER FIELD

1918 • 1921-1929

"I never saw anyone with his ability to cover ground. He could go farther than Tris Speaker to get a fly ball. For covering ground, Mostil was in a class by himself. I never saw his equal."

~ *White Sox manager Eddie Collins*

Johnny Mostil was the American League's premier defensive centerfielder during most of the Roaring 20s. The fleet-footed Mostil hit a career .301 and was the original Go-Go Sock. South Side crowds chanted "Steal! Steal!" whenever he got on. The homegrown Chicagoan was one of the few bright spots for a franchise in decline following the 1919 Black Sox Scandal.

A superb leadoff man, the popular Mostil was the catalyst for the Sox offense, topping the AL in runs scored once, steals twice and hit-by-pitch three times. A patient hitter with a great eye, he could get on base many ways. His 135 runs scored in 1925 is still a club record.

Ted Lyons said it was "like turning a rabbit loose" when the ball was hit near Mostil. Among AL flycatchers, he still ranks first all-time in highest range factor (average putouts & assists per game). Only two NL outfielders, Taylor Douthit and Richie Ashburn, grade higher.

Mostil made an unprecedented play in a 1925 spring training game at Nashville's Sulphur Dell Park. From center field, he caught a fly ball in foul territory, beating his left-fielder to the ball. It remains the only time in history that a centerfielder has ever caught a foul ball.

★ ★ ★ ★ ★

John Anthony Mostil was born on June 1, 1896 to Barbara and Caspar Mostile (spelled with an e) in Chicago, Illinois. His parents were both German émigrés. Enthralled with baseball from the start, Mostil grew up in Chicago Wards 5 and 6 with three sisters and a brother.

He played for years on the Chicago sandlots, but was still undiscovered at 22. In early 1918, a cab driver who had spent minor league time was so impressed with his speed and play at second base he drove him to Comiskey Park and arranged a tryout. The White Sox signed him.

Because manager Eddie Collins also played second base, Mostil debuted only as a pinch runner on June 20, 1918. Al-

though Mostil normally would have gone directly to the minors, Collins joined the Marines in August and the still unpolished Mostil was tabbed to fill in.

After the short audition, the Sox sent him down to the Double-A Milwaukee Brewers of the American Association. Mostil spent the 1919 and 1920 seasons in Wisconsin learning to play center field. He showed his upside, hitting .318 in 1920 with 190 hits- 45 of them for extra-bases.

By 1921, eight top White Sox, including centerfielder Happy Felsch and the legendary Shoeless Joe Jackson, had been banned permanently from baseball for conspiring to throw the 1919 World Series. Mostil filled the void as the regular centerfielder for the injured franchise.

On April 30, 1922, Sox hurler Charlie Robertson faced the Tigers at Navin Field. In left field, Mostil preserved a no-hitter with a diving catch of a liner early. With Robertson's perfect game on the line in the ninth, Johnny Bassler hit a line shot just inside the left field line. Near the chalk, Mostil dove headlong, snaring the ball fully stretched out, to dramatically save the gem.

The 5'8" 168-pound Mostil had his best years in 1925 and 1926. His live *Louisville Slugger* and Gold Glove-style glove earned him runner up in the 1926 AL MVP voting behind Cleveland's George Burns. He reached career-highs with 197 hits, 41 doubles, 15 triples, a .328 average and .415 OBA. He also slugged .467 while stealing 35 bases and scoring 120 runs.

On August 21, 1926, Ted Lyons walked the first Red Sox batter Johnny Tobin. With one out, Baby Doll Jacobson smoked a 2-0 pitch to center. Mostil came on quickly for a spectacular shoestring catch on the sinking line drive and then threw to double off Tobin at first. From there, Lyons went on to pitch a no-hitter while Mostil lined out four hits with three RBI in support.

Mostil arrived for 1927 spring training in Shreveport, Louisiana with high blood pressure, a throbbing dental

G	AB	R	H	2B	3B	HR	RBI	SB	BB	SO	BA	OBP	SLG	TB
972	3507	618	1054	209	82	23	375	176	415	336	.301	.386	.427	1496

condition, and neuritis inflaming his nerves in his jaw and left shoulder, causing unrelieved, sharp pain. He was then hit in the chest in his first round of batting practice.

On March 8, Mostil attempted suicide with a razor and pocket knife, inflicting 13 stab and slash wounds to his chest, left wrist, neck and legs. He was found in a hotel room, bleeding heavily. Teammates got him to the hospital where he was administered the Catholic last rites.

Mostil later confided to his family that he could not explain his actions. He was released from the hospital on March 28, but he had sliced the tendons extending to the second and third fingers of his left hand. Mostil made it back on September 1, but was never the same ballplayer.

Early in his 1928 comeback on May 24, attempting to break up a double play, Mostil was hit between the eyes and knocked unconscious by Tigers shortstop Chick Galloway's relay to first. He persevered but had lost a step, swiping just 23 bags in 43 attempts, and hit only .270.

His 1929 year was star-crossed from the onset. Mostil developed an infection in his right foot and then broke his thumb. He fractured his right ankle after just 12 games, tripping on home plate on the front end of an uncontested double steal. He never played again in the major leagues.

Mostil was cut by the Giants in spring 1930 and was sent to play for Casey Stengel's Toledo (OH) Mud Hens for two years. He took a turn with the 1932 Little Rock (AR)

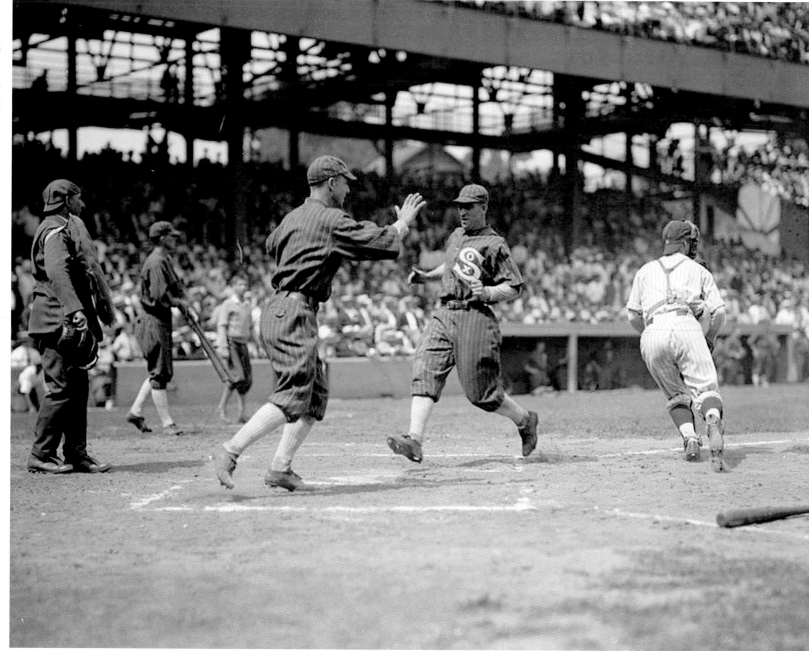

Travelers, and then was five years as the Class-D Northern League Eau Claire (WI) Bears player-manager.

Mostil skippered the Northern League's Grand Forks (ND) Chiefs in 1938 and 1939; the 1940 Jonesboro White Sox (Northeast Arkansas League); and finished with the 1942 Waterloo (IA) Hawks (Indiana-Illinois-Iowa League)

before going into scouting for nearly two decades.

After his long tenure as a White Sox scout, he retired because of poor health to his home at 73 in Whiting, Indiana. Mostil was in a Midlothian (IL) nursing care facility at age 74 when he passed away after a long illness on December 10, 1970. He was a bachelor his entire life.

EDDIE ROMMEL

PHILADELPHIA ATHLETICS
RIGHT-HANDED PITCHER

1920-1932

"The ball does not seem to do its stuff until it is about six feet from the plate. If it made a one-way hop the batter would be able to set himself and be able to familiarize himself with the break. But that's just where Rommel's success comes in. It goes down one time and the next will take an upward break."

~ George Sisler

Eddie Rommel is known as the "father of the modern knuckleball." He was the ace of the early Roaring 20s Philadelphia teams and a relief star for the 1929 and 1930 World Series Champions. Rommel then went on to serve as an American League umpire for over two decades.

He led the AL twice each in wins (1922 & 1925), won/lost percentage (1927 & 1929), games (1922-23), and assists (1923-24). His stock-in-trade was pinpoint control of his fastball and curve. His off-speed, fluttering, darting knuckleball confounded even the best of hitters.

★　★　★　★　★

Edwin Americus Rommel was born of German lineage to Louisa B. and Frederick A. Rommel on September 13, 1897 in Baltimore, Maryland, the youngest of seven. Rommel began pitching for the semi-professional Seaford (Delaware) team in the Peach League in 1916 where the Seaford first baseman, Cutter Druery, showed him his knuckleball technique.

In 1918, the 20-year-old Rommel leapfrogged directly to the Double-A Newark (NJ) Bears of the International League. After he won a dozen games with a 2.42 ERA, the Giants purchased his contract on an option. The next spring, he survived until the last big-league cut just before Opening Day.

Back at Newark that May, Rommel hurled a no-hitter against Toronto. Bears manager Earle Mack sent for his father, Philadelphia Athletics owner Connie Mack. Rommel was knocked out early in both ends of a twin bill with Mr. Mack present. After he won 22 games, however, the Athletics were still impressed enough to buy his contract.

Philadelphia finished dead last in the American League out of eight teams each year from 1915 to 1921, a horrible seven-year stretch. Rommel became a key element of their rebuilding process in the early 1920's, along with future Hall of Famers Mickey Cochran, Jimmie Foxx, Lefty Grove and Aloysius Simmons.

Debuting on April 19, 1920, he went on to win seven games, tossed two shutouts, relieved in 21 appearances, and sported a 2.85 ERA. Pitching for a 53 win-100 loss team in 1921, he topped the American League with 23 losses and 21 home runs allowed, but also led the Athletics with 16 wins and 285⅓ innings pitched.

Indeed, 1921 was the first of five years consecutively that Rommel led the staff in victories, winning an even 100 games during those years. The 6'2" 197-pound workhorse threw no fewer than 261 innings pitched in that stretch and faced more batters (1,154) in 1925 than any other American League pitcher.

Using his knuckleball more effectively in 1922, Rommel finished second to American League Most Valuable Player George Sisler, winning a league-best 27 games which represented over 41 percent of his team's 65 victories. It took 50 years to eclipse the feat. The Phillies' Lefty Carlton won 27 of 59 (46 percent) in 1972.

In front of President Calvin Coolidge at the District of Columbia's Griffith Stadium on Opening Day 1926, Rommel and the great Walter Johnson locked horns in a pitching duel for the ages for 15 innings. The Nationals barely outlasted the Athletics, 1-0, though Rommel chose not to throw a single knuckleball.

He hurled a colossal 2,358⅔ innings over his first nine professional seasons through 1926, but never threw 200 innings again. Mostly out of the bullpen because his arm could no longer stand the strain, Rommel went 52-19 and paced the American League in relief wins three times from 1927 to 1931 as the resurgent Ath-

G	IP	W	L	PCT	SHO	SV	GS	CG	H	ER	SO	BB	ERA
501	2557	171	119	.590	18	30	249	145	2729	1006	599	724	3.54

letics finished no lower than third place.

At Shibe Park in the 1929 Fall Classic Game 4, the Athletics trailed the Cubs, 7-0. Rommel worked the seventh frame and gave up a lone run. His team came roaring back in one of the most epic rallies in history, scoring ten times in the inning, and won, 10-8. The A's took the Series title in five games to become one of the most distinguished teams in baseball history.

Pennsylvania's blue laws precluded baseball on the Sabbath, so on Sunday, July 10, 1932, the team had to travel to Cleveland for a single game. To save train faire, the penurious Mack took only two hurlers- Rommel and rookie Lew Krausse. After pitching batting practice, he saw Krausse get shelled for seven runs in the first inning. The only pitcher left, Rommel came on to throw over 500 pitches in 17 innings over four hours. Though he gave up a record 29 hits, 14 runs and nine walks, he got the victory, 18-17. The Indians amassed 33 hits, nine by Johnny Burnett- still both big-league records. It was Rommel's last win and effectively ended his career.

He hurled his final game on September 17, 1932. After handing him his release at season's end, Mr. Mack brought him back as a coach (1933 & 1934). Rommel then managed and pitched for the Class-B Richmond (VA) Colts, leading them to the 1935 Piedmont League title.

Rommel apprenticed as an umpire in the New York-Penn and International Leagues, and was promoted to the AL in 1938, working through 1959. He umpired two World Series to become only the third man to appear as both player and umpire. He called six All-Star Games.

Rommel and his wife Emma raised a son and a daughter. After baseball, he was an aide to Maryland Governor J. Millard Tawes. Rommel passed away on August 26, 1970 in Baltimore, Maryland after a lengthy illness. He is buried in Baltimore's New Cathedral Cemetery.

PIE TRAYNOR

PITTSBURGH PIRATES
THIRD BASE

1920-1937

"If I had to pick the greatest team player in baseball today – and I have some of the greats on my own club – I would have to pick Pie Traynor."

~ *Giants manager John J. McGraw*

Pie Traynor was the finest third baseman in baseball for the first half of the 20th century. One of the best players of the Roaring 20s, he was voted *The Sporting News'* top third baseman seven times. Traynor drove in over 100 runs in seven campaigns, finishing with 1,278 RBI and an impressive .320 career average.

The graceful Traynor was blessed with quick reflexes, soft hands, a fast release and a strong arm. He was a magician at charging bunts and slow rollers bare-handed and firing accurately to first on the run from any angle. Traynor could dash to his left to cut off certain hits and had a flair for making back-handed stops on shots down the line. He had 6,134 chances and participated in 308 double plays at third base, leading the National League in putouts a record seven times, four straight years in double plays, and three times in assists. He still holds the NL mark of 2,288 putouts at the hot corner, playing a record 1,864 games there.

★ ★ ★ ★ ★

Harold Joseph Traynor was born on November 11, 1898 to Lydia Maud and James Henry Traynor in Framingham, Middlesex County, Massachusetts. His large family moved to Somerville outside of Boston when he was five.

Soon the boy gravitated to the sandlots, where Father John Nangle, a clergyman and shopkeeper, frequently watched and gave pointers. When the boys came into his corner store after games, he would offer them treats. Harold would invariably say, "I'll take pie Father." The amused priest took to calling him "Pie Face," and the name stuck.

Traynor signed with Portsmouth Truckers of the Virginia League in May, 1920. The Pirates quickly saw his potential, signed him, and put him in a big-league game on September 15. He hit .336 in 131 games in the Southern Association for the Birmingham (AL) Barons in 1922. By

1923, he was a full-fledged Pirate star, batting .338 with 108 runs scored, 208 hits, 19 triples and 101 RBI and NL-leading 191 putouts and 310 assists.

He credited Rogers Hornsby with advising him to switch to a heavier bat, forcing him to use the entire field and leading to ten .300 plus seasons. Swinging for the fences was foolish at Forbes Field which measured 435 feet to left-center, 428 to dead center and 395 with a high screen to right-center. It was a perfect park for triples. The 6' 170-pound Traynor had nearly three times as many three-baggers as home runs.

The 1925 Pirates won the pennant and the Pie Man enjoyed a storybook year, playing 150 games with 114 runs, 189 hits, 39 doubles, 106 RBI and a .320 average. He led all third basemen in fielding, chances, putouts, assists and a record 41 double plays. In Game 1 of the World Series against the Nationals, he homered and singled off Walter Johnson and made a dramatic diving catch. Despite losing three of the first four, the Bucs persevered to win in seven with Traynor hitting .346 and handling 24 chances flawlessly.

He was an unrepentant bat forager, seeking any discarded bat with hits left in it. The 6' 170-pound Traynor swung a single scavenged 42-ounce *Louisville Slugger* for the entire 1927 season. Batting in his usual cleanup spot, he hit .342, played in 149 games, and drove in 106 runs. His game-winning, bases-loaded single on the final day clinched the pennant, but the Bucs were swept in the Fall Classic by the Ruth and Gehrig Yankees.

One of the toughest outs ever, Traynor struck out only 278 times in 7,559 career at-bats and never went down on strikes more than 28 times in any season. In 1928 and 1929 combined, he struck out a mere 17 times in 1,109 at-bats. Traynor hit .337, .356 and .366 respectively in 1928,

G	AB	R	H	2B	3B	HR	RBI	SB	BB	SO	BA	OBP	SLG	TB
1941	7559	1183	2416	371	164	58	1273	158	472	278	.320	.362	.435	3289

1929 and 1930, driving in 351 runs with just 16 home runs. As a hardworking player in a blue collar town, he had become the pride of the Steel City.

Traynor was named the Pirates player-manager in 1934, the year he was involved in a career-altering play. Sliding into home, he missed the plate attempting to evade the tag of Phillies backstop Jimmie Wilson. As he reached back to touch home, the catcher fell heavily on his right arm. Traynor never was able to throw the same again.

His active career almost over, Traynor concentrated on his managerial duties, giving himself only cameo playing roles through 1937. His best chance for a pennant was in 1938, but in late September Gabby Hartnett launched his fabled "Homer in the Gloaming" as darkness fell at Wrigley Field to beat the Pirates and win the pennant for the Cubs. Traynor's career as a manager ended in 1939 with a 457-406 ledger.

After World War II, he became a virtual "Mr. Pittsburgh," traveling throughout western Pennsylvania, speaking to local organizations as a popular civic ambassador. He also served as a sports broadcaster for Radio KQV. Anyone who lived in Pittsburgh probably saw him walking downtown as he never learned to drive a car. Traynor enjoyed talking baseball with everyone, taking up to twenty minutes to go a single block.

He was enshrined in the National Baseball Hall of Fame in Cooperstown on June 13, 1949. During the 1969 centennial gala, Traynor was voted baseball's "Greatest Third Baseman of All-Time." His uniform #20 was retired by the Pirates, and he was honored with his own United States postage stamp. Traynor passed away on March 16, 1972 and is interred in Homewood Cemetery in Pittsburgh, Pennsylvania.

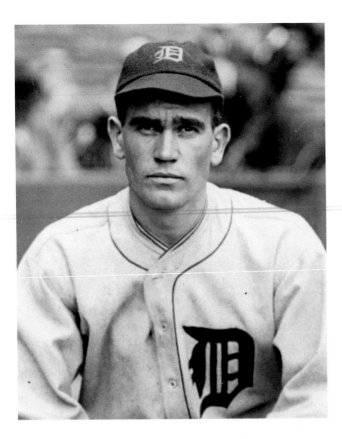

LARRY WOODALL

DETROIT TIGERS
CATCHER

1920-1929

"He had been one of [Detroit's] best catchers and one of the best-hitting catchers in the league. But Woodall will be remembered chiefly by other ball players and persons who knew him as a thorough sportsman. His gentlemanly qualities on and off the field gained him many admirers..."

~ sportswriter Sam Greene

Larry Woodall had a major league career that spanned one of the most thrilling and important periods in baseball history- the Golden Era of the Roaring 20s. He performed in the American League at a time when the game was the most popular sport in America.

The American League was composed of the same eight stable franchises during Woodall's entire major league career- the Boston Red Sox, Chicago White Sox, Cleveland Indians, Detroit Tigers, New York Yankees, Philadelphia Athletics, St. Louis Browns (now the Baltimore Orioles), and the Washington Nationals (now the Minnesota Twins).

Batting right-handed, the stocky 5'9" 165-pound Woodall hit over .300 in three seasons (1921, 1922 & 1924). He shared backstop duty with receiver Johnny Bassler, the best catcher in the AL for many years. Known for his agility, sure-handedness and accurate arm, he made just 26 errors while throwing out 158 base runners for an outstanding 36 percent success rate.

★ ★ ★ ★ ★

Charles Lawrence Woodall, Jr. was born on July 26, 1895 in Staunton, Virginia to Fannie Lawton and Charles Lawrence Woodall, Sr. He was born in the Shenandoah Valley only three decades removed from the devastation, ruin and bitterness caused by the systematic torching of the "Breadbasket of the Confederacy" by Union General Philip Sheridan during the Civil War.

His father "Charlie" dubbed him "Larry" from the start to avoid confusion. Woodall grew up in rural Virginia with an older sister and brother and attended Wake Forest University in Winston-Salem, North Carolina in 1912 and 1913, playing on the Demon Deacons team. He then transferred to the University of North Carolina at Chapel Hill for the 1914 collegiate season. The 1915 Tar Heels baseball captain, he graduated in June of that year.

At the end of the 1915 UNC collegiate season, Woodall

inked a professional baseball contract with the Asheville Tourists of the Class-D North Carolina State League. He then spent the 1916 through 1919 seasons learning his craft with the Fort Worth Panthers of the Class-B Texas League. For the first three of those four years, Fort Worth had no relationship with any major league team. In 1919, however, the Panthers became affiliated with the Detroit Tigers.

Woodall enlisted in the U.S. Army in 1918 and served 11 months mostly on the battlefields of France with the 36th Infantry Division, returning to baseball on July 4, 1919. After the 1919 campaign, the Tigers bought Woodall's Fort Worth contract and manager Hughie Jennings gave him his big-league debut on May 20, 1920. That spring, the American League had introduced a more lively *Spalding* baseball which effectively ushered out the Deadball Era.

Woodall was shuttled between the Tigers and the Toledo (OH) Mud Hens of the Double-A American Association in 1920, appearing in 40 games for Toledo and 18 for Detroit. Ty Cobb was appointed Tiger manager in 1921 and was at the helm through 1926. A long and close friendship between Woodall and Cobb began at the 1921 Detroit training camp and Woodall credited the "Georgia Peach" with practical hitting tips that helped him hit .363 that season.

In 1927, the year of the Great Bambino's historic 60 circuit clouts, Woodall played a career-high 86 games at catcher under first-year manager George Moriarty. He hit .280 in 291 plate appearances and fielded .997, setting a Junior Circuit record for catchers. While committing just one error, he gunned down 43 percent of attempted base stealers.

Woodall played his last game for the Motor City on May 9, 1929, but his active career was far from over. Taking advantage of the great weather and equivalent salaries, he played a decade more in the Pacific Coast League- at that time called the third major league. From 1929 to 1931,

G	AB	R	H	2B	3B	HR	RBI	SB	BB	SO	BA	OBP	SLG	TB
548	1317	161	353	52	15	1	161	16	159	67	.268	.347	.333	438

Woodall caught for the Portland (OR) Beavers, taking a turn as player-manager in 1930.

While with Portland in 1929, Woodall mentored young pitchers like Roy Mahaffey. He taught him a slow curve and a changeup to complement his live fastball. Woodall educated him on how to mix his pitches to keep hitters off balance and Mahaffey became much more effective.

He caught for the Sacramento (CA) Senators in 1932 and 1933 and then played six more seasons with the San Francisco Seals from 1934 to 1939. There in 1934 and 1935, Woodall witnessed Seals teammate Joe DiMaggio tear up the PCL before going to fame in New York.

Finally retiring as an active professional player at the age of 45, Woodall served as a Seals coach in 1940 and 1941. In 1941, he taught Larry Jansen a new pitch- the slider. Jansen was one of the first hurlers to utilize the slider and helped popularize it at the major league level.

Woodall then worked for more than two decades for the Red Sox. He was Boston's first base coach from 1942 to 1947, which included the 1946 AL pennant winners, led by Ted Williams. After serving as the Red Sox Director of Public Relations, he became a scout.

In 1949, Woodall scouted Willie Mays of the Birmingham Black Barons in the Negro American League and reported to the Boston brass that Mays "was not the Red Sox's type of player." The evaluation was one of the most egregious scouting blunders in history. Boston was the last team to have an African American on its big-league roster in 1959 in Pumpsie Greene.

Woodall and his wife, Dorothy Buckley, raised a daughter and a son and resided in Cambridge, Massachusetts. He remained a Red Sox scout until he passed away on May 6, 1963 at the Santa Maria Hospital in Newton (MA) from complications of cirrhosis of the liver. He is interred at the Gate of Heaven Cemetery in Silver Spring, Montgomery County, Maryland.

ROSS YOUNGS

NEW YORK GIANTS
RIGHT FIELD

1917-1926

"Everybody has Cobb,
Ruth and Speaker on his
all-time outfield. But,
somehow, I've got to find
a place for Pep Youngs.
Don't ask me to take one
out, I've just got to put
Pep in there somewhere."

~ Ford C. Frick

Ross Youngs was the key offensive catalyst of the Roaring 20s Giants and one of the 20th century's most colorful and tragic figures. With Youngs as the igniter, the Giants won the National League pennant four straight years starting in 1921 and garnered championships in 1921 and 1922. He was manager John J. McGraw's favorite outfielder.

Youngs' competitive makeup was one of the finest ever. Averaging almost 90 runs scored over nine full seasons, he was so aggressive on the base paths with his relentless hustle and hard slides that his teammates took to calling him "Pep."

Displaying a beautiful left-handed stroke, the 5'8" 162-pound Youngs batted over .300 eight times, and over .350 twice. Regularly ranked among the National League batting leaders, he hit a lifetime .322 while drawing 160 more walks than he struck out.

McGraw praised him as the best rightfielder in the NL. He matured into a superb fly chaser using his explosive speed and howitzer right arm to lead the league in assists three times. He was expert at playing the carom off the Polo Grounds' right field wall.

★　★　★　★　★

Ross Middlebrook Youngs was born to S.J. and Henrie Middlebrook Youngs on April 10, 1897 in Shiner, Lavaca County, Texas, out on the west Texas plains. He graduated from the Texas Military Institute in San Antonio where he starred as a football halfback, ran track and also played baseball.

After a lackluster 10-game stint in 1914, Youngs was released from an Austin team, but was undeterred. He played with little distinction at Bartlett (Mid-Texas League) and Waxahachie (Central Texas League) in 1915. Both leagues folded during the season.

Youngs finally caught fire in 1916, playing second base for the Class-D Sherman (TX) Lions, and led the Western Association with a .362 average, 195 hits and 103 runs scored in 539 at-bats. He was discovered there by Giants scout Dick Kinsella.

Youngs' contract was acquired by the Giants in early 1917. He played most of the year for the Rochester (NY) Red Wings under manager Mickey Doolan. Youngs' errant throws from second prompted his move to right field, but McGraw already saw stardom.

The 20-year-old Youngs hit .356 in 506 at-bats before debuting with the Giants on September 25, 1917. He hit .346 in short duty. Youngs played his first full season in 1918, batting .302 and striking out a minimal 49 times in 582 plate appearances.

After topping the NL with 31 doubles and hitting .311 in 1919, Youngs finished runner up to Rogers Hornsby in the 1920 batting race, hitting .351 with 204 hits, 75 walks, a .427 on-base percentage, 92 runs scored, 18 steals and 78 RBI.

After driving in 102 runs in the regular 1921 season, he became the first to collect two hits in one World Series inning, slashing a double and a triple in the seventh inning of Game 3 against the Yankees. He lined out 200 hits in 1923, leading the NL with 121 runs scored and reached career highs in 1924 with 10 round trippers and a .356 average.

Youngs was Nationals ace Walter Johnson's nemesis in the 1925 World Series. In his first Fall Classic start, "The Big Train" lost Game 1 on Youngs' bases loaded single in the twelfth inning, 4-3. Johnson came back to win Game 7, but was so wary of Youngs that he walked him intentionally twice to get to future Hall-of-Famer Highpockets Kelly.

G	AB	R	H	2B	3B	HR	RBI	SB	BB	SO	BA	OBP	SLG	TB
1211	4627	812	1491	236	93	42	592	153	533	501	.322	.399	.441	2101

In the spring of 1926, he was diagnosed with Bright's disease, a terminal kidney inflammation now known as nephritis. Some suggested that his ailment stemmed from his habit of diving into bases head first or from collisions on the base paths. With a full-time caretaker traveling with him, Youngs courageously hit .306 in 95 games, but had to leave the team after playing his final game on August 10, 1926. He was completely spent.

Youngs would never play again and regressed rapidly. One of the last to visit him was his signing scout, Dick Kinsella, who was stunned at his physical deterioration. He weighed less than 100 pounds and died on October 22, 1927, in San Antonio, Texas. He left his wife, Dorothy Peinecke Youngs, and three-year old daughter Caroline.

In Youngs' funeral service, which was attended by thousands, McGraw eulogized, "...he was the easiest man I ever knew to handle. In all his years with the Giants, he never caused one minute's trouble for myself or the club." McGraw never quite got over Youngs' passing. He kept framed photos of Christy Mathewson and Youngs, his two surrogate sons, in his Polo Grounds office until his own death in 1934.

Ross Youngs was inducted posthumously into the National Baseball Hall of Fame in 1972 after being elected by the Committee on Baseball Veterans. A plaque was

installed at the Polo Grounds in 1928 to honor him which read: "A brave untrammeled spirit of the diamond, who brought glory to himself and his team by his strong, aggressive, courageous play. He won the admiration of the nation's fans, the love and esteem of his friends and teammates, and the respect of his opponents. He played the game." Youngs is interred at the Mission Burial Park South in San Antonio.

CHAPTER THREE

THE DEPRESSION 30s & WORLD WAR II

1931-1945

Wrigley Field –
Chicago, Illinois

LUKE APPLING

CHICAGO WHITE SOX
SHORTSTOP

1930-1943 • 1945-1950

"Like my old coach, Luke Appling, said here, he told me if you're going to be lucky you've got to think lucky."

~ hitting pupil
Dusty Baker

Luke Appling overcame a host of feigned and actual ailments to be chosen the "Greatest Living White Sox" during Professional Baseball's Centennial Celebration in 1969. Although an affable gentleman and a popular teammate, he was nicknamed "Old Aches and Pains" for his nonstop complaining about a variety of maladies.

Honored as the most outstanding major league shortstop by *The Sporting News* three times, the 5' 10" 183-pound Appling is the White Sox all-time leader in games, at-bats, runs, hits, doubles and walks. He hit over .300 16 seasons, made seven All-Star teams, and won two AL batting titles, but never saw action in a World Series.

He was the consummate leadoff man, topping .400 in on-base percentage eight times, and drew close to three walks for every time he struck out. Handling his *Louisville Slugger* like a magic wand, he used the whole field line-to-line to find the gaps.

With his keen eye, he could foul off pitch after pitch before selecting a good ball to hit or patiently just accept a walk. He was renowned for wearing out opposing pitchers. Manager Jimmy Dykes labeled him the most dangerous hitter in the AL with two strikes.

Guilty of kicking routine ground balls and erratic throws early, he developed to pace AL shortstops in chances three years and assists seven years straight. He set records for games played and double plays and AL marks for chances, putouts and assists.

★　★　★　★　★

Lucius Benjamin Appling, Jr. was born to Dola Sappenfield and Lucius Benjamin Appling, Sr. in High Point, North Carolina on April 2, 1907. He grew up the oldest son in a brood of seven. The family moved to Atlanta, Georgia where the young Appling played football, ran track, and

was an All-City shortstop for the Fulton High Cardinals.

A three-sport star at Oglethorpe College as well, he once hit four home runs in a college game and signed with the Atlanta Crackers after his second year in 1930. Already a first-rate hitter, he batted .326 and was the best shortstop in the Southern Association.

The White Sox bought Appling's Crackers contract for $20,000 and soon gave him his major league debut on September 10, 1930. The club waited two years for their pricey investment to pay dividends, but he finally turned the corner, batting .322 in 1933.

In 1934, new manager Jimmy Dykes counseled Appling to stay within himself and refrain from trying to hit homers out of spacious Comiskey Park. His new disciplined approach would make him one of the most successful hitters in the Depression Era.

Appling was the 1936 AL batting champion with a lofty .388 average- the highest ever by a shortstop. He also put together a club-record 27-game hitting streak and set career highs with 204 hits, 111 runs, 128 RBI, a .474 OBA, and a .508 slugging average.

There was nothing feigned about the injury he sustained during a spring training game on March 27, 1938. Appling broke his right leg in two places sliding. It shelved him for half the season and cost him speed and range. When he finished second in the 1940 AL batting race, his .348 was just three infield hits short of Joe DiMaggio's .352.

His average plummeted to .262 in 1942, which he attributed to the fact that he was completely healthy all year. His aches and pains returned in 1943, which led to another batting title at .328 and a league-leading .419 on-base percentage.

G	AB	R	H	2B	3B	HR	RBI	SB	BB	SO	BA	OBP	SLG	TB
2422	10254	1319	2749	440	102	45	1116	179	1302	528	.310	.399	.398	3528

Appling entered the Army in January 1944 and soon was assigned to the reconditioning service at Lawson General Hospital near Atlanta. He was discharged on August 30, 1945, missing almost two full major league seasons.

In 1949 at age 42, Appling was baseball's oldest shortstop and still hit .301. He retired after the next year to become the manager of the Southern Association's Memphis (TN) Chickasaws and was *The Sporting News* 1952 Minor League Manager of the Year.

Appling also skippered the 1962 American Association Champion Indianapolis (IN) Indians and coached the Indians, Tigers, Orioles, A's and White Sox. He was also a late stand-in as the 1967 Kansas City Athletics manager after Alvin Dark was let go.

The affable Appling and his wife, the former Faye Dodd, moved to Cumming, Georgia when he was hired on with the Atlanta Braves as a hitting instructor in 1976. There the couple raised two daughters, Linda and Carol, and a son, Lucius III.

Luke Appling was inducted into the National Baseball Hall of Fame in 1964 by a special writers' runoff vote. The White Sox franchise retired his uniform #4 in 1975 and he was a posthumous finalist to Major League Baseball's 1999 All-Century Team.

In the first annual Cracker Jack Old Timers Classic at RFK Stadium on July 19, 1982 in Washington, D.C., the 75-year-old Appling, never a power hitter, blasted a towering home run off Warren Spahn. As he circled the bases, Spahn applauded.

Two days after he retired from the Braves, Appling suffered an abdominal aneurysm and died during emergency surgery on January 3, 1991 at age 83. Old Aches and Pains was laid to rest at the Sawnee View Gardens Cemetery in Cumming.

TOMMY BRIDGES

DETROIT TIGERS
RIGHT-HANDED PITCHER
1930-1943 • 1945-1950

"A hundred and fifty pounds of courage. If there ever is a payoff on courage this little 150-pound pitcher is the greatest World Series hero."

~ Tigers manager
Mickey Cochrane after
the 1935 World Series

Tommy Bridges was one of baseball's elite pitchers during the Depression Era 30s. An American League All-Star six times, he had 194 regular season victories, four World Series wins, and one in the 1939 All-Star game for 199 career victories and 33 complete game shutouts.

His sharp-breaking, down-and-out curveball was one of the best ever by a right-hander. He possessed long, slender fingers that enabled him to spin the ball so tightly that his curve broke like it was dropping off a table. Bridges' curveball set up his fastball.

At 5'10½" and 155 pounds, he was one of the hardest throwers of his day, one that Junior Circuit hitters had to respect. His manager and battery mate Mickey Cochrane maintained that he won more games with his fastball than with his curve.

Bridges was among the league leaders in earned run average ten times between 1932 and 1943 and finished in the American League Top 10 in strikeouts a dozen times. If he had an Achilles heel, it was his sporadic control problems. He issued over 100 walks six times.

★　★　★　★　★

Thomas Jefferson Davis Bridges was born December 28, 1906, in Gordonsville, Smith County, Tennessee to Florence Davis and Joe Gill Bridges. His father, a country doctor, named him for U. S. President Thomas Jefferson and Confederate President Jefferson Davis.

Coming from several generations of physicians, Bridges studied for four years at the University of Tennessee to follow in his father's footsteps. However, he left without a degree in 1929 to sign with the Tigers. Scout Billy Doyle had observed him pitching for the Volunteers.

Bridges began his pro career in mid-1929 with the Wheeling (WV) Stogies of the Class-C Middle Atlantic League, going 10-3, and striking out 20 in a game. In 1930 he went to the Class-B Evansville (IL) Hubs (Three-I League) and put up a 2.96 ERA with 189 strikeouts.

The Tigers were so impressed Bridges was given his debut in relief on August 13, 1930. He induced Babe Ruth to ground out on his first major league pitch and later struck out Lou Gehrig. He secured a spot in the Tigers' regular pitching rotation in his first full year in 1931.

Versus Washington on August 5, 1932, Bridges came within an out of hurling a perfect game. Nats manager Walter Johnson, behind 12-0, sent top pinch hitter Dave Harris to hit for his pitcher Bobby Burke. Harris singled to break up the perfecto. He retired the next batter easily.

Bridges came back with another one-hitter against Washington on May 24, 1933. The lone safe hit was a circuit smash by Joe Kuhel. It was the first time in American League history that a pitcher had surrendered a home run and still polished off a one-hitter.

Later in that season Bridges again reached the ninth inning with a no-hitter on September 24. This time, he gave up a pair of hits but still beat the St. Louis Browns, 7-0. For the season, Bridges had a 3.08 ERA, second in the American League only to Mel Harder of the Indians.

Coincident with the arrival of new catcher-manager Mickey Cochrane, Bridges went 22-11 in 1934 with 23 complete games to rally the Tigers to their first AL flag in 25 years. He added a win in World Series Game 2 over Dizzy Dean, 3-1, but Detroit lost to St. Louis in seven.

Stellar again in 1935, his line was 21-10 with 23 complete games and a win in Fall Classic Game 6. With the score at 3-3 in the top of the ninth, Bridges gave up a lead-off triple to Stan Hack, but retired the next three Cubs, stranding Hack, to lock up Detroit's first world title.

In a nationwide poll, Bridges was named the Number 2 sports hero of 1935, behind University of Notre Dame halfback Andy Pilney. When he led the AL in 1936 with

G	IP	W	L	PCT	SHO	GS	CG	H	ER	SO	BB	ERA
424	2826.1	194	138	.584	33	362	200	2675	1122	1674	1192	3.57

23 wins and 175 Ks, he had finished off a magnificent run in which he won 66 games in just three seasons.

Bridges was involved in one of the legendary pitching duels of all time on August 11, 1942. Indians ace Al Milnar had a no-hitter until Doc Cramer singled with two out in the ninth. Milnar and Bridges battled to a 14-inning 0-0 tie, until the game was called because of darkness.

He entered the U. S. Army in late 1943, leaving behind a weakened wartime AL in 1944. Upon returning in 1945, he contributed to a Tigers pennant. When he came on in relief in World Series Game 6, he joined Hank Greenberg as the only two Tigers to play in four Fall Classics.

Bridges hurled for the Tigers in 1946, throwing his last major league pitch on July 20 and finished as a coach. He toiled for the PCL's Portland (OR) Beavers from 1947 to 1949, getting his no-hitter in 1947 versus the San Francisco Seals, and led the PCL with a 1.64 ERA at age 40.

Bridges had married Carolyn Jellicorse in 1930 and the couple raised one daughter. The intelligent, well-bred, sensitive Bridges began to struggle with a drinking problem during his stint in the military. It turned into a full-fledged bout with alcoholism and a subsequent divorce.

Bridges re-married Iona Veda Kidwell on May 17, 1950 and finished out with the Seals and Seattle Rainers. He was both a coach and scout for the 1951 Reds and also scouted for the Tigers (1958-60) and the Mets (1963-68). He was a tire salesman in Detroit when not in baseball.

Bridges' distinguished career accomplishments have not yet met the voting criteria for him to be elected into the National Baseball Hall of Fame, yet he favorably matches up with many pitchers who have already been enshrined. Bridges passed away on April 19, 1968, in Nashville, Tennessee at age 61 and is buried in Ridgewood Cemetery in Carthage, Tennessee.

FRANKIE CROSETTI

NEW YORK YANKEES
SHORTSTOP

1932-1948

*"Frank Crosetti had a
legendary career with the
Yankees starting as a player
with Babe Ruth through
Gehrig and DiMaggio, and
remaining as a coach.
He was a true Yankee."*

~ Rick Cerrone

Frankie Crosetti was the fine-fielding bellwether shortstop for the Yankees during their Second Dynasty from 1932 to 1943. He played for the Bronx Bombers for 17 seasons and then coached third base for another 20 years. Wearing Yankee pinstripes through four decades and 37 straight seasons, Crosetti has the longest tenure stretch of any individual in franchise annals.

Crosetti was called "Crow," certainly an abbreviation of his last name, but also because he was the "holler guy" with his high-pitched, shrill shouts from the dugout. As a player, he was a member of nine World Series squads. As a third base coach, he took part in 14 more, giving him the singular distinction of participating in 23 Fall Classics- 17 of them as World Champions.

The team began giving Crosetti engraved shotguns instead of title rings. His 23 World Series paychecks totaled only $142,989.30. Although a significant sum for those times, it reveals how much the economics of the game have changed, even since the 1960s.

Crosetti began his career as a teammate of Babe Ruth in 1932. He drove Joe DiMaggio from San Francisco to his first Yankee training camp in Florida in 1936. He observed Lou Gehrig make his "Luckiest Man" speech at Yankee Stadium in 1939. He shook Roger Maris' hand at third base after his 61st home run in 1961. He coached Mickey Mantle for his full career.

The 1927, 1936 and 1939 Yankee teams are still ranked as three of the greatest in the history of the game. Crosetti was an important part of the 1936 and 1939 Yankees clubs as an All-Star both years. A marvelous fielder always among the American League defensive leaders, the 5'10" 165-pound Crosetti topped the AL in putouts and double plays twice each.

As the Yankees' leadoff hitter, he was a masterful bunter and drew his fair share of walks. The resourceful Crosetti paced the league in hit-by-pitches eight times and got plunked a career 114 times. He crossed the plate over 100 times a year during a four-year stretch from 1937 to 1940 and set a major league 154-game schedule record with 747 plate appearances in 1938.

* * * * *

Francesco Paolo Giuseppe Crosetti was born on Oct. 4, 1910 to Rachel Montever and Dominico Crosetti in San Francisco. While his father was born in Italy, his mother was a native Californian. He and his brother John were raised in North Beach near Fishermen's Wharf, the neighborhood where his future teammate Joe DiMaggio later grew up on the same sandlots.

Crosetti starred in baseball at Prep High School in Santa Clara, California, a Jesuit-run private Catholic school now known as Bellarmine College Preparatory High School. At 17, he signed a contract with his hometown San Francisco Seals in the Double-A Pacific Coast League.

In his first summer, he played third base. He then moved over to shortstop for the next three years to play 556 games in the long 200-game PCL schedules of 1929, 1930 and 1931. Crosetti hit a combined .330 in 2,300 at-bats with 759 hits, 168 doubles, 26 triples and 44 home runs. The Yankees purchased his contract in late 1930 for the extraordinary sum of $75,000. The team wanted him to spend one more year in the PCL to get ready for 1932 spring training.

Crosetti was assigned uniform #5 and given his debut with the Yankees on April 12, 1932. Making an immediate impact, he played in 116 games at third base, shortstop and second base under manager Joe McCarthy. He helped the Yankees to 107 victories plus a World Series sweep of the Cubs highlighted by Babe Ruth's "Called Shot" at Wrigley Field off Charlie Root.

Crosetti had his best offensive season in 1936, hitting .288 with 15 home runs, 90 walks and 18 stolen bases while scoring a career-high 137 runs. The Yankees of 1937

G	AB	R	H	2B	3B	HR	RBI	SB	BB	SO	BA	OBP	SLG	TB
1683	6277	1006	1541	260	65	98	649	113	792	799	.245	.341	.354	2225

reclaimed the pennant in DiMaggio's rookie year (he took over Crosetti's #5) with Hall of Famers Gehrig, DiMaggio, Bill Dickey and Tony Lazzeri. Crosetti was the Series Game 2 catalyst, going 3-for-5 and scoring four runs as the Yankees beat the Giants, 18-4, on their way to the title.

In 1938, after leading the AL in 157 games played, 757 plate appearances and 27 steals, Crosetti flashed some leather in the 1938 World Series. He made three game-saving plays in Game 1 and blasted a game-winning eighth inning homer off Dizzy Dean in Game 2. The Cubs never recovered and the Bombers went on to sweep. Crosetti could have been the Series MVP.

He led the AL in 1939 with 737 plate appearance and 656 at-bats, but his bat speed began to slow down in 1940, hitting just .194. Crosetti mentored future Hall of Fame shortstop Phil Rizzuto in 1941 instead of shunning the young man who would replace him at shortstop.

In 1942 World Series Game 3, third baseman Crosetti argued vehemently after umpire Bill Summers signaled safe on a close play at third. Crosetti shoved Summers... and Summers shoved back. Suspended for the first month of 1943, he returned in June and the Yankees won the pennant, but ran into a hot Cardinal club that dispensed them again, 4-1, as they had in 1942.

In his last two seasons in 1947 and 1948, Crosetti only got 15 at-bats as a player-coach. After his final game on October 3, 1948, Crosetti became the Yanks' third base coach for 20 years, taking part in 15 more Fall Classics. Working mostly under Casey Stengel and Ralph Houk, he was an expert at stealing signs. After his final season with the Yankees in 1968, he also coached for the 1969 Seattle Pilots and then the 1970 Minnesota Twins before retiring in 1971.

Frankie Crosetti was inducted into the PCL Hall of Fame in 2004. He and his wife Norma were married for 63 years and lived in Stockton, California later in life. They had a son and a daughter, three grandchildren and two great-grandchildren. Crosetti passed away on February 11, 2002 in Stockton at age 91 and was laid to rest at the Holy Cross Cemetery in Colma, California.

HARRY DANNING

NEW YORK GIANTS
CATCHER

1933-1942

> *"Danning will be the best catcher in the National League this year, possibly in baseball, and I include Hartnett and Dickey."*
>
> ~ Giants manager
> Bill Terry before the 1939 season

Harry Danning was the greatest Jewish catcher in major league history. A four-time All-Star, he earned the distinction of being the third-best all around receiver of his era behind only Hall of Famers Bill Dickey of the Yankees and Gabby Hartnett of the Cubs.

The 6'1" 190-pound Danning hit .300 or better each season from 1938 to 1940 while catching at least 120 games. He was known as "Harry the Horse" after the Damon Runyon short story and Broadway character. The nickname stuck because of his workhorse durability.

Danning fielded a career .985 as one of the great defensive catchers of his day, steadying a Big Three starting staff of Carl Hubbell, Hal Schumacher and Freddie Fitzsimmons. He paced NL backstops in putouts three times, assists twice, and base-runners-caught-stealing twice.

The popular fan favorite Danning was behind home plate when Lou Gehrig hit his final Fall Classic home run; when Joe DiMaggio hit his first World Series circuit clout; and when Ted Williams hit his famous walk-off four-bagger in the 1941 Midsummer Classic.

A powerful right-handed line-drive hitter, Danning used a noticeably closed stance that he felt allowed him to pull an inside fastball and still drive outside pitches to right field. His career 162 doubles and .415 slugging percentage bear out his strong middle-of-the order offense.

★　★　★　★　★

Harry Danning was born in Los Angeles on September 6, 1911 to Jenny Goldberg and Robert Danning- both Russian Jewish émigrés. He grew up with two brothers- Ike and Curtis Ben- and a sister Leah. His older brother Ike later caught briefly for the 1928 St. Louis Browns.

The teenage Danning played sandlot baseball and then starred for the Los Angeles Polytechnic High baseball team, graduating in 1927. He went to work in the car-

pet and rug business while playing in semi-pro leagues where he was scouted and signed by the Giants.

In 1931, his rookie year in baseball, Danning caught for the Bridgeport (CT) Bears of the Class-A Eastern League, hitting .324. New Giants manager Bill Terry decided to bring him up to the big club in early June of 1932. He was told the news as he took the field in Bridgeport. In that game, a line drive broke his jaw as a base runner at third base. His promotion was delayed.

Mentored by catching great Ray Schalk, the 1933 Buffalo (NY) Bisons manager, he refined his craft in the International League, hitting .349. Danning got his debut with the Giants on July 30, but mostly rode the bench and didn't get into the Fall Classic win over the Nationals.

In his first four seasons, Danning was Gus Mancuso's understudy. His hitting suffered because of sparse playing time, but by 1937, he was catching 93 games for the NL Champions. In Game 4 he went 3-for-4 in the lone win over the Yankees, despite a broken bone in his hand.

After Mancuso fractured a finger early the next year, Danning emerged as the regular catcher, hitting .306 in 120 games. Honored as the NL's best catcher in 1939, he hit .313 in 135 games, including 16 bombs and 249 total bases, while pacing all NL receivers in fielding at .991.

He was the best catcher in baseball in 1940, hitting .300 for the third year in a row with 34 doubles and 91 RBI. Hitting for the cycle versus the Pirates in June, his inside-the-park homer traveled 460 feet and landed in front of the Giants' clubhouse behind the Eddie Grant Memorial.

From 1938 to 1940, Danning had finished in the top ten in the NL MVP balloting each year. Although he was a 1941 All-Star, he played that year and the next beset with injuries and his *Louisville Slugger* was not as dangerous. He played his last game before turning 31 years old.

In late 1942, Danning was drafted into the military

G	AB	R	H	2B	3B	HR	RBI	SB	BB	SO	BA	OBP	SLG	TB
890	2971	363	847	162	26	57	397	13	187	217	.285	.330	.415	1232

and entered service with the U. S. Army Air Corps on April 6, 1943. During World War II, he attained the rank of Sergeant in the 6th Ferrying Group, Air Transport Command USAAF at the Long Beach (CA) Army Air Base.

Danning regularly played for the 6th Ferrying Group baseball squad during his tour of duty. By May of 1945, his knees had had enough. Doctors advised him that continuing to play the game could cause lasting damage. He decided to hang up the tools of ignorance for good.

After the war, Danning coached a season with the Hollywood (CA) Stars in the Pacific Coast League. He also was a car dealer for a time, then worked in circulation at the *Daily News Los Angeles*. He settled in as an insurance agency manager with Metropolitan Life in Millbrae, California.

Danning retired in 1976 and lived in Chesterton, Indiana with his wife of 38 years, the former Diane Nygord, until she passed away in 1978. He resided with his only daughter, Viktoria, her husband and three grandchildren for the rest of his life in Valparaiso, Indiana.

Danning still ranks ninth all-time in career hits among Jewish major league players. He was issued a Silver Lifetime Pass by Major League Baseball to attend any game and remained connected with the National Pastime through a steady volume of letters he received from fans.

An inductee of the New York, National, and International Jewish Sports Halls of Fame, Danning was the oldest living Jewish major leaguer in 2003. Wheelchair bound and in poor health, he was unable to attend a Hall of Fame event in Cooperstown to honor Jewish players.

The last surviving member of the 1933 World Series Champion Giants, The Horse passed away of pneumonia in Valparaiso on November 29, 2004 at age 93. His ashes were strewn about Harry Danning Field located at the old Porter County Fairgrounds in Valparaiso.

BILL DICKEY

NEW YORK YANKEES
CATCHER

1928-1943 • 1946

"There is only one Bill Dickey. Bill isn't fast. But he is the best handler of pitchers I ever saw. Beyond which, he is the greatest clutch hitter I ever saw, not only for a catcher but for anyone else in baseball."

~ rival Roger Bresnahan

A member of eight World Series Championship Yankees teams, Bill Dickey is considered the greatest major league catcher in the first half of the 20th century and the soul of the Yankee Dynasty. He bridged the Babe Ruth, Lou Gehrig and Joe DiMaggio eras as a player, and the Mickey Mantle era as a coach.

An 11-time All-Star, Dickey was the best hitting catcher of his time and the most dangerous clutch hitter on the Bronx Bombers according to his manager Joe McCarthy. Starting in 1929, the left-handed hitting backstop batted over .300 ten out of 11 seasons.

Dickey was thin, rangy and agile at 6'1½" and 185 pounds. He was known for his strong, laser-accurate throwing arm and his ability to handle pitchers, especially the mercurial Lefty Gomez. Dickey caught 125 games in 1931 without a single passed ball.

He was also a fierce competitor. After a ferocious home plate collision on July 4, 1932 with the Nationals' Carl Reynolds, the normally mild-mannered Dickey broke Reynolds' jaw with one punch and was suspended for a month.

Dickey never played a big-league game at any position other than catcher and received in over 100 games 13 straight seasons (1929-1941), a mark matched only by Johnny Bench. He caught in a record 38 World Series games- six of them in 1936 with his glove hand broken in two places. Despite the injury, he launched a Game 4 home run.

* * * * *

William Malcolm Dickey was born on June 6, 1907 in Bastrop, Morehouse Parish, Louisiana to Laura and John Dickey. The Scots-Irish family with seven children soon moved to Kensett, Arkansas. His railroad brakeman father and older brother Gus were semi-pro stars and his older brother George was a Red Sox and White Sox catcher.

After starring for Searcy High and Little Rock Junior College, he had a short audition with the 1925 Little Rock (AR) Travelers of the Class-A Southern Association. Dickey began his first full season in pro baseball with the 1926 Class-C Muskogee (OK) Athletics of the Western Association, finishing the last 17 games with the Travelers. He caught the eye of Yankee scout Johnny Nee playing for the Class-D Jackson (MS) Senators of the Cotton States League in 1927 and subsequently signed with the Yankees.

Dickey hit exactly .300 in 60 games for Little Rock, then had a brief stopover with the Double-A Buffalo (NY) Bisons (International League) before getting his debut on September 27, 1928. He played only ten games and saw no action in the World Series.

As a rookie in 1929, he immediately embarked on a six-season stretch where he hit .300 or better. Dickey put up some of the finest offensive seasons ever by a catcher from 1936 to 1939, hitting over 20 home runs (102 total) and driving in over 100 runs every year. He posted a career-high .362 in 1936, the highest average by a catcher until Joe Mauer hit .365 more than six decades later in 2009. He followed with a .332 mark and a personal-best 29 home runs in 1937, including grand slams on successive days.

On July 26, 1939, he walloped three straight homers against the Browns. In the four-game World Series sweep against Cincinnati, Dickey poled two circuit clouts and drove in five runs, including a walk-off home run in the bottom of the ninth in Game 1.

His average and power both waned in 1940 and 1941 with only 16 home runs. In 1942 and 1943, he caught a total of just 167 games, but accounted for all the runs with a two-run clout in the 1943 World Series Game 5 finale victory over the Cardinals.

G	AB	R	H	2B	3B	HR	RBI	SB	BB	SO	BA	OBP	SLG	TB
1789	6300	930	1969	343	72	202	1209	36	678	289	.313	.382	.486	3062

At the end of the season, Dickey enlisted in the U. S. Navy and served two years in the Pacific. He came back for a final season in 1946, appearing in only 54 games before taking over for manager Joe McCarthy, who was hired by the Red Sox. He led the Yankees to a 57-48 mark, good for third in the league, but resigned in September.

In 1949, Dickey returned under Casey Stengel as first base and catching coach. He taught a young Yogi Berra the intricacies of the catching position. Berra had inherited his #8, so Dickey graciously wore #33 until he turned in his pinstripes after the 1957 season. He scouted for the Yankees one year in 1959 before retiring.

As Gehrig's longtime roommate, Dickey was the first Yankee to find out about Gehrig's illness. Still an active player, he appeared as himself in the 1942 film *The Pride of the Yankees* with Gary Cooper and again in *The Stratton Story* in 1949.

Dickey was inducted into the National Baseball Hall of Fame in 1954 as was Berra in 1972, the year the Yankees retired #8 to honor both men. On August 22, 1988, both were paid homage with plaques in Monument Park at Yankee Stadium.

Dickey was named to *The Sporting News'* 1999 list of "Baseball's Greatest Players" and was a nominee for baseball's All-Century Team. He is currently the only Yank with a retired number not yet featured on the YES Network series *Yankeeography*.

Dickey spent part of his retirement residing in the Yarborough Landing community on the shores of Millwood Lake in southwestern Arkansas. He remained an avid hunter, fisherman and golfer until he passed away in Little Rock in 1993. He was laid to rest at the Roselawn Memorial Park in Little Rock.

JOE DiMAGGIO

"DiMaggio was the greatest all-around player I ever saw. His career cannot be summed up in numbers and awards. It might sound corny, but he had a profound and lasting impact on the country."

~ Ted Williams

Joe DiMaggio established himself as one of baseball's greatest players, admired for his effortless classic swing and the ease with which he patrolled center field. His sensational 56-game hitting streak remains the most untouchable record in sports.

DiMaggio led the Bronx Bombers to ten pennants and nine World Series titles. A three-time American League MVP, he was an All-Star in each of his 13 major league seasons and an eight-time member of *The Sporting News* Major League All-Star team.

With his wide stance, short stride and long fluid swing, the 6'2" 195-pound DiMaggio twice won AL batting crowns and twice topped his league in home runs, RBI and slugging percentage. He struck out just eight times more than he hit a home run.

DiMaggio was also the graceful "Yankee Clipper," never appearing to strain or lunge for a ball and always in the right spot to catch it. He covered the expansive Yankee Stadium outfield with style and used his powerful arm to cut down many a base runner.

An intensely private person, DiMaggio always comported himself with dignity in the glare of the New York spotlight, bringing class to his Yankee team. He even wore stylish, tailored suits to Yankee Stadium, upholding the Yankees' corporate image of that period.

★ ★ ★ ★ ★

Giuseppe Paolo DiMaggio, Jr. was born on November 25, 1914 to Rosalia Mercurio and Giuseppe Paolo DiMaggio, Sr. in Martinez, California. He grew up in a large Sicilian Catholic family in San Francisco's North Beach section. His father was a fisherman.

DiMaggio quit Galileo High in 1931 to join the semi-pro Sunset Produce team and hit .632. His older brother Vince was playing for the Double-A San Francisco Seals

when the club signed him at 17 and had him fill in at shortstop for the last three games of 1932.

With the Seals in 1933, DiMaggio put together a 61-game hitting streak, a Pacific Coast League record that attracted national interest. Poised for stardom and hitting .341 in August of 1934, DiMaggio tore ligaments in his left knee stepping out of a jitney bus.

The only big-league team willing to take a gamble on the injured 19-year-old was the Yankees. They bought his contract and sent him back to the Seals. He responded by batting an imposing .398 with 34 home runs and 154 RBI as the PCL's 1935 MVP.

DiMaggio made his debut on May 5, 1936 and hit .323 with 132 runs scored, 206 hits, 29 home runs and 125 RBI. He led the AL with 15 triples and 22 assists and capped one of the best rookie years ever by batting .346 in a World Series win over the Giants.

Lou Gehrig was felled by ALS in early 1939 and DiMaggio stepped forward with a phenomenal year, winning the batting crown at .381 as the AL MVP and *The Sporting News* Major League Player of the Year. He also paced the Yankees to a Fall Classic win.

After earning a second consecutive batting title in 1940, DiMaggio captivated the nation in 1941 by hitting safely in a 56 straight games while striking out just five times. He was stopped with two fielding gems behind third base by Ken Keltner on July 17.

Joltin' Joe went on to hit safely in 72 of 73 games, while batting .357, and struck out only 13 times in 622 plate appearances. In his first seven seasons, he averaged .339, 123 runs scored, 193 hits, 31 homers and 133 RBI with six pennants and five world titles.

He enlisted in the U. S. Army Air Force on February 17, 1943 and requested combat duty, but was turned

G	AB	R	H	2B	3B	HR	RBI	SB	BB	SO	BA	OBP	SLG	TB
1736	6821	1390	2214	389	131	361	1537	30	790	369	.325	.398	.579	3948

down and remained stateside. DiMaggio joined the military at 28 and mustered out at 31, losing three prime athletic years in the middle of his career.

After a year readjusting to major league competition, DiMaggio won the 1947 AL Most Valuable Player award, hitting .315 and committing only one error the entire year. He topped the Junior Circuit in 1948 with 39 home runs and 155 RBI while hitting .320.

A right heel bone spur in 1949 put him out until June 28 when he hit four homers, drove in nine, and made a game-saving catch during a three-game sweep of the Red Sox. The Yanks won the pennant by a single game and defeated Brooklyn in the World Series.

After a virtuoso 1950 season, DiMaggio's skills began to erode. He hit a mere .263 in 1951 and though the three-time World Series Champion Yankees offered him another big contract, he decided to retire at 36, no longer able to meet his own high expectations.

He wed glamorous movie star goddess Marilyn Monroe on January 14, 1954 in the celebrity marriage of the 20th century. Although the union did not last, Miss Monroe and DiMaggio maintained a close relationship up until her tragic death in 1962.

The Yankees retired his #5 in 1952 and the National Baseball Hall of Fame hailed him in 1955. DiMaggio

was honored in the 1969 baseball centennial as the "Greatest Living Ballplayer." Gerald Ford awarded him America's highest civilian honor in 1976, the Presidential Medal of Freedom. He is a member of baseball's All-Century Team.

Joe DiMaggio passed away of lung cancer at his Hollywood, Florida home on March 8, 1999 and was interred in the Holy Cross Cemetery in Colma, California. That year the Yankees dedicated a fifth Stadium monument to him and wore his #5 on their sleeves.

BOB FELLER

CLEVELAND INDIANS
RIGHT-HANDED PITCHER

1936-1941 • 1945-1956

"Many athletes are great. Bob Feller was seminal. In the long-ago time, unlike nowadays, it was unheard of for teenagers to succeed in the big top of athletics. Feller dressed in the uniform of the major league Cleveland Indians, striking out – fanning! – American demigods ... in the only professional team sport that mattered then in the United States."

~ writer Frank Deford

Flame-throwing Bob Feller was the greatest player ever to wear an Indians uniform. He was a 17 year old prodigy, the first pitcher to win 20 games before he turned 21. He would have earned the Cy Young Award in 1939, 1940 and 1941 if it had existed.

With the primitive speed devices of his day, Feller's fastball was clocked at as high as 105 mph. The 6' 190-pounder started his motion with a full pump of his arms, and then a huge kick, helping him hide the ball until it was suddenly on the hitter.

An eight-time All-Star, "Rapid Robert" Feller won 20 games six times and threw a record 12 one-hitters and three no-hitters. He paced the AL in strikeouts seven times, in wins and complete-games six times, and in innings pitched five times. He is the Indians' all-time leader in innings pitched, complete-games, wins, strikeouts, shutouts and walks.

* * * * *

Robert Andrew William Feller was born on November 3, 1918, to Lena E. Forret and William Andrew Feller near Van Meter, Dallas County, Iowa, deep in the Midwest corn country. He put in many a full day of summer chores on his father's farm and credited his powerful arm strength to milking cows, baling hay and picking corn.

His father encouraged his baseball by building him a homemade ball field and played catch with him after his chores were finished. At age 12, Feller hurled for the Adel (IA) American Legion, tossing five no-hitters facing older teenagers and grown men.

In 1934, Feller threw for the Iowa State Champion West Des Moines American Legion and starred for the semi-pro Farmers' Union Insurance team in 1935. There he was first spotted by Indians chief scout Cy

Slapnicka who signed him at age 15.

While the Indians kept him hidden on a minor league roster, he hurled five no-hitters for Van Meter High in early 1936. Kenesaw Mountain Landis could have deemed the young phenom a free agent, but his parents insisted that he remain with Cleveland.

Feller never pitched in the minor leagues. The Indians brought him up as a 17 year old to make his debut in a relief appearance on July 19, 1936 against the Nationals in Griffith Stadium. The action made him the youngest player to pitch in a major league game.

Feller received his first major league start on August 23, struck out 15 St. Louis Browns, and won, 4-1, in the greatest pitching debut ever. Later, Feller set the AL record by fanning 17 A's on September 13. His fastball was already the "Van Meter Heater."

In 1937, the year he graduated from high school, he struck out 150 AL batters. On October 6, 1938, Feller set the big-league standard by striking out 18 Tigers. He went 17-11, topped the AL with 240 strikeouts and walked 208 batsmen, still a major league high.

After posting a 24-9 mark in 1939, Feller threw his first no-hitter on April 16, 1940 against the White Sox. It is still the only Opening Day no-no in big-league history. He went on to be *The Sporting News* 1940 Major League Player of the Year at 21.

Before he turned 23, Feller had already won 109 games and had three 20-game seasons. Proud and patriotic, he was intensely affected by the bombing of Pearl Harbor on December 7, 1941. He enlisted the next day- the first major league player to do so.

Feller served as an anti-aircraft gun crew chief for 26 months in the Pacific and North Atlantic on the battleship *USS Alabama*. He earned five campaign ribbons

G	IP	W	L	PCT	SHO	GS	CG	H	ER	SO	BB	ERA
570	3827	266	162	.621	44	384	279	3271	1384	2581	1764	3.25

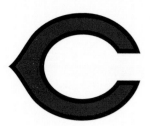

studded with eight battle stars, sacrificing four years between 24 and 28 at the peak of his powers.

In his first full season after the War in 1946, Feller had his finest year, going 26-15 with a 2.18 ERA. He threw his second no-hitter at Yankee Stadium on April 30, finished 36 of 42 starts, rang up 348 hitters in 371⅓ innings, and hurled 10 shutouts.

In 1947, despite slipping off a wet mound and injuring his back, Feller led the AL in strikeouts for his seventh straight season. The 1948 Tribe won the World Series title with Feller going 6-1 during the tight pennant race. He was the Fall Classic Game 1 starter, but lost a 1-0 two-hitter to the Braves before the Indians prevailed in six games.

The Sporting News 1951 AL Pitcher of the Year, Feller paced the league with 22 victories, pitching alongside Early Wynn, Mike Garcia, and Bob Lemon in one of the best rotations ever. He achieved his third no-hitter on July 1, beating the Tigers, 2-1.

In his last five years, Feller went only 36-31. After his last season, the Indians retired his #19 in 1957 and he was voted a first-ballot National Baseball Hall of Famer in 1962. In the 1969 baseball centennial, he was deemed the "Greatest Living Right-Handed Pitcher." He was honored with a statue at the opening of Jacobs Field in 1994.

Feller was long a fixture in the Progressive Field press box for decades. He would proffer his opinions on current events and give his take on how the Indians were playing. He maintained excellent health into his early 90s, but was diagnosed with leukemia in 2010, then pneumonia. Bob Feller passed away on December 10, 2010 at age 92 and was interred at the Gates Mills North Cemetery, Cuyahoga County, Ohio near his home.

LOU GEHRIG

NEW YORK YANKEES
FIRST BASE

1923-1939

Lou Gehrig's courage and humility have been an inspiration to generations of Americans. He became the legendary "Iron Horse," baseball's greatest first baseman, while establishing an incredible record of 2,130 consecutive games played.

Because Gehrig hit cleanup behind Babe Ruth, he was given the number "4." The flamboyant Bambino and the reserved Gehrig were personality opposites but great teammates, and formed the heart of the Yankees' "Murderers' Row" from 1925 to 1934.

A relentless RBI machine, Gehrig averaged 147 runs batted in per year. He owns half of the top six seasonal RBI marks ever, including his AL record 184 in 1931. He drove in a staggering 509 runs during a three-year run from 1930 to 1932.

The brawny 6'1" 220-pound Gehrig swung his 40-ounce *Louisville Slugger* with a vengeance, hammering line shots to all fields. He earned a record five seasons with 400 total bases, hit over .350 six times and finished eight years with 200 or more hits.

Gehrig accumulated 13 straight years with 100 runs and 100 RBI. He boomed a record 23 grand slams and was the first hitter to blast four home runs in a single game. He took part in eight World Series championships, hitting a Fall Classic record .361.

★　★　★　★　★

The son of poor German immigrants Anna Christina Fack and Wilhelm Heinrich Gehrig, Henry Louis Gehrig was born June 19, 1903 in Manhattan's Yorkville section. He weighed 14 pounds at birth and was the only sibling of four to survive an early age.

Already full grown with broad shoulders and massive thighs as a junior at the High School of Commerce in 1920, he stunned a Wrigley Field crowd of over 10,000 by launching a grand slam completely out of the park versus Chicago's Lane Tech High.

Gehrig went on to attend Columbia University where he played football and baseball. He struck out 17 hitters in one game, later powered a 450-foot shot out of the Lions' South Field and soon signed a hometown Yankee contract.

The young slugger debuted in the big time as a ninth inning replacement on June 15, 1923, but manager Miller Huggins sent him to Hartford for seasoning in 1923 and 1924. On June 2, 1925, Gehrig replaced the slumping Wally Pipp for good at first base.

The 24-year-old phenom unleashed one of the greatest offensive seasons in 1927. Gehrig hit .373 with 218 hits, 52 doubles, 18 triples, 47 home runs and 175 RBI. His 117 extra-base hits and 447 total bases are among the most ever. Ruth hit 60 home runs, but Gehrig was *The Sporting News* American League Most Valuable Player.

In his prime in the early 1930s, Gehrig helped establish new manager Joe McCarthy in 1931 when he hit .341 and led the AL with 163 runs, 211 hits, 46 home runs, 184 RBI and 410 total bases. In 1934, he earned the AL Triple Crown, hitting .363 with 49 bombs and 165 RBI, and was chosen *The Sporting News* AL MVP again.

Combining with rookie sensation Joe DiMaggio in 1936 to form a new pinstripe power-hitting tandem, Gehrig hit .354, pounded 49 home runs and drove 167 runs across the plate as the Bronx Bombers won their first of four straight World Series titles.

After another stellar season in 1937 in which the strongman slugged .643, his constitution began to erode in 1938 in the middle of the season. By the time he began spring training in 1939, it was evident that

G	AB	R	H	2B	3B	HR	RBI	SB	BB	SO	BA	OBP	SLG	TB
2164	8001	1888	2721	534	163	493	1995	102	1508	790	.340	.447	.632	5060

his game had deteriorated ominously.

After another weak performance in early May, Gehrig benched himself in Detroit before a game at Briggs Stadium. He had remained in the lineup for 14 years straight, doggedly playing through all sorts of injuries big and small, including three major concussions and broken bones in every finger on both hands.

Gehrig would never play baseball again. As his strength ebbed, he visited the Mayo Clinic where Dr. Harold Harbein diagnosed his condition as amyotrophic lateral sclerosis (ALS), known forever after as "Lou Gehrig's Disease."

Lou Gehrig Appreciation Day was proclaimed on July 4, 1939. A crowd of 61,808, along with many of his 1927 teammates, bade him a poignant farewell. Delivering what is now considered baseball's *Gettysburg Address*, Gehrig declared to a hushed stadium, "Today, I consider myself the luckiest man on the face of the earth..."

The Yankees retired his uniform #4, the first player to be so honored. In late 1939, Gehrig was elected unanimously to the National Baseball Hall of Fame after the waiting period was waived. He was chosen the greatest first baseman of all time in 1969 and received the most fan votes of any player for baseball's 1999 All-Century Team.

Lou Gehrig passed away at his home in the Bronx on June 2, 1941. He was only 37 years old. People lined up for blocks to view his casket before the funeral at Christ Episcopal Church of Riverdale. Gehrig was interred at Kensico Cemetery in Valhalla, New York. His wife of six years, Eleanor Grace Twitchell, never remarried and devoted the rest of her life to supporting an ALS cure. The first Yankee captain was also the first Yankee player to be honored with a monument in center field at Yankee Stadium a month later.

CHARLIE GEHRINGER

DETROIT TIGERS
SECOND BASE
1924-1942

"Gehringer says 'hello' on opening day and 'goodbye' on closing day, and in between he hits .350."

~ *teammate and Tigers manager Mickey Cochrane*

Charlie Gehringer is considered by many the greatest all-around second baseman of all-time. Dubbed "The Mechanical Man" for his reliable excellence and taciturn air, he led the Tigers to three pennants and a World Series title, letting his *Louisville Slugger* do the talking. He completed 14 seasons over .300, achieved the 200-hit plateau seven times, scored 100 runs 12 times, belted 30 doubles ten times and drove in 100 runs seven times.

The left-handed hitting Gehringer may have been the best two-strike hitter ever, never striking out more than 42 times. So durable, he built two consecutive game streaks of over 500 games and played every inning of the first six All-Star games. He remains the All-Star batting king at .500 (10-for-20). In 81 World Series at-bats, he hit a superb .321.

The 5'11" 180-pound Gehringer was also a splendid defensive second baseman, making difficult plays look easy with his long graceful strides, sure hands and accurate arm. He led the AL in fielding seven times, putouts three times, and assists a record seven times. His 7,068 career assists still rank second all-time and are a testament to his range.

* * * * *

Charles Leonard Gehringer was born on May 11, 1903 outside of Fowlerville, Michigan, a rural farming town 57 miles north of Detroit. The youngest son of German immigrants Therese Hahn and Lenard Gehringer, he starred for his town and school teams, and earned a scholarship to nearby University of Michigan at Ann Arbor.

Gehringer was invited to Detroit to work out for Tigers manager Ty Cobb in late 1923. Cobb convinced owner Frank Navin to sign him and never allowed anyone to alter his classic erect hitting style. Gehringer spent 1924 with the London (ON) Tecumsehs and debuted with the Tigers on September 22, hitting .462 in five games.

After another year of seasoning with the Triple-A Toronto (ON) Maple Leafs, he earned his spot as the Tigers second baseman in 1926 and tried to fit into Cobb's small ball-oriented offense. He hit a pedestrian .277 with a career-high 27 sacrifice bunts.

Gehringer's brilliant 1929 is a gauge of how complete a ballplayer he had become. He hit .339 with 106 RBI and led the American League with 155 games played, 131 runs scored, 215 hits, 45 doubles, 19 triples and 27 steals while pacing all Junior Circuit second basemen in fielding and putouts.

Charlie Gehringer Day was planned in his honor on August 14, 1929. His nonchalant response was to deposit the first pitch thrown to him over the right field wall, bang out three more hits, handle ten chances perfectly and steal home to win the game.

The Tigers won their first pennant in a quarter of a century in 1934. Gehringer batted .356 with a career-best 127 RBI and paced the American League with 134 runs scored and 214 hits. In the World Series loss to the Cardinals, he hit .379 with a Game 5 home run off future Hall of Famer Dizzy Dean.

Seeking redemption in 1935, the Tigers won their first World Series title, besting the Cubs, 4-2. Gehringer hit .330 with 123 runs scored and 108 RBI and starred in the Fall Classic, hitting a dazzling .375 with clutch hits in Games 2 and 4, and scored the winning run in Game 6.

The Mechanical Man was a virtual metronome in 1936, playing in every game and hitting .354 with 116 RBI. He had career-highs with 227 hits, 87 extra base hits and slugged .555. While striking out a career-low 13

G	AB	R	H	2B	3B	HR	RBI	SB	BB	SO	BA	OBP	SLG	TB
2323	8860	1774	2839	574	146	184	1427	182	1186	372	.320	.404	.480	4257

times, he set season records for second basemen with 60 doubles, 144 runs scored and 356 total bases, and anchored the defense.

Gehringer's encore was to wallop his way to the 1937 American League batting championship (.371) and the Most Valuable Player award. He collected 209 hits, drove in 96 runs and scored 133 times while posting a career-high .458 on-base percentage.

Not at full strength in 1940, he still helped the Tigers win a pennant, hitting .313. In 1941, Gehringer hit a disappointing .220 and retired. He was persuaded to return, but played only sparingly and retired for good to be commissioned as a U.S. Navy lieutenant.

After the War, Gehringer became wealthy as a manufacturer's agent, purveying auto accessories in the Motor City. Tigers owner Walter "Spike" Briggs hired him back as general manager for 1951 and 1952 and then as a vice president (1955-59).

Throughout his career, Gehringer took care of his diabetic mother and remained a bachelor. When he did marry, he missed his own induction into the National Baseball Hall of Fame in 1949, planning his wedding to Josephine Stillen.

During the 1969 Baseball Centennial Celebration, Charlie Gehringer was selected baseball's "Greatest Living Second Baseman." He was ranked #46 on *The Sporting News* 1999 list of the "100 Greatest Baseball Play-

ers." The Tigers retired Gehringer's uniform #2 in 1983 and dedicated a magnificent statue of him completing a double play which was erected beyond left-center field at Detroit's new Comerica Park.

The Mechanical Man suffered a stroke in December

1992 and passed away peacefully on January 21, 1993 in Bloomfield Hills, Michigan at age 89. He is buried at the Holy Sepulchre Mausoleum in Southfield, Oakland County, Michigan.

STAN HACK

CHICAGO CUBS
THIRD BASE

1932-1947

"Hack came closest to an earthly manifestation of the ideal third baseman of the day. Tall, slender, handsome, confident – Hack was the idol of every sandlot urchin playing third base in a pair of torn knickers."

~ author William Curran

Stan Hack was the finest third baseman of his generation and one of the greatest players in Cubs history. A five-time All-Star and career .300 hitter, he played on four National League Championship teams, but never a World Series Champion. *The Sporting News* named Hack the top third baseman in baseball three times. When he retired, he ranked only behind Cap Anson on the Cubs all-time lists in games played, at-bats and hits. A perennial fan favorite, Hack was a handsome, good-natured player with a famous smile.

★ ★ ★ ★ ★

Stanley Camfield Hack was born in Sacramento, California on December 6, 1909. After graduating from Sacramento High, he went to work as a bank clerk and played semi-pro baseball on weekends. The hometown Sacramento Solons of the Double-A Pacific Coast League signed him in 1931 where he hit .352, registering 232 hits and scoring 128 runs. So impressed was Cubs general manager Bill Veeck, Sr., he traveled to California and signed Hack himself for a $40,000 bonus.

The left-handed hitting Hack was the preeminent leadoff catalyst of the 1930s. He was an adept contact hitter, becoming particularly skillful at swinging late and lining the ball into left field. He scored 100+ runs in seven seasons and was known as an expert bunter. Hack led the NL three times in plate appearances and times-on-base; twice in hits and stolen bases. He never struck out more than he walked and still holds the Cubs record of 1,092 free passes. His career on-base percentage of .394 was the highest by any third baseman until Wade Boggs finished in 1999 at .415. Pie Traynor was the only National League third baseman with more hits, doubles and total bases when Hack hung 'em up.

He broke into the big-leagues in 1932 at age 22. Two years later he was well-established at Wrigley Field as the league's best third baseman. At an agile 6' 170 pounds, he was a stylish fielder with an accurate throwing arm and a quick release. The sure-handed Hack led the NL five times in putouts; three times in double plays; and twice in fielding percentage and assists. At the time of his retirement, he ranked runner-up to Traynor at the hot corner all-time in games (1,836), putouts (1,944), assists (3,494) and total chances (5,684). Hack had a hand in 255 double plays, third in NL history.

By 1935, he had achieved true star status throughout the Senior Circuit. One day 21-year-old Bill Veeck, Jr. (later baseball's most outrageous promoter) walked through the Wrigley Field bleachers selling a souvenir featuring a grinning photo of Hack with "Smile with Stan" printed on it and a mirror on the reverse. In a bizarre scene, mischievous Cubs fans immediately started shining the mirrors into rival batters' eyes. The umpires suspended the game and threatened to declare a Cubs forfeit.

Hack batted a stellar .348 in four World Series with 24 hits, five doubles and five RBI. The Cubs were swept by the Yankees in 1932 and 1938. In Game 6 of the 1935 Series against Detroit with the score tied, 3-3, Hack stepped up and hit a clutch triple to lead off the ninth inning. But he was stranded there and the Cubs went down to defeat.

With today's rules, Hack would have been declared the 1940 National League batting champion with his .317 average in 603 at-bats. However, little known Debs Garms of the Pirates (.355) was handed the honor with only 358 at-bats.

Roughhewn old catcher Jimmie Wilson was hired to manage the Cubbies in 1941. The unqualified Wilson

G	AB	R	H	2B	3B	HR	RBI	SB	BB	SO	BA	OBP	SLG	TB
1938	7278	1239	2193	363	81	57	642	165	1092	466	.301	.394	.397	2889

seemed unable to communicate with Hack, who decided he'd had enough and retired following the 1943 season. The organization finally came to its senses ten games into the 1944 campaign, relieving Wilson and giving back the reins to Hack's old friend "Jolly Cholly" Grimm, who soon convinced him to return.

In 1945, Hack enjoyed his greatest season, helping the Cubs to a National League pennant. He hit a career-high .323 with a .420 on-base percentage, 193 hits, 110 runs scored and 99 walks. Hack led the National League with 195 putouts, a .975 fielding average and a record 54 consecutive errorless games. He was selected an All-Star.

Facing elimination against the Tigers in Game 6 of the 1945 Fall Classic at Wrigley, he came to the plate in the twelfth inning with the score tied. With two out and a man on, he delivered his fourth hit, an electrifying walk-off double to even the Series, but Hack's dream season came up one game short when the Cubs dropped the finale. It would be the last time Wrigley Field would host a Series in the 20th century.

Hack's final campaign was 1947. He quickly transitioned into a managerial role, leading three different minor league teams between 1948 and 1953. Hack was named the Cubs manager in 1954, leading Chicago through three unexceptional campaigns. He also managed the Cardinals to a 3-7 mark in the last ten games of 1958, concluding his managerial career at 199-272. Thereafter, he managed in the minors and retired after his tenure with Dallas-Fort Worth in 1966. His first wife, Dorothy Weisel, was a nationally-ranked amateur tennis player. He later became a restaurant manager with his second wife, Gwen. Hack passed away on December 15, 1979 at his home in Dixon, Illinois.

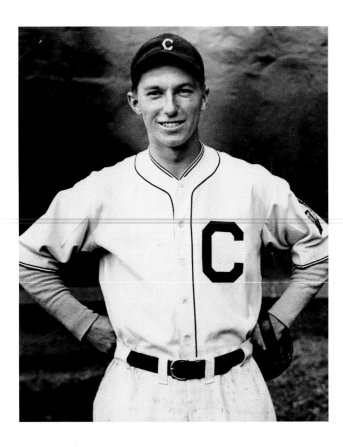

MEL HARDER

CLEVELAND INDIANS
RIGHT-HANDED PITCHER

1928-1947

"The biggest thing that ever happened to me in baseball was Mel Harder. He taught me fundamentals, so I could find the trouble when my curve and slider weren't breaking. Harder made me realize that nothing concerns a pitcher except the player at bat. Mel Harder made me a pitcher."

~ Early Wynn

Mel Harder played more seasons in an Indian uniform than any man in history and spent 36 straight summers in Cleveland as a pitcher and coach. He is the single individual in major league annals to have enjoyed both 20-year playing and coaching careers.

Despite his important contributions to baseball as an extraordinary pitcher, a master teacher and an admired role model, he remains the lone star to have played 20 years for a single franchise who is not in the National Baseball Hall of Fame.

Called "The Chief," he was one of the most effective and dependable pitchers of the Depression Era. He ranked in the AL top ten in both wins and ERA six times and set Cleveland franchise marks with 223 victories, 433 starts and 3,426$\frac{1}{3}$ innings pitched. He still holds the club mark of 582 games pitched, yet he never threw in a World Series.

The 6'1" 195-pound Harder was a brilliant All-Star, appearing in all four games from 1934 to 1937 and pitching a record 13 straight shutout innings. He came on in the 1934 game to blank the National Leaguers on one hit in the last five innings for the win.

Harder earned double-figure victory totals 13 times. His repertoire included a sinking fastball, a devastating 12-to-6 overhand curveball, an elusive change, and razor-sharp control. He helped his own cause by leading AL moundsmen in putouts four times.

* * * * *

Melvin Leroy Harder was born on October 15, 1909 to Clara Skala and Claus Harder on their farm outside Beemer, Cuming County, Nebraska. He grew up in Omaha slow to take to athletics because he was nearsighted.

However, by the time he had graduated from North Omaha's Tech High in 1927, he had become a full-fledged pitching star. Indian scout Cy Slapnicka signed him and he was sent up the street to the Omaha (NE) Buffaloes of the Single-A Western League.

The 18-year-old Harder debuted at Cleveland's old League Park on April 24, 1928. He was used sparingly, mostly in relief, in his first two campaigns with the Indians. Harder also pitched briefly in the minor leagues with the Single-A New Orleans (LA) Pelicans of the Southern Association in 1929 to polish his curveball.

Manager Roger Peckinpaugh assigned him the number four rotation spot in 1930. He also picked him to start the inaugural game at the new Municipal Stadium on July 31, 1932. He lost a classic duel, 1-0, to Athletics ace Lefty Grove before 80,184 fans.

Probably his finest pitching campaign was in 1933 when he led the American League with a 2.95 ERA, worked 253 innings and walked just 67 batters. Despite his performance, the Indians gave him limited run support and he settled for a 15-17 record.

Harder went 20-12 in 1934 with a 2.61 ERA and tied for the AL lead with six shutouts. In 1935, despite a painful case of shoulder bursitis and a sore elbow, he was 22-11 with a 3.29 ERA, finishing second in the AL in wins and innings pitched (287$\frac{1}{3}$).

He put up eight straight seasons with 200+ innings and 15+ wins (1932-39). His arm was deteriorating by 1941, yet on May 14, the day before Joe DiMaggio began his famous 56-game streak, The Yankee Clipper went 0-for-3 against him. DiMaggio called Harder the most difficult pitcher he ever faced, hitting a career .180 against him.

Harder was released that September. After off-season surgery, he was invited back and won another 47 games.

G	IP	W	L	PCT	SHO	GS	CG	H	ER	SO	BB	ERA
582	3426.1	223	186	.545	25	433	181	3706	1447	1161	1118	3.80

He threw his final pitch on September 7, 1947 ranked eighth in games pitched among AL all-time leaders, ninth in wins, and tenth in starts.

As he was finishing up his active career, he began mentoring Bob Lemon in 1946. In Harder's initial year as the Indians pitching coach, Lemon had his first 20-win season, dominating as the ace of Cleveland's 1948 World Series Champion pitching staff.

He served under a dozen Tribe skippers and mentored seven pitchers who won 20 games a total of 17 times. Another protégé, Early Wynn, teamed with Lemon, Mike Garcia and Bob Feller to form the 1954 Indian "Big Four" rotation which combined for 78 of Cleveland's record 111 wins. He also had major impact on the careers of Mudcat Grant, Tommy John, Sudden Sam McDowell, Jim Perry, Herb Score and Luis Tiant.

Indians general manager Gabe Paul chose not to renew Harder's contract after the 1963 season, but he continued to have strong influence as the pitching coach for the 1964 Mets, the 1965 Cubs, the 1966-68 Reds and the 1969 Royals. The reserved, soft-spoken Harder often could be seen sitting quietly in hotel lobbies talking with his young pitchers.

The Indians retired his uniform jersey #18 in 1990. Sixty-one years after he pitched Municipal Stadium's Opening Day, he was asked to toss out the ceremonial first pitch at the ballpark's last game on October 3, 1993 as the team moved to Jacobs Field.

Harder retired to his residence in Chardon, Ohio with his wife Sandy. The "Pride of the Indians" passed away at home on October 20, 2002 at age 93. His ashes were scattered over Mel Harder Park, the local baseball field that was named in his honor.

CARL HUBBELL

NEW YORK GIANTS
LEFT-HANDED PITCHER

1928-1943

"He had the greatest

screwball I ever looked at.

He'd drop one in for a strike,

then really explode one when

you thought sure you had him."

~ rival hitter Joe Cronin

Carl Hubbell was one of the greatest left-handed pitchers in history. A two-time NL MVP and nine-time All-Star, he still holds the major league mark of 24 consecutive victories. Known as "The Meal Ticket," he rang up five straight 20-win seasons (1933-37), possibly the best five-year stretch any pitcher ever had. The 6' 170-pound Hubbell helped his Giants to three pennants and the 1933 World Series title. In six Fall Classic starts, he was 4–2 with a 1.79 ERA and his 1934 All-Star game performance is legendary.

Using a slow, cartwheel-like delivery, Hubbell utilized his fastball, curve and change to set up his signature screwball. His "screwjie," delivered with the same overhand motion as his fastball, darted in on left-handers and tailed away from righties.

* * * * *

Carl Owen Hubbell was born on June 22, 1903 in Carthage, Jasper County, Missouri to Margaret Ann Delilah Upp and George Owen Hubbell. He was the fourth of six brothers who grew up on the family pecan and cotton farm near Meeker, Oklahoma.

In his second pro year, he won 17 games for the Western League's Oklahoma City Indians in 1925. The Tigers picked up his contract, but Detroit manager Ty Cobb sent him to the Double-A Toronto Maple Leafs for 1926 with orders to discard the pitch.

Hubbell was relegated to the Class-B Decatur (IL) Commodores of the Three-I League in 1927. He won 14 games there, but the Tigers sold him outright to the Texas League's Beaumont Exporters where he was encouraged to throw his screwball again.

Giants scout Dick Kinsella, attending the 1928 Democratic National Convention in Houston, saw Hubbell throw 11 impressive innings against the Houston Buffaloes. A month later, the Giants' John J. McGraw paid

$30,000 for the rights to his contract.

McGraw promptly gave Hubbell his major league debut on July 26, 1928 against the Pirates. Effective from the start, Hubbell tossed his only no-hitter on May 8, 1929 in an 11-0 drubbing of the Bucs at the Polo Grounds. Averaging over 15 wins a season in his first five years, he won 77 games while the Giants languished without a pennant.

Under new player-manager Bill Terry, the revamped 1933 Giants rode a rotation of Hubbell (23-12), Hal Schumacher (19-12), Freddie Fitzsimmons (16-11) and Roy Parmelee (13-8) to a title. Facing the potent Cardinals on July 2, Hubbell threw an epic 18-inning, six-hit 1-0 shutout. He fanned 12 with no walks and tossed 12 perfect frames. By August he had stifled NL hitters for a record $46\frac{1}{3}$ consecutive scoreless innings.

On his way to the MVP award, Hubbell turned in another clutch gem in late September, pitching a ten-inning 2-0 shutout over the Braves without walking a single batter or even getting to a full count. He finished with ten shutouts and a 1.66 ERA.

In the 1933 World Series Game 1, he struck out the side in the first inning of a 4-1 win. He was also triumphant in the 11-inning, 2-1, Game 4 thriller. The Giants beat the Nationals in five games with stalwart glove work and a hitting attack led by Mel Ott.

Hubbell's prowess in the 1934 All-Star Game at his home Polo Grounds is still held in awe. He struck out five straight Hall of Famers- Babe Ruth, Lou Gehrig, Jimmie Foxx, Al Simmons and Joe Cronin. Each hitting star fell victim to his illusive screwball.

Hubbell had his finest year in 1936, winning a career-high 26 games as the NL's first unanimous MVP. He captured his last 16 decisions and led all NL pitchers in wins, and ERA. In the 1936 Fall Classic against the Yankees, Hubbell won Game 1 without allowing an out-

G	IP	W	L	PCT	SHO	GS	CG	H	ER	SO	BB	ERA
535	3590.1	253	154	.622	36	433	260	3461	1188	1678	724	2.97

field chance, but he lost Game 4 as the cross-town rivals prevailed in six games. Joltin' Joe DiMaggio said he was one of the toughest pitchers he had ever faced.

King Carl's 24-game win streak came to a halt when he lost on Memorial Day 1937 to the Dodgers, but he went on to pace the NL with 22 wins and 159 strikeouts. In the rematch World Series, his Game 4 victory was the only bright spot in a Yankees rout.

Hubbell's vaunted screwball pitch that baffled so many hitters also put serious stress on his elbow. The pain had become excruciating by 1938. While working in a loss to the Dodgers on August 18, Hubbell left the game in agony and a bone chip was removed days later. He was out for the season and was never the same pitcher. Hubbell was left with a deformed left palm which faced out instead of in toward his body.

But he showed flashes of his former brilliance. On Memorial Day 1940, Hubbell hurled a one-hitter versus Brooklyn, facing only 27 batters. The only runner was erased on a double play. In his final season, he one-hit the Pirates on June 5, 1943 after which Giants owner Horace Stoneham promptly made him Director of Player Development.

King Carl Hubbell was elected to the National Baseball Hall of Fame in 1947. He was the first NL player ever to have his uniform number retired. His #11 appears on the upper deck facing in the left field corner of San Francisco's AT & T Park.

Hubbell held his player development position for 35 years until felled by a stroke in 1977. He continued as a part-time scout for the San Francisco Giants for his last 11 years. Hubbell died of injuries sustained in an auto accident in Scottsdale, Arizona, on November 21, 1988. He was laid to rest at Meeker-Newhope Cemetery in Meeker.

ARNDT JORGENS

"I think I've sent Huggins a real coming catcher. He's a little fellow, like Schalk and Ruel, but he's built of iron. He's a Norwegian, and you know how those fellows are built. They never tire and he can catch every day. He hits the ball, too; he is a sweet right-handed hitter."

~ *Yankees scout Eddie Herr*

Arndt Jorgens stood in the shadow of the great Hall of Fame catcher Bill Dickey as his understudy for a dozen years. While Dickey caught every inning of 23 World Series games, Jorgens saw zero playing time. He cashed five World Series titlist paychecks to hold the record for a player who was eligible ... but never appeared in a single Fall Classic game.

Known as "Arnie" or "Red" to his teammates, the compact 5' 9" 160-pound Jorgens came up one year after Dickey arrived at Yankee Stadium. He was a longtime teammate of such baseball immortals as Babe Ruth, Lou Gehrig, Joe DiMaggio, Tony Lazzeri and Lefty Gomez.

On perennial championship teams in the center of the baseball universe, he saw action in just 307 contests and only caught 150 complete games during his years on the Yankees roster. Jorgens is still one of only three major leaguers in history to have been a native Norwegian.

One of the game's best catchers, the underrated Jorgens could have started on most other AL teams. He had a strong, accurate throwing arm with a quick release, pitchers liked his smarts and energy, and he was an expert at watching an opposing hitter's feet to guess his intentions.

Jorgens cashed $29,530 in World Series paychecks and $60,000 in regular season salary checks to become the highest paid player per hour of actual service in his era by far. He bided his time in the Yankee dugout, tutoring young pitchers or warming up relievers down in the Yankee bullpen. The popular Jorgens was virtually another coach for the Bronx Bombers.

Jorgens holds the curious title of wearing the most Yankee uniforms later retired. During his career, he wore #9 (Roger Maris), #10 (Phil Rizzuto), #15 (Thurman Munson) and #32 (Elston Howard) and finally settled on #18 while earning four of his five World Series championship rings from 1936 to 1940.

★ ★ ★ ★ ★

Arndt Ludwig Jorgensen was born on May 18, 1905 to Helma "Helen" Strand and Andreas "Andrew" Jorgensen in the tiny village of Amot near Modum, Buskerud County, Norway near Oslo. The family immigrated in 1907 and settled in Rockford, Illinois, near Chicago. His father soon shortened the family name and started work as a railroad fireman.

The oldest of three children, Jorgens started playing baseball at age six and gravitated toward catching almost immediately. His younger brother Orville, born three years later in Rockford, eventually grew up to pitch for the Phillies in 1935, 1936 and 1937.

His family moved to Chicago where Jorgens attended Albert Grannis Lane Manual Training High, an all-boys magnet school. He starred in baseball and then caught on with the semi-pro Rogers Park team, playing on weekends in 1924 and 1925.

Jorgens started his professional career at age 20 in 1926 when Percy Gray, one of his semi-pro skippers, landed the manager's job with the Rock Island (IL) Islanders of the Class-D Mississippi Valley League. He hit .302 in 121 games for the Islanders.

The young catcher graduated to the Class-A Oklahoma City (OK) Indians of the Western League in 1927 and 1928. Hitting .335 for the Indians in 1928, he contributed 114 hits in 115 games with 20 doubles while playing a solid defensive game behind the plate.

Yankees scout Eddie Herr took notice of his performance and bought out his contract from Oklahoma City on August 24, 1928. Jorgens put up the highest Yankees batting average in 1929 spring training. Yankees manager Miller Huggins gave him his big-league debut on April 26, 1929, spelling catcher Johnny Grabowski in the late innings in a 5-2 loss to the A's. But, Huggins wanted him to

G	AB	R	H	2B	3B	HR	RBI	SB	BB	SO	BA	OBP	SLG	TB
307	738	79	126	31	5	4	89	3	85	73	.238	.317	.310	229

get regular work and sent him to the Double-A Jersey City (NJ) Skeeters.

He spent most of 1929 and 1930 in the International League catching an aggregate 166 games and hit a robust .367 in 1930 in his abbreviated stay with the Yankees. Although his best season may have been 1931 when he batted .270, Jorgens' career-high in games played for the Yankees was 1934. After a home plate collision, regular catcher Dickey broke the jaw of an opposing base runner and was suspended indefinitely.

Dickey's punch gave Jorgens the opportunity to see action in 58 games and set career-highs with 38 hits and 20 runs batted in. A highlight in that year came on September 23 when Jorgens drove in the only run against the Red Sox's George Hockette to assist Lefty Gomez in posting his 26th victory with a 1-0, three-hit shutout.

One of his best friends on the Yankees was Gehrig. On January 18, 1934, Jorgens and Modelyn Jone Schultz were married after meeting during spring training in St. Petersburg, Florida. The couple would take Gehrig with them for dinner and dancing before he was married. The Iron Horse was shy around women and would sometimes end up dancing with Modelyn.

Jorgens' final game action with the Yankees was on August 2, 1939, scoring as a pinch runner. He was on the Yankee active roster through the rest of 1939 and during the entire 1940 campaign, yet did not get in another game. It remains another major league record.

After Jorgens retired, he became an executive in a Midwestern grocery store chain owned by his father-in-law and resided in New Tier, Cook County, Illinois with his wife and their daughter, Barbara Rhey. Jorgens passed away in Wilmette, Illinois at the age of 74 on March 1, 1980 and was interred in the Memorial Park Cemetery in Skokie, Illinois.

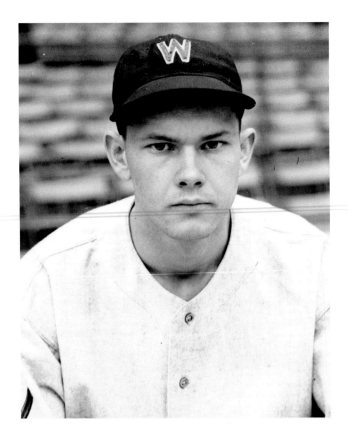

BUDDY LEWIS

WASHINGTON NATIONALS
THIRD BASE • RIGHT FIELD

1935-1941 • 1945-1947 • 1949

An All-Star at both third base and right field, Buddy Lewis was the most dangerous Nationals hitter through the late 1930s before losing four prime years to World War II. One of the most popular players in D.C. annals, he was a strong favorite of team owner Clark Griffith.

The left-handed hitting 6'1" 175-pound Lewis collected over 170 hits six times, hit over .300 four times, scored over 100 runs four times, and ranked among AL leaders in triples seven times. He also had a keen batting eye, drawing a walk 270 more times than he struck out.

★　★　★　★　★

John Kelly Lewis, Jr. was born on August 10, 1916 to Ada May Jenkins and John Kelly Lewis, Sr. in Gastonia, Gaston County, North Carolina. He was raised with five sisters and two brothers and played his first hardball at 12 with the Gastonia American Legion Post 23 team.

Lewis developed for five years as the third baseman for Gastonia Legion starting in 1929, earning a regional reputation for his potent bat. He was chosen for the North Carolina State Legion All Star Team twice and was a key component in leading Gastonia to the 1933 state title.

After a year at Wake Forest College, Lewis signed a professional contract with the Chattanooga (TN) Lookouts of the Southern Association in 1934. His uneven glove work and wild throws at third base were more than offset by his strong flair with a *Louisville Slugger*.

Chattanooga manager Clyde Milan recommended Lewis to Washington scout Zinn Beck. Beck signed him prior to the 1935 Single-A Southern Association season. At age 18, Lewis hit .303 with 179 hits in 154 games to earn his major league debut on September 16, 1935.

Lewis tore up 1936 spring training, hitting .450, and earned the starting job at third base. He continued his hot hitting into May, appearing in 143 games, and finished at .291, with 175 hits, 100 runs scored, 21 doubles and 13 tri-

ples. Teammate Buddy Myer spent so much time tutoring him that the veteran's nickname rubbed off. Lewis also became known as "Buddy."

By 1937, Lewis had become one of the best young hitters in the Junior Circuit. In an AL record 156 games, he batted .314 with 210 hits and 107 runs scored and paced the league with 668 at-bats and 162 singles. In four straight games between July 25 and 28, he lined out 15 hits.

From the #2 spot in the order in 1938, the 21-year-old Lewis batted .296 with 122 runs scored and 91 RBI. He started at third base for the 1938 AL All-Star squad along with seven future Hall-of-Famers. With Myer's tutoring, Lewis mastered the drag bunt dropped down between the mound and second to exploit his foot speed. He led the AL in bunt hits in 1938.

Although he had the most assists (329) and double plays (32) of any AL third baseman in 1938, he also topped the league with 47 errors. Lewis came back in 1939 to post career-bests in average (.319) and slugging percentage (.478) while legging out a league-high 19 triples.

Manager Bucky Harris moved him to right field in 1940. Using his fleet feet and strong arm, he went on to lead AL rightfielders in assists four times, double plays twice, and putouts once. Lewis hit .317 that year with 190 hits, 101 runs scored, 38 doubles and 74 free passes.

He was drafted in April 1941, but contended that his income was the sole support for his parents. Granted deferments for the season, Lewis hit .297 with 97 runs scored. After six major league campaigns, he had more career hits at age 24 than any other player except Ty Cobb.

Lewis enlisted in the U.S. Army Air Corps on November 18, 1941 and flew 342 World War II combat missions as a C-47 pilot in the Burma War Theater. He hauled supplies and flew the wounded over the Himalayas between India, Burma and China. A First Air Commando Group

"My good friend Buddy Lewis left for war and missed four years of baseball. He left a dark-haired man and came back to us at the end of 1945 with a full head of white hair and some hair-raising stories."

~ teammate George Case

G	AB	R	H	2B	3B	HR	RBI	SB	BB	SO	BA	OBP	SLG	TB
1349	5261	830	1563	249	93	71	607	83	573	303	.297	.368	.420	2211

W

captain, he was awarded three Distinguished Flying Crosses and three Air Medals.

On July 23, 1945, Lewis was discharged from the US-AAC. When he returned to the Nats four days later, he arrived ready to play. Hitting #3 in the order, he batted .333 with a .423 OBA and slugged .465 in 69 games to help extend the AL Champion Tigers to the season's final day.

The starting AL outfield for the 1947 All Star Game was Ted Williams, Joe DiMaggio and Buddy Lewis. Late in that season, he injured his hip seriously in a collision with Stan Spence near the outfield wall at Griffith Stadium. He finished at an atypical .261 in only 140 games. It was becoming apparent that Lewis' war experiences had taken a harsh toll on his young body.

Lewis' career average stood at an even .300 on exactly 1500 hits at the end of 1947. His injury and concerns for his auto dealership in Gastonia led him to retire. Griffith convinced him to come back after a year off, but he hit only .249 to see his lifetime average dip just below .300.

Lewis confirmed his decision to retire for good in a February 15, 1950 letter to Griffith. Back home in Gastonia, he successfully operated his Ford auto dealership for 35 years and served as an area commissioner, coach and athletic officer for American Legion baseball. With former major leaguer Crash Davis, he led his old Post 23 to state and regional titles in 1954.

Buddy Lewis was inducted into the North Carolina American Legion Baseball Hall of Fame in 1967 and the North Carolina Sports Hall of Fame in 1975. The City of Gastonia named the baseball field at Sims Legion Park the John K. "Buddy" Lewis Jr. Field in 2003.

Lewis and his wife, Frances Oates, were married 59 years and raised two daughters and a son. He passed away at age 94 in his home after a battle with cancer on February 18, 2011. His nephew, former big-leaguer Hal Morris, named his youngest son John Kelly in Lewis' honor.

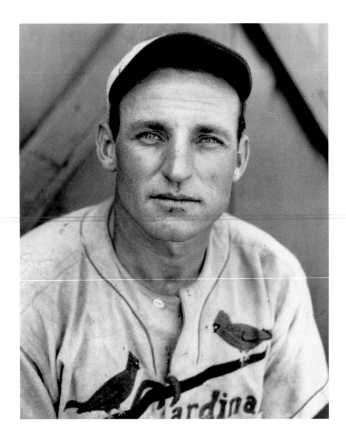

PEPPER MARTIN

St. Louis Cardinals
Third Base • Outfield
1928 • 1930-1940 • 1944

"To a whole generation, Pepper Martin was the red blood of baseball, the spirit of the game. He was a symbol of hope for all young men in the Great Depression, when there were no jobs, and for many, little to eat... Martin was the hope of the finer future. He was the ordinary guy who thumbed his nose at VIP's and made them all seem stuffed shirts. He was a guy who could bounce fallen spirits sky high..."

~ writer Joe King

Pepper Martin was the most colorful of the legendary Gas House Gang Cardinals of the Depression Era, one of the fiercest competitors in baseball history. Martin found a way to win with his heart and hustle, approaching every game as if it were his last. Nobody played any harder. He hit .300 four times, topped his league in steals three seasons, scored 120 runs three times and led the Cardinals to two World Series titles.

A rawboned 5'8" and 170 pounds, Martin was bow-legged and had a barrel chest, massive shoulders and long arms. Cradling his *Louisville Slugger* bat in the crook of his right arm, he took a muscle-bound swing, often driving the ball to right field. Martin's trademark was to charge around the bases like a stampeding animal and then dive head first with his exaggerated belly flop slide. His uniform was invariably stained with dirt, grass, chalk and *Beech Nut* tobacco juice, making him the "dirtiest player" in baseball.

★ ★ ★ ★ ★

Johnnie Leonard Roosevelt Martin was born the youngest of seven children to Celia and George Martin in rural Temple, Cotton County, Oklahoma on leap year, February 29, 1904. When severe drought wiped out their farm when Martin was six, the family moved to Oklahoma City. He never finished school and worked itinerantly until his first year of professional baseball in 1924 with the Class-D Greenville (TX) Hunters of the East Texas League. It would be a seven-year minor league odyssey.

Cardinals head scout Charley Barrett reported his upbeat makeup and upside potential and St. Louis (then featuring an expanded 26-team farm system) picked up his contract. Martin's first stop was the Fort Smith (AR) Twins of the Class-C Western Association. The team's owner noted his exuberance and nicknamed him "Pepper."

Martin spent 1926 with the Syracuse (NY) Stars and went to the Houston (TX) Buffaloes in 1927 to learn the outfield. He made the big club's roster the next April, hit .308 in 39 at-bats, and pinch-ran in the World Series versus the Yankees. But he was sent back to Houston for further seasoning in 1929. With the 1930 Rochester (NY) Red Wings, he batted a ferocious .363, running everywhere, and was christened "The Wild Horse of the Osage" by a local sportswriter. He was ready for the Big Time.

Martin roamed center field and hit .300 with 32 doubles for the 1931 Cardinals. He then became a part of Cardinal lore in the Fall Classic, dominating one of the greatest Philadelphia Athletics teams. Martin stole five bases, scored five runs, drove in five runs and made a number of diving catches. He hit .500 including a record 12 hits, five doubles and a home run. He had quickly become one of America's most famous sports figures.

A fun-loving character, he unnerved the Cardinals brass with his reckless style. Martin played semi-professional football, trapped snakes for the St. Louis Zoo and hunted wild hogs and mountain lions in the off season. He was a fascinating paradox, known for his heartfelt sincerity and homespun honesty but also as an incurable practical joker. He was a mischievous cheat on the field, yet deferential to umpires and a gentleman in social situations.

Martin's 1933 season was a comeback success as he led the National League with 122 runs scored and 26 steals and batted a strong .316 with 189 hits, 40 doubles and 14 triples. A four-time All-Star, he came to the plate as the first hitter in All-Star history on July 18, 1933.

G	AB	R	H	2B	3B	HR	RBI	SB	BB	SO	BA	OBP	SLG	TB
1189	4117	754	1227	270	75	59	501	146	369	438	.298	.358	.443	1824

Again an All-Star in 1934, he led the Senior Circuit with 32 stolen bases.

Martin next burnished his World Series legend, scoring eight times and batting .355 on 11 hits, three doubles and a triple in the 1934 World Series to lead a narrow seven-game triumph over the Tigers. Martin's Fall Classic career batting average of .418 (23-for-55) remains the *highest ever* for a player with 50 or more at-bats.

Martin was named team captain in 1939 and the Cardinals' usually unsentimental general manager Branch Rickey vowed never to trade him. But he was unable to temper his hard-charging play as injuries limited his last five years to less than 100 games each.

After the 1940 season, Rickey named Martin the player-manager of the Double-A Sacramento (CA) Solons, which he piloted to the 1942 Pacific Coast League title. He managed the Double-A Rochester (NY) Red Wings in 1943.

In his last hurrah, Martin was asked to come back to the 1944 Cardinals and was influential in that championship year as the club's oldest player. He never forgot that playing baseball was a privilege, always cultivating goodwill with teammates and fans.

Martin enjoyed a succession of managerial stints and also landed a coaching job with the Cubs in 1956 before his

final coaching position with the Tulsa (OK) Oilers. He was a proud inductee of the Oklahoma Sports Hall of Fame.

Pepper Martin retired to his 960-acre cattle ranch on Lake Overholser near Oklahoma City. He and his wife

Ruby raised three daughters and doted over their eight grandchildren. The Wild Horse of the Osage died of a heart attack on March 5, 1965 in McAlester at age 61 and was laid to rest in Oklahoma City's Memorial Park Cemetery.

JO-JO MOORE

NEW YORK GIANTS
LEFT FIELD

1930-1941

*"Stop throwing at
Joe or I'll break every
bone in your body!"*

*~ teammate Hank Leiber,
threatening Dizzy Dean
for head-hunting Moore*

Jo-Jo Moore was the finest National League left-fielder of the Depression Era. He made the journey from the little Central Texas hamlet of Gause to the bright lights of the Big Apple, playing superbly. In support of Giants Hall of Fame teammates Bill Terry, Mel Ott, Travis Jackson and Carl Hubbell, Moore was a six-time All-Star in his nine seasons as a regular.

Known as the "Gause Ghost" for his hometown, his running speed, and his slender 5'11" 155-pound physique, the left-handed-hitting Moore was the Giants' leadoff man, batting over .300 five years, scoring over 100 runs three seasons, and lining out over 200 hits twice.

Setting the table for the Giants sluggers, Moore was an impatient free-swinging contact hitter who rarely walked, but was almost impossible to strike out. He never was rung up more than 37 times in a season and fanned only 247 times- just 4.6 percent of his official at-bats.

Moore was known to be a notorious first-ball hitter. Opposing managers, such as the Reds' Charlie Dressen, would fine their pitchers if Moore got a hit on the first pitch. He often had to duck or sprawl to the ground on an opening delivery to avoid being hit.

A well-respected, almost flawless defensive leftfielder, Moore had an especially strong right arm and made many a scintillating catch. With seemingly effortless movements toward the ball, he had great range with his agility and instinctual quickness off the bat.

★ ★ ★ ★ ★

Joe Gregg Moore was born in Gause, Milam County, Texas on Christmas Day, 1908 to Rowena Gregg and Charles William Moore, their only child. Gause was a farming community near the Brazos River that was especially hard hit by the Dust Bowl of the Depression 30s.

Moore started off with the Class-D Coleman Bobcats of the West Texas League at 19. He batted an aggregate .327

in 750 at-bats for 1928 and 1929. After averaging .329 for the Class-A San Antonio Indians in the Texas League, he earned his Giants debut on September 17, 1930.

But dogmatic manager John J. McGraw made the irrevocable decision that Moore was too small for the majors. Moore continued to make his case in 1931 with the Class-A Bridgeport (CT) Bears (.359 in 30 games) and Double-A Newark (NJ) Bears (.347 in 79 games). He was given another big-league "cup of coffee" in September, but McGraw just didn't believe in him.

Bill Terry replaced McGraw as Giants manager in June of 1932 and, without hesitation, brought Moore up from the Double-A Jersey City (NJ) Skeeters and installed him as his regular leftfielder over Freddy Leach. Moore strung together a 20-game hitting-streak and hit .305.

The following year, the Giants captured the National League pennant with Moore leading the club's outfielders with a .292 average. Paced by Carl Hubbell's sterling pitching, the Giants ousted the Nationals in five-games to become the 1933 World Series champions. Moore stroked out two singles in the third inning of Game 2 ... both on first pitches.

He hit a career-high .331 in 1934, riding his hot *Louisville Slugger* bat to a 23-game hitting streak. An All-Star for the first of five straight years, he had 106 runs scored, 192 hits, 37 doubles, and finished third in the poling for NL MVP behind Dizzy Dean and Paul Waner.

In 1935, Moore was a member of the big-leagues' only outfield triumvirate to score over 100 runs each. He crossed home plate 108 times; centerfielder Hank Leiber scored 110; and rightfielder Ott added 113. Moore hit .295 with 201 hits, nine triples, 15 home runs and 71 RBI.

He paced the 1936 pennant-winning Giants with 205 hits in a NL-high 681 at-bats. The club met its rivals from across the Harlem River in the Series, but the Gehrig and DiMaggio-led Bronx Bombers were too much. The Giants

G	AB	R	H	2B	3B	HR	RBI	SB	BB	SO	BA	OBP	SLG	TB
1335	5427	809	1615	258	53	79	513	46	348	247	.298	.344	.408	2216

pitching staff could only manage a 6.79 ERA.

The Giants won the NL title again in 1937 as Moore hit .310 with 37 doubles. In his best postseason, Moore led all hitters with a robust .391 (9-for-23) in the five-game series. His nine hits tied a Series record, but the Giants hit only .237 and lost convincingly to the Yankees again.

Moore had another rock-solid year in 1938, hitting .302 and making his fifth consecutive All-Star squad. He would be an All-Star a final time in 1940, but by 1941, the Giants were getting old and the 32-year-old Moore had just had his third subpar campaign in a row.

His final appearance in the Big Time was on September 21, 1941. The Giants replaced Terry with Ott as manager and began making changes. Moore was sold to Cincinnati on December 10. Reds manager Bill McKechnie did not see a fit so Moore went to the minors to play for the Double-A Indianapolis (IN) Indians of the American Association in 1942 and 1943.

With World War II raging, he mustered into the military in 1944. Part of his duty was playing baseball with and against other professionals through the end of the War at Waldron Field, Texas. He finished his pro baseball career in 1947, hitting .419 in only 26 games, mostly as a pinch-hitter, for the nearby Bryan (TX) Bombers in the Class-C Lone Star League.

Moore retired with his wife, Jewell Ely, to live in the rambling brick home they built after the 1933 World Series with his winner's share of $4,259. He worked his ranch, served as a deacon for the Gause First Baptist Church, and raised their son, Joe Gregg Moore, Jr.

Moore was enshrined in the Texas Baseball Hall of Fame in 1988. Sabermetrician Bill James ranked "The Gause Ghost" as the #77 best leftfielder of all-time. For the last years of his life, Moore was the oldest living Giants everyday player. A leadoff hitter with perfect timing, Jo-Jo Moore made it safely home on the first day of the baseball season, passing away on April 1, 2001 in Bryan, Texas at the age 92. He and his wife are buried in the Gause Cemetery.

TERRY MOORE

St. Louis Cardinals
Center Field

1935-1942 • 1946-1948

"Terry Moore was a real Gashouser. In him burned the fire and determination of a crusader. A warrior. He asked no quarter and gave none."

~ *Cardinals general manager Branch Rickey*

Popular centerfielder Terry Moore served as the captain of two Cardinals World Series title teams. A four-time All-Star, he captained squads that included Hall of Famers Dizzy Dean, Frankie Frisch, Ducky Medwick, Johnny Mize, Stan Musial and Enos Slaughter. The trio of Moore, Slaughter and Musial undoubtedly composed the best Cardinals outfield of all-time.

A home-grown Cardinal, Moore was a key element in the transition from the 1930s Gas House Gang to the powerhouse Redbirds of the 1940s. He took over for Pepper Martin in center field and supplied energy and leadership for the 1942 and 1946 World Championship clubs.

The classy Moore was known for being a great centerfielder with speed and a howitzer arm – certainly one of the best in the game's history. He patrolled Sportsman's Park with abandon, crashing into walls, diving for balls, and catching almost anything hit out of the infield.

Moore enjoyed playing shallow in order to turn dying-quail singles into outs. He had the sixth sense to anticipate the direction of the ball and break even before the crack of the bat to run down drives hit over his head. And he had a strong throwing arm to go with his great glove.

The well-built 5'11" 190-pound Moore was never a slugger, but hit a solid .280 for his career. He walked more than he struck out and ranked in the top ten in the National League in stolen bases six times, doubles three times and home runs twice.

★　★　★　★　★

Terry Bluford Moore, Jr. was born on May 27, 1912 to Etta and Terry Bluford Moore, Sr. in rural Vernon, Lamar County, Alabama near the Mississippi border. His family moved to Memphis, Tennessee when he was six, then to St. Louis when he was ten. He played on the sandlots and semi-pro leagues until 1932 and was scouted by a Mr. DeWitt of the Cardinals.

Moore began his pro career with the 1932 Columbus (OH) Red Birds of the Double-A American Association, but played in just three games. In 1933, the Cardinals offered him a contract for only $75 per month and he turned it down to work outside of baseball.

After the hiatus, Moore went back with the Class-A Elmira (NY) Red Wings in the New York-Penn League and hit .316. Promoted back to Columbus, Moore batted .328 with 183 hits, 36 doubles, 11 triples and 14 home runs, helping the team win the 1934 Little World Series.

His showing earned him a spot on the Cardinals roster a year after the Gas House Gang took the 1934 World Series. At 22, he was given his major league debut on April 16, 1935 and gradually took centerfielder Ernie Orsatti's job away. Moore had one game where he slammed two doubles and powered two homers, and several weeks later went 6-for-6 in another.

Still learning the nuances of big-league hitting from 1936 to 1938, he hit .264, 267 and .272, respectively. Beginning in 1939, he was chosen a National League All-Star four straight years — a stretch in which he hit an aggregate .295, twice slugging 17 home runs.

Moore was hit behind the ear by a fastball thrown by the Braves' Art Johnson in Boston on August 20, 1941. He spent ten days in a Boston hospital and then was flown back to St. Louis for more hospitalization. He didn't return from the serious concussion until September 14.

The highly-respected Moore was the oldest player on Billy Southworth's young 1942 Redbirds at 30 and was named team captain. He hit in 20 consecutive games and posted a .288 average while the Cards were winning 43 of their last 51 to edge the Dodgers for the pennant.

In the World Series, St. Louis was a heavy underdog to the vaunted Bronx Bombers of Joe DiMaggio, Bill Dickey, Joe Gordon, Tommy Henrich, King Kong Keller and Phil Rizzuto. Red Ruffing had a no-hitter after 8²/₃ in-

G	AB	R	H	2B	3B	HR	RBI	SB	BB	SO	BA	OBP	SLG	TB
1298	4700	719	1318	263	28	80	513	82	406	368	.280	.340	.399	1877

nings in Game 1 before Moore broke it up with a single to right. The Cardinals could not pull off a Game 1 victory, but went on to shock the baseball world by upending the Yankees four straight games to win the World Series title. Moore hit .294.

After the Fall Classic triumph, Moore entered the military in late 1942. For a time, he was stationed in the Panama Canal Zone and played for the Colon team there. He returned to the Cardinals when he was 34 for the 1946 season and remained a top defensive centerfielder, but his *Louisville Slugger* seemed rusty in the early going.

He was able to play only 91 games because of an old knee injury. The 1946 World Series went to a Game 7. When Red Sox shortstop Johnny Pesky hesitated for a split second in the bottom of the eighth on the relay, Slaughter slid home after his daring "Mad Dash" from first.

In 1947, a healthy 35-year-old Moore made a marvelous comeback. He pounded out nine consecutive hits at one point and rebounded for a .283 average in 127 games, but was frequently replaced in the late innings. When Moore was reduced to a backup role in 1948, he could see the writing on the wall and played his final game on September 24 at age 36.

Moore became a Cardinals coach from 1949 to 1952. He worked as a Phillie scout in 1953 and 1954 before managing the Phillies for the second half of the 1954 campaign. Moore replaced Steve O'Neill on July 15, managing for exactly half a season, winning 35 of 77 games as the interim skipper. Moore then returned to the Cardinals coaching staff from 1956 to 1958.

One of the most underrated Cardinals of all-time, Moore might have been Hall of Fame bound if not for the three years he spent defending his country in World War II during his prime. He and his wife Patricia settled in Collinsville, Illinois where he passed away on March 29, 1995 at age 82. Moore was laid to rest in the Holy Cross Lutheran Cemetery in Collinsville.

MEL OTT

NEW YORK GIANTS
RIGHT FIELD • THIRD BASE

1926-1947

O ne of the most popular men ever to play the game, Mel Ott became the first National Leaguer to surpass 500 home runs. His final total was over 200 more than any other Senior Circuit slugger and was exceeded only by Babe Ruth and Jimmie Foxx.

Ott set NL career records for runs scored, walks and RBI. He hit .300 ten times, scored 100 runs and drove in 100 runs nine times each, and was the first NL hitter to post eight straight seasons with 100 or more runs batted in. He led the NL in walks six times.

At 22 in 1931, the left-handed hitting 5'9" 175-pound Ott became the youngest ever to hit 100 home runs. With his head still and his *Louisville Slugger* slung low, he lifted his right foot high before the pitch. His unique style created extra power to exploit the 258-foot right field porch at the Polo Grounds. Ott won six NL home run titles.

A remarkable all-around player, the 12-time All-Star also earned a reputation as the NL's finest rightfielder. Deftly negotiating caroms off the Polo Grounds wall and showing a gun for a right arm, he posted double-digit assist totals in 11 seasons.

★　★　★　★　★

Melvin Thomas Ott was born on March 2, 1909 to Carrie and Charles Ott in the New Orleans suburb of Gretna, Jefferson Parish, Louisiana. He had the benefit of learning from his father and two uncles, all of whom played semi-professionally.

At age 16, Ott signed on as a 5'7" 150 pound catcher for the semi-pro Patterson (LA) Grays. Grays Owner Harry Williams urged his friend, Giants manager John J. McGraw, to give the youngster a look and purchased Ott a train ticket to New York City in late 1925. McGraw was thrilled with the young prodigy from his first turn at bat.

McGraw signed Ott in January of 1926. During spring training, he converted him to the outfield. Rather than sending him out to a minor league skipper who might ruin his natural swing, McGraw kept him close. Ott never played an inning in the minor leagues.

The veteran manager nurtured him slowly. When the teenager wasn't in the game, he sat awkwardly on the bench listening to McGraw's profane rants. The New York writers began calling him "Master Melvin" because of his age and naïve appearance.

Ott broke out at 20 in 1929 with 138 runs scored, 37 doubles, 42 homers, 151 RBI, and slugged .635. He only struck out 38 times and set still current NL road marks of 79 runs scored and 87 RBI. He piled up 26 assists and initiated a record 12 double plays.

Ott led the 1933 pennant winners with 23 home runs and 103 RBI, and then took over in the World Series, hitting .389 against the Nationals. After going 4-for-4 in the Game 1 win, he clinched the Fall Classic with a two-out, tenth inning bomb in Game 5.

In a move that propelled the team to the 1937 NL title, Ott shifted to third base mid-season. Playing great hot corner defense, he tied Ducky Medwick for the home run title at 31. The Giants succumbed to the Yankees in both the 1936 and 1937 Series.

"Ottie" was named team captain in 1939 and Giants President Horace Stoneham convinced him to become a player-manager in 1942. In 1943, the Giants were depleted by star players going to war and finished last. Each of Ott's 18 home runs came at home.

Still very popular, he was *Sport Magazine's* "Sports Father of the Year" with his daughters Barbara and Lyn. In 1944, he was chosen the most popular sports hero of all-time, beating out Ruth, Lou Gehrig, Christy Mathewson, Joe Louis and Jack Dempsey.

Ott regained his form in 1944 and on August 1, 1945,

"I never knew a baseball player who was so universally loved. Why even when he was playing against the Dodgers at Ebbets Field he would be cheered and there are no more rabid fans than in Brooklyn."

~ Leo Durocher

G	AB	R	H	2B	3B	HR	RBI	SB	BB	SO	BA	OBP	SLG	TB
2730	9456	1859	2876	488	72	511	1860	89	1708	896	.304	.414	.533	5041

he launched his 500th home run. He went on to lead his team in homers for the 18th straight year- a big-league record. In early 1946, he injured his knee diving for a fly ball and played little from there.

Ott appeared in his last four games as a player in 1947. In July of 1948, Stoneham also asked him to step away as skipper and replaced him with the controversial and acerbic Leo Durocher. During his managerial tenure, Ott had compiled a 464-530 record.

He assisted his long time friend and teammate Carl Hubbell in running the Giants minor league system through the 1950 season. In 1951, Ott left the Giants after 25 years of service to manage the Oakland (CA) Oaks of the Pacific Coast League through 1952.

Mel Ott's uniform #4 was retired by the Giants in 1949 and he was a first ballot National Baseball Hall of Fame selection in 1951. His number is still displayed on the left field corner upper deck facade at the San Francisco Giants' AT&T Park.

Ott worked with a Louisiana building firm in 1953, but joined the Mutual Network's "Game of the Day" radio team in 1955 and then announced Tigers games on radio and TV in 1956 with Van Patrick. With his friendly Southern style, he was a hit.

On November 14, 1958, Ott and his wife, Mildred Mattigny, were driving toward their home in Metairie (LA) through Mississippi in a dense fog, when they were hit head-on by a driver who had drifted over the line. One of baseball's true gentlemen passed away a week later at the young age of 49 and was laid to rest in the Metairie Cemetery.

Ott was ranked #42 on *The Sporting News'* 1999 list of the "100 Greatest Baseball Players" and was featured on a 2006 U.S. postage stamp. He was among several baseball legends portrayed in Ray Kinsella's Iowa cornfield during the film *Field of Dreams*.

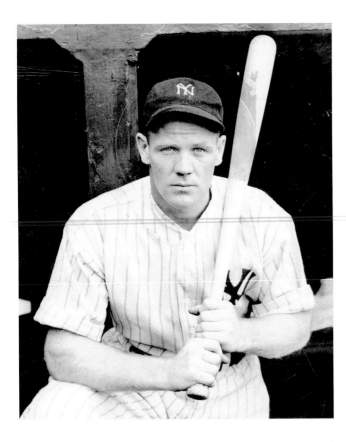

RED ROLFE

New York Yankees
Third Base

1931 • 1934-1942

"Long before he was ready to hang up his glove, he was recognized as the leading third baseman of his era and one of the greatest in the long and colorful history of the American League. There is no challenging his right to the number one post among Yankee third sackers. Red stands alone."

~ writer Ed Rumill

Red Rolfe was a major contributor to six Yankees pennants and five World Series titles in his seven years as a Yankees regular from 1935 to 1941. From 1936 to 1939, the Bronx Bombers averaged over 102 wins and took all four World Series, losing only three games. Rolfe excelled in six Fall Classics, hitting .284 (33-for-116) and striking out just nine times.

Nicknamed "Red" because of his full head of ginger-colored hair, Rolfe was perhaps the most prominent player ever to come out of New Hampshire. He was reliable at the hot corner with great reflexes, sure hands and a strong arm, leading the Junior Circuit in fielding twice.

The 5'11½" 170-pound Rolfe was a left-handed line drive hitter who hit .300 or more four times. He batted second in the Bronx Bombers lineup mainly behind Frank Crosetti and in front of Hall of Famers Joe DiMaggio, Lou Gehrig and Bill Dickey. In 1939, Rolfe set a major league record by scoring in 18 consecutive games. He crossed home plate at least 100 times every year he was a regular and averaged an incredible 138 runs per year from 1937 to 1939.

* * * * *

Robert Abial Rolfe was born on October 17, 1908 in Penacook, Merrimack County, New Hampshire to Lucy E. Huff and Herbert Wilson Rolfe. He had one brother and four sisters. His English roots went back eight generations in New Hampshire and Massachusetts.

Rolfe starred in football, basketball and baseball at Penacook High and graduated second in his class before entering Phillips Exeter Academy. Excelling in three sports at Dartmouth College, Rolfe was the Ivy League batting champion as a sophomore under baseball coach Jeff Tesreau and an NCAA All-American shortstop as a senior, batting .359.

He graduated in 1931 with an English degree and signed directly with the Yankees. The club gave him a one game big-league cameo debut at shortstop on June 29 (He did not get a plate appearance) before sending him down to the Albany (NY) Senators in the Eastern league.

Rolfe played shortstop for the Newark (NJ) Bears in the International League in 1932 and 1933. Hitting an aggregate .328 in 303 games (390-for-1,190), he claimed 1933 International League Most Valuable Player honors, showing he was ready for major league pitching.

As a rookie in 1934, Rolfe hit .287 and earned a regular spot at third base. Secure in his position in 1935, he hit an even .300 in 705 plate appearances and batted .319 in 1936 with a major league-leading 15 triples. After he hit .400 (10-for-25) in the exciting World Series victory, he and "Isabel" Africa were married on October 12 in Manchester, New Hampshire.

Rolfe led the majors with 741 plate appearances in 1937 and was an AL All-Star for the first time. He hit .276, walked 90 times and hit .300 (6-for-20) in the Fall Classic. Again an All-Star in 1938, Rolfe batted .311 while leading the Junior Circuit with 151 games played at third.

The 1939 Yankees were one of the greatest teams in history. Even without the ill Gehrig, the team started the most players ever in any All-Star Game- Dickey, DiMaggio, Joe Gordon, Rolfe, Red Ruffing and George Selkirk. Rolfe had his finest year. He played 152 games and set career-highs in most offensive categories, hitting .329 with 14 home runs, ten triples and 84 RBI. He led the major leagues with 213 hits and 139 runs scored and paced the AL with 46 doubles.

During the winter of 1940, Rolfe began his struggle with chronic ulcerative colitis at age 31. He and the Yankees both had down years in 1940 although he made his fourth and final American League All-Star team. His average slipped to .250- a significant 79-point slide.

The summer of '41 would be Rolfe's last as a regular.

G	AB	R	H	2B	3B	HR	RBI	SB	BB	SO	BA	OBP	SLG	TB
1175	2322	942	1394	59	8	69	497	10	489	514	.289	.356	.373	866

He earned his fifth and final World Series title ring, batting .300 (6-for-20) in the World Series triumph over the Dodgers. A part-timer in 1942, he hit only .219 and played his last regular season game on September 27. In his last hurrah, he had an impressive Fall Classic, hitting .353 (6-for-17) in the loss to the Cardinals.

Rolfe served as the Yale University Bulldogs basketball coach from 1942 to 1946 and Yale's baseball coach from 1943 to 1945. In the closing weeks of the 1946-47 basketball season, he coached the Toronto Huskies of the Basketball Association of America, a predecessor to the NBA.

Rolfe returned to coach the Yankees in 1947 under his former teammate Bill Dickey and then joined the Tigers as 1948 farm system director. He succeeded Steve O'Neill as Tigers manager in 1949. His Bengals narrowly missed an upset of the powerful Yankees in 1950, winning 95 games and finishing three games back of the eventual World Series Champions. Rolfe was awarded *The Sporting News* 1950 American League Manager of the Year.

His Tigers slipped to 73 wins in 1951, finishing fifth place, and completed the skid in 1952, going a dismal 23-49 to begin the season. After one of his pitchers, Fred Hutchinson, replaced him on July 5, the club went on to finish 50-104. It was the first time any Tigers team had lost 100 games. Rolfe's final managerial record stood at 278-256.

Rolfe returned to his alma mater as athletic director from 1954 to 1967. The Big Green's baseball facility is named Red Rolfe Field in his honor. The Ivy League's northern division, composed of Harvard, Yale, Brown and Dartmouth, is now designated the Red Rolfe Division.

During the 1969 Baseball Centennial celebrations, Rolfe was voted the best Yankees third baseman ever. A lifelong Granite State resident, Rolfe died in Gilford at age 60 from chronic colitis on July 8, 1969. He was laid to rest in Penacook's Woodlawn Cemetery.

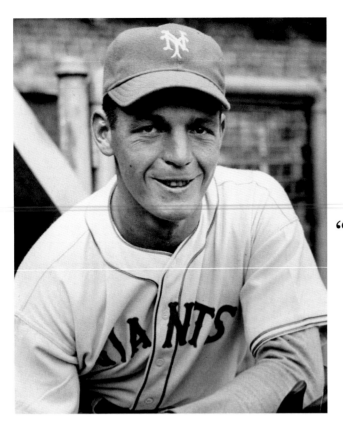

HAL SCHUMACHER

NEW YORK GIANTS
RIGHT-HANDED PITCHER

1931-1942 • 1946

"*P*rince Hal" Schumacher was the ultimate warrior for Giants teams that won three pennants and a World Series title during the Depression Era 1930s. Schumacher was the right-handed counterpart to left-hander "King Carl" Hubbell. The regal twosome formed one of the most formidable pitching tandems in New York baseball history.

A 6' 190-pound workhorse, Schumacher pitched almost a thousand innings before he was 25 years old. He showed great command with a heavy sinking fastball, a marvelous biting overhand curve, and later a deceptive palm ball.

* * * * *

Harold Henry Schumacher was born on November 23, 1910, in Hinckley, Oneida County, New York, to Magdalena Anstett and Andreas Schumacher, recent émigrés from Merzalben, Germany. He was the youngest of nine. The big Catholic family soon moved to Dolgeville, a village up against the Adirondack Mountain foothills, where his father was a shoe maker.

Even at 15 he doubled as a pitcher and shortstop for the Dolgeville town team and starred for the nearby Little Falls semi-pro squad. Scouts from the Cardinals, Giants and Yankees were all tracking him as he graduated from Dolgeville High School in 1928.

Instead, Schumacher pursued a college degree at Saint Lawrence University in upstate Canton where he stood out in football, basketball and baseball as Central New York's best all-around athlete. In early 1931, he relented and signed with the Giants.

Giants manager John J. McGraw liked Schumacher's look and started the 20-year-old in the second game of the year on April 15, 1931. Afterward, he was sent down to learn how to pitch with the Bridgeport (CT) Bears and Rochester (NY) Red Wings.

New York was mired in the cellar when the aging McGraw stepped down after 40 games in 1932. Schumacher's roommate Bill Terry took the reins, yet only gave him 13 more starts. He went 5-6, but worked diligently to perfect his sinker and curve.

Schumacher earned the #2 starter role in 1933 behind Hubbell. The Giants were in first place on his June 12 graduation day at Saint Lawrence. Terry and the entire Giant squad traveled north to Canton to attend the ceremony. Schumacher went on to support Hubbell, the NL MVP, with 19 victories, a 2.16 ERA (third in the league), 21 complete games and seven shutouts. The Giants rode their two aces to the pennant.

He hurled a nifty five-hitter in World Series Game 2 versus the Nationals. In the Game 5 final, his two-run single in the second put the Giants ahead, but he left in the sixth with the game tied. Ott's homer in the tenth won the World Series for the Giants.

Prince Hal followed up in 1934 with a superb 23-10 mark in a career-high 297 innings pitched. He also set a NL record for a pitcher with six home runs, adding five doubles and 15 RBI. Despite 93 wins, the Giants finished second by two games.

On April 28, 1935 Schumacher threw a no-hitter, facing only 29 hitters ... or so he thought. The next day he found out that the official scorer had ruled a second inning error to be a scratch hit. In the 1935 All-Star Game, he gave up a lone run in four frames.

Later in July on a sweltering hot St Louis afternoon, Schumacher collapsed with no pulse after pitching the sixth inning. The Cardinals physician, Robert Hyland, saved his life by packing him in ice in the clubhouse. He recovered to go 19-9 with a 2.89 ERA.

On February 1, 1936, Schumacher and his high school

"*Hal Schumacher was another man who matched his era — like Bill Terry, confronted with a tough situation, he had worked hard and come out well.*"

~ writer Peter Williams

G	IP	W	L	PCT	SHO	GS	CG	H	ER	SO	BB	ERA
391	2482.1	158	121	.566	26	329	138	2424	926	906	902	3.36

sweetheart, Alice Clifford Sullivan, were married at St. Joseph's Church in Dolgeville. The Giants were NL champs that year, but his pitching arm was already starting to deteriorate and he went just 11-13.

Schumacher was shelled in a World Series Game 2 loss to the Yankees, but in the clutch performance of his career in Game 5 he came back to hurl a ten-strikeout ten-inning gem at Yankee Stadium. Working his way out of a no-out, bases-loaded mess in the third, he struck out Joe DiMaggio and Lou Gehrig, and then induced Bill Dickey to fly out.

All the innings, his herky-jerky delivery, a sore shoulder, bone fragments in his elbow- all eroded his fastball. He used guile to win 13 games each year from 1937 to 1940, and threw a one-hitter in 1938 versus Brooklyn, but he was no longer the same.

After the 1942 season, Schumacher joined the United States Naval Reserves, serving aboard an aircraft carrier. He returned to the Giants in 1946, started 13 games, appeared in 24 and posted a 4-4 record. He'd had enough and headed home to Dolgeville.

From late 1946 until 1967, Schumacher worked with a local Dolgeville firm later known as the Adirondack Bat Company and promoted his brand at spring training camps. Giant greats Bobby Thomson, Willie Mays and Willie McCovey all swung *Adirondacks*.

The Schumachers adopted a son William and a daughter Mary. Schumacher was venerated in Dolgeville and the region. The unassuming retiree enjoyed a family summer home on nearby Canada Lake and was an excellent golfer, sometimes breaking 70.

Prince Hal Schumacher entered Cooperstown's Mary Imogene Bassett Hospital in early 1993 with advanced stomach cancer. He passed away in Cooperstown on April 21 at age 82 and is buried in St. Joseph's Church Cemetery in his hometown of Dolgeville.

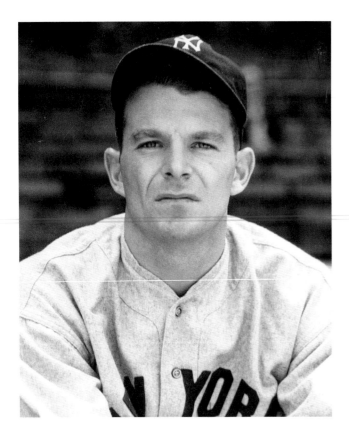

GEORGE SELKIRK

NEW YORK YANKEES
RIGHT FIELD

1934-1942

"He is serious and intent on his baseball, always seeking efficiency. And it didn't help him that he was named as the successor to Babe Ruth, was even assigned the same number and, in his early big league days, was faced with the burden of crowd comparison between the former wearer of No. 3, Ruth, and the current one."

~ *writer Arthur Siegel*

George Selkirk had the unenviable role of following Babe Ruth as the Yankees' rightfielder. He finally won over the Gotham fans to become the greatest Canadian-born player of the first half of the twentieth century. Selkirk might as well be known as the "Canadian Mr. October." He saw action in more World Series games (21), had more hits (18), more RBI (10), more walks (11) and more championship rings (5) than any other Canadian before or since.

The left-handed hitting 6'1" 182-pound Selkirk was an important part of Joe McCarthy's Yankee Dynasty teams, playing for five World Series champions and six Yankee pennant-winners. A two-time All-Star, Selkirk produced five .300 seasons and drove in 100 runs twice.

Suiting up alongside baseball immortals like Lou Gehrig, Joe DiMaggio, Bill Dickey and Lefty Gomez, Selkirk more than held his own. His physical strength was well-respected inside the Yankees clubhouse. He was the only Yankee who could wrestle a healthy Gehrig to a draw.

★   ★   ★   ★   ★

George Alexander Selkirk was born of Scottish lineage on January 4, 1908 to Margaret "Maggie" Dykes and William Selkirk in Huntsville, Ontario, Canada. His father moved the family to Rochester, New York in 1913 where he started a funeral parlor. A three-sport star at Rochester Technical High, Selkirk first captured the attention of scout Herb Moran as a catcher.

He began his professional career at age 18 with the 1927 Cambridge (MD) Canners of the Class-D Eastern Shore League. His minor league career featured tours with the American Association's Columbus (OH) Red Birds (1932) and the International League's Jersey City (NJ) Skeeters (1928-31); Newark (NJ) Bears (1932-36), Toronto (ON) Maple Leafs (1932); and his hometown Rochester Red Wings (1933). Selkirk's eight-year minor league average was .303.

He was hung with the nickname "Twinkletoes" by his Jersey City teammates because he ran on the balls of his feet. Selkirk was hitting .357 after 106 games in 1934 when the Yankees summoned him. He made his debut on August 12 after Earle Combs was injured severely in a game in St. Louis. He hit .313 in 46 games, playing the outfield, sometimes in place of Ruth.

The Great Bambino was released by the Yankees on February 26, 1935. When Selkirk arrived in Fort Lauderdale, McCarthy informed him he was going to be the club's starting rightfielder and would be assigned the same #3 jersey that Ruth had made famous. Selkirk hit over .300 in his first four years with the club but was not immediately embraced by the Yankee fans.

In 1936, Selkirk batted .308 with 18 home runs and 107 RBI as one-third of an all-.300 hitting outfield with DiMaggio and Jake Powell. In his Fall Classic debut on September 30, he drilled a Carl Hubbell screwball over the right field wall at the Polo Grounds in his first at-bat, joining only 33 other players (and the only Canadian) to homer in their inaugural at-bat. His eight hits, two home runs and a triple helped the Bronx Bombers beat the cross-town Giants.

In 1937, the underrated Selkirk was hitting .344 and tied for the AL lead in circuit clouts when he fractured his collarbone diving for a fly ball on Canada Day- July 1. He only played in 78 games, but hit .328 with 18 home runs and slugged .629, nearly as high as Gehrig's .643. He knocked in six runs and scored five more in the Series, as the Yanks again subdued the Giants.

After a down 1938, Selkirk came back to have his finest campaign in 1939. He batted .306 with 21 bombs and 101 RBI and led the Yankees with 103 walks to finish with a .452 OBA. He had his weakest postseason, but the Bombers swept the Reds for their fourth straight title.

Selkirk was seeing reduced playing time by 1940.

G	AB	R	H	2B	3B	HR	RBI	SB	BB	SO	BA	OBP	SLG	TB
846	2790	503	810	131	41	108	576	49	486	319	.290	.400	.483	1347

With a group of Yankee fly chasers including DiMaggio, Tommy Henrich and King Kong Keller, he only got into 118 games. In 1941 and 1942, he played even less, but pinch-hit three times in the two Fall Classics.

Volunteering to do his patriotic chore for his adopted country in World War II, Selkirk joined the U.S. Navy on November 24, 1942. After serving as an aerial gunner until 1945, he came back to baseball at age 38 but couldn't reprise his former skills after the three-year hiatus.

Nevertheless, the Yankees did hire him to manage three of their minor league affiliates – the Triple-A Newark (NJ) Bears (1946-47) and Kansas City (MO) Blues (1951-52) as well as the Class-A Binghampton (NY) Triplets (1948-50). He then skippered two Milwaukee Braves affiliates – the Triple-A Toledo (OH) Sox (1953-55) and Triple-A Wichita (KS) Braves (1956).

After his 11-year minor league managerial career, he worked as the player personnel director for the Kansas City Athletics from 1957 to 1961 and the player development director of the Baltimore Orioles for a single year in 1962. Selkirk was named the general manager of the expansion franchise Washington Senators in late 1962.

He served as the Senators' general manager from 1963 to 1969. The death of one of the team's key owners forced the sale of the team after the 1968 season, and Selkirk was a casualty during the transition, losing his job. He returned to the Yankees as a scout in 1970.

Selkirk was inducted into the International League Hall of Fame in 1958 and the Canadian Baseball Hall of Fame in 1983. He and his wife Norma, a registered nurse, raised a daughter and eventually retired to their home in Pompano Beach, Florida. He passed away at age 79 on January 19, 1987 in Fort Lauderdale, Florida. His wife died just eight months later. Selkirk was laid to rest in the Siloam United Methodist Cemetery in Harrisonville, Pennsylvania.

VIC SORRELL

DETROIT TIGERS
RIGHT-HANDED PITCHER

1928-1937

"I might be from the sticks stranger, but I've been on railroad trains, have seen street cars and even airplanes, so if you have any more jokes to tell you might walk down to the barber shop. Someone down there might listen to you."

~ Vic Sorrell to Tigers scout Billy Doyle
thinking it was a prank

Vic Sorrell was a workhorse starter for the Tigers in the Depression 30s, helping Detroit to win two AL pennants and their initial World Series title in 1935. He pitched backed by such Hall of Famers as Mickey Cochrane, Charlie Gehringer, Goose Goslin and Hank Greenberg. The modest 5'10" 180-pound right-hander was nicknamed "Lawyer" and "The Philosopher" as one of the first big-league hurlers to wear eyeglasses. His spectacles enhanced his thoughtful look.

★　★　★　★　★

Victor Garland Sorrell was born on April 9, 1901 to Lela Frances "Fannie" McGee and Julius Judson "Bug" Sorrell in Morrisville, Wake County, North Carolina. He grew up with two older brothers and a younger sister on a 400-acre plantation devoted to growing cotton and corn.

Sorrell first gained notice as a star pitcher for Wake County's Cary High as a sophomore. As a junior, he pitched the Clayton High Comets, southeast of Raleigh, to a North Carolina state title. Back at Cary High as a senior, he fanned 21 Raleigh High hitters in a single game.

Matriculating at Wake Forest College, Sorrell pitched for both the freshman and varsity teams his first year and led the Demon Deacons to Big Five Conference championships as a sophomore and junior. He won his last eight games as a junior, surrendering only three runs.

Sorrell's eligibility was questioned before a game on April 13, 1925 at North Carolina State College because he had pitched for a coal mining company team in Bluefield, West Virginia and was on its payroll the previous summer. He threw a 12-inning, 5-4 victory before a record North Carolina State crowd of over 8,000. After the game, he was declared ineligible.

Sorrell caught Tigers scout Billy Doyle's attention and was sent to the Toronto (ON) Maple Leafs of the Double-A International League. The 1926 Maple Leafs won the International League title and Sorrell was key, going 8-0 with a 3.08 ERA. When he won his first four games for Toronto in 1927, he was undefeated in his initial 12 decisions as a professional pitcher.

In 1927, Sorrell finished at 14–8 with a 3.98 ERA. He signed with Detroit on January 19, 1928. Months later, he earned his major league debut at the advanced age of 27 on April 22, 1928, pitching four scoreless innings in relief against the Chicago White Sox.

In his rookie season, Sorrell registered a memorable strikeout against Ty Cobb. The longtime Tiger great at the end of his career with the Philadelphia Athletics fouled off two of Sorrell's offerings and then was buckled by a sharp-breaking curveball that nipped the corner. The cantankerous Cobb argued the call for ten full minutes.

From 1928 to 1933, Sorrell was a vital hurler in the Detroit starting rotation. He was given the starting call 175 times during his first six seasons and registered 80 complete games. Sorrell's finest year was in 1930 when he finished eighth in the American League with 16 wins and seventh with a 3.86 ERA. He was also tenth in the Junior Circuit with 99 strikeouts in 1931.

On August 13, 1933, Sorrell started at Comiskey Park and pitched an epic 17-inning complete game. After the ninth inning, neither team could score until Detroit went ahead, 6-5, in the top of the 17th. Sorrell shut down the White Sox in the bottom half for the win. He faced 69 batters, allowed 17 hits (15 singles and two doubles), walked four, and threw over 250 pitches.

The 1934 Tigers had the best season in franchise history, posting a 101-53 record to run away with the pennant by seven games over the Yankees. Sorrell was the third starter behind 20-game winners Tommy Bridges and Schoolboy Rowe. With only 28 starts and just $129\frac{2}{3}$ innings pitched, he went 6–9 and did not pitch against the Gas House Gang Cardinals in the Fall Classic.

G	IP	W	L	PCT	SHO	GS	CG	H	ER	SO	BB	ERA
280	1671.2	92	101	.477	8	216	95	1820	823	706	619	4.43

By 1935, the 34-year old veteran's arm was starting to suffer the effects of almost 1,500 major league innings over the previous seven seasons. The Tigers won their first World Series Championship in franchise history against the Cubs, but Sorrell could only start eight games.

On July 23 however, he bested future Hall of Famer Lefty Gomez at Yankee Stadium with a nifty eight-hitter, 3-1, frustrating a lineup that featured future Hall of Famers Earle Combs, Lou Gehrig, Bill Dickey and Tony Lazzeri. Three of his four wins were against the Bronx Bombers, but Sorrell saw no action in the 1935 Fall Classic, the first in Tigers franchise history.

He tossed his final game at age 36 on June 3, 1937. After retirement, Sorrell skippered the Class-D Bluefield (WV) Blue-Grays of the Mountain State League in 1939 and 1940. With the start of World War II, he left baseball to work in the Wilmington, North Carolina shipyards.

Sorrell became the head baseball coach of North Carolina State University in 1946, a post he held until 1966. His 21-year tenure was the longest in Wolfpack history. Playing only 20 games a year and getting only nominal scholarship help, his teams compiled a 223-196-5 record.

NCSU went 96–89 in 13 years under Sorrell in the Atlantic Coast Conference. He mentored 29 All-ACC players and three NCAA All-Americans. More than 50 former players came out to tip their hats to him on Vic Sorrell Day before his last home game in 1966.

Sorrell remained a member of the NCSU athletic staff and resided in Raleigh in later years with his wife, the former Willa Elizabeth Garner. His son, Victor, Jr., played shortstop under him from 1963 to 1965 and later became a golf professional in Bluefield, West Virginia.

Sorrell passed away at his home in Raleigh at age 71 on May 4, 1972 and was laid to rest at the Raleigh Memorial Park. Sorrell was a posthumous inductee of both the North Carolina Sports Hall of Fame in 1999 and the Wake Forest University Athletics Hall of Fame in 2003.

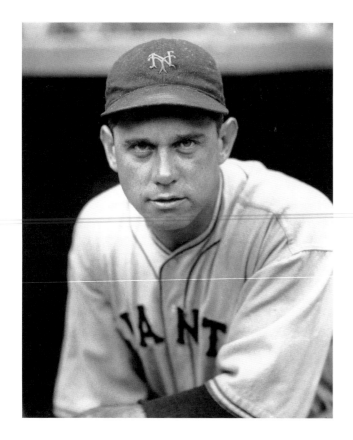

BILL TERRY

NEW YORK GIANTS
FIRST BASE

1923-1936

> *"He once hit a ball
> between my legs so
> hard that my center
> fielder caught it on
> the fly backing up
> against the wall."*
>
> ~ Dizzy Dean

Bill Terry will be remembered as the National League's last .400 hitter. He was a left-handed offensive wrecking crew, wielding his heavy 35" *Louisville Slugger* to lace doubles and triples into the spacious left and right field power alleys at the Polo Grounds.

Terry completed his career hitting a cool .341 including four seasons over .350 and nine consecutive years hitting above .320. He amassed 200 hits six times, scored 100 runs seven times, and drove in 100 runs in six straight seasons.

Defensively, the 6'2" 210-pound Terry was the premier first baseman of his day, once playing 468 straight games. He fielded a stylish .992, leading NL first basemen in double plays and putouts five times, assists three times, and fielding percentage twice.

⭐   ⭐   ⭐   ⭐

William Harold Terry was born in Atlanta, Fulton County, Georgia on October 30, 1898 to Bertha Blackmon and William Thomas Terry. He spent his hard scrabble youth in Memphis, Tennessee hindered by an unhappy, unstable home. His parents separated for the last time when he was 15, and he went to work to support his mother.

Terry began his pro career at Newnan, Georgia in 1915, and then played for the Shreveport (LA) Gassers in the Texas League for two years. He married Memphis belle Elvena Sneed after the 1916 season but finances got so grave in Louisiana that he had to pawn his new wife's wedding ring. He quit organized ball after the 1917 season, going to work for the Standard Oil Company of Memphis, and organized the company team.

In 1922 and 1923, Terry starred for the Toledo (OH) Mud Hens where he was scouted by Giants manager John J. McGraw. McGraw had his first experience with Terry's

bargaining style. Three weeks of talks inked Terry to a $5,000 a year contract.

Less than a week later "Memphis Bill" debuted in the big time on September 22, 1923. His apprenticeship would last three more years until Highpockets Kelly was traded to the Cincinnati Reds. Terry took over at first base full time in 1927, hitting .326 with 121 RBI, but most of his baseball legend would be burnished after he turned 30.

The NL used hitter-friendly, lowered-stitch *Spalding* baseballs in 1930. Taking full advantage, Terry played every game, recorded 139 runs scored, 23 home runs, 129 RBI, a .452 on-base average and slugged .619. He matched the NL record of 254 hits and hit .401- both unequaled since. He was the obvious 1930 *The Sporting News* National League Most Valuable Player.

Terry's cold glare and bluntness showed that he viewed baseball as a serious business. He and McGraw wrangled about everything from salary to field strategy. Terry just missing the NL batting title again in 1931 at .3486 to Chick Hafey's .3488. In early 1932, he sent his contract back and told the writers he was "thoroughly disgusted."

Terry would become a perennial holdout. McGraw was so piqued with Terry's negotiating, he wrote him back to negotiate a trade for himself to another team. Yet, when "The Little Napoleon" selected his managerial successor just six months later, he picked Terry- the first time they had spoken to each other in almost two years.

Terry took the reins from the ailing McGraw in June of 1932 and grew into an effective manager while finishing his playing career. Terry inherited a collection of long-in-the-tooth veterans and yet guided them to the 1933 World Series championship over the Nationals. He went on to

G	AB	R	H	2B	3B	HR	RBI	SB	BB	SO	BA	OBP	SLG	TB
1721	6428	1120	2193	373	112	154	1078	56	537	449	.341	.393	.506	3252

compile an 823-661 record, winning three NL pennants.

Terry gained a place in Giants and Dodgers lore during the busy 1934 winter meetings. Noting the Dodgers hadn't participated in any trades, he remarked playfully, "Is Brooklyn still in the league?" It became a rallying cry for the Flatbushers who portrayed the throw-away joke as disrespectful of their on-field performance and defeated the Giants twice on the season's last weekend, depriving them of the NL pennant.

Terry considered himself a Giant "first and last" and rejected several proposals by other teams to be a dual field and general manager. He handed over the Giants helm to Mel Ott in 1942 to become general manager and then served as minor league director. In the 1950s, he even tried unsuccessfully to buy the club in order to keep it in New York.

The baseball writers branded Terry as hostile and arrogant and made him wait 13 years for his rightful induction into the National Baseball Hall of Fame in 1954. But he never showed any resentment and became a regular at the annual Cooperstown festivities where he always signed baseballs with ".401" beneath his signature.

The Giants retired Terry's uniform jersey #3 in 1984. It is now displayed on the left field upper deck façade at San Franciso's AT&T Park. He was ranked #59 on *The Sporting News* 1999 "100 Greatest Baseball Players" list and was nominated for Major League Baseball's All-Century Team.

Terry made a fortune in oil and cotton speculation after returning to Memphis. He then concentrated on a successful automobile distributorship in Jacksonville, Florida with one of his sons. Terry was an avid golfer and fisherman. He passed away on January 9, 1989 in Jacksonville and is buried at the Evergreen Cemetery.

CECIL TRAVIS

WASHINGTON NATIONALS
SHORTSTOP • THIRD BASE

1933-1941 • 1945-1947

*"Hell, in 1941,
Cecil Travis was just
as good as either of us!
Cecil Travis is one
of the five best
left-handed hitters
I ever saw."*

~ Ted Williams

Cecil Travis was the finest all-around shortstop ever to play in Washington, D.C. He set the American League record for the highest career batting average for a shortstop at .314, third behind National Leaguers Honus Wagner at .327 and Arky Vaughan at .318. More than any other major league star, he sacrificed his would-be Hall of Fame career for his country in World War II.

Travis hit over .300 in eight of his first nine seasons. A true gentleman and fan favorite, the three-time American League All-Star played shortstop and third base for the Nats six years each, showing solid range, a strong accurate throwing arm and sure hands.

★   ★   ★   ★   ★

Cecil Howell Travis was born on August 8, 1913, the youngest of ten children to Ada and James Travis on a 200-acre farm outside of Atlanta in Riverdale, Clayton County, Georgia. Farm work and baseball occupied his time. He was persuaded to attend a baseball school for young players at Atlanta's Ponce de Leon Park in the winter of 1930-1931. Proprietors Kid Elberfeld and Tubby Walton noted his natural, smooth swing.

Walton eventually persuaded Nats scout Joe Engel to sign him. Travis batted .429 in 1932 for the Single-A Chattanooga (TN) Lookouts in 13 games. He then hit .362 in 152 games in 1933 with 203 hits, 88 RBI and a Southern Association-leading 17 triples.

Travis just missed making the 1933 Washington roster on Opening Day, but soon got his debut on May 16. Spelling the injured Ossie Bluege at third, he lined out five hits, tying Fred Clarke's 1894 record. He hit .302 in 43 at-bats before being sent back down.

But in 1934 at age 20, the angular 6'1½" 185-pound Travis took over the third base job for the Nationals. He

drove the ball to the opposite field often, finishing at .319, and quickly grew into a young star. From 1935 to 1938, he hit .318, .317, .344 and .335 respectively, with 705 hits and only 105 strikeouts while learning to pull the ball and use the power alleys to run out doubles and triples. It culminated in an All-Star berth in 1938.

With two bouts of the flu in 1939, Travis struggled and only raised his average to .292 in the last two months. Disappointed, he reported in 1940 ultra fit and 20 pounds heavier which translated into 37 doubles, 11 triples, a .322 average and All-Star honors.

The sweet-swinging Georgian had a banner year in 1941 and credited a friend for part of his success. Ben Chapman was let go by the Nats in May, but not before he had loaned Travis his choice 36", 36-ounce *Louisville Slugger*. He used it the rest of the year.

In the campaign's first two weeks, he smashed seven doubles, four triples, four home runs, hit a torrid .526 (30-for-57), scored 14 runs and knocked in 20. In June and July, his 24-game hitting streak unfolded at the same time as Joe DiMaggio's famous record 56-game run. He hit .420 (42-for-100) during his streak with 13 multi-hit games.

Travis finished with a league-best 218 hits and cemented his reputation as the game's top shortstop. In the batting race, his .359 average was second only to Ted Williams' .406. Travis posted career-highs of 106 runs scored, 39 doubles, 19 triples, seven home runs, 101 RBI and slugged .520. He struck out only 25 times in 152 games.

Before World War II, Travis had earned a career average of .327 as the best offensive shortstop in baseball. In his physical prime at 28 years old, Travis was poised to finish off a 3,000-hit career and punch his ticket to the National Baseball Hall of Fame in Cooperstown, but then came the bombing of Pearl Harbor by Japan.

G	AB	R	H	2B	3B	HR	RBI	SB	BB	SO	BA	OBP	SLG	TB
1328	4914	665	1544	276	67	43	657	23	723	515	.314	.370	.416	2290

 **W**

He enlisted to do his patriotic duty. During Ardennes Forest combat in the winter of 1944 and 1945, Travis went days without food or water and his feet were frozen during the Battle of the Bulge. He was one of the 76th Infantry Division heroes, "The Battered Bastards of Bastogne," who held on until Allied reinforcements arrived to doom the Third Reich's final offensive drive.

Immediate surgery prevented amputation of his frostbitten feet, but he had sustained permanent damage. He received the United States Army's Bronze Star for Valor for his heroism and never expressed any regret about the high personal cost of his service to his country, but Travis would never be the same ballplayer.

Upon his return on September 8, 1945, he received a standing ovation from Washington fans including President Harry S Truman. Although Travis never made excuses, his damaged feet had eroded his balance and timing. In 1946, he hit only .252 despite a six-hit game against the Cleveland Indians in early May.

Travis faded to .216 in 1947. Before he retired, the Nationals hosted Cecil Travis Night at Griffith Stadium on August 15. With his wife, Helen Hubbard, and two sons, he was overwhelmed with gifts and appreciation. The ceremony featured encomiums by Five Star General Dwight D. Eisenhower, other top military brass, Nationals owner Clark Griffith and Philadelphia Athletics owner Connie Mack.

Travis returned to run the family farm in Riverdale while scouting for the Nationals in the Atlanta area until 1956. He was inducted into the Georgia Sports Hall of Fame in 1975. A true American hero, Travis passed away on December 16, 2006 of heart failure at his Riverdale farm. He is buried at the Crest Lawn Memorial Park in Atlanta.

CHAPTER FOUR

THE POST WAR GOLDEN ERA

1946-1957

Ebbets Field –
Brooklyn, New York

JOE ASTROTH

PHILADELPHIA & KANSAS CITY ATHLETICS
CATCHER

1945-1946 • 1949-1956

J oe Astroth was such a well-suited battery mate that he became Bobby Shantz's personal catcher in 1952, the year the diminutive 5'6" 139-pound Shantz pitched 255 innings and went 24-7 with a 2.48 ERA as the American League's Most Valuable Player. Astroth caught almost every inning and ran the game for him. Astroth and Shantz became lifelong friends.

The stocky 5'9" 187-pound Astroth was primarily known for his defensive play. With his bazooka throwing arm, he retired after ten years in the major leagues with one of the all-time best "caught stealing" percentages of 48 percent. His career fielding average was an elite .987 with 2,057 putouts, 233 assists, 46 double plays and only 33 errors.

* * * * *

Joseph Henry Astroth was born on September 1, 1922 in East Alton, Madison County, Illinois to Austrian émigré Mary Guardia and August Henry Astroth. Playing athletics with competitive older brother Levere and younger siblings Margaret and Robert, he grew up in Alton and nearby Roxana with aspirations of becoming a professional ballplayer from the age of six.

Astroth was an all-round star at tiny East Alton-Wood River High School. He played football and basketball and captained the Oilers baseball team, despite competing without nails on his right ring and pinky finger due to an industrial factory accident when he was age 17.

Astroth planned to become a high school coach and teacher like his brother Levere and followed him to the University of Illinois at Urbana-Champaign where he excelled in football, basketball and baseball in 1939, 1940 and 1942. One of his teammates was future 12-year major league outfielder Hoot Evers.

However, Astroth was called into military service with the United States Coast Guard in 1942. Stationed at the Coast Guard Academy at New London, Connecticut, he played for Babe Young's Coast Guard Dolphins baseball squad and was first noticed by Athletics scout Tom Fleming. Dodgers scout and Hall of Famer George Sisler offered him a contract while there.

Astroth left military service in mid-1945 and immediately signed with the Athletics. Former catcher Connie Mack, the miserly A's owner and manager, was famous for his frugal ways. He put the young backstop under contract with a $500 bonus plus a $300 monthly salary.

Without a single minor league game for seasoning, Astroth was given his major league debut on August 13, 1945 at Comiskey Park, pinch-hitting for Mayo Smith against the White Sox's Earl Caldwell. He appeared in ten games in 1945 and only four more in 1946.

Astroth was sent down to the Class-B Lancaster (PA) Red Roses in the Interstate League in 1946 and hit .289 in 301 at-bats. After the IL season, he was promoted to the Toronto (ON) Maple Leafs to get a look at Triple-A International League competition, but only got three at-bats.

Astroth hit .280 for the 1947 Class-A Savannah (GA) Indians of the South Atlantic League and really showed his talent in 1948 both in the batter's box and behind the plate with the Double-A Memphis (TN) Chickasaws. He batted .352 for the Chicks as a Southern Association All-Star and plainly demonstrated he was ready for his second tour of duty with Philadelphia.

Astroth enjoyed a career day on September 23, 1950 versus the Nationals when he launched a grand slam home run off Julio Morena and a two-run single for six RBI in the sixth inning. The Athletics scored a dozen runs in that inning and won going away, 16-5. Astroth was the fifth man in modern baseball history to accomplish this major league record. He went on to hit a career-high .327 that year, leading the Athletics in hitting.

On September 2, 1952, in the second game of a double-

> *"Joe caught every ball I threw for the A's in 1952. He ran the game for me. I never shook him off. We were very close at the time and we still are."*
>
> *~ battery mate Bobby Shantz*

G	AB	R	H	2B	3B	HR	RBI	SB	BB	SO	BA	OBP	SLG	TB
544	1579	163	401	51	10	13	156	6	177	124	.254	.334	.324	511

header, Astroth turned out to be the spoiler. Just up from the Havana Cubans, Nationals rookie Mike Fornieles was making his major league debut and hurled a one-hit 5-0 shutout. Astroth was the only Athletic to hit safely with an early second-inning single.

Chicago real estate entrepreneur Arnold Johnson bought the Athletics in 1954 and moved the franchise from Philadelphia to Kansas City for the 1955 campaign. Missouri fans turned out in support in record numbers for that time, drawing 1,393,054 to Municipal Stadium in 1955. It would be Astroth's last full year in Major League Baseball.

He played his final game in the Big Time on May 13, 1956 at age 33. Astroth was given his unconditional release after only eight games and spent the rest of that season with the San Diego Padres, a Cleveland Indians affiliate in the Pacific Coast League.

Despite feeling the wear and tear of 16 pro seasons behind the plate, he caught for two more years for the Buffalo (NY) Bisons, the Athletics' Triple-A entry in the International League, retiring in 1958. Astroth's minor-league totals included 553 games and a .281 average.

He went on to enjoy a flourishing career in business, though baseball remained an abiding interest. He and his former battery mate Shantz owned and operated the "Pit Catcher" Bowling Lanes & Dairy Bar for many years in Chalfont, Pennsylvania, a Philadelphia suburb. It was not catcher Tim McCarver who first used the line that he and Lefty Carlton should be buried 60' 6" apart. It was originally associated with the early 1950s Astroth and Shantz battery.

Astroth and his wife of over 60 years, Marjorie, retired in Boca Raton, Florida in St. Andrews Estates South. The couple raised four children- August, Joe Jr., Brian and Janet- and had ten grandchildren. He served as an ambassador for the Philadelphia Athletics Society until his death at age 90 on May 3, 2013 in Boca Raton.

AL BRAZLE

St. Louis Cardinals
Left-Handed Pitcher

1943 • 1946-1954

"Old Alfie was a terrific relief pitcher because he was a lefthander with good control and a great natural sinker that dipped better the more he worked and the more tired he became."

~ teammate Stan Musial

Al Brazle spent almost eight years and labored over 1,200 innings in the minor league backwaters before finally getting his chance to pitch for the Cardinals at the advanced age of 29. After a superb rookie season, he lost two years of a burgeoning baseball career in his prime, fighting for his country during World War II in infantry combat in Europe.

The wiry 6'2" 180-pound Brazle was a member of two National League pennant-winners and one World Series Champion. Becoming solely a relief specialist in later years, he was 41-23 as a career fireman, topping the National League in saves in 1952 and 1953.

Popular with St. Louis fans and affectionately referred to as "Alfie" by his teammates, the herky-jerky sidearmer finished in the National League's top 10 in a dozen pitching categories. Brazle ranked in the league's higher echelon in games pitched seven times; saves six times; games finished five times; winning percentage four times; and ERA three times.

★ ★ ★ ★ ★

Alpha Eugene Brazle was born to Fannie and William Eugene Brazle near Loyal, Kingfisher County, Oklahoma on October 19, 1913. He grew up in the nearby township of Lone Mound in Caddo County, working on the family farm along with his older brother and sister. He was not formally educated beyond his grammar school years.

Pitching in the local semi-pro and town team leagues, the 23-year-old Brazle was discovered by the Red Sox in 1936, signed to a contract, and sent to the Little Rock (AR) Travelers of the Class-A1 Southern Association. He was with Class-A Hazelton in 1937 in the New York-Pennsylvania League, but back with Little Rock for 1938, 1939 and 1940.

At the end of the 1940 season, the Red Sox traded Brazle to St. Louis for pitcher Mike Ryba. The Redbird farm system then consisted of 31 affiliate teams, making the competition to get to the majors unusually difficult. He threw for the Class-1A New Orleans (LA) Pelicans (Southern Association) and Class-1A Houston Buffaloes (Texas League) in 1941. Hurling for Houston again in 1942, he was still only 8-13 with a 3.45 ERA in 175 innings pitched.

However, Brazle gained newfound command and success in 1943 with the Sacramento (CA) Solons. He won 11 games, sporting a 1.69 ERA as the Pacific Coast League ERA champ. His performance punched his ticket to the Big Time. Brazle got his debut at age 29 on July 25 and finished at 8-2 with a microscopic 1.53 ERA, hurling eight complete games in nine starts.

Manager Billy Southworth gave Brazle the ball in Game 3 of the 1943 World Series at Yankee Stadium. In front of a crowd of 69,990 on the biggest stage, he and the Yankees' Hank Borowy engaged in a classic pitchers' duel through seven innings. Leading 2-1 going into the bottom of the eighth, Brazle tired. Billy Johnson's bases loaded triple was the deciding blow. By the time he had been relieved, the damage had been done and the Bronx Bombers prevailed, 6-2.

The day after the 1943 World Series ended, Brazle and teammate Harry "The Hat" Walker were inducted together into the United States Army at Jefferson Barracks, Missouri. Both were sent to the Cavalry Replacement Training Center (CRTC) at Fort Riley, Kansas.

Brazle and Walker were assigned to the 65th Reconnaissance Troop (Mechanized) of the 65th Infantry Division and combat trained. On March 19, 1945, the 65th breached the Siegfried Line, the Nazi defense system spanning 390 miles with 18,000 bunkers, tunnels and tank traps.

Meeting heavy Nazi resistance at Oppenheim in late March, Brazle and his 65th Division fought their way to the Danube River below Regensburg in late April. They

G	IP	W	L	PCT	SHO	GS	GF	CG	SV	H	ER	SO	BB	ERA
441	1376.2	97	64	.602	7	178	178	47	60	506	878	554	492	3.31

took Passau, forcing the Germans to surrender *en masse*, and were in Austria when World War II ended on May 8.

War heroes Brazle and Walker returned to the Cardinals and re-invigorated Major League Baseball in 1946. Brazle came back in good form, posting an 11-10 record with a 3.29 ERA. The 1946 Cardinals were strong, featuring a lineup which included future Hall-of-Famers Stan Musial, Red Schoendienst and Enos Slaughter. The club won the pennant by prevailing in two straight playoff games against the Brooklyn Dodgers, the first playoff series in baseball history.

In 1946 World Series Game 5 at Fenway Park, manager Eddie Dwyer pulled Howie Pollet with one out in the first inning in favor of Brazle. Adroitly escaping jams in the early going, Brazle maneuvered his way through six innings.

In the seventh, two doubles, two intentional walks and a Marty Marion error on a sharply-hit grounder led to three runs and a loss, 6-3. Although the defeat put the Cardinals down 3-2 in the Series, Harry "The Cat" Brecheen won his third game of the Fall Classic in Game 7 to bring home the title to St. Louis.

Brazle was 14-8 with a 2.84 ERA in 1947 and threw a career-high 206 innings in 1949 with a 3.18 ERA, winning 14 games. Used in relief in his last years, he was 12-5 with a 2.72 ERA in 1952, leading the league with 16 saves and followed with an NL-high 18 saves in 1953.

In 1954, at age 40, he was the oldest player in the Senior Circuit, pitching his last big-league game on September 24 before being given his release at the end of the season. He ended his professional career with the Sacramento Solons in 1955, appearing in 19 games.

Brazle and his wife, the former Helen Blankenship,

lived in Cortez, Colorado in later years. Brazle passed away on October 24, 1973 at the Veterans Hospital in Grand Junction at age 60 after suffering a long illness, perhaps due in part to his severe combat experience in World War II. He is buried in the Fairview Cemetery in Yellow Jacket, Montezuma County, Colorado.

ROY CAMPANELLA

BROOKLYN DODGERS
CATCHER

1948-1957

"I've never seen a more enthusiastic guy on a ball field, one who got more sheer joy out of playing."

~ Dodgers manager
Walter Alston

One of the greatest all-around catchers ever, Roy Campanella was also the first black receiver in major league history. One of the most respected and beloved stars of his generation, he anchored five National League Champion Dodger teams and earned NL Most Valuable Player honors three times. Campy's passion, grit and intelligence made him the heart and soul of the Brooklyn *Boys of Summer* teams of the 1950s.

The powerfully-built 5'9" 200-pound Campanella was the complete defensive catcher. He led the NL in fielding five times, putouts six times and caught 100 or more games a record nine straight years. He pounced on bunts with catlike quickness and gunned down two out of three would-be base stealers with his pinpoint accurate arm.

* * * * *

Roy Campanella was born November 19, 1921 in Homestead, Allegheny County, Pennsylvania to Ida Mercer and John Campanella, the youngest of four children. His mother was of African descent and his father was an immigrant from Sicily. When he was seven, his family moved to Nicetown, a working class section of North Philadelphia.

Already competing on weekends at 15 for the Baltimore Elite Giants in the Negro National League, Campanella left Simon Gratz High the next summer to play full time. He became the Elites starting catcher in 1939 and, like most black ballplayers of his era, barnstormed the country in buses and spent winters playing in Mexico and the Caribbean. Campy would reign as the best catcher in segregated black baseball during the 1940s.

Dodger president Branch Rickey signed the first three African American ballplayers before the 1946 season. Jackie Robinson was slotted for Montreal to prepare for his historic 1947 debut. Campy signed next, and with Don Newcombe was sent to Nashua, New Hampshire in the Double-A New England League- the first pro team to be racially integrated within the United States. Under Walter Alston, he became the NEL Most Valuable Player and the next year in Montreal was the International League MVP.

Campanella made his major league debut on April 20, 1948, but was up for only three days before Rickey dispatched him to St. Paul, Minnesota to integrate the American Association. He ransacked the league for 35 games, hitting .325 with 39 RBI. Half of his 40 hits went for extra bases, including 13 home runs. He was recalled in June for good.

In 1949, Campy's 22 home runs helped to ensure a Dodger pennant and started an eight-year run where he averaged over 28 home runs. One of the first four black All-Stars, he went on to play a record 55 straight innings in eight All-Star games in a row.

After narrow second place finishes to the Phillies in 1950 and to the rival Giants in the 1951 playoff final, the Dodgers came back to earn two league titles in a row. Campanella's best season was 1953 as the consensus NL MVP. He hit .312 with 103 runs scored and set records for a catcher with 42 home runs, 142 RBI and 807 putouts.

In the 1955 World Series title year, Campanella was a force as MVP. After the Dodgers had slipped to 0-2 in the Series, he greeted the Yankees with a first inning home run in Game 3 and launched another bomb in a Game 4 victory. He also guided young lefty Johnny Podres through Game 7 to bring home the only Big Trophy to Flatbush.

The 1957 season would be the Dodgers' last in Brooklyn and Campanella's last as a player. Driving home to

G	AB	R	H	2B	3B	HR	RBI	SB	BB	SO	BA	OBP	SLG	TB
1215	4205	627	1161	178	18	242	856	25	533	501	.276	.360	.500	2101

Glen Cove, Long Island after closing his liquor store in Harlem late on January 28, 1958, his car skidded on an icy road, struck a telephone pole and turned over. Suffering fractured fifth and sixth cervical vertebrae and a nearly severed spinal cord, he would be confined to a wheelchair the rest of his life.

The Los Angeles Dodgers hosted Roy Campanella Night on May 7, 1959 at the Memorial Coliseum to raise money for his medical expenses. A record crowd of 93,103 fans saluted him before the Yankees and Dodgers took the field for the exhibition game.

Campy was an inspiration to many for the way he approached his life in a wheelchair. Never complaining about his fate, he was gifted at cheering people up and enjoyed two decades as a mentor at the annual Dodger spring training site in Vero Beach, Florida. Campy's Corner outside the old Dodgertown clubhouse was the place for young Dodger players to receive encouragement and hear his stories.

Campanella was inducted into the National Baseball Hall of Fame in 1969 and the Dodgers retired his jersey #39 in 1972 as one of the greatest Dodgers of them all. In 2006, he was featured on a United States postage stamp and a Roy Campanella Award was created for the Dodger who best exemplified his leadership and spirit each year.

He and his wife Roxie Doles founded The Roy and Roxie Campanella Physical Therapy Scholarship Foundation in 1991 to support those with spinal cord injuries and fund physical therapy student scholarships. Roy Campanella died of a heart attack on June 26, 1993 at his home in Woodland Hills, California. The Dodger Stadium flags flew at half mast the following day as the scoreboard streamed highlights of his legendary career and the fans listened to Louie Armstrong's recording of *What a Wonderful World*. Campy was laid to rest at Forest Lawn in Hollywood Hills, California.

SPUD CHANDLER

New York Yankees
Right-Handed Pitcher

1937-1947

"Spud Chandler

was the best pitcher

I ever saw."

~ battery mate
Bill Dickey

Spud Chandler is the all-time leader in winning percentage among hurlers with at least 100 victories. He remains the only Yankee pitcher ever to win the MVP Award and the only pitcher besides Babe Ruth to post a winning record every season in a career of at least ten years.

The Sporting News 1943 Major League Player of the Year, Chandler was a four-time AL All-Star, a two-time 20-game winner, and the author of 26 career shutouts. In four World Series, he earned a 1.62 ERA in $33\frac{1}{3}$ innings and was a member of six World Series titlist teams.

The rugged 6' 181-pound Chandler's sinking fastball resulted in plenty of ground ball outs. He also threw a tight overhand curve and late-breaking "slurve." His overhand sinker put undue stress on his pitching arm and limited his innings and effectiveness for much of the 1930s.

⋆   ⋆   ⋆   ⋆   ⋆

Spurgeon Ferdinand Chandler was born on September 12, 1907 to Olivia Catherine Hix and Leonard Ferdinand "Bud" Chandler in Commerce, Jackson County, Georgia. Raised in a farming community with three brothers and four sisters, he went by "Spurge" early, which in time became "Spud." The Yankees were always his favorite team, even from early boyhood.

His father moved the family over to Franklin County when he was a young boy to be closer to his school. He pitched and played football at Carnesville High School with such intense ferocity that he intimidated teammates and opponents alike before graduating in 1928.

Chandler stood out for the University of Georgia Bulldogs as a major college halfback for three seasons. In the Sanford Stadium dedication game in 1929, he threw a famous fourth quarter 22-yard touchdown pass in the 15-0 upset over powerhouse Yale University. UGA visited his future baseball home of Yankee Stadium in 1931 to play NYU and he starred in the 7–6 victory.

Chandler also competed on the Bulldog track team and pitched four years for UGA before earning his Bachelor of Science in agriculture in 1932. He soon inked a contract with Yankee scout Johnny Nee and went a combined 12-1 for the Binghamton (NY) Triplets of the Class-B New York-Penn League and Springfield (MA) Rifles of the Class-A Eastern League.

Though slowed by a shoulder injury sustained on the college gridiron, he worked his way up the Yankee system with the Newark (NJ) Bears and Syracuse (NY) Chiefs of the Double-A International League; the Minneapolis (MN) Millers of the Double-A American Association; and the Oakland (CA) Oaks and Portland (OR) Beavers of the Double-A Pacific Coast League.

Chandler began the 1937 campaign at Newark, but earned his major league debut on May 6, pitching two innings in relief versus the Tigers at Navin Field. In $82\frac{1}{3}$ innings that summer, he went 7-4 with a 2.84 ERA, but saw no World Series action in the win over the Giants.

With a potent 1938 Bronx Bomber lineup featuring Lou Gehrig, Joe DiMaggio and Bill Dickey, Chandler went 14-5 with a 4.29 ERA, fighting elbow tenderness the entire season. After his fourteenth win on September 5, he appeared only once more and the team shut him down.

Chandler fractured his ankle in 1939 spring training. By the time he recuperated in late July, the Yanks had virtually sewed up the AL pennant, but he got three wins in 19 relief innings with no losses. Chandler married Frances Virginia Willard on October 19 after the World Series.

He continued to be plagued by injuries in 1940 and 1941, posting records of 8-7 and 10-4. Chandler rebounded in 1942 with a 16-5 mark and 2.38 ERA while getting the win in the 1942 All-Star Game. He had one start each in the 1941 and 1942 World Series, but lost both times.

Chandler's signature year was 1943. He paced the Junior Circuit in almost every major category including victories (20), winning percentage (.833), complete games

G	IP	W	L	PCT	SHO	GS	CG	S	H	ER	SO	BB	ERA
211	1485	109	43	.717	26	184	109	1327	1327	468	614	463	2.84

(20), shutouts (5), and ERA (1.64). His ERA was the lowest in Yankee annals and the lowest of any pitcher from 1920 to 1967. In 253 innings and 30 starts, he allowed only 54 free passes, 46 earned runs, five home runs and four losses as the league's MVP. Chandler finished off his greatest campaign with two complete-game Fall Classic wins. His Game 5 shutout gem closed out the Cardinals.

After only one game in 1944, Chandler enlisted in the Army on April 28 at Atlanta's Fort McPherson Reception Center and was assigned to the Headquarters Company of the 65th Infantry Division at Camp Shelby, Georgia. He pitched very little during his 16 months of active duty.

Discharged in early September 1945, Chandler got his first start before a crowd of 72,152 partisans at Yankee Stadium on September 9. Matched up against the Indians' Bob Feller, he showed some rust in a 10-3 defeat, but the fans were energized to have him back in pinstripes.

Chandler's only great postwar season was 1946 at age 38. He won 20 and lost eight with a microscopic 2.10 ERA second only in the American League to Detroit's Hal Newhouser. An All-Star that year, he fanned a career-high 138 batters while accumulating 20 complete games.

Chandler finished the 1947 season at 9–5 and was the league ERA Champion at 2.46. He threw for the last time in the 1947 Fall Classic in relief against the Dodgers in Game 3. After undergoing surgery to remove elbow bone chips, he attempted a comeback in 1948, but failed.

Chandler served as the Athletics pitching coach in 1957 and 1958 and then worked for the Yankees as a scout and minor league manager. He scouted for the Athletics, Indians and Twins before retiring in 1984. Chandler is a member of the Georgia Sports Hall of Fame (1969); Franklin County Sports Hall of Fame (1997); and University of Georgia Ring of Honor (2000).

Chandler and his wife raised two sons. In September 1989, he fell and broke his shoulder. Complications set in and he died of heart failure at South Pasadena, Pinellas County, Florida on January 9, 1990 at age 82. He was interred at St. Petersburg's Woodlawn Memory Gardens.

JERRY COLEMAN

New York Yankees
Infield

1948-1957

Jerry Coleman spent over seven decades in baseball as a player, executive, manager and broadcaster. His World War II service delayed his path to the majors, yet he played on eight pennant-winners, appeared in six Fall Classics, and won six World Series rings. He is one of only 12 Yankees to have played on each of five straight Series titlist teams from 1949 to 1953.

One of the best defensive second basemen of all time, the 5'11" 165-pound Coleman was dependably sure-handed with a strong arm and a quick release, committing only 89 errors in 3,168 chances and turning 532 double plays. He did not often hit for power, but was an expert bunter and hit-and-run artist. He made consistent contact, fanning just 218 times in his career.

Coleman remains the only major league player to see combat in two wars. His brilliant military record includes 120 missions, two Distinguished Flying Crosses, 13 Air Medals and three Navy citations. He retired from the U. S. Marine Corps at the rank of lieutenant colonel.

★　★　★　★　★

Gerald Francis Coleman was born on September 14, 1924 in San Jose, Santa Clara County, California to Theresa Viola Pearl Beaudoin and Gerald Griffin Coleman. His mother left his abusive father when he was eight. Shortly afterward, he shot her, almost killing her and leaving her crippled. After Coleman and his sister and mother lived on relief for two years, his father came back to support them. The family-of-convenience weathered the Great Depression.

Coleman met Charlie Silvera when they were ten years old playing on the Big Rec ballfield in San Francisco's Golden Gate Park. Bobby Brown later joined them. The three future teammates went on to play together on a semi-pro winter league team sponsored by the Yankees.

Coleman excelled in two sports at James Russell Lowell High School. An All-City basketball guard, he was offered a scholarship to play hoops and baseball at USC, but

when Japan bombed Pearl Harbor in December of his senior year, it changed his priorities.

After graduating from high school in 1942, the 17-year old Coleman signed with Yankees scout Joe Devine, as did Silvera. The two friends were assigned to the Class-D Wellsville (NY) Yankees of the Pennsylvania-Ontario-New York League. Coleman hit .304 in 83 PONY League games, while marking his time to enlist as a Marine fighter pilot as soon as he turned 18.

He joined the Corps on October 23, 1942, as a naval aviation cadet in the V-5 program. Trained to fly the Douglas SBD Dauntless Dive Bomber, Coleman was sent to Guadalcanal in the Solomon Islands in August of 1944 and assigned to the VMSB-341 "Torrid Turtles." He flew 57 dangerous close air support combat missions in the Solomons and the Philippines.

With the end of the Pacific War, he was deactivated in January of 1946 and married his school sweetheart, Louise Leighton. After missing three seasons in his athletic prime, he would spend another three years of seasoning in the minors before arriving in the Big Apple for good.

Coleman was placed on the Yankees roster for the last weeks of the 1948 season but did not get any playing time. Earning his debut on April 20, 1949, he appeared in 128 games, pacing all AL second basemen in fielding while teaming with double-play partner Phil Rizzuto.

The 1949 AP AL Rookie of the Year, Coleman culminated his summer with a bases-loaded eighth inning double to beat the Red Sox in the final game to ice the pennant. His three doubles and four RBI then helped the Yanks best the Dodgers in a five-game Fall Classic.

In 1950 he hit a solid .287 in 153 games and was chosen an All-Star. His stellar October defense and game-winning hits in Games 1 and 3 earned him the Babe Ruth Award as the World Series Most Valuable Player. Despite only scoring 11 runs, the Yankees swept the Phillies.

"I've been watching second basemen for 50 years and nobody could play the position the way Jerry Coleman could. He was the best ever at turning the double play."

~ teammate Bobby Brown

G	AB	R	H	2B	3B	HR	RBI	SB	BB	SO	BA	OBP	SLG	TB
723	2119	267	558	77	18	16	217	22	235	218	.263	.340	.339	719

Coleman appeared in 121 games for the 1951 Yankees and after hitting .405 in 11 1952 games, he was called back to active duty in Korea. With the VMF-323 "Death Rattlers," he flew 63 F4U and AU1 Corsair combat missions in close air support, interdiction and strike operations.

Coleman was transferred back to the USA in August 1953 and placed on the reserve list. He was back playing second base for the Yankees later that month and was feted on September 13 with Jerry Coleman Day at Yankee Stadium in front of over 48,000 appreciative fans.

After his combat tour in Korea, "The Colonel" was never the same player, appearing in only 321 more games. Repeatedly injured and relegated to spot duty, he retired after the 1957 season, but finished with a flourish, hitting .364 (8-for-22) in the World Series loss to the Braves.

Coleman began his broadcast career at the suggestion of friend Howard Cosell with CBS TV in 1960, conducting *Game of the Week* pregame interviews. Behind the mic for the Yankees (1963-69) and the Angels (1970 -71), he also called broadcasts for CBS radio for 22 seasons.

From 1972, Coleman was the iconic radio voice of the San Diego Padres, with a brief respite as the 1980 Padres manager. His trademark call was "Oh doctor, you can hang a star on that baby!" He was also the "Master of the Malaprop" for his endearing verbal gaffes at the mic.

Jerry Coleman is a member the San Diego Padres Hall of Fame (2001), the Bay Area Sports Hall of Fame (2007), and the National Radio Hall of Fame (2007). The National Baseball Hall of Fame inducted him into its broadcasting wing with the prestigious Ford C. Frick Award in 2005. He is also a member of the United States Marine Corps Sports Hall of Fame (2005).

The Padres paid homage to Coleman with his own statue at Petco Park on September 15, 2012. A true American hero, Coleman died at Scripps Hospital in La Jolla on January 6, 2014 at age 89 after suffering head injuries in a fall. He left behind his second wife, the former Maggie Hay, his three children (Diane, Jerry, Jr. and Chelsea), and many grandchildren.

JOE COLLINS

NEW YORK YANKEES
FIRST BASE • RIGHT FIELD

1948-1957

*"If I can't be a Yankee
I'd rather not play
ball. So I'm retiring."*

*~ Joe Collins,
Spring 1958*

Joe Collins competed on seven World Series stages, collected six title rings and blasted four circuit clouts. Each homer was hit at Yankee Stadium and led to a victory. At his retirement, Collins had played more Yankee games at first base than anyone except the great Lou Gehrig.

A left-handed pull-hitter perfectly suited for the short right-field porch at old Yankee Stadium, the muscular 6' 190-pound Collins hit the low-pitch extremely well and consistently wore out White Sox and Indians pitching. He was known for being formidable in the clutch.

The affable Collins was popular with teammates, fans and the press. Although he experimented with a variety of batting stances throughout his career, Collins was always a hitter with a great eye, finishing his career with 75 more free passes than strikeouts.

He was one of manager Casey Stengel's favorite players for his willingness to play either first base or the outfield and for his positive influence in the clubhouse. The left-handed throwing Collin played 715 regular-season games at first and 114 games in the outfield.

★　★　★　★　★

Joseph Edward Kollonige was born on December 3, 1922 to Nellie and George Kollonige in Scranton, Lackawanna County, Pennsylvania. His Russian-Greek father and Polish mother raised him with an older brother and younger sister. Collins was still only 140 pounds at age 15, but grew a year later and caught on with the Minooka 20th Warders- a first-rate semi-pro team.

That summer, the 16-year-old Collins was invited to work out with the Wilkes-Barre (PA) Barons. Instead, he practiced with the visiting Binghamton (NY) Triplets, a Yankee affiliate, and subsequently signed with them in 1939. He appeared in just 14 games combined with Easton (PA) of the Eastern Shore League and Butler of the Pennsylvania State League.

Back with Butler in 1940 at age 17, Collins hit .320 (122-for-381) with nine home runs, then progressed to Class-C Akron (OH) in 1941. Continuing his development in 1942, he was with the Class-C Amsterdam (NY) Rugmakers and the Class-B Norfolk (VA) Tars.

After playing for the 1943 Class-A Springfield (MA) Rifles, Collins entered the U. S. Naval Air Corps. He trained to be a pilot while stationed in Hawaii and served aboard the USS Henry until December 1, 1945, but didn't play a baseball game for two years. Collins married his high school sweetheart, Peg Reilley, in 1945 and the union produced three sons and a daughter.

Collins had to start all over when he returned to professional baseball for the 1946 season with the Double-A Beaumont (TX) Exporters and the Triple-A Newark (NJ) Bears. In 1947, Collins crashed 23 homers and hit .316 between Newark and the Birmingham (AL) Barons and followed in 1948 to hit .317 and power 23 round trippers for Newark and the Kansas City Blues.

After his exceptional season with the Blues, the Yankees called him up and gave him his debut on September 25, 1948. The team sent him back to Kansas City for more seasoning in 1949. He batted .319 with 20 long balls and again merited a late-season audition with the Yankees. After seven years of apprenticeship, he would never go back to the minor leagues.

Collins shared first base duties in 1951 with Johnny "Big Cat" Mize, hitting .286 in 125 games. His home run in Game 2 of the 1951 World Series off New York Giants ace Larry Jansen ensured a 3-1 victory and set the stage for a Yankee Fall Classic triumph.

The regular Yankees first baseman from 1952 through 1954, his best year was 1952 when he hit .280 with a career-best 18 home runs and 59 runs batted in. One of his home runs was a majestic 475-foot shot into the right-field upper deck at Yankee Stadium versus the Indians.

In the 1952 World Series Game 7, Collins was indi-

G	AB	R	H	2B	3B	HR	RBI	SB	BB	SO	BA	OBP	SLG	TB
908	2329	404	596	79	24	86	329	27	338	263	.256	.350	.421	981

rectly involved in one of the most dramatic fielding plays in postseason history. The Yankees' Vic Raschi loaded the bases in the seventh inning at Ebbets Field. With two out, Dodger second baseman Jackie Robinson lifted a high pop fly which should have been Collins' defensive responsibility at first base, but he was blinded by the sun. At the last possible moment, Billy Martin sprinted in all the way from second base and lunged to make the famous World Series-saving catch.

Batting second in the lineup in Game 1 of the 1953 Fall Classic, Collins hit a circuit clout deep into Yankee Stadium's right field bleachers off Brooklyn Dodger reliever Clem Labine. The game-winning bomb broke a seventh inning 5-5 tie. The Yankees won going away, 9-5. Collins went 2-for-4 with two runs scored and two runs batted in.

Hitting fifth in the lineup in the 1955 Series opener, Collins poled a pair of long home runs off Don Newcombe in the 6-5 win. He went 2-for-3 with three RBI and three runs scored to do most of the damage. However, Brooklyn recovered to win its only world title in seven games.

Collins played his final major league game on September 29, 1957. In 1958 spring training, the Yankees sold his contract to the Phillies for $20,000. The man Stengel once called his "meal ticket" promptly announced his retirement, desiring to end his career as a Yankee.

After his baseball career, Collins worked as a public relations executive for People's Express Trucking in Newark, New Jersey and also represented the Union Center National Bank in Union, New Jersey where he raised his family in a neighborhood which included homes owned by Yankee teammates Phil Rizzuto, Gil McDougald, Yogi Berra and Gene Woodling.

Shortly before his passing, a local baseball field and small park off of Liberty Avenue was named in his honor for his years of community service in the Newark area. Joe Collins died of natural causes at his Union Township home at age 66 on August 30, 1989. He was laid to rest in Fairview Cemetery in nearby Westfield, New Jersey.

DOMINIC DiMAGGIO

BOSTON RED SOX
CENTER FIELD

1940-1942 • 1946-1953

"I think Dom DiMaggio was the best fielding center fielder of all time. He lived in the shadows of his brother Joe but he was the best leadoff hitter I ever saw. He should be in the Hall of Fame."

~ teammate Mel Parnell

Dominic DiMaggio was the most underrated star of his era, playing in the shadow of his teammate Ted Williams and his older brother Joe DiMaggio. The finest leadoff hitter in the American League, he is one of only three men to average over 100 runs scored per season throughout his career. For the decade he played, he led all of Major League Baseball in hits.

The 5'9" 168-pound DiMaggio played outfield boldly, charging hard to hold runners from taking the extra base. He had speed and the instincts to anticipate a play. Getting such an exceptional jump off the bat resulted in his average of 2.98 chances per game- an AL record.

A seven-time All-Star, DiMaggio paced the AL in assists three times and in putouts and double plays twice. His 1948 totals of 503 putouts and 526 total chances stood as AL records for nearly three decades. DiMaggio's eight seasons with over 400 putouts is a major league standard.

★　★　★　★　★

Dominick Paolo DiMaggio was born on February 17, 1917 in San Francisco, California to Sicilian immigrants Rosalia Mercurio and Giuseppe DiMaggio. He grew up near Fishermen's Wharf in the North Beach-Telegraph Hill section of the city, the youngest son of nine children.

His father was a fisherman who never spoke English well and found the American game of baseball frivolous. His mother made alibis for her boys so that they could play and three DiMaggio brothers- Vince, Joe and Dominic- went on to roam center field in the major leagues.

As a senior at Galileo High, DiMaggio pitched and played shortstop, hitting .400. He was a math whiz and was offered a scholarship to nearby Santa Clara College, but chose baseball. He attended a San Francisco Seals tryout and was immediately offered a contract.

In 1937, DiMaggio started with the Seals in the Pacific Coast League. After adding 20 pounds of muscle in 1939

and absorbing the instruction of manager Lefty O'Doul, he hit .360 with 239 hits to finish second in the batting race. At season's end, DiMaggio was chosen the PCL's MVP, prompting the Red Sox to purchase his contract for the huge price of $75,000.

He earned his major league debut on April 16, 1940 and went on to hit .301 in 108 games. In the summer of 1941, he scored 117 runs, got his first All-Star nod, and was nicknamed "The Little Professor" because of his diminutive stature, his sober air and his spectacles.

An All-Star again in 1942, DiMaggio scored 110 runs with 36 doubles and 272 total bases. After the season, he again pursued military enlistment despite an initial rejection by the Navy due to his eyesight. He was accepted by the Coast Guard and left for a three-year tour.

DiMaggio returned to baseball in 1946, along with his close friends and longtime teammates Williams, Johnny Pesky and Bobby Doerr. In that historic Boston year, the Red Sox finished 104-50 to win its first pennant in 28 years. DiMaggio hit .316 and again was an All-Star.

With two out in the top of the eighth of World Series Game 7 at St. Louis' Sportsman's Park, DiMaggio slammed a line shot off the right-center field wall, driving in two runs to tie the score at 3-3. Hustling to get his triple, he pulled a hamstring and limped in lame to third base.

DiMaggio was removed for pinch runner Leon Culberson, who also replaced him in center field. It was a pivotal moment. In the bottom of the ninth, Harry Walker doubled to center with Enos Slaughter scoring from first in his Mad Dash to win the game and Series.

If DiMaggio had remained in the game, he might have been able to catch Walker's liner. Even if the hit had dropped, his rifle arm could have held Slaughter at third. Slaughter later admitted that he would not have attempted to score had DiMaggio still occupied center field.

DiMaggio scored 127 runs in 1948 and posted career-

G	AB	R	H	2B	3B	HR	RBI	SB	BB	SO	BA	OBP	SLG	TB
1399	5640	1046	1608	308	57	87	618	100	750	571	.298	.383	.419	2363

bests of 101 walks, 87 RBI and 40 doubles. In the summer of 1949, he batted .307 on 186 hits with 126 runs and 34 doubles. From June 26 to August 7, he spaced out a Boston Red Sox franchise record 34-game hitting streak.

DiMaggio enjoyed his greatest year in 1950, hitting a career-high .328 with 193 hits and topping the league with 131 runs scored and 15 steals. He followed in 1951 with 189 hits and an AL-leading 113 runs scored, stringing together a 27-game hitting streak from May 12 to June 7.

After being relegated to the bench early in 1953 by new Boston manager Lou Boudreau, he saw action in just three games before deciding to call it quits on May 9. After such an accomplished career, he had no interest in accepting the role of a demoted substitute at age 36.

DiMaggio founded a firm in 1953 that produced padding for a variety of products including automobile seats. In 1961, he merged two companies to form the Delaware Valley Corporation which made products for the construction, marine, medical and RV industries.

DiMaggio was a founding partner of the old American Football League Boston Patriots- now the National Football League's New England Patriots. He was appointed a board trustee of New Hampshire's Saint Anselm College and assisted in the school's expansion for four decades.

The three years in the prime of his playing career lost to serving his country in World War II may have cost DiMaggio his place at Cooperstown in the National Baseball Hall of Fame. He has been a member of the Boston Red Sox Hall of Fame since 1995.

DiMaggio married his wife of 60 years, the former Emily Alberta Frederick, in 1949. The DiMaggio's had three children- Dominic, Jr., Peter and Emily. Surrounded by his family at his home in Marion, Massachusetts, "The Little Professor" passed away on May 8, 2009 after a short battle with pneumonia. He was laid to rest at the Newton (MS) Cemetery & Crematory.

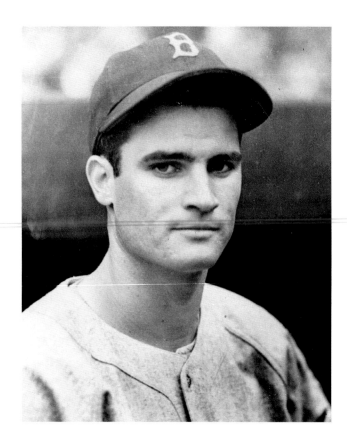

BOBBY DOERR

BOSTON RED SOX
SECOND BASE

1937-1944 • 1946-1951

The quiet leader of the Red Sox, Bobby Doerr was the best fielding second baseman of the 1940s. Admired by teammates and rivals alike for the honest way he played the game, his most revealing metrics were his six seasons driving in 100+ runs. Teammate Ted Williams insisted he was the one indispensable Red Sock of the 1940s.

A nine-time All-Star, he enjoyed success at Fenway Park, hitting .315 with 145 home runs. An up-the-middle hitter upon joining the Sox, the right-handed 5' 11" 175-pound Doerr learned to pull the ball to put the Green Monster left field wall into play.

He never played another position other than second base and led the AL in double plays five times, putouts and fielding four, and assists three. When he retired, Doerr was the all-time big-league second base leader in fielding at .980 and double plays with 1,507.

★　★　★　★　★

Robert Pershing Doerr was born to Frances Herrnberger and Harold Doerr on April 7, 1918 in Los Angeles, California, the second of three children. His middle name was a tribute to General John J. Pershing, U. S. military commander in World War I.

Doerr learned baseball playing with some talented friends. His 1932 California Champion Leonard Wood Post American Legion team of 14 year olds sported a future big-league infield of George McDonald (1B), Mickey Owen (SS) and Steve Mesner (3B).

With his brother Hal already catching in the Pacific Coast League, he performed on his father's winter league team as a 15 and 16-year-old. Competing capably against players that had professional experience, he gained confidence and got noticed.

Doerr had already been working out with the PCL's Hollywood (CA) Sheiks when he was offered a no-cut two-year contract in 1934. He appeared in 67 games for

the Sheiks that summer, and played 172 games in 1935, hitting .317 with 22 doubles.

The Sheiks moved south to become the San Diego Padres early in 1936. Doerr hit .342 with a PCL-leading 238 hits, 100 runs scored, 37 doubles and 12 triples. That July, Boston scout Eddie Collins had come to evaluate the team and bought Doerr's contract.

Only 18, Doerr sparkled in Red Sox spring training in 1937 and earned his debut as the leadoff hitter on Opening Day, going 3-for-5. Hitting in a powerful 1938 lineup with Joe Cronin and Jimmie Foxx, he learned to bunt and led the AL with 22 sacrifices.

Doerr welcomed Williams to the club in 1939 and improved to .318. A year later, Boston featured Cronin, Foxx, Williams and Doerr, all with 100+ RBI. He pounded out 37 doubles and 22 homers and led the AL with 118 double plays and 401 putouts.

Doerr was an ironman in 1943, appearing in all 155 Red Sox games while topping AL second basemen in most fielding categories. He had been rejected for World War II service during that year because he was married with a son and had a perforated eardrum.

However, the country needed more men as the war dragged on. He received his draft orders in early 1944 to report in early September. When the date arrived, Doerr departed for duty with the team only four games back of the Browns. The Sox couldn't keep pace without him and faded to fourth. He had closed out at .325 and slugged an AL-best .528 to become *The Sporting News* 1944 American League Player of the Year.

After undergoing combat training at Camp Roberts (CA), Army Staff Sergeant Doerr and his unit were ready to be shipped out for the invasion of Japan. When it was decided to drop the Bomb, it saved him and thousands of other U.S. military personnel.

> "Bobby Doerr is
> one of the very few
> who played the game
> hard and retired
> with no enemies."
>
> ~ Tommy Henrich

G	AB	R	H	2B	3B	HR	RBI	SB	BB	SO	BA	OBP	SLG	TB
1865	7093	1094	2042	381	89	223	1247	54	809	608	.288	.362	.461	3270

Back in a Sox uniform in 1946, he led the AL in putouts, assists, double plays and fielding and had 116 RBI. *The Sporting News* 1946 All-Star second baseman, Doerr hit safely in all seven games (9-for-22 .409) in the Fall Classic loss to the Cardinals.

He set a Junior Circuit record in 1948 by handling 414 chances in a row over 73 games without an error and put up a BoSox second base mark for fielding percentage at .993. It took 58 years for Mark Loretta to edge that established standard in 2006 at .994.

He averaged 110+ RBI from 1946 to 1950 with a high of 120 in '50 while pacing the AL in triples. After trying to return from a back injury sustained in August, he took himself out after his first at-bat on September 7, 1951 and retired to his Oregon farm.

In 1957, he came back as a roving Red Sox minor league coach and scout until hired as the first base coach for the 1967 Impossible Dream season. Doerr mentored Carl Yastrzemski, who belted 44 home runs and won the Triple Crown although he had never hit more than 20 circuit clouts before at any level.

He also served as the hitting coach for the Blue Jays from 1977 to 1981. As the ultimate career honor, Doerr was voted into the National Baseball Hall of Fame in 1986 by the Veterans Committee and the Red Sox retired his uniform #1 on May 21, 1988.

He lives in Oregon since marrying Monica Terpin in 1938, a union that lasted 65 years. He was devoted to her care for many years as her multiple sclerosis eventually placed her in a wheelchair. She passed away in 2003 after suffering a series of strokes.

Doerr continues to live a quiet lifestyle on his 160-acre spread bordering the scenic Rogue River near Junction City. He regularly fishes for steelhead salmon and other large game fish and enjoys time with his son Don who lives in Eugene.

CARL ERSKINE

BROOKLYN & LOS ANGELES DODGERS
RIGHT-HANDED PITCHER

1948-1959

*"On Carl and Betty Erskine's fifth
wedding anniversary, the Dodgers
made it a game of fives, winning Game
5 of the World Series on October 5 by
a score of 6-5 in a game where the
Yankees scored their five runs in the
fifth inning before yielding to Brooklyn
at 5:05 in the afternoon of the fifth."*

*~ Dodgers radio announcer
Vin Scully, 1952*

Prominent among the celebrated *Boys of Summer* Brooklyn Dodgers of the 1950s, Carl Erskine won 122 games with a .610 percentage as one of the aces of the staff. The Dodgers were National League pennant winners in fully half of Erskine's dozen years with the team.

He contributed to their only World Series title in Brooklyn in 1955, as well as their first Big Trophy in Los Angeles in 1959, appearing in 11 games in five Fall Classics. Affectionately known as "Oisk" by the Brooklynite faithful, he was one of the most popular Dodgers ever.

With his straight overhand fastball and devastating 12-to-6 curve ball, the slight 5'10" 165-pound Erskine was particularly sensational from 1951 through 1956, accumulating a 92-58 record. He was a 1954 National League All-Star and hurled two of the Senior Circuit's seven no-hitters during the Decade of the 1950s.

★ ★ ★ ★ ★

Carl Daniel Erskine was born on December 13, 1926, in Anderson, Madison County, Indiana of Scottish descent to Bertha and Matthew Erskine. Introduced to the game early by his father, he pitched in American Legion competition and starred for Coach Charles Cummings' Anderson High School nine all four years.

Erskine was drafted into the U. S. Navy in 1945 and stationed at the Boston Navy Yard. A recreation officer snubbed him for the base team, so he resorted to pitching for a semi-professional squad. He was soon noticed by Dodger scout Stanley Feezle and Branch Rickey inked him to a bonus contract.

After pitching nine games for Danville (IL), Commissioner A.B. "Happy" Chandler voided Erskine's contract because he was still active in the service. He received

a second bonus when the habitually stingy Rickey had to re-sign him shortly after his Navy discharge in 1946.

Erskine toiled the entire 1947 year at Danville, going 19-9, with 191 strikeouts and a 2.34 ERA, while appearing in a Three-I League-high 233 innings. That year, he married his high school sweetheart, the former Betsy Palmer, on October 5. The couple would raise four children.

After his two Danville tours and a turn in the Cuban winter leagues, Erskine was invited to Dodgers spring training in 1948. The great Jackie Robinson faced him in a five-inning stint and told him, "You're going to be with us real soon." It began a lifelong alliance and friendship.

The 21-year-old Erskine quickly accumulated 15 wins for the Fort Worth (TX) Cats and earned his debut on July 25, 1948. Shuttled up and down because of arm trouble, he spent part of 1949 in Texas and 1950 in Montreal, but went 21-10, mostly in relief, with the big club.

Erskine completed his first full season with Brooklyn in 1951, earning 19 starts. He also appeared 27 times in relief, going 16-12. For the next five seasons he was indispensable to the rotation, especially in 1952 and 1953, when Don Newcombe was serving his time in the army.

Against the Cubs on June 19, 1952, Erskine pitched a no-hitter, the only blemish a walk to rival pitcher Willy Ramsdell. He finished the year at 14-6 with a career-low 2.70 ERA, and then triumphed in a World Series Game 5 masterpiece. After Erskine was cuffed around in the fifth for five runs, manager Charlie Dressen came out to the mound to pull him, but suddenly changed his mind. "Oisk" went on to retire 19 consecutive Yankees, winning 6-5 in 11 innings.

In his best year, he paced the NL in 1953 with a .769 winning percentage (20-6). His 187 strikeouts and 16

G	IP	W	L	PCT	SHO	GS	CG	H	ER	SO	BB	ERA
335	1718.2	122	78	.610	14	216	71	1637	763	981	646	4.00

complete games were career-bests as Brooklyn won 105 games. Erskine's signature performance came in World Series Game 3 with a complete-game, 3-2 victory at Ebbets Field, striking out a record 14 batters including the entire Yankee side in the ninth.

He won 18 games in 1954 on career-highs of 37 starts and $260\frac{1}{3}$ innings and won 11 more in 1955. On May 12, 1956 against the Giants, on his way to 13 wins, he tossed his second no-hitter after reading an article quoting Giants Scout Tom Sheehan saying he was "washed up."

The team headed to California after the 1957 season. Though he started and won the first game at the Los Angeles Memorial Coliseum on April 18, 1958, his career was already winding down. He threw his final pitch on July 14, 1959, but stayed on to coach in the Dodgers' successful World Series championship run.

Only 33, Erskine went back to Anderson to raise his family in 1960. He has been particularly devoted to his youngest son Jimmy, born with Down's syndrome, and has worked diligently on behalf of the Special Olympics. He is also a founding member of the Fellowship of Christian Athletes.

Erskine went on to enjoy successful careers as a life insurance agent, a banker and a baseball coach. As the head coach of the Anderson University Ravens for 12 years, he won four Hoosier College Conference titles and a berth in the NAIA College World Series.

A 6-foot bronze statue has been erected in front of the Carl D. Erskine Rehabilitation & Sports Medicine Center in Anderson. Erskine was inducted into the Indiana National Baseball Hall of Fame in 1979. As an affectionate tribute from his adopted town, Erskine Street in Brooklyn was created in his honor in 2002.

WHITEY FORD

NEW YORK YANKEES
LEFT-HANDED PITCHER

1950 • 1953-1967

"I don't care what the situation was, how high the stakes were- it never bothered Whitey. He pitched his game. Cool. Crafty. Nerves of steel."

~ teammate Mickey Mantle

Whitey Ford was the greatest pitcher in Yankee history. A member of 11 pennant-winning Yankees teams and an eight-time All-Star, he won 69 percent of his games, the best among twentieth century pitchers with 200 or more decisions. His career 2.75 ERA is the lowest of any post-World War II starting pitcher with at least 1,500 innings.

Ford was also possibly the best Big Game pitcher who ever lived. When he retired, he was ranked first all-time with ten World Series wins, 146 innings, eight opening day starts, 22 games started and 94 strikeouts. He tossed 33 consecutive scoreless innings over three Fall Classics to break Babe Ruth's record of 29$^2/_3$ innings.

The unflappable Ford was known as the "Chairman of the Board" for his ability to take charge as the consummate money pitcher. The crafty left-hander dominated games with his moxie and pinpoint control. Hitters had to contend with Ford's varied assortment of moving fastballs, sharp-breaking curveballs and disappearing changeups.

★   ★   ★   ★   ★

Edward Charles Ford was born in Queens, New York on October 21, 1928 to Edith and James Ford. He grew up in Astoria Queens, just miles from Yankee Stadium and graduated from the Manhattan High School of Aviation in Sunnyside, Queens.

The Yankees signed him in October of 1946. He scintillated at every minor league level with 16 wins for Butler (PA) in 1947; 16 wins for the 1948 Norfolk (VA) Tars; and an Eastern League-low 1.61 ERA for the 1949 Binghamton (NY) Triplets.

Ford got his big-league debut on July 1, 1950 after a short stint with the Kansas City (MO) Blues. The 22-year-old started explosively, winning nine straight before a loss in relief and was *The Sporting News* 1950 AL Rookie of the Year. In the World Series, he pitched 8$^2/_3$ innings without an earned run to win the finale in a sweep over the Phillies.

Ford spent 1951 and 1952 in the U.S. Army stationed in the Signal Corps at Fort Monmouth, New Jersey. He returned to win 18 in 1953 and 16 more in 1954. By 1955, Ford was the Yankees ace with an AL-best 18 wins and 18 complete games, hurling two straight one-hitters in September. He was *The Sporting News* Major League All-Star left-handed pitcher and would have been the Cy Young Award winner had the trophy existed.

The following year he was even better, going 19-6 to lead the AL in winning percentage and ERA at 2.47 and tying his previous AL record for six consecutive strikeouts. Ford was picked again to *The Sporting News* Major League All-Star team.

He won the ERA title in 1958 at 2.01 and topped the American League with seven shutouts, but only went 14-7. The 5'10" 178-pound lefty was rested by manager Casey Stengel at least four days between starts and had more than 30 appearances only once in his nine years under Stengel. "The Ol' Perfessor" apparently thought he was not up to it.

Although Ford pitched two shutouts in the 1960 World Series, the highly favored Yankees succumbed to Pittsburgh in a seven-game classic. Inexplicably, Stengel had not started his ace in the opener so he could not get three starts. It cost Stengel his job.

New skipper Ralph Houk installed Ford in a regular four-man rotation in 1961. He thrived, leading the AL with 39 starts and 283 innings pitched to earn the Cy Young Award. His 25-4 line led the majors in wins

G	IP	W	L	PCT	SHO	GS	CG	H	ER	SO	BB	ERA
498	3170.1	236	106	.690	45	438	156	2766	967	1956	1086	2.75

and percentage. Especially adept at keeping runners close with his pickoff move, Ford pitched a record 243 straight innings without allowing a stolen base and topped off his year as the World Series MVP against the Reds.

In 1963, he again paced the AL in wins, percentage, starts and innings, going 24-7. Although he was edged by Sandy Koufax for the single Cy Young Award, Ford was *The Sporting News* AL Pitcher of the Year. The two aces faced off in Fall Classic Games 1 and 4 with Ford taking the loss both times. In Game 4, he lost a two-hitter on an error.

Toward the end of Ford's career there were rumors that he was doctoring the baseball. He was accused at various times of throwing a spitball, a mudball or a scuffball. His catcher Elston Howard helped out by cutting the baseball on his shin guards.

After going 17-6 in 1964 as baseball's first ever pitcher-coach and 16-13 in 1965, Ford broke down with shoulder problems. He had surgery in August of 1966 to correct a circulatory blockage in his left shoulder and endured a painful bone spur in his elbow. He lasted just one inning in his final start on May 21, 1967, and retired at age 38.

Whitey Ford and his close friend and teammate Mickey Mantle were inducted into the National Baseball Hall of Fame together in 1974. The Yankees retired his uniform #16 that year and he returned one last summer to be the Yankees pitching coach. On August 2, 1987, a plaque was dedicated in Yankee Stadium's Monument Park, calling Ford "one of the greatest pitchers ever to step on a mound."

Ford ranked 52nd on *The Sporting News'* 1999 list of "Baseball's 100 Greatest Players" and was a nominee for Major League Baseball's All-Century Team. He and his wife, the former Joan Foran, raised a daughter and two sons. Ford is a keynote speaker and comes back often as a Yankees spring training instructor in Tampa, Florida.

DICK FOWLER

PHILADELPHIA ATHLETICS
RIGHT-HANDED PITCHER

1941-1942 • 1945-1952

"If you put a pennant contender behind Dick Fowler, he'd be a 20-game winner in a breeze. You just can't believe the balls that dribble through the infield because of lackadaisical effort. He's a great pitcher."

~ teammate Carl Scheib

Dick Fowler was the anchor of the late 1940s Athletics pitching staffs. With teams that never finished higher than fourth, he never won more than 15 games, garnering little run-support. Fowler remains the first and only Canadian to ever throw a major league no-hitter.

The imposing 6'4½" 195-pounder sported a live fastball, an effective curve, a change-up, and a fork-slider. He toiled 200 innings plus and tossed at least 14 complete games from 1946 to 1949 and finished in the top ten in shutouts in the Junior Circuit from 1947 to 1949.

★ ★ ★ ★ ★

Richard John Fowler, Jr. was born on March 30, 1921 to Mary Gould and Richard John Fowler, Sr. in Toronto, Ontario, Canada. The son of a sawmill operator, he was raised with seven sisters. He began pitching for Toronto Catholic Youth Organization (CYO) teams at an early age.

Fowler quit school at 16 to tryout with the Toronto Maple Leafs. He was given his break by scout Dan Howley and began his pro pitching career with the Cornwall (ON) Maple Leafs of the Class-C Canadian-American League in 1939. He hurled just three games before being sent down to the Class-D Batavia (NY) Clippers of the Pennsylvania-Ontario-New York League.

Back in the Canadian-American League in 1940 with the Oneonta (NY) Indians, Fowler met his future wife Joyce Howard while going 16-10 in 209 innings pitched. He debuted for his hometown Maple Leafs of the International League late in 1939 for one game and then was a workhorse in 1941, just missing a no-hitter and posting a 10-10 mark with a 3.30 ERA.

Connie Mack gave the 20-year-old his major league debut on September 13, 1941. He pitched in four games, winning one and losing two. One of those losses came in the season's last game versus the Red Sox. Fowler faced Ted Williams in his first two plate appearances and was touched for a single and a long circuit clout. The Splen-

did Splinter finished famously at .406.

Fowler was a mainstay for the 1942 cellar-dwelling A's, hurling in 31 games and going 6-11. His highlight was a 16-inning complete-game gem versus the Browns, although he took the loss, 1-0. The stint brought on a case of bursitis, which dogged him for the rest of his career.

Fowler enlisted for military duty in 1943 and served for three years with the 48th Light Highlanders in the Royal Canadian Infantry. While on maneuvers, he was injured and assigned to a military post office job in Nova Scotia. Scheduled to be deployed to Europe, Fowler was given his discharge early because his wife had become seriously ill.

Fowler is best known for pitching a no-hit, no-run game just 25 days after returning to the Athletics after his military duty. In the nightcap of a doubleheader on a rainy afternoon at Shibe Park on September 9, 1945, he out-dueled St. Louis Browns ace Johnny "Ox" Miller, 1-0.

Relying on his change and curveball, Fowler faced only 29 defending AL-Champion Browns hitters, punching out six, walking four and allowing only five soft fly balls to the outfield. The last batter, Lou Finney, hit into a double play, but extra innings, darkness and a curfew loomed when the A's came to bat in the bottom of the ninth with the game still tied. A triple by Hal Peck, followed by a walk-off single by Irv Hall sealed the victory. Fowler had his classic gem for the ages as the first Athletics hurler to throw a no-hitter since Bullet Joe Bush in 1916. It was also his first complete-game shutout and his only win of the season.

In 1945, the Athletics would finish dead last, 34½ games behind the champion Tigers and 17 games behind the seventh place Red Sox. Fowler was one of three Athletics pitchers to lose a league-high 16 games in 1946 with another cellar-dwelling club, even with his 3.28 ERA.

The easy-going, affable hurler became one of the stalwarts of Mr. Mack's pitching staff over the next three

G	IP	W	L	PCT	SHO	GS	CG	SV	H	ER	SO	BB	ERA
221	1303	66	79	.455	11	170	75	4	1367	595	382	578	4.11

years, when the team finished fifth, fourth and fifth. In 1947, he was 12-11 with a 2.81 ERA (third best in the AL), including eight straight complete games between July 10 and August 27. He and 19-game winner Phil Marchildon were the top two hurlers on the staff.

In 1948, the Athletics made their first serious run at a pennant since the early 1930s and drew their all-time franchise attendance record of 945,076 fans. The A's staff was headed by 15-game winner Fowler and three 14-game winners- Carl Scheib, Joe Coleman, and Lou Brissie. The team was in contention until September but was derailed ultimately by injuries.

In 1949, he became an American citizen while reprising his 15-win total of 1948, along with four shutouts and a 3.74 ERA. Fowler set an American League record on June 9 with seven putouts for an extra-inning game during a 1-0 victory over the White Sox in 12 innings.

Fowler continued to pitch even though his chronic shoulder bursitis made throwing a baseball agonizing. In 1950, as the team fell apart, his bursitis got worse and his record was 1-5 in only 11 games. In 1951, Fowler was 5-11 in 22 games and in 1952 was 1-2 in just 18 games.

His final major league action came on September 1, 1952. After a two-season comeback try with the Charleston (WV) Clippers of the American Association, Fowler retired to Oneonta, where he and his wife raised a son and a daughter. He worked in a department store, served as the Oneonta Community Hotel night deskman, and coached one of the town's first Little League teams.

Dick Fowler passed away at the Aurelia Osborn Fox Memorial Hospital in Oneonta on May 22, 1972 from complications of both liver and kidney disease. He was only 51. Fowler is interred at the Oneonta Plains Cemetery. The classy right-handed fireballer was inducted into the Canadian Baseball Hall of Fame posthumously on August 7, 1985.

CARL FURILLO

BROOKLYN & LOS ANGELES DODGERS
RIGHT FIELD

1946-1960

"I always thought he was the most underrated of all the Dodgers. Carl did more things to win games for us than he ever got credit for. No two outfielders ever communicated better than we did. It was a pleasure playing alongside him."

~ teammate Duke Snider

The quintessential blue collar player, Carl Furillo played a consistently brilliant right field for the Brooklyn Dodgers during their glory years of the late 1940s and 1950s. A two-time All-Star, he was the 1953 National League batting champion, hitting .344.

Furillo was a mainstay for seven NL titlists, hitting over .290 in 14 seasons. He also launched over 20 homers three times, drove in over 90 runs six times, and slugged over .500 three times. He was just a lone hit short of batting an even .300 for his career.

The muscular 6' 190-pound Furillo was a marvelous, fluid outfielder with the strongest, most accurate outfield throwing arm in baseball in the late 1940s and early 1950s. Known as "The Reading Rifle," he had nine or more assists in 11 campaigns, twice leading the NL, and even threw out seven runners that rounded first too widely.

Enemy base runners effectively stopped testing Furillo's howitzer throwing arm after his 18 assists in 1950 and his phenomenal career-high of 24 in 1951. He also was a master at negotiating caroms off Ebbets Field's high right field wall and tricky right field corner. Furillo and centerfielder Duke Snider routinely denied opposing hitters the extra base. He fielded a stellar career .979 with 151 assists and only 74 errors in 3,547 chances.

★ ★ ★ ★ ★

Carl Anthony Furillo was born in rural Stony Creek Mills near Reading, Berks County, Pennsylvania on March 8, 1922 to Italian immigrant parents Philomena Petroci and Michael Furillo. After the eighth grade, he dropped out of school and worked in a woolen mill among other jobs and played baseball constantly. When he was 18, his mother passed away, leaving him free to make a profession out of the game he loved.

Furillo split his 1940 rookie minor league season between the independent Class-D Pocomoke (MD) Chicks and his hometown Class-B Reading Chicks. After the season the Dodgers purchased the Reading franchise, including Furillo and 19 other players.

Furillo hit .313 for the newly-christened 1941 Reading Brooks in the Class-B Interstate League. He slugged .490 and earned 25 assists playing center field. In 1942, still only 20 years old, Furillo hit a solid .281 for the Double-A Montreal (QC) Royals.

He would lose three seasons serving in the Army to World War II. Furillo was wounded in combat in the Pacific and received three battle stars. After the War, he made his big-league debut on Opening Day April 16, 1946, going 2-for-4 versus the Braves.

In the historic 1947 season when Jackie Robinson broke the color line with the Dodgers, Furillo played mostly center field. He batted .295 with 88 RBI, helping Brooklyn to the NL pennant, and led all Dodger starters in the World Series, hitting .353.

Furillo's 1953 campaign was his finest, but when he won the batting crown, he was on the disabled list with a broken finger. In an early September contest at the Polo Grounds, Furillo was at bat against the Giants' Ruben Gomez. Rival manager Leo Durocher was screaming, "Stick it in his ear!" The next pitch plunked Furillo on the right wrist, and he ambled to first. After the count went full to the next hitter, he charged the Giants dugout and began choking Durocher. In the ensuing brawl along the first base side, Monte Irvin stepped on his hand, breaking a knuckle on his little finger.

Furillo was an indispensable part of the Brooklyn Dodgers' only World Series title in 1955. He finished seventh in the NL at .314 with a career-high 26 home runs

G	AB	R	H	2B	3B	HR	RBI	SB	BB	SO	BA	OBP	SLG	TB
1806	6378	895	1910	324	56	192	1058	48	514	436	.299	.355	.458	2922

and 95 RBI. Furillo took part in seven Fall Classics, all but one a Subway Series with the Yankees. In 40 games, he had 34 hits, nine doubles, two home runs and 13 runs batted in.

Coming west with the Dodgers in 1958, he hit .290 with 18 home runs. In the final game of the 1959 National League playoff series against the Milwaukee Braves, Furillo beat out a ground ball in the twelfth inning to score Gil Hodges, for a walk-off pennant-winning hit.

The 37-year-old veteran also delivered in Game 3 of the 1959 World Series facing the Chicago "Go Go" White Sox, the first Fall Classic game ever played in California. His bases loaded, pinch-hit single in the seventh inning drove in two runs for the margin of victory, 3-1. The game drew a record 92,394 to the Los Angeles Memorial Coliseum.

Early in the 1960 season, Furillo had appeared in only eight games before tearing a calf muscle. The Dodgers abruptly handed him his release. Irritated with the team for waiving him while he was still injured, Furillo maintained that his release was issued so the Dodgers could avoid paying him a higher pension and medical expenses.

Furillo decided to take legal action against the Dodgers and was awarded $21,000. Commissioner Ford C. Frick came out with a public statement saying that baseball had not blacklisted him, but he was never able to get employment again in the game he loved.

Furillo and his wife, the former Fern Reichart, moved back to Stony Creek Mills. When Roger Kahn finally located him in 1970 to interview him for his milestone book *The Boys of Summer*, Furillo was installing Otis Elevators in the World Trade Center twin towers. He died at his home in Stony Creek Mills of a heart attack on January 21, 1989 at 66. Furillo is buried in the Forest Hills Memorial Park in Reiffton, Pennsylvania.

ORVAL GROVE

CHICAGO WHITE SOX
RIGHT-HANDED PITCHER

1940-1949

"A groan went up from the crowd as Grove approached so close to diamond immortality, only to fail. The youngster, who was notching his seventh victory without a defeat, whizzed over a strike before Gordon swung from his heels to ram that double down the left field line."

~ James P. Dawson

Homegrown Chicagoan Orval Grove was an American League All-Star pitcher and a White Sox workhorse. A mainstay in the Chicago rotation for many years, he got his start during World War II when many major league moundsmen were in the military.

The 6'3" 200-pound Grove threw a natural sinking fastball that led to frequent ground ball outs. He was one of the first pitchers to come out of the White Sox minor league farm system established in 1939 where he acquired a sharp-breaking curve and valuable changeup.

★ ★ ★ ★ ★

Orval Leroy Grove was born on August 29, 1919 to Jewell and Edward M. Grove in West Mineral, Cherokee County, Kansas. He grew up in Maywood, Proviso Township, Illinois just outside of Chicago and by eighth grade had already decided he wanted a career in baseball.

He pitched for the Proviso East High team as a freshman- the school's first ever varsity freshman. During his prep career, Grove lost only two games, notched two one-hitters and threw a no-hitter against Evanston High. He also starred for football and basketball champion teams.

In his junior year in 1937, Grove attracted the attention of White Sox scout Doug Minor and was invited to work out with the big-leaguers at Comiskey Park. He threw batting practice a number of times and was persuaded to sign with the White Sox later in 1937 for a $2,500 bonus.

Grove spent his first year with the Class A1 Dallas Steers (Texas League) and then the Class-C Longview Cannibals (East Texas League), winning ten games. For the 1939 Oklahoma City Indians (Texas League), he threw 158 innings, among them a strange no-hitter in Tulsa.

A lightning storm knocked the Oiler Park lights out three times while Grove was gradually walking the bases loaded in the ninth. He was pulled, but his reliever walked the next batter to force in the winning run. Grove took the loss, 1-0, though he had just tossed a no-hitter.

After a solid spring training, he made Chicago's 1940 Opening Day roster and got his debut on May 28, but soon was optioned back to Oklahoma City. Pitching under manager Rogers Hornsby on August 11, he threw a 12-inning 1-0 victory over the Tulsa Oilers' Dizzy Dean.

Grove threw briefly for the 1941 White Sox, but fought control problems and was sent to the Texas League's Shreveport (LA) Sports on May 19. In route to a 17–7 mark in 201 innings pitched with a 2.73 ERA, he incurred a knee injury and later hurt his other knee in a car accident.

Grove finally got his shot with the White Sox in 1942, but a July medical exam revealed torn cartilage in his left knee, ending his year. In the fall, an abscess on the back of his knee required another operation. Because of his knees, Grove was classified "4-F" in early 1943.

The Sox signed him to a one-dollar 1943 contract to wait and see. Grove reeled off nine wins in a row to start, equaling a franchise record set in 1917 by Lefty Williams. The highlight was on July 8, when he took a no-hitter into the ninth versus the Yankees in front of over 31,000 home fans. With two out, Joe Gordon hit a sharp grounder down the third base line just fair that nicked the diving Jimmy Grant's glove for a double. He then finished off an epic one-hitter.

The youngest pitcher on the staff, he was the White Sox's ace with over 216 innings pitched, 18 complete games, 15 victories, three shutouts, a 2.75 ERA and 76 strikeouts. After the successful year, he married the former Catherine Sloan in the off season on January 8, 1944.

The Opening Day starter on April 19, 1944, Grove opposed Indians ace Al Smith and won, 3-1. He shut out the Yankees on May 18, the first time the pinstriped sluggers had been whitewashed all season. Chosen an All-Star, he finished with 14 wins on 234 innings pitched.

G	IP	W	L	PCT	SHO	GS	CG	H	ER	SO	BB	ERA
207	1176.2	63	73	.463	11	152	66	1237	494	374	444	3.78

The staff workhorse, Grove felt that he should be paid for it. He held out, finally signing only weeks before Opening Day 1945 for $8,500. Proving his value, he paced the Sox with 33 games, 30 starts and four shutouts and registered 16 complete games, 14 wins and a 3.44 ERA.

Grove threw in 33 games in 1946 for the ChiSox and started 26. On August 3, he gave up three hits and a walk but faced a minimum 27 Washington batters as each runner was erased with a double play. Grove had eight wins and a 3.02 ERA, but unleashed an AL-high ten wild pitches.

He began the 1947 season as part of a starting quartet of Eddie Lopat, Joe Haynes and Frank Papish, but briefly lost his spot after struggling with his command in the middle months. Getting only 19 starts, Grove went 6-8 with just six complete games and a telltale 4.44 ERA.

He relinquished his starting job in 1948, posting a subpar 2-10 mark with a 6.16 ERA in only 11 starts. Grove pitched the final game of his big-league career against the Indians on April 27, 1949, allowing four runs on four hits, a walk and a hit batsman in two-thirds of an inning.

After the game, he was sent down to the Sacramento (CA) Solons. Grove quickly became a part of one of the most vaunted rotations in Pacific Coast League history, joining Ken Holcombe, Bob Gillespie and Frank Dass. He would win 17 games in 1950 while eating up 309 innings in the long 200-game Pacific Coast League schedule.

Grove was traded to the Portland (OR) Beavers after the 1952 season, but decided to retire and settle in Sacramento. He enjoyed pitching in the local semi-pro circuits while operating a car wash business for 20 years, raising four children and taking pleasure in four grandchildren.

Grove and Joe Gordon, the Hall of Famer who broke up his 1942 no-hitter, became close friends in Sacramento. Grove died on April 20, 1992 in Carmichael, California at age 72 and is buried alongside his wife at the Calvary Catholic Cemetery & Mausoleum in Sacramento.

TOMMY HENRICH

NEW YORK YANKEES
RIGHT FIELD

1937-1942 • 1946-1950

"He was at his best in the big games, and he never made a mistake in the outfield. And as he grew older, he was very helpful to younger players."

~ teammate Bobby Brown

New York City's demanding partisan fans embraced Tommy Henrich as one of their most popular Yankees ever. A proud man of high character, he personified pinstripe class, contributing to eight pennants and seven World Series championships in an 11-year truncated career interrupted by three years of military service.

The five-time American League All-Star had a penchant for delivering the key hit when the game was in the balance. Yankee Broadcaster Mel Allen nicknamed him "Ol' Reliable" for his dependability and his teammates referred to him as "The Clutch."

Perhaps the finest Yankee rightfielder ever, the 6' 180-pounder was respected for his rifle arm and good judgment, rarely making a throw to a wrong base. He studied hitters' tendencies and wind currents and fielded ground balls like a middle infielder.

* * * * *

Thomas David Henrich was born on February 20, 1913 to Mary Elizabeth Dressler and Edward M. Henrich in Massillon, Stark County, Ohio. One of six children growing up in a German family, he played only softball because of a shortage of fields.

The Indians signed him in late 1933. He began at Class-D Monessen (PA), and then moved up to Class-C Zanesville (OH). In 1935 and 1936, Henrich played for the New Orleans (LA) Pelicans, hitting a lusty .346 with 100 RBI in his second season there.

He averaged .339 over three minor league seasons, but was denied a promotion. Henrich filed a grievance with Commissioner Kenesaw Mountain Landis in early 1937, alleging that Cleveland was illegally concealing him in the Indians farm system.

Judge Landis ruled that he had been wrongfully denied an opportunity to play in the major leagues, and he could sign with any team. As baseball's first free agent and a Yankee fan since early boyhood, he chose the Yankees after an eight-team bidding war and received a substantial $25,000 bonus.

Henrich debuted on May 11, 1937. He platooned with George Selkirk and King Kong Keller in 1938, but still had 22 home runs and 91 runs batted in. Manager Joe McCarthy hit him third in the lineup against the Cubs in the World Series sweep, and he belted one of his four Fall Classic homers.

It was in World Series Game 4 at Ebbets Field that he became a key factor in one of baseball's most unlikely rallies. With a full count and two out in the ninth with the Dodgers leading, 4-3, he swung and missed on a sharp-breaking Hugh Casey curveball.

But the game wasn't over... Catcher Mickey Owen had been fooled by the pitch and the alert Henrich saw the ball carom away, hustling to first. Three hits and a walk later, the Yankees had won stunningly, 7-4. They then put Brooklyn away the next day.

Henrich was called to serve in the U. S. Coast Guard in September, 1942. Before his last at-bat, he was given one of the grandest ovations in Yankee Stadium history. He missed the postseason and three prime years stationed in Grand Haven, Michigan.

Henrich reunited with Keller and Joe DiMaggio in 1946 to reprise one of the greatest outfields of all-time. He was a force in the middle of the Bronx Bomber lineup in 1947 with 98 RBI, 109 runs scored, 35 doubles and a league-leading 13 triples.

The offensive star of the 1947 Series, Henrich drove in two runs in the victory over the Dodgers in Game 1, and clouted a Game 2 solo shot. With the score tied, 2-2, bases loaded and two out, he drove in the Game 7 clincher. He hit .323 (10-for-31).

G	AB	R	H	2B	3B	HR	RBI	SB	BB	SO	BA	OBP	SLG	TB
1284	4603	901	1297	269	73	183	795	23	712	383	.282	.382	.491	2261

Henrich followed with his finest overall campaign in 1948, leading the AL with 138 runs scored, 14 triples and 81 extra base hits. He clubbed 25 homers, added 42 doubles, 326 total bases and 100 RBI. His four grand slams tied a Junior Circuit record.

Ol' Reliable came through with 24 home runs and slugged .526 in 1949, supplying crucial hits repeatedly in September. In the pressure-packed 154th game finale against Boston at Yankee Stadium, he blasted a dramatic pennant-clinching home run.

In yet another Subway Series opener, Brooklyn's Don Newcombe and Allie Reynolds dueled in the sun for eight scoreless innings. Leading off the last of the ninth inning, Henrich drove a laser into the right-field seats for the first walk-off home run in Fall Classic history.

"The Clutch" indeed... He was an All-Star in each of his last four seasons, but retired after an injury-riddled final year in 1950 when he hit only six homers. Henrich's last curtain call was October 1 before the start of the World Series against the Phillies.

He spent 1951 as a Yankees coach, tutoring highly-touted rookie Mickey Mantle, who would put on the same uniform #7 that Henrich wore before World War II. He later coached for the Giants (1957) and Tigers (1958-59), and worked as a sports broadcaster.

Henrich was joyful in retirement, devoted to his wife of 68 years, Eileen, three daughters and two sons. He loved to play the piano and sing in the church choir. His pastor led the effort to rename a street in his honor- Tommy Henrich Boulevard.

Ol' Reliable received the 1987 Pride of The Yankees Award as a significant person in the franchise's history. Weakened by several strokes in his last years, Henrich passed away on December 1, 2009 at the age of 96 in his Beavercreek, Ohio home.

FRED HUTCHINSON

DETROIT TIGERS
RIGHT-HANDED PITCHER

1939-40 • 1946-1953

Fred Hutchinson is remembered for his pitching tenacity as well as his dignity and courage. He was the first nationally recognized sports figure out of his hometown of Seattle, Washington and also achieved distinction as a manager for the Tigers, Cardinals and Reds.

Hutchinson's cool, no-nonsense demeanor on the mound earned him the sobriquet "The Iceman." Although never a flamethrower, he had excellent command and featured a repertoire which included a natural sinking fastball, a choppy curveball and a disappearing change-of-pace.

The 6'2" 190-pound Hutchinson could also be a temperamental pitcher with a quick temper. Notwithstanding, he garnered wide respect for his intelligence and leadership skills and was known all over the American League as a fierce competitor with an intense will to win.

Hutchinson was also one of the best hitting pitchers of his era. Wielding his *Louisville Slugger* from the left side, he was asked frequently to pinch-hit and batted over .300 in four separate years. His career average was a sturdy .263 with 171 hits, four home runs and 83 RBI.

★ ★ ★ ★ ★

Frederick Charles Hutchinson was born on August 12, 1919 to Nona Burke and Dr. Joseph Lambert Hutchinson in Seattle. His parents were Wisconsin natives who migrated to southeast Seattle where his physician father set up a medical practice. Both of his older brothers went on to play baseball for the University of Washington. Bill captained the 1931 Pacific Coast Conference Champion Huskies and John later played in the Browns organization.

Hutchinson excelled for two American Legion clubs, starred on Franklin High's 1934 to 1937 championship teams that went 60-2, and pitched for the semi-pro 1937 Yakima (WA) Indians of the Northwest League, going 16-2. At age 19, he signed with the newly-named Seattle Rainiers and wowed the 1938 Pacific Coast League in his rookie professional season.

Hutch posted a 25-7 mark with 29 complete games and a 2.48 ERA as the PCL's MVP and *The Sporting News* 1938 Minor League Player of the Year. Now a hot commodity, he was traded to the Tigers in December for $50,000 and four players- a major deal for a minor leaguer.

Hutch was given his debut on May 2, 1939 at Detroit's Briggs Stadium. After struggling in that game, he was sent to the Double-A Toledo (OH) Mud Hens and split 1940 between the Buffalo (NY) Bisons and Detroit. He was ready for full time big-league duty after toiling the entire 1941 summer in Buffalo where he ruled the International League, registering a 26-7 record with 31 complete games and 171 strikeouts. As the IL Most Valuable Player, he also batted .385.

Hutch joined the Navy on October 24, 1941 and served on active duty for four years in World War II., rising to lieutenant commander. He married his school sweetheart Patsy Finley in St. Augustine, Florida in 1943 where she was stationed in the Women's Army Auxiliary Corps.

After the War in 1946, he quickly earned a spot in the Tigers starting rotation with Dizzy Trout, Hal Newhouser and Virgil Trucks and began a streak of six straight seasons with 10+ wins, going 87-57. Hutch was 18-10 in 1947 and ranked fourth in the AL with a 2.96 ERA in 1949. He went 17-8 in 1950 and was a 1951 All-Star, pitching three innings at Briggs Stadium.

Hutchinson's Tigers teammates elected him their team player representative in 1947 and he was voted the American League's player representative from 1948 until 1952. Hutch took over the manager's reins for the cellar-dwelling Tigers on July 5, 1952 through the 1954 season.

He went back home to manage the Rainiers to the 1955 PCL pennant and was hired by the Cardinals for the 1956 season. The next year, he steered St. Louis to a runner-up finish behind the World Series Champion Milwaukee Braves as the 1957 NL Manager of the Year.

> *"If I needed one game upon which my whole season was based, if my career depended on that one victory, I'd pick Hutch to pitch it for me."*
>
> ~ Tigers manager
> Steve O'Neill, 1946-48

G	IP	W	L	PCT	SHO	GS	CG	H	ER	SO	BB	ERA
242	1464	95	71	.572	13	169	81	1487	606	591	388	3.73

He landed back with the Reds-owned Seattle Rainiers yet again in 1959 as both general manager and field manager. By July, the parent club was floundering and Hutch was summoned to replace Reds manager Mayo Smith. He immediately put the franchise on the upswing.

Hutchinson's Reds put together an historic 1961 season, winning 93 games, and he was named NL Manager of the Year again. The World Series pitted Cincy against the powerful 1961 Yankees of Roger Maris, Mickey Mantle and Whitey Ford. The Reds could muster just one win.

In late 1963, a lump on his neck was diagnosed by his physician brother Bill as malignant thymoma. A heavy cigarette smoker since his Navy days, Hutchinson faced a grim prognosis with tumors already present in his lungs and neck. His cancer advanced rapidly. At a 45th birthday tribute on August 12, a weak Hutchinson told the fans, "What a lucky man I am." A day later, first base coach Dick Sisler took over for him. The Reds almost pulled off an inspired upset, finishing just a game behind the eventual World Series Champion Cardinals.

Hutch retreated to Anna Maria Island near Bradenton, Florida, his permanent home since 1959. He formally resigned as manager on October 19 and succumbed on November 12, 1964, at a hospital near his home. He was laid to rest at Mount Olivet Cemetery in Renton, Washington.

Hutchinson was honored as *Sport Magazine's* 1964 Man of the Year. The team retired his Reds uniform #1 and he was inducted into the Cincinnati Reds Hall of Fame in 1965. *The Seattle Post-Intelligencer* named him Seattle's Athlete of the 20th Century in 1999.

Hutchinson's life and courage were honored in 1965 when his brother, Dr. William B. Hutchinson, founded the world-class Fred Hutchinson Cancer Research Center in his native Seattle. Major League Baseball's Hutch Award was established in 1965 and is still given yearly to the major league player who best exemplifies Hutchinson's honor, courage and dedication.

BOB LEMON

"I have to rate Lemon as one of the very best pitchers I ever faced. His ball was always moving, hard, sinking, fast-breaking. You could never really uhm-mmph with Lemon."

~ Ted Williams

Bob Lemon is the only 20th century Hall-of-Famer to start his career as a hitter and earn induction as a pitcher. He began as a left-handed-hitting third baseman, starred as a right-handed hurler, and finished as a three-time AL Manager of the Year.

Lemon was named to seven straight All-Star teams and ranked among league leaders in wins nine straight years. *The Sporting News* AL Pitcher of the Year in 1948, 1950 and 1954, he was the fourth hurler in AL history to win 20 games seven times.

The 6' 185-pound Lemon was incapable of throwing a straight fastball. His offerings would dip or take off sideways. He had an impressive curveball and a tight slider taught him by coach Mel Harder. Both pitches complemented his sinking fastball.

Durable and strong, Lemon led the American League in complete games five times, innings pitched four times, and wins three times. His 188 complete games in 350 starts are remarkable considering his relatively late conversion to the pitchers' mound.

Lemon was a Gold Glove-quality fielder, drawing on his experience playing third base. He set a still existing major league record in 1953, participating in 15 double plays as a pitcher, and was often a Junior Circuit leader in putouts, assists and total chances.

One of the best hitting pitchers of all-time, Lemon drove in 147 runs and slugged 37 home runs- only one behind the all-time leader for pitchers, Wes Ferrell. As a pinch-hitter, Lemon averaged a solid .284 (31-for-109) for his career.

★　★　★　★　★

Robert Granville Lemon was born to Ruth and Earl Lemon in San Bernardino, California on September 22, 1920. He developed into the 1938 California Baseball Player of the Year as a shortstop and pitcher out of Long Beach's Woodrow Wilson High.

The young 17 year old was discovered by Indians scout John Angel who signed him in 1938 for $100 per month. He spent five years apprenticing in the minor leagues as an infielder and outfielder with short "cups of coffee" in the Big Time in 1941 and 1942.

Lemon enlisted in the U. S. Navy in early 1943 and played for the Navy military team. He was directed to pitch when injuries had depleted the team's staff. Another Navy man, Tigers catcher Birdie Tebbetts, later tipped off Indians manager Lou Boudreau.

Lemon was the Indians' centerfielder and #2 hitter in the lineup when Bob Feller threw his no-hitter on April 30, 1946. Boudreau began to pitch him in relief, gradually converting him. Assigned his first start on July 31, 1947, he immediately won ten straight games.

In his first year as a full-time starter in 1948, Lemon hurled a 2-0 no-hitter against the Tigers at Briggs Stadium on June 30- the first no-no pitched at night. After topping the AL with 293²/₃ innings, 20 complete games and ten shutouts, he was stellar in the Fall Classic. He out-dueled the Braves' Warren Spahn in Game 2, 4-1. In the Game 6 finale, he went 7²/₃ innings to pick up the win. His Series ERA was 1.65 for the world champs.

Lemon led the AL in 1950 with 23 wins, 170 strikeouts and 288 innings. He paced the AL in 1954 with 23 wins and 21 complete games to lead one of the greatest pitching staffs in baseball history including Early Wynn, Mike Garcia and Bob Feller.

Tops again in the AL with 18 wins in 1955, he won 20 more in 1956 but struggled with a leg injury in 1957 and elbow trouble in 1958. His last outing with the Tribe was on July 1, although he did pitch briefly with the Triple-A

G	IP	W	L	PCT	SHO	GS	CG	H	ER	SO	BB	ERA
460	2850	207	128	.618	31	350	188	2559	1023	1277	1251	3.23

San Diego Padres before retiring.

He was the pitching coach for the 1960 Indians and 1961 Phillies and managed the Angels' Pacific Coast League entry, starting in 1964. He skippered the Seattle Angels to the 1966 PCL title and was *The Sporting News* Minor League Manager of the Year.

Lemon was promoted to Angels pitching coach in 1967 and 1968 and had the same role for the 1970 Royals. Instated as Royals manager in midseason 1970, he guided Kansas City to its first winning season in 1971, earning AL Manager of the Year honors.

Lemon managed the 1974 PCL Sacramento (CA) Solons of the Triple-A Pacific Coast League and the 1975 Richmond (VA) Braves of the Triple-A International League. While serving as pitching coach for the 1976 American League Champion Yankees, he was inducted into the National Baseball Hall of Fame that summer in Cooperstown.

White Sox owner Bill Veeck hired him on as his manager in 1977, and Lemon improved the team's record by 26 full games to win his second AL Manager of the Year award. In spite of this, Veeck cut him loose after the team started 34-40 in 1978.

Lemon was soon hired as Yankees manager to replace Billy Martin by President Al Rosen, his Indians teammate. After winning the AL East in sudden death, the Yankees beat the Royals in the ALCS, and then slipped by the Dodgers as 1978 World Champs.

Owner George Steinbrenner replaced him after the team stumbled out of the gate in 1979. Lemon came back for a third time in late 1981 and led them to another pennant. He was relieved of his duties again early in 1982 but continued as a scout.

The Indians organization retired his uniform jersey #21 on June 20, 1998 at Jacobs Field. Married to the former Jane McGee in 1944, Lemon and his wife lived out their final years in Long Beach, California until he passed away on January 11, 2000.

MICKEY MANTLE

NEW YORK YANKEES
CENTER FIELD

1951-1968

"He has more speed than any slugger and more slug than any speedster- and nobody has ever had more of both of 'em together. This kid ain't logical. He's too good. It's very confusing."

~ Yankees manager
Casey Stengel

Mickey Mantle was the greatest power-hitting switch-hitter of all-time and one of the most gifted and charismatic players in history. A 16-time All-Star, he manned the premier position on the premier team in professional sports during baseball's Golden Era.

Possessing spectacular power from both sides of the plate, Mantle blasted titanic home runs extraordinary distances. Also the fleetest runner of his time, he could beat out a drag bunt to first base in 3.1 seconds and circle the bases in a dazzling 13.9 seconds.

The essence of pinstripe glamour, Mantle led his Yankee Dynasty teams to 12 World Series and seven world titles in his first 14 years in New York City on the biggest baseball stage. He still holds Fall Classic records of 65 games played, 42 runs scored, 43 walks, 54 strikeouts, 26 extra base hits, 18 home runs, 40 RBI and 123 total bases.

* * * * *

Mickey Charles Mantle was born in Spavinaw, Mayes County, Oklahoma on October 20, 1931 to Lovell Richardson and Elven Charles Mantle. After his shift in the mines, his father pitched to him, starting at age four, to mold him into a switch hitter.

Mantle was only 90 pounds as a freshman at Commerce High, but matured into a three-sport star. During prep football, he was kicked in the left shin which resulted in a severe case of osteomyelitis. Only the new drug penicillin saved his leg from amputation.

Yankees scout Tom Greenwade drove to Kansas in 1948 to observe the Baxter Springs Whiz Kids. After watching Mantle launch bombs from each side into the Spring River way beyond the field, he knew he had just seen every scout's fantasy in the flesh.

The Yankees signed him after graduation in 1949 and sent him to Class-D. By the time he had won the 1950 West-ern Association batting title at .383 playing for the Joplin (MO) Miners, he was a full-fledged phenom celebrated as the "Commerce Comet."

In a pre-season 1951 exhibition game on campus against the USC Trojans, Mantle powered an epic left-handed 656-foot missile that left the park and sailed completely over a nearby football field. Casey Stengel gave him his debut in the Big Apple on April 17.

The 19-year-old prodigy pressed early and was sent down. But he overwhelmed Triple-A pitching with the Kansas City (MO) Blues and soon rejoined the Yankees. Playing right field in World Series Game 2, he pulled up to avoid an outfield collision with Joe DiMaggio, caught his spikes in a drainage cover, and blew out his right knee.

Without current surgical methods to treat the grave damage to his knee, Mantle played in constant pain the rest of his career. Despite his blacksmith-strong forearms, improbably broad back and 18" neck, the 5'11" 200-pounder was strangely injury-prone.

DiMaggio left big shoes to fill when he retired and New York fans did not quickly embrace Mantle. Yet there were glimpses of future greatness, such as the rocket he hit out of Griffith Stadium from the right side on April 17, 1953 that traveled some 565 feet.

"The Mick" finally put it all together in 1956. As the AL Most Valuable Player, he won the Triple Crown and remains the last man to lead both leagues in all three categories (.353 average - 52 home runs - 130 RBI). Mantle is the only switch-hitting Triple Crown winner ever. He repeated as the 1957 MVP, hitting a personal-best .365.

In their first year together in 1960, Roger Maris and Mantle finished 1-2 in the MVP voting. Against Detroit at Briggs Stadium on September 10, Mantle put a ball into orbit left-handed that cleared the right field roof. It was

G	AB	R	H	2B	3B	HR	RBI	SB	BB	SO	BA	OBP	SLG	TB
2401	8109	1676	2415	344	72	536	1509	153	1733	1710	.298	.421	.557	4511

measured at a stunning 643 feet.

Babe Ruth's record of 60 home runs was in jeopardy in 1961 as the "M & M Boys" made their run. Mantle was now the fan favorite, but was derailed at 54 home runs by an abscessed hip. He hit .317 with 128 RBI and led the AL with 132 runs scored, 126 walks and a .687 slugging average. He followed with his third MVP Award in 1962.

On May 22, 1963, Mantle nearly became the only man ever to belt a fair ball out of Yankee Stadium. His line drive was still rising when it hit inches from the top of the 110-foot high third deck facade. Unimpeded, it might have traveled over 700 feet. He called the mammoth walk-off shot the hardest ball he ever hit.

Injuries and dissipation began to take their toll by 1965. Mantle's legs were gone and with them the Yankee Dynasty. He hit an aggregate .253 his last four years and saw his career mark erode to .298, but went out playing more games than any other Yankee.

The Yankees retired his uniform #7 on Mickey Mantle Day, June 8, 1969. At that point, the only other retired uniform numbers were #3, #4 and #5, honoring Ruth, Lou Gehrig and DiMaggio respectively. In his first year of eligibility in 1974, Mantle and his great friend and teammate Whitey Ford were inducted into the National Baseball Hall of Fame together, the first teammates to be so honored on the same day in Cooperstown.

After a liver transplant revealed inoperable cancer, he formed the Mickey Mantle Foundation to raise awareness for the organ donor program. He passed away at Baylor University Hospital on August 13, 1995 and was laid to rest in Sparkman-Hillcrest Memorial Park in Dallas, Texas. A tribute shrine was dedicated in Monument Park at Yankee Stadium in 1996 which bears the words: "*A Great Teammate. A Magnificent Yankee who left a Legacy of Unequaled Courage.*"

GIL McDOUGALD

NEW YORK YANKEES
SECOND BASE • THIRD BASE • SHORTSTOP
1951-1960

*"Gil was one tough ballplayer.
He could also be hard-headed.
I'll always remember that crazy
stance of his and he didn't want
to change. He was a great guy to
have playing behind you.
He played all of those positions
and played them well."*

~ teammate Whitey Ford

Gil McDougald was the superstar of role players in the 1950s for one of baseball's greatest dynasties. A six-time All-Star, he contributed to eight American League pennants and earned five World Series Championship rings in his decade in pinstripes. Yet he may be most remembered for his line drive that forever altered the promising career of pitcher Herb Score.

The 6' 175-pound McDougald's versatility, reliable fielding and knack for getting on base made him a significant asset in the Yankees lineup. He was not only known for his stellar glove and clutch bat, but also for his character and being a consummate teammate.

McDougald paced AL infielders in double plays at third base (1952), second base (1955) and shortstop (1957). He was an All-Star at third base (1952), shortstop (1957), and second base (1958). He and Pete Rose are the only two men to have been an All-Star at three positions.

McDougald was known for his inelegant-looking batting stance, once described as having the appearance of a broken banana stick. With his arms slumped awkwardly, he hit out of an exaggerated wide open position, dangling his *Louisville Slugger* below the plane of his hands.

Aesthetics aside, he hit over .300 in 1951 and 1956, his two finest campaigns. Those two Yankee teams are still considered among the best in franchise history. In 53 World Series games, he accumulated 45 hits, walloped seven home runs and drove in 24 runs.

★　★　★　★　★

Gilbert James McDougald was born of Scottish descent on May 19, 1928 to Ella Corrine McGuire and William James McDougald in San Francisco, California. Learning his baseball on the sandlots with his brother, he matured into a standout multi-sport athlete at Commerce High.

McDougald starred two years for the University of San Francisco Dons in baseball and basketball. After taking a realistic look at his future as a pro hoopster in the new NBA, he chose baseball and signed with the Yankees' West Coast Scouting Director Joe Devine in 1948.

It took McDougald only three summers in the minors to prove he was ready for the Big Time. He hit .340 for the 1948 Class-C Twin Falls (ID) Cowboys; then .344 for the Class-B 1949 Victoria (BC) Athletics; and finally .336 for the 1950 Double-A Beaumont (TX) Roughnecks.

The Yankees gave the 22-year-old McDougald his debut on April 20, 1951. Against the Browns on May 3, he had six RBI in the ninth inning on a grand slam and two-run triple. He went on to pace the Yanks in hitting at .306 while slugging 14 home runs. In World Series Game 5, McDougald launched a grand slam off Giant hurler Larry Jansen, the first ever by a rookie.

McDougald spent 1951 in effect backing up starters Jerry Coleman, Phil Rizzuto and Bobby Brown. Casey Stengel recognized he had the luxury of mixing and matching his infield to almost any opponent. In the AL Rookie of the Year voting, McDougald beat out Minnie Minoso.

His finest year was 1956 when he hit .311 and pounded out seven hits in the Fall Classic victory over Brooklyn. Early in Game 5, McDougald deprived Jackie Robinson of a hit. The liner bounced off Andy Carey's mitt at third base, but McDougald snared the carom at short and fired to first, nipping the fleet Robinson. Don Larsen went on to hurl his historic perfect game.

On May 7, 1957, McDougald came up against young Indians ace Herb Score. He flicked his *Louisville Slugger* at a low-outside fastball, driving a hard smash back through the box that hit Score in the right eye and broke bones in his face. The injury altered Score's career forever.

Feeling blame for the incident, McDougald visited Score in the hospital after the game and remained in touch with him over the years. Score regained his full vision and came

G	AB	R	H	2B	3B	HR	RBI	SB	BB	SO	BA	OBP	SLG	TB
1336	4676	697	1291	187	51	112	576	45	559	623	.276	.356	.410	1916

back to pitch for Cleveland in late 1958, but arm troubles led to a premature end to his promising career.

In the 1958 All-Star Game, McDougald drove home Frank Malzone with the winning run. Later in World Series Game 6, he swatted a clutch game-winning bomb in the tenth inning off the Braves' Warren Spahn. The 1958 Lou Gehrig Memorial Award went to him as "the player who best exemplified the character and integrity of Gehrig both on and off the field."

McDougald's last major league action was in the historic Game 7 of the 1960 World Series. As a ninth-inning pinch runner, he scored on Yogi Berra's grounder to tie the score. Playing third base in the fateful bottom of the ninth inning, he watched as Bill Mazeroski's walk-off home run sailed over the left field wall at Forbes Field for the Pirate victory.

McDougald and his wife Lucille had just had their fourth child. He could see that his bat speed and playing time were diminishing. Shortly after World Series Game 7, he decided to retire to build his new company, Yankee Corporate Maintenance, which eventually flourished.

McDougald also served as head coach at New York City's Fordham University from 1970 to 1976, leading the Rams to a 21-11 mark in 1975 — the most wins for a Fordham team since 1926. During his seven-year run he had five winning seasons and a record of 100-79-4.

McDougald was hit behind his left ear in a batting practice incident in 1955 which eventually caused his hearing to deteriorate during his Fordham years. However, his hearing loss was largely restored by a cochlear implant received surgically at the NYU Medical Center in 1994. Later he became the national spokesman for the manufacturer, Cochlear Americas.

A devout Roman Catholic, McDougald could be seen frequently at Mass even during midweek. He died of prostate cancer at his home in Wall Township, New Jersey, at age 82. Gil McDougald left behind his wife Lucille, their seven children, 14 grandchildren and seven great-grandchildren. He was laid to rest in St. Catherine's Cemetery in Sea Girt, New Jersey.

BOB MILLER

PHILADELPHIA PHILLIES
RIGHT-HANDED PITCHER

1949-1958

"I haven't seen such poise in a young pitcher. And on top of that, Miller is unbelievably fast. His quick one takes off about 10 to 15 feet from the plate and shoots like a bullet."

~ umpire Frank Dascoli, June 7, 1950 after Miller shut out the Reds

Bob Miller was a key member of the 1950 National League Champion Phillies "Whiz Kids" team. He had a successful, yet star-crossed career in which two freak, off-the-field accidents curtailed his chances to fulfill the spectacular beginning to his career.

The lanky, hunch-shouldered 6'3" 194-pound Miller had an unconventional delivery and two extraordinary pitches. He had fine control of a knuckler and sinker and delivered both with an unusual push delivery in which his arm seemed to come to home plate before the ball. As a result, the hitter's timing was often disrupted. He threw many a double play ground ball.

★　★　★　★　★

Robert John Miller was born on June 16, 1926 to Helen Margaret Walling and Albert Joseph Miller in Detroit, Michigan. The oldest of four with two brothers and a sister, he was raised in a Catholic home. Miller pitched on the same American Legion team as future Phillies teammate Stan Lopata and starred at Detroit's Saint Mary's of Redford Catholic High School.

Following graduation in 1944 and barely 18 years old, Miller joined the Army infantry in World War II. After a month of combat in Luzon during a half-year stationed in the Philippines, he also fought in New Guinea. When his 26 months of service ended, he remained in the Pacific and played baseball in Japan in the summer of 1946.

Following his discharge, he won three games in a national amateur tournament in Youngstown, Ohio in 1947 and then enrolled at the University of Detroit Mercy. He was pitching for UDM when Phillies scout Eddie Krajnik signed him to a pro contract in 1948.

With the Class-B Terre Haute (IN) Phillies in 1949, Miller led the Three-I-League in wins, going 19-9. He also paced the circuit with a 2.72 ERA, 25 complete games, 255 innings pitched, 1,018 batsmen faced, and 207 strikeouts. He was honored as the Three-I-League MVP.

Miller was called up by the Phillies and enjoyed his major league debut on September 16, 1949. He threw 2⅔ innings of scoreless relief that year. The following season, the 23-year-old rookie became a member of the Phillies' young pitching staff which included Curt Simmons (21), Robin Roberts (23), Bubba Church (25) and Russ Meyer (26).

He came out of the gate ferociously as a freshman sensation. With a fastball that exploded across the plate, he beat the Braves' Vern Bickford, 2-1, in his first start on April 29, 1950. He then shut out the Pirates and Reds, stringing together 22⅔ scoreless innings in a row and ran his mark to 8-0 as the odds-on favorite to win the NL Rookie of the Year award.

Manager Eddie Sawyer sent him ahead to Boston to rest up for his next start. Bounding up the stairs two-by-two to the platform in the North Philly Railroad Station with his bags in his hand, he missed his footing, lurched to one side and wrenched muscles and tendons in his right shoulder. He was incapacitated for a month and went 3-9 thereafter in a Jekyll and Hyde season.

The Phillies secured the pennant on the last day and Miller finished with 22 starts, 35 appearances, an 11-6 record and a 3.57 ERA. He ranked third on the staff in innings and fourth in wins with seven complete games but was nudged by Sam Jethroe for NL Rookie of the Year.

With his parents in attendance for the first time, he got the start in the 1950 World Series Game 4. Miller gave up two hits and two runs in a third of an inning and was knocked out of the box by a Joe DiMaggio double. He took the 5-2 loss that finalized a Yankees four-game sweep.

Miller's back and shoulder problems were slow to mend. He requested to be sent down to the Class-B Wilmington (DE) Blue Rocks in the Interstate League

G	IP	W	L	PCT	SHO	GS	CG	H	ER	SO	BB	ERA
261	822	42	42	.500	6	68	23	889	362	263	247	3.96

in 1951 to start over. His 12-9 mark and 2.35 ERA for the 1952 Baltimore Orioles of the Triple-A International League signaled that he had regained his confidence.

The Phillies began to recognize that he might be better coming out of the bullpen because he could not sustain his stuff more than six innings. In the final seasons of his career, he was used mostly out of the bullpen, making 131 relief appearances between 1955 and 1958.

A second off-the-field accident late in his career led to his retirement from the game. Miller tripped on his three-year-old son's toys late in the 1958 season, landed heavily on his right wrist and broke it. As it turned out, his last major league game was on August 10, 1958.

After a short audition early in 1959 with the Buffalo Bisons, a Cardinals affiliate in the International League, Miller was returned to the Phillies. His subsequent stay with the Montreal Royals in the International League was also short and he hung up his spikes for good.

Miller returned to Detroit to enter the insurance business and started his long 33-year career as an insurance agent for the New England Life Insurance Company. His college coach, Lloyd Brazil, needed an assistant in 1963 and Miller decided join the baseball staff part time.

He became the head baseball coach of the UDM Titans in 1965 and served until 2000. Two of his sons played for him at UDM. His son Pat now serves as an assistant coach at Walled Lake (MI) Central High and his son Bob, Jr. is the baseball coach at Redford Union (MI) High.

Miller's 896-780-2 UDM career record ranks him in the top 30 all-time for victories. He was inducted into the UDM Titans Sports Hall of Fame (1979) and the Michigan State Sports Hall of Fame (1999). He and his wife, the former Maureen Maher, were married in 1954 and raised their three sons and a daughter in the Detroit area where they continue to reside.

PAT MULLIN

Detroit Tigers
Outfield • Pinch Hitter
1940-1941 • 1946-1953

"Rookie of the Year? Detroit has the sensational Patrick Mullin in center field but elsewhere in the American League, one looks in vain for an overshadowing recruit. Mullin, batting .362, is easily the pick of the newcomers on form shown to date."

~ writer Sam Greene, June 1941

Pat Mullin was a two-time American League All-Star who spent four of his prime athletic years in the service of his country during World War II. His career was also seriously derailed by a shoulder injury that limited his playing time and eventually diminished his defensive value.

The 6'2" 190-pound left-handed-hitting Mullin enjoyed one of the most impressive individual offensive performances of any major league slugger in the Decade of the 1940s. He accumulated 13 total bases in a single game against the New York Yankees in 1949.

Throwing right-handed, the young Mullin roamed center field, running like a gazelle and showing off an exceptionally strong, accurate throwing arm. One of the fastest outfielders in the AL, he charged ground balls like an infielder and ran the bases with speed and good judgment.

★ ★ ★ ★ ★

Patrick Joseph Mullin was born on November 1, 1917 to Margaret Moore and Francis Edward Mullin in Trotter, Fayette County, Pennsylvania. His parents were both Irish émigrés. The oldest of seven, Mullin grew up in tiny Grindstone about 45 minutes south of Pittsburgh.

While his father worked as a boss in the soft coal mines, the youngster played baseball all day, dreaming of major league stardom. Later he spent two summers with the high-level semi-pro Flint (MI) Buicks and was discovered by chief Detroit Tigers scout A.J. "Wish" Egan.

Mullin starred for the Redstone Township High Black Hawks as an All-Fayette County running back and punter, hoopster and catcher. He considered a football scholarship offer to attend the University of Notre Dame, but signed with the Tigers in August before his senior year.

After he graduated in 1937, the Tigers assigned him to the Lake Charles (LA) Skippers in the Class-D Evangeline League. With his foot speed, Mullin was soon converted to

the outfield never to play a single inning as a pro catcher. He hit a strong .383 with 17 triples and 16 homers.

Advanced to the Beaumont Exporters of the Class-A1 Texas League for 1938 and 1939, Mullin batted a combined .277 in 1,159 at-bats. After he hit 15 homers against International League pitching in 1940 for the Double-A Buffalo (NY) Bisons, he was ready for The Show.

Mullin was called up for his major league debut on September 18, 1940 as a pinch hitter during a 14-0 shellacking of the Athletics. After his cameo with the AL Champion Tigers, he started 1941 back with Buffalo. When Hank Greenberg left for the Army, Mullin was recalled.

As the centerfielder standing in for the injured Barney McCosky, he was the rookie sensation of the league, hitting an impressive .345 in 54 games with a .400 on-base percentage, and slugged .509. He scored 42 runs and had 76 hits, 21 of them for extra bases.

His season was cut short on July 2 in Chicago when he got tangled up with White Sox pitcher Bill "Bullfrog" Dietrich on a play at first base. Trying to avoid Dietrich, he tripped and went airborne, landing heavily on his right shoulder, dislocating it, and was out for the year.

Mullin enlisted in the Army on March 13, 1942 and managed the New Cumberland (PA) Reception Center team for two years. He was then sent to Alabama Special Services H.Q. where his team won the Alabama title. He was also named to Mickey Cochran's All-Service team.

Honorably discharged as a first lieutenant in early 1946, Mullin struggled to re-acclimate with the Tigers. However, he came back to be chosen as a 1947 All-Star, sporting a .470 slugging average and .829 OPS, and was also among American League leaders with 28 doubles and 49 extra base hits.

His finest campaign was 1948. Mullin was the American

G	AB	R	H	2B	3B	HR	RBI	SB	BB	SO	BA	OBP	SLG	TB
864	2848	381	676	106	43	87	385	20	330	312	.271	.358	.453	1129

League All-Star starting centerfielder and leadoff hitter. He hit .288 with 80 RBI and was among the league leaders with 22 triples, 23 homers and 21.6 at-bats per bomb. He slugged .504 and registered a .889 OPS.

On June 26, 1949, Mullin achieved a home run hat trick in front of 62,382 fans at Yankee Stadium. He homered off Vic Raschi... singled... walked... homered off Spec Shea... walked... and homered again off Shea. On deck when the game ended, he had an astounding 13 total bases.

Starting in 1949, Mullin played mostly as a reserve outfielder and pinch hitter because of his shoulder. He made 57 appearances exclusively as a pinch hitter in 1953, his final season. Rookie Al Kaline wore #25 that year, but asked Mullin if he could have his #6 after the season.

Mullin was player-coach for the 1954 Little Rock (AK) Travelers (Southern Association) and player-manager of the 1955 Idaho Falls (ID) Russets (Pioneer League) and 1956 Jamestown (NY) Falcons (Penn-Ontario-New York League). All three teams were Tigers affiliates.

Mullin scouted for the Tigers from 1957 to 1963 when he began a four-year tenure as Detroit's first base coach. After 26 years in the Tigers organization, he was hired to be Joe Adcock's Indians hitting coach for 1967 and then as an Indians scout in 1968. Mullin then worked for the Expos as either a scout or a minor league hitting instructor from 1969 until 1978. He had

a strong influence on Gary Carter and Andre Dawson early in their careers and as Montreal's hitting coach from 1979 to 1981. He called it quits in 1985 after 48 years in the game.

Mullin and his wife, Geraldine Wensing, enjoyed a long marriage and raised three sons. He was inducted into the

Mid-Monongahela Valley All Sports Hall of Fame (1952) and the Fayette County Sports Hall of Fame (2012). Mullin died of lung cancer on August 14, 1999 in Brownsville, Pennsylvania at age 81 and is buried at Brownsville's Lafayette Memorial Park.

STAN MUSIAL

St. Louis Cardinals
Outfield • First Base

1941-44 • 1946-63

> "No man has even been
> a perfect ballplayer.
> Stan Musial, however, is the
> closest thing to perfection
> in the game today.
> ... He's certainly one of the
> great hitters of all time."
>
> ~ Ty Cobb

The greatest player ever to wear a Cardinal uniform and one of the iconic immortals of the game, Stan Musial was the most feared batsman in the Senior Circuit, leading his league in more hitting categories than anyone but Babe Ruth or Ty Cobb.

The sweet-swinging Musial owned 29 NL and 17 big-league records when he retired and still holds Cardinal marks for hits, homers and RBI. In 20 All-Star games, he hit .317 (20-for-63) with a record six home runs, eight extra-base hits and 40 total bases.

The left-handed 6' 175-pound Musial attained seven NL batting crowns, three NL MVP awards and three World Series title rings with his trademark peek-a-boo batting stance described as like a boy peeking around a corner to see if the police were coming.

Famous for his consistency and sustained brilliance, Musial recorded 1815 hits at home and 1815 hits away. He did not dip below .310 in his first 17 seasons. He respected his gift and appreciated it profoundly, missing only 16 games in his first 13 full years.

The most obliging of superstars, Musial was a warm, gregarious gentleman with a perpetually sunny disposition. His grace and humanity set Musial apart, as much as his virtuosity with his M159 *Louisville Slugger*. The game's most beloved player, he was a selfless teammate, never questioned umpires, and was never tossed out of a single game.

★ ★ ★ ★ ★

Stanislaus Francis Musial was born in Donora, Pennsylvania in the Monongahela Valley on November 21, 1920. He was the 5th child of six and first son of Mary Lancos, a Catholic Czech émigré, and Lukasz Musial, a steelworker born in Poland.

In his first outing as a 1937 Donora High junior, Mu-

sial struck out 17 batters in a seven inning game. Months later, he signed with the Cardinals and spent the next two summers with the Williamson (WV) Colts in the Class-D Mountain States League.

He wed his high school sweetheart, Lillian Labash, on May 25, 1940 (They would be married almost 72 years and raise four children). That pivotal year he posted an 18-5 pitching record for the Class-D Daytona Beach Islanders of the Florida State League.

After Musial injured his shoulder badly in August on a diving outfield play, manager Dickie Kerr converted him to the outfield. He went from Class-C Springfield to Double-A Rochester to his debut on September 17, 1941, and went on to hit .426 in 12 games.

Musial played a key role in his 1942 rookie year as the Redbirds dumped the Yankees in the Fall Classic. In 1943, he hit .357 to win his first batting title, fanning only 18 times, and led the NL with 220 hits, 48 doubles and 20 triples as the NL's MVP.

The Cardinals were World Series champs again in 1944 as Musial topped the NL with 51 doubles and 197 hits, batting .347. After serving in the Navy in 1945, he returned to lead his team to another Series title with his second MVP and batting title, hitting .365.

Musial's 1948 was a year for the ages. Missing a Triple Crown by one rained-out home run, he led in *every other major offensive category*, hitting .376, with a .450 OBA, 135 runs, 230 hits, 46 doubles, 18 triples, 131 RBI, 429 total bases, while slugging .702.

He was so phenomenal in 1948 versus the Dodgers, repeatedly firing lasers off the Ebbets Field right field scoreboard and lining home runs over it, that the partisan Brooklynites started referring to him as "that Man." Musial had become "Stan the Man."

G	AB	R	H	2B	3B	HR	RBI	SB	BB	SO	BA	OBP	SLG	TB
3026	10972	1949	3630	725	177	475	1951	78	1599	696	.331	.417	.559	6134

He continued to rule the Senior Circuit, winning batting titles from 1950 to 1952. On May 2, 1954, The Man hammered five home runs in a twin bill against the Giants at Sportsman's Park to set a major league record for most round trippers in a single day.

Before the 1957 season, owner Gussie Busch announced that no other Cardinal would ever wear his #6 again. After garnering his last batting title in 1957 at .351, he hit a mortal .283 his last five seasons. However, in his penultimate 1962 year, he revived his old stroke to hit .330 at age 41. Musial singled in his last at-bat on September 29, 1963.

President Lyndon Johnson appointed him the National Director of the President's Council on Physical Fitness in 1964. Abidingly loyal to his franchise, Musial was in the Cardinals' front office for 25 years and GM for the 1967 World Series Champions.

He was a presence in countless St. Louis civic and charitable endeavors. He might pull out his harmonica and play "Take Me Out to the Ball Game" or quickly jump into his patented stance while greeting fans with his familiar "whatayasay, whatayasay."

Musial was only the 4th player in history to be voted into the Baseball Hall of Fame on the first ballot in 1969. He received 317 votes out of 340 (92.3%), bringing into question what the other 23 hapless writers were thinking. In 2010, he was awarded the Presidential Medal of Freedom, the highest honor an American civilian can receive.

There are two statues of Musial outside the new Busch Stadium. Below the older statue are etched the words of Ford Frick: *"Here stands baseball's perfect warrior. Here stands baseball's perfect knight."* One of baseball's great ambassadors and the most cherished Cardinal of them all, Stan "The Man" Musial passed away at 92 on January 19, 2013, at his home in Ladue, Missouri surrounded by his family.

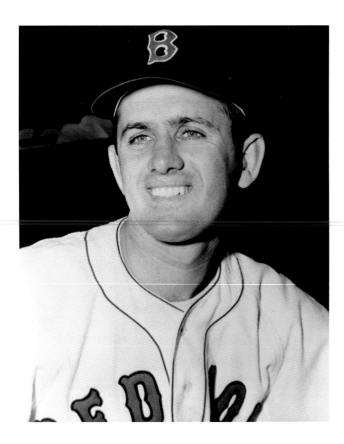

MEL PARNELL

BOSTON RED SOX
LEFT-HANDED PITCHER

1947-1956

"With a little luck, Mel would have had 200 victories easily and if he hadn't been plagued with his injuries during the 1954-55-56 seasons, Mel would have had 250 victories. He was a great pitcher as far as I'm concerned."'

~ teammate Ted Williams

Stylish Mel Parnell has more wins, more innings pitched, and more games started than any southpaw in Red Sox history, ahead of Hall of Famers Babe Ruth and Lefty Grove. He was the rare lefty who could be successful at Fenway Park, going 71-30. Parnell's win total ranks second in Red Sox annals behind only Roger Clemens and Cy Young - each with 192 victories.

With its intimidating Green Monster left field wall less than 300 feet from home plate, Fenway has been a nightmare for most left-handed pitchers. With an effortless delivery, Parnell served up an array of darting inside sliders, split-fingered fastballs, and off-speed screwballs. His slider looked like a fastball, moving in on hitters' fists to shatter many a *Louisville Slugger*.

Parnell consistently helped his cause as a good-hitting pitcher. Batting over .300 twice, he sometimes appeared as high as seventh in the lineup. Manager Lou Boudreau allowed him to stay in games longer because of his hitting prowess and even used him as a pinch hitter.

After one of his many victories at Fenway where shortstop teammate Johnny Pesky had hit the deciding round tripper near the short right field foul pole, Parnell baptized the stanchion "Pesky's Pole." It remains a cherished part of Fenway Park and Red Sox lore to present day.

★ ★ ★ ★ ★

Melvin Lloyd Parnell was born to Anna May Trauth and Patrick Parnell on June 13, 1922 in New Orleans, Louisiana. He was a hitting and pitching star for Samuel Jarvis Peters High on one of the best prep baseball teams ever assembled in the Crescent City area. Future big-league shortstop George Strickland, Parnell and five others went on to play professional baseball.

Red Sox scout Ed Montague signed Parnell in 1941 and sent him to Class-D Centreville (MD) in the Eastern Shore League. He made a statement for the 1942 Class-C Canton (OH) Terriers (Middle Atlantic League), going 16-9 with a 1.59 ERA in 204 innings. On August 31, Parnell persevered in an 18-inning victory over Zanesville, throwing over 300 pitches.

With World War II raging, Parnell enlisted in the Army Air Force and was based stateside as part of a flight training command. Re-entering baseball with Class-A Scranton of the Eastern League in 1946, he went 13-4 with a 1.30 ERA and seemed ready for the Big Time.

After a cameo with the Triple-A Louisville Colonels in the American Association, Red Sox manager Joe Cronin gave him his major league debut on April 20, 1947. His first win came ten days later over Tigers pitcher Hal Newhouser, 7-1, and he appeared in 15 games as a rookie.

Now experienced and brimming with confidence, Parnell posted 15 victories in 1948. Going deep into most of his starts because the team lacked a reliable closer, he completed 16 games and pitching 212 innings. Despite a 96-win year, Boston finished runner up to the Indians.

Although the Cy Young Award had not yet been instituted, Parnell's 1949 season was that kind of masterpiece. It was his best campaign, as he paced the league with 27 complete games, 25 wins and 295⅓ innings. He put up a career-low 2.77 ERA with four shutouts and was chosen the AL's All-Star game starter, finishing fourth in the MVP balloting.

The Red Sox were one game ahead of the Yankees with two games to go. Each team had two aces. Boston brought Parnell (25-7) and Ellis Kinder (23-6) and the Yankees countered with Allie Reynolds (17-6) and Vic Raschi (21-10). The Yankees won both games in a classic series.

Junior Circuit All-Star manager Casey Stengel oddly left him off the 1951 team, although he was 5-0 versus Stengel's Yankees and the leading pitcher in all of baseball with a 12-4 mark at the break. He finished at 18-10 and followed with another 18-win year as a 1951 All-Star.

G	IP	W	L	PCT	SHO	GS	CG	H	ER	SO	BB	ERA
289	1752.2	123	75	.621	20	232	113	1715	682	732	758	3.50

Parnell's last great year was 1953 when he delivered a superb 21-8 record, a 3.06 ERA and a career-high 136 strikeouts. In early 1954 at the plate against former teammate Mickey McDermott (traded to the Washington Senators the previous winter), Parnell was hit by his friend's pitch, breaking the ulna bone in his left arm. Ironically, McDermott and Parnell were scheduled to have dinner together that evening. The injury resulted in elbow problems and led to two operations in the last three years of his career.

During his final season on July 14, 1956, Parnell pitched a no-hitter at Fenway versus the White Sox, winning 4-0. It was the first for a Red Sox hurler since Howard Ehmke in 1923. It would be over a half century until another Red Sox lefty threw a no-hitter (Jon Lester in 2008). The no-hitter would prove to be the final highlight of his career. Fighting a torn muscle in his pitching arm, he made his last major league appearance on September 29, 1956.

Parnell went on to be the head coach of the 1958 Tulane University Green Wave and served as the general manager of his hometown New Orleans Pelicans of the Double-A Southern Association in 1959. He skippered a series of Red Sox minor league clubs from 1961 to 1963.

The always gracious Parnell went behind the microphone as a radio announcer with the Red Sox (1965-68), working mostly with Curt Gowdy, and with the White Sox in 1969, teaming with Jack Drees. He later was a popular guest at autograph signings and was mentioned in Terry Cashman's 1981 nostalgic song "Talkin' Baseball." Parnell was inducted into the Louisiana Sports Hall of Fame in 1963 and the Boston Red Sox Hall of Fame in 1997.

Parnell and his wife, Velma Buras, raised four children and enjoyed three grandchildren over 61 years of marriage. Residing in Lakeview, New Orleans, he passed away on March 20, 2012, following a long bout with cancer. He is interred at the Lake Lawn Metairie Cemetery.

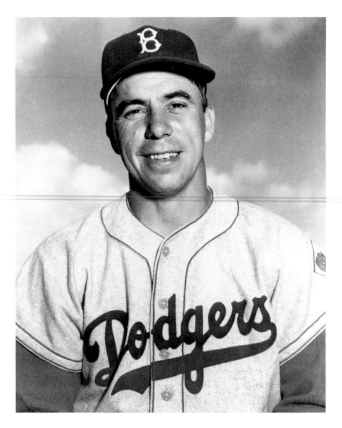

PEE WEE REESE

Brooklyn & Los Angeles Dodgers Shortstop

1940-1942 • 1946-1958

"[Reese] came over and stood beside me for a while. He didn't say a word but he looked over at the chaps who were yelling at me through him and just stared. He was standing by me, I could tell you that. I will never forget it."

~ teammate Jackie Robinson on the "Crosley Field Gesture"

The captain leader of the legendary *Boys of Summer* Brooklyn teams, Pee Wee Reese was the heart and soul of seven National League champion teams and the 1955 World Series titlist. He played every inning in seven Fall Classics. No player outside of the Yankees has ever seen action in more Series for the same team. He gained lasting acclaim for his support of Jackie Robinson in his mission to break baseball's color line.

A ten-time All-Star, Reese was the premier National League shortstop in baseball's post World War II Golden Era. A rock solid fielder who averaged 148 games per year in his first full 13 seasons, he led the National League in putouts four years and still ranks high all-time in putouts and double plays.

The prototype leadoff hitter with great bat control, pitch selection and bunting acumen, Reese was also a clutch home run threat. One of the smartest base runners of his time, he scored more runs than any Dodger in franchise history and stole 252 bases.

★ ★ ★ ★ ★

Harold Henry Reese was born to Emma and Carl Reese on July 23, 1918 in Meade County, Kentucky on a farm. His father became a detective for the Louisville & Nashville Railroad and moved the family to segregated Louisville when he was seven. He became a marbles champion at 14, and the handle "Pee Wee" (a small marble) stuck.

As a 5'4" 120-pound senior at DuPont Manual High, Reese was too small to be a pro prospect. After graduating in 1936, he took a job splicing cable for the Kentucky Telephone Company and played on the New Covenant Presbyterian Church team. In late 1937, the now 5'10" 155-pound Reese, signed with his hometown Louisville Colonels.

The Colonels were purchased along with a Red Sox working agreement in 1938. Boston shortstop-manager

Joe Cronin was sent to scout Reese, but wasn't ready to yield his job and undervalued him. Reese was sold to the Brooklyn Dodgers on July 18, 1939.

Manager Leo Durocher gave him his big-league debut on April 23, 1940, but injuries relegated him to only 84 games. Reese started for the 1941 NL Champs, showed inexperience, but emerged as a 1942 All-Star, leading the NL in putouts and assists.

He enlisted in the Navy in early 1943 and shipped out to the Pacific Theater in the 3rd Marine Division. Brooklyn struggled during his years in the service, but upon Reese's return, the 1946 team rebounded to finish just two games behind the Cardinals.

When the influential Reese met Jackie Robinson in early 1947, it was the first time he had ever shaken hands with a black man. Yet, the soft-spoken Dodger leader rejected a spring training player boycott petition and loyally defended him as his friend.

On May 13, 1947 at Crosley Field, Robinson was enduring sadistic verbal taunts and threats from fans and some Cincinnati players during infield practice. Reese suddenly stopped and walked slowly across the infield to first base to stand with Robinson. He put his left arm around Jackie's shoulder and just starred at the hecklers. This clear gesture of support silenced the Reds bench-jockeys *and* the crowd and was a turning point.

Reese went on to hit .284 in 1947 with 16 homers, a National League-high 104 walks, and a career-high .426 slugging percentage. By 1948, he and Robinson had formed one of the most dynamic double play combinations in baseball history.

He paced the NL with 132 runs scored in 1949 and 30 steals in 1952, the year he enjoyed his finest Fall Classic, batting .345. The 1953 team won 105 games and Reese

G	AB	R	H	2B	3B	HR	RBI	SB	BB	SO	BA	OBP	SLG	TB
2166	8058	1338	2170	330	80	126	885	232	1210	890	.269	.366	.377	3038

scored 108 runs, but the Dodgers once more came up short against the Bronx Bombers.

Again battling the Yankees in the 1955 World Series, Reese helped save the title in Game 7. He fielded the cut-off throw from Sandy Amoros after his famous catch, spun from short left field, and rifled a throw to first to double off the sliding Gil McDougald.

Reese gave way to Charlie Neal as the starting short-stop in early 1957, but joined the Dodgers for one last season in California. He played in 59 games and then retired to coach his team for one year, the 1959 championship season, earning a second ring.

Reese did television broadcasting for CBS and NBC in the 1960s, as well as radio play-by-play of the World Series in 1967 and 1968 and for the Cincinnati Reds in 1969 and 1970. Hillerich & Bradsby, the makers of *Louisville Slugger* bats, later hired him as Director of the College & Pro Baseball Staff.

He earned the Lou Gehrig Memorial Award in 1956 for his character and integrity on and off the field. Reese was elected to the National Baseball Hall of Fame by the Veterans Committee in 1984. The Dodgers retired his uniform #1 and now display it below the Dodger Stadium pavilion roof beyond left field.

A bronze statue of the "Little Colonel" stands at the main entrance to Louisville Slugger Field, home of the Louisville Colonels. At the Brooklyn Cyclones' KeySpan Park on Coney Island, a bronze sculpture pays homage to his "Crosley Field Gesture."

Pee Wee Reese valiantly battled lung and prostate cancer during his waning years. He finally succumbed on August 14, 1999 at his Louisville home at age 81. He was laid to rest at the Resthaven Memorial Park Cemetery in Louisville.

PHIL RIZZUTO

New York Yankees
Shortstop

1941-1942 • 1946-1956

"Phil Rizzuto serves as the ultimate reminder that physical stature has little bearing on the size of a person's heart. Nothing was ever given to Phil, and he used every ounce of his ability to become one of the greatest Yankees to ever wear this uniform."

~ Derek Jeter

Phil Rizzuto was an offensive sparkplug and defensive stalwart for New York Yankee teams that marched to ten American League pennants and seven World Series championships. *The Sporting News'* top major league shortstop for four straight years from 1949 to 1952, Rizzuto was a five-time All-Star who perfected the bunt as an offensive weapon. He became known as "The Scooter" for the way he scampered the base paths, emblematic of his hustling, heads-up style of play.

★　★　★　★　★

Philip Francis Rizzuto was born September 25, 1917 in Brooklyn, New York. After trying out with the hometown Dodgers in 1935, Brooklyn manager Casey Stengel dismissed him as too small, saying, "Go get a shoeshine box, kid, you can't play." When he auditioned for the Yankees in 1937, scouts saw vital intangibles, signed him, and by 1940, the gritty Rizzuto was *The Sporting News* Minor League Player of the Year.

With invaluable mentoring by incumbent shortstop Frankie Crosetti, he debuted in the major leagues on April 14, 1941. Joe DiMaggio's roommate during the Yankee Clipper's historic 56-game hitting streak, Rizzuto hit .307 in 133 games. He and second baseman Joe Gordon quickly jelled into a formidable double play combo as the Yankees beat the Dodgers in the 1941 Fall Classic. In the 1942 World Series, he led all hitters with eight hits and a .381 average before devoting three prime years to the United States Navy.

Upon his return in 1946, the sure-handed 5'6" 150-pound Scooter became the bellwether of the Yankees infield, leading the American League three times in double plays; twice in fielding and putouts; and once

in assists, and committing only 263 errors. He took part in 1,217 double plays (second all-time) and finished second in the AL all-time in fielding at .958 with 8,148 total chances, 3,219 putouts and 4,666 assists.

His peak years were 1949 and 1950, when he flourished at leadoff. Before the 1949 campaign, Stengel was appointed Yankee manager, who watched Rizzuto excel and finish second in the MVP balloting. His pinnacle was 1950 when he established many personal-bests, hitting .324 with 125 runs scored, 200 hits, 36 doubles, 66 RBI, 92 walks, a .418 on-base percentage and a .439 slugging average. Defensively, Rizzuto went 58 consecutive games without an error. He was the American League Most Valuable Player and *The Sporting News* Major League Player of the Year. Stengel would later admit, "He is the greatest shortstop I have ever seen in my entire baseball career..."

The most dramatic exhibition of his bunting genius came on September 17, 1951. With just a dozen games to go and the Bombers and Indians tied for the league lead, Rizzuto came to bat facing right-handed Indians ace Bob Lemon in the bottom of the ninth inning, game tied, 1-1. With DiMaggio on third base, Rizzuto took a called strike and argued the call, all the while signaling Joltin' Joe that a squeeze play was on.

On the next pitch, DiMaggio sprinted down the line too early and Lemon detected the play, throwing a high, hard fastball behind Rizzuto. When he bunted the ball, he was airborne, body contorted, and would have been hit in the face had he not made contact. Rizzuto had put his *Louisville Slugger* up just in time to lay down a fair bunt toward first base, allowing DiMaggio to cross the plate with the winning run. Stengel labeled it, "the

G	AB	R	H	2B	3B	HR	RBI	SB	BB	SO	BA	OBP	SLG	TB
1661	5816	877	1588	239	62	38	563	149	651	398	.273	.351	.355	2065

greatest play I ever saw."

The next month, Rizzuto hit a clutch .320 in the 1951 World Series and won the Babe Ruth Award as the top player. Overall, he holds Fall Classic records at shortstop for games played, putouts, assists and double plays and ranks in the top ten with 21 runs scored, 45 hits, 30 walks and ten stolen bases. Rizzuto competed in a World Series Game 7 three times (1947, 1952 & 1955), hitting an incredible .455 in those ultimate games.

The diminutive warrior began to wear down after a strong 1953 championship year, and he became a part-time player in 1955 and 1956. Rizzuto was released without warning on Old-Timers' Day, August 25, 1956 but wisely masked his irritation at the way it was handled. Almost immediately the Yankees offered him a broadcasting job. For the next four decades, Rizzuto earned a devoted following with his quirky style and high-pitched trademark call, "Holy Cow!" He was a folksy storyteller whom fans loved as they would a delightful, eccentric uncle.

The Scooter's uniform #10 was retired at Yankee Stadium in 1985 and a plaque in the Stadium's Monument Park immortalizes his career. After a persuasive presentation by Ted Williams before the Veterans Committee, Rizzuto was inducted into the National Baseball Hall of Fame in 1994.

Rizzuto and his beloved wife Cora Anne lived a wonderful life with countless friends. Among other charities, he raised millions of dollars for St. Joseph's School for the Blind, donating the proceeds from many of his ventures. Rizzuto died of pneumonia at 89 in West Orange, New Jersey on August 13, 2007.

JACKIE ROBINSON

BROOKLYN DODGERS
INFIELD

1947-1956

*"He was the greatest
competitor I have ever seen.
I've seen him beat a team
with his bat, his ball, his
glove, his feet, and, in
a game in Chicago one
time, with his mouth."*

~ teammate Duke Snider

A true American icon, Jackie Robinson changed baseball forever as the first African American to play in the major leagues in the 20th century. He became a symbol of hope and pride for his people and had a major cultural impact beyond the playing field. Robinson gave momentum and inspiration to the Civil Rights Movement of the 1960s.

In his short epic career, he sparked six National League pennant winners, hit over .300 six consecutive years, and was named to six straight NL All-Star squads. Robinson was also the second baseman on four *The Sporting News* Major League All-Star teams.

The most aggressive base runner of his time, he disrupted entire defenses with his daring leads. Robinson was thrown out just 30 times in his career, while stealing home an amazing 19 times. A regular at four positions, he was one of the most versatile players ever to wear a major league uniform.

* * * * *

Jack Roosevelt Robinson was born on January 31, 1919 in rural Albany, Dougherty County, Georgia to Mallie and Jerry Robinson. His father abandoned the family when he was six months old and his mother, a woman of character, moved her five children to Pasadena, California shortly thereafter. He was raised in relative poverty.

Robinson excelled in football, basketball, baseball and track & field at John Muir Technical High, Pasadena City College and as UCLA's first four-sport star. He was the greatest all-around athlete in UCLA history as a 5'11½" 195-pound All-American halfback, NCAA long-jump champion and two-time conference hoops scoring leader.

Doing his patriotic duty in World War II, Robinson was finally commissioned as an U. S. Army second lieutenant stationed at Fort Hood, Texas. Never one to back down, he refused to move to the back of a military bus and was arrested and court-martialed, but later acquitted of all charges.

After his honorable discharge in late 1944, Robinson played shortstop for the 1945 Negro League Kansas City Monarchs and started emulating the bold base running style of Cool Papa Bell. Brooklyn Dodger president Branch Rickey first saw his fierce competitive fire there and noted his clean lifestyle which included no tobacco or alcohol. Sensing Robinson was right for the noble experiment, Rickey signed him in late 1945, but not before he promised Rickey he would not react in the face of racial taunts.

He took withering abuse from fans and players in the 1946 Florida spring camp and performed poorly. However, when his Montreal (QC) Royals opened against the Jersey City (NJ) Giants, he went 4-for-5 with a homer and hit in ten of his first 12 games. He went on to win the International League batting crown (.349) and the MVP award.

At the age of 28, Robinson debuted in the big time on April 15, 1947. A group of teammates signed a petition demanding his removal. Opposing players threatened to boycott the Dodgers. Base runners purposely spiked him. He received death threats. In his first 37 games, he was hit by six pitches and knocked down in almost every game.

But others defended him, including Commissioner A.B. "Happy" Chandler, National League president Ford C. Frick, slugger Hank Greenberg and Dodger captain

G	AB	R	H	2B	3B	HR	RBI	SB	BB	SO	BA	OBP	SLG	TB
1382	4877	947	1518	273	54	137	734	197	740	291	.311	.409	.474	2310

Pee Wee Reese. In one poignant episode on June 21 in Cincinnati when bench jockeys and fans were spewing insults at Robinson, Reese stopped the workout, slowly walked over to first base, and put his arm around his valiant teammate in un-ambiguous support.

Robinson used this bigotry to fuel his drive, summoning all of his powers to pace his team to a pennant. As the inaugural 1947 Major League Rookie of the Year, he hit .297 with 12 home runs, 19 bunt hits, 125 runs scored and an NL-leading 29 stolen bases.

Starting in 1948, he led NL second basemen in fielding and double plays for four consecutive years. He reached the height of his prowess with his thick-handled *Louisville Slugger* in 1949, winning the batting title (.342) and the NL Most Valuable Player award.

Compelled by his example, the Dodgers were National League Champions in four of Robinson's last five seasons. The Boys of Summer elevated their games and brought Brooklyn and Ebbets Field its only World Series Championship in 1955.

Robinson was dealt to the rival Giants in January of 1957 but decided not to accept the trade and retired. Devoting his time to business and social causes, he helped establish the black-owned Freedom National Bank and was a spokesman for the NAACP.

Jackie Robinson was inducted into the National Baseball Hall of Fame in 1962 as its first African American member. On the 50th anniversary of his debut in 1997, all baseball paid him tribute and honor by permanently retiring his uniform #42.

Robinson died of a heart attack on October 24, 1972 in Stamford, Connecticut. The great man often stated, "A life is not important except in the impact that it has on others." His life will be remembered as one of the most influential in American history.

AL ROSEN

CLEVELAND INDIANS
THIRD BASE

1947-1956

"That young feller, that feller's a ball player. He'll give you the works every time. Gets all the hits, gives you the hard tag in the field. That feller's a real competitor, you bet your sweet [curse] life."

~ *Yankees manager Casey Stengel*

One of the greatest Jewish American baseball stars, Al Rosen was the unanimous 1953 American League MVP, missing the immortality of a Triple Crown on the last day of the season. A four-time All-Star, he led the AL twice each in home runs and RBI, driving in 100 or more runs five straight years. His five All-Star circuit clouts matched a record set by Ted Williams.

He was the first top Jewish player to decline to play on the Jewish High Holy Days. Yet as an expert boxer, the 5'10" 185-pound Rosen stood his ground on the playing field. When someone on the opposing bench spewed anti-Semitic invective in his direction, his style was to walk calmly over to the dugout and call out the taunter. No one ever accepted his invitation.

* * * * *

Albert Leonard Rosen was born in Spartanburg, South Carolina on leap year February 29, 1924, to Rose and Louis Rosen. After his father abandoned the family, his mother moved farther south to Florida to provide her asthmatic three-year old and his little brother with a drier climate.

Raised by his mother, aunt, and grandmother, he grew up in rough southwest Miami, now the heart of Little Havana. His was the only Jewish family in the neighborhood so he grew up engaged in countless fisticuffs defending his heritage. His nose was broken 11 times.

After starring for Florida Military Academy in St. Petersburg, Rosen was a standout for the University of Florida Gators in 1941 and 1942. Following the 1942 collegiate season, he signed with the Indians and hit .307 for Class-D Thomasville of the North Carolina State League.

Late in 1942, Rosen enlisted in the U. S. Navy, and spent almost four years fighting in the South Pacific during World War II. At Okinawa, he navigated an assault boat in the initial landing in one of the War's bloodiest battles. He left the Navy as a lieutenant.

Rekindling his baseball career with the 1946 Pittsfield (MA) Electrics of the Class-C Canadian-American League, Rosen went from a substitute to hitting .323 and leading the C-AL with 16 home runs and 86 RBI. He was called the "Hebrew Hammer" as the league's top rookie.

In 1947, Rosen produced perhaps the finest MVP season in Texas League history. At Oklahoma City, he led the Double-A circuit with a .349 average, 186 hits, 47 doubles, 83 extra-base hits and 141 RBI to earn himself a big-league debut on September 10 at age 23.

Indians third baseman Ken Keltner was still entrenched in 1948 so Rosen played for the Triple-A Kansas City (MO) Blues. He hit five consecutive home runs in late July as the American Association Rookie of the Year, was called up late, and earned a World Series ring.

After a solid 1949 with the San Diego Padres in the Pacific Coast League, Rosen finally got his chance in 1950. He paced the AL with 116 RBI, 100 runs scored and 37 bombs- a Junior Circuit rookie record that lasted 37 years. And he topped AL third basemen with 322 assists.

Rosen competed in a league-high 154 games in 1951 and tied a record with four grand slams, but he was unhappy with his .265 average. Over the winter, he worked out hard and came back to lead the AL with 105 RBI and 297 total bases and hit .302 with 38 home runs.

Still this was only a prelude to Rosen's magnificent 1953 MVP year. His 43 home runs and 145 RBI assured him AL titles, but he lost the batting crown in his last at-bat. Rosen had ostensibly beaten out a hit, but was called out for missing first. His 3-for-5 final put him at .3355592 just behind Mickey Vernon at .337171. Rosen also led the AL with a .613 slugging average, 115 runs scored, 367 total bases, as well as an AL-high 338 assists and 38 double plays.

The loaded 1954 Indians set an all-time record with 111 wins. Rosen was a central figure in that success. He hit an

G	AB	R	H	2B	3B	HR	RBI	SB	BB	SO	BA	OBP	SLG	TB
1044	3725	603	1063	165	20	192	717	39	587	385	.285	.384	.495	1844

even .300 with 24 home runs and 102 RBI, despite playing most of the year with a broken finger. He also drilled consecutive homers as the 1954 All-Star Game MVP.

In a head scratcher, Cleveland minority owner and general manager Hank Greenberg, Rosen's boyhood idol, rewarded Rosen's fifth straight 100 RBI season by cutting his salary from $42,500 to $37,500 for 1955. Although he went on to hit 21 home runs, it left a bad taste.

Rosen hit only .267 with 15 home runs in 1956 due to nagging injuries. There were also the press insinuations that it was improper that a Jewish player was allowed to play through a slump on a Jewish-owned team. At the young age of 32, a proud Rosen decided to retire when Greenberg sought to slash his salary another $5,000 after the season.

He began a 17-year career as a stockbroker, but kept his hand in as an Indians batting instructor and sat on the club's board of directors. Back in baseball as the Yankees president in 1978, he let go "Bronx Zoo" manager Billy Martin after his infamous remarks about George Steinbrenner and Reggie Jackson and then hired ex-teammate Bob Lemon. The Yankees went on to win, but when the micro-managing "Boss" rehired Martin, Rosen resigned on July 19. 1979.

After five turbulent years as the Astros GM, Rosen was appointed president and GM of the last-place Giants for 1986. Finally given autonomy, he revived the franchise, winning the 1987 NL West and 1989 pennant. He was 1987 Major League Baseball Executive of the Year.

The Indians hosted a special tribute at Jacobs Field in 1994 honoring Rosen's *magnum opus* of 1953. He is a member of the Cleveland Indians Hall of Fame (2006) as well as the Cleveland, Jewish Sports, and Texas League Halls of Fame. He and his second wife Rita Kallman lived in Rancho Mirage, California until he passed away there at 91 on March 13, 2015.

SIBBY SISTI

Sibbi Sisti was one of the first true utility players in major league history, having played every position except pitcher and catcher. His hard-nosed play, his affability and his perseverance in the face of numerous injuries made him an all-time Boston Braves fan favorite.

The 5' 11" 175-pound Sisti was a total team player. Never a star but always critical to the success of the Braves over the long 154-game big-league grind, he came ready to play and worked hard to master the game's nuances-traits that won him the confidence of his managers.

Sisti brought value as a skillful bunter and utilized his marvelous speed offensively, but his livelihood was dependent on his ability to play seven positions well, at times with no notice. He dealt well with the pressure of knowing that his career rode on his excellent glove work.

★ ★ ★ ★ ★

Sebastian Daniel Sisti was born to Rose E. Caruso and Daniel J. Sisti in Buffalo, Erie County, New York on July 26, 1920. He was the only child of parents of Italian descent, growing up of modest means in Buffalo near Niagara Falls just south of the Canadian border.

Sisti starred in football, basketball and baseball at Buffalo's Canisius High School and later was chosen the Crusaders Athlete of the Decade. As a 17-year-old junior, Sisti signed with Boston Bees Buffalo-area scout Jack Onslow and agreed not to play football his senior year.

After graduating in the spring of 1938, he began in professional baseball as a third baseman with the Hartford (CT) Chiefs of the Eastern League where he batted .293. Asked to play full time at second base in 1939, Sisti hit a solid .312 (62-for-199) in 54 games.

In June, Bees shortstop Eddie Miller and centerfielder Aloysius Simmons had collided chasing a blooper into short center with Miller fracturing his ankle. When others went down as well, the 18-year-old Sisti unexpectedly found himself the youngest player in the major leagues.

On July 21, he got his first at-bat in the ninth inning versus the Cubs in front of a sparse Braves Field crowd of only 2,797. He attempted an unsuccessful drag bunt off veteran Charlie Root but went on to see action in 63 games, playing second base, third base and shortstop.

Manager Casey Stengel chose him as his starting third baseman for 1940 and 1941. Sisti batted .251 and .259 respectively. In 1941, the Bees changed their name back to the Braves but it didn't prevent the team from finishing seventh again out of eight National League teams.

Sisti started 124 games at second base in 1942 before enlisting in the United States Coast Guard on December 11. He served at the Coast Guard Station in Seattle, Washington, played on the Repair Yard baseball team, and was honorably discharged in October of 1945.

Sisti was sent to the Triple-A Indianapolis (IN) Indians after only one game with the Braves in 1946. The American Association batting champion at .343 and league leader with 203 hits and 14 triples, he added 99 runs scored and 86 runs batted in as *The Sporting News* 1946 Minor League Player of the Year.

Sisti had more than earned his way back to Boston and enjoyed a great start in 1947. Lunging for a grounder in a July game against the Reds, he landed awkwardly on his left shoulder, suffered ruptured ligaments, and was out for over a month. He hit .281 in 56 games.

The fully recuperated Sisti and rookie Alvin Dark battled for the Braves shortstop job in early 1948 before skipper Billy Southworth handed Dark the post. However, on July 8 second baseman Eddie Stanky sustained a broken ankle. The ready Sisti patiently awaited his call.

On July 31, the first place Braves trailed the Cardinals, 6-4, at Braves Field in the bottom of the ninth with one out. With bases jammed, Sisti pinch-hit against

> *"On the few occasions when [Sisti] seemed to have a job wrapped up and won, he got hurt. When Sisti gets hurt, he does the job completely. The most sewn-up athlete in baseball, he carries the scars of 75 stitches on his carcass, giving him the title of 'The Embroidered Man.'"*
>
> ~ *sportswriter Al Hirshberg*

G	AB	R	H	2B	3B	HR	RBI	SB	BB	SO	BA	OBP	SLG	TB
1016	2999	401	732	121	19	27	260	30	283	440	.244	.313	.324	972

pitcher Jim Hearn and hammered the ball to deep right-center for a dramatic walk-off, three-run triple.

The clutch three-bagger got him his old job back at second. Sisti was a major factor in the team's first NL pennant since 1914, making only six errors in 44 games and batting close to .300. But when Stanky came back, Sisti saw almost no action in the Fall Classic against the Indians.

He remained with the Braves when they moved to Milwaukee in 1953 and retired on June 6, 1954 to be a Braves coach. He managed the 1955 Provincial League Quebec Braves, 1956 Big State League champion Corpus Christi Clippers, 1957 Texas League Austin Senators, the 1958 Pacific Coast League Sacramento (CA) Solons, and the 1959 Sally League Jacksonville (FL) Braves. He also coached for his hometown Buffalo Bisons and the 1969 AL Seattle Pilots.

Sisti had a cameo role in the 1984 film *The Natural* starring Robert Redford which was filmed in Buffalo's old War Memorial Stadium. He played the Pittsburgh Pirates manager and was also a technical advisor to make certain it depicted the true feel of 1940s baseball.

Sisti was a lifelong resident of Buffalo where he raised five children with his wife Norine. In retirement, Sisti kept connections with his former colleagues and appeared in golf events with former major-leaguers where he enjoyed reminiscing and telling baseball stories.

"The Pride of Buffalo," Sisti is a member of the Buffalo Baseball Hall of Fame and the Greater Buffalo Sports Hall of Fame. He was one of four 1994 charter inductees into the Boston Braves Hall of Fame along with Johnny Sain, fellow Buffalo native Warren Spahn and Tommy Holmes. Sibby Sisti passed away on April 24, 2006 at the age of 85 in Amherst, New York near Buffalo, and was interred in the Mount Calvary Cemetery in Cheektowaga, New York.

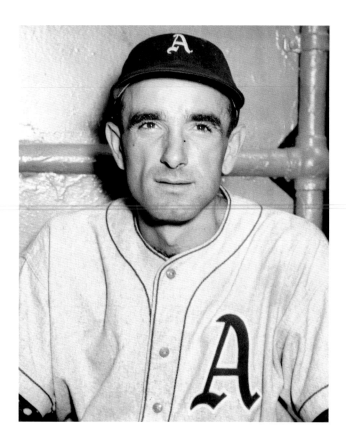

PETE SUDER

PHILADELPHIA & KANSAS CITY ATHLETICS
INFIELD

1941-1943 • 1946-1954

"A long time from now when
they're telling of how so and
so could 'get two' with no
strain, we'll think of the days
of Connie Mack's A's and of
*Joost and **Suder** and Fain."*

~ closing stanza of the poem
by Dick Armstrong

Pete Suder was best known as a marvelous defensive second baseman. He was so agile, he acknowledged that no base runner ever took him out sliding into second to break up a double play. Connie Mack's legendary Athletic infield of third baseman Hank Majeski, shortstop Eddie Joost, second baseman Suder and first baseman Ferris Fain combined to set the season double play record of 217 in 1949, still as yet unbroken. Only ten infields in history have ever turned over 200 double plays in a year, even with the advent of expansion and the 162-game schedule. Three of those were Athletics infields (1949, 1950 and 1951) with Suder as the keystone man.

"Pecky" Suder (his nickname a word play on the wood "pecky cedar") was extremely versatile, playing second, third and shortstop. Second base, however, was his natural position and he led the American League in fielding percentage there in 1947 and 1951. His career fielding average at second base was .982 with only 75 errors in 4,246 total chances and 613 double plays. Counting his work at all four infield positions, he was involved in 803 double plays in his 12-year career. The *Rawlings* Gold Glove award for fielding excellence did not exist until 1957. If it had, he would have won a number of gold gloves in the 1940s and early 1950s.

The underrated Suder was a contact hitter who put the ball into play and could move runners over with 92 career sacrifice hits. Despite his superior running speed, he established the all-time Athletics record for hitting into double plays (158). Suder's *Louisville Slugger* produced mostly line drives and sharply hit ground balls. He almost never struck out and walked even less.

* * * * *

Peter Suder was born of Serbian lineage in Aliquippa, Beaver County, Pennsylvania just northwest of Pittsburgh on April 16, 1916 to Smilja Segan and Bozidar Sucevic Suder.

Raised with five brothers and four sisters, he was a basketball star by age 14, excelling for the champion Shooting Stars basketball team in 1930.

After standing out at Aliquippa High School in baseball and basketball under Coach Nate Lippe, Sudor signed as an amateur free agent with the Yankees before the 1935 season. Directed to play the hot corner for the Washington (DC) Generals of the Class-D Pennsylvania State Association, he hit .294 in 98 games. For the 1936 Akron (OH) Yankees of the Class-C Middle Atlantic League, Suder played shortstop and batted .309 with 18 home runs. In 1937 he played third for the Class-B Norfolk (VA) Tars, hitting .300 with 22 homers as a Piedmont League All-Star.

Promoted to the Class-A Binghamton (NY) Triplets in 1938, Suder helped them to the pennant by hitting .278 with ten homers as the Eastern League All-Star third baseman. Back again with the Triplets in 1940 at third base for 140 games, he hit .301 with 16 homers as Binghamton won the Eastern League title again. Suder was an All-Star, won the batting title, and earned the EL Most Valuable Player award. Despite his six increasingly productive seasons in their system, the Yankees let him slip away in the Rule 5 Draft on October 1, 1940.

Suder debuted with the A's on April 15, 1941 and collected his first hit off Red Ruffing at Yankee Stadium, a double past centerfielder Joe DiMaggio. As a rookie, he struck out only 47 times in 558 plate appearances, walked just 19 times and led the AL, hitting into 23 double plays.

Suder would have three valuable years averaging over 500 trips to the plate each year with the Athletics before entering the U. S. Army in March of 1944. He received his honorable discharge in January, 1946. During spring training, the 1946 *Who's Who in Baseball Guide* stated, "Suder has been in the service for a couple of years. He's an in-

G	AB	R	H	2B	3B	HR	RBI	SB	BB	SO	BA	OBP	SLG	TB
1421	5085	469	1268	210	44	49	541	19	288	456	.249	.290	.337	1713

fielder- not too promising." The review couldn't have been farther off the mark. Suder played every infield position with consummate skill while hitting .281 in 128 games.

The keystone combination of shortstop Eddie Joost and second baseman Suder in 1949 was crucial to the Athletics finishing 81-73, good for fifth in the AL. The 87-year old Connie Mack was managing his 49th Athletics team and declared that his 1949 infield was better defensively than the famed A's "$100,000 Infield" of the early century. Suder contributed solidly at the plate with career-highs in doubles (24) and RBI (75). He also had a fine year in 1953 when he matched his season high with 130 hits in 115 games and hit a career-best .286.

Suder was at second base in 1954 and drove in the last two runs in Philadelphia's Connie Mack Stadium against the Yankees before the team departed for Kansas City. He was in the Athletics Opening Day lineup in Kansas City in 1955, his last year in the big time. After 1,421 major league games, he played his final game on May 30, 1955, retiring at age 39.

After his playing days were over, Suder managed in the minor leagues in the Washington Senators organization with the 1957 Kinston (NC) Eagles and the 1958 Fox Cities (WI) Foxes, but never managed again after that. He also scouted for the Senators.

A private personality, Pete went back to Aliquippa where he served on the school board and later as the warden at the Beaver County Jail. He was inducted into the Beaver County Sports Hall of Fame in 1976. Once back in Aliquippa, he left town rarely, venturing out only once to attend a 1997 Philadelphia Athletics Reunion in Philly. The popular Suder always remained accommodating to his fans with autographs and photos. He passed away on November 14, 2006 in Aliquippa at age 90 and was laid to rest in Aliquippa's St. Elijah Serbian Cemetery.

WES WESTRUM

NEW YORK GIANTS
CATCHER

1947-1957

"Pitching was what took us over the hill in this race and it was Wes's handling of the pitchers that played a tremendous part in their success. ... I think he's the best defensive catcher in baseball."

~ Coach Eddie Stanky on the 1951 Giants season

Wes Westrum was one of the finest defensive catchers of his time with a Gold Glove-worthy .985 fielding percentage, gunning down 47 percent of would-be base stealers to rank ninth all-time. Twice an NL All-Star, he caught the most games (902) in Giants franchise history.

Before the modern hinge catchers' gloves, Westrum used the old pillow mitt and had to receive with both hands. Although he worked at keeping his bare right hand out of harm's way, he still sustained eight broken fingers and countless jammed, split and sprained fingers.

When not injured, the burly 5'11" 185-pound Westrum was a powerful right-handed offensive threat in the middle of the lineup. His numerous hand injuries inevitably affected his hitting. Often he had difficulty even gripping his *Louisville Slugger* at the plate.

★ ★ ★ ★ ★

Wesley Noreen Westrum was born on November 28, 1922 to Mable Robinson and Harry Westrum in Clearbrook, Clearwater County, Minnesota. He was the oldest of four children, growing up in the tiny hamlet of Clearbrook, about 250 miles northwest of Minneapolis.

Westrum was a standout in football, basketball, and baseball at Clearbrook-Gonvick High. He was notable as a hard-nosed fullback, but chose baseball as his profession while still a prep junior, catching 56 Northern League games for the Crookston (MN) Pirates in 1940.

Westrum was the 1941 Northern League All-Star catcher for the Class-C Eau Claire (WI) Bears, hitting .330 with 70 RBI. After spending 1942 with the Little Rock (AK) Travelers, he was drafted and spent three years first in the Army's Airborne Division as a paratrooper and then worked security at a state prison housing military prisoners near Poughkeepsie, New York.

While in Poughkeepsie, Westrum was introduced to his future wife Josephine and settled there after their marriage. Returning from the War, Westrum was a 1946 South Atlantic League All-Star for the Class-A Jacksonville (FL) Tars. With the 1947 Minneapolis (MN) Millers, he was the American Association All-Star catcher, hitting .295 with 24 homers and 87 RBI.

He earned his debut in Chicago on September 17, 1947, going 2-for-4 against the Cubs. Giants farm director Carl Hubbell was effusive in his praise, describing him as the best young catcher to come into the National League in years, but his 1948 season was injury-marred.

The Giants even optioned him to Triple-A Jersey City in 1949. In 51 International League games, he hit .308 with 15 homers and hammered five grand slams. Upon his June 14 recall, the gritty Westrum caught Larry Jansen's 2-0 shutout of the Reds despite a broken finger.

As the Giants' regular backstop in 1950, he set a big-league mark, fielding .999 in 139 games with one error in 680 chances. He was in on 21 double plays- the 11th highest total ever for a catcher- and led NL backstops with 31 runners thrown out (54.4 percent) and 71 assists.

Westrum also launched 23 home runs that year and drove in 71 runs with his 103 hits. His finest game was on June 24 at the Polo Grounds. Hitting cleanup, he went 4-for-4 with three homers, a triple, 15 total bases, four RBI and five runs scored in a 12-2 blitz of the Reds.

Westrum played a pivotal role in the Giants' miracle pennant-winning season of 1951. He contributed 20 home runs with 70 RBI, 104 walks and a career-high .400 OBA while pacing all NL catchers again in runners-caught-stealing. The Giants trailed the Dodgers by 13 games on August 12, but tied them at the wire and won on Bobby Thomson's walk off homer in sudden death. Westrum caught each of the six 1951 Fall Classic games in the defeat to the Yankees.

He continued his excellence in 1952, catching 54 of the first 55 games, with 12 home runs, but then broke a finger,

G	AB	R	H	2B	3B	HR	RBI	SB	BB	SO	BA	OBP	SLG	TB
919	2322	302	503	59	8	96	315	10	489	514	.217	.356	.373	866

re-injured it, broke a thumb, and then suffered a split finger. He caught only 112 games, but still finished runner up to Cardinals catcher Del Rice in assists.

Still the starting catcher through the 1954 season, Westrum was featured on the inaugural August 16 cover of *Sports Illustrated* with Braves Hall of Famer Eddie Mathews and umpire Augie Donatelli. That fall, he worked all four games in the Giants' Series sweep of the Indians.

By that time, Westrum's damaged hands had become a liability. He was relegated to backup duty behind Ray Katt in 1955, Bill Sarni in 1956, and Valmy Thomas in 1957. When the Giants moved to California in 1958, manager Bill Rigney said he preferred him to be a coach.

Westrum decided to retire at age 34 and coached for the Giants from 1958 to 1963. He then was involved in the only trade of coaches in history for the Mets' Cookie Lavagetto and became the manager of the Mets on August 30, 1965, succeeding the legendary Casey Stengel.

His 1966 Mets escaped the NL cellar for the first time in their history, but talented young hurlers Tom Seaver, Jerry Koosman, Jon Matlack and Tug McGraw matured too late to save him in 1967. He resigned with 11 games to go, just missing the 1969 Miracle Mets' title magic.

Westrum served at the Giants' first-base coach (1968-71) and major league scout (1972) before being given the reigns to succeed Charlie Fox as San Francisco's manager on June 28, 1974. His 1975 Giants finished one game under .500 and Stoneham replaced him with Rigney.

Westrum worked as an Atlanta Braves scout out of his Mesa, Arizona home from 1977 until the 1994 work stoppage. An approachable, humble gentleman his entire life, Westrum passed away from complications of cancer at 79 on May 28, 2002 in Clearbrook, where he had maintained a summer lake home. He is interred in Clearbrook's Silver Creek Cemetery.

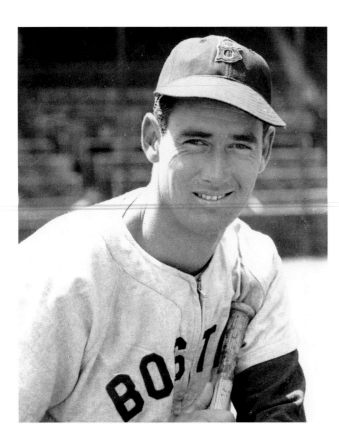

TED WILLIAMS

BOSTON RED SOX
LEFT FIELD

1939-1942 • 1946-1960

"No other player visible to my generation concentrated within himself so much of the sport's poignance, so assiduously refined his natural skills, so constantly brought to the plate that intensity of competence that crowds the throat with joy."

~ writer John Updike

Ted Williams may be the greatest hitter of all time. His .344 lifetime average is the highest of any player with more than 500 home runs and the best of anyone who spent his entire career in the post-1919 Liveball Era. Williams was a six-time AL batting champion and a five-time *The Sporting News* Major League Player of the Year. His .483 on-base average is unrivaled and his .634 slugging average is second only to Babe Ruth.

Williams drew 2,021 free passes (the equivalent of four full seasons) and struck out only 709 times, a 3-to-1 walks-to-strikeout ratio, unimaginable for a hitter of his devastating power. He was the consummate hitting master, wielding his 31-ounce, boned *Louisville Slugger* bat. His discipline to wait for *his* pitch was legendary.

★ ★ ★ ★ ★

Theodore Samuel Williams was born in San Diego, California on August 30, 1918, to Mae Venzer and Samuel Stuart Williams. His mother was so zealous for the Salvation Army, she was known as "The Angel of Tijuana." Both of his parents were regularly absent, so he virtually raised himself. The young Herbert Hoover High star caught the Yankees' eye, but his mother said he was too young to be away from home.

Instead, he excelled for the hometown San Diego Padres of the Pacific Coast League in 1936 and 1937 before the Red Sox bought out his contract. Williams' bravado did not play well with the veteran Red Sox in 1938. "Ted the Kid" was sent down to the Minneapolis (MN) Millers, where he led the American Association in average, runs scored, home runs, and RBI. A Red Sox regular in 1939, he hit .327 and set a rookie record of 145 runs batted in.

Williams' 1941 year at 23 would be one for the ages.

Before the season's final day, Williams' average stood at .39955. Manager Joe Cronin suggested he sit out the twin bill. "The Splendid Splinter" never considered it, going 6-for-8 for a .406 finish and a record .551 on-base percentage. He followed with his first Triple Crown in 1942.

After serving in World War II for three years, Williams returned to lead the pennant-winning 1946 Red Sox as MVP. Lou Boudreau's "Williams Shift" was initiated that year, placing six fielders on the right side, and then was employed by the Cardinals in the World Series. An injured Williams hit just .200 in an agonizing seven-game loss.

Williams won his second Triple Crown in 1947. Two years later, he led the American League in round trippers, reached base in a record 84 consecutive games and tied teammate Vern Stephens for the RBI title. "The Thumper" narrowly missed his third Triple Crown in the closest batting race ever in 1949, finishing at .34275 to the .3429 of Detroit's George Kell.

Williams' two MVP awards and two Triple Crowns were earned in four separate seasons. The outspoken Williams referred to Hub beat writers derisively as the "Knights of the Keyboard," but the jaded journalists got even through the MVP balloting. His feud with the press also seeped into his relationship with the fans. He chaffed at the smattering of Fenway boos directed at him and stopped his practice of tipping his cap altogether.

Williams spent 1952 and 1953 serving as a Marine Corps fighter pilot. Early in 1953, flying as part of a jet bomber squadron north of Korea's 38th parallel, enemy flak knocked out his hydraulics. Maneuvering his crippled F-9 back to safety, he crash-landed and skidded over a mile before escaping the flames. Williams went on to fly

G	AB	R	H	2B	3B	HR	RBI	SB	BB	SO	BA	OBP	SLG	TB
2292	7706	1798	2654	525	71	521	1839	24	2021	709	.344	.483	.634	4884

39 combat missions. He was awarded the Air Medal and was welcomed back a war hero, having spent five prime years in defense of his country.

Williams' popularity soared as he hit at least .345 his first four years back. At age 39 in 1957, he batted .388 while powering 38 home runs, falling short of .400 by five hits. He reached base a record 16 consecutive times and averaged .453 over the last half.

In his final career at-bat on September 28, 1960 at Fenway, "Teddy Ballgame" hit a home run in the most dramatic finale in baseball history. The crowd's extended standing ovation did not prod him to tip his cap circling the bases or leave the dugout.

Williams was asked to manage the Washington Senators in 1969 and led them to 86 wins as the AL Manager of the Year. He always enjoyed discussing his hitting craft with active players. Williams' other great love was fly and deep-sea fishing. His talent was so rare he was voted into the International Game Fishing Association Hall of Fame.

Williams was a first ballot National Baseball Hall of Fame inductee in 1966 and his Red Sox uniform jersey #9 was retired forever in 1984. Major League Baseball named the All-Star Game Most Valuable Player trophy in his honor and *The Sporting News* chose him Player of the Decade for the 1950s.

He gradually mellowed into the game's beloved grand old man. Williams was triumphantly driven into Fenway's infield prior to the 1999 All-Star Game and finally waived his cap to the appreciative throng. His support of the Jimmy Fund, combating children's cancer in New England, was well-known and came from the heart. The last man to hit .400 passed away of heart failure in Crystal River, Florida on July 5, 2002.

THE SINGLE FRANCHISE
HALL OF FAME
FRATERNITY

The list of player names is located on page 390.

CHAPTER FIVE

THE EXPANSION ERA

1958-1974

Tiger Stadium at the Corner –
Detroit, Michigan

GENE ALLEY

PITTSBURGH PIRATES
SHORTSTOP
1963-1973

"Alley's got good baseball instincts. He's got a good head. He backs up plays well, he goes to his spots well. He does everything well – he's complete. He was the best hit-and-run man on the club, a good bunter, one of the better base runners."

~ Pirates manager Harry "The Hat" Walker

Gene Alley was one of the finest fielding shortstops of his era with two *Rawlings* Gold Glove awards. A member of the 1971 World Series Champion Pittsburgh Pirates, he was twice voted a National League All-Star and *The Sporting News* National League All-Star shortstop.

Alley teamed with Bill Mazeroski to form one of the most dazzling double play combos in history, setting a major league record of 161 double plays in 1966 that still stands. Maz could field a ball up the middle with no one on and flip it to Alley knowing he had the stronger throw.

The 6' 165-pound Alley was a rock-steady shortstop with exceptional range and an accurate throwing arm. Although he only had above average foot speed in the straightaway, his first step was super quick getting to the ball and he was elusive in avoiding the runner at second.

Alley did not hit for power or high average consistently, but he compensated by doing all of the little things necessary to win. With excellent bat control, he learned to hit the ball to right field, especially in hit-and-run situations. He was also an accomplished, dependable bunter.

★ ★ ★ ★ ★

Leonard Eugene Alley was born of German ancestry on July 10, 1940 in Richmond, Virginia to Helen and Claude Alley. His father was killed in an auto accident shortly after he was born but a widow's railroad pension allowed his mother to stay home to raise her four children.

Alley grew up playing Pony and American Legion baseball and took All-City honors in basketball and baseball at Richmond's Hermitage High. He captained both squads as a senior in 1958, batting .429 for the Panthers. Pirates scout Joe Bowen signed him in February of 1959. That year with the Dubuque (IA) Packers in the Class-D Midwest League, he injured his arm.

Alley did not play his natural shortstop position for three years. He was a third baseman in 1960 with the Class-C Grand Forks (ND) Chiefs, winning the Northern League MVP award. He also played with the Class-B Burlington (IA) Bees and the Triple-A Columbus (OH) Jets.

Alley played mostly second base in 1961 with the Class-A Asheville (NC) Tourists in the Sally League and split time between Columbus and Asheville in 1962. He was back at shortstop for Columbus in 1963. His stellar glove and 19 home runs earned him a late season call-up.

Alley earned his big-league debut on September 4 versus the Braves in Milwaukee against Warren Spahn and got into 17 games. He made the 1964 team as a backup for starting shortstop Dick Schofield and hit his first career homer off Cardinals ace Ernie Broglio on May 3.

In March of 1965, Bill Mazeroski broke his foot, and Alley filled in for him in the season's first 40 games. Upon Maz's return, manager Harry Walker moved Alley to shortstop, replacing Schofield. He responded by fielding .968 overall at the two positions in 153 games.

His best year was 1966. In 147 games Alley batted .299 with 28 doubles- both career highs. He also scored 88 runs along with 173 hits and ten triples. His 20 sacrifice hits ranked second in the NL. With Mazeroski, he helped the Bucs turn a NL record 215 double plays.

Alley fielded .979 in 1966 with 235 putouts, 472 assists and just 15 errors. He was himself involved in a club record 128 double plays and was awarded his first *Rawlings* Gold Glove at shortstop. He finished 11th in the National League Most Valuable Player voting.

Just days before the 1967 All-Star game, Alley threw a ball in from the outfield during batting practice and felt a stabbing pain in his shoulder. He was the NL's starting shortstop in the All-Star game at Angel Stadium, but the shoulder injury hampered him the rest of his career. Alley finished 1967 at .287 with 158 hits in 152 games.

G	AB	R	H	2B	3B	HR	RBI	SB	BB	SO	BA	OBP	SLG	TB
1195	3927	442	999	140	44	55	342	63	300	622	.254	.310	.354	1392

The pain recurred each time he threw, but he had 257 putouts, 500 assists and 105 double plays to earn his second straight Gold Glove. He repeated as a 1968 National League All-Star with a fielding percentage of .974.

Alley was on the disabled list for 29 days in 1969, but his defense continued to scintillate. He added in a 21-game hitting streak that began on August 13 in San Francisco and ended on September 9. During the streak Alley hit .366 with 15 runs scored, eight home runs and 21 RBI.

The Pirates won the 1970 NL East pennant with Alley playing in 121 games and fielding .975. On September 2, he hit a rare inside-the-park grand slam at Montreal's Jarry Park Stadium. Facing Carl Morton, he laced a sinking line drive to center field in front of Boots Day, who slipped on the wet grass. The ball rolled all the way to the wall and everyone scored.

In the historic 1971 season, Pittsburgh went 97-65 to win the NL East again. An 11-game winning streak in July was the turning point. Alley played in 114 games and contributed, but the cumulative effect of thousands of throws was starting to take its toll on his shoulder and knees.

Pittsburgh dispensed with the Giants in four games in the 1971 NLCS and faced the Orioles in the Fall Classic. Led by a transcendent Roberto Clemente, the Bucs beat Baltimore in seven games. The injured Alley only saw action in two games with three plate appearances.

The Pirates won their third straight divisional title in 1972. A diminished Alley hit .248 in 119 games in 1973 and ended with a .203 average in 76 games during his final major league campaign. He played his last game on September 27 at the relatively young age of 33.

Married since 1962, Alley and his wife, the former Elizabeth Ann Tilley, live in Glen Allen, Virginia near Richmond where they raised two daughters. Alley enjoys golf, hunting, fishing and coin collecting. He was inducted into the Virginia Sports Hall of Fame in 1989.

BOB ALLISON

WASHINGTON SENATORS & MINNESOTA TWINS
OUTFIELD • FIRST BASE

1958-1970

*"Allison is a great clutch hitter.
I like to see him up there in
a crucial spot. That's when
he seems to deliver the best."*

~ Twins manager Sam Mele

Bob Allison is one of the most celebrated Twins sluggers of the 20th century and one of the most popular players in Minnesota baseball annals. The 1959 American League Rookie of the Year and a three-time All-Star, he teamed with his friend Harmon Killebrew to form one of the most dangerous slugging duos in baseball history.

Allison boomed 30 or more home runs three times and 20 or more eight times, ranking in the AL top ten in homers eight seasons. He struck out often, but earned his title "Mr. Clutch" for coming through time and again in late inning pressure at-bats.

Playing all three outfield positions, Allison displayed a sensationally strong throwing arm, cutting down 14 runners in 1961 alone and totaling double figures in six seasons. He ran extremely well for a big man and got an outstanding jump off the bat.

The fiercely competitive powerful 6'4" 230-pound Allison was the most physical base runner in the league. Middle infielders could hear him thundering down the line and were acutely aware that he would be sliding hard to break up the double play.

* * * * *

William Robert Allison was born on July 11, 1934 in Raytown, Jackson County, Missouri outside of Kansas City to Frances Louise and Robert Louis Allison. The oldest of three children, he learned to play baseball in the sandlots, on an American Legion team, and in semi-professional ball because Raytown High had no baseball.

A superb all-around athlete, Allison attended Kansas University at Lawrence on a football scholarship where he starred as a bruising fullback. He also was a sprinter in track and a centerfielder in baseball.

Signed by Senators scout Ray Baker in early 1955, Allison progressed steadily, if not spectacularly, through the farm system. He improved with the Class-B Hagerstown (MD) Packets (1955) and the Class-A Charlotte (NC) Hornets (1956), and hit .307 with the Double-A Chattanooga (TN) Lookouts in 1958 to earn his debut on September 16.

In his first full campaign in the big time in 1959, Allison parlayed a fast start to hit 30 home runs (one short of Ted Williams' rookie record), top the AL with nine triples, and knock in 85 runs. He was named an AL All-Star and garnered top rookie honors.

Owner Calvin Griffith relocated the franchise to Minnesota in 1961. Allison and his new wife, the former Elizabeth Jane Shearer, were the first to move to the Twin Cities where they would raise their two sons. The good-natured slugger at once was a folk hero, signing autographs at Metropolitan Stadium and genuinely engaging the fans.

Allison's 1963 campaign may have been his finest. While hitting cleanup, he led the AL with 99 runs scored and lined out 25 doubles and 35 home runs with 91 RBI. He swung his heavy 36-ounce *Louisville Slugger* to hit three bombs in one game on May 17 against Cleveland. Allison and Killebrew lived up to their nickname "The Home Run Twins" on July 18. They both hit grand slams in the first inning against the Indians.

He came back in 1964 with 32 circuit clouts and 86 RBI and was selected for his third All-Star game. Allison, Tony Oliva, Jimmie Hall and Killebrew combined to hit four consecutive home runs in the seventh inning of a game in Kansas City on May 3.

Manager Sam Mele's 1965 American League Champions registered 102 victories. In the fifth inning of

G	AB	R	H	2B	3B	HR	RBI	SB	BB	SO	BA	OBP	SLG	TB
1541	5032	811	1281	216	53	256	796	84	795	1033	.255	.358	.471	2271

World Series Game 2, Allison pulled off the greatest catch in Twins history. He made a spectacular diving backhanded grab after a long sprint, sliding head long across the left field foul line. It turned around the game's momentum and the Twins upset Dodgers ace Sandy Koufax, 5-1. Allison also blasted a 373-foot game-winning home run in Game 6, but the Twins could not get past Koufax in Game 7, losing 2-0.

The next year, Allison was hit by a pitch and sustained a broken left hand, missing 91 games. He came back to hit 22 and 25 home runs respectively in 1967 and 1968, but declined thereafter and played his last game on September 29, 1970.

Participating in a 1987 Metrodome Old-Timers Game, Allison first noticed he had difficulty running and catching the ball. He began to walk haltingly, and his speech soon became slurred. Two years later he was finally diagnosed with a condition called progressive sporadic ataxia. Allison battled the rare degenerative neurological disease for eight long years. He eventually lost his ability to talk, walk, write or even feed himself. He passed away in Rio Verde, Arizona on April 9, 1995 at age 60.

Established in 1991 and supported faithfully by his family, the Bob Allison Ataxia Research Center at the University of Minnesota continues to fund research and raise public awareness of ataxia to ultimately find a cure for the dread disease.

Bob Allison was inducted into the Minnesota Twins Hall of Fame posthumously in 2003. In final tribute, the Twins honored his life and character by creating the Bob Allison Award in 2008 for the Minnesota player who best exemplifies his leadership, determination, hustle, tenacity and competitive spirit- both on and off the field.

ERNIE BANKS

CHICAGO CUBS
SHORTSTOP • FIRST BASE

1953-1971

"He never complained about his team's bad luck or bad talent, never stopped playing the game with joy, never stopped giving his all, never lost his proud demeanor, and never acted like anything but a winner. He was a symbol of the Cub fan's undiminishing resilience. If he could be happy to come to the park each afternoon, then so could we."

~ actor Joe Mantegna

Ernie Banks was the greatest player in Chicago Cubs history. He has been such a strong icon of the franchise, both on and off the playing field, he will always be known as "Mr. Cub," the most popular player ever to play on Chicago's North Side. His career became synonymous with the joy of playing the national game.

The Cubbies were rarely in contention despite Banks' brilliance, yet his optimism was never dampened. His mantra was, "What a beautiful day for a ballgame. Let's play two!" Wrigley Field was the only unlighted major league park, and Banks savored playing in the sunshine within the "friendly confines," a term he coined and popularized.

An 11-time All-Star, Banks hit more than 20 homers 13 times, 40 or more home runs five times, and drove in over 100 runs eight times. He is the all-time Cubs leader in games played, at-bats, extra base hits and total bases; and second in hits, home runs and runs batted in. Banks led the Senior Circuit in extra base hits four seasons and in home runs and RBI twice. He was also the author of a dozen career grand slam home runs.

The slender 6' 1" 165-pound Banks generated his power at the plate from amazingly quick and active wrists, strong forearms and a compact stroke. His offensive power numbers were a quantum leap beyond the shortstops of his day. The first slugger to use a light bat, he held his 31-ounce *Louisville Slugger* high, waggling it rhythmically, coiled for his pitch. Banks belted 248 homers and drove in 694 runs from 1955 to 1960, the most in baseball. He reached his peak in 1958 and 1959 with back-to-back National League Most Valuable Player awards.

* * * * *

Ernest Banks was born on January 31, 1931 in Dallas, Texas, the eldest son of 12 children born to Essie Van-

essa and Eddie Banks. He was raised in a hardworking, close-knit family which imbued good character and high standards. His high school didn't have baseball, but Banks was noticed playing softball, and invited to barnstorm with a summer Negro semi-pro team before his senior year, which showcased his raw talent.

Hall of Famer Cool Papa Bell scouted and signed Banks in 1950 with the Kansas City Monarchs of the Negro American League, managed by Buck O'Neil. Fortunately, the kindly O'Neil drew out the shy youngster and gently coaxed him out of his shell. The new Banks could be seen smiling, shaking hands and cheerfully learning his craft.

He returned to the Monarchs in early 1953 after a two-year U. S. Army hitch in Germany. As soon as the Monarchs season was over, the Cubs dealt for him. The right-handed hitting Banks bypassed the minor leagues altogether, making his big-league debut in September as the first African American ever to play for the Cubs.

Banks topped the National League in 1958 with 47 home runs, 129 runs batted in and a .614 slugging percentage. His .313 batting average, 119 runs scored, 193 hits and 11 triples were career-highs. His 1959 was just as impressive as he led the Senior Circuit with 45 home runs and 143 RBI, hitting .304 and slugging .596.

As a young player, Banks' fielding lacked consistency. But by 1959, he had become an accomplished shortstop, committing only 12 errors and fielding .985, both major league records. Banks also registered a National League-best 519 assists while playing in every game. He won the 1960 *Rawlings* Gold Glove award with the fewest errors in baseball and led NL shortstops in fielding in both 1960 and 1961.

G	AB	R	H	2B	3B	HR	RBI	SB	BB	SO	BA	OBP	SLG	TB
2528	9421	1305	2583	407	90	512	1636	50	763	1236	.274	.330	.500	4706

Because his range had been eroded by leg injuries, Banks moved to first base in 1962, bringing smooth footwork and soft hands to his new position. He went on to lead the National League in putouts at first base five times.

Leo Durocher became manager in 1966 as the Cubs rebuilt. By 1969, the team had pre-season prospects to win the NL pennant. Despite Banks' 23 home runs and 106 RBI in 155 games, the contentious Durocher's fatigued club nosedived at the wire, watching the Miracle Mets rush past. The debacle of 1969 ensured that Banks owned the major league record for most games played without a single postseason appearance.

On May 12, 1970, Banks lined his 500th home run over Wrigley's ivy-covered walls into the left field bleachers. After he retired in 1971, the Cubs honored him by hoisting a pennant with his uniform #14 atop Wrigley Field's left field foul pole.

Banks was elected into the National Baseball Hall of Fame in his first year of eligibility in 1977 and became the first Cubs player to have his number retired in 1982. He was voted onto Major League Baseball's 1999 All-Century Team. A statue in Banks' likeness was dedicated outside Wrigley Field in 2008. He was honored in 2013 with the Presidential Medal of Freedom, the country's highest civilian award.

Twice Chicagoan of the Year, Banks and his wife Eloyce had residences in Los Angeles and Chicago. Ernie Banks International and Ernie Banks Live Above & Beyond Foundation provided support to underprivileged children. Mr. Cub passed away at 83 on January 24, 2015 in Chicago and was laid to rest in Chicago's Graceland Cemetery.

JOHNNY BENCH

CINCINNATI REDS
CATCHER

1967-1983

"Bench is the greatest athlete who ever has played the game. It's almost pitiful that one man should have so much talent."

~ Reds manager Sparky Anderson

Johnny Bench was the greatest catcher of the 20th century, defining the standard by which all future receivers would be measured. A 12-time All-Star, he earned ten consecutive *Rawlings* Gold Gloves for his fielding brilliance. The ultimate intimidator with a *Louisville Slugger* in his hands, he drove in 1,013 runs during the Decade of the 1970s- the most by any major league hitter.

A central gear in Cincinnati's Big Red Machine, Bench caught 100 or more games for a record 13 straight years and revolutionized the tools of ignorance. Capable of holding seven baseballs in his hand at once, he popularized the larger hinged catcher's mitt with a one-handed style and began applying sweeping tags like an infielder.

Bench used his powerful throwing arm and agility to gun down 469 base runners and allowed only 94 passed balls. "The Little General" took charge with swagger and a keen knowledge of the strengths and weaknesses of his pitchers and the opposing hitters.

★　★　★　★　★

Johnny Lee Bench was born in Oklahoma City, Oklahoma on December 7, 1947 of Cherokee descent. His parents, Katy and Ted Bench, moved their four children to the nearby small town of Binger when he was five. Bench began playing American Legion baseball at age 14 with boys much older. During practice sessions, his father extended second base to twice the normal distance of over 250 feet to enhance his arm strength.

The valedictorian of his senior class, Bench received college scholarships for both baseball and basketball. He went a combined 84-3 as a pitcher for Binger High and Legion but was chosen as a catcher in the second round by Cincinnati in the 1965 draft.

The 6'1" 210-pound prodigy enjoyed a meteoric rise through the minors as the 1966 Double-A Carolina League Player of the Year for the Peninsula (VA) Grays, and the 1967 Minor League Player of the Year for the Triple-A Buffalo (NY) Bisons of the International League. He was called up for his debut at Crosley Field on August 28, 1967.

In Bench's first full year in the National League in 1968, he slammed 40 doubles, hit 15 homers and drove in 82 runs. Catching a rookie record 154 games, he became the first receiver to win the NL Rookie of the Year Award. The next spring, Ted Williams autographed a baseball for him that read, "To Johnny Bench, a Hall of Famer for sure."

New skipper Sparky Anderson arrived just in time in 1970 to savor Bench's finest year. He led the NL with 45 home runs and 148 RBI as the Reds won the pennant by 14½ games. The clear NL MVP, he was *The Sporting News* Major League Player of the Year.

Although Bench suffered through an injury-laden, slump-ridden 1971 season, he atoned for it in 1972 with his second MVP award, leading the NL with 40 home runs and 125 RBI. He hit the greatest clutch home run in Reds history in the final NLCS game, leading off the bottom of the ninth to tie the game and set the stage to beat the Pirates.

Bench won another NL RBI title in 1974, but the Queen City was still looking for its first World Series trophy in over three decades. Despite sustaining a serious left shoulder injury in 1975, he keyed Cincinnati to 108 victories, the most in the Senior Circuit since the 1909 Pittsburgh Pirates. After a sweep of the Pirates for the pennant, the Reds achieved a dramatic seven-game victory over the Red Sox in a classic World Series.

G	AB	R	H	2B	3B	HR	RBI	SB	BB	SO	BA	OBP	SLG	TB
2158	7658	1091	2048	381	24	389	1376	68	891	1278	.267	.345	.476	4044

REDS

The encore 1976 Big Red Machine rolled on as one of the best teams in history, triumphing in seven consecutive playoff games- the first team ever to do so. In the World Series sweep of the Yankees, Bench went 8-for-15 with six RBI, slugged 1.133 and shut down a fast Bronx team on the base paths. His impact was so profound it became known as the Johnny Bench World Series. In his 45 career postseason games, he allowed only two stolen bases and supplied eight doubles, ten home runs, 20 RBI and slugged .527.

Bench walloped his 314th homer in July of 1979, breaking Yogi Berra's home run record for catchers. In his last three seasons, he caught only 13 games as his legs began to age, but he seized the moment before a record 53,790 grateful Riverfront fans on Johnny Bench Night September 17, 1983 and hit his 389th and last home run.

After he retired as a player, Bench spent nine years announcing CBS Radio's Game of the Week, the All-Star game and the playoffs. He appeared on ESPN and FSN television often and did play-by-play on the Reds local station WLWT.

The great catcher became the eighteenth first year-eligible player to be elected into the National Baseball Hall of Fame in 1989. His uniform jersey #5 was retired forever during his induction into the Cincinnati Reds Hall of Fame in 1989. Bench was the highest-ranking catcher in *The Sporting News* 1999 "100 Greatest Baseball Players" list and is a member of Major League Baseball's elite All-Century Team.

Bench has championed many medical causes, visited U.S. Desert Storm troops and sang with the Cincinnati Pops. He has been a scratch golfer, competing in several PGA Senior Tour and celebrity golf events. Bench is married to the former Laura Cwikowski. The couple resides in the Cincinnati area.

STEVE BLASS

PITTSBURGH PIRATES
RIGHT-HANDED PITCHER

1964 • 1966-1974

"Clemente was great all right, but if it hadn't been for Mr. Blass, we might be popping the corks right now!"

~ Orioles manager Earl Weaver after the 1971 World Series

Steve Blass was one of the Senior Circuit's most effective starting pitchers from 1968 to 1972, winning 78 games and becoming a National League All-Star. He was the author of a clutch complete game victory in the pressure cooker of Game 7 of the 1971 World Series.

Blass' herky-jerky, unorthodox motion was once described as like a "barn full of owls coming at you." Changing speeds and exploiting hitters' weaknesses with his razor-sharp control, Blass displayed a 90-mile-per-hour fastball, a change-up curve and a biting slider. He had such belief in his slider that he threw it even when he was behind in the count.

At the close of 1972 season, the 6'2" 180-pound Blass could boast a 100-67 record for a superb .598 percentage with 867 strikeouts and only 508 walks. It would rank him among the top hurlers in NL annals, but then came the tragic unraveling and demise of his career in 1973.

* * * * *

Stephen Robert Blass was born on April 18, 1942 in rural Canaan, Litchfield County, Connecticut to Rose and Robert Blass. He starred in cross country, basketball and baseball for the Housatonic Valley Regional High Mountaineers, throwing five no-hitters, three as a senior as he went 14-2 with 164 strikeouts. Pirates scout Bob Whalen signed him as he graduated in 1960.

Blass really started to show his potential with the 1962 Class-B Kinston (NC) Eagles. He was a Carolina League All-Star, sporting a 17-3 line with a 1.97 ERA and 209 strikeouts. Pirates pitching instructor Don Osborne became a mentor, teaching him to trust his stuff and compete.

Soon after Blass married his high school sweetheart Karen Lamb in late 1963, the couple traveled to the Dominican Winter League so he could pitch for the Cibaenas Eagles. He built confidence in his newfound slider, throwing it to quality hitters such as the three Alou brothers.

When the Pirates broke from spring training in 1964, Blass was sent down to the Triple-A Columbus (OH) Jets, but was called back for his major league debut in relief on May 10. In his first start on May 18, he hurled a complete game victory over Dodgers ace Don Drysdale, 4-2.

After learning the ropes in 1966 and 1967, he became the ace of the Pirates staff. Blass went 18-6 to lead the NL in percentage in 1968 with a career-best 2.12 ERA. Three of his career-high seven shutouts and nine straight winning starts came in the heat of the pennant race.

Playing their first full season in Three Rivers Stadium in 1971, the Bucs fielded six Latin American and seven African American players with multiracial talent and positive leadership. Blass produced a 15-8 year with a 2.85 ERA and tied for the NL-lead with five shutouts.

He was magnificent in the Fall Classic, hurling two complete-game victories against the Orioles. He crafted a Game 3 three-hitter, winning 5-1, to best Mike Cuellar. The decisive Game 7 match-up featured Blass and Cuellar again. Blass gutted out a four-hit, 2-1 nail-biter to take Game 7 and earned runner up honors to Clemente for World Series Most Valuable Player.

Blass followed with his best season. Second in the Cy Young Award derby to Lefty Carlton, he claimed 19 wins with a 2.49 ERA while lifting the Pirates to the NL West title. The Pirates lost the pennant to the Reds, though Blass was superb, posting a microscopic 1.72 ERA.

Despite being in great shape and experiencing no arm troubles at the start of 1973 spring training, Blass began having difficulty locating his pitches. He was hit hard, walked batters and let loose with wild pitches, often throwing behind hitters. Virdon shut him down in August. Although Danny Murtaugh replaced Virdon and gave

G	IP	W	L	PCT	SHO	GS	CG	H	ER	SO	BB	ERA
282	1597.1	103	76	.575	16	231	57	1558	644	896	597	3.63

him the ball in September, Blass was unreliable and finished with a miserable outing against the Mets. He went 3-9 with a 9.81 ERA, walked 84 batters in 88²/₃ innings, struck out only 27, and led the NL with 12 hit batsmen.

The most bewildering part of the ordeal was that when he threw alone with a catcher, he performed with the same command that he had had for so many years. He tried everything to overcome his psychological block- psychotherapy, transcendental meditation, optometherapy, hypnosis. Nothing worked. The wheels had completely come off.

"Steve Blass Disease" now defines a pitcher's sudden loss of the ability to accurately throw a baseball. Blass pitched only one game in 1974 on April 16 at Wrigley Field. He came on in the fourth inning behind 10-4, tossed five innings, gave up eight runs, and walked seven Cubs.

The Pirates sent Blass to the Triple-A Charleston (SC) Charlies to work things out. It got worse. He walked 103 batters in 61 innings. He tried one last spring comeback, but was still confounded by the problem. After issuing 25 free passes in 14 innings, he retired.

The loquacious Blass went to work for the class ring company *Jostens* in the 1970s. In 1983, he was invited to join the Pirates' TV and radio broadcast team as a fill-in color commentator and went full-time in 1986. With play-by-play icon Bob Prince, the popular duo became an institution broadcasting Pirates games for Home Sports Entertainment Cable TV.

Blass has overcome his perplexing ordeal with upbeat good cheer. His second act as an engaging broadcaster and affable raconteur has made him an enduring favorite in Pittsburgh. Blass' life is testimony that a man can triumph over even the most devastating setback. The Pirates honored his 50ᵗʰ year with the club in 2009. Blass and his wife have lived in the same home in Upper St. Clair, Pennsylvania for over 40 years where they raised their two sons.

GATES BROWN

"In high school I took a little English, some science, some hubcaps and some wheel covers."

~ Gates Brown

One of the most redemptive stories in baseball history, Gates Brown lifted himself from prison to major league stardom as the American League's all-time pinch-hit king. First on the major league career list with 414 pinch-hit at-bats, he holds the Junior Circuit marks for pinch hits (107) and pinch home runs (16). Brown will always be remembered for his prominent role on the 1968 World Series Champion Detroit Tigers.

★ ★ ★ ★ ★

William James Brown was born in Crestline, Ohio on May 2, 1939 to Phyllis James and John Brown. His father played for the Homestead Grays in the Negro National League before raising his three boys and three girls working for the Pennsylvania Railroad.

His mother began calling him "Gates" as he was always at the gate of the family farm at age five. Brown grew up in the small blue collar community and was a three-sport star at Crestline High, but he was arrested for burglary at 17 and sent to the Ohio State Reformatory in Mansfield, the same prison depicted in the well-known film *The Shawshank Redemption*.

The prison athletic director, Chuck Yarman, noting Brown's muscular 5'10" 215-pound physique, urged him to try out for the prison baseball team. The left-hander's natural flair with a *Louisville Slugger* was unmistakable from the beginning and soon Tigers scout Pat Mullin drove up from Detroit to observe him thump a tape-measure home run on the prison grounds.

The Tigers helped Brown obtain early parole, signed him, and sent him to the Duluth-Superior Dukes in 1960. He seized the opportunity with 104 runs scored, 13 triples and 30 steals. Brown next dealt with playing for the 1961 Durham (NC) Bulls as a black ex-convict. In front of hostile crowds, he won the Carolina League batting title (.324) and turned his hecklers into fans.

The 22-year-old Brown batted .300 for the Triple-A Denver (CO) Bears of the American Association in 1962. After a short stay with the Triple-A Syracuse (NY) Chiefs (International League) in 1963, he earned his major league debut on June 19. Brown was the 11th man ever to homer in his first at-bat, crashing a 400-foot shot into Fenway Park's right field seats.

Brown's only year as a starter was 1964. He put up career-highs of 116 hits, 65 runs scored, 22 doubles, six triples, 15 home runs, 54 RBI and 11 steals. Making only a $12,000 salary, he supported his wife, the former Norma Jean Sterling, and infant daughter Pamela Ann, as a furniture salesman in the off season. The couple also had a son, William James, Jr., in 1965.

The Boston Red Sox edged Detroit on the final day of 1967 season. Brown had an off year, hitting only .187. In 1968 spring training, the Tigers even considered trading him briefly but the day after the opener, he hit a game-winning pinch-hit home run in the ninth inning.

It would become his calling card. The resurgent Brown came off the bench to lift the 1968 Tigers with stunning regularity, pounding out an American League record 18 hits and averaging .450. The mark would be third best all-time among players with 35+ pinch-hit at-bats.

Brown could also be a source of comic relief. In the fifth inning of an early August contest, he grabbed two clubhouse hot dogs. Mayo Smith suddenly called him to pinch-hit, so he stuffed the full dogs down his uniform to avoid detection, strode to the plate, and lined a double into the gap. After sliding head first into second, he noticed mustard, ketchup, hot dogs and buns smashed all over his uniform front. The fielders and his teammates doubled up with laughter.

Days later, Brown thrilled the home crowd in a Sunday twin bill against the Red Sox. In the opener, he connected for a pinch hit walk-off bomb in the 14th inning to send Tiger Stadium into delirium. In the nightcap, he pinch hit

G	AB	R	H	2B	3B	HR	RBI	SB	BB	SO	BA	OBP	SLG	TB
2262	1051	330	582	78	19	42	322	30	242	275	.257	.330	.420	950

in the ninth and drilled a walk-off single to right field. Even the great Al Kaline admitted he had never heard the crowd cheer like they did that day.

An essential ingredient on Detroit's road to the 1968 World Series title, Brown hit .370 with a .442 on-base percentage and a phenomenal .685 slugging percentage. He averaged an extra-base hit *every six at-bats* as the only full-season Tiger to hit .300. In the "Year of the Pitcher," the overall 1968 American League batting average was an anemic .230.

Brown became Detroit's first-ever designated hitter in 1973, a role made for him. He played his final game on September 26, 1975 at 36. Only three weeks later, the Tigers hired him as a scout to evaluate college and pro talent and instruct the Tigers' Gulf Coast League rookies.

Brown became the Tigers' hitting coach in 1978 and helped the team jump from eighth to second in the American League in hitting. Working with Sparky Anderson from the beginning of 1979, Brown developed young hitters such as Kirk Gibson, Lance Parrish, Alan Trammell and Lou Whitaker. After the 1984 title season, he resigned over a contract dispute and left the Tigers after a quarter century of service.

Although he lived in Detroit, Brown frequently returned to his hometown to speak with the city's largely low income youth. Known as the "Pride of Crestline," he was relentlessly positive, promoting education, personal responsibility and hard work. Brown also did unsolicited charity work, quietly helping Crestliners who had fallen on hard times or who had suffered a loss. Crestline High's baseball complex was renamed Gates Brown Field in his honor in 2009.

He was inducted into the Michigan Sports Hall of Fame in 2002. Gates Brown's climb from prison cell infamy to national radio and television interviews with Joe Garagiola, Bob Hope and Ed Sullivan is an incredible odyssey. Coaching at the Tigers Fantasy Camp in Lakeland, the jovial Brown remained popular with one and all. He passed away on September 27, 2013 and is buried in East Crestline's Greenlawn Cemetery.

ROBERTO CLEMENTE

PITTSBURGH PIRATES
RIGHT FIELD

1955-1972

"I never thought about being a writer when I grew up; a writer wasn't something to be. An outfielder was something to be. Most of what I know about style I learned from Roberto Clemente."

~ novelist John Sayles

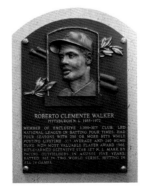

They called him "Roberto El Magnifico." Roberto Clemente was the greatest baseball player ever to come out of Latin America. Transcending his sport to become legendary, Clemente played the game with such intensity, passion and pride that his name will be forever writ large in his native Puerto Rico and across the Americas.

Handsomely cut in his Pirates uniform for 18 summers, Clemente was a portrait of solemn dignity with his defiant jaw and soulful eyes. As then baseball commissioner Bowie Kuhn intoned, "He had a touch of royalty."

Clemente was a four-time National League batting champion and the 1966 NL Most Valuable Player. An 11-time All-Star, he batted over .300 13 times and played in more games than any other Pirate. Yet the way that Clemente competed, and the impact he had on his teammates and the game itself, cannot be reduced to statistics.

Recognized as the greatest defensive rightfielder ever, Clemente earned a record 12 straight *Rawlings* Gold Gloves for outfield excellence. Even though enemy base runners were cautious because of his spectacular throwing arm, Clemente led all Senior Circuit outfielders in assists a league-high five times with a peak of 27. His laser throws cut down many an unsuspecting runner- even running to first base. Clemente's magnificent throwing arm is still the gold standard by which major league scouts judge every other outfield prospect even to the present day.

Clemente displayed his unique style not only in the field but also at bat. Early in his career, Clemente learned to keep his hands back and drive balls to the opposite field in cavernous Forbes Field. In other home parks, the sinewy-strong Clemente would have hit many more than his career 240 home runs. Some called him a bad ball hitter, but he consistently selected a ball that looked good to him and slashed it hard wherever it was pitched. Anyone who ever saw Clemente run from first base to third base on a single to right field never forgot his intensity and flair.

* * * * *

Roberto Clemente Walker was born on August 18, 1934 in Carolina, Puerto Rico to Luisa Walker and Melchor Clemente. He was signed by the Brooklyn Dodgers at age 18 and spent his only minor league season in 1954 sequestered in Montreal, getting little chance to showcase his talents. The Dodgers didn't fool the Pirates general manager Branch Rickey who acquired him first in the Rule 5 draft.

As a Latino of African descent, Clemente came to the United States speaking only halting English and feeling the prejudice from the press. When writers branded him a hypochondriac for speaking about his injuries, he felt misunderstood and disrespected.

Eventually overcoming the language barrier, Clemente spoke out with courage against the discrimination he experienced. He was such an eloquent pioneer advocate for Latin Americans that there is currently a movement to have all major league teams retire his uniform #21. Clemente has had the most meaningful impact of any player for Latinos in baseball history.

He carried the Pirates to glory in two World Series. Against the 1960 New York Yankees and 1971 Baltimore Orioles, Clemente averaged .414 and hit safely in every one of his 14 World Series games. The Most Valuable Player of the 1971 Fall Classic, he thoroughly dominated the Orioles with clutch home runs in Games 6 and 7 and

G	AB	R	H	2B	3B	HR	RBI	SB	BB	SO	BA	OBP	SLG	TB
2433	9454	1416	3000	440	166	240	1305	83	621	1230	.317	.359	.475	4492

missed another by only inches. Defensively, two marvelous running catches and his thunderbolt throws from right field compelled the world to take note of his greatness.

On September 30, 1972, Roberto Clemente reached exactly 3,000 career hits, pounding out a line drive double off the left field wall at Three Rivers Stadium off New York Mets ace Jon Matlack. It was his last career hit in his final regular season at-bat.

Clemente perished that year on New Year's Eve off the coast of Isle Verde in Puerto Rico when his overloaded DC-7 airplane crashed into the sea. He was leading a mercy flight to provide humanitarian aid to victims of a major earthquake in Nicaragua. Adding to the Clemente myth, his body was never found.

He was voted into the National Baseball Hall of Fame without the usual five-year wait 11 weeks later, the first Latino ever inducted. When Major League Baseball announced its Latino Legends Team in 2005, Clemente was the leading vote getter.

Clemente's Pirates now play in the stylish new PNC Park, perhaps the finest of the new major league ballparks. The right field fence stands exactly 21 feet high in homage to his retired uniform jersey #21. Beyond center field, an enormous dramatic statue has been erected in his honor adjacent to the Roberto

Clemente Bridge, spanning the Allegheny River into downtown Pittsburgh.

In tribute to his life, Major League Baseball annually sponsors the prestigious Roberto Clemente Man of the Year Award, given to the current player who best exemplifies his humanitarianism and sportsmanship. Clemente loved and respected his Pittsburgh fans and they in turn made him the most popular Pirate ever.

JIM DAVENPORT

SAN FRANCISCO GIANTS
THIRD BASE

1958-1970

*"Jim was a human
vacuum at third base,
and a hell of a major
league prospect.
A great teammate.
I liked him right away."*

~ Orlando Cepeda 1957

An original San Francisco Giant as a 1958 rookie, Jim Davenport quickly became one of the franchise's most popular players. Although never the offensive threat of National League contemporaries Ron Santo of the Cubs or Ken Boyer of the Cardinals, he surpassed them with his glove work, leading the league in fielding three times to become the Giants' best fielding third baseman ever. A *Rawlings* Gold Glove winner, Davenport patrolled the hot corner with style and consistency year after year, demonstrating sure hands, quick reflexes and a powerful, accurate throwing arm.

★　★　★　★　★

James Houston Davenport was born to Helen Virginia Wooten and Walton Stewart Davenport August 17, 1933 in rural Siluria, Alabama. His father, a textile mill overseer, had to labor tirelessly to provide for his brood of ten. The youngster grew up a natural athlete, excelling at baseball and football. He was a high school quarterback and attended the University of Southern Mississippi on a full ride football scholarship in 1952. His focus was to become a high school football coach.

Fate intervened while he was playing semi-professional baseball in Birmingham, Alabama during the summer of 1955. He caught the eye of New York Giants scout Dickie Martin. Married with two children at the time, Davenport elected to sign with the Giants and forego his last year on the college gridiron.

After hitting .363 for the El Dorado (AK) Oilers of the Class-C Cotton States League in 1956, he marched through the Giants' minor league system, advancing to the Double-A Texas League's Dallas Eagles in 1956 and then on to the Triple-A American Association's Minneapolis (MN) Millers in 1957.

There he met the young Puerto Rican slugger Or-

lando Cepeda, and the two became fast friends. Both youngsters impressed Giants player personnel director Carl Hubbell and were invited to major league spring training the following year.

The 24-year-old Davenport and "The Baby Bull" made their debuts on Opening Day April 15, 1958 at Seals Stadium in the first major league game ever played in California. Davenport was the Giants' first hitter, striking out against the Dodger ace Don Drysdale. He went on to impress manager Bill Rigney with his glove work all season while hitting .256 with 12 home runs, 41 RBI and a NL-leading 17 sacrifice hits. His work earned him a spot on *The Sporting News* National League All-Rookie Team.

Davenport was a solid 5' 11" and 180 pounds by 1962, a year he reached career-highs in batting average (.297) and home runs (14). A National League All-Star, he helped the Giants capture the NL pennant in a three-game playoff with the Dodgers. In the penultimate match up at the new Dodger Stadium, Davenport worked a clutch ninth inning walk from Stan Williams with the bases loaded and the game tied. It would be the eventual pennant-winning RBI and a great cap to his best campaign.

However, Davenport's dream season ended just short of perfection. After alternating victories, the Giants and Yankees saw the World Series come to a climax at Candlestick Park in Game 7. With two out in the ninth inning, Willie McCovey's laser shot line drive was stopped by Yankee second baseman Bobby Richardson. The Giants' potential winning run had been stranded at second base in the person of Willie Mays.

Davenport set a major league record in 1966 by playing 97 consecutive errorless games while accepting 209

G	AB	R	H	2B	3B	HR	RBI	SB	BB	SO	BA	OBP	SLG	TB
1501	4427	552	1142	177	37	77	456	16	382	673	.258	.318	.367	1624

total chances at the hot corner. His defensive work was all the more astonishing in chilly, windswept Candlestick Park, perhaps the most challenging ballpark in history. But Davenport chose to look at it as an advantage as he and his teammates learned to read the wind currents swirling from left to right field.

Although his career was winding down, he played errorless ball in 65 straight games in 1967, fielded 1.000, and averaged .370 as a pinch hitter. Upon his retirement as an active player in 1970 at 37, the Giants tapped him to manage the Pacific Coast League Phoenix (AZ) Giants from 1971 to 1973. He also served as the Giants third base coach from 1976 to 1982 and advance scout in 1983-84.

Davenport's chance to manage the Giants finally came in 1985, but his team went a mediocre 56-88 before he was replaced with Roger Craig by owner Bob Lurie in September. He eventually served as the third base coach for four other major league teams- the Padres (1974-75), Phillies (1987), Tigers (1988) and Indians (1989).

Davenport has served the Giants loyally for over 40 years as a player, scout, instructor, coach and manager, including his stint as skipper of the 1998 PCL Southern Division Champion Fresno (CA) Grizzlies during their inaugural year. He helped players such as Bill Mueller and Pedro Feliz improve their skills in the minor leagues.

The fans voted Jim Davenport as the third baseman on the Giants 25th Anniversary Dream Team in 1982. He has been enshrined in the Mississippi Sports Hall of Fame (1983) and the Alabama Sports Hall of Fame (2006). Davenport resided in San Carlos, California with his wife Betty until his death in Redwood City at age 82 on February 18, 2016.

DON DRYSDALE

BROOKLYN & LOS ANGELES DODGERS
RIGHT-HANDED PITCHER

1956-1969

"I've never seen a pitcher so unafraid of batters."

~ Dodgers manager
Walter Alston

DONALD SCOTT DRYSDALE
BROOKLYN N.L. 1956-1957
LOS ANGELES N.L. 1958-1969
HARD-THROWING SIDE-ARMER NOTED FOR
INTIMIDATING STYLE AND DURABILITY. HAD 209-166
RECORD WITH 2.95 ERA AND 2,486 STRIKEOUTS.
LED N.L. IN STRIKEOUTS 3 TIMES AND HURLED 49
SHUTOUTS. WAS 25-9 IN 1962 AND WON CY YOUNG
AWARD. THREW 6 SHUTOUTS IN A ROW IN 1968,
SETTING RECORD WITH 58 CONSECUTIVE SCORELESS
INNINGS. PITCHED IN RECORD 8 ALL-STAR GAMES.

Don Drysdale was a ferocious competitor, combining a sizzling sidearm fastball with exceptional command to star for five pennant winners and three World Series champions. A tireless workhorse, he led the NL in games started four times and strikeouts three times, sustaining teams that didn't show much offense. He holds All-Star Game records with eight games pitched, five starts, 19$\frac{1}{3}$ innings pitched and 19 strikeouts.

Although known for his congeniality off the field, "Big D" was an intimidating presence on the mound with his 95-mile-per-hour fastball, knocking down batters at will. He drilled a record 154 NL hitters and led the league in hit batsmen a record five times.

Drysdale also helped his own cause as one of the best hitting pitchers of any era. His 29 career home runs rank second only to Warren Spahn among all NL pitchers. Often used as a pinch-hitter, he twice tied the NL record of seven home runs by a pitcher.

★ ★ ★ ★ ★

Donald Scott Drysdale was born on July 23, 1936 to Verna and Scott Drysdale in Van Nuys, Los Angeles County, California. His father had pitched in the Pacific Coast League and was a Dodger scout, but refused to let him pitch until his senior year. He became a prep phenom overnight, going 9-1 to lead Van Nuys High to the 1954 Los Angeles City Championship. Dodger scout Lefty Phillips signed him right afterward.

The young prodigy didn't grow to his full height of 6'6" until after high school, sprouting up over four inches. It took him just two summers to work his way to the major leagues. He had only a stop with the Class-C Bakersfield Indians (California League) and then a promotion to the Triple-A Montreal (QC) Royals (International League) in 1955.

The 19-year-old Drysdale made a veteran Dodgers club in 1956. His locker was placed next to Sal "The Barber" Maglie who gave many a hitter a close shave. Drysdale was a willing student. He won his debut against the Phillies on April 17 and went 5-5.

In the Brooklyn Dodgers' last year, Drysdale became their stopper, going 17-9. He hurled the first major league game in California history in 1958 against the Giants, but lost and pitched poorly all year, pressing too much in front of family and friends.

Drysdale settled down in 1959, winning 17, and paced the National League with 242 strikeouts and seven shutouts. He was the All-Star Game Most Valuable Player at Forbes Field, and won World Series Game 3 over the White Sox at the Los Angeles Memorial Coliseum, the first Fall Classic game ever in the state of California.

Drysdale's best campaign was 1962 when he was the Major League Player of the Year, *The Sporting News* Pitcher of the Year, and baseball's Cy Young Award winner. He led the NL with 25 victories, 41 starts, 287 strikeouts and 314$\frac{1}{3}$ innings pitched.

Drysdale struck out 251 batters in 1963 and pitched perhaps his finest game in World Series Game 3, a 1-0 masterpiece over the Yankees at the newly-minted Dodger Stadium. In 1965, he was the only Dodger .300 hitter, pulling off the feat of winning 23 games and hitting .300 in the same year. He also beat the Twins in the Fall Classic.

After the season, Drysdale and Sandy Koufax jointly held out for $1.05 million, challenging the reserve clause. Just before Opening Day, each settled for six figures- the first time for any pitcher. Their holdout was the start of collective bargaining in baseball.

The signature event of Drysdale's career came in 1968

G	IP	W	L	PCT	SHO	GS	CG	H	ER	SO	BB	ERA
518	3432.1	209	166	.557	49	465	167	3084	1124	2486	855	2.95

when he broke Walter Johnson's 1913 record with 58²/₃ consecutive scoreless innings. He threw six shutouts in succession and then blanked the Phillies for four innings before his streak ended.

Drysdale retired in midseason in 1969, succumbing to a torn right rotator cuff. He was a young 32, the last active Dodger to have played in Brooklyn. He had pitched 14 eventful years for Walter Alston, the longest tenure for any player under one skipper.

During his career, the handsome Drysdale appeared in an array of Hollywood television cameos including *The Rifleman, The Brady Bunch* and *Leave It to Beaver*. The Disney car character *Herbie* sported the number "53" in tribute to Big D.

Drysdale enjoyed a distinguished 22-year career in radio and television. He broadcasted for the Expos, Rangers, Angels, White Sox, and finally for the Dodgers starting in 1988. He also announced nine years for ABC Sports in a variety of TV roles.

Don Drysdale was inducted into the National Baseball Hall of Fame in 1984 and his uniform #53 was officially retired by the Dodgers on July 1, 1984. It still can be seen displayed underneath the Dodger Stadium pavilion roof behind the right field fence.

On November 1, 1986, he married his second wife, UCLA basketball All-American and network broad-

caster Ann Meyers. It was the first time that a married couple each became members of a hall of fame in their respective sports.

Drysdale died of a heart attack in Montreal on July

3, 1993, where he had been announcing a Dodgers game. His radio partner Vin Scully announced the news on the air. His body was cremated at Forest Lawn Memorial Park Cemetery in Glendale, California.

BILL FREEHAN

DETROIT TIGERS
CATCHER • FIRST BASE
1961 • 1963-1976

"What makes [Freehan] so extraordinary is that he plants his two big feet firmly in the ground, doesn't bother giving the base runner barreling down on him from third base so much as a sidelong glance and plain refuses to budge even when said base runner hits him at midship like a torpedo. For that he has the respect of ballplayers everywhere. They know they don't make catchers like Freehan anymore."

~ *writer Milton Richman*

Bill Freehan was the finest catcher in Detroit Tigers history and the premier backstop in the game for the Decade of the 1960s. He caught more games than any other Tiger and his 11 selections as an All-Star are the most by any eligible player who is not in Cooperstown.

A warrior who put on the "tools of ignorance" in 100+ games for nine straight seasons, Freehan was rock solid defensively. He led AL backstops in putouts six times, in fielding three times and set all-time marks with 10,734 chances, 9,941 putouts and a .9933 fielding average.

The 6'2" 205-pound Freehan was thunder in the middle of the lineup and is still in the Tigers Top 10 in six categories. His 200 homers and 2,502 total bases put him behind only two other AL catchers, and he is Top 5 in hits, runs scored, extra base hits and slugging percentage.

★ ★ ★ ★ ★

William Ashley Freehan was born November 29, 1941 in Detroit, Michigan to Helen Morris and Ashley Freehan. He grew up in suburban Royal Oak and moved with his family to St. Petersburg, Florida when he was 14. There he starred in football, basketball and baseball before graduating from the all-boys Bishop Barry High School in 1959. His summers were spent in Detroit playing sandlot ball where Tigers scout Louis D'Annunzio discovered and followed him.

Freehan earned a scholarship to the University of Michigan to play football and baseball. An NCAA All-American for the 1961 Big-Ten Champion Wolverines, he set the conference record, hitting .585. After the NCAA playoffs, he signed with his hometown team for $125,000. Following stints with the Class-C Duluth-Superior Dukes (.343) and the Single-A Knoxville (TN) Smokies (.310), he made his big-league debut on September 26 at 19. Detroit then gave him another 392 at-bats to season him with the Triple-A Denver (CO) Bears in 1962.

As a rookie the next year, Freehan split duty, catching

73 games and profited from Hall of Famer Rick Ferrell's mentoring. He came of age in 1964, becoming the first Tigers backstop to hit .300 since Mickey Cochran in 1935 while blasting 18 homers. Freehan committed only seven errors, logged 517 innings in a row in the final 56 games, and was chosen an All-Star.

His hands were banged up from foul tips in 1965 and 1966 affecting his hitting, but his glove work and game-calling skills kept improving. He won his first of five straight *Rawlings* Gold Gloves in 1965, paced the league in fielding in 1966, and led the AL both years in putouts.

Freehan moved closer to the plate in 1967 to hit .282 with 20 home runs in 158 games as the Tigers were nipped by the Red Sox on the last day. He was honored as the 1967 Tiger of the Year by the Detroit Chapter of the Baseball Writers Association of America.

Now the field general, he adeptly managing the pitching staff in 1968 while breaking his own American League records with 971 putouts and 1,050 total chances. He also set a new AL mark, being hit by 24 pitches. With career-highs of 25 homers and 84 RBI, he finished second to battery-mate Denny McLain in the MVP voting. The Tigers won the pennant by 12 games.

Freehan was a key figure in one of the most pivotal plays in World Series history. In Game 5, the Cardinals had the Tigers on the ropes in the fifth inning, leading the Series, 3-1, and the game, 3-2. Lou Brock attempted to score from second as Freehan speared leftfielder Willie Horton's one-hop throw and blocked the plate. Brock barreled into Freehan, trying to jar the ball loose, but the big man held on. Detroit rallied to win and went on to triumph in Games 6 and 7.

During the 1969 season, he wrote a book detailing his experiences called *Behind the Mask: An Inside Baseball Diary*. His candid excerpts regarding Denny McLain's self-

G	AB	R	H	2B	3B	HR	RBI	SB	BB	SO	BA	OBP	SLG	TB
1774	6073	706	1671	241	35	200	758	24	626	753	.262	.340	.412	2502

indulgent clubhouse behavior ruffled some Motown fans, but all was forgiven in 1971 when he paced AL catchers with a .277 average, 21 home runs, 71 RBI and a durable 144 games receiving.

An All-Star again for the 1972 AL Eastern Division ti-tlists, he recovered from a hairline fracture of his thumb to double and homer in the ALCS Game 3 victory. In Game 4, he drove in the first of three runs in the 10th inning in a clutch come-from-behind 4-3 win at Tiger Stadium.

In 1974, Freehan was shifted to first base. Unfazed, he hit .297 with 18 home runs and slugged .479. The veteran moved back behind the plate for 113 games the following year and earned his 11th All-Star berth. He was relegated to a reserve role in 1976, catching just 61 games, and played his final big league game on October 3, 1976 at age 35.

After his active playing career, he was a principal in Freehan-Bocci & Company, an auto manufacturers' rep-resentative agency, in suburban Detroit. He also enjoyed serving as a color analyst for Seattle Mariners TV (1979-80) and for Tiger broadcasts (1984-1985).

In 1989, Freehan returned to Ann Arbor as the Michi-gan head baseball coach, working seven seasons to bring back a moribund program. Early on, he had mentored rookie catcher Lance Parrish. The Tigers coaxed him back again as a catching instructor from 2002 to 2005.

Freehan is unarguably a better player than many of the catchers in the National Baseball Hall of Fame, and the best receiver not in Cooperstown. Sabrematrician Bill James ranks him the 12th best catcher ever. Freehan was enshrined in the Michigan Sports Hall of Fame in 1982.

Today he lives in the southern Detroit suburb of Bloom-field Hills with his high school sweetheart and wife, the former Patricia O'Brien. In 1999, Motor City fans voted Freehan as the catcher on the All-Time Detroit Tigers Team. He remains one of the most popular Tigers ever.

JAKE GIBBS

New York Yankees
Catcher

1962-1971

"Any sports Hall of Fame in Mississippi has to start with Jake Gibbs. Jake is one of the all-time great guys, just a wonderful human being. I love Jake Gibbs."

~ *Yankee teammate and Hall of Fame manager Bobby Cox*

J ake Gibbs became the first two-sport NCAA All-American in University of Mississippi history before signing a bonus contract with the Bronx Bombers. Although he never reached the stardom of Yankee catchers before and after him, he was a proud Yankee in the best tradition.

The 6' 185-pound left-handed hitting Gibbs was a superb defensive catcher but was plagued by injuries throughout his career, probably in part from the pounding he took as a three-year Southeastern Conference quarterback, leading the Rebels to a 29-3-1 record.

A popular teammate and a genuine Southern gentleman, Gibbs served as an extra coach on the field, in the dugout, and in the bullpen. He never developed at the plate to the Yankees' projections, which resulted in a backup catcher role for most of his career.

★　★　★　★　★

Jerry Dean Gibbs was born on November 7, 1938 to Ruby Morgan and Ben Frank Gibbs in Grenada, Mississippi. He excelled in baseball and football at Grenada's John Rundle High where Yankee scout Atley Donald first noticed him as a senior in 1957 and followed him to the University of Mississippi.

Gibbs accepted his Ole Miss football scholarship offer because the school gave him the green light to compete in both his sports. A three-time All-SEC third baseman, he led the Rebels to their first SEC title in 1959 and a repeat in 1960. He was selected an NCAA All-American in 1960 and 1961 and his .384 career average still ranks high in Rebels baseball history.

In his junior football year, Gibbs led the SEC in passing and total offense in 1959. He is remembered for punting the ball to Louisiana State University's Billy Cannon with the #3-ranked Rebels ahead of the #1-ranked Tigers, 3-0. Heisman Trophy winner Cannon fielded the football on one bounce at his own 11-yard line and rambled 89 yards for the game's only TD.

The 7-3 loss cost Ole Miss a chance at the wire service national title since those polls were voted upon prior to bowl games. The system at that time did not take into account the Rebels' 21-0 drubbing of LSU in the Sugar Bowl 62 days later. Gibbs was All-SEC that year.

As a senior co-captain, Gibbs led Ole Miss to a national title with a 10−0−1 record. Ole Miss went on to defeat Rice University in the 1961 Sugar Bowl, 14-6, with Gibbs scoring both touchdowns as the game's Most Outstanding Player. He was a consensus NCAA All-American quarterback, the 1960 SEC Player of the Year, and third in the Heisman Trophy voting.

Despite being drafted in 1961 by the AFL's Houston Oilers and the NFL's Cleveland Browns, Gibbs opted for professional baseball, signing with the Yankees for a reported $105,000 bonus, and started with the Richmond Virginians of the Triple-A International League.

In his professional debut he accumulated five hits in a twin bill and had hits in his first eight games. The Yankees optioned him again to Richmond in 1962 where he hit .284 in 490 at-bats and was rewarded with his major league debut on September 11. He scored two runs and played third base in the only game of his career he didn't play catcher.

Manager Ralph Houk, a former catcher, suggested Gibbs learn to play catcher in 1963. He was initially resistant, but Houk convinced him that he would reach full-time status in the major leagues faster and extend his career longer. The plan was to have Gibbs succeed Elston Howard as the regular catcher. He worked hard to learn his new craft at Richmond.

With Yogi Berra's retirement before the 1964 season, Gibbs became Howard's full-time understudy after another year of seasoning in Richmond. He was called up again but was unable to appear in the 1964 World Series against the

G	AB	R	H	2B	3B	HR	RBI	SB	BB	SO	BA	OBP	SLG	TB
538	1639	157	382	53	8	25	146	28	120	231	.233	.289	.321	526

Cardinals due to broken fingers.

The Yankees traded the aging Howard to the Red Sox during the 1967 season, at which point Gibbs became the starting Yankee catcher in 1967 and 1968. He got 871 plate appearances in 240 games in those two campaigns, but 1969 marked the arrival of a young Thurman Munson.

Munson quickly established himself as the Yankees' starting catcher and went on to be the AL Rookie of the Year. Ironically, Gibbs' best year was as Munson's backup in 1970. He batted .301 with a career-high eight four-baggers that year. In June of 1971, Gibbs announced his retirement, effective at the end of the season and played his final game on September 29, 1971.

During the Yankees' off-seasons starting in 1965, Gibbs had already started to return in the fall to his alma mater in Oxford as an assistant football coach. He mentored the quarterbacks, including Heisman Trophy finalist and future National Football League great Archie Manning.

Following his retirement, Gibbs took the reins of the Ole Miss baseball program for 19 years (1972-1990). In 1972, he coached Ole Miss to the SEC title as the SEC Coach of the Year. The Rebels set an SEC mark for consecutive wins and went to their first College World Series.

He also guided the Rebels to the 1977 SEC Championship and SEC Tournament Title as the SEC Coach of the Year. Gibbs retired with 485 wins, the most of any Ole Miss coach up until that time. In 1993, he was the Yankees bullpen catcher under manager Buck Showalter and skippered the Tampa (FL) Yankees in the Class-A Florida State League in 1994 and 1995.

Gibbs was a 1995 inductee into the College Football Hall of Fame. Earlier, he had been enshrined in the Mississippi Sports Hall of Fame in 1976 and the Ole Miss Sports Hall of Fame in 1989. Gibbs has homes in both Oxford, Mississippi and Tampa, Florida. His beloved wife of many years, the former Patricia Ann Monteith, passed away in 2012. They had raised three sons. Gibbs continues to appear at the Yankee Old-Timers Days on a regular basis.

BOB GIBSON

ST. LOUIS CARDINALS
RIGHT-HANDED PITCHER

1959-1975

"He was an intimidating, arrogant-looking athlete. The arrogance he projected toward batters was fearsome. There was no guile to his pitching, just him glaring down at that batter. He wanted the game played on his terms."

~ battery mate Tim McCarver

With his fierce competitive drive, legendary intensity and toughness, Bob Gibson was almost certainly the most intimidating pitcher in history. He is still the winningest Cardinals pitcher and the second hurler behind Walter Johnson to reach 3,000 strikeouts.

Gibson led the National League in shutouts four times, struck out 200 hitters nine times, threw a no-hitter, and averaged over 19 wins from 1963 to 1972. He overwhelmed hitters with superb command, an explosive fastball, a sharp-breaking slider and a slow-looping curve. He also could bury a pitch into a hitter's ribs to re-establish who was boss.

An eight-time All-Star, the sleek 6'2" 195-pound Gibson excelled with his arm, legs, bat and glove. An agile, sure-handed athlete with nine consecutive *Rawlings* Gold Gloves, he also blasted 24 home runs with 144 RBI and could pinch hit and pinch run.

Gibson was at his best in the hot spotlight of the World Series, reeling off seven consecutive victories and hurling eight straight complete games. He is second only to Whitey Ford in Fall Classic victories with a 1.89 ERA in 81 innings of work.

★　★　★　★　★

Pack Robert Gibson was born on November 9, 1935 to Victoria and Pack Gibson in Omaha, Douglas County, Nebraska. His father died of tuberculosis three months before he was born. The youngest of seven children, he was sickly as a young boy with rickets, asthma and a heart murmur.

Gibson eventually starred in basketball, baseball and track at Omaha Technical High. Creighton University offered him a basketball scholarship as its first black hoops star. He also played center field as one of the best all-around athletes in Nebraska history.

Gibson inked contracts with both the Cardi-

nals and the world-famous Harlem Globetrotters in 1957. Omaha Cardinals manager Johnny Keane saw his potential as a pitcher right away and took him under his wing. That winter he became popular with the Trotters for his reverse dunks, but Cardinals GM Bing Devine paid him not to play again.

Gibson began 1958 at Omaha with Keane's positive influence and soon was moved up to the Rochester (NY) Red Wings. He debuted in the majors on April 15, 1959, but two trials yielded only a 6-11 record and a lukewarm appraisal by the Cardinals brass.

Fortuitously, Keane was tapped to manage St. Louis in 1961 and he immediately placed the young fireballer into the starting rotation. Gibson responded with 13 wins, then struck out 208 hitters in 1962, and broke out in 1963 with a fine 18-9 record.

He carried the team for the last two months of the 1964 season as the Cardinals caught the fading Philadelphia Phillies. In the World Series against the powerful Yankees, Gibson won Games 5 and 7 to take Most Valuable Player honors with 31 strikeouts and a 3.00 ERA in 27 innings pitched.

Enjoying another banner year in 1967 after his first two 20-game win seasons, in July the Cardinals ace was struck in the right shin by a shot off the bat of Roberto Clemente. He faced three more hitters before collapsing with a fractured fibula.

Gibson came back and took over, beating the Red Sox three times in the 1967 Fall Classic to become a Gateway City icon. He bested Jose Santiago in Games 1 and 4 and outlasted Jim Lonborg in Game 7, hitting a clutch home run, as the runaway MVP.

Gibson's 1968 campaign was a magnificent masterpiece. His 13 shutouts were the most since Grover Cleve-

G	IP	W	L	PCT	SHO	GS	CG	H	ER	SO	BB	ERA
528	3884.1	251	174	.591	56	482	255	3279	1258	3117	1336	2.91

land Alexander's record 16 in 1916. In one stretch, he allowed only two earned runs in 92 frames, hurled 47 straight scoreless innings and won 15 games in a row. He toiled 303²/₃ innings, finished 28 of 34 starts, fanned 268 and walked just 62.

The NL MVP and Cy Young winner, Gibson's ERA was 1.12, the best ever for 300+ innings. He lost five 1-0 games or his 22-9 finish would have even been better. In Series Game 1, Gibson shut out the Tigers to beat Denny McLain while fanning a record 17. He also won Game 4 and crashed a home run. His 35 strikeouts are still the standard.

Baseball responded by lowering the mound from 15 to ten inches in 1969. The measure had little effect on Gibson. He went 20-13 with a 2.18 ERA and 28 complete games and won his second Cy Young Award in 1970, going 23-7 with a 3.12 ERA.

He tore up his right knee in late 1973, ending his great run. Upon his retirement on September 1, 1975, Busch Stadium hosted Bob Gibson Day. His jersey #45 was retired forever by the Cardinals and 48,435 fans gave him a ten-minute standing ovation.

Gibson became only the sixth pitcher to be elected a first ballot National Baseball Hall of Famer in 1981. He is ranked #31 on *The Sporting News* 1999 list of "100 Greatest Baseball Players" and was voted onto Major League Baseball's elite All-Century Team.

Gibson resides in the Omaha suburb of Bellevue with his wife, the former Wendy Nelson. Just north of Omaha's Rosenblatt Stadium, the former home of the NCAA College World Series for decades, the City of Omaha has designated Bob Gibson Boulevard in honor of its favorite son. Gibson still serves as a special instructor pitching coach for the St. Louis Cardinals.

JUNIOR GILLIAM

Brooklyn & Los Angeles Dodgers
Infield • Outfield

1953-1966

"What a great team player he was. He'd hit behind Maury [Wills], take pitch after pitch after pitch. And when Maury got to second, he'd give himself up by hitting the ball to the right side, even with two strikes, which most hitters won't do."

~ teammate Jeff Torborg

Junior Gilliam played a key role in the two most glorious eras in Dodger franchise history. As one of Brooklyn's Boys of Summer that dominated the National League in the 1950s and as a mainstay for the Los Angeles Koufax Dodgers, Gilliam helped his team to seven World Series and its first four Big Trophies ever, the only position player to do so. He was widely admired for his character and the way he played the game.

No Dodger has ever been more difficult to strike out and only Pee Wee Reese has drawn more walks. Just three Dodgers have played in more games or scored more runs in history and he resides third on the all-time Dodger list with 8,299 plate appearances.

The multi-talented, versatile 5'10½" 175-pound Gilliam did all the little things to win. He was an adept bunter, an excellent hit-and-run man and a master at hitting behind the runner. A smart base runner and base stealer, he played consistently strong defense and was a positive influence in the clubhouse with his tension-cutting humor.

* * * * *

James William Gilliam, Jr. was born October 17, 1928 in Nashville, Davidson County, Tennessee to Katherine Mitchell and James William Gilliam, Sr. Raised by his grandmother after his father passed away when he was only six months old, he dropped out of Pearl High School as a senior to join the Nashville Black Volunteers of the new Negro Southern League in 1945.

After one season, he signed with the Baltimore Elite Giants. As the youngest Elite, Gilliam was dubbed "Junior" by coach George Scales and jelled with shortstop Pee Wee Butts to form one of the great double play combos in Negro League history. Scales made him a switch-hitter, and he was a Negro NL East All-Star from 1948 to 1950.

The Brooklyn Dodgers bought Gilliam's contract on April 16, 1951. Playing for the Montreal (QC) Royals in a home doubleheader, he reached base all 11 times with eight hits and three walks and hit a grand slam in his last at-bat. Gilliam led the league in runs scored twice and was voted the 1952 International League Most Valuable Player.

Clearly ready for the Big Time, Gilliam debuted on April 14, 1953 at second base, replacing Jackie Robinson who moved to third. He had instant impact with a NL-leading 710 plate appearance and 17 triples, 125 runs scored, 21 steals and a NL rookie record 100 walks. Gilliam was the National League Rookie of the Year, the fourth African American Dodger to be so honored in the award's first seven years. He also stood out in the 1953 World Series with three doubles and home runs from both sides of the plate.

Gilliam crossed home plate at least 100 times in each of his first four seasons and topped the Dodgers in steals his first six years. He hit .300 as a 1956 All-Star, paced the NL with 277 times-on-base, and finished second with 95 walks and 21 stolen bases.

In 1957, the Dodgers last season in Ebbets Field, Gilliam led the Senior Circuit in fielding and putouts and placed second in steals. Always popular for his hustling play, he became a fan favorite in the team's 1958 inaugural in California, playing 147 games at five positions and leading the team with 145 hits, 25 doubles, 18 steals and 78 walks.

Manager Walter Alston's first Los Angeles teams were built on great pitching, solid defense and small ball. Playing third base for the 1959 World Champions, Gilliam was first in the NL with 96 walks and second with 23 steals. Alston moved him to second in the order when

G	AB	R	H	2B	3B	HR	RBI	SB	BB	SO	BA	OBP	SLG	TB
1956	7119	1163	1889	304	71	65	558	203	1036	416	.265	.360	.355	2530

base stealing catalyst Maury Wills arrived. Gilliam unselfishly fouled off pitches if Wills got a poor jump, took hittable pitches when Wills had a base stolen, and discreetly used the barrel of his *Louisville Slugger* to obscure the catcher's view.

Gilliam batted .282 in the 1963 pennant year, placed sixth in that year's NL MVP vote, and helped the Dodgers to a World Series sweep over the powerful Yankees. Alston named him his third base coach after the 1964 season as one of the first African American coaches in the Big Time. However, because of team injuries, he was called back into action at third base. Gilliam hit .280 for the 1965 World Champions as part of the only all switch-hitting infield in history with Wes Parker, Jim Lefebvre and Wills.

He retired again in 1966 but Alston pressed him into duty one last time to ensure a Dodger pennant. Gilliam's last curtain call was in Game 2 of the 1966 Fall Classic before becoming a full-time coach in 1967. As part of three more NL Champions, he was well-known for schooling young Dodgers on how to act and dress as major leaguers.

Gilliam suffered a brain hemorrhage at his home on September 15, 1978. He lapsed into a coma following surgery, never regained consciousness and died on October 8 at Daniel Freeman Hospital in Inglewood with his wife of almost twenty years, Edwina Shields, at his side. The Dodgers had clinched the 1978 NL pennant the day before.

Jim Gilliam's sudden passing stunned Dodger fans on both coasts and the team wore black arm-bands with "19" on them during the World Series. The Dodgers retired his uniform #19 now displayed underneath the Dodger Stadium pavilion roof behind the left-center field fence. He is interred in the Inglewood Park Cemetery.

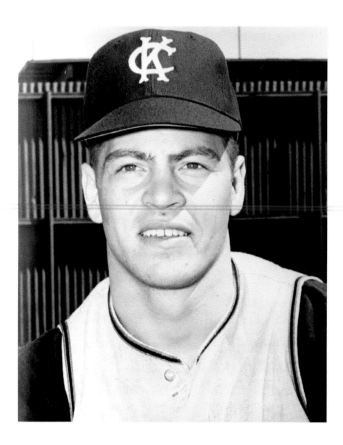

DICK GREEN

Kansas City & Oakland Athletics
Second Base

1963-1974

"Green became a human highlight reel at second base, making one sensational sprawling play after another. Had he not gone 0-for-13 at the plate, he, not Fingers, would have been the World Series MVP."

~ writer Ron Bergman
on the 1974 World Series

Dick Green was a marvelous defensive second baseman for the Kansas City and Oakland Athletics for a dozen years. He was a significant member of the Athletics dynasty that achieved the World Series Championship hat trick in 1972, 1973 and 1974. No American League second baseman had better hands. None turned the double play as efficiently.

The 5'10" 180-pound Green displayed respectable power, hitting ten or more home runs four times. He shined brightest under the intensity of the Fall Classic. His six double plays during the 1974 Series tied the mark for most twin-killings in a five-game series.

★ ★ ★ ★ ★

Richard Larry Green was born on April 21, 1941 to Leanne Singleton and Larry Green in Sioux City, Iowa. His first five years were in Sioux City before his family moved to Yankton, South Dakota where he attended grammar school. Green went to Mitchell High School in nearby Mitchell where he began to be noticed as an up-and-coming baseball talent.

Green was All-South Dakota in football and also excelled in baseball, basketball and track. As a 1959 senior, he was chosen the South Dakota High School Athlete of the Year and then played shortstop for the Mitchell Kernels in the Basin League in the summer. Green was scouted there and signed a bonus contract with the Athletics before the 1960 season.

The A's assigned him to the Class-D Sanford Greyhounds of the Florida State League for 1960, getting him 417 at-bats. He was then sent to the Class-B Lewiston (ID) Broncs in the Northwest League for 1961. Playing under manager Johnny McNamara, he batted .273.

Green advanced to the Double-A Albuquerque (NM) Dukes in the Texas League in 1962, hitting .285 with ten home runs while playing mostly third base. He continued to improve, manning second base in the Triple-A Pacific

Coast League for the Portland (OR) Beavers in 1963. Green acquitted himself so well at second the A's gave him a call up. He earned his big-league debut on September 9, seeing action in 13 games, and hit his first homer in The Show.

In 1964, Green's first full year in the bigs, he made only six errors in 130 games at second and finished the season fielding .990. He continued to play superb defense in the Athletics' last three years in Missouri, but in 1967, his average fell below the Mendoza Line.

After the 1967 season, Athletics owner Charles O. Finley decided to relocate the franchise west to Northern California. The decision proved to be a renaissance for Green. In Oakland, he put up better numbers the next two seasons. His high-water mark as a hitter was 1969 when he reached career-bests, batting .275 with 12 homers, 61 runs scored and 64 RBI.

By the time the 1972 season arrived, the Oakland A's had taken on a new team persona with gold and kelly green uniforms and white cleats instead of the more customary black ones. They also featured a rowdy hirsute look with 19 of the 25 A's growing some sort of facial hair.

The egotistical Finley was almost universally disliked by the fans, who even failed to fill the Oakland Coliseum for the World Series. Finley's players fought him and fought each other in a case of unhealthy clubhouse chemistry. Nevertheless, the A's were talented with great balance, winning 93 games and finishing runner up in the AL in runs scored (604), runs allowed (457), and defense (.732 defensive efficiency rate). Green, however, battled injuries all season long.

Oakland defeated the Tigers in a five-game ALCS, earning the right to play Cincinnati's Big Red Machine in the World Series. The Reds mirrored the Athletics' team balance, but their image and persona were the polar opposite-clean cut, no facial hair allowed, old school.

G	AB	R	H	2B	3B	HR	RBI	SB	BB	SO	BA	OBP	SLG	TB
1288	4007	427	960	145	23	80	340	26	345	785	.240	.303	.347	1391

Second only to World Series MVP Gene Tenace, Green hit .333 (6-for-18) during the epic battle between the two evenly matched teams that ended in a narrow seven-game victory for the Athletics. Two cities and 41 years later, the Athletics had finally won a Fall Classic again.

In the 1973 Fall Classic, Oakland met a relatively weak 82-79 Mets. Led by Series MVP Reggie Jackson, the A's eked out another seven-game win to make it two straight world titles. Afterward, Athletics manager Dick Williams quit in disgust because of Finley's meddling.

Green had a major influence over the first ever All-California Fall Classic versus the Dodgers in 1974. He tied a Series record in Game 3 by starting three double plays, the first two by doubling up runners after catching line drives. The third was a ground ball to end the game.

Green also started a game-ending double play in Game 4. In the eighth inning of the Game 5 finale at the Oakland Coliseum, he gunned down the Dodgers' Billy Buckner with a perfect peg to third to preserve the 3-2 victory. It would be Green's last game as a major leaguer.

Although future Hall of Famer Rollie Fingers was named World Series MVP, Green was honored with the 1974 Babe Ruth Award given annually by the New York Chapter of the Baseball Writers Association of America to the "World Series Most Outstanding Player." He received this prestigious award for his incredible fielding, despite not registering a single hit.

For several years previously, Green had made an annual rite of announcing his imminent retirement, but had stayed on each time for one more year. He made the decision to retire on top after experiencing the satisfaction of earning his third straight World Series title ring.

Rapid City has been Green's home not only during his major league career but after it as well. He operated a moving company in Rapid City, which he eventually sold to his partner. He is now retired and continues to reside in Rapid City with his wife Jenny.

TERRY HARMON

PHILADELPHIA PHILLIES
INFIELD

1967 • 1969-1977

Terry Harmon was one of the most respected and valuable utility infielders in Phillies history and a key player in the franchise's renaissance. He started his career with second division Philly clubs in the late 1960s and finished as a member of two straight NL East champion teams.

The reliable 6'2" 185-pound Harmon probably could have been the starting shortstop on half dozen other big-league squads but settled into a "Super Sub" role, playing second base, shortstop and third base. He was also the Phillies' player rep for three years (1971 to 1973).

Harmon always seemed to come up with the timely pinch-hit, bunt or great fielding play. He was one of those rare players who could sit on the bench for weeks and then, when called upon suddenly, could step on the field and play rock-solid defense at three infield positions.

★ ★ ★ ★ ★

Terry Walter Harmon was born to Janie Radabaugh and Walter M. Harmon on April 12, 1944 in Toledo, Lucas County, Ohio. He grew up in Toledo and attended Thomas A. DeVilbiss High School where he graduated in 1962 after excelling in football, basketball and baseball.

Harmon went on to play at Ohio University and led the Tigers to the 1964 Mid-American Conference title while hitting .420 to rank eighth in the NCAA University Division. He also keyed the Tigers to the 1965 MAC title and later was inducted into the Ohio University Sports Hall of Fame in 1978.

Harmon was taken in the fifth round by the Phillies in the June amateur free agent draft. After hitting .322 for the semi-pro Bloomington Bobcats, good for third in the Central Illinois Collegiate League batting race that summer, he signed with scout Tony Lucadello in September.

Harmon spent 1966 with the Bakersfield Bears of the California League and 1967 with the Tidewater (VA) Tides where he paced all Carolina League shortstops in fielding at .960. It earned him his major league debut on July 23, when he was sent in to pinch-run at Connie Mack Stadium versus the Reds. It would only be a two at-bat cameo and a quick trip back to the minors.

With the 1968 Buffalo (NY) Bisons of the Triple-A International League on July 20, Harmon suffered a shoulder separation in a head-first slide into second base. On the disabled list for the balance of the season, he had nonetheless impressed the Phillies brass with his versatility.

Harmon made the Philadelphia roster for good in 1969. Called up the night before Opening Day at Wrigley Field, he drilled a pinch-hit single up the middle in the seventh off Cubs ace Ferguson Jenkins. Harmon went on to appear in 88 games and logged 227 plate appearances.

In 1970, Harmon played in 71 games, making only two errors in the field while again splitting time in three positions. By 1971, Larry Bowa was the Phillies' regular shortstop and the team began employing the sure-handed Harmon more at second base.

Harmon set a post-1900 major league record with 18 chances at second in a nine-inning game on June 12, 1971. He accepted all of the chances with seven putouts and 11 assists, fielding eight grounders and getting in on three twin killings started by third baseman Bobby Pfeil.

He and his good friend and roommate Denny Doyle shared second base duties in 1972. The left-handed hitting Doyle started against right-handed pitching and Harmon played against lefties. He batted a team-high .284 in 218 at-bats and fielded .996 in 50 games at second base. Harmon also smacked his first homer, an inside-the-parker, at the Astrodome on August 30.

The 1973 and 1974 seasons would be a test of his renowned upbeat attitude. In 1974, three of the four Nation-

> *"They don't make too many Terry Harmons. It's a pleasure to have a guy like that around. Some guys don't play and pretty soon they become clubhouse lawyers. They've had a few of them here the last couple of years. Terry isn't like that. He's an asset on the field and off the field."*
>
> ~ *Phillies manager Frank Lucchesi*

G	AB	R	H	2B	3B	HR	RBI	SB	BB	SO	BA	OBP	SLG	TB
547	1125	164	262	31	12	4	72	17	117	175	.233	.311	.292	329

al League ironmen who appeared in all 162 games were his Phillies teammates- third baseman Mike Schmidt, second baseman Dave Cash, and shortstop Bowa. Harmon saw action in only 27 games.

By 1975, Philadelphia was contending and up-and-coming teams need great role players like Harmon. Despite only one official at-bat in the first 41 games, he performed in 33 games at shortstop after Bowa broke his thumb and sparkled in the field with only one defensive miscue.

Harmon hit a career-high .295 in 1976 after a year long slump in 1975, yet his fielding seemed to regress (.960 at short and .958 at second). The Phillies finally won the division in 1976, but were swept in the NL Championship Series by Cincinnati's Big Red Machine.

The Phillies won their second consecutive NL Eastern Division title in 1977, Harmon's last year in the major leagues. This time the club played the Dodgers in the NLCS, but lost in four games. Harmon fielded better in 1977 but he had progressively lost some of his bat speed.

As much as the Phillies appreciated Harmon's contributions over the years, the team was pointing toward its first World Series championship and his production had fallen off precipitously. As it turned out, Harmon's last major league game was on October 7, 1977.

After struggling in Phillies spring training in Clearwater, Florida, Harmon was given his release before Opening Day on April 13, 1978. His only coaching job was the following year with the Oklahoma City (OK) 89ers of the Triple-A American Association in 1979.

After baseball, Harmon worked for the Philly cable sports channel PRISM, QVC home shopping, and Jewelry TV in Tennessee. He and his wife, the former Kay Gernheuser, reside in South Jersey. He still keeps tabs on the Phillies and enjoys hunting and fishing.

JOHN HILLER

DETROIT TIGERS
LEFT-HANDED PITCHER

1965-1970 • 1972-1980

"Considering the physical problems he had to overcome and the era in which he pitched, John Hiller should be regarded among the elite relief pitchers in baseball history."

~ *battery mate Lance Parrish*

After nearly dying of several heart attacks, John Hiller fought back to author the finest season by a reliever in major league history. He retired with 125 saves and 545 games pitched, more than any other Tiger. Hiller is the Detroit leader with 7.51 strikeouts-per-nine-innings.

The 6'1" 185-pound Hiller logged 962²/₃ career innings in relief, employing a devastating three-pitch repertoire featuring a low-90s fastball with movement, a darting slider, and a baffling change-of-pace. He and Rollie Fingers changed the way the game valued the relief ace.

★ ★ ★ ★ ★

John Frederick Hiller was born in Toronto, Ontario, Canada to Ethel Cassis and Donald Hiller on April 8, 1943. The son of an auto body repairman, he grew up in nearby Scarborough with his brother Jim, playing ice hockey as a goaltender and hanging around Maple Leaf Gardens as a diehard hockey fan.

As a junior at Scarborough High, in a seven-inning game he struck out an amazing 22 hitters (one man advanced to first base on a wild pitch after fanning). He also pitched in Toronto semi-pro leagues where Tigers scout Cy Williams discovered him and signed him in June 1962.

Hiller began his career with the Jamestown (NY) Tigers of the New York-Penn League in 1963 with 14 wins. After posting a 2.53 ERA for the 1965 Montgomery (AL) Rebels (Southern League), he received a September 6 major league call up, but pitched most of 1966 with the Syracuse (NY) Chiefs (International League), and began 1967 with the Toledo Mud (OH) Hens.

Detroit Tiger manager Mayo Smith recalled him in late August and made him a starter. Hiller tossed against the Indians and A's and won a third straight start, almost shutting out the Angels. As a rookie he sported a 2.63 ERA and a stellar 49-to-9 strikeout-to-walk ratio.

Hiller played a key role on the Tigers' 1968 World Series titlist team. Pitching mostly in relief, he was also an effective starter. Hiller rang up the first six Cleveland batters he faced to tie a big-league record on August 6; whitewashed Chicago on August 20; and came on in the eighth at Yankee Stadium to pitch nine shutout innings on August 23. With two complete-game wins in September, Hiller finished with 39 appearances, 12 starts, a 9–6 line and a 2.39 ERA. He was the top reliever in a corps that combined for 24 of the Tigers' impressive 103 wins.

Pitching coach Johnny Sain worked with Hiller in 1969 to polish a new slider. He pitched in relief in 1970 except for four starts in September. In the season finale, he punched out seven Cleveland hitters in a row to tie an AL record on his way to a 1-0 two-hitter, striking out 11.

Hiller had put on 35 pounds since 1968, engaged in only spotty conditioning over each winter, and smoked heavily. He suffered three heart attacks on January 11, 1971 at only 27 and almost died. His recovery goes down as one of the greatest comeback stories in baseball annals.

Against all odds, Hiller was back running, lifting and stretching three hours a day by November. While serving as a minor league pitching instructor, he learned a more deceptive change-up from coach John Grodzicki. The new third pitch added to his effectiveness, but he only went north initially as a batting practice pitcher.

When two starters went down with arm trouble in July, Hiller finally got his chance. He went on to throw in 24 games with a fine 2.03 ERA and a strikeout-to-walk ratio of 26-to-13. In the 1972 ALCS Game 4, Hiller won in relief, shutting Oakland down after the A's had scored two runs in the tenth inning. He earned the win when Detroit got three in the last of the tenth.

Hiller had the greatest single season for a closer in baseball history in 1973, the American League's first year using the designated hitter rule when the league ERA climbed from 3.06 in 1972 to 3.82. Tiger Stadium was one of the most hitter-friendly ballparks in the AL at that time.

G	IP	W	L	PCT	SHO	GS	CG	SV	H	ER	SO	BB	ERA
545	1242	87	76	.534	6	43	13	125	1040	391	1036	535	2.83

Averaging almost two innings per game, Hiller pitched 125⅓ innings in a major league-high 65 games, finished 60 games and struck out 124 with a superb 1.44 ERA. His record 38 saves were 11 more than the AL runner up. Hiller was the AL Fireman of the Year, Comeback Player of the Year, and won the Hutch Award for his fighting spirit and competitive desire.

Pitching for a club that finished in the AL East cellar in 1974, Hiller threw 150 innings all in relief and went 17-14 to set a new Junior Circuit standard for most relief decisions in a season. His 17 relief victories were just one shy of the record of 18 set by Pirates fireman Elroy Face in 1959.

Hiller's 1975 year was halted when he pulled a muscle in late July. He returned in 1976 to resume his role as the Tigers' most reliable reliever. After hurling 55 games out of the bullpen, he started the season's finale and blanked the Brewers on four hits for his 12th victory.

His 92⅓ innings in 1978 were his fewest in a full campaign since his rookie year, even though he pitched in 51 games. Hiller was 9-4 with a 2.34 ERA and 15 saves, but with seven blown saves. By 1979, it had become evident that he was nearing the end of the trail.

Early in the 1980 schedule, Hiller pitched ineffectively in 11 games. His final appearance was on May 27 when he was hit hard by the Yankees. The 38-year-old veteran retired on May 30 as the oldest Tiger and the last link to the celebrated 1968 championship team.

Hiller returned to the organization as a roving pitching coach in Lakeland, Florida, but a circulatory blockage behind one knee demanded he step away. Today he remains in great health and is still committed to all the heart-related charities he became involved in when he pitched.

Hiller and his second wife Linette have been married since 1985 and reside in Iron Mountain on Michigan's Upper Peninsula. He is a member of the Canadian Baseball Hall of Fame (1985), Canada's Sports Hall of Fame (1999), and the All-Time Detroit Tigers Team.

AL KALINE

DETROIT TIGERS
RIGHT FIELD

1953-1974

"I have always referred to Al Kaline as Mr. Perfection. He does it all- hitting, fielding, throwing, running- and he does it with that extra touch of brilliancy that marks him as a super ballplayer."

~ Tigers manager Billy Martin

Al Kaline had one of the most sublime careers in history, coming to Detroit as a shy 18-year old boy and leaving 22 years later as the legendary "Mr. Tiger." He played more games and hit more home runs than any other Tiger, but it was his character, class and leadership that made him the most popular in franchise history. *The Sporting News* Player of the Year in 1955 and 1963, Kaline kept working to perfect his skills to become one of the finest all-around players ever to grace a major league field.

The versatile Kaline played in 100 plus games a record 20 straight seasons, while hitting better than .300 nine times and produced 25 or more home runs seven times. A star among stars, he averaged .324 in 16 All-Star games. His understated style and work ethic seemed to blend perfectly with the blue collar character of the Motor City.

The 6'2" 184-pound Kaline is still heralded as one of the finest rightfielders of any era, earning ten *Rawlings* Gold Gloves. He turned playing right field into an art form with his fluid, silky smooth style. Kaline had a quick first step, sure hands, great reflexes, excellent speed, and a cannon throwing arm that was accurate. He once cut down two runners at home in the same inning and performed in 242 straight games without an error.

Kaline was a proud, dignified gentleman. The definitive team player, he was a credit to his adopted city and his franchise. He supported his managers in the clubhouse and was attentive and respectful to Tiger fans. Kaline's teammates paid him the ultimate tribute. They simply referred to him by his uniform number- "Six."

★ ★ ★ ★ ★

Albert William Kaline was born in Baltimore, Maryland on December 19, 1934 to Naomi and Nicholas Kaline. He was born with baseball in his blood as his grandfather, father, and two uncles all played semi-professionally on Maryland's Eastern Shore.

Kaline drew scouts from all 16 major league teams at Baltimore Southern High School while hitting .333, .418, .469, and .488 respectively, making the All-Maryland prep team each year. Upon graduation, Kaline signed with Detroit for $30,000 and debuted with the Tigers a week later as a bonus baby required to be on the major league roster for two years.

Already a polished defender, he won over teammates with his talent and dedication and would never play in the minor leagues. Still only 20 years old in the spring of 1955, he hit safely in 23 of his first 24 games and went on to become the youngest American League batting champion ever. Kaline finished at .340 with 27 home runs, 102 runs batted in, and a league-leading 200 hits, establishing himself as one of the baseball's brightest stars before he was even eligible to vote.

Kaline followed with another dazzling season, batting .314 with 196 hits, 27 homers and a career-high 128 RBI. From 1957 to 1967, his consistency was remarkable as he hit between .280 and .300 each year with 18 to 25 homers and 70 to 100 RBI.

Detroit finally earned its first pennant in the Kaline era in 1968. The Tigers lost three of their first four World Series games and were pushed to the brink of elimination by the Cardinals. In the defining moment of the Fall Classic in Game 5, down 3-2 in the seventh inning with the bases loaded, Kaline delivered a game-

G	AB	R	H	2B	3B	HR	RBI	SB	BB	SO	BA	OBP	SLG	TB
2834	10116	1622	3007	498	75	399	1583	137	1277	1020	.297	.376	.480	4852

winning line shot to right-center, driving in two runs. Also referred to as "The Line," he had come through with *everything* on the line, igniting a roaring Tigers comeback that gave Detroit its first world title since 1945. He led all Tigers at .379 with 11 hits and eight crucial runs batted in.

After an injury-marred 1971 season, he earned glorious redemption when he led the Tigers to the 1972 AL playoffs in one of his finest performances. In September Kaline carried his teammates on his back with key hits in game after game, finishing at .313 and leading his team all the way to the AL Championship Series with Oakland.

In Baltimore on September 24, 1974, Kaline powered a double off Dave McNally to become the twelfth man to reach 3,000 hits. At the end of his storybook career a week later, Kaline and Ty Cobb were the only players to spend two full decades as a Tiger.

He was the 1973 recipient of the prestigious Roberto Clemente Award in recognition of his humanitarianism, character and integrity. In 1980, Kaline became the tenth man ever elected on the first ballot to the National Baseball Hall of Fame and his uniform #6 was retired that same summer at Tiger Stadium. A statue of Kaline now stands above left-center field at the Tigers' beautiful new Comerica Park.

He has remained active within the Detroit organization, serving as a color commentator on the Tigers WWJ-TV broadcasts from 1975 to 2002. Since 2003, Kaline has been a special assistant to the Detroit Tigers' brass and has worked as a coach. "Mr. Tiger" continues to live in Bloomfield Hills near Detroit with his wife, the former Louise Hamilton. He is an avid golfer and works in a variety of charitable causes.

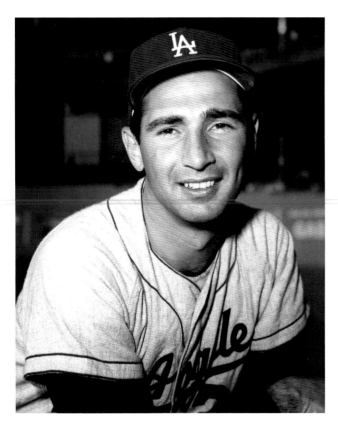

SANDY KOUFAX

BROOKLYN & LOS ANGELES DODGERS
LEFT-HANDED PITCHER

1955-1966

*"If Sandy Koufax
did not exist, we
would have had
to invent him."*

~ poet Robert Pinsky

The incomparable Sandy Koufax has often been referred to as the greatest left-handed pitcher in baseball history. A flame thrower with a classic style and an unassuming genteel bearing, his astonishing achievements in his last half dozen years on center stage have continued to inspire admiration in the afterglow of his brilliant career.

Koufax is one of only five pitchers with more strikeouts than innings pitched. He fanned ten or more batters in a game 97 times and topped the NL in strikeouts four times. Koufax won two MVP awards and three Cy Young awards, all unanimously.

A seven-time All-Star, Koufax is the only hurler ever to lead the NL five straight years in ERA. He earned three Major League Triple Crowns (wins, strikeouts & ERA). Under the national spotlight, Koufax was twice the World Series Most Valuable Player.

Koufax possessed the best rising fastball and finest overhand curve ball in the game. It was known that he tipped his pitches, but his stuff was so overpowering it didn't matter. Batters knew what was coming and Koufax was still unhittable.

* * * * *

Sanford Braun was born on December 30, 1935 to Evelyn Lichtenstein and Jack Braun in Brooklyn, New York. His parents divorced when he was five. His mother married attorney Irving Koufax when he was nine and he took his stepfather's name.

The family moved to Brooklyn's Bensonhurst section before his sophomore year at Lafayette High. There he was better known for his basketball skills, scoring 165 points in ten games as the senior captain. He played mostly first base on the baseball team.

Koufax walked on to the University of Cincinnati to play basketball and later earned a partial scholarship when he made the 1954 varsity. After his frosh year, Dodger scout Al Campanis gave the 19-year-old a tryout at Ebbets Field and signed him to a $20,000 bonus. The contract required Koufax to be on the big-league roster for two years.

At 6'2" and 210 pounds, Koufax was blessed with exciting talent, but the young prodigy was not able to harness a fastball that was clocked at upwards of 102 miles per hour. For six long, frustrating years, he saw limited action while learning how to pitch.

In early 1961, Koufax received some advice from Norm Sherry. His battery mate contended that he need not throw as hard as he was able. If he would throttle back a few miles an hour, it might lead to better control. Koufax leveraged Sherry's observations and broke out with 18 wins and a NL record 269 strikeouts. His progress continued in 1962. He won 14 games before suffering a serious circulatory problem in his left index finger.

Koufax became baseball's premier pitcher in 1963. He won 25 games, struck out 306, finished 20 complete games, hurled 11 shutouts, and won two World Series games in the sweep over the Yankees. He was the NL's MVP and the Cy Young Award winner.

After 19 victories in 1964, another arm injury once more ended his campaign prematurely. Hurling almost 1,000 innings in four years, the great left-hander had traumatic arthritis in his pitching arm and was faced with pain killers and cortisone shots.

The Dodgers' 1965 season was anchored by their courageous ace's 26 victories, a record 382 strikeouts in $335^{2}/_{3}$ innings, and a microscopic 1.94 ERA. Koufax added a perfect game, his record fourth no-hit no-run gem in as many years. In a pitching duel for the ages, he bested Cubs pitcher Bob Hendley, who himself threw a one-hitter.

G	IP	W	L	PCT	SHO	GS	CG	H	ER	SO	BB	ERA
397	2324.1	165	87	.655	40	314	137	1754	713	2396	817	2.76

In October, Koufax earned lasting respect when he announced that he would not pitch on Yom Kippur, the Jewish Day of Atonement. He sent the clear signal that the High Holy Day meant more to him than Game 1 of the 1965 World Series. Although Koufax lost Game 2, he rebounded heroically to win Games 5 and 7 against the Twins.

He made his last year his finest. Koufax threw 323 innings in 1966, won a career-high 27 games, completed a stunning 27 starts, and struck out 317. He had mastered his art with a combination of natural ability, an almost perfect mental makeup, and a competitive heart. He had become pitching's 20th century Michelangelo.

At the final act, a subdued Sandy Koufax called a press conference and stoically announced his retirement at the young age of 31, citing his damaged arm. As author Jane Leavy noted, "No other sports hero had retired so young, so well, or so completely."

His Dodger uniform #32 was retired in 1972 just months before he became the youngest player ever to be inducted into the National Baseball Hall of Fame at age 36. He was honored as baseball's Player of the Decade for the 1960s and one of only 30 legends on Major League Baseball's prestigious All-Century All-Star Team.

After his career, Koufax tried his hand as a sportscaster and has continued to work with the young Dodger pitching talent. A true master of his craft, Koufax still becomes animated when he breaks down the art of pitching for his spellbound young charges.

But outside the sanctuary of his baseball family, his natural reticence has made him an enigma to the press. Ironically, Koufax's desire to maintain his privacy has only added to his legend. The innate dignity of the gentleman has become even more evident as the years have passed. He currently lives a private life in Bucks County, Pennsylvania.

ED KRANEPOOL

NEW YORK METS
FIRST BASE

1962-1979

"The Mets have as much of a chance to win the World Series as man has of landing on the moon."

~ Ed Kranepool,
spring training 1969

Ed Kranepool became the only player to compete in each of the New York Metropolitans' first 18 seasons. No other Met has ever played as long for the club. Kranepool's career spanned the ineptitude of the expansion Amazin' Mets of 1962 through the glory of the 1969 Miracle Mets and a decade beyond.

★ ★ ★ ★ ★

Edward Emil Kranepool III was born November 8, 1944 in the Bronx, New York to Emily and Edward Emil Kranepool, Jr. Upon graduation from high school, he signed a bonus contract with the Mets for $85,000. While still 17 years old on September 22, 1962, Kranepool got his first big-league at-bat against the Cubs at the old Polo Grounds.

Manager Casey Stengel, "The Ol' Perfessor," started him at first base the next day in place of the celebrated "Marvelous Marv" Throneberry, perhaps the most infamous of the hapless Amazin' Mets. However, Kranepool's contribution to the team that set the modern Major League Baseball season record of 120 losses was minimal.

In the following two years, Kranepool continued to improve while he was learning to play at the big-league level. Despite Throneberry's popularity with the Mets fans, his lackluster play finally relegated him to the Triple-A Buffalo (NY) Bisons. That left Kranepool with the first base job if he could hold it but Kranepool himself was farmed out in July of 1963.

With the Mets' acquisition of future Hall of Famer Warren Spahn in 1965, Kranepool relinquished his uniform #21. With his new #7 and a new maturity, Kranepool was chosen a National League All-Star, performing in 153 games and hitting .253 with 133 hits, 24 doubles,

ten home runs and 55 runs batted in.

As Kranepool continued to develop, so did the Mets. They were no longer the bumbling Mets of Stengel. Gil Hodges was now at the helm with good young talent in their early to mid-20s including Tommie Agee (26), Jerry Grote (26), Bud Harrelson (24), Cleon Jones (26), Jerry Koosman (25), Kranepool (24), Tug McGraw (24), Nolan Ryan (22), Tom Seaver (24), Art Shamsky (27), Ron Swoboda (24) and Al Weis (24).

By 1969, Mets fans were guardedly optimistic that their team would put together at least a winning season, something that had not yet happened in seven campaigns. Not only did astronaut Neil Armstrong walk on the moon on July 20, 1969, but the Mets, against even greater odds, won 100 regular season games and the World Series title.

It was the most unlikely, whimsical, underdog scenario in baseball history. The thrilling, magical season of 1969 was one for the ages that will never be forgotten in New York. And Kranepool played his part, hitting a home run in World Series Game 3.

He finished poorly in 1969 and Kranepool was about to encounter the most important crucible of his career. Despite his eight-year tenure, the Mets banished him unceremoniously to the Tidewater (VA) Tides in the Triple-A International League in early 1970. A disconcerted Kranepool seriously considered retirement as he spent almost the entire year with Tidewater.

To his credit, Kranepool showed resiliency and enjoyed his best season in 1971. He hit .280 with 14 home runs and 58 runs batted in while leading the National League with a near perfect .998 fielding percentage. Kranepool had turned his demotion into a time to develop professionally. From then on, he

G	AB	R	H	2B	3B	HR	RBI	SB	BB	SO	BA	OBP	SLG	TB
1851	5436	536	1418	225	25	118	1058	15	454	581	.261	.316	.377	2047

made himself valuable as a first baseman, outfielder and pinch hitter.

Between 1974 and 1978, Kranepool became one of baseball's premier pinch hitters, batting .396. He hit .486 in that role in 1974, still the all-time major league season record for pinch hitters with 35 or more at-bats. Kranepool remains the Mets record holder with 90 career pinch hits. He had not only become popular with Mets fans, but he was also a favorite with Mets owner Joan Payson who rejected all bids to trade him.

Thereafter, with the exception of his 455 plate appearances in 1976, Kranepool experienced a diminishing role with his team. While he was the youngest player in the major leagues in 1962 when he broke in, he also retired relatively young at the age of 34. This was hastened by the purchase of the Mets by Fred Wilpon and Nelson Doubleday. Kranepool had been a part of a competing consortium which offered a legitimate bid, but lost out in the end, and he no longer had the benefaction of Mrs. Payson.

While "The Krane" was never destined to be a Hall of Famer, he finished his career as the New York Mets all-time leader in eight offensive categories. Before the 2015 season, he still leads in games played and ranks second only to David Wright in at-bats, plate appearances, hits, single, doubles, times-on-base, sacrifice flies, outsmade, and double-plays-grounded-into.

Kranepool played in 1,853 games, more games than any Met in history. He was inducted into the New York Mets Hall of Fame in 1990. As testament to his continuing popularity, Mets baseball is still celebrated on the internet through the Eddie Kranepool Society. He currently resides in New York as a stockbroker and restaurateur.

VERNON LAW

PITTSBURGH PIRATES
RIGHT-HANDED PITCHER

1950-1951 • 1954-1967

"Not only is Law magnificent in his chosen field of endeavor, but one who is also a living symbol of all that is good and clean in this troubled world. No athlete better exemplifies the kind of man every youngster should aspire to be than the tall handsome Mormon from Boise, Idaho."

~ Pittsburgh Post-Gazette 1965

Vernon Law was baseball's 1960 Cy Young Award winner while leading the Pirates to their first World Series championship since 1925. The 6'3" 200-pound right-hander was at his best when his team needed him the most with precision command and a sneaky-fast fastball.

Law is a member of the ordained priesthood of the Church of Jesus Christ of Latter-Day Saints (LDS) Church. Former Pirates teammate Wally Westlake nicknamed him "Deacon" in the 1950s and Pirate broadcaster Bob Prince later popularized it in the Steel City.

★　★　★　★　★

Vernon Sanders Law was born in rural Meridian, Ada County, Idaho on March 12, 1930 to Melva Christina Sanders and Jesse Law. He and his two brothers grew up working on the farm, bailing hay and doing physical field work. After he graduated from Meridian High in 1948, scouts from nine major league clubs descended on tiny Meridian to vie for his services.

Idaho Senator Herman Welker had mentioned the young hurler to his friend, singer and Pirate minority owner Bing Crosby. Bucs scout Babe Herman arrived with roses and chocolates for Law's mother. Halfway through the meeting, the phone rang with Crosby on the line.

It sealed the deal for the Pirates and the team sent him to Santa Rosa (CA) of the Class-D Far West League. He went 8-5 before being promoted to Davenport (IA) of the Class-B Three-I League, where he sported a 2.94 ERA in 144 innings pitched in 1949.

With the 1950 New Orleans (LA) Pelicans of the Double-A Southern Association, Law threw 81 innings by early June. His 2.67 ERA earned him his debut in the Big Time on June 11. The next year, Law tore a rotator muscle after he hurled in both ends of a rain delay.

A stint in the military during the Korean War (1952-53) allowed him to heal. Law's arm had recovered so

fully by 1955 that he tied an NL record by pitching 18 innings in a game. From 1954 through 1957, he and Bob Friend anchored a young pitching corps on mediocre teams.

The Bucs steadily assembled a strong core with the emergence of players such as Roberto Clemente, Bill Mazeroski, Dick Groat and Bill Virdon. Law and Friend both came of age in 1958 and the Pirates climbed to second. Law pitched 266 innings in 1959 and won 18 games.

He was the indispensable Pirates ace in their 1960 World Series Championship season. He finished with a 20-9 record with a NL-high 18 complete games in 35 starts. He was an ironman in an era of four-man rotations and without relief specialists as we know them today.

During the pennant-clinching celebration in Milwaukee, a teammate grabbed at his shoe and Law locked up his foot and leg to brace himself for the twisting. It resulted in a severe ankle injury that forced him to alter his pitching delivery in the 1960 World Series.

Pittsburgh followed a formula of losing big and winning close in the Fall Classic. In Game 1 at Forbes Field, Law took a 6-2 lead into the eighth inning before stepping aside for reliever Elroy Face in the Bucs' 6-4 victory. In Game 4, Law helped his own cause with two hits, an RBI double and a run scored. Face relieved him again in the seventh to preserve the win, 3-2.

In the white hot pressure of Game 7, Law checked the Bronx Bombers early. Manager Danny Murtaugh thought he saw Law's ankle weaken and pulled him for Face in the sixth in a 4-1 game. The Pirates won in the ninth on Mazeroski's walk-off home run. They were outscored 55-27 and out hit 91-60. In the four games Law didn't start, New York averaged almost 11 runs.

His ankle injury led to three years of shoulder woes. He missed most of 1961 with another torn rotator muscle. Law took to carrying a red spiral notebook entitled

G	IP	W	L	PCT	SHO	GS	CG	H	ER	SO	BB	ERA
483	2672	162	147	.524	28	364	119	2833	1118	1092	597	3.77

Words to Live By and filled it with aphorisms. He wrote, "Difficulty can be the means of opening up a new opportunity." He entered two other famous quotes: "A winner never quits and a quitter never wins" and "Experience is a hard teacher because she gives the test first, the lesson afterwards."

Pitching in pain during 1962, Law rebounded to go 10-7, but was hurt in the spring of 1963. He worked his way back in May, but only appeared in 18 games the entire season. With so many arm setbacks, he asked the Bucs to put him on the voluntarily retired list in August.

The winter caused him to re-think his decision. Law returned in 1964, winning 12 games with a 3.61 ERA. Despite losing his first five starts in 1965, he came on to win eight straight and then another nine in a row. With a two-hitter and three three-hitters, he paced the Bucs with 17 wins and a 2.15 ERA to earn the Lou Gehrig Memorial Comeback Player of the Year Award.

After an injury-laden final two years, Law appeared for the last time as a major league hurler on August 20, 1967. He started serving as a Brigham Young University assistant baseball coach in 1969 and spent two decades as a coach for a variety of organizations before moving on to corporate sales.

When his son Vance, a former 11-year major leaguer, was appointed BYU head coach in 2000, Law helped the Cougars' program by sharing pitching tips and throwing batting practice. He has been the pitching coach for the Provo High nine across from the BYU campus.

Law and his wife of over 50 years, the former VaNita McGuire, raised a daughter, VaLynda, and five sons — Veldon, Veryl, Vance, Vaughn and Varlin. The couple has 29 grandchildren and nine great-grandchildren who frequently visit their Grandview Hill home.

After seven-way bypass heart surgery in early 2005, the 75-year-old Law was swinging a golf club within weeks before giving in to family pleas to adhere to a proper recovery period. Law has since returned to his two favorite spots — the golf course and the pitching mound.

BILL MAZEROSKI

PITTSBURGH PIRATES
SECOND BASE

1956-1972

""Bill Mazeroski's defensive statistics are probably the most impressive of any player at any position."

~ baseball analyst
Bill James

Bill Mazeroski was the greatest defensive second baseman in the history of baseball. Yet his enduring reputation was assured in one dramatic moment on October 13, 1960 when he became the only man to hit a Game 7 World Series walk off home run.

"Maz" was awarded eight *Rawlings* Gold Glove awards for fielding excellence, posting a sparkling .983 career average despite playing on the rough Forbes Field infield. He led the National League in assists nine times, double plays eight times and chances accepted eight times- all of the totals are highest in Senior Circuit history for a second baseman. Maz registered at least 500 assists in five campaigns to tie the NL mark.

Total Baseball has given Mazeroski a 36.3 player rating, ranking him 62nd best all-time. His 1,706 double plays are the most ever and his quick feet, marvelous soft hands, lightning quick transfer and accurate arm all contributed to hundreds of saved runs. Maz was dubbed "No Touch" for his ability to redirect the ball from his glove to his hand. Pirates broadcaster Bob Prince referred to Mazeroski simply as "The Glove."

A seven-time NL All-Star, the stocky 5'11" 183-pound Maz was also dangerous with his bat. From 1957 to 1968, he drove in 608 runs, the most of any middle infielder. He hit over twice as many homers in away parks as he did at cavernous Forbes Field. Yet he was still one of the top home run hitters among NL second basemen of his era.

★　★　★　★　★

William Stanley Mazeroski was born to Mayme and Lew Mazeroski in Wheeling, West Virginia on September 5, 1936. He grew up not far from Pittsburgh in Tiltonsville, Ohio where he was encouraged by a father who loved the game. Maz attended Warren Consolidated High School there, starring in baseball and basketball. As a fresh-

man, he was already a force as a shortstop and pitcher. The Pirates signed him upon graduation.

In 1954, Maz spent his first pro summer with the Double-A Williamsport (PA) Grays and his second year with the Hollywood (CA) Stars of the Pacific Coast League. He debuted in the big-leagues on July 7, 1956, turning his first double play off the bat of Willie Mays. However, he didn't begin to flourish until 1958 when he played in his first All-Star game, won his first *Rawlings* Gold Glove, and bombed a career-best 19 home runs.

He was a major factor in the 1960 World Series from beginning to end. Against the favored Bronx Bombers of Mickey Mantle and Roger Maris, Maz provided the margin of victory with a two-run round tripper in Game 1 and turned three double plays. He also laced a two-run RBI double in the Game 5 victory.

However, his lasting fame came with one swing of his *Louisville Slugger* bat. The stage was set as he led off the bottom of the ninth inning in Game 7 with the score tied, 9-9. After taking a pitch, Mazeroski drove a high fastball from Ralph Terry over the left field wall to give the Steel City its first World Series title since 1925.

Pandemonium broke out as he leapt around the bases and was mobbed by fans and teammates at home plate. He earned the Babe Ruth Award as the World Series Most Outstanding Player and was *The Sporting News* 1960 Major League Player of the Year.

The middle infield of Mazeroski and Dick Groat was the foundation of the 1960 title run. Maz took over as Pirate captain in 1963 and worked with shortstop Dick Schofield for two years. Then in 1965, he and Gold Glove shortstop Gene Alley teamed as one of the best keystone combinations in baseball annals. The Bucs turned a NL record 215 double plays in 1966 and Maz

G	AB	R	H	2B	3B	HR	RBI	SB	BB	SO	BA	OBP	SLG	TB
2163	7755	769	2016	294	62	138	853	27	447	706	.260	.299	.367	2848

took part in 161- the most ever for a second baseman.

He suffered from pulled muscles in both legs in 1967, yet refused to come out of the lineup and set a NL record with 163 games played at second. The durable Maz also set the league mark with 392 consecutive games played by a second baseman that year.

His leg problems took him out of the lineup in 1969 as Dave Cash took over at second. Mazeroski played no more than 70 games in each of the 1969, 1971 and 1972 seasons in a utility role. He retired officially on October 24, 1972 to become a member of manager Bill Virdon's coaching staff, but only stayed a year.

Mazeroski's uniform jersey #9 was retired forever by the Pirates on August 7, 1987. He was elected to the National Baseball Hall of Fame in 2001 by the Veterans Committee. Maz had intended to deliver a prepared speech on induction day, but had to stop because the honor moved him so profoundly. Apologizing, he sat down to a loud standing ovation from the audience and his fellow Hall of Famers.

Today a portion of the left field brick wall from Forbes Field remains as a memorial on the University of Pittsburgh campus. A plaque where Mazeroski's homer cleared the wall marks the spot. Visitors to PNC Park can view a statue of the Pirate great perma-

nently displayed at the end of a cul-de-sac on Mazeroski Way near the right field entrance. It depicts him jubilantly nearing home plate after his legendary home run.

Mazeroski is retired in Panama City, Florida with his wife Milene Nicholson. They raised two sons. He continues to host his annual charity golf tournament and attends spring training in Bradenton, Florida as a special infield instructor for the Pirates.

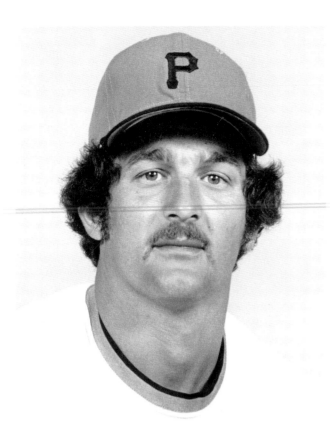

BOB MOOSE

PITTSBURGH PIRATES
RIGHT-HANDED PITCHER

1967-1976

"He pitches like he's been around for awhile. He isn't overpowering but he throws strikes. And he showed me a good slider."

~ *Henry Aaron in 1968 after going 0-9 against Moose*

Born and raised right outside of Pittsburgh, Bob Moose was a no-hit pitcher and member of the Pirates' legendary 1971 World Series championship team, but a multitude of injuries and his tragic early demise preventing him from fulfilling his larger promise of superstardom.

A fierce competitor, he had five straight campaigns with 11+ wins, threw more than 200 innings twice, and led all NL pitchers in winning percentage in 1969. Moose was respected and admired by his Pirates teammates, coaches and opponents and was extremely popular with fans.

The stocky 5'11" 195-pound Moose featured an animated sinking fastball, a moving curve, an absurdly deceptive slider and great command. A poised, confident hurler, Moose was also one of the game's better fielding pitchers with one of baseball's best pickoff moves.

★　★　★　★　★

Robert Ralph Moose, Jr. was born on October 9, 1947 to Molly Cardoni and Robert Ralph Moose, Sr. in the borough of Export, Westmoreland County, Pennsylvania just 20 miles east of Forbes Field. His father was a Pittsburgh bus driver. He grew up competing in the Franklin Township Little League, Pony League and on the Export American Legion team.

Moose was a three-sport athlete at Franklin Regional High in nearby Murrysville, also excelling in football and basketball. With three no-hitters and only two losses in his four-year prep career, he was taken by the Pirates in the 18th round of the 1965 June amateur draft.

Moose signed and began with the Salem (VA) Rebels of the rookie Appalachian League, making the All-Star team. He spent 1966 with two Class-A affiliates, the Raleigh (NC) Pirates of the Carolina League and the Gastonia (SC) Pirates in the Western Carolina League.

Assigned to the Triple-A Columbus (OH) Jets of the International League in early 1967, Moose was soon sent down to the Macon (GA) Peaches of the Double-A Southern League. He went 6-2 and was called back up to Columbus, where he won another four of five games.

After accumulating an overall minor league pitching mark of 29-10, Moose earned his major league debut on September 19, 1967- still three weeks shy of his 20th birthday. He threw $5^2/_3$ strong innings against the Astros at Houston's Astrodome in the Pirates victory.

Moose married Alberta Duriscoe, his high school sweetheart in February of 1968. He made the Pirates' roster at age 20 and had seven relief appearances before getting his first start against the Braves on May 9. He left for a pinch-hitter, trailing 2-1 in the seventh inning.

Moose came closer than anyone to pitching a no-hitter at Forbes Field– a feat never accomplished in its 60-year history. Versus the Astros in just his fifth start, he threw $7^2/_3$ hitless frames on June 14, 1968. Within four outs of a perfecto, he had to settle for a two-hit 3-0 victory.

Moose's best campaign was 1969, performing both as a starter and reliever for a 14–3 record, the NL's best .824 winning percentage, and a 2.91 ERA. On September 20, Moose no-hit the Mets in New York's last loss at home the year they won their first world title. His no-hitter was preserved with a leaping catch by Roberto Clemente off the right field fence to close out the sixth. Moose faced only 30 batters in the first no-hitter thrown by a Pirates pitcher in ten years.

Moose appeared twice in relief in the 1971 World Series and was asked to start Game 6 after the Pirates had swept the middle three games played in Pittsburgh. He pitched five solid innings opposite future Hall-of-Famer Jim Palmer, but got a no-decision in the loss.

Moose won 13 games in 1972 with a 2.91 ERA in 226 innings pitched for the National League East titlists. His year's work was eclipsed by events in the deciding game of the NL Championship Series. In relief of Dave Guisti after Johnny Bench tied the game in the ninth inning with a home run,

G	IP	W	L	PCT	SHO	GS	CG	H	ER	SO	BB	ERA
289	1303.2	71	76	.495	13	160	35	1308	827	827	387	3.50

he threw a low and away breaking ball that got by catcher Manny Sanguillen, scoring George Foster and sending the Reds to the World Series.

Moose's first outing of 1974 showed that he had no residual psychological ill-effects from the wild pitch, hurling a four-hit shutout against the Cubs. Yet in late May, after he had lost five straight with a fat 7.50 ERA, he was diagnosed with a life-threatening blood clot under his right shoulder. His top right rib was removed in surgery to free the clot in a rare procedure. After a second operation when his lungs filled with blood, he was on the shelf for the rest of the year.

A badly bruised thumb in July of 1975 set him back again. General manager Joe Brown suggested that he work himself back into shape with the Triple-A Charleston (SC) Charlies. He was recalled in early September and was the Bucs' most effective hurler for the last month.

On April 11, 1976, Moose pitched four innings of two-hit, shutout ball in relief of Bruce Kison. In his first six relief stints, Moose had three saves and allowed no runs. With ten saves in 53 appearances for the year, he seemed the natural successor to injured relief ace Dave Guisti.

Moose was killed in an accident on his 29th birthday, October 9, 1976, traveling from Bill Mazeroski's golf course in Rayland, Ohio where he earlier had played in a tourney Maz had hosted. He was on his way to a dinner at a restaurant owned by Mazeroski with some teammates.

The two-car head-on collision occurred in a light rain about halfway between Yorkville and Martins Ferry at 9:35 p.m. His northbound sports car slid onto the bank of the heavily traveled Ohio Route 7, swerved back left of center and hit another vehicle head-on.

Moose and his family resided in Monroeville just east of Export at the time of his death. He left behind his wife Alberta and five-year old daughter April, then a kindergartener. Moose was laid to rest in the Twin Valley Memorial Park in Delmont, Pennsylvania near Export.

THURMAN MUNSON

"We both thought we were the best catcher in the league and we tried to prove it to one another that each of us was better than the other. There was no such thing as hatred between us. I really had the utmost respect for him as a person."

~ *rival Red Sox catcher Carlton Fisk*

The heart and soul of his Yankee teams, Thurman Munson was one of the game's best catchers and arguably the top AL hitter with men on base. He anchored his teams to three pennants and two World Series titles, hitting a stout .373 (25-for-67) in three Fall Classics.

The burly 5' 11" 191-pound Munson earned three straight *Rawlings* Gold Gloves for fielding excellence from 1973 to 1975. Branded as "Squatty Body," he was one of the quickest catchers ever, pouncing on bunts and throwing out 44 percent of would-be base stealers.

★　★　★　★　★

Thurman Lee Munson was born on June 7, 1947, in Akron, Stark County, Ohio to Ruth Myrna Smylie and Darrell Vernon Munson. His father was a stern tough World War II veteran and long-distance trucker. His mother acknowledged Thurman, the youngest of her four children, was her favorite.

Munson met his future wife, Diana Dominick, in elementary school when he was 12. The two shared a paper route and played catch in the summers regularly. He was a three-sport star at Canton's John H. Lehman High, batting .581 his senior year as an All-Ohio State shortstop.

Although offered a number of football scholarships, he chose Kent State University for a full ride in baseball. As the 1968 NCAA All-American catcher, Munson hit .413 and set Golden Flash marks with 38 hits, ten doubles and six triples before metal bats and longer schedules.

The Yankees selected him fourth overall in the first round of the 1968 amateur draft and sent him to the Double-A Binghamton (NY) Triplets. He flunked a military physical during the season because of an ankle bone spur, but still led the Eastern League with a .301 average.

Munson and Diana married in the offseason. He took a second physical, passed and spent four months in the Army Reserve at Fort Dix, New Jersey. When not on reserve duty, he played 28 games for the 1969 Syracuse (NY) Chiefs of the Triple-A International League, hitting .363.

Munson earned his debut on August 8 against the A's, going 3-for-6 with a home run before returning to Fort Dix. His reserve duty expired on August 30 and three days later he was back to stay with the Yankees. Munson spent a grand total of only 99 games in the minors.

In his first full big-league season, the 23-year-old backstop was the runaway American League Rookie of the Year, hitting .302. He topped all 1971 AL catchers in fielding with a .998 average and attained career-highs with 20 home runs in 1973 and a .318 average in 1975.

A leader on and off the field, he was named captain by manager Billy Martin in 1976, only the second captain in Yankee history behind Lou Gehrig. Munson hit .302 with a career-best 105 RBI as the 1976 American League Most Valuable Player and the club won the AL East.

Munson batted .435 in the ALCS to help the Yankees upend the Royals in five games, but Cincinnati's Big Red Machine swept New York in the Fall Classic in four straight. Reds catcher Johnny Bench batted .533 (8-for-15) with Munson right with him at .529 (9-for-17).

During the following winter owner George Steinbrenner signed Reggie Jackson. Jackson made controversial comments about Munson in *Sport Magazine* that ignited mistrust and bad clubhouse chemistry. From there it descended into the most fractious year in Yankee history now known as the Bronx Zoo. Munson still hit .308 with 100 RBI as the first Yankee since DiMaggio to bat .300 and drive in 100 runs three years in a row. He hit .320 in the victorious Fall Classic.

Munson was an All-Star for the sixth straight year in 1978. After his Yankees beat the Red Sox in the division tiebreaker, they routed the Royals in the ALCS. Behind 5-4 in the vital Game 3 in the eighth, he powered a two-run blast off Doug Bird that traveled over 440 feet.

The Dodgers and Yankees then butted heads for the

G	AB	R	H	2B	3B	HR	RBI	SB	BB	SO	BA	OBP	SLG	TB
1423	5344	696	1558	229	32	113	701	48	438	571	.292	.346	.410	2190

second consecutive year in the World Series. New York dropped the first two games but battled back to win the last four. The ever-intense Munson rose to the occasion once again, hitting .320 with three doubles and seven RBI.

In early July of 1979, Munson bought a new powerful high-speed Cessna Citation 501 twin engine jet to commute to Canton on his days off to be with his wife, two daughters and son. On August 2, 1979 at the pinnacle of his exceptional career, he perished in a tragic plane crash.

Practicing touch-and-go landings at the Akron-Canton Regional Airport in his new jet, Munson came up short of runway 1-9. Seconds after impact, Munson asked passengers David Hall and Jerry Anderson if they were all right and then requested help. Due to fire and intense heat inside the cockpit, neither friend could unhook Munson's seat belt before they escaped.

Munson was suddenly gone at only 32. The entire stunned Yankee team and front office attended the funeral at the Canton Civic Center along with many baseball dignitaries and former teammates. Munson was laid to rest in the Sunset Hills Burial Park near his home in Canton.

Bench, Munson and Fisk were the three finest receivers of their generation. Munson compares favorably with Hall of Fame catcher Roy Campanella, hitting a career .292 to Campy's .276, but as yet has not been inducted into the National Baseball Hall of Fame.

The Yankees honored him by immediately retiring his uniform #15, and dedicated a memorial plaque as a lasting tribute in Yankee Stadium's Monument Park. In 1998, Munson was selected the *The Sporting News* American League catcher for the Decade of the 1970s.

Munson's locker has never been given out to any other player and was moved to the new Yankee Stadium when it was opened. A replica of his locker is on display in Cooperstown, complete with his jersey and catcher's gear — a fitting homage to the beloved Yankee captain.

TONY OLIVA

MINNESOTA TWINS
OUTFIELD • DESIGNATED HITTER

1962-1976

"Everybody says Rod Carew
was the best left-handed
hitter in the American League
in the 1960's and '70's.
But Tony Oliva could
hit like Carew and he
did it with power."

~ Bill Melton

Tony Oliva was one of the most feared hitters of his generation and the best of all of the Cuban players of the 1960s. In his prime, he was almost certainly the finest all around player the Minnesota Twins ever produced. If not for his balky knees, Oliva would already be in the National Baseball Hall of Fame.

He became the first player to win a batting crown and a Rookie of the Year award in the same year. Oliva earned his first batting titles in his initial two seasons and finished in the top three in the AL seven times. A three-time *The Sporting News* American League Player of the Year, he led his circuit in hits five times and doubles four times. Oliva batted over .300 six seasons, struck out only 645 times in 6,301 career at-bats, and was chosen an All-Star eight consecutive years, surpassing the great Joe DiMaggio's record.

His 15-year career with Minnesota is the longest of any player who ever played exclusively for the Twins. Distinguishing himself in all aspects of the game, Oliva earned the lasting respect of his organization, teammates and fans.

★ ★ ★ ★ ★

Pedro Oliva, Jr. was born on July 20, 1938 in Pinar del Río, Cuba to Maria López and Pedro Oliva, Sr., the oldest of four boys and the third of ten children. After signing with the Twins in 1961, he could not locate his birth certificate and decided to use his brother Antonio's identification to pass through U.S. Customs. When it was finally discovered, he chose to remain as Tony Oliva and later formally changed his name.

In a puzzling administrative decision, Minnesota released him after a strong spring showing in 1962. Unwilling to return to Fidel Castro's repressive Cuba, Oliva went to North Carolina to work out with a friend who played for the Twins affiliate there. Soon the Twins were reminded of his quick wrists and upside power and re-signed him. Oliva promptly demolished the Appalachian League, hitting .410 on the way to winning the *Silver Louisville Slugger* as the leading hitter in all of professional baseball.

However, Oliva would have to wait for his coming out party until 1964 when he led the Junior Circuit with 109 runs scored, 217 hits, 43 doubles, 84 extra base hits, 374 total bases and a .323 average. His hit total set a major league record for a first year player, and his total bases tied Hal Trosky's rookie mark from 1939.

In 1965, Oliva won his second straight batting title, leading Minnesota to the American League pennant and into a memorable World Series with the Dodgers. He also won a *Rawlings* Gold Glove for his fielding excellence, a testament to his ball hawking abilities and his powerful, accurate arm. His 1965 season was a magnificent highlight reel, leaving the young sensation's teammates to marvel at his five-tool talent.

The sweet-swinging Oliva hit .337 to win his third and final batting title in 1971, the sixth American Leaguer to do so. He resigned himself to his third knee surgery, three months after re-injuring the knee diving for a ball in Oakland in June. Oliva was never the same ballplayer again, eventually requiring seven operations.

Always a positive influence in the Twins clubhouse, Oliva befriended and roomed with Rod Carew soon after he broke in. Hall of Famer Carew gave credit to Oliva as his early career hitting mentor. From 1964 to 1975, the left-handed hitting roommates Carew and Oliva combined to win the American League batting championship eight times. Carew remembered his roommate groaning and icing his aching knees often

G	AB	R	H	2B	3B	HR	RBI	SB	BB	SO	BA	OBP	SLG	TB
1676	6301	870	1917	329	48	220	947	86	448	645	.304	.353	.476	3002

in the middle of the night.

Oliva became the Twins first designated hitter in 1973 when owner Calvin Griffith cast the decisive vote for the adoption of the designated hitter rule the previous winter. His conversion to DH was instant, leading the Twins with 92 RBI. As his career wound down, he batted .500 as a pinch-hitter in 1975, raising his career mark to .403.

To reward Oliva for what he had meant to the team, the Twins named him player-coach for 1976. In his final curtain call, he was limited to only 67 at-bats. Through all of the frustration, his teammates remember most his gratitude for being able to play at all.

After retiring, Oliva served the Twins as hitting and first base coach, scout and minor league instructor. He exerted considerable influence over a young Kirby Puckett, proposing that he employ a front leg kick at the plate for additional weight shift and power. Puckett went on to lead the next Twins generation.

Over the years the impact that Oliva has had on the Minnesota Twins franchise cannot be overestimated. He left a lasting legacy as a great hitter and a consummate teammate. Oliva's #6 Twins jersey was retired in 1991 and he was made a charter member of the Minnesota Twins Hall of Fame in 2000. In 2014, he was one Veterans Committee vote shy of induction into the National Baseball Hall of Fame.

Oliva has continued to work as an ambassador for his team in the Twin Cities community. In 2010 when the Twins opened Target Field, their beautiful new downtown outdoor ballpark, Gate #6 was named in his honor with a bronze statue depicting him in mid-swing. Still a popular figure, he resides in Bloomington with his wife Gordette.

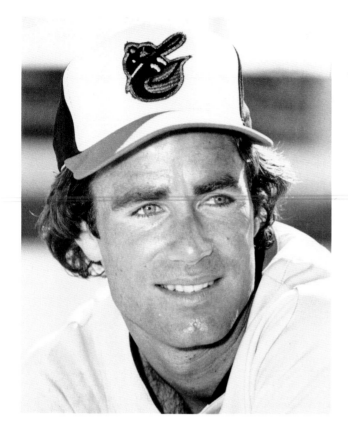

JIM PALMER

BALTIMORE ORIOLES
RIGHT-HANDED PITCHER

1965-1967 • 1969-1984

Jim Palmer was the greatest pitcher in Orioles history. An icon of Baltimore's glory days, he is the only Oriole to appear in all six World Series and wear three title rings. His 186 victories and 44 shutouts during the 1970s were the most in all baseball.

A six-time All-Star, the stylish 6'3" 195-pound Palmer was known for his fluid effortless delivery. Along with Roger Clemens, Greg Maddux, Pedro Martinez and Tom Seaver, he is one of only five right-handers to have won at least three Cy Young Awards.

Repeatedly derailed by arm, shoulder and back problems, Palmer overcame it all to win 20 games in eight seasons, toiling four years with over 300 innings. He led the AL in victories three times, ERA twice, and was a four-time *Rawlings* Gold Glove winner.

Palmer established Oriole standards for most wins, strikeouts, shutouts and complete games. His career 2.856 ERA is second only to Koufax and Whitey Ford (both at 2.75) in the Liveball Era. He never allowed a grand slam or back-to-back home runs.

Palmer registered an 8-3 postseason line with a 2.61 ERA and two shutouts in six AL Championship Series and World Series. He set records with six complete games and 90 strikeouts and is the only hurler to win Fall Classic games in three separate decades.

★ ★ ★ ★ ★

James Alvin Palmer was born on October 15, 1945 in New York City, but never knew his biological parents. Polly and Moe Wiesen (a well-to-do garment industry executive) adopted him soon after birth. When Mr. Wiesen passed away in 1955, the family relocated to Beverly Hills, California where he starred in Little League Baseball.

His mother married actor Max Palmer in 1956 and the family soon moved to Arizona. Palmer garnered all-

state prep honors in football, basketball and baseball, going 10-0 as a senior at Scottsdale High in 1963. Although offered a basketball scholarship to attend UCLA, he signed with the Orioles for a reported $50,000 bonus on August 16.

After a single minor league season with the Aberdeen (SD) Pheasants of the Class-A Northern League in 1964, the 19-year-old prodigy was given his Orioles debut against Boston on April 17, 1965. He registered his first victory on May 16, stopping the Yankees at Memorial Stadium while walloping the first of his three big-league homers.

Palmer's team-high 15th win was the 1966 pennant clincher. In World Series Game 2 at Dodger Stadium, he became the youngest hurler to win a complete-game shutout, out-dueling Sandy Koufax with a four-hitter. His effort initiated a record-setting 33 1/3 straight scoreless innings by Orioles pitchers to highlight a Fall Classic sweep.

Palmer fought through a rotator cuff injury for the next two years. He threw just 49 innings in 1967, underwent surgery, rehabbed in the fall, and then did a turn in the Puerto Rican Winter League. Remarkably, the Orioles left Palmer unprotected in the 1969 expansion draft and both the Royals and Pilots passed on a future Hall of Famer.

Four days after coming off the disabled list again on August 13, 1969, he threw a no-hitter versus the Athletics. Palmer finished at 16-4 with a 2.34 ERA and began the verbal jousting with fiery new manager Earl Weaver that lasted his entire career.

The 1970 and 1971 O's ranked among the finest teams of all-time. Mike Cuellar, Dave McNally and Palmer each notched 20 wins in 1970. McNally, Palmer, Cuellar and Pat Dobson all won 20 in 1971 to match the

> *"Jim had one of the most beautiful deliveries I've ever seen. It was almost like watching ballet."*
>
> ~ Orioles pitching coach Ray Miller

G	IP	W	L	PCT	SHO	GS	CG	H	ER	SO	BB	ERA
558	3948	268	152	.638	53	521	211	3349	1253	2212	1311	2.86

1920 White Sox with four 20-game winners.

After winning 21 games with a 2.07 ERA and 184 strikeouts in 1972, he backed it up with a 22-9 year and 2.40 ERA to earn his initial Cy Young Award. Undermined by elbow problems for two months in 1974, the resilient Palmer bounced back in 1975 to pace the American League with 23 wins, a 2.09 ERA and ten shutouts to earn his second Cy Young. With 22 wins and a 2.51 ERA, he completed his Cy Young hat trick in 1976.

The veteran put up 20 wins in 1977 and 21 in 1978, but over the last half dozen seasons of his career he was hampered by arm weariness and nagging injuries. Though clearly in decline, he brought a steady professional influence to the Orioles pitching staff.

In the crucial Game 3 of the 1983 World Series, Palmer came on in relief of Mike Flanagan, worked carefully through the Phillies' loaded lineup, and allowed no runs in two innings pitched. It would be his final major league victory. He asked for his release on May 12, 1984.

While still active, he gained national recognition as a model for *Jockey* brand men's briefs. Palmer appeared in Jockey ads and billboards in Times Square. Later, he teamed with Al Michaels and Tim McCarver to form a popular ABC TV broadcast team.

Jim Palmer's #22 was retired by the Orioles in 1985, and he was a first ballot National Baseball Hall of Famer in 1990. Ranked #64 on *The Sporting News* 1999 list of "100 Greatest Baseball Players," Palmer was a finalist for baseball's All-Century Team.

Palmer has become a near scratch golfer when not engaged as a keynote speaker, broadcaster or philanthropist. He has homes in Juno Beach (FL), California, and a condo in Baltimore's Little Italy which he uses when doing the Orioles' MASN TV broadcasts.

RICO PETROCELLI

BOSTON RED SOX
SHORTSTOP • THIRD BASE

1963 • 1965-1976

*"The pitch is looped toward
shortstop. Petrocelli's back.
He's got it! The Red Sox win!
And there's pandemonium
on the field! Listen!"*

*~ broadcaster Ned Martin's call
on the end of the 1967 season*

A leader on Boston's celebrated pennant-winning teams of 1967 and 1975, Rico Petrocelli was one of the finest fielders in Red Sox history and one of the most feared power hitters of his generation. With a swing tailored for Fenway's Green Monster, he hit 97 homers and knocked in 289 runs from 1969 to 1971 to top all Boston players. His nine career grand slams are second only in the Hub City to Ted Williams.

The 6' 175-pound Petrocelli was respected as one of the American League's most adept and consistent infielders for over a decade, leading the AL in fielding three times and at two positions- twice at shortstop (1968-69) and once at third (1971).

★　★　★　★　★

Americo Peter Petrocelli was born in Brooklyn on June 27, 1943, the youngest of Louise and Attilio Petrocelli's seven children. His family ran a tool sharpening shop in Manhattan's Garment District. When it became apparent he had bona fide talent, his four older brothers each worked double-time, sacrificing so he could concentrate on his game.

A star hurler and outfielder at Brooklyn's Sheepshead Bay High, he pitched in the 1961 city championship on a cold day and hurt his right elbow. Most teams shied away, but Boston super scout Bots Nekola offered him a tryout and then signed him on the spot.

After stints at Winston-Salem in 1962 and Reading in 1963, he earned his big-league debut on September 21, 1963, doubling off the Green Monster in his first at-bat.

With a solid year at Seattle in 1964, he was installed as the Sox shortstop for 1965. Coach Pete Runnels advised him to pull the ball to take advantage of Fenway's left-field wall.

Manager Billy Herman's autocratic approach with the youngster in 1966 led to a rift that became irreparable when Petrocelli left during a game to attend to his ill wife. Herman wanted him suspended, but the front office levied a stiff $1,000 fine instead.

The Red Sox began 1967 at 100-1 odds to win the pennant. New manager Dick Williams started over with Petrocelli. He hired the low-key Eddie Popowski to coach and be his locker mate. Popowski helped to re-build his confidence with daily talks.

At Yankee Stadium on June 21, both benches cleared after the blood rivals exchanged bean balls. The fiery Petrocelli and Joe Pepitone, friends who had grown up together in Brooklyn, were key figures in the brawl that quickly turned ugly and exploded into a full scale melee. It required a dozen stadium security guards to restore order. One was Petrocelli's brother David, who dragged him out from under a pile of Yankees.

The fight, coupled with Carl Yastrzemski's clutch hitting, ignited the team to finish 60-39 for an Impossible Dream season. He was a solid team leader as an All-Star starter, finishing with 17 home runs, and fielded brilliantly. Petrocelli's two round trippers against the Cardinals in World Series Game 6 set the standard for a shortstop.

After an elbow injury in 1968, he spent that winter building up his arms and wrists. It resulted in 1969 career-highs of .297, a shortstop-record 40 home runs, and a .589 slugging average. He went 44 straight games without a miscue, fielded a Boston record .981, including 103 double plays, and received more votes than any other All-Star.

Following 1970 when he amassed a personal-best 103 RBI with 29 home runs, Boston GM Dick O'Connell asked him if he would be willing to move to third base to accommodate the acquisition of shortstop Luis Aparicio. He readily endorsed the idea, reported early and worked long

G	AB	R	H	2B	3B	HR	RBI	SB	BB	SO	BA	OBP	SLG	TB
1553	5390	653	1352	237	22	210	773	10	661	926	.251	.332	.420	2263

hours with former BoSox third sacker Frank Malzone.

The results were phenomenal. Petrocelli played an all-time record 77 straight errorless games at the hot corner, and led the AL in fielding with a team record .976 (11 errors in 463 total chances). He also added 28 circuit clouts and 12 game-winning hits.

On September 15, 1974, he was beaned by a pitch thrown by the Brewers' Jim Slaton. The injury would taint the rest of his career, causing an inner ear condition that upset his equilibrium and made it difficult to focus on the ball. His hitting declined.

With the aid of medication, Petrocelli returned to form in time for the 1975 ALCS, hitting a home run in Game 2 to help sweep the Athletics. Against the Reds in a classic Series, he hit .308 with four RBI, contributing several fielding gems at third.

Petrocelli's defensive play at third base remained splendid in 1976, but he had to discontinue his medication due to allergic reactions. His balance problems returned, he hit only .213 and manager Don Zimmer lost faith in his bat. It would be his last year.

He was the Red Sox 1979 radio color commentator and later was a radio and television analyst for the Mariners. Petrocelli went on to skipper the White Sox's Single-A Appleton (WI) Foxes (1986); the Double-A Birmingham (AL) Barons (1987-88), and the Triple-A Pawtucket (RI) Red Sox (1992). After spending six years as a Red Sox roving instructor, he remains a frequent guest on Boston sports programs and hosts a sports talk show on Boston's AM 1510.

Petrocelli was enshrined in the Boston Red Sox Hall of Fame on September 7, 1997. He lives in Nashua, New Hampshire with his wife, the former Elsie Schmidt. They have raised four sons. He continues his longtime support for the Jimmy Fund.

BOBBY RICHARDSON

NEW YORK YANKEES
SECOND BASE

1955-1966

Bobby Richardson was a perennial clutch performer during one of the Bronx Bombers' most triumphant runs in their glorious history. Although an eight-time All-Star and five-time *Rawlings* Gold Glove winner, he remains one of the most underrated Yankees of all time.

In seven Fall Classics, he averaged .305 while slugging .405. He still holds World Series records of 30 consecutive games played, 12 runs batted in, and six runs batted in during a single Series game. He is tied for most hits in a five-game series (9); most hits in a seven-game series (13); and most runs in a seven-game series (8).

A tough out, Richardson struck out only 243 times in 5,783 plate appearances and hit into only 100 double plays in his entire career. He batted over .300 twice while leading the AL in at-bats three times and sacrifices twice. An expert bunter, he laid down 98 career sacrifice bunts.

Fielding a lifetime .979, the 5'9" 170-pound Richardson was half of one of the most elite keystone combos along with shortstop Tony Kubek, taking part in 963 career double plays. In his last seven seasons, he averaged 111½ twin killings and led the Junior Circuit four of those years.

* * * * *

Robert Clinton Richardson, Jr., was born in Sumter, South Carolina on August 19, 1935 to Willie Owens and Robert Clinton Richardson, Sr. Raised in a Southern Baptist home, he had a Christian conversion experience when he was 14 that profoundly influenced the rest of his life.

The young Richardson emerged as the star shortstop for Edmunds High and the 1952 Sumter American Legion State Champion team. Norfolk (VA) Tars manager Mayo Smith and Yankees scout Bill Harris both loved his makeup, signing him upon his graduation day in 1953.

Already a rock-solid infielder by 1954, he was the Eastern League's MVP, hitting .310 for the Binghamton (NY) Triplets. As the American Association's All-Star second

baseman in 1955 and 1956, he hit .296 and .328 respectively under the tutelage of manager Ralph Houk.

Although Richardson was called up for his debut on August 5, 1955, he didn't start until 1957 when he was picked as an All-Star. In 1959, Coach Bill Dickey suggested he use a heavier *Louisville Slugger* which resulted in his Yankee-best .301 average and a 19-game hitting streak.

Richardson's 1960 Fall Classic performance against the Pirates was nothing short of phenomenal. He hit .367 with 12 RBI, slugging .667 with a Game 3 grand slammer, fielded flawlessly, and earned the World Series Most Valuable Player award- the only time in history that honor was bestowed on a member of the losing team.

Now a workhorse, in 1961 he played in all 162 games (23 doubleheaders) and led the American League with 413 put-outs and 136 double plays to earn his first *Rawlings* Gold Glove. His nine hits and 23 at-bats both tied marks for a five-game Series as the Yankees beat the Reds.

Richardson had his best year in 1962 when he hit .302 with 99 runs scored, 38 doubles, 59 RBI and struck out only 24 times. He led the AL with personal-bests of 754 plate appearances, 693 at-bats and 209 hits. An All-Star, he won his second *Rawlings* Gold Glove and was runner up to teammate Mickey Mantle in the Most Valuable Player balloting.

World Series Game 7 at Candlestick Park featured one of baseball's most dramatic plays. With the Yankees ahead by a single run, two Giants in scoring position and two outs in the ninth inning, Richardson snared Willie McCovey's laser line drive for the final pressure-packed out.

The Yankees enjoyed their fifth consecutive World Series appearance in 1964. The Fall Classic against the Cardinals was hard fought with St. Louis prevailing. Richardson went 7-for-14 against MVP Bob Gibson while leading the Bronx Bombers with a 13 hits and hitting. 406.

With Kubek retiring after the 1965 season, the Yan-

> *"Bobby Richardson is the best second baseman I have ever known and the type of person I think that all fathers would like to see their children grow up to be."*
>
> ~ Yankees manager
> Ralph Houk

G	AB	R	H	2B	3B	HR	RBI	SB	BB	SO	BA	OBP	SLG	TB
1412	5386	643	1432	196	37	34	390	73	262	243	.266	.299	.335	1804

kees offered him a five-year contract to play one more year and then assist the club in non-playing duties for the remaining four years. On August 31, 1966, Richardson announced his retirement and the Yankees responded by honoring him with Bobby Richardson Day at Yankee Stadium on September 17.

Richardson became the University of South Carolina's coach in 1970. His teams won over 70 percent of the time in his seven years there. His 1975 Gamecocks (51-6) were College World Series finalists. He also coached at Coastal Carolina College and Liberty University.

At President Gerald Ford's suggestion in 1976, Richardson ran as a Republican for a seat in the United States House of Representatives from South Carolina's Fifth Congressional District. He lost to incumbent Democrat Kenneth Holland by less than 3,000 votes.

Now a minister, Richardson continues to deliver his powerful Christian message across the country. He is the man Mantle called to his hospital bed to confirm that he had accepted Jesus Christ as his Lord just before he died and asked him to deliver the eulogy at his funeral.

Richardson married Betsy Dobson in 1956. Together they raised three boys and two girls and now enjoy 15 grandchildren. The couple has been inducted into the Palmetto Family Council Hall of Honor (2003) together as one of South Carolina's most commendable families.

He was a 1963 Lou Gehrig Memorial Award recipient, given annually to the player who best embodies the character of the great Gehrig. He was also inducted into the South Carolina State Hall of Fame in 1996 and the University of South Carolina Athletic Hall of Fame in 2004.

Bobby Richardson has been a wonderful role model, having led a rich, balanced and victorious life on and off the baseball field. He was "Mr. Clutch" for the Yankees in the postseason, a magician on the field, and a truly exceptional family man and human being off it.

BROOKS ROBINSON

BALTIMORE ORIOLES
THIRD BASE

1955-1977

"There is not a man who knows him who wouldn't swear for his integrity and honesty and give testimony to his consideration for others. He's an extraordinary human being, which is important, and the world's best third baseman of all time, which is incidental."

~ *writer John Steadman*

Brooks Robinson was the finest fielding third baseman of the 20th century. In his record 23 seasons with Baltimore, he became renowned as the legendary "Human Vacuum," earning 16 consecutive *Rawlings* Gold Gloves and 15 straight starting berths as an American League All-Star. Robinson led the Orioles from mediocrity into perennial contention and two World Series titles as one of the greatest Orioles of them all.

The stylish Robinson's career was one long defensive highlight reel. Although the possessor of only ordinary running speed and an average throwing arm, he had a flare for the dazzling fielding play. Robinson used lightning fast reactions to a hard hit ball and a quick throwing release to lead the American League in assists eight times and fielding 11 times. He set career marks at the hot corner with 2,870 games, 9,165 chances, 6,205 assists, 2,697 putouts, 618 double plays and a .971 fielding average.

★ ★ ★ ★ ★

Brooks Calbert Robinson, Jr. was born on May 18, 1937 in Little Rock, Pulaski County, Arkansas to Ethel Mae Denker and Brooks Calbert Robinson, Sr. His fireman father had played for the minor league Little Rock Travelers and passed on his affection for the game to his son. Little Rock High didn't have a baseball team, so the youngster starred for the three-time American Legion state champion Little Rock Doughboys.

After graduation in 1955, Robinson weighed bids from 12 of the 16 major league clubs before choosing the Orioles. He hit .331 with 11 home runs for the Class-B York (PA) White Roses (Piedmont League) and enjoyed his big-league debut on September 3.

After a full year with the 1956 Double-A San Antonio (TX) Missions (American Association), Robinson steadily improved under the guidance of aging O's third baseman George Kell. He played 50 games for the big club in 1957 and started briefly in 1958, but never really got untracked. Six months of military reserve duty truncated his 1959 season.

The 6'1" 180-pound Robinson came of age in 1960, hitting .294 with 14 home runs and 88 RBI. It was a year the Birds were perched in first place as late as September and served notice of the approaching Oriole dynasty built around pitching and defense.

By 1964, Robinson's bat and glove work were the talk of baseball. Wearing his trademark short-billed batting helmet, he posted career-highs, hitting .317 with 28 home runs and an AL-best 118 RBI. Robinson was the 1964 All-Star Game MVP, the American League MVP, and *The Sporting News* Major League Player of the Year.

He again was named the All-Star Game MVP in 1966, getting three hits, and helped the Orioles sweep to their first World Series title in October. Robinson's presence at third discouraged an experienced Dodger team from utilizing its usual bunting game.

The 1970 season was a benchmark for Robinson. He gathered his 2,000th hit, 1,000th RBI and 200th home run. The postseason became his personal showcase known as the Brooks Robinson World Series. He dominated the Fall Classic making so many preposterous defensive plays the Reds called him "Hoover." Robinson won Game 1 with a seventh inning solo homer, unloaded another in Game 4 and hit .429. It earned him the 1970 Hickok Belt as Professional Athlete of the Year and would be the capstone of many great postseasons.

G	AB	R	H	2B	3B	HR	RBI	SB	BB	SO	BA	OBP	SLG	TB
2896	10654	1232	2848	482	68	268	1357	28	860	990	.267	.322	.401	4270

He hit .303 in four Fall Classics with five home runs and fielded .986.

As his career wound down, Robinson was in debt because of failed investments. Despite his eroding skills, the Orioles kept him active out of respect for his character and contributions. His Oriole uniform #5 was retired on his day at Memorial Stadium, September 18, 1977, before the largest regular season crowd in its history.

Robinson was the second recipient of baseball's coveted Roberto Clemente Award for community service and humanitarianism in 1972. He was a first ballot National Baseball Hall of Famer in 1983 and his induction ceremony drew one of the largest crowds ever. In 2008 he was voted to the All-Time *Rawlings* Gold Glove Team.

Robinson was elected to Major League Baseball's elite All-Century Team and was one of the first two charter inductees enshrined in the Baltimore Orioles Hall of Fame. A nine-foot tall statue of Robinson was unveiled in 2011 outside Oriole Park at Camden Yards depicting him at third base preparing to throw out a runner.

As a color commentator for the Orioles TV broadcasts, he put his financial woes behind him and now serves as an executive for a counseling firm that supports athletes professionally, financially and personally. Robinson has supported the Boy Scouts of America and has been the MLB Players Alumni Association president since 1999.

A truly generous and kind gentleman, Robinson continues to reside in the Baltimore area where he and his wife, the former Connie Butcher, raised their four children. He is a beloved Baltimore icon and a community role model, so much so that many Baltimoreans have named their sons after him.

MICKEY STANLEY

DETROIT TIGERS
CENTER FIELD • FIRST BASE • SHORTSTOP
1964-1978

"He really is a throwback to the old-timer who played the game for the sheer joy of it. Stanley simply signed his contract and never complained about playing time. He accepted his manager's decision about where to play and was loyal to his team. He is just there, day after day, doing his job and having fun."

~ writer Joe Falls

One of the finest all-around athletes ever to wear a Tigers uniform, Mickey Stanley was a virtuoso defensive outfielder, earning four *Rawlings* Gold Glove awards. With his .991 career outfield fielding percentage, he ranks just under the all-time career high of .993 by Terry Puhl.

Stanley combined outstanding foot speed with an almost clairvoyant ability to get a jump on a batted ball even before the hitter made contact. He possessed a rifle arm as a young player, sure hands, and the ability to leap at the fence to haul down many a would-be home run.

In 1967, 1968 and 1970, the 6' 185-pound Stanley led all major league outfielders in fielding with perfect 1.000 percentages. He was also one of the most versatile players in Tigers history, playing seven different positions and designated hitter during his 15-year tenure.

Stanley was a streaky right-handed hitter, but made up for any shortcomings at the plate with his defensive skills and his approach to the game. He simply loved to play for the pure joy of the experience... the first player to arrive at the ballpark and the last to leave each day.

* * * * *

Mitchell Jack Stanley was born on July 20, 1942 to Betty and James Stanley in Grand Rapids, Kent County, Michigan. He was the middle child of five and a Tigers fan from the start. His bakery truck driver father encouraged his baseball interest, often playing catch with him.

Stanley was a standout at Ottawa Hills High in baseball, basketball, and football, showing his versatility early by manning several gridiron positions. While also pitching, he won the 1959 Grand Rapids City League batting title (.523) and was chosen the GRCL's top athlete in 1960.

After graduation, Stanley starred for the Grand Rapids Sullivan-Polynesians, a team that won the 1960 National Baseball Congress championship in Wichita, Kansas. The head coach, Detroit scout Bob Sullivan, persuaded him to

sign after the tournament for a $10,000 bonus.

After his first pro season with the 1961 Duluth (IL) Commodores (Class-C Northern League) and the Decatur (IL) Dukes (Class-D Midwest League), Stanley married his high school sweetheart, Ellen Ann Terrell. Back with Duluth in 1962, he batted .285 and was an All-Star.

Stanley moved up to the 1963 Double-A Knoxville (TN) Smokies and spent most of the 1964 season there as well, hitting .304 as a Southern League All-Star. He earned a cameo major league debut on September 13 at Tiger Stadium, but was sent down for a second tour with the Syracuse (NY) Chiefs in 1965. He figured out Triple-A pitching, batting .281 with 152 hits and 73 RBI as a 1965 International League All-Star and was again called back up by the Tigers.

Stanley hit his first big-league home run on September 3, 1966 at Tiger Stadium- a 400-foot shot off the Senators Marshall Bridges and played superb defense, flawlessly handling 174 chances. He competed in 145 games in 1967, but the Tigers lost to the Red Sox on the last day.

Stanley made one of the greatest catches in Motor City annals on June 15, 1968. Sprinting 60 yards back diagonally across Comiskey Park's right-center field, he dove for a Tom McCraw liner, tumbled onto the gravel track, bounced up, and doubled off Luis Aparicio at first.

The Tigers of 1968 amassed 103 wins, including 31 by pitcher Denny McLain. Stanley had his finest year with career-highs of 151 hits and 88 runs scored in a pitching-dominated year. He fielded 1.000 with 308 chances in center field to win his first *Rawlings* Gold Glove.

Mayo Smith looked for a way to keep Al Kaline in the World Series lineup. In one of the boldest moves in history, he shifted Stanley to the key position of shortstop. Tested by leadoff hitter Lou Brock's grounder in Game 1, he gunned down the speedster on a bang-bang play.

With the Tigers down 3–0 in the do-or-die Game

G	AB	R	H	2B	3B	HR	RBI	SB	BB	SO	BA	OBP	SLG	TB
1516	5022	641	1243	201	48	117	500	44	371	564	.248	.298	.377	1891

5, Stanley led off the fourth with a clutch triple to begin a two-run rally. Kaline's single in the seventh knocked in two more runs for the 5-3 victory. After a Game 6 win, Detroit took the final game, 4–1, beating Bob Gibson. Stanley handled 30 of 32 chances at short successfully. His outfield stand-in Kaline had eight RBI.

Even with a pre-season injury to his throwing arm, Stanley led the Tigers in 1969 with 149 games and had a career-high 70 RBI. When the team traded for Tom Tresh to play shortstop in June, he returned to center and registered a Tigers record 220 straight errorless outfield games.

In 1970, Stanley led Detroit in runs scored, hits, triples and steals and again topped major league outfielders in fielding with a 1.000 percentage to earn his third *Rawlings* Gold Glove. Stanley was a mainstay in the outfield for the next three campaigns under Billy Martin.

He hit a career-best .292 in 1971 and topped his team in 1972 with 18 go-ahead RBI as the Tigers clinched the AL East title in the penultimate game. The veteran Stanley paced the 1973 Tigers in at-bats, runs scored and hits while winning his final *Rawlings* Gold Glove.

His tenure as the Tigers regular centerfielder ended abruptly on July 30, 1974, when a pitch broke his hand. Ron LeFlore was immediately called up and Stanley finished the campaign on the disabled list. Thereafter, manager Ralph Houk utilized him as a role player.

During his last four seasons, Stanley played every position except pitcher and catcher. He saw action in only 53 games in 1978, but made the last play at the original Yankee Stadium on September 30, gathering in a fly ball hit by Mike Hegan for the final out of the season.

After his retirement, Stanley has partnered with his son Scott to develop real estate subdivisions. An enthusiastic golfer, he participates in numerous charity events. Stanley and his wife have eight grandchildren by their son and daughter Karen. They live in Brighton, Michigan.

WILLIE STARGELL

PITTSBURGH PIRATES
LEFT FIELD • FIRST BASE

1962-1982

> *"I never have seen a batter who hits the ball any harder. For sheer crash of bat meeting ball, Stargell simple is the best."*
>
> ~ Pirates manager
> Harry "The Hat" Walker

One of the greatest left-handed sluggers ever, Willie Stargell was legendary for hitting titanic blasts into the stratosphere. The franchise leader in home runs, RBI and extra base hits, he helped his Pirates seize six NL East and two World Series titles.

A seven-time All-Star, the 6' 3" 235-pound Stargell personified the ultimate menacing figure at the plate, pin-wheeling his 36½" *Louisville Slugger* until the pitcher started his windup. He slammed more homers than anyone in the Decade of the 1970s.

Stargell tagged seven of the 16 balls that completely left Forbes Field. He slugged four of the only six shots ever to reach Three Rivers Stadium's upper deck and hit two of the four fair balls that have sailed out of Dodger Stadium. Stargell's majestic 507 foot blast off Alan Foster in 1969 was the longest. He also struck out a NL record 1,936 times.

One of the most popular figures in Pittsburgh sports history and one of baseball's true gentlemen, the effervescent Stargell brought a joyful approach and lasting impact on the field, in the clubhouse and in the Steel City community.

★   ★   ★   ★   ★

Wilver Dornel Stargell was born on March 6, 1940 to Gladys Vernell and William Stargell near Earlsboro, Pottawatomie County, Oklahoma of African and Seminole descent. His father left the family before he was born, leaving his paternal grandfather to take the responsibility for raising the young Stargell.

The family relocated to the Alameda Public Housing Projects near Oakland, California where he attended Encinal High and earned eight letters in football, basketball, baseball and track. A rawboned teenager, he hit some balls a long way, but was only the third best player on a team featuring future big-leaguers Tommy Harper and Curt Motton.

Pirates scout Bob Zuk signed him as a project in August of 1958. When Stargell reported to Class-D Roswell (NM) in 1959, he was met with the humiliation of Jim Crow bigotry, but determined baseball was his way out of the greater indignities of the ghetto.

After tours with the 1960 Class-C Grand Forks (ND) Chiefs and the 1961 Class-A Ashville (NC) Tourists, Stargell started to show his muscle, ripping 27 homers for the 1962 Triple-A Columbus Jets. The Pirates gave him his debut on September 16.

He was a streaky hitter early on before exploding for 27 homers in 1965 and 33 more in 1966. After two down years, he was counseled by Captain Roberto Clemente in 1969 to use a heavier 37-ounce bat. He quit trying to pull the ball and was a better hitter.

Part of his challenge had been learning how to hit in Forbes Field, a home run graveyard.

In 1971, his first full season in the Pirates' new Three Rivers Stadium, Stargell paced the NL with 48 big hits, drove in a career-high 125 runs, and led Pittsburgh to the NL pennant. The team went on to win the "Clemente World Series" in seven games.

With the terrible news of Clemente's loss on New Year's Eve of 1972, it was Stargell who quietly stepped into the breach. Appointed captain in early 1973, he came out to lead the NL in doubles (43), home runs (44), RBI (119) and slugging (.646).

By 1978, "Pops" Stargell was a father figure to a new group of young teammates. He started awarding small embroidered black stars to his teammates after a great play or big game. The players fastened "Stargell's Stars" to their old-fashioned pillbox caps. It was his favorite team, which pressed the Phillies for the NL East pennant before yielding in the penultimate game. He was *The Sporting News* NL Comeback Player of the Year.

The hit song *We Are Family* by Sister Sledge became

G	AB	R	H	2B	3B	HR	RBI	SB	BB	SO	BA	OBP	SLG	TB
2360	7927	1195	2232	423	55	475	1540	17	937	1936	.282	.360	.529	4190

Stargell's anthem for the 1979 Pirates. His clutch hitting in many come-from-behind wins earned him a share of the 1979 NL MVP award. The inspired squad won the pennant on the season's last day.

After his NLCS MVP performance in a sweep of the Reds, he rallied the Bucs in a Cinderella World Series comeback. Stargell's thrilling two-run blast in the sixth inning of Game 7 off Oriole ace Scott McGregor was the deciding blow. His .400 average with three homers, four doubles and record 25 total bases made him the unanimous MVP.

Stargell is the only man ever to have won this MVP trifecta in one year. He was also the Major League Baseball Player of the Year; *The Sporting News* Man of the Year; *Sports Illustrated* Sportsman of the Year; and *Associated Press* Male Athlete of the Year.

After a season-long farewell tour through the National League in 1982, Stargell saw his #8 retired in a ceremony on September 6. Manager Chuck Tanner soon hired him as a hitting coach and in 1986 brought him over with him when he became the Braves manager. There he had a strong early impact on a young Chipper Jones.

In 1988, Willie Stargell became the 17th man to be elected to the National Baseball Hall of Fame on the first ballot. He was ranked 81st on *The Sporting News* 1999 "100 Greatest Baseball Players" list and was a finalist for baseball's All-Century Team. In 2012, the U.S. Postal Service issued a forever stamp featuring Willie Stargell.

Stargell died of a massive stroke at the New Hanover Regional Medical Center in Wilmington, North Carolina on April 9, 2001. That afternoon was the inaugural game at the Pirates' elegant new PNC Park, the very day a magnificent 12-foot bronze statue of Stargell's likeness was unveiled on Federal Street right outside the ballpark.

MEL STOTTLEMYRE

Mel Stottlemyre was the Yankees dependable ace who served as one of the few players with links to a more successful time. The Yankees did not appear in a single postseason after his rookie year in the most barren period in franchise history since before the Babe Ruth era.

A five-time All-Star, the stylish Stottlemyre relied on the command of his trademark natural sinking fastball and a hard slider to fashion a superb career 2.97 ERA. He won 15 or more games seven times, collected three 20-win seasons and threw an amazing 40 shutouts.

★ ★ ★ ★ ★

Melvin Leon Stottlemyre, Sr. was born on November 13, 1941 to Lorene Ellen Miles and Vernon Stottlemyre in Hazleton, St. Louis County, Missouri. His pipefitter father was itinerant until Stottlemyre was in eighth grade, when the family settled in the small town of Mabton in south central Washington. He and his younger brother Keith pitched to each other constantly.

He lost only one game in four years pitching for Mabton High before graduating in a class of only 24 in 1959. Hurling in American Legion, as well as at Yakima Valley Community College, he was touted by Yankees scout Eddie Taylor, who signed him on June 10, 1961.

After splitting his first pro year between the Harlan (KY) Smokies (Appalachian Rookie League) and Class-D Auburn (New York-Penn League), Stottlemyre broke out in 1962 to go 17-9 with a 2.50 ERA, hurling eight shutouts, for Greensboro in the Class-B Carolina League.

He leapfrogged to the Triple-A International League in 1963, but pitched himself out of the rotation with the Richmond Virginians and had to return in 1964. Learning how to set up hitters by getting them to think slider and then throwing his sinker, he reeled off ten straight wins as a starter. His 1.42 ERA and final line of 13-2 earned him his ticket to the big time.

Called up midsummer in the middle of a tense pennant race, Stottlemyre made his major league debut on Aug. 12, 1964. He induced 19 ground ball outs while hurling a 7-3 complete-game victory over the White Sox with the support of two long Mickey Mantle home runs.

The 22-year-old rookie went 9-3 to help the Yankees win their fifth straight pennant and suddenly was featured on the cover of *The Sporting News*. With less than two months in the big-leagues, he was about to duel the Cardinals ace Bob Gibson three times in the 1964 Fall Classic.

Stottlemyre tossed a complete-game gem in Game 2 over Gibson to even the Series, winning 8-3 with 18 ground ball outs. Pitching well in Game 5 versus Gibson, he allowed only two runs in seven innings but got no decision in an extra inning loss. In the decisive Game 7, he took the rubber on two days rest only to surrender three runs during the fourth inning when he jammed his right shoulder on a play covering first. He had to be taken out and absorbed the loss.

In the 18 years from 1947 to 1964, the Yankees had won 15 American League pennants and ten World Series championships. The youthful Stottlemyre assumed the pinstripe dynasty would continue indefinitely, but the franchise fell into the "Great Yankee Depression."

Stars Jim Bouton, Clete Boyer, Whitey Ford, Elston Howard, Mantle, Roger Maris, Bobby Richardson and Tom Tresh all seemed to get old or injured overnight and the Yankees farm system ran dry. Even as the club unraveled around him in 1965, Stottlemyre sparkled, going 20-9 with a 2.63 ERA, and topped the AL with 291 innings pitched and 18 complete games.

He pitched at least 250 innings in each of his nine full seasons and posted only two losing campaigns. Supported by second-rate teams, he led the AL with 20 losses in 1966, and tied for most losses with 18 in 1972. The team's only winning season was 1970 when it won 93 games.

> *"He has a good sinker and the courage and control to use it right. I would recommend signing him for a small bonus, or a larger bonus contingent on performance."*
>
> ~ Yankees scout
> Eddie Taylor in his report

G	IP	W	L	PCT	SHO	GS	CG	H	ER	SO	BB	ERA
360	2661.1	164	139	.541	40	356	152	2435	878	1257	809	2.97

Just before the Yankees began a new run of success, Stottlemyre was forced into retirement with a torn rotator cuff in his pitching shoulder suffered on June 4, 1974. He pitched his last major league game on August 16 and the team gave him his release on March 29, 1975.

Stottlemyre started a five-year stint as a Mariners roving instructor in 1977. He was the Mets pitching coach from 1984 to 1993 including the 1986 title year. During his tenure, he oversaw the conversion of power pitcher Dwight Gooden to a craftier, more durable hurler.

Following a two-year hitch as the Astros pitching coach (1994-95), Stottlemyre was hired by new Yankees manager Joe Torre as the team's pitching coach. Under his tutelage, the Yankees staff progressively lowered its ERA from 4.65 (1996) to 3.84 (1997) to 3.82 (1998).

After ten seasons and four World Series rings, he resigned his coaching position on October 12, 2005 on the heels of the Yankees' ALDS defeat at the hands of the Angels. He cited personal disagreements with meddlesome owner George Steinbrenner among his reasons.

Stottlemyre spent one year as the Seattle Mariners pitching coach in 2008, appointed under manager John McLaren at the start of the season. He was kept on by interim manager Jim Riggleman after McLaren's dismissal.

Stottlemyre has been diagnosed with multiple myeloma, a rare form of bone marrow cancer, which is now in remission. He has been enshrined into the State of Washington Sports Hall of Fame (1989), the Tri-Cities Sports Council Hall of Fame (2000) and the Department of Washington American Legion Baseball Hall of Fame (2012). The Yankees honored him with his own bronze plaque in Yankee Stadium's Monument Park in 2015.

Stottlemyre now resides in Issaquah, Washington with his wife, the former Jean Mitchell. His youngest son Jason died of leukemia at the age of 11 in 1981. His two older sons, Todd and Mel, Jr., both followed in their father's footsteps to become major league pitchers.

ROY WHITE

NEW YORK YANKEES
LEFT FIELD

1965-1979

"If you really don't watch him, and you really don't figure out what he does, he can easily be overlooked. But his biggest asset to the club, is that here's a guy who's going to do his job and not make mental mistakes, a guy who will bunt, hit a grounder to the other side to advance a runner, hit a sacrifice fly, get you a quiet single and get on base."

~ teammate Reggie Jackson

Roy White was the reserved, dignified star whose career bridged the gap between the 1960s Yankee dynasty teams and the 1970s renaissance of three pennant-winners and two World Series champions. A switch-hitter, he had the distinction of batting cleanup behind two of history's greatest sluggers. White was perhaps the only Yankee #4 hitter to choke up on his *Louisville Slugger*, yet he went yard from both sides of the plate in the same game five times.

A 5'10" 160-pound, two-time All-Star, White accumulated a career .988 fielding percentage as a leftfielder. He topped all AL leftfielders in putouts eight times, fielding five times and double-plays twice. He was the first Yankee to play an errorless season in 1975.

* * * * *

Roy Hilton White was born on December 27, 1943 to Margaret King and Marcus White in Compton, Los Angeles County, California. His parents split when he was five years old, leaving his mother to support him and his younger brother. White grew up poor in one of the toughest Southern California areas, but played baseball year around.

He excelled in football and baseball for Compton's Centennial High. Playing second base next to shortstop Reggie Smith (a future big-league star), the two preps formed an exceptional double play combination. Showing sensational speed, he batted over .400 as a senior in 1961.

White decided to sign with Yankees scout Tuffy Hashem on July 1, 1961 and was sent to Class-D Fort Lauderdale in 1962. He hit .286 before being advanced to Greensboro. Back at Class-A Greensboro in 1963, he solved Carolina League pitching, hitting .309 in 554 at-bats.

Promoted to the Double-A Columbus (OH) Clippers in 1964, he scuffled there, but came back to bat .300 with 14 triples and 19 home runs and was chosen the 1965 South-

ern League MVP. His performance landed him his major league debut at age 21 on September 7, 1965.

White's arrival coincided with the team's descent from five straight AL pennants to sixth place and then the AL cellar in 1966. He worked to find a solid hitting approach but the short Yankee Stadium right field porch seduced him into pulling the ball more as the year unfolded.

White was sent to Spokane in early 1967 to regain his stroke but was brought back up midseason. By August of 1968, he was the regular leftfielder and manager Ralph Houk inserted him as cleanup hitter, moving Mickey Mantle to #3. Protecting Mantle, he hit 17 home runs.

Now in his prime, White hit .290 in 1969 and closed 1970 at .296 with 22 home runs, 109 runs scored, 94 RBI and 24 steals. He followed up in 1971 at .292 with 19 home runs and 84 RBI while setting a league mark with 17 sacrifice flies. He paced the AL with 99 walks in 1972.

George Steinbrenner purchased the Yankees from CBS in early 1973, a year in which White topped the AL in games played, plate appearances and at-bats but had a mediocre year. When he started slowly in 1974, manager Bill Virdon decided to make him a designated hitter.

That experiment was brief as Virdon was fired in July of 1975. Billy Martin quickly re-instated White in left field and hit him in the #2 slot. Batting between Mickey Rivers and Thurman Munson in 1976, White led the AL in runs scored and the Yankees won the pennant.

In the American League Championship Series Game 1, he drilled a game-winning, two-run double in the top of the ninth inning to beat the Royals. With the Series tied in Game 5, his two walks, a single and two runs scored laid the groundwork for Chris Chambliss' dramatic walk off home run in the bottom of the ninth inning to seal the pennant for the Yankees.

The Yankees were swept by the Reds in the 1976 Fall

G	AB	R	H	2B	3B	HR	RBI	SB	BB	SO	BA	OBP	SLG	TB
1881	6650	964	1803	300	51	160	758	233	934	708	.271	.360	.404	2685

Classic, but came back to clinch the 1977 pennant on the next to the last day. White was a key engine in the Yankees' first World Series title in 15 years. Reggie Jackson's three Game 6 bombs finished off the Dodgers.

White was platooned with Lou Piniella in left field in 1978, but was stalwart in the tight September pennant race, playing 24 games and hitting .337 with a .400 OBA. The Red Sox and Yankees finished the season in a dead heat to set up a one-game playoff at Fenway.

With the Yankees down 2-0 in the seventh inning, White singled with Chambliss on first to set up Bucky Dent's famous home run for the 5-4 win. He went on to hit .313 in the ALCS versus the Royals with a home run, and averaged .333 in the Fall Classic with a home run against the Dodgers to earn his second World Series championship ring.

White played his last game in pinstripes on September 27, 1979 at age 35. He stunned the baseball world by signing a contract to play for the Yomiuri Giants of the Japanese Central Professional League, a club that featured the great Sadaharu Oh in the final season of his career.

White hit fourth behind Oh, batting over .300 with 29 home runs and 106 RBI as an All-Star. In 1981, he blasted 23 bombs as the Giants won the Japan World Series versus the Nippon Ham Fighters. White retired in 1982, and was hired as the Yankees hitting coach (1983-86).

He then spent a decade in the Yankees front office and as a minor league instructor and was influential in the scouting and signing of Hideki "Godzilla" Matsui. As hitting coach for the Athletics' PCL entry, the Sacramento River Cats, White won two Triple-A titles in five years.

He and his wife Linda Hoxie created the Roy White Foundation, a non-profit that provides financial aid to young people in the New York area to further their education. Married in 1966, they live in Toms River, New Jersey and have raised a daughter Loreena and a son Reade.

DON WILSON

HOUSTON ASTROS
RIGHT-HANDED PITCHER

1966-1974

"Don has a great arm. He has a high-riding fast ball and a short, hard slider...He won 10 games for us when he didn't know what it was all about. He's young, strong and eager. He should be a dandy."

~ Astros manager
Grady Hatton 1968

Fireballer Don Wilson enjoyed spectacular highs in his career, hurling two no-hitters, and was only deprived of a third perfecto when he was removed for a pinch-hitter after eight full innings. He also established the Houston Astros record for a single game with 18 strikeouts.

Early in his career Wilson was one of the hardest throwers in the National League. With his loose arm and effortless, easy motion, his live 93-mile-per-hour fastball exploded out of his hand. A little prone to wildness, he also threw a hard sharp slider, a curve and a changeup.

His fastball also had extraordinary movement- diving or sailing or darting sharply out on a right-handed hitter. Wilson had the best high fastball in the NL. He could aim the ball in the strike zone at the hitter's belt and by the time it reached the plate it would be shoulder high.

* * * * *

Donald Edward Wilson was born on February 12, 1945 to Lizzie Newman and Felton Wilson in Monroe, Ouchita Parish, Louisiana. He grew up in Compton, California, playing Little League with future major league stars Reggie Smith and Roy White.

Even in junior high, Wilson's pitching was already attracting dozens of scouts, but he hurt his arm before his senior year at Centennial High. He rehabbed while at Compton College and the Houston Colt 45s re-discovered him pitching in a local semi-professional league.

Wilson signed with Houston as a free agent after graduating from junior college in 1964. The rangy 6'2" 195-pound right-hander began his professional career with the Colts of the Cocoa Florida Rookie League, appearing in only ten games as a 19-year-old rookie.

He made great strides with the 1965 Cocoa Astros of the Class-A Florida State League, going 10-8 with a 1.44 ERA in 181 innings. Wilson then went 18-6 with a 2.21 ERA and 197 strikeouts for the 1966 Amarillo Sonics as the Double-A

Texas League's Pitcher of the Year.

The Astros gave Wilson his major league debut on September 29 against the Reds. He was brought on in the third inning and tossed six frames, allowing only two runs on five hits, walking one and striking out seven. Turk Farrell came on in the ninth to save his first victory.

As a 22-year-old rookie, Wilson pitched the first no-hitter in Astros history, 2–0, against the Braves at the Astrodome on June 18, 1967. Henry Aaron was the last out and his 15th strikeout victim. Wilson's fastball and slider were so unhittable he threw only one changeup and one curveball. It was the first no-hitter ever pitched in a domed stadium or on artificial turf.

In his rookie year he won ten games, sported a 2.79 ERA, and broke an Astros record by pitching 25 scoreless innings in a row. Wilson fanned 18 Reds on July 14, 1968 to join the likes of Bob Feller and Sandy Koufax as the only men to strike out 18 batters in a nine-inning game.

Wilson established career-highs in 1969 with 225 innings pitched, 34 starts and 16 victories, even without much run support. He struck out 235 and had ten games with ten or more strikeouts. Wilson tossed his second no-hitter on May 1, 1969, beating the Reds again, 4-0.

He finally became a finished pitcher in 1971. An All-Star, he went 16-10 with a 2.45 ERA to rank third in the NL. As the Astros workhorse and MVP, he pitched 268 innings and led the league in hits-per-nine-innings at 6½. With run support, he would have easily won 20 games.

Wilson enjoyed another stellar season in 1972, going 15-10 with a 2.68 ERA. He was often magnificent, fanning 12 Cubs on July 22, then ringing up 12 Giants on August 12, and 14 Phillies on August 20. He gave up only one run to the Giants in 13 innings on September 7.

Due to arm trouble, Wilson was given just one start in the first 30 games of 1973 by manager Preston Gomez. He

G	IP	W	L	PCT	SHO	GS	CG	H	ER	SO	BB	ERA
266	1748.1	140	92	.531	20	245	78	1479	611	1283	640	3.15

didn't get his second start until May 12 but punched out 14 Reds to return to the rotation. Wilson's 3.20 ERA that year was compiled in a career-high 37 games.

On July 8, 1974, he worked eight frames not allowing a single Reds hit. Although he had allowed two unearned runs, Wilson was within three outs of his third no-no (only Koufax had achieved three in the NL). Gomez removed him for a pinch hitter and the home crowd booed.

He completed what would be his last campaign with back-to-back impressive gems against the Atlanta Braves. He allowed a lone run in eight innings on September 22 and then pitched a two-hit, 5–0 shutout on September 28 in which he did not have a single strikeout.

In the final eight starts of his impressive career, Wilson posted a miniscule 1.02 ERA and held batters to an anemic .158 batting average. He was successfully re-inventing himself, mixing in his breaking pitches with great accuracy and confidence.

After beginning his offseason with a full schedule as part of the Astros Speakers Bureau, Wilson was the victim of carbon monoxide poisoning on January 5, 1975. He was found lifeless, slumped in the passenger seat of his 1972 Ford Thunderbird inside the garage of his Fondren Southwest Houston home. The garage was below where his family slept so the toxic gas also took the life of his five-year-old son Donald Alexander. His wife Bernice discovered their nine-year-old daughter Denise in a coma. She was hospitalized in critical condition, but survived.

Wilson's uniform #40 was retired by the Astros on April 13. A black circular patch with his number in white was worn on the left sleeve of the 1975 Astros rainbow jerseys in tribute to their fallen teammate. Wilson is remembered on the Astros Wall of Honor at Minute Maid Park. He and his son are buried together in the Forest Lawn Memorial Park in Covina Hills, California.

CARL YASTRZEMSKI

BOSTON RED SOX
LEFT FIELD

1961-1983

*"For that one season
there could not
have been a better
baseball player."*

~ rookie manager
Dick Williams, 1967

Carl Yastrzemski played 23 seasons with Boston – the longest of any single-team player along with Brooks Robinson. An 18-time All-Star, he was the first AL hitter ever to amass 400 home runs and 3,000 hits and ranks second to Pete Rose in games played.

The durable Red Sox captain is first in games played with one team and trails only Ty Cobb and Derek Jeter in hits with one team. He appears on many all-time lists including at-bats, hits, RBI, doubles, bases on balls, extra base hits and total bases.

The 5'11" 182-pound Yastrzemski was well-known for his distinctive left-handed stance. He held his C271 34½" *Louisville Slugger* especially high, giving his swing a stylish dramatic arc. Yaz led the AL in 23 major offensive categories during his career.

He was a superstar leftfielder, mastering Fenway Park's 37-foot high Green Monster and its erratic caroms. With his strong, accurate arm, Yaz led the AL in assists a record seven seasons and won seven *Rawlings* Gold Gloves for his fielding excellence.

* * * * *

Carl Michael Yastrzemski was born on August 22, 1939 to Hattie Skonieczny and Karol Yastrzemski in Southampton, Suffolk County, New York. He grew up Polish Catholic, working on his family's potato farm outside of Bridgehampton, Long Island.

At Bridgehampton High, Yastrzemski set the Long Island prep basketball record with 628 points in 1957. He also hit .512 for his high school career and pitched a no-hitter in his last game for the Suffolk County championship, striking out 18 of 21 batters.

Yastrzemski attended the University of Notre Dame on a basketball and baseball scholarship before turning pro. He signed with Red Sox scout Frank "Bots" Nekola for a

$108,000 bonus in late 1958 without ever playing a varsity inning for the Fighting Irish.

Yaz was sent to the Class-B Raleigh (NC) Capitals in 1959. Playing shortstop, he hit .377, 64 points higher than any other Carolina League batter, and was league MVP. He was given a year to learn to play left field in 1960 with the Minneapolis (MN) Millers as Ted Williams' replacement. He hit .339 and sported a 30-game hitting streak.

The 21-year-old Yastrzemski made his debut on Opening Day April 11, 1961, against the Kansas City A's, singling in his first at-bat, but felt the pressure of replacing his renowned predecessor and hit only .266. He settled in to win the 1963 AL batting crown (.321) while playing a brilliant left field. He also paced the AL in hits, doubles and walks.

After finishing ninth in 1966, Boston was a 100-to-1 long shot in 1967. Yaz put the Red Sox on his back and carried them to an Impossible Dream pennant. In the last 12 games, he hit .523 (23-for-44) with five home runs, 14 runs scored and 16 RBI.

Boston had to win the last two games against Minnesota to avoid a tie with the Tigers and Twins. Yastrzemski went 7-for-8 with a three-run blast in the first game. He also killed a Twin rally by throwing out Bob Allison at second on a certain two-bagger.

In one of the most heroic seasons in baseball history, Yastrzemski won the Triple Crown (.326 average - 44 home runs - 121 RBI) as the AL MVP. He also topped the circuit with 112 runs scored, 189 hits, 360 total bases, .418 OBP, 1.040 OPS and slugged .622.

Despite Yaz's .400 average and three bombs, the Red Sox lost a hard-fought World Series to the Cardinals, 4-to-3. He was *Sports Illustrated's* Sportsman of the Year, *AP* Male Athlete of the Year, and won the Hickok Belt as the top pro athlete of the year.

In the Year of the Pitcher 1968, Yastrzemski earned his

G	AB	R	H	2B	3B	HR	RBI	SB	BB	SO	BA	OBP	SLG	TB
3308	11988	1816	3419	646	59	452	1844	168	1845	1393	.285	.379	.462	5539

second straight batting title. His .301 average was the lowest of any batting champion in history. He was the only hitter in the league to bat .300 that year. Yaz also paced the AL in OBA and walks.

He went 4-for-4 as the 1970 All-Star MVP in a losing cause and batted a career-high .329 that year with 40 home runs, but Alex Johnson took the batting title by .001. He led the AL with 125 runs scored, a .452 OBA, slugged .592 and had an OPS of 1.044.

After playing first base for most of the year, Yaz returned to left field in the 1975 ALCS against the A's, made several dazzling plays, and hit a torrid .455. While he hit .310 In the Fall Classic versus the Reds, he flew out to center for the final out in Game 7.

In the 1978 AL East tiebreaker, Yaz opened the scoring with a home run off Cy Young winner Ron Guidry. It would be the only round tripper hit off the left-handed ace by a left-handed hitter that entire season. He fouled out to third base to end the season.

Yastrzemski stroked his 3,000th hit on September 12, 1979 against the Yankees, stinging a Jim Beattie fastball into right field for a clean single. He was still a regular in the Red Sox lineup at 41 and played his last game on October 2, 1983 at age 44.

Yaz was a first ballot National Baseball Hall of Famer in 1989 and his #8 was retired forever. A replica was unveiled on Fenway's right field roof facing and a statue was dedicated in 2013 outside depicting him raising his helmet before his last at-bat.

He and Carol Ann Casper married in 1960 and raised three daughters and a son. Yastrzemski and his second wife Nancy Benson currently reside in North Boston. The taciturn Red Sox legend is a roving instructor, assisting young hitters to improve their craft. He continues to deflect attention from himself and his renown.

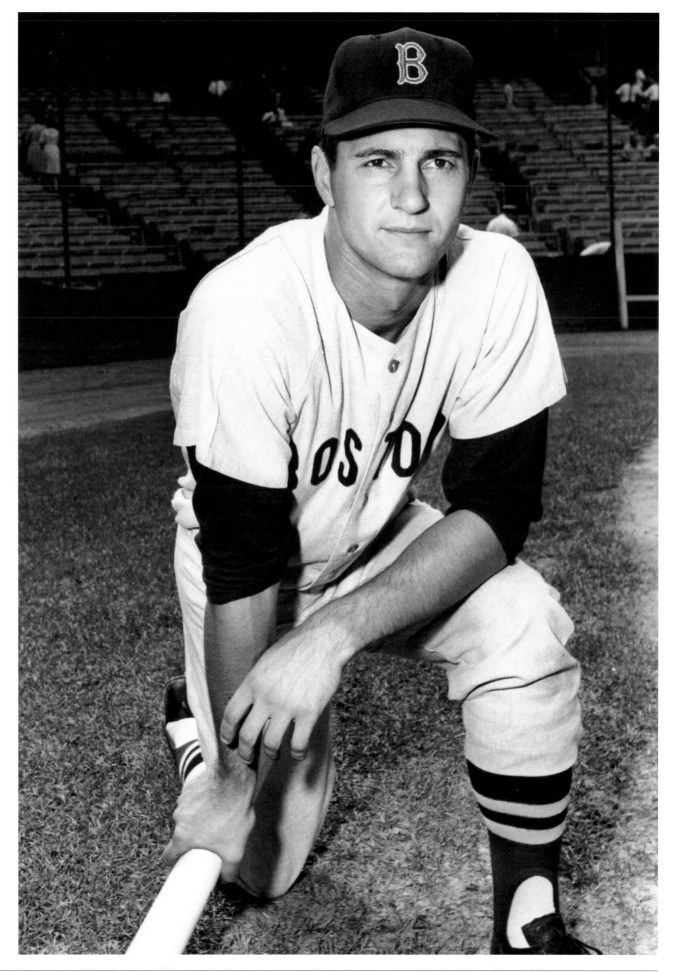

CHAPTER SIX

FREE AGENCY AND THE MODERN ERA

1975-1990

JERRY AUGUSTINE

MILWAUKEE BREWERS
LEFT-HANDED PITCHER

1975-1984

"I like the way he goes about his job out of the bullpen. He walks out there, grabs the ball and says, 'Let's go.' Also, you have to have an arm that responds to pitching every day. His does. It bounces back every day. He just goes about his job well."

~ *Brewers manager George Bamberger*

Jerry Augustine pitched as a starter, long reliever, set up man and closer, finishing his career ranked in the Top 10 in eight major pitching categories for his hometown Brewers. He is still ranked sixth on the all-time Brewers lists in games pitched, ninth in shutouts, tenth in complete games, 12th in innings pitched, and 12th in victories.

The 6' 183-pound Augustine was a member of the 1982 American League Champion Brewers, nicknamed "Harvey's Wallbangers" after their manager Harvey Kuenn. A strong-armed left-hander with a good curveball, he completed 27 career starts including six shutouts.

* * * * *

Gerald Lee Augustine was born on July 24, 1952 to Elerene Gibson and Donald Augustine in Green Bay, Brown County, Wisconsin. He grew up with five brothers and a sister in the nearby small town of Kewaunee on the northwestern shore of Lake Michigan. Augustine attended Kewaunee High, a school with an enrollment of less than 350 students. He was a three-sport star for the Storm, playing quarterback, point guard and pitcher.

Augustine pitched three years for the University of Wisconsin at La Crosse, graduating in 1974. A star on the 1972 and 1973 Wisconsin State University Conference titlist squads, he was all-WSUC in 1973 with a 4-0 mark and led the conference with 49 strikeouts and a 2.91 ERA.

Augustine was picked in the 15th round of the June 1974 free agent draft and signed by Brewers scout Emil Belich. He started with the Danville (IL) Warriors of the Class-A Midwest League and went to the Sacramento (CA) Solons of the PCL in 1975. Pitching in Hughes Stadium and its left field curtain only 200 feet from home plate, his ERA was 4.78.

Notwithstanding, the Brewers liked what they saw and gave him a September call up. Augustine was given his debut on September 9 and earned his first victory against the Yankees on September 16 at Milwaukee's County Stadium, giving up only two runs in 8$\frac{1}{3}$ innings.

With 20 starts as a regular in the Brewers' 1976 rotation, he went 9-12 with a 3.30 ERA in 171$\frac{2}{3}$ innings. Augustine was the left-handed starting pitcher on the 1976 AL *Topps* All-Rookie Team and the Milwaukee Baseball Writers Association Brewers Rookie of the Year.

During his rookie summer on July 20, 1976, his teammate Henry Aaron hit his 755th and last career round tripper off the California Angels' Dick Drago. Augustine gave up only five hits in seven innings in that game to earn the victory, 6-2.

He finished the 1977 year topping the staff with 12 wins and ten complete games in a career-high 209 innings pitched, but his best overall performance may have come on August 28, 1978. Augustine held a strong Tigers lineup to two hits in a 10-1 victory and ultimately accrued a career-high 13 victories that year. In his three seasons in the Brewers rotation, he won 34 games. He was also elected to serve as the Brewers player representative starting in 1977.

Augustine made a successful shift from the rotation to the bullpen in 1979, with nine wins and five saves, setting a personal-high in winning percentage. He posted a 0.95 ERA with five victories during the seven weeks of the season he pitched out of the bullpen. His performance made him the Brewers "*Rolaids* Man of the Year."

As the 1980 season began, Augustine had been rewarded with a five-year contract and was poised to be the ace of the bullpen but Rollie Fingers joined the Brewers in 1981 and Augustine was moved back to set him up. Milwaukee went to the postseason in 1981 and

G	IP	W	L	PCT	SHO	GS	CG	H	ER	SO	BB	ERA
279	944	55	59	.482	6	104	27	1028	444	348	340	4.23

1982. Fingers was the 1981 AL Most Valuable Player and Cy Young Award winner, but Bob McClure was given the closer role with Fingers' injury in the '82 "Suds World Series" with the Cardinals.

During his last two full years in 1982 and 1983, Augustine finished with an ERA of over 5.00. He pitched his final major league game on April 11, 1984 and then was sent down to the Vancouver (BC) Canadians, Iowa Cubs, and Louisville (KY) Redbirds, but had limited success.

Augustine was granted free agency by the Brewers on November 8, 1984. He kept trying to make a comeback for another two seasons with the Columbus (OH) Clippers and Rochester (NY) Red Wings in the Triple-A American Association before retiring for good from baseball.

Augustine became head baseball coach of the University of Wisconsin at Milwaukee in 1995. In a dozen seasons, his Panthers won five conference tournament or regular season titles and qualified for the NCAA tournament in 2001 while finishing second in the nation in hitting.

A three-time Midwestern Collegiate Conference Coach of the Year, Augustine's teams won at least 20 games every year and won 30 or more games six times. His 347-297-1 career record give him the most victories by any coach in UWM's Division I athletics history.

Augustine was inducted into the University of Wisconsin at La Crosse Hall of Fame in 1984. He has also been elected to the Milwaukee Brewers Wall of Honor located at the Hot Corner Entrance to Miller Park along with other Brewers greats such as Henry Aaron, Rollie Fingers, Paul Molitor and Robin Yount.

Augustine opened his American Family Insurance Company in 1986, in West Allis, Wisconsin and still runs his business full-time. He is also a popular television analyst for the Milwaukee Brewers on Fox Sports Wisconsin (FSW). Augustine and his wife Nancy currently reside in Muskego, Wisconsin outside of Milwaukee. They have raised five children.

BRUCE BENEDICT

ATLANTA BRAVES
CATCHER

1978-1989

"Benedict has improved so much that there is only one catcher [Montreal's Gary Carter] whose arm is stronger and more accurate. But his most valuable trait is his intelligence. He doesn't have a full year's experience in the big leagues, but he already calls the best game for our pitchers. They love him back there."

~ Braves manager Bobby Cox

Bruce Benedict was a two-time National League All-Star and superb defensive catcher. His work behind the plate enabled the Braves to find another position for future National League Most Valuable Player Dale Murphy and the Braves soon thereafter became pennant contenders.

Benedict displayed excellent footwork, a lightning quick release and a laser accurate throwing arm. Pitchers appreciated the intelligent way he called the game. Hall of Fame knuckleballer Phil Niekro maintained Benedict was the best battery mate he ever had.

The hometown crowd at Fulton County Stadium habitually chanted "BRUUUUCE!!" whenever he came to bat. Thanks to the Braves' popular national TV presence on the Turner Broadcasting System (TBS), Benedict became familiar to baseball fans all over the country.

Although not primarily known for his offense, the 6'1" 185-pound Benedict made good contact and drove the ball to all fields. A right-handed, line-drive hitter, he stood away from the plate and focused on hitting the ball hard where it was pitched.

* * * * *

Bruce Edwin Benedict was born on August 18, 1955 to Kathryn and David Eugene Benedict in Birmingham, Jefferson County, Alabama. His father pitched in the Yankees and Cardinals systems for ten years, reaching the Triple-A level. The family moved to Omaha, Nebraska and the young Benedict started catching when he was ten years old. He excelled in basketball and baseball at Omaha's Millard High School before graduating in 1973.

Benedict caught for coach Virgil Yelkin's University of Nebraska at Omaha Mavericks from 1974 to 1976. He was the UNO Male Athlete of the Year in 1975 and was twice named to the All-NCAA Division II District and North Central Intercollegiate Athletic Conference teams.

Benedict was taken in the fifth round of the 1976 draft and signed by Braves scout Al LaMacchia. After only weeks in the Appalachian League at Kingsport (TN), he was shipped to Greenwood (SC) in the Western Carolinas League and then to Double-A Savannah (GA).

Back with Savannah in 1977, Benedict was the *Topps* Double-A All-Star and Southern League All-Star catcher, leading all SL receivers with 770 putouts and 112 assists. In August, Braves farm director Henry Aaron declared that he was ready to catch in the major leagues.

Benedict began the 1978 season #3 on the catchers' depth chart behind Dale Murphy and Biff Pocoroba. The Braves sent him to Triple-A Richmond (VA) in the International League to get him more playing time. He was called up for his major league debut on his 23rd birthday.

Murphy was set to be manager Bobby Cox's catcher for the 1979 season with Benedict being used mostly against left-handed pitchers. However, when Murphy kept firing his throws to second into center field, Cox decided to start Benedict and relocate Murphy to the outfield.

Benedict threw out 44 would-be base stealers in 1980 for an NL-leading 37 percent caught-stealing rate. He did it again in 1981, gunning down 48 runners at a 37 percent clip with 73 assists, topping all Senior Circuit backstops. He was chosen a 1981 National League All-Star.

In 1982, he led all NL receivers in fielding at .993 while appearing in 118 games for manager Joe Torre. From August 23 through September, he hit a clutch .389 to help Atlanta win the NL West title. In his only postseason, the Braves were swept by the Cardinals in the NLCS.

In late May of 1983, Benedict was still leading the NL in hitting at .338 and earned All-Star honors again. He hit a career-best .298 in 134 games with a solid .385 on-base percentage. His .992 fielding average was second

G	AB	R	H	2B	3B	HR	RBI	SB	BB	SO	BA	OBP	SLG	TB
982	2878	214	696	98	6	18	260	12	.242	251	.242	.320	.299	860

only to Hall of Famer Gary Carter among NL catchers.

Benedict's batting average dropped in 1984 and Alex Trevino began receiving more of the work. Rick Cerone got most of the playing time at catcher in 1985 and Benedict backed up Ozzie Virgil from 1986 to early 1988, appearing in only about one-third of the games.

However, he returned to a key catching role when former catcher Russ Nixon assumed the Braves' reins. Benedict saw action in 50 of Nixon's first 81 games as manager. He also had a role in building young Atlanta pitching talent, catching almost all of Hall of Famer Tom Glavine's starts in his initial three years and catching for John Smoltz in his first win in 1988.

Benedict appeared in his final game at age 34 on September 11, 1989, and retired at the end of the season. He managed the 1993 Danville (VA) Braves (Appalachian League); the 1994 and 1995 Double-A Greenville (SC) Braves (Southern League); and Mets' affiliate Triple-A 1986 Norfolk (VA) Tides (International League). He became the Mets' catching coach in 1997.

As manager Bobby Valentine's bench coach, Benedict stood in for him on June 16, 1999. The day before, Valentine had been ejected, but remained in the Mets dugout tunnel, donning a faux mustache and sunglasses. Benedict served as a Mets major league advance scout until 2006.

He began refereeing junior high, high school and junior college basketball games in 1985. By 1990, he was an NCAA Division 1 college basketball official, working up to 65 games per year in six collegiate conferences, including the SEC, traveling all over the South.

Benedict and his wife, the former Kathleen Ann McCormick, reside in Dunwoody, Georgia where they raised two sons and a daughter. Benedict is currently a Chicago White Sox scout and operates his Bruce Benedict Baseball Academy in Norcross, Georgia.

GEORGE BRETT

KANSAS CITY ROYALS
THIRD BASE

1973-1993

"With most great players on other teams, you notice how great they are, but when they become teammates and you see them everyday, you notice the flaws. It is exactly the opposite with George Brett."

~ teammate Jim Sundberg

George Brett wreaked havoc on American League pitching for 21 years as the most feared hitter of his time and one of the most complete baseball players ever to wear a uniform. Brett's approach was all out every day with a maximum focus on his team.

A .300 hitter 11 times, he was one of the classic line drive hitters in baseball history. Brett led the Royals to seven playoff berths, two pennants and the 1985 World Series title. He earned a career postseason average of .344 in 43 games with 56 hits, ten home runs and 23 RBI while slugging .638 as one of the best October hitters ever.

A 13-time All-Star, Brett is the only hitter to win a batting title in three separate decades (1976, 1980 & 1990). He is also the only man to amass 3,000 hits, 600 doubles, 100 triples, 300 homers and 200 stolen bases. As a third baseman, Brett's great hands, range and throwing arm were recognized when he won the 1985 *Rawlings* Gold Glove.

*　★　★　★　★　★*

George Howard Brett was born in Glen Dale, West Virginia on May 15, 1953 to Ethel Johnson and Jack Brett. He grew up in Hermosa Beach, California, the youngest of four brothers. His brother Ken was a major league pitcher. Brett starred in football and baseball for El Segundo High and was drafted by the Royals as a shortstop in June, 1971.

That summer, he hit .291 for the Class-A Billings (MT) Royals and made the All-Pioneer League team. Playing for the San Jose (CA) Royals in 1972, he led all California League third basemen in assists. At Omaha in 1973, he hit .284 and made the American Association All-Star squad, leading to his major league debut on August 2.

Brett became the most famous protégé of hitting sage Charley Lau, melding his great talent with hard work and Lau's weight shift theories. The 6' 190-pound left-handed hitter had never averaged .300 in the minor leagues, but Lau taught him to hit every type pitch and to use the entire field, foul line to foul line.

By 1975, Brett was polished, batting .308 and leading the AL with 195 hits and 13 triples. He led the AL in three-baggers again in 1976 and set a big-league record of six straight games with three or more hits (May 8-13) on the way to his first batting crown.

In 1979, the left-handed hitting Brett went for the cycle on May 28 and became one of only five players to accumulate at least 20 doubles, 20 triples and 20 home runs in one season. He posted a .329 average and paced the AL with 212 hits and 20 triples.

Brett's high water mark was 1980 when he hit a cool .390 - the best since Ted Williams' .406 in 1941. Sporting a 37-game hitting streak, he raised his average to a high of .407 and was above .400 as late as September 19. His 118 RBI in 117 games made him the first hitter in three decades to have more runs batted in than games played. He was the runaway American League Most Valuable Player with a .664 slugging percentage and .461 on-base average. He was *The Sporting News, Sport Magazine* and *Associated Press* Major League Player of the Year.

Perhaps the most publicized event in Brett's career was the "Great Pine Tar Incident" of July 24, 1983. Facing Yankees nemesis Goose Gossage at Yankee Stadium in the top of the ninth inning, Brett clubbed a clutch home run to put the Royals ahead, 5-4. Yankees manager Billy Martin immediately complained that Brett had applied pine tar above the label of his *Louisville Slugger* and umpire Tim McClelland called him out for a rules violation.

When Brett heard the adverse decision, his fierce

G	AB	R	H	2B	3B	HR	RBI	SB	BB	SO	BA	OBP	SLG	TB
2707	10349	1583	3154	665	137	317	1595	201	1096	908	.305	.369	.487	5044

indignation spoke volumes about his will to win. The normally mild-mannered Brett raged out of the dugout, had to be restrained, and was ejected from the game. After the Royals' formal protest, the decision was overruled by AL president Lee MacPhail and the Royals went on to win.

His team's emotional leader, he finished in the 1985 AL Top Ten in ten major offensive categories. Five of Brett's career-high 30 home runs came in the last six wins to give the Royals the AL West pennant. He also was the ALCS MVP versus the Blue Jays and was brilliant in the Fall Classic, hitting .370. The Royals won their only World Series title in the 20th century in 1985 against the Cardinals in an all-Missouri match up.

Brett became the 18th hitter to reach 3,000 hits when he singled off lefty Tim Fortugno on October 1, 1992 at Angel Stadium. He finished with 3,154 career hits- the most ever by a third baseman. Brett ended his career ranking fifth on the all-time doubles list with 665, trailing only Tris Speaker, Pete Rose, Stan Musial and Ty Cobb. He also ranks high all-time in hits, extrabase hits and total bases and holds the AL mark with 229 intentional walks.

George Brett was inducted into the National Baseball Hall of Fame in 1999 after being named on over 98 percent of all ballots. Brett's uniform #5 will never be worn again by another Royal. His career has been commemorated with a statue beyond the center field fountains at Kauffman Stadium, depicting him hitting in full launch position.

Brett will forever be "The Franchise" as the best player in Royals history. Working in the Royals front office, he remains active as a beloved icon in his adopted hometown. Brett lives in Prairie Village, Kansas with his wife Leslie and three sons.

RANDY BUSH

MINNESOTA TWINS
OUTFIELD • PINCH HITTER • DESIGNATED HITTER

1982-1993

"Many people can't do it. It is very difficult. And you don't want to go up there and try to pull everything, but just hit it someplace. I believe that's what Bush does. He's ready, excited to go and hit at the end of the game. He has a beautiful swing, especially when he gets in a groove and isn't lunging. He's a pro who knows what he has to do."

~ Twins coach Tony Oliva
on pinch-hitting

Randy Bush was one of only seven Twins to win two World Series Championship rings in 1987 and 1991. A left-handed slugger with tremendous power, he embraced what would become a career-long role as a designated hitter, bench bat and reserve outfielder.

The 6'1" 190-pound Bush reached double figures in homers five times despite never having 400 at-bats. As the Twins' pinch hitter extraordinaire, he twice had 13 pinch-hits in a season, once launched two straight pinch-hit home runs, and paced the AL in pinch hits in 1991.

The difference in his success hitting left-handed pitching versus right-handed pitching was as extreme as any major league player in history. He hit .255 against righties with a .422 slugging percentage. Facing lefties, he hit .152 and slugged .232. Under managers Billy Gardner and Tom Kelly, Bush was placed in spots that allowed him to succeed. Against left-handers, he averaged fewer than ten trips to the plate per season (118 career plate appearances total).

He had particular success hitting at home in the Metrodome with a .796 OPS in Minneapolis as opposed to .699 in away games. He also performed better in the clutch, putting up a .801 OPS with runners in scoring position, versus a pedestrian .711 OPS with bases empty.

* * * * *

Robert Randall Bush was born on October 5, 1958 in Dover, Kent County, Delaware. Growing up in the Miami suburbs, he attended Carol City High and was all-Florida State in baseball. At Miami-Dade Community College North, Bush hit .454 as a 1978 junior college all-star.

He competed one year for the University of New Orleans in 1979. Hitting .369, Bush set a school record with eight triples, and led the Sun Belt Conference champion Privateers with 18 home runs and 77 runs batted in. UNO went 49-14 and qualified for the NCAA playoffs.

He was selected in the second round of the 1979 amateur free agent draft and signed by Twins scout Ed Dunn. Assigned to the Orlando (FL) Twins of the Double-A Southern League, he moved up to the Toledo (OH) Mud Hens of the Triple-A International League in 1980.

Bush broke through with Orlando in 1981 to hit .290 with 22 home runs and 94 RBI. It earned him his debut on May 1, 1982 against the Brewers at age 23. He pinch-hit for Sal Butera to lead off the bottom of the ninth inning. Hall of Fame reliever Rollie Fingers struck him out.

In the first game of a doubleheader at the end of his rookie year on September 28, Bush played the role of spoiler. Blue Jays ace Jim Clancy retired 24 straight hitters before Bush broke his *Louisville Slugger* with a single in the ninth. It was the only safe hit that Clancy allowed.

In the 1987 World Series Game 2, Bush contributed to the Twins victory by hammering a clutch two-run double off Cardinals hurler Danny Cox. He later crossed the plate on a head-first slide, evading catcher Tony Pena's tag. The Twins went on to win in seven for their first title.

Bush had a monster game on May 20, 1989 against the Texas Rangers. Batting cleanup and playing first base in place of Kent Hrbek, he produced a run-scoring single in the first inning, a sacrifice fly in the seventh inning and three-run homers in the eighth and ninth innings for eight runs batted in. His performance tied a Twins franchise record for RBI in one game.

Minnesota finished dead last in the American League West in 1990 with a 74-88 mark, but came back to win the division the next year with 95 wins. During the Cinderella 1991 season, Bush hit a career-high .303 with a .401 OBA and .886 OPS. He also ranked fifth in the AL with ten intentional walks. Bush led the Junior Circuit with 13 pinch-hits that season, batting .318 as a pinch hitter. From July through August 19, he tied an AL record with seven con-

G	AB	R	H	2B	3B	HR	RBI	SB	BB	SO	BA	OBP	SLG	TB
1219	3045	388	763	154	26	96	409	33	348	505	.251	.334	.413	1257

secutive pinch hits. He also hit .378 with a .622 slugging percentage in "close and late" at-bats.

Bush appeared in three 1991 Fall Classic games, providing a hit in the classic Game 7 Metrodome duel between the Twins' Jack Morris and the Braves' John Schmoltz. Minnesota won its second title in ten innings, 1-0. It turned out to be Bush's last productive season.

He hit .214 in 1992 but not before pounding a home run off the Yankees' Scott Sanderson on May 2 in the fifth inning. His teammates Hrbek, Shane Mack and Kirby Puckett also hit home runs off Sanderson in that inning, making him the 12th pitcher in history to surrender four circuit clouts in a single frame. The Twins needed all of the bombs to win, 7-6.

Bush retired after Minnesota gave him his release on June 27, 1993. He batted only .146 in 32 games. After serving as a minor league hitting coordinator for the Cubs in 1999, Bush was appointed head coach of the University of New Orleans Privateers from 2000 through 2004.

He guided UNO to the 2000 Sun Belt Conference title with a 38-25 record and an appearance in the NCAA South II Regional in Baton Rouge, Louisiana. Bush's record over five seasons was 144-145. He was the first baseball inductee of the UNO Athletic Hall of Fame.

Bush was named the special assistant to the Cubs general manager in early 2005, during which time he served as an advance scout, charting other major league teams and players as well as the Cubs' own organizational players. He was promoted to Cubs assistant GM in late 2006.

On August 19, 2011, Bush was named the Cubs interim general manager, replacing Jim Hendry. Bush was retained by new general manager Theo Epstein. Continuing in his assistant GM role, he is involved in the hiring process of the field staff as well as the scouting staff. Randy Bush and his wife Catherine Vogel reside in the New Orleans area. They have two sons.

LARRY CHRISTENSON

PHILADELPHIA PHILLIES
RIGHT-HANDED PITCHER

1973-1983

"I have to admit seeing Larry go nine full innings and winning his first time out has to be the highlight of my managing career thus far."

~ rookie manager
Danny Ozark, April 13, 1973

Larry Christenson was a stalwart on Philadelphia teams that won three straight National League East pennants from 1976 to 1978. He pitched in four postseasons and was a mainstay in 1980 on the only Philly World Series championship team in the 20th century. His single franchise tenure is the most for any Phillies hurler and second only to Mike Schmidt's 18 seasons.

The big 6'4" 215-pound Christenson was a right-handed flamethrower, displaying dominant strikeout stuff. To compliment his sizzling fastball, he also displayed a curve, slider and change. And he had some pop in his bat with 11 big-league home runs and two in one game.

* * * * *

Larry Richard Christenson was born on November 10, 1953 to Mary Ruth Aanderud and Arnold Benjamin Christenson in Everett, Snohomish County, Washington. He starred in football, basketball, baseball and cross-country at nearby Marysville High. As a 1972 senior, he threw fastballs at nearly 100 mph, striking out 143 in just 72 innings with a 0.28 ERA. The Phillies grabbed him third overall in the free agent draft and scout Bill Harper signed him immediately.

Philadelphia was unaware that Christenson had adjusted his delivery to compensate for a birth defect condition called spinal stenosis that would later cause recurring back problems. He was sent to the Pulaski (VA) Phillies of the short season rookie Appalachian League for 1972.

Well-intentioned Pulaski coach Bunky Warren changed his mechanics to a more conventional style, unaware of his back condition. Christenson went along with it, but was only able to pitch 38 innings over five starts before landing in the hospital with serious arm issues.

Fortunately by the next spring, he had recovered. The Phillies' strategy was to have him learn his craft in the minors before exposing him to the Big Time. But Christenson was so imposing in his spring audition that new manager

Danny Ozark assigned him to be a starter in his rotation along with newly acquired rookie Dick Ruthven.

Only 19 years old, Christenson was given his major league debut on April 13, 1973 at Veterans Stadium. He dispatched the Mets, 7-1, with a complete game five-hitter as the youngest player in baseball (18-year-old David Clyde of the Texas Rangers didn't debut until June 27).

Later Christenson was sent down to the Eugene (OR) Emeralds in the Triple-A Pacific Coast League. He posted a 5.13 ERA in 100 innings pitched before requiring surgery on his right elbow over the winter for bone chips. He also spent part of 1974 with the Triple-A Toledo (OH) Mud Hens of the International League, gaining further seasoning in 172 innings pitched.

Christenson pulled a rib muscle in 1975 spring training and was optioned to Toledo for rehab and tutoring by manager Jim Bunning. Soon recalled for good, Christenson went 11-6 with a 3.67 ERA in 26 starts over 171²/₃ innings as one of the top starters for the 86-victory NL East runner up. The year proved to be a harbinger of strong Philly teams to come in the late 1970s.

Christenson's finest campaign was in 1977. He had a 19-6 line in 34 starts and 219¹/₃ innings pitched, winning 15 of his last 16 decisions. He was a key figure in the team's winning the NL East title, although the Phillies were upended by the Dodgers in four games in the NLCS.

Christenson pitched well in 1978 although his 13-14 record didn't reflect it, posting a career-best 3.24 ERA. Ozark tabbed him as the Game 1 starter against the Dodgers in the NLCS but he was shelled, lasting only 4¹/₃ innings and giving up seven hits and six earned runs.

By 1979, injuries had begun to hobble Christenson's career. He started the season on the disabled list with elbow problems and was sidelined for the first month. In June, he fractured his collarbone participating in a charity bike-a-thon caravan, missed several more weeks, and

G	IP	W	L	PCT	SHO	GS	CG	H	ER	SO	BB	ERA
243	1402.2	83	71	.539	6	220	27	1401	591	781	395	3.79

finished the year throwing only 106 innings and winning only five of his 15 decisions.

In 1980, Christenson started out on an upswing, going 3-0, but went on the disabled list again to undergo another surgery on his pitching elbow. He recovered to finish the year 5-1 in a minimal 73 1/3 innings pitched. Against the Astros in the NLCS Game 3, he came back to pitch six strong innings, allowing only three hits and no runs, but got no decision in a 1-0 Astrodome loss.

Christenson started Game 4 of the 1980 World Series, but was knocked out of the box in the first inning by the Royals and took the defeat. The Phillies recovered and took home the franchise's only World Series championship trophy of the 20th century.

Christenson was only able to accumulate a 4-7 record in 1981. His finest performance was his victory in Game 4 of the NL Divisional Series against the Expos. In the 6-2 win, he scattered four hits over six innings, allowing only one run, and struck out eight Montreal hitters.

Christenson's last injury-free season was 1982, when he made 32 starts and went 9-10. He pitched his last major league game on June 3, 1983. After a 2-4 start, he went under the knife for elbow surgery for the final time. As a result, he failed to make the postseason roster. The Phillies gave him his unconditional release after the playoffs on November 10, his 30th birthday.

Christenson spent several years back in Washington attempting to rehab his pitching arm. His arm just never responded and he came to the realization that his pitching career was over. He owns Christenson Investment Partners, doing institutional investing, and lives in Malvern, Pennsylvania, twenty miles from Philadelphia. Christenson is still connected with the Phillies and is well known for his work on behalf of local charities including diabetes, heart disease, leukemia and multiple sclerosis foundations. He has two daughters, Libby and Claire.

DAVE CONCEPCION

CINCINNATI REDS
SHORTSTOP

1970-1988

"Maybe somewhere there has been a man who played shortstop as well as he does, but I assure you there has never been a man who can cover the amount of ground he covers."

~ *manager Sparky Anderson*

Dave Concepción excelled at a premier position on the 1975 and 1976 World Series Champion Big Red Machine teams, two of the greatest clubs of all-time. A nine-time National League All-Star, he was the finest shortstop in the game during the 1970s, winning two *Louisville Slugger* Silver Slugger awards and five *Rawlings* Gold Gloves.

The versatile Dave Concepción played over 2,100 games at shortstop. Blessed with a powerful arm and unmatched range, he could make the acrobatic play, as well as the routine one. He and Joe Morgan formed one of the finest double play duos in history.

Concepción was masterful on the hard artificial turf at Cincinnati's Riverfront Stadium and throughout the league. Playing a deep shortstop, he was the first to use the one-bounce throw to first and perfected the skill working with first baseman Tony Perez.

★ ★ ★ ★ ★

David Ismael Concepción Benitez was born to Ernestina Benitez and David Concepción on June 17, 1948 in Ocumare de la Costa, Aragua State, Venezuela. He grew up idolizing Venezuelan shortstops Chico Carrasquel and Luis Aparicio.

Primarily a pitcher at Aragua Escuela and Augustin Codazzi College, he was taken by the Reds in the 1967 amateur free agent draft and assigned to the Tampa Tarpons in the Single-A Florida State League for the 1968 season. Manager George Scherger tried Concepción out at shortstop and realized the Reds had something special.

After hitting .341 in the American Association for the Indianapolis (IN) Indians in 1969, the 6'2" Concepción looked like he was ready even though reed-thin at 155 pounds. First-year skipper Sparky Anderson started him in his debut against the Expos on Opening Day

April 6, 1970. The young Venezuelan was still unable to speak English.

After sharing duty with Woody Woodward and Darrel Chaney for his first three seasons, Concepción blossomed in 1973 and made his first National League All-Star roster. Two days before the All-Star game, he broke the fibula of his left leg sliding into third base. When he was placed on the disabled list, he was hitting .287 with eight home runs, 46 runs batted in, and 22 stolen bases.

Concepción missed the rest of the season, but returned in 1974 to play 160 games in his best campaign, hitting .281, with 14 home runs and 82 RBI to go with his first *Rawlings* Gold Glove. He stole 41 bases and was caught only six times.

The Big Red Machine's celebrated "Great Eight" starting lineup of Johnny Bench, Perez, Morgan, Pete Rose, Concepción, George Foster, César Gerónimo, and Ken Griffey, Sr. became legendary in 1975 and 1976. Concepción hit .455 in the 1975 NLCS, leading the Reds over the Pirates. He also went off in the 1979 NLCS, batting.429.

The durable Concepción outlasted all of his Great Eight teammates. As a result, later in his career he often batted third in the order on teams that lacked the firepower of the Big Red Machine. He was the Reds Most Valuable Player in 1981, batting .306 with 129 hits, 28 doubles and 67 RBI. He paced the NL with 14 game-winning hits.

In the 1982 All-Star game, the first played beyond the borders of the United States, Concepción's two-run homer helped the Senior Circuit to a 4-1 victory at Olympic Stadium in Montreal. He was named the Midsummer Classic's Most Valuable Player.

Debilitated by an elbow injury and shoulder surgery in 1982, Concepción had two down years in 1983 and 1984.

G	AB	R	H	2B	3B	HR	RBI	SB	BB	SO	BA	OBP	SLG	TB
2488	8723	993	2326	389	48	101	950	321	736	1186	.267	.322	.357	3114

While serving as the Reds' captain, he helped to groom Barry Larkin who replaced him in 1986, and became a dependable handyman at all four infield positions. His final game was September 15, 1988.

Concepción also played more than two decades in Maracay for the Tigres de Aragua of the Venezuela Winter League. The Tigres retired his #13 jersey and honored him with a monument that hangs in center field at Estadio Jose Perez Colmenares. Even after he was a big-league star, he still worked relentlessly on his game in the winter.

Dave Concepción was inducted into the Cincinnati Reds Hall of Fame in 2000. His uniform jersey #13 was retired on August 25, 2007 before a game with the Marlins at Cincinnati's new Great American Ballpark. He was also part of the charter class of inductees into the Latino Baseball Hall of Fame in 2010.

The 2011 National Baseball Hall of Fame Expansion Era Veterans Committee cast their ballots for long retired players active in 1973. In Concepción's first year of eligibility, he received eight votes of the required 12 for election- the most of any player.

Although his admission seems inevitable, Concepción has been upstaged by the dazzling style of the other great shortstop of his era, Ozzie Smith. Voters will eventually see that Concepción hit well over three times as many home runs as "The Wizard."

Concepción and his wife Dilia Montenegro continue to reside in Maracay, Venezuela where he is beloved and treated like royalty. The people in his hometown call him "Rey David" — King David. In fact, younger Venezuelan infielder stars such as Omar Vizquel, Ozzie Guillen and Edgardo Alfonzo all chose uniform #13 in honor of Concepción, their boyhood hero.

RICH DAUER

BALTIMORE ORIOLES
SECOND BASE • THIRD BASE

1976-1985

*"I walked into Double-A and
Cal Ripken, Sr. grabbed me by
the throat and he threw me up
against the wall, and he said,
'I don't care where you went to school.
I don't care what round you got
drafted in. I don't care who you are,
and I don't care if you hit .300. But if
you play and you give me 110 percent,
then we're going to get along fine.'"*

~ Rich Dauer

Rich Dauer teamed with Mark Belanger and then later with Cal Ripken, Jr. to form two superb Orioles double play combinations. He never played for a losing Baltimore team and is one of the few players to win a College World Series and a Major League World Series. He is also one of a handful of men to have participated in a Fall Classic as both a player and a coach.

The scrappy 6' 180-pound Dauer was a reliable fielder and an intelligent contact hitter who was almost impossible to strike out, leading the AL twice in at-bats to strikeouts ratio. An expert bunter, he was successful in 54 of 55 sacrifice bunt attempts during his career. Manager Earl Weaver favored him for his steady defense on teams built around strong pitching.

★　★　★　★　★

Richard Fremont Dauer was born on July 27, 1952 of German lineage to Nellie Sweany and Charles W. "Bud" Dauer in San Bernardino, California. He grew up in Colton where Euliss Hubbs, father of former Cubs star Kenny Hubbs, was one of his first baseball coaches and also helped him in the Punt, Pass & Kick competition. Dauer was a basketball shooting guard for the Colton High Yellowjackets, playing alongside Gary Hubbs, Kenny's younger brother. He was also an All-CIF Southern Section shortstop in 1970.

Dauer starred at San Bernardino Valley College under coach Steve Smith in 1971 and 1972. Named the 1972 California Junior College Player of the Year, he landed a scholarship to the University of Southern California where he played on teams that earned USC's fourth and fifth consecutive national collegiate baseball titles. Dauer was coach Rod Dedeaux's MVP shortstop for the 1974 College World Series Champion Trojans, defeating the Miami Hurricanes.

An NCAA All-American in 1974, Dauer produced 108 hits, 24 doubles, 92 RBI and 181 total bases in the NCAA's first year allowing aluminum bats. In both of his seasons with the Trojans, he led the team in hitting, averaging an aggregate .376 with a .617 slugging percentage.

The June 1974 amateur free agent draft produced just 725 draft choices, the fewest in draft history, and only 300 were college ballplayers. Baseball scouts were apparently unconvinced that the metal bat batting averages could translate to wood. The Orioles took Dauer in the first round and 24th overall.

That summer playing for Double-A Asheville (NC) of the Southern League, Dauer hit .328 with 11 home runs in 53 games. He split 1975 between Asheville and the Rochester (NY) Red Wings. After a stellar 1976 at Rochester where he averaged .336 and shared the International League MVP award, he made his major league debut on September 11.

In his first two Orioles years, he split playing time with Billy Smith at second base, and also filled in for the chronically-injured Doug DeCinces at the hot corner. Manager Earl Weaver would pinch-hit him in the late innings and bring in Lenn Sakata to finish the game at second.

However, by 1978, Dauer had replaced Bobby Grich at second base for the Orioles. From July 18 to 28, he posted ten straight games with at least two hits- still a franchise record. During the hot streak, he batted .583 (28-for-48). That year Dauer set big-league defensive records by playing 86 straight errorless games and handling 425 chances without an error. He made his lone error of the season in the final game on September 30, a 5-4 loss to the Detroit Tigers.

After playing 142 regular season games as a rock-solid contributor to an AL East title, Dauer helped the Orioles to defeat the California Angels in the 1979 ALCS in four games. Against the Pirates in the World Series, he hit .294 (5-for-17) including a clutch early circuit blast off Jim

G	AB	R	H	2B	3B	HR	RBI	SB	BB	SO	BA	OBP	SLG	TB
1140	3829	448	984	193	3	43	372	6	297	219	.257	.310	.343	1312

Bibby in Game 7 that gave Baltimore a lead before Willie Stargell's game-winning home run.

In the 1983 World Series commonly known as the "I-90 Series," the Orioles defeated the Phillies in five games which resulted in Dauer earning his only World Series championship ring. His average dropped precipitously to .202 in 1985 and he played his last game on September 11.

Dauer managed the Class-A San Bernardino Spirit of the California League in 1987. His number has been retired with the current incarnation of the Spirit, called the Inland Empire 66ers. Dauer directed traffic as third base coach for the Indians' Triple-A Colorado Springs (CO) Sky Sox in 1988 and 1989 and moved up to coach third base for the Indians in 1990 and 1991.

He spent the 1992 season

as an Orioles minor league roving infield instructor. After a season as a coach for the Triple-A Omaha (NE) Royals, Dauer worked as a Royals roving infield instructor from 1994 to 1996 and was in the Royals' third base coaching box from 1997 to 2002.

As Brewers bench coach from 2003 to 2005, he assisted manager Ned Yost. During the Orioles managerial search in 2004, he was a finalist before Lee Mazzilli was ultimately chosen. From 2006 to 2008, Dauer served as a Rockies roving minor league infield coordinator. In 2009 he joined the Rockies as the third base coach, a role he played until the end of the 2012 season.

In 2010, Dauer was honored with the Distinguished Athlete Award from the San Bernardino Valley College Alumni & Athletic Hall of Fame. In 2012, he became the 12th member of the 1983 Orioles title team to be elected to the Baltimore Orioles Hall of Fame. Rich Dauer Park has been named in his honor in Colton at the corner of Cottonwood & Torrey Pines Drive. Dauer lives with his wife, the former Christin King, in Highlands Ranch, Colorado. They have raised three children — Casey, Kelsey and Katie.

TIM FLANNERY

San Diego Padres
Second Base • Third Base

1979-1989

*"Tim is like a
two-sport star with
his music and baseball.
He can do it very well."*

*~ country music star
Garth Brooks*

Tim Flannery was an all-time Padres fan favorite, earning a reputation as a scrappy infielder who would do anything to help his team win. He played 972 games for the Padres, the fourth most in history behind Tony Gwynn, Dave Winfield and Garry Templeton.

The 5'11" 175-pound Flannery was so popular with the hometown fans for his hustle and enthusiasm that Padres organist Danny Topaz greeted Flannery's at-bats with the heroic strains of German composer Richard Wagner's opus *Ride of the Valkyries*. The crowds went wild.

The hardnosed Flannery established his value by playing almost every position on the field. At second base, he fielded a career .977. He is one of only four men in history to be in uniform for both of the Padres' Fall Classic appearances- in 1984 as a player and in 1998 as a coach. He was also an All-Star coach in 1999 (Fenway Park), 2011 (Arizona's Chase Field), and 2013 (Old Yankee Stadium).

★ ★ ★ ★ ★

Timothy Earl Flannery was born to Joyce Smith and Ragon Flannery on September 29, 1957 in Tulsa, Oklahoma. His ancestors emigrated from County Cork, Ireland and settled in the Appalachian Mountains of Kentucky. Flannery grew up with the Celtic influences of mountain music played by all his family. His father was a Christian minister. His mother's brother was Hal Smith, who hit a clutch eighth inning three-run home run in Game 7 of the 1960 World Series.

After the family moved to Southern California, Flannery became known as a fiery competitor, earning All-Empire League honors at shortstop for the Anaheim High Colonists. He also was a hustling basketball guard, a member of the Mozart Choir and an avid surfer.

Flannery starred for Chapman College in Orange, California from 1976 to 1978, leading the Panthers twice to NCAA Division II West Regional berths. He was an NCAA All-American, set school records for hits (90) and batting average (.435), and finished with a career average of .399. He was taken by the Padres in the sixth round of the June 1978 amateur free agent draft.

In his first summer in pro baseball, Flannery hit .350 for the Single-A Reno (NV) Silver Sox of the California League. And then in 1979, he hit .345 for the Double-A Amarillo Gold Sox of the Texas League with six home runs and 71 RBI to merit a September call-up by the Padres.

Hitting leadoff and playing second base at San Diego Stadium against the San Francisco Giants in his major league debut on September 3, 1979, Flannery went 1-for-3 and drove in the second run in the Padres' 3-0 victory. However, he slumped in 65 at-bats the rest of the way.

Flannery split the 1980 season between San Diego and the Triple-A Hawaii Islanders. He batted .346 in the Pacific Coast League, but hit only .240 in the National League that year. In 1981, he appeared in just 37 National League games, hitting .254.

"Flan's" first full big-league campaign was 1982. He hit his first home run in 1983- a solo shot off the Cubs' Chuck Rainey. On August 3, 1983, Nolan Ryan pitched his ninth career one-hitter, striking out ten in a 1-0 win. Flannery's third inning single was San Diego's only hit.

He played a key role off the bench for the 1984 National League Champion Padres. In his lone postseason, he made three NLCS plate appearance trips and reached base each time. In Game 4 trailing 3-2, he led off the fifth inning with a single and came around to score the tying run in a 7-5 victory over the Cubs. In Game 5, he reached base on a grounder that famously went through the legs of first baseman Leon Durham to score the tying run. In his only World Series at-bat, Flannery stroked an eighth inning pinch-hit single off the Tigers' Jack Morris in Game 4.

As the Padres regular second baseman in 1985, he batted .281 with 50 runs scored and 40 RBI- all career-highs.

G	AB	R	H	2B	3B	HR	RBI	SB	BB	SO	BA	OBP	SLG	TB
792	2838	255	631	77	25	9	209	22	277	293	.255	.355	.317	785

In 1986, he set a Padres second base franchise record with a .993 fielding percentage, but relinquished his job to Joey Cora in 1987, and then to Roberto Alomar in 1988.

Flannery finished out his playing career on his 32nd birthday, September 29, 1989. The sellout crowd greeted his first at-bat with a standing ovation so extended that play had to be stopped. After the game, radio talk shows discussed whether his #11 should be retired. Later Flannery was honored in 2003 as one of the Top 35 players in Padres history.

He went to work as a local Channel 8 CBS news feature reporter before returning to baseball in 1993 as the manager of the Spokane (WA) Indians, the Padres' Northwest League affiliate. He skippered the 1994 Rancho Cucamonga Quakes to a California League title and was promoted to manage the Triple-A Las Vegas Stars of the Pacific Coast League in 1995.

Padres manager Bruce Bochy chose him to be his third base coach in 1996 and he remained on Bochy's coaching staff through 2002. After two stints as a Padres broadcaster in 2005 and 2006, he reunited with Bochy when his close friend was appointed the Giants manager for 2007. Flannery was a major contributor from his third base coaching box as the Giants took three World Series titles in five years between 2010 and 2014. He retired from baseball after the 2014 season.

He is also an accomplished musician and gifted songwriter, having released 11 CDs. Flannery's bluegrass band *The Lunatic Fringe* has shared the stage with such stars as Jackson Browne, Jimmy Buffett, Judy Collins, Merle Haggard, Bruce Hornsby, Willie Nelson, Bonnie Raitt, Linda Ronstadt and Dwight Yoakam. Flannery's shows have been so beloved by his audiences they have been called traveling medicine shows. He and his wife Donna have a son Danny and two daughters Virginia and Kelly. The Flannerys live in Encinitas, California.

JIM GANTNER

MILWAUKEE BREWERS
SECOND BASE

1976-1992

*"I was drawn to Jim Gantner.
I was drawn by his passion,
his love of the game, his
energy, the way that he played
the game with an all-out style.
He was a guy that I could
really relate to. I tried to play
the game as hard as he did."*

~ Brewers teammate
and manager Ned Yost

A Wisconsin baseball icon, Jim Gantner played Little League, collegiate and major league baseball all in his native state. He was a vital part of the stellar Brewers infield in the 1980s with first baseman Cecil Cooper, third baseman Paul Molitor and shortstop Robin Yount.

The 6' 180-pound Gantner was nicknamed "Gumby" for his ability to contort around the keystone base. One of the most dependable and consistent second basemen in baseball history, he was extraordinary at turning the double play. In Gantner's 1,449 games at second base, he fielded .985, leading the Junior Circuit in chances three times, putouts twice, and assists once.

The Brewers trio of Gantner, Molitor and Yount held the professional sports record of 15 straight seasons (1978-92) by three teammates before the Yankees' Derek Jeter, Jorge Posada and Mariano Rivera surpassed it in 2011. The same Brewer triumvirate collected 6,399 hits, the most ever by three teammates. Hitting left-handed, Gantner batted over .280 seven times and is still among the Brewers career leaders in hits, runs scored, doubles and runs batted in.

* * * * *

James Elmer Gantner was born to Erma Cappozzo and Elmer Edward Gantner on January 5, 1953 in Fond du Lac, Wisconsin. He grew up in Fond du Lac County in the nearby village of Eden, attending Campbellsport High and starring for the Cougars' athletic teams.

He excelled as a two-time All-Wisconsin Intercollegiate Athletic Conference shortstop for the University of Wisconsin at Oshkosh Titans, a fifth place finisher in the 1974 NCAA Division III College World Series. He was enshrined into the Titans Hall of Fame in 1984.

Longtime Brewers scout Emil Belich observed Gantner's progress through college. The Brewers signed the native Wisconsinite after drafting him in the 12th round of the 1974 June amateur free agent draft. Belich was also the scout responsible for signing Paul Molitor.

Gantner methodically worked his way through the Brewers' system. He had stops with the 1974 Single-A Newark (NJ) Co-Pilots (New York-Penn League); and with the Eastern League's 1975 Thetford Mines (QC) Miners and 1976 Double-A Berkshire (MA) Brewers. With the 1977 Triple-A Spokane (WA) Indians (Pacific Coast League), he hit .281 with 35 doubles.

Gantner was given his big-league debut against the Tigers' Mark "The Bird" Fidrych on September 3, 1976, going 2-for-4. His teammates included a 20-year-old Yount and a 42-year-old Henry Aaron. He pinch-ran for Aaron in the great man's final game on October 3, 1976.

Eminently versatile, Gantner also played 360 games at third, seven at shortstop, three at first, nine as a designated hitter, and even pitched for an inning on August 29, 1979. He mopped up for an inning in relief in a blowout loss to the Royals, allowing two hits and no runs.

Gantner alternated with Don Money at third base in 1980 while hitting his first grand slam home run on June 23. Manager Harvey Kuenn named him his starting second baseman in 1981, the first of eight seasons in which Gantner would appear in over 100 games at second.

Harvey Kuenn's renowned Wallbangers won the 1982 AL pennant. Gantner scored the winning run in the bottom of the seventh of the decisive Game 5 of the ALCS, scampering home on Cecil Cooper's RBI single. In a close Fall Classic, he hit .333 batting eighth in the lineup, with four doubles and five runs scored as the Brewers were edged in seven by the Cardinals.

Now in the prime of his career, Gantner hit .282 in 1983 with personal-bests of eight triples, 11 home runs and 74 runs batted in. The following season, he was chosen the Milwaukee Brewers Most Valuable Player after

G	AB	R	H	2B	3B	HR	RBI	SB	BB	SO	BA	OBP	SLG	TB
1801	6189	726	1696	262	38	47	568	137	383	501	.274	.319	.351	2175

hitting .282 with 173 hits, 27 doubles, and 56 RBI.

In early 1988, Brewers manager Tom Trebelhorn switched Molitor to second base and Gantner to the hot corner. Although he had previously never stolen more than 13 bases, that year Gantner stole 20 bases for the first time at age 35. He swiped 20 bags again in 1989 before being roll-blocked at second base by the Yankees' Marcus Lawton attempting to complete a double play. He suffered a serious knee injury, returned after successful surgery, and competed for three more campaigns.

Gantner hit his final home run in dramatic fashion on August 14, 1992 at County Stadium. The walk off bomb in the bottom of the 13th inning off Boston's Jeff Reardon was famously called by broadcaster Bob Uecker: "Here's the pitch to Gantner. He hits one to right and deep. Get up. Get up. Get outta here – gone! A dinger for Klinger! And this game is over. Woah, Jimmy Gantner!"

Gantner's last game was October 3, 1992. He served as the Brewers first base coach in 1996 and 1997 and was voted onto the Brewers Walk of Fame in 2004. Fans can view his large home plate-shaped granite monument in Miller Park's home plate plaza. He joined former Brewers Aaron, Molitor and Yount in 2005 in the Wisconsin Athletic Hall of Fame.

In tribute to the affable infielder, "Gantner's Garden" has been established as the prime location in the Miller Park parking lot for tailgating before Brewers games. Private spaces can be rented out in this special area which has generators, tents, concessions and restroom access.

Gantner was the field manager of the 2007 and 2008 Wisconsin Woodchucks, playing out of Wausau, an entry in the Northwoods League, a collegiate summer wood bat circuit. He and his wife Jeannine have moved back to his hometown of Eden, about an hour north of Milwaukee near Fond du Lac, where he is part owner of the historic bar and grille called "Scuds Buds."

SCOTT GARRELTS

SAN FRANCISCO GIANTS
RIGHT-HANDED PITCHER

1982-1991

*"In fact, former Giants
pitcher Scott Garrelts had
the best splitter I ever saw.
It was absolutely electric
because he could throw
it 90 miles per hour."*

~ Tony Gwynn

The devastatingly effective Scott Garrelts was the finest Giants right-handed pitcher in the Decade of the 1980s. He performed as the top bullpen specialist for the Giants from 1984 to 1988 and assumed a key starting role on San Francisco's pennant-winning team of 1989.

At 6'4" and 210 pounds, Garrelts sported perhaps the best split-finger fastball ever. He was the most prominent Giants pupil of split-finger guru and manager Roger Craig. In the late 1980s and early 1990s, Craig had almost his entire staff throwing the pitch.

⋆　⋆　⋆　⋆　⋆

Scott William Garrelts was born on October 30, 1961 in Urbana, Champaign County, Illinois to Mary L. Hull and Lonnie W. "Spyder" Garrelts. He grew up in the small rural farming community of Buckley, Iroquois County, Illinois. Garrelts pitched for Coach Walt Simmons' Buckley Loda High, a school so tiny that there were only 38 seniors in his 1979 graduating class.

Garrelts received national recognition as a junior by striking out 22 batters, one over the normal maximum number, in a seven-inning game against Wellington High. Two batters reached base on dropped third strikes. A tall, lanky 16 year old, he was already bringing his fastball at 93 miles per hour, and was throwing a well-developed curve, drop and knuckler. He also pitched in the summer for the semi-pro Buckley Dutch Masters of the Eastern Illinois League.

The young phenom was drafted in the first round by the Giants in the June 1979 amateur free agent draft. Hurling for Class-A Clinton (IA) in 1980, he led the Midwest League with 159 strikeouts and 149 walks in 176 innings pitched. Garrelts allowed only two home runs, a testament to the natural heavy movement on his sinker.

He spent 1981 and 1982 with the Shreveport Captains of the Double-A Texas League, hurling a combined 221⅓ innings with 232 strikeouts. Garrelts was given his major league debut with a two-inning cameo on October 2, 1982 as the youngest player in the NL at age 20.

As one of the brightest young star pitchers in baseball, Garrelts had almost unlimited potential. In his first major league start in 1983, he went eight innings to pick up a 2-1 win over the Braves. Eighteen days later he hurled a five-hit shutout in Houston, besting Nolan Ryan.

Yet for years he struggled with his control. Finally switching from a full windup to setting up from a stretch, Garrelts went from a 22-year-old walking 7.1 batters per nine innings to giving free passes to only 3.8 batters per nine at 24. He bounced between the Giants and Triple-A Phoenix in the Pacific Coast League in 1983 and 1984 before sticking for good.

In 1985, Garrelts led the cellar-dwelling Giants with nine wins, 13 saves and a 2.30 ERA- all in relief. The only Giant National League All-Star that year, he had a streak of 24 straight scoreless innings and averaged over a strikeout per inning in his first full big-league campaign.

Still primarily a reliever in 1986, he also made 18 starts and finished second on the Giants in wins and strikeouts. That year Garrelts was reported to have thrown pitches at 102 and 103 miles per hour. Despite missing the month of September in 1987 with a broken finger tip, he was still second on the club in saves. Healthy again in 1988, he paced the Giants with 12 saves.

Garrelts was asked to be a starter in 1989 and went 14-5 in 29 starts and 193⅓ innings pitched. He won the National League earned run average title at 2.28 and also paced the Senior Circuit in winning percentage (.737) and WHIP (walks + hits per innings pitched) at 1.009.

After leading the Giants to the NL pennant, Garrelts was given the ball in NLCS Game 1. He beat the Cubs' Greg Maddox with seven strong innings at Wrigley Field. In a rematch with Maddox in Game 4, neither starter got the decision, but the Giants emerged with the victory.

G	IP	W	L	PCT	SHO	GS	CG	SV	H	ER	SO	BB	ERA
352	959.1	69	53	.566	6	89	9	48	815	351	703	413	3.29

The Giants were swept in four games in the Bay Bridge World Series against the Oakland Athletics from across the bay. Garrelts absorbed losses in both Games 1 and 3, which were almost two weeks apart because of delays caused by the horrific Loma Prieta Earthquake that devastated much of the San Francisco Bay Area on October 17, 1989.

On July 29, 1990 before a capacity Candlestick Park crowd of 55,792, Garrelts took a no-hitter into the ninth inning against the Cincinnati Reds. He had only to retire Paul O'Neill to complete his bid for immortality, but O'Neill drove a single over shortstop Jose Uribe's outstretched glove. Garrelts finished off his 4-0 one-hit gem in only two hours and 15 minutes.

His strikeout rate plummeted the rest of the year, but he still finished second on the Giants with 12 victories and 80 strikeouts. In an era before pitch counts, Garrelt's workload far exceeded the expectations of today's hurlers. Now the splitter, his out pitch, is less frequently employed because of the strain it places on a pitcher's arm. Garrelts' arm was spent by 1991 when he threw his last 20 innings in the major leagues. His final game was on September 28.

Convinced he was not quite finished, Garrelts attempted a comeback in 1992, making brief appearances with Single-A San Jose (CA), Double-A Shreveport (LA) and Triple-A Phoenix (AZ). After pitching with little effectiveness for the Single-A Rancho Cucamonga (CA) Quakes and the Triple-A Las Vegas (NV) Stars in 1993, he rested his arm for a year.

Garrelts finally hung his spikes up for good after a brief three-inning fling with the Omaha (NE) Royals in 1995. The quiet, slow-talking Garrelts currently makes his home in Shreveport, Louisiana. He and his wife, the former Kathryn Mixon, have raised one daughter. His career has been celebrated on the San Francisco Giants Wall of Honor with a plaque outside of AT & T Park on the third base side on The Embarcadero.

MIKE GREENWELL

BOSTON RED SOX
LEFT FIELD

1985-1996

"Jose Canseco admitted he cheated his entire career. Everything he ever did should be wiped clean. I think his 1988 MVP should go back and should go to the runner up."

~ Curt Schilling

Mike Greenwell was the left field successor to Red Sox greats Ted Williams, Carl Yastrzemski and Jim Rice. He performed splendidly, hitting a career .303, but the expectations at that position were so high that anything less than Ruthian results never seemed to be enough.

Possessing a smooth fluid left-handed batting stroke patterned after George Brett, Greenwell hit .300 in seven of his 12 seasons, averaging 93 RBI per year. He was a line drive hitter, consistently bruising Fenway Park's Green Monster left field wall with doubles. He was a most difficult hitter to strike out, with only 364 career whiffs weighed against 460 career walks.

★　★　★　★　★

Michael Lewis Greenwell was born July 18, 1963 in Louisville, Jefferson County, Kentucky to Martha and Leonard Greenwell. He attended North Fort Myers High in Florida, the same school as Deion Sanders and Jevon Kearse. After being taken in the third round of the 1982 amateur free agent draft, Greenwell was signed on June 9, 1982 by Red Sox scout George Digby.

Making his way through the minor leagues, he played for the Low-A Elmira (NY) Pioneers of the New York-Pennsylvania League in 1982, followed by a two-year stint with the Single-A Carolina League's Winston-Salem (NC) Spirits, finishing at .306 for the 1984 season.

After advancing to Triple-A Pawtucket (RI), he improved greatly and earned a September 5 call up for 17 games in 1985. His big-league debut came as a pinch-runner for Jim Rice against the Indians. His first hit was a game-winner in the 13th-inning at Toronto on September 25.

After batting an even .300 with 18 home runs at Pawtucket in 1986, Greenwell got into 31 games with the Red Sox at the end of a tight pennant race. The 22 year old made the postseason roster and played in both the ALCS and Fall Classic, mostly as a pinch hitter. He batted for

Roger Clemens in the eighth inning of World Series Game 6, striking out, as Boston went on to lose the disastrous "Billy Buckner Game." Greenwell entered his prime in 1987, hitting .328 with 19 homers and 89 RBI and finished fourth in the AL Rookie of the Year voting.

In his finest season in 1988, he led Boston to the American League East title, hitting .325 with 22 home runs and 119 RBI, striking out only 38 times. Greenwell topped the Junior Circuit in intentional passes and burnished his year by hitting for the cycle on September 14. He was runner-up in the MVP voting and won the *Louisville Slugger* Silver Slugger Award.

Nicknamed "The Gator" because he liked to wrestle alligators in his adopted home state of Florida, Greenwell was an All-Star again in 1989, hitting .308 with 14 homers and 95 runs batted in. He also had the longest hitting streak of his career at 21 games.

Against the Yankees at home on September 1, 1990, he hit a rare inside-the-park grand slammer and closed out the season at .297, but endured a dreadful ALCS as the Sox were swept by the A's. A knee injury derailed his 1992, but he came back in 1993 to hit .315 with 72 RBI.

On Opening Day at Fenway in 1994, Greenwell injured his left shoulder but gamely soldiered on. He was finally placed on the disabled list on August 4 and underwent arthroscopic surgery to repair torn shoulder cartilage just before the baseball strike interrupted play.

Even toward the end of his career when his power numbers started to tail off, he would continue to average near .300. Greenwell clubbed 15 homers in his last full season in 1995 while batting .297 to help Boston to its fourth American League East title during his Hub City tenure.

He slowed in 1996, hitting .295 in only 77 games, but on September 2, Greenwell left his calling card in a game for the ages. In Boston's 9-8 win over the Mariners in the

G	AB	R	H	2B	3B	HR	RBI	SB	BB	SO	BA	OBP	SLG	TB
1269	4623	657	1400	275	38	130	726	80	460	364	.303	.368	.463	2141

Kingdome, he had nine RBI. No other player has ever driven in nine or more runs for his team's total score.

Greenwell declared as a free agent at the end of the 1996 campaign. Courted by the Hanshin Tigers of Japanese Professional Baseball, he negotiated the largest contract ever for a Hanshin player, worth about $2.5 million.

His stellar career in Major League Baseball heightened expectations in Japan, but he hurt his back in 1997 spring training and then fractured his left foot with a foul tip a week after returning. Greenwell's entire Japanese career consisted of only seven games before he retired.

He came home to his 890-acre ranch in Alva, Florida to grow fruit and vegetables. Greenwell gave coaching a try with the Cincinnati Reds in 2001, but it only lasted a single year. He now owns and operates a family amusement park in Cape Coral, Florida called "Mike Greenwell's Bat-A-Ball & Family Fun Park" opened in February of 1992. Greenwell also is a real estate developer and a volunteer baseball coach with Riverdale High School in Fort Myers.

In 2005, he got back into the headlines. When Jose Canseco released his book *Juiced*, confirming that his whole career was fraudulently built on the use of performance enhancing drugs, Greenwell suggested that Canseco should relinquish his 1988 AL MVP Award.

Greenwell had always enjoyed driving late-model stock cars. In May of 2006, he made his debut in the Craftsman Truck Series at Mansfield Motorsports Speedway for Green Light Racing. Greenwell raced competitively for four years before retiring in 2010.

He and his wife Tracy raised two sons, Bo and Garrett. Bo currently plays outfield in the Red Sox minor league system. His younger son Garrett is a 6' 235-pound first baseman who has played baseball for Oral Roberts University. Mike Greenwell was inducted into the Boston Red Sox Hall of Fame in 2008.

RON GUIDRY

NEW YORK YANKEES
LEFT-HANDED PITCHER

1975-1988

*"Every hitter in
baseball should've
taken a contract out on
Sparky Lyle for teaching
Guidry that slider."*

~ *rival Amos Otis*

Ron Guidry was the personification of dignity and class as he secured his place as one of the greatest pitchers in New York Yankees history. Leading all of baseball in pitching victories from 1977 to 1986, he earned a 170-91 career record with one of the highest winning percentages in the history of the game.

The fiercely competitive Guidry was a three-time 20-game winner while hurling 95 complete games and 26 shutouts. He was named *The Sporting News* American League All-Star left-handed starting pitcher four times. Guidry's 1978 pitching masterpiece was one of the most dominating single season performances in baseball annals.

The down to earth self-effacing Guidry thrived in the postseason glare with three complete games, five victories, a 3.02 ERA and 51 strikeouts. He remains high on the all-time Yankee lists for games pitched, innings pitched, strikeouts, wins and shutouts.

Guidry was the Yankees' best athlete, running the 40-yard dash in 4.2 seconds and the hundred-yard dash in 9.7 seconds. "Gator's" strong legs, quickness and agility garnered him five consecutive *Rawlings* Gold Gloves for fielding excellence.

★   ★   ★   ★   ★

Ronald Ames Guidry was born on August 28, 1950 in Lafayette, Jefferson Parish, Louisiana to Mary Grace and Roland Guidry. He starred in football, basketball and track at Northside High and played American Legion baseball in the summer. After starring for two seasons at the University of Southwestern Louisiana at Lafayette, Guidry was drafted by the Yankees in the third round of the 1971 amateur free agent draft.

The Yankee approach then was to acquire proven pitchers through trades and free agency. As a result, Guidry was unable to crack the starting rotation until

age 26. Because he was a wiry 5' 11" and 155 pounds, his managers consistently questioned his durability despite his strong legs. Guidry's angst reached its peak when he was sent down to Syracuse (NY) Chiefs in 1976. He almost quit baseball in despair.

In early 1977, Yankee bullpen aces Sparky Lyle and Dick Tidrow taught him to throw a slider. By June, manager Billy Martin had made him a starter and he finished 16-7 for the eventual World Series Champions. Guidry had honed the wicked, devastating slider that would become his signature "out" pitch.

To be a Yankee fan was a roller coaster ride in 1978. By mid-July, the team was mired 14 games out of first behind the Red Sox. When strife and feuding erupted between the press, the team and Martin, the Yanks were tagged "The Bronx Zoo." Despite all of the distractions, Guidry serenely reeled off 13 consecutive victories to begin the season.

Without their steady ace, the Yankees would have been adrift- 15 of his wins followed a Yankee loss. On June 17, 1978, Guidry set a franchise record striking out 18 California Angels. The fans began their practice of standing and clapping on all of his two-strike counts and broadcaster Phil Rizzuto acclaimed him "Louisiana Lightning."

Relying on a 95-mile-per-hour fastball and a disappearing slider for a heavy-duty $273^2/_3$ innings, Guidry finished the regular season at 25-3 with a microscopic 1.74 ERA. He matched Babe Ruth's AL pitching record of nine complete-game shutouts by a southpaw and set a single season Yankee standard with 248 strikeouts. Bewildered American League hitters could do no better against him than a .193 batting average.

The *coup de grace* of Guidry's dream season was his 25th victory in the sudden death AL East playoff. In

G	IP	W	L	PCT	SHO	GS	CG	H	ER	SO	BB	ERA
368	2392	170	91	.651	26	323	95	2198	874	1778	633	3.29

leading his team to a World Series title, Guidry was honored unanimously with the 1978 American League Cy Young award. He was also chosen *The Sporting News* Major League Player of the Year and the *AP* Male Athlete of the Year.

Always the consummate team player, Guidry volunteered to go to the bullpen in 1979 when closer Goose Gossage was injured. He still won 18 games, leading the AL with a 2.78 ERA. Guidry again showed his bionic endurance in 1981 by topping the Junior Circuit with 21 complete games and going 21-9. His last 20-victory season was 1985 when he posted a 22-6 record, pacing the AL in wins and winning percentage again.

The Yankees rewarded Guidry by naming him co-captain in 1986, but arm troubles finally began to affect his performance as he struggled in his last three seasons. Guidry was slow to recover from elbow surgery after the 1988 season and retired from baseball on July 13, 1989 when he could no longer perform to his own high standard.

He was honored by baseball in 1984 with the prestigious Roberto Clemente Award for his community service and humanity. On Ron Guidry Day, August 23, 2003, he joined 15 other legendary Yankees when his uniform #49 was retired and his plaque was erected in Yankee Stadium's Monument Park. Whitey Ford and Guidry still remain the only two Yankee pitchers in the 20th century to have their uniform numbers retired.

He served as a Yankee spring training instructor and then as Joe Torre's pitching coach for two years before retiring to his farm on the Lafayette bayou. Guidry and his wife Bonnie Lynn Rutledge have raised three children. He enjoys hunting and fishing and the close family ties that are the hallmark of the Acadian lifestyle.

RON HODGES

NEW YORK METS
CATCHER • PINCH HITTER

1973-1984

"If Yogi [Berra] was Casey Stengel's 'boy' with the Yankees, Hodges is Yogi's 'boy' with the Mets. It was Yogi who asked for him, got him, played him and was not embarrassed by him."

*~ writer Jack Lang
after the 1973 season*

Ron Hodges was the quintessential team player with the second longest exclusive tenure with the Mets behind only Ed Kranepool. An excellent handler of pitchers, he reinvented himself later in his career as a quality pinch hitter. Hodges was a stoic, homespun Virginia gentleman, a class act who was always attentive and accommodating with the fans.

The 6'1" 185-pound Hodges was a left-handed hitting catcher, a scarce commodity in the game which made him valuable coming off the bench. A reliable backup catcher and pinch hitter, Hodges' patience with a *Louisville Slugger* in his hand also allowed him to draw an abundance of free passes, making him more effective than his average might have indicated.

★　★　★　★　★

Ronald Wray Hodges was born on June 22, 1949 in Rocky Mount, Franklin County, Virginia to Daisy and Tony Hodges. Growing up with eight brothers and sisters in the small town along the Pigg River, he starred in Little League and American Legion baseball.

Hodges graduated from Rocky Mount's Franklin County High School in 1968 after captaining the baseball team his junior and senior years and the football team as a senior. He was an All-Piedmont Conference quarterback and three-time All-Piedmont Conference catcher.

Hodges played baseball at Appalachian State University in Boone, North Carolina. He was taken by the Orioles in the sixth round of the 1970 amateur draft but decided not to sign. Instead Hodges went back to ASU to captain the 1971 Mountaineers as an NAIA All-American, batted .714 in the NAIA World Series, and made the All-NAIA Tournament team.

He was the Royals' 15th pick in the first round of the 1971 January secondary phase amateur draft and the Braves' first round draft choice (tenth overall) in the 1971 June amateur draft (secondary phase active). He finally signed with Mets scout Bill Herring after being selected in the second round of the 1972 January secondary phase draft.

Hodges began his pro baseball career that summer with the Pompano Beach Mets in the Class-A Florida State League, leading the team with 15 home runs in 112 games. Although no relation to the great Mets manager Gil Hodges, he and Gil Hodges, Jr. were roommates that year.

Hodges was promoted to the Memphis (TN) Blues of the Double-A Texas League in 1973. He was batting just .173 in 47 games when he got the call. With catchers Jerry Grote and Duffy Dyer both injured, Mets manager Yogi Berra preferred a left-handed hitting catcher and regarded Hodges as the best defensive catcher in the Mets minor league system.

Not yet 24 years old, he made his debut on June 13, 1973, catching future Hall of Fame right-hander Tom Seaver. In the seventh inning, Hodges got his first major league hit. Two days later, he blasted his first home run, a game-winner into the Shea Stadium right field bullpen off the Padres reliever Bill Grief.

Hodges found himself in charge of a Mets pitching staff which included Seaver, Jerry Koosman, Jon Matlack and Tug McGraw. He figured prominently in the greatest regular season game in Mets annals on September 20, featuring the wild "Ball Off the Wall" miracle play.

In the top of the 13th inning with two out and the Pirates' Richie Zisk on first base, Dave Augustine walloped a Ray Sadecki offering high and deep to left field. The ball hit the pointed edge of the wall, bounced straight up and miraculously came down right in left-fielder Cleon Jones' glove. Jones turned and hurled the ball to shortstop Wayne Garrett. The relay to Hodges barely nipped the sliding Zisk in a close play. With the tie preserved, Hodges then lined a game-winning sin-

G	AB	R	H	2B	3B	HR	RBI	SB	BB	SO	BA	OBP	SLG	TB
666	1426	119	342	56	2	19	147	10	224	217	.240	.342	.322	459

gle to center in the bottom of the inning, plating John Milner for a dramatic 4-3 win.

Hodges caught in 45 games before Grote returned from the disabled list. He played just one game in the 1973 World Series, drawing a walk against Athletics ace Rollie Fingers in his only plate appearance to finish with a career 1.000 on-base percentage in the Fall Classic.

Although it was an exciting, productive freshman year, in retrospect he was rushed into the major leagues out of Double-A and it set him back. Manager Joe Torre submerged him behind John Stearns and Alex Trevino. By the time new manager George Bamberger noticed, the die had been cast and Hodges spent the majority of his major league career as a backup catcher.

On April 23, 1978, he tied a record for receivers by taking part in three double plays in an extra-inning game. Early in the 1981 season, Hodges was involved in a freak play. On Mets pitcher Craig Swan's fifth pitch of the game (all called balls), the runner on first base, Tim Raines, took off for second base on an attempted steal. Hodges' throw down to second pelted Swann in the back, fractured his rib, and put him on the disabled list.

Hodges caught a career-high 96 games in 1983 and appeared in 110 games as a result of an injury to John Stearns. By that time, he was a veteran, not unlike an assistant coach on the field and in the dugout. He had a number of clutch hits during the 1984 pennant race, but played his last game on September 30, the last survivor of the Mets 1973 NL titlist team. The Mets decided not to pick up his option for 1985, paid him a $50,000 buyout, and gave him his release.

Hodges married the former Peggy Jarrett in 1974 and the couple raised four sons. He has been a Realtor since 1985 with Mountain to Lake Realty in Rocky Mount. Hodges enjoys hunting and fishing and being an American Legion baseball manager.

KENT HRBEK

MINNESOTA TWINS
FIRST BASE

1981-1994

"I got you here.
I'm going to be at home
taking care of Mom. You
keep going with what
you are doing here."

~ Ed Hrbek to his son
after his 1981 ALS diagnosis

One of the most popular players in Twins history, Kent Hrbek is admired as a key leader in Minnesota's World Series championships of 1987 and 1991. He ranks among all-time Twins leaders in almost every offensive category. Only Harmon Killebrew has hit more home runs or has driven in more runs while wearing a Twins uniform.

Hrbek was a charismatic, bubble gum-chewin', sunflower seed-spittin' throwback character, tossing out a continuous stream of feigned invective around the batting cage. He was the consummate teammate and a hardscrabble competitor.

At 6'4" and 244 pounds, Hrbek supplied upper deck power yet showed great plate discipline, struck out less than he walked, and never fanned more than 87 times in a season. A career .994 fielding first baseman with agility, sure hands and a wide wingspan, he had 13,725 putouts, 1,049 assists, 1,331 doubles plays and only 87 errors.

★　★　★　★　★

Kent Allen Hrbek was born May 21, 1960 to Justina Kiminski and Edward John Hrbek in Minneapolis, Minnesota. He grew up in Bloomington within blocks of the Twins' Metropolitan Stadium and matured into a prep star at Bloomington Kennedy High School. He was chosen in the 17th round by the Twins in the 1978 amateur draft.

Hrbek's career got on track in 1981 at Visalia in the California League. He hit .379 to win the league batting title and hit 27 home runs with 111 RBI. It punched his ticket directly to the bigs. Hrbek debuted at Yankee Stadium on August 24 with a game-winning home run and played briefly in aging Metropolitan Stadium in its last year.

The big, affable slugger was an instant homegrown favorite, christening the Metrodome with its first two home runs on April 3, 1982 in an exhibition against the Reds. Coiled from the left side in his signature low crouch with the barrel of his *Louisville Slugger* behind his ear, Hrbek went on to hit .301 with 23 bombs and 92 RBI. He was selected a 1982 All-Star and the runner up to Rookie of the Year Cal Ripken, Jr.

Hrbek followed up in 1984 with an even better year. Second in the American League Most Valuable Player balloting, he was the Twins Most Valuable Player, hitting .311 with 27 home runs, a career-high 107 RBI and a strong .522 slugging average.

By 1987 "Herbie" was part of a dynamic duo, batting cleanup behind Kirby Puckett. He set a Metrodome record by smashing 20 of his personal-best 34 home runs at home and put up career-highs in on-base (.392) and slugging (.545) percentages. The Twins won only 87 games while overcoming the Tigers on their way to the AL crown.

With Minnesota on the verge of elimination in Game 6 of the World Series, Hrbek stepped to the plate in the bottom of the sixth with bases loaded and two out and hammered a first-pitch fastball that rattled Metrodome seats some 439 feet away. The Twins fed off this lightening bolt clutch grand slam and completed their run to a world title the next day. Unfazed by it all, Hrbek went duck hunting early before Game 7.

He contributed 20 home runs and 84 RBI during the 1991 season, rallying the Twins from last place the previous year to their second Big Trophy. He put his imprint on the Fall Classic in a tight Game 2. With two outs in the top of the third, the Braves' Ron Gant singled and took a big turn. As a slightly off-balance Gant scurried back to beat a hard throw, Hrbek applied the tag as

G	AB	R	H	2B	3B	HR	RBI	SB	BB	SO	BA	OBP	SLG	TB
1747	6192	903	1749	312	18	293	1086	37	838	798	.282	.367	.481	2976

Gant's leg came off the base. Umpire Drew Coble called him out, citing forward progress, ending the inning and the Twins prevailed, 3-2.

In Game 7 with no score in the eighth inning, Hrbek initiated a rare first base-to-catcher-to-first base bases-loaded double play with catcher Brian Harper, killing the Braves' biggest threat. The Twins eventually triumphed, 1-0, in the tenth behind Jack Morris' historic pitching gem.

Hrbek retired on his own terms as the players strike ended the 1994 season. He cited nagging injuries and his desire to spend more time with his wife Jeanie Marie Burns and daughter Heidi. In his final game, fans stood clapping on his every at-bat, all with bases loaded against the Red Sox. He responded with a home run and four RBI.

Hrbek's legacy in Minnesota with the Twins is secure. His uniform #14 was retired formally in 1995, and he was inducted into the Minnesota Sports Hall of Fame in 1996. In the charter class of the Minnesota Twins Hall of Fame in 2000, he was enshrined with Rod Carew, Calvin Griffith, Killebrew, Tony Oliva and Puckett. Gate 14 at Target Field is named as a tribute to him and a Hrbek statue was dedicated outside in 2014.

Hrbek's father died of *amyotrophic lateral sclerosis* in his rookie year, and he has since worked to increase awareness of the disease. He has sponsored golf and fishing tournaments which have raised over a million dollars for ALS research. The Kent & Jeanie Hrbek Foundation supports ALS research and youth sports in Minnesota.

Hrbek can be seen hosting *Kent Hrbek Outdoors*, an outdoor sports program on KARE TV-11 Minneapolis and meets the local crowds with a sincere handshake and a warm smile. The rest of his time is spent hunting and fishing. Hrbek still lives in Bloomington where the four-field Valley View baseball complex of his youth has been renamed in his honor.

DENNIS LEONARD

KANSAS CITY ROYALS
RIGHT-HANDED PITCHER

1974-1983 • 1985-1986

*"He was the guy
I identified with.
And I still do.
He was such a gamer.
Tough, competitive,
hated to lose."*

~ pitcher David Cone

Dennis Leonard was the winningest right-handed pitcher in Major League Baseball from 1975 to 1982. He is the only Royals hurler in history to win 20 or more games in a season more than once (1977, 1978 and 1980) and still holds all-time Royals career records in complete games and shutouts. Only Paul Splittorff has more pitching victories.

A true workhorse, Leonard owns Royals single season marks of 294²/₃ innings pitched, 40 games started, 27 complete games and 244 strikeouts. He toiled 200+ innings seven consecutive years (1975-81) and took the rubber in 30+ starts six straight years (1975-80). Leonard paced the AL in starts three times and was the Royals Pitcher of the Year in 1975, 1977 and 1979.

The durable 6'1" 205-pound Leonard had 103 career complete games. By comparison, Clayton Kershaw led the NL in 2014 with six complete games and Dallas Keuchel paced the AL with five. Both of these league leaders combined had fewer then Leonard had in 1977 and 1978.

*   *   *   *   *

Dennis Patrick Leonard was born on May 8, 1951 to Catherine Kawara and William Aloysius Leonard in Brooklyn, New York. He spent his early life in New York City and grew up in Oceanside, a hamlet located in the southern part of the town of Hempstead, Nassau County, New York.

After pitching for the Oceanside High School Sailors, Leonard went on to pitch three years for Iona College in New Rochelle. He was an All-Metropolitan Conference pitcher for the 1971 MC champion Gaels that reeled off 17 consecutive wins in route to a 19-7 campaign.

Leonard was a second round pick in the 1972 free agent amateur draft. He got valuable work that summer at Kingsport in the Appalachian Rookie League and at Waterloo in the Class-A Midwest League, going a combined 6-4 in 89 innings with a 3.13 ERA and 94 strikeouts.

In 1973, Leonard thrived with the San Jose Bees in the California League, winning 15 games, and was promoted to Omaha (NE) in the American Association in 1974. After winning 12 games with a 3.47 ERA in 223 innings pitched, he earned himself a call up to the parent club.

Leonard got his big-league debut with the Royals on September 4, 1974. During his first full season in the major leagues in 1975, he emerged as one of the club's top young pitchers, winning 15 games on a 91-victory team and helping begin the franchise's path to its glory years.

Leonard would become a stalwart in the Royals starting rotation on four Royals championship teams, spanning from 1976 to 1980. He won 17 games in 1976 and was chosen as the right-handed pitcher on the *United Press International* All-American League team.

The first of Leonard's three 20-win seasons came in 1977 when he finished fourth in the AL Cy Young Award voting. He won 21, 14 and 20 games from 1978 to 1980 and was the 1980 World Series Game 4 starter and winner, hurling seven strong innings versus the Phillies.

Leonard remained stellar through 1981 when he won 13 games in the strike-shortened season and paced the AL in innings pitched. But starting in 1982, he had major stretches of breakdown due to injuries. The worst of those occurred on May 29, 1983, when he stumbled off the mound and ruptured his right patella tendon while facing the Orioles' Cal Ripken, Jr.

Kansas City had one of baseball's best starting rotations during its 1985 World Series Championship season despite not having the services of Leonard during what should have been the prime of his great career. Notwithstanding, he was a major spiritual contributor to the team.

For two and a half seasons, Leonard fought through

G	IP	W	L	PCT	SHO	GS	CG	H	ER	SO	BB	ERA
282	1597.1	103	76	.575	16	231	57	1558	644	896	597	3.63

many setbacks to return to his previous high standard of performance on the mound. He underwent four knee operations and worked through a grueling rehabilitation regimen with the aid of Royals trainer Mickey Cobb.

One of the most memorable non-championship moments in Royals history was his storybook comeback on April 12, 1986. Scheduled starter Danny Jackson couldn't go so manager Dick Howser handed Leonard the ball in a surprise start for the first time in years.

He bravely shut out the Blue Jays, 1-0, on a three-hit gem that was viewed by a national television audience on NBC's Game of the Week. Leonard gave the credit – and the game ball – to the always encouraging Cobb who had stood by him throughout his entire rehab process.

By mid-June, Leonard had won six games with a 2.60 ERA, but he was unable to sustain his early season success, ending the year at 8-13 with a 4.44 ERA. His final game was September 27; the Royals gave him his release on December 22; and he retired on February 2, 1987.

In honor of his courageous struggle to return to the game, Leonard was awarded the 1987 Fred Hutchinson Award, given annually to the major league player who best exemplified the fighting spirit and competitive desire of "Hutch," persevering through adversity.

Leonard pitched briefly for the Fort Myers (Florida) Sun Sox in the Senior Professional Baseball Association in 1989, posting a 4-1 record with a serviceable 4.76 ERA. The SPBA dissolved after the 1990 season due to a lack of attendance.

Dennis Leonard was inducted into The Iona College Athletics Hall of Fame in 1984, the Kansas City Royals Hall of Fame in 1989, and the Missouri Sports Hall of Fame in 2003. He and his wife Audrey have lived in Blue Springs, Missouri, a suburb of Kansas City, since 1974 where they raised their two sons Dennis, Jr. and Ryan.

DON MATTINGLY

NEW YORK YANKEES
FIRST BASE

1982-1995

Don Mattingly became one of the most admired athletes in New York history, a true Yankee icon who achieved legendary stature for his modest demeanor and class. A six-time American League All-Star, he was known as "The Hit Man" for his ability to hit for both high average and fence-busting power.

Mattingly wielded his T141 *Louisville Slugger* as well as any Yankee in history from 1984 to 1989 when he hit .327, collected at least 186 hits each season and led all baseball with 684 runs batted in. He was also one of the best defensive first basemen ever, finishing with a near perfect .996 fielding average and nine *Rawlings* Gold Gloves.

* * * * *

Donald Arthur Mattingly was born on April 20, 1961 in Evansville, Indiana to Mary and William Mattingly. At Reitz Memorial High School, he excelled at point guard, quarterback and as the leader of the state champion baseball team as a junior. However, he was taken in the 19th round behind 489 other players in the 1979 amateur draft.

Signed by Yankee scouts Gus Poulos and Jax Robertson, the 6' 175-pound lefty averaged .332 in his minor league career, but there was little in his profile to suggest the power he would later unveil. He was platooned in his 1983 rookie year while he studied how to recognize pitches he could drive into Yankee Stadium's short right field porch.

His thorough preparation and hard work produced breakout results in 1984 as he batted third and started at first base. Mattingly paced the AL with 207 hits, knocked in 110 runs, and hit .400 with runners in scoring position. He displayed real power with a .537 slugging average, 23 home runs, 324 total bases, and an AL-best 44 doubles. On the final day, he edged teammate Dave Winfield for the batting title, finishing at .343.

"The Hit Man" came back with an extraordinary encore in 1985. He hit .324, registered 211 hits, scored 107 times and recorded a career-high 35 bombs. Mattingly led the Junior Circuit with his 48 doubles, .567 slugging percentage, 370 total bases and 145 runs batted in. He was the overwhelming choice as the 1985 American League Most Valuable Player.

With a technician's efficiency, he dismantled AL pitching in 1986, setting new franchise marks with 53 doubles and 238 hits- his third straight 200-hit season. Mattingly had 31 circuit clouts with 113 RBI and led the league in total bases (388) and slugging (.573). The hits kept coming in 1987 as Mattingly hit six grand slam home runs to break Ernie Banks' mark and mashed home runs in eight straight games to match Dale Long's record. He tweaked his back in June but still hit .327 with 30 homers and 115 RBI.

Mattingly's back problems flared in 1990 and he landed on the disabled list in July, ruining his year. But as the team's valued leader, he was named the tenth Yankee captain in early 1991. Despite undergoing extensive rehabilitation in his final six years, he hit only 58 home runs. His bad back had robbed him of much of his power, although his defense remained stalwart as he led the AL three straight years starting in 1992.

The greatest Yankee star never to play in a World Series, his career precisely spanned the longest Fall Classic drought in franchise history. His aspirations for the postseason hit a new roadblock in 1994. The Yanks were in first place, and Mattingly was hitting .304, but a labor strike in August caused the World Series to be cancelled.

His perseverance finally was rewarded when he led the Bombers to a 1995 American League wild card berth at the wire. In pre-game introductions before the ALDS

> *"I'm glad I don't have to face*
> *that guy every day.*
> *Don Mattingly has that*
> *look that few hitters have.*
> *I don't know if it's his stance,*
> *his eyes or what, but you can*
> *tell he means business."*
>
> ~ *pitcher Doc Gooden*

G	AB	R	H	2B	3B	HR	RBI	SB	BB	SO	BA	OBP	SLG	TB
1785	7003	1007	2153	442	20	222	1099	14	588	444	.307	.358	.471	3301

against the Mariners, the capacity partisan crowd gave him a lengthy, emotional ovation. Mattingly reacted by hitting .417 with six RBI including a clutch home run in Game 2 and a go ahead two-run double in Game 5 before the Yankees lost a heartbreaking finale.

While he was contemplating retirement that winter, the Yankee brass asked his consent to negotiate for his replacement, a tribute to the respect held for him as a leader. When the team signed Tino Martinez, he unofficially retired, waiting to see if his back would heal. By the end of 1996, it was clear that his comeback would never be.

Mattingly relished playing in New York but only wanted to be known for his on-field accomplishments. The ultimate gamer, he competed with the heart of a warrior. Rival Kirby Puckett, noting his hard-nosed intensity, hailed him as "Donnie Baseball." Only a bad back and bad timing has made his election to Cooperstown less than certain.

Mattingly served as a Yankee spring training hitting instructor for many years. Manager Joe Torre chose him as his hitting coach from 2004 to 2006 and as his bench coach in 2007. When Torre was hired by the Dodgers in 2008, he asked Mattingly to join his staff. He was chosen Torre's successor as Dodger manager in 2010 and led the team to three straight National League West titles (2013-15) before becoming the manager of the Miami Marlins.

The Yankees formally retired Mattingly's uniform jersey #23 in 1997 and dedicated his plaque within Monument Park. He is one of the most popular players ever to wear pinstripes, always receiving the loudest, most appreciative ovations when introduced at Yankee old-timers games. To the Bronx faithful, "Donnie Baseball" will forever be the personification of the best of New York Yankee pride and tradition.

SCOTT MCGREGOR

BALTIMORE ORIOLES
LEFT-HANDED PITCHER

1976-1988

"If you watch him warm up, you feel like grabbing a bat and running up to home plate. Many batters do exactly that, then grumble and mumble after he beats them."

~ from a 1984 Scouting Report

For seven seasons from 1978 through 1984, Scott McGregor was the only pitcher in Major League Baseball to post a winning record each and every year. He was a major piece in several great Baltimore Orioles starting pitching staffs alongside Mike Boddicker, Storm Davis, Mike Flanagan and Jim Palmer.

Accumulating 138 regular season career victories, McGregor pitched 34 innings in World Series competition with a 2.12 ERA and hurled 15²/₃ innings in the American League Championship Series, posting a microscopic 0.57 ERA. The ultimate big game ace, his overall postseason earned run average was a phenomenal 1.63 in 49²/₃ innings pitched.

The 6'1" 190-pound left-hander was a finesse pitcher who had impeccable command of his off-speed pitches and a deceptive motion that hid his pitching arm until the horsehide was right on the plate. Yielding few walks and pitching to contact, the crafty McGregor kept hitters off-balance with his disappearing curve, which was especially tough on left-handed hitters. He also had a formidable pickoff move which stymied many a would-be base stealer.

★　★　★　★　★

Scott Houston McGregor was born January 18, 1954 in Inglewood, Los Angeles County, California to Frances E. and Eric Scott McGregor. With future Hall of Fame third baseman George Brett playing behind him, he pitched the El Segundo High School Eagles to 51 wins against only 4 losses. The Yankees picked McGregor 14th overall in the first round of the June 1972 amateur draft and signed him immediately.

He started that summer with Fort Lauderdale in the Florida State League. McGregor was promoted to West Haven (CT) of the Double-A Eastern League in 1973. Hurling for the Triple-A Syracuse (NY) Chiefs, Mc-

Gregor was the 1974 International League Most Valuable Pitcher with a 13-10 line in 27 starts and a 3.44 ERA in 199 innings pitched. He continued to toil for the Chiefs through early 1976 where he was strongly influenced by his pitching coach, Cloyd Boyer. Amid other advice, Boyer suggested that he attend Baseball Chapel on a regular basis.

In midseason 1976, the Yankees traded McGregor, Rick Dempsey, Tippy Martinez, Rudy May and Dave Pagan to the Orioles for Ken Holtzman, Doyle Alexander, Grant Jackson, Elrod Hendricks and Jimmy Freeman. It proved to be a windfall for Baltimore as McGregor established himself as a top-of-the-rotation starter, Dempsey became a team leader, and Martinez emerged as a stopper in relief. All three played substantial roles on the Orioles 1983 World Series Championship club.

McGregor made his major league pitching debut on September 19, 1976. After manager Earl Weaver inserted him into the Birds' starting rotation in 1978, he won 15 games. In June of 1979, however, McGregor experienced such severe pain in his left elbow he couldn't even toss the ball up to home plate. The diagnosis was tendonitis. With rest, he recovered in time and finished the season at 13-6, but the incident pointed up that his career could end at any moment.

McGregor won the deciding Game 4 of the 1979 ALCS with a complete game whitewash of the Angels, 8-0. After hurling a nine-inning World Series victory in Game 3 at Three Rivers Stadium, he was saddled with the Game 7 loss at Memorial Stadium on Willie Stargell's sixth inning homer despite yielding only two runs in eight innings to the World Champion Pirates.

On the final day of the 1980 season, McGregor reached the 20-win plateau for the only time in his career, working 252 innings. In the strike-shortened 1981 campaign, he was chosen an All-Star and won 13 of 18 decisions.

G	IP	W	L	PCT	SHO	GS	CG	H	ER	SO	BB	ERA
356	2140.2	138	108	.561	23	309	83	2245	949	904	518	3.99

His 1978 to 1981 earned run average lines were astonishingly consistent... 3.32 ...3.35 ...3.32 ...and 3.26.

McGregor fought an arm injury in 1982, going 14-12 with a 4.61 ERA, and struggled the entire year. He recovered in 1983 to pace all Oriole starters with 260 innings pitched, 36 starts, 12 complete games, 18 wins and a .720 winning percentage. His earned run average dropped back down to his previous steady levels at 3.18.

After losing Game 1 of the 1983 American League Championship Series to the White Sox, 2-1, McGregor pitched a five-hit Game 1 gem in the Fall Classic against the Phillies, but lost again, 2-1. In the Game 5 clincher before over 67,000 rabid Philly fans, he got redemption, hurling another five-hitter. This time he authored a 5-0 complete game shutout victory.

McGregor won 15 games in 1983, but then fell off precipitously after turning 30 in 1984. After the Orioles lost 23 of their first 25 games in 1988, including his four consecutive ineffective starts, he was released by the Orioles on May 2. At the time he left baseball, he had won more major league games than all but four other pitchers from 1980 forward.

A devout Christian, the affable McGregor became an ordained Pentecostal minister and served as a youth pastor in the Baltimore area from 1988 through 1991. He was first an associate pastor and then senior pastor in nearby Dover, Delaware from 1992 to 2001. He and his wife Cara and their children currently live in Towson, Maryland outside of Baltimore.

McGregor has had coaching duties with Orioles affiliates the Aberdeen (MD) IronBirds (New York-Penn League), the Frederick (MD) Keys (Carolina League), the Bowie (MD) BaySox (Eastern League), and with the Orioles. He is ranked #26 on "The 40 Greatest Orioles of All-Time" list. McGregor was inducted into the Baltimore Orioles Hall of Fame in 1990.

BOB MONTGOMERY

BOSTON RED SOX
CATCHER

1970-1979

Bob Montgomery labored nine years in the minors before becoming synonymous with Red Sox Baseball during the 1970s, 1980s and 1990s first as a player and then a broadcaster. He was a proud member and significant contributor to the 1975 American League Champions.

The strong 6'1" 203-pound Montgomery was known as "The Hammer" and was one of the best hit-and-run specialists of his era. His fielding average as a receiver was .983 with 136 assists and only 31 errors. He cut down a third of all the runners who attempted to steal on him.

*   *   *   *   *

Robert Edward Montgomery was born on April 16, 1944 to Rosa and Carl Montgomery in Nashville, Davidson County, Tennessee. He grew up in a baseball family. His father was a semi-pro pitcher and his younger brother Gerald pitched briefly in the Red Sox organization.

Called "Monty" from an early age, he was All-Tennessee State at Nashville's Central High School in football, basketball and baseball. Baseball was always his favorite sport although he didn't play catcher in school. He starred as a pitcher, first baseman and outfielder.

The 18-year-old Montgomery signed with Red Sox scout George Digby soon after graduation on June 9, 1962. He was assigned to play third base for the Class-D Olean (NY) Red Sox of the New York-Pennsylvania League. With the Waterloo (IA) Hawks of the Class-A Midwest League in 1963, manager Len Okrie suggested he convert to catcher.

Okrie gave him work behind the plate that year and then inserted him as the team's catcher for 1964. He made the transition from infielder to backstop with ease to become the Midwest League All-Star catcher, yet it would take him five more years to see big-league time.

He rose slowly through the system with Winston-Salem (NC) of the Class-A Carolina League (1965); Pittsfield (MA) of the Double-A Eastern League (1966); Toronto (ON) Ma-

ple Leafs of the Triple-A International League (1967): and Louisville (KY) Colonels (1968-1970).

Montgomery hit a solid .292 for Louisville, was voted the 1969 International League All-Star catcher, and repeated as the IL All-Star catcher again in 1970. In 131 games for the Colonels, he batted .324 with 30 doubles, 14 home runs and 89 runs batted in.

Montgomery was called up and got his major league debut on September 6, 1970 at Fenway Park. He struck out looking in his first at-bat, but then singled off the Orioles' Dave McNally. Five days later, he drilled his first home run off of future Hall of Famer Jim Palmer.

Backing up hard-working future Hall of Famer Carlton Fisk in 1972, Monty appeared in 24 games, hitting .286. The Red Sox lost the American League pennant race by a mere half game in a campaign marred by a players' strike that shortened the schedule to 145 games.

Fisk continued to handle most of the Red Sox catching choirs in 1973, although Monty got into 34 games with 128 at-bats, hitting .320 and slugging .563. When Pudge sustained a serious injury on June 28, 1974, Montgomery filled in capably, catching 88 games.

During 1975 spring training in Fort Myers, Florida, Fisk sustained a broken arm. At the beginning of the season, Montgomery contributed the game-winning RBI in four of the Red Sox's first 11 wins. Fisk hurt a finger in August and Monty got added playing time, also playing first base six times before season's end. He appeared in 62 games and played rock solid defense.

After the Red Sox won the AL pennant, Montgomery did not get into the ALCS sweep of the Athletics and was also absent from the 1975 World Series lineup until Game 7. He pinch-hit in the bottom of the ninth against Will McEnaney with one out and the Reds ahead, 4-3, but grounded out to the shortstop. Carl Yastrzemski then flied to center to end an epic Fall Classic.

> *"Bob Montgomery*
> *was probably the*
> *premier backup*
> *catcher in the major*
> *leagues throughout*
> *the seventies."*
>
> ~ *writer Herb Crehan*

G	AB	R	H	2B	3B	HR	RBI	SB	BB	SO	BA	OBP	SLG	TB
387	1185	125	306	50	8	23	156	6	64	268	.258	.296	.372	441

The team relieved field manager Darrell Johnson in the middle of the 1976 season and hired Don Zimmer. Fisk was healthy in 1976 and 1977 so Montgomery got little playing time, crouching behind the plate in only 31 games in 1976 and just 17 in 1977.

In 1978, Fisk was so durable that Montgomery found action in only ten games the entire year. More than half of his hits came in a single game. He went 4-for-5 in the second half of a May 21 doubleheader at Tiger Stadium, including an RBI triple in the ninth inning against Fernando Arroyo. The Red Sox would lose the pennant in a one game playoff with the Yankees.

Montgomery hit a career-high .349 in 86 at-bats in his last campaign in 1979. Baseball had mandated that all players wear protective batting helmets in 1971. Active players such as Montgomery were allowed to bat without a helmet. He availed himself of the privilege, although he did line the inside of his hat with protective padding. On September 9, Montgomery went 1-for-2 in his finale as the last major league player to bat without wearing a batting helmet.

In 1980 and 1981, Monty worked in sports radio, doing Red Sox games as backup. In 1982, he was hired to do the color on Red Sox telecasts for Boston's WSBK-TV and worked with Red Sox play-by-play man Ned Martin for 14 years until 1995 when the Sox's contract with Channel 38 expired. He won eight Emmy Awards for telecasting Red Sox Baseball.

Montgomery now owns and operates Big League Promotions which produces game boards using pro sports licensing. He is a color analyst for NESN and Cox Sports New England for minor league Red Sox affiliates the Portland (MA) Sea Dogs and Pawtucket (RI) Red Sox.

Outside of work, Montgomery enjoys golf, mostly teeing it up with former Red Sox teammates Jim Rice and Luis Tiant. He also enjoys model railroading. Montgomery resides in Saugus, Essex County, Massachusetts with his wife Ann Sujko and daughter Loren.

MIKE NORRIS

OAKLAND ATHLETICS
RIGHT-HANDED PITCHER

1975-1983 • 1990

"Get your glove and go to the clubhouse, because you just embarrassed yourself. You threw two pitches inside the whole night, and those were by mistake. You gotta have some guts."

~ fellow Black Ace Bob Gibson
challenging Norris to
intimidate hitters in 1979

Mike Norris gained fame as a member of The Black Aces, an exclusive fraternity of 15 African American pitchers who have won 20 or more games in a season. His magnificent 1980 year was the high water mark of an only too brief career derailed by injury and drug addiction.

At the height of his prowess, the 6'2" 175-pound right-hander threw an explosive fastball along with a devastating screwball with such tight spin and quick darting motion that hitters missed the ball by as much as two feet. The two pitches rendered him almost unhittable.

Norris was known for his distinctive green fielding glove which he used to win two *Rawlings* Gold Glove awards for fielding excellence. He pounced on bunts and slow rollers with extraordinary agility and reacted with cat-like reflexes to hard hit balls through the box.

★   ★   ★   ★   ★

Michael Kelvin Norris was born on March 19, 1955 to Lula Mae Norris and Elma Hall in San Francisco, California and grew up in the projects of the Fillmore District, or Western Addition. When he was seven, his father was killed in a knife fight. Norris' first insights into baseball were through his mother as the two sat watching Giants games on television.

In Norris' junior year at Polytechnic High, he starred in football, basketball and as an All-City pitcher. Polytechnic was closed for earthquake retrofitting his senior year, so he went to Balboa High and was the San Francisco Public School Baseball Player of the Year, going 7-0.

The World Champion A's took Norris as their last pick in the first round of the 1973 draft and offered him a nominal bonus. Unimpressed, he enrolled at the City College of San Francisco. The A's tendered a new offer for $25,000 and soon he moved his mother out of the projects.

Assigned to the Class-A Burlington (IA) Bees (Midwest League), he went 8-4 with a 2.21 ERA, tossing a no-hitter and a one-hitter. After a 1974 tour at Double-A Birming-

ham (Southern League), the 20-year-old prodigy debuted against the White Sox on April 10, 1975 and hurled a complete-game shutout. He hurt his elbow in his third start, but his ERA for the year was zero.

Trying in vain to capture the magic of his debut for the next three years, Norris bounced between the A's and the minors, hurling in the Pacific Coast League for the Tucson (AZ) Toros, San Jose (CA) Missions and Vancouver (BC) Canadians, and Jersey City in the Eastern League.

Back with the A's in 1979, he threw a one-hitter over the Orioles on May 9, but was still looking for the key to more consistent success. Bob Gibson, now a broadcaster, offered Norris some career-changing advice later that year. Gibson suggested that he pitch aggressively inside to the best hitters because if they could be intimidated, then so could the rest of the order.

When Billy Martin was appointed manager of the A's in 1980, his starting rotation of Matt Keough, Brian Kingman, Rick Langford, Steve McCatty and Norris averaged only 25 years of age. The five overworked young aces would go on to lead the majors with 94 complete games.

Norris paced the AL with just 6.8 hits allowed per nine innings. He finished second with 284⅓ innings pitched, 22 wins, 24 complete games, 180 strikeouts and a 2.54 ERA. He was arguably the AL's best pitcher, but the Cy Young Award went to the Orioles' Steve Stone.

During 1980, Norris faced a daunting 1,135 batters. The extended pitch counts and heavy workload were plainly harmful to his pitching arm. In one ill-advised outing on June 11, Martin left him in to throw 168 pitches in a marathon 14-inning 6-2 victory over the Twins.

The next year, his 9-3 start helped the A's to the best record in the first half of the strike-shortened season and a spot in the ALDS. He pitched in the All-Star Game, but couldn't shake off the rust in the second half and faded to finish at 12-9 with an AL-high 14 wild pitches.

G	IP	W	L	PCT	SHO	GS	CG	H	ER	SO	BB	ERA
201	1124.1	58	59	.496	7	157	52	972	486	636	499	3.00

Showing his mettle, Norris tossed a four-hit shutout in the AL Divisional Series Game 1, working himself out of two bases-loaded jams, to start a sweep over the Royals. He took the ball again in the American League Championship Series Game 1. Allowing three Yankee runs in the first inning, he absorbed a tough 3-1 loss.

Norris dealt with arm tendinitis in 1982 and had a 21-day disabled list stay. By 1983, his arm was shredded. He blew out his shoulder midseason so completely that he couldn't even pick up a baseball. Norris underwent surgery and was on the DL for the rest of 1983 and all of 1984.

By 1985, he had become addicted to cocaine and tested positive for codeine. The A's put him on the Alcohol & Drug Rehabilitation List and then granted him free agency in November. He put in three long years in exile toiling for the unaffiliated San Jose Bees and in the Caribbean.

On April 11, 1990, Norris came back to work two scoreless innings in relief of Mike Moore to seal a 3-0 win over the Twins. On April 17 in relief, he earned his first major league victory since May 16, 1983. It was the third longest length between victories in baseball history.

His final big-league appearance was July 4. After a wrangle with pitching coach Dave Duncan about his fitness for a starting role, Norris was put on waivers on July 15. Although the Athletics signed him to another minor league contract later, he never pitched in the majors again.

In 1999, Norris began to suffer from cervical myelopathy, a narrowing of his spinal cord due to arthritic buildup. After two surgeries, he now has partial paralysis of his legs. Norris walks with a walker, but still exercises by playing golf, which is therapeutic for his condition.

He is currently using the hard lessons of his life to help young people. The big-hearted, genial Norris is directing the Reviving Baseball in Inner Cities (R.B.I.) outreach program in Oakland, where he is teaching youngsters life skills while they also learn about baseball.

RON OESTER

CINCINNATI REDS
SECOND BASE

1978-1990

"I don't know that anybody's quicker turning the double play than Ron. For a big guy [6'2", 192], he's very agile. He's especially good coming in on the ball."

~ Reds Coach Tommy Helms

Hometown Queen City product Ron Oester was the ultimate competitor. Known for his hustling style of play, he earned a World Series championship ring in his final season in 1990. Oester was the rare player who began as a late draft pick but later starred in the major leagues.

Starting his career two years after the heyday of the Big Red Machine, Oester appeared in 1,171 games at second base, more than all but two players- Joe Morgan and Brandon Phillips- in the storied history of baseball's first professional team. Cincy's starting second baseman for six consecutive years, Oester was a quiet, efficient player who always seemed to be underrated.

In his prime, Oester may have had the best throwing arm of any infielder in the National League. He didn't show exceptional speed, but had great agility and soft sure hands with pivot work on the double play as smooth as silk. He was dependable, durable and tough.

Oester was not a slugger, but more of a line drive hitter who used the whole field to line out singles and doubles. Particularly clutch with teammates in scoring position, he normally hit in the sixth or seventh spot in the Reds batting order. Oester was old school as one of the few major league hitters who did not wear batting gloves. He perpetually developed blisters on his hands, and according to his teammates they would develop into deep wounds on his palms.

★　★　★　★　★

Ronald John Oester, Jr. was born on May 5, 1956 in Cincinnati, Ohio to Mary and Ronald John Oester, Sr. Like thousands of other Cincinnati youngsters, Oester grew up adulating homegrown hero Pete Rose. Rose slid headfirst, so Oester followed. Rose's father taught him to switch-hit at nine years old. Oester's father taught him to switch-hit starting at four.

He starred for Coach Tom Chambers' Withrow University High Tigers at shortstop before graduating in 1974.

Oester was drafted by the Reds in the ninth round of the 1974 draft. After hitting .311 that summer playing for the Billings (MT) Mustangs in the Pioneer Rookie League, Oester slumped in 1975 for the Tampa Tarpons in the Single-A Florida State League.

After that lost season, he spent the 1976 year with the Trois-Rivieres (QC) Aigles of the Double-A Eastern League. Playing for the Indianapolis (IN) Indians of the Triple-A American Association from 1977 to 1979, he returned to switch hitting, got over 500 plate appearances each year and improved. He was twice an American Association All-Star shortstop.

Oester got his major league call up and debut with the Reds on September 10, 1978. Although he wore #14 in honor of Rose in the minor leagues, as a major leaguer he took #16 out of respect for him. Until Oester came up to Cincy, he had always been a shortstop, but switched to second base as the slick-fielding Dave Concepcion was already entrenched at short.

The 24-year-old Oester stuck for good with the Reds in 1980, the year after Rose began playing for the Phillies. He requested Rose's vacated locker. That year he hit .277 in 100 games, finished fourth in NL Rookie of the Year balloting, and made the *Topps* All-Star Rookie Team.

In 1984, Oester spaced together a 21-game hitting streak and in 1985, he hit a career-high .295 as a regular. On July 5, 1987, during a game at Riverfront Stadium, the Mets' Mookie Wilson slid aggressively into second to break up a double play. During the slide, Oester collided with Wilson, his cleats got caught in the turf, and his left anterior collateral ligament was torn.

Oester did not return to action until July 16, 1988, but his resilience and ability to come back and thrive is one thing fans took away from his career. Although he lost his second base job to Mariano Duncan in 1990, Oester was one of the club's top pinch hitters, averaging .299.

G	AB	R	H	2B	3B	HR	RBI	SB	BB	SO	BA	OBP	SLG	TB
1276	4214	458	1118	190	33	42	344	40	369	681	.265	.323	.356	1500

Cincinnati would become the Cinderella Reds in 1990 and go on to beat the Pirates in the NL Championship Series in six games. One of Oester's biggest moments came when he crossed the plate as the winning run in the Reds' NLCS-clinching game. He hit .333 in the NLCS.

His last action was in World Series Game 2 at Riverfront Stadium on October 17, 1990. In his only Fall Classic at-bat, pinch-hitting for pitcher Scott Scudder with two out, he stroked a hard groundball single up the middle off A's ace Bob Welch to score Joe Oliver from second base in the fourth inning. The Reds won 5-4 and went on to sweep the Athletics in four games.

Oester managed the Reds' Southern League affiliate, the Chattanooga (TN) Lookouts, in 1992 and came back to the Reds as first base coach in 1993. He was the first base coach for the Tigers in 1996 before returning again to the Reds in the same position from 1997 to 2001.

Oester was on manager Jack McKeon's staff and was considered the favorite for the job after McKeon announced his retirement at the end of the 2000 season. While Oester was negotiating his offer to take over as manager in October, Reds general manager Jim Bowden balked at paying him more than $300,000. Oester and Bowden had a falling out and the job was abruptly offered to Bob Boone. Oester was not brought back by Boone after the 2001 season.

He served as a minor league infield instructor with the Philadelphia Phillies in 2002 and 2003 and then came back with the Reds in 2004. He has served as the Chicago White Sox's infield instructor since 2009. Ron Oester Field was dedicated as the home field of his alma mater, Withrow University High School, in 2015.

Ron Oester was inducted into the Cincinnati Reds Hall of Fame on August 9, 2014. He continues to reside in Cincinnati with his wife Jacqueline Ann. They have raised two daughters and two sons. His son Jake signed with the White Sox in 2010 and plays third base.

BIFF POCOROBA

ATLANTA BRAVES
CATCHER • THIRD BASEMAN • PINCH HITTER
1975-1984

B iff Pocoroba was a National League All-Star catcher, but after several excellent seasons, a rotator cuff injury to his throwing arm put a damper on his burgeoning career as a young backstop. After a brief trial at third base, he was ultimately relegated to pinch hitting duties.

Pocoroba threw out 26 percent of would-be base stealers and boasted a career .985 fielding percentage. He was a battery mate for noteworthy Atlanta pitchers such as Jim Bouton, Mike Marshall, Andy Messersmith, John "The Count" Montefusco, Donnie Moore, Phil Niekro, Gaylord Perry, Al "The Mad Hungarian" Hrabosky and Dick Ruthven.

A 5'10" 175-pound switch hitter, Pocoroba made contact with the pitched ball most the time, striking out only 109 times in 1,457 at-bats while drawing 182 bases on balls. He only had one season in which he struck out more than he walked.

★ ★ ★ ★ ★

Biff Benedict Pocoroba was born on July 25, 1953 to Ida Geraldine Bellini and Victor Raymond Pocoroba in Burbank, Los Angeles County, California. His birth certificate reflects "Biff" as his first name. Pocoroba is the only major league player in history to have an *onomatopoeic* sound found more often in a *Batman* comic book than on a birth certificate.

He grew up in Canoga Park, California with his two brothers, Joe and Steve. Pocoroba was eight years old when Dodger Stadium was christened in 1962 about 25 miles away. He attended scores of games there at the Los Angeles Dodgers' new home in Chavez Ravine. The Dodgers became his favorite team. In fact, his brother Joe later signed with the Dodgers and was a minor league infielder in 1978 and 1979.

After starring as a catcher for the Canoga Park High School Hunters, he graduated in 1971 and was drafted by the Atlanta Braves in the 17th round of the June free agent amateur draft. Signed by Braves scout Ed Roebuck at only 17 years old, Pocoroba was assigned to the Wytheville (VA) Braves of the Appalachian Rookie League and hit .298 in 42 games.

He paced the Western Carolina League with a .979 fielding average in 1972 while hitting .259 for Greenwood (SC) in 75 games. Pocoroba caught for Savannah (GA) in the Double-A Southern League the entire 1974 season, handling the catching chores and hitting .311.

During the Braves' 1975 spring training in Kissimmee, Florida, Pocoroba turned some heads when he threw out 11 straight base runners in a row attempting to steal. It got him his big-league debut on April 25 as a defensive replacement against the Padres in San Diego at age 21.

Pocoroba spent the 1975 season as a backup for starting catcher Vic Correl. Appearing in 67 games, he threw out only 17 percent of base stealers and was charged with 13 passed balls. His defensive skills improved rapidly and he moved into a starting role, throwing out 34 percent of the base runners attempting to steal the next two seasons.

The highlight of his young career came on May 17, 1977 at Atlanta-Fulton County Stadium. With Braves trailing the Expos, 6-5, Pocoroba came to the plate with bases loaded and two out in the bottom of the ninth inning. The pitcher-batter duel went to a full count before Pocoroba hammered Bill Atkinson's fastball for a grand slam home run and a dramatic walk-off Braves victory, 9-6. He posted career-bests that year with 123 games played, 387 plate appearances, 24 doubles, eight home runs, 44 runs batted in, and a .290 average.

The Braves were impressed with their 24-year-old catcher and tendered a six-year, million dollar contract to him that winter. Pocoroba continued on the upswing in 1978 when he led all National League catchers with a

"I wanted something distinctive. I didn't want him going through life having to answer to Herman, or something like that."

~ Pocoroba's father Victor on naming his son

G	AB	R	H	2B	3B	HR	RBI	SB	BB	SO	BA	OBP	SLG	TB
596	1457	132	374	71	2	21	172	6	182	109	.257	.339	.351	512

6.29 range factor (putouts + assists per games played).

Chosen as a National League All-Star for the game played at San Diego Stadium on July 11, Pocoroba caught the last inning with his future Hall of Fame battery mate on the mound, knuckleballer Phil Niekro. Niekro polished off the American Leaguers for a 7-3 win.

Less than a month later on August 9, Pocoroba was placed on the disabled list with a highly inflamed right shoulder. He had been making the long throws to second base too often at too young of an age. He went under the knife with world-renowned orthopedic surgeon Dr. Frank Jobe in December of 1978 to repair a torn rotator cuff.

Pocoroba appeared in only 28 games in 1979 and came to the plate just 46 times. The injury to his shoulder never completely healed, ultimately forcing him from behind the plate to third base. From 1979 to 1983, Pocoroba was only able to catch 96 games.

From 1979 until the end of his career in 1984, he appeared in only 119 games. Pocoroba played a total of 23 games at third base in 1981 and 1982, but with limited success. He also brought his *Louisville Slugger* into the batters' box as a pinch hitter, but only from the right side.

After going 2-for-4 in four games as a pinch hitter, Pocoroba played his final game on April 20, 1984. He received his unconditional release from the Braves on April 24, 1984 and retired from professional baseball at the young age of 30.

Pocoroba and his two brothers have built a great business making custom and specialty sausages. He is president of Sausage World Incorporated domiciled in Lilburn, Georgia. The restaurant supply business in the metropolitan Atlanta area sells a huge variety of meat from all over Europe and America including sweet basil Italian sausage, links of pepperoni, bratwurst, kielbasa and andouile. He continues to reside in the Atlanta area.

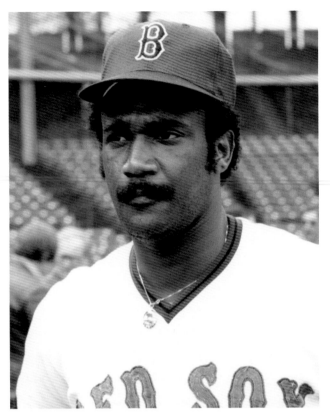

JIM RICE

BOSTON RED SOX
LEFT FIELD • DESIGNATED HITTER

1974-1989

"I have been in this game thirty years. I have seen all of the power hitters in that time. Nobody can hit a baseball as hard or as far as Jim Rice."

~ Don Zimmer

Jim Rice took the torch from Boston legends Ted Williams and Carl Yastrzemski to complete a great triumvirate of lifelong Red Sox leftfielders extending over half a century. An eight-time All-Star, he ended his career ranked third on the all-time Red Sox rolls in hits, home runs, total bases and runs batted in, trailing only his two predecessors.

A 6'2" 220-pounder, Rice displayed a distinctive blend of ferocious power and hitting artistry. He used powerful wrists and a disciplined stroke to hit 20 homers 11 times, post 100 RBI eight times, hit .300 seven times and collect 200 hits four times. Rice led his league in total bases four times, home runs three times; and RBI and slugging twice. He was so strong he once broke his *Louisville Slugger* on a checked swing.

★ ★ ★ ★ ★

James Edward Rice was born to Julia May and Roger Rice on March 8, 1953 in the northwestern South Carolina rural community of Anderson. When integration was mandated at his formerly all-white Hanna High School, the introspective young black man's leadership and up-beat nature helped ease any potential racial tension. Rice was an all-state football star, as well as a basketball and track standout, but his best sport was baseball and he was taken in the first round by Boston in the 1971 free agent draft.

Rice's assault on minor league pitching was devastating. He took the Double-A Eastern League batting crown at Bristol in 1973. At Pawtucket, he was the 1974 Triple-A International League Triple Crown winner (.337 average - 25 home runs - 95 RBI), Most Valuable Player and baseball's "Minor League Player of the Year."

The 22-year-old Rice and fellow rookie Fred Lynn were the most celebrated Sox newcomers of 1975, chris-tened "The Gold Dust Twins." Rice batted .309 with 174 hits, 22 home runs and 102 RBI before a pitch broke his left hand in late September. He had to sit out the historic 1975 Series won by Cincy's "Big Red Machine." To this day, Red Sox Nation asserts that their cleanup hitter's presence would have made all of the difference.

In 1977, he began a run of three straight years record-ing at least 35 homers and 200 hits, the only player ever to do so. The 1978 American League Most Valuable Play-er, Rice batted .315 and led all of baseball with 213 hits, 15 triples, 46 home runs, 139 RBI, 406 total bases and a slugging average of .600. That year he became the first American League hitter to amass over 400 total bases since Joe DiMaggio in 1937. Despite all of his contribu-tions, the Red Sox crumbled late and lost in a playoff to the Yankees.

Starting another string of four exceptional years, Rice hit .305 in 1983 and led the American League with 39 home runs and 126 RBI. With him as its cleanup hit-ter and captain, Boston returned to the postseason in 1986. He hit .324 with 200 hits, 20 home runs and 110 RBI. In 14 postseason games, Rice scored 14 runs, col-lected 14 hits and crushed a three-run homer against the Angels to clinch the AL Championship Series in Game 7. In his only Fall Classic, he batted .333 (9-for-27) in the painful loss to the Mets.

Jim Rice was the premier hitter in baseball from 1975 to 1986. Twenty ballplayers have batted .300 with at least 350 home runs over *any* dozen-year period. Rice was the *only* player of his era to do so. Over that stretch, he led the AL in home runs, slugging percentage and hits, set-ting himself apart by averaging a stout .304. With decep-tive foot speed for a big man, he also legged out the most triples (73) with his galloping style.

G	AB	R	H	2B	3B	HR	RBI	SB	BB	SO	BA	OBP	SLG	TB
2089	8225	1249	2452	373	79	382	1451	58	670	1423	.298	.352	.502	4129

Working to become a quality outfielder, Rice mastered the caroms off Fenway Park's elevated left field wall. With 137 career assists and a .980 fielding average, he ultimately made himself into the most dangerous outfielder in the league to run on. Many a surprised runner was tagged out because of his shrewd decoys off the Green Monster.

As his career wound down, Rice became a designated hitter, continuing to hit near .300 and average over 20 home runs. Hampered by an elbow injury, off-season knee surgery and vision problems, Rice's production began to fall in 1987. These concerns plagued him through 1989, prompting his release at age 36.

Since 1992, Rice has served his Red Sox in a variety of capacities including batting coach and hitting instructor while earning a solid reputation as an incisive baseball analyst for the New England Sports Network.

Rice was inducted into the Boston Red Sox Hall of Fame in 1995 and the Ted Williams Hitters Hall of Fame in 2001. As the years went by, it became increasingly evident that Rice's power numbers compare favorably even with those sluggers who may have benefited from performance-enhancing drugs in baseball's "Steroids Era."

Despite his clashes at times with a critical Hub press and the fourth estate in general, Jim Rice was finally elected into the National Baseball Hall of Fame in 2009 in his 15th and final year of eligibility. Two days after his Hall of Fame induction, his Red Sox uniform jersey #14 was formally retired at Fenway Park on July 28, 2009.

Rice continues to support an array of charitable organizations including The Jimmy Fund and Major League Baseball's RBI (Reviving Baseball in Inner Cities) program. He and his wife Corrine have resided in Andover, Massachusetts since 1975.

J.R. RICHARD

HOUSTON ASTROS
RIGHT-HANDED PITCHER

1971-1980

J. R. Richard had one of the most tragic careers ever chronicled, a career that seemed destined for immortality in Cooperstown. One of the most talented, dominant pitchers in the National League, he was unable to come back after being felled by a stroke in his prime.

With his 100-mile-per-hour fastball and 93+ slider, the 6'8" 250-pound Richard was one of the hardest throwers in history. Hitters stepped in with trepidation because he did not always know where the ball was going. He led the Senior Circuit in wild pitches and walks three times.

Richard topped the National League once in ERA, twice in strikeouts, and three times in fewest-hits-allowed-per-nine innings. His 313 strikeouts in 1979 remain an Astros franchise record. He also set the club's standard for career strikeouts, eventually broken by Nolan Ryan.

★ ★ ★ ★ ★

James Rodney Richard was born on March 7, 1950 to Lizzie Frost and Clayton Richard in Vienna, Lincoln Parish, Louisiana. The big athletic youngster was a man among boys at Lincoln High. He never lost a game he started and allowed no runs his senior year. Despite over 200 basketball scholarship offers, he signed with the Astros as the 1969 second overall pick.

After a summer in the Appalachian League with the Covington (VA) Astros and a season with Cocoa of the Florida State League, he leapfrogged to the Triple-A Oklahoma City 89ers in 1971. There he went 12-7 and led the American Association with 202 strikeouts.

The 21-year-old Richard earned his big-league debut on September 5, 1971. Using a devastating fastball and slider combination, he notched his first victory, 5-3, and matched Karl Spooner's first start record of 15 strikeouts, including three punchouts of the great Willie Mays.

However, periodic wildness continued to plague him and he bounced between Houston and the minors for several years. In 1974, Richard posted a zero ERA in 33 innings

pitched for the Triple-A Denver (CO) Bears, convincing the Astros to keep him on their roster for good.

In his first full season in 1975, he became the #3 starter behind Larry Dierker and Dave Roberts. He was still wild, leading the NL with 138 walks and 20 wild pitches, but posted the only winning record (12-10) among Astros starters and topped the club with 176 strikeouts.

Now at his peak, Richard finished **1976** at 20–15 with 14 complete games, 214 strikeouts and a 2.75 ERA. The Astros MVP, he had qualified as the ninth member of the Black Aces, an elite group of African American big-leaguers who have won at least 20 games in a season.

In 1977, Richard hurled seven complete game victories in the first half of the campaign. He finished by winning nine of his last 12 games to lead the Astros staff with 18 wins, 13 complete games, 267 innings pitched, 104 walks and 214 strikeouts. His ERA was a fine 2.97.

Richard was the 1978 July NL Pitcher of the Month on his way to winning 18 games with a 3.11 ERA. His 303 strikeouts set a new league standard for a right-hander. He was only the third NL hurler ever to reach 300 Ks, all while issuing a NL-high 141 walks and 16 wild pitches.

Richard closed the 1979 year as the September NL Pitcher of the Month, winning his 11th game in a row versus the Dodgers. He claimed the National League earned run average title at 2.71 and pitched an Astros record 86 straight innings without requiring help from the bullpen.

With 313 strikeouts, he joined Sandy Koufax and Nolan Ryan as the only men to strike out 300 batters two seasons in a row. In October, the club signed him to a new four year contract. Going into 1980, Richard had already achieved more success than any Astros pitcher in history.

He was the 1980 April NL Pitcher of the Month and went 10–4 during the first half with 115 Ks, a 1.96 ERA and a start in the All-Star Game. During his last outing on July 14, Richard struck out the side in the second inning, but

> *"He had the greatest stuff*
> *I have ever seen and*
> *it still gives me goose*
> *bumps to think of what*
> *he might have become."*
>
> ~ *teammate Joe Morgan*

G	IP	W	L	PCT	SHO	GS	CG	H	ER	SO	BB	ERA
238	1606	107	71	.601	19	221	76	1227	562	1493	770	3.15

had difficulty seeing catcher Alan Ashby's signs. He left the game in the fourth inning after his right arm "went dead" with numbness in his fingers.

Richard was placed on the 21-day disabled list. Tests were run at Methodist Hospital. The blood pressure in his left arm was normal but nearly absent in his right arm due to an obstructed artery. On July 25, doctors decided no surgery was needed after they checked his neck arteries.

While playing catch before an Astros game on July 30, Richard suffered a major stroke and collapsed in the outfield. He was rushed to the hospital for emergency surgery to remove a life-threatening blood clot in his neck. It would be a sudden end to his brilliant career at age 30.

The stroke had slowed down Richard's reaction time and hurt his depth perception. He worked out diligently in 1981 with the Astros and at TCU, but saw no action. He spent the next two years in the minors with little success and the Astros gave him his release in April of 1984.

With the loss of his livelihood, Richard's personal life spiraled downward. He lost over $300,000 when he was scammed on a Louisiana oil business deal. Later, he lost $669,000 in a divorce settlement. A second marriage also dissolved, costing him his suburban Houston home.

Richard was penniless by late 1994, living many nights under the Highway 59 overpass at Beechnut Road in Houston. Fortunately, he became eligible for his baseball pension in 1995 and started his road back from despair by appearing in an Old-Timers Game at the Astrodome.

A short time later, he began attending the Now Testament Church in Houston and sought counsel from its minister, Reverend Floyd Lewis. Richard later came back to the church as a Christian minister. He has since engaged himself in the Houston community, working to set up baseball programs for Houston youth. He is also on the platform as a national motivational speaker. J.R. Richard's career will always be remembered for what it might have been.

STEVE ROGERS

MONTREAL EXPOS
RIGHT-HANDED PITCHER

1973-1985

"He's trying to reach perfection in a game where that's impossible. Even after a great game, you don't see him all smiles, because he's seen things he hasn't been pleased with."

~ teammate Scott Sanderson

Steve Rogers was the most successful pitcher in Montreal history and a key contributor in lifting the expansion Expos franchise from an also-ran status to a respected organization. He is the team's all-time leader in victories, innings pitched, strikeouts, complete games and shutouts.

Averaging over 13 wins per season from 1973 and 1983, Rogers led the National League once in ERA and twice in shutouts. A five-time All-Star, he authored an amazing 129 regular season complete games and 37 shutouts, while going 3-1 with a 0.97 ERA in postseason play.

Known for his deceptive delivery, Rogers seemed to almost stumble in his follow-through. A crafty pitcher with a full repertoire, he had solid command of his fastball, curveball, slider and changeup. His career 3.17 ERA is lower than 16 pitchers enshrined in Cooperstown.

* * * * *

Stephen Douglas Rogers was born on October 26, 1949 to Connie and W. L. Douglas Rogers in the capital of Missouri, Jefferson City. The eldest of six children, he was raised in Springfield, Missouri, growing up playing baseball with his siblings at a local park most days.

Rogers led his Glendale High School Falcons to the Missouri State semi-finals, only to be upended, 2-0, by future pitching rival Jerry Reuss. Legendary scout Tom Greenwade had the Yankees pick him in the 60th round of the 1967 draft, but then counseled him to go to college.

After his freshman year hurling for the University of Tulsa, Rogers grew three inches to 6'2". He was 10-2 for the 1969 College World Series finalist Golden Hurricane, and went 12-2 to lead TU to a third place CWS finish as a 1971 NCAA All-American. His college line was 31-5. Rogers was drafted fourth overall by Montreal in the secondary phase of the 1971 draft.

The Expos sent him to their top Triple-A International League affiliate, the Winnipeg (MB) Whips. After only 378 minor league innings, Rogers got his debut in Houston on July 18, 1973. He gave up two runs on four hits in eight innings, then pitched his first win, a 4-0 one-hitter at Veterans Stadium over Lefty Carlton. Next he blanked the Mets, 1-0, at Shea Stadium. With three shutouts, a 10-5 mark and 1.54 ERA, Rogers was *The Sporting News* 1973 National League Rookie of the Year. His teammates started calling him "Cy" for Cy Young and it stuck.

It is a baseball axiom that to lead the league in losses, a pitcher must be a workhorse and have quality stuff. His managers kept giving Rogers the ball for marginal Expos teams. He had the most NL losses in two of the next three years with an aggregate 3.63 ERA in 735⅓ innings.

The 27-year old Rogers got a fresh start in 1977, going 17-16 with a 3.10 ERA, when the Expos moved to the more spacious Olympic Stadium. In his first 22 starts in 1978, he was given little support, averaging fewer than three runs per game. He was 13-10 despite a low 2.47 ERA.

The young Expos of Gary Carter, Andre Dawson, Larry Parrish and Ellis Valentine came of age in 1979, winning 95 games, and battled the Pirates for the National League East title until the last weekend. Though Rogers struggled to adapt to authoritarian manager Dick Williams' style, he came back from elbow surgery to win 13 games and top the league with five shutouts.

He and Williams reached détente in spring training and Rogers flourished. Rogers' 1980 line was 16-11 with a 2.98 ERA and a NL-high 14 complete games. He was a monster down the stretch with a 4-2 mark, two shutouts, five complete games and another win over Carlton. His team went scoreless in each loss. One was to his old rival Jerry Reuss and the Dodgers, 2-0.

Rogers played an integral role off the field in 1981 as one of four player representatives negotiating with Major League Baseball's owners during the midyear players strike. The work stoppage was settled with the winning

G	IP	W	L	PCT	SHO	GS	CG	H	ER	SO	BB	ERA
399	2837.2	158	152	.510	37	393	129	2619	1001	1621	876	3.17

teams of each half facing each other in a divisional series.

Montreal made the postseason for the only time in its history and defeated the Phillies in the NLDS. Rogers was the putative MVP, going $8^2/_3$ innings in Game 1 to beat Carlton, 3-1, and bested the future Hall of Famer again in Game 5 on a six-hitter, 3-0, while driving in two runs.

In the NLCS Game 3, Rogers finally got his payback against Reuss, pitching a seven-hit victory, 4-1. The Game 5 finale was played on a drizzly cold Quebec Monday afternoon. In the ninth, manager Jim Fanning called Rogers out of the bullpen to retire Rick Monday. Fatigued, he gave up the game-winning home run. That day is still referred to in Montreal as *Blue Monday*.

Rogers returned in 1982 to have his best campaign with a first-rate 19-8 mark and was the NL ERA champion at 2.40. He started and won the All-Star Game played in Montreal and finished second in the Cy Young Award voting behind only Carlton with his 23 wins and 3.10 ERA.

Rogers sustained his excellence in 1983, finishing with a 17-12 record and a 3.23 ERA, and again led the NL with five shutouts. He made his fifth and final All-Star squad and placed fourth in the Cy Young Award voting. It would be his last healthy, successful campaign.

Prior to 1984, Rogers had labored almost 3,000 professional innings. His right shoulder finally wore out, yielding a subpar 6-15 1984 record. The Expos gave him his release on May 21, 1985. After short cameos with Edmonton (Angels) and Buffalo (White Sox), he retired.

Because of his experience as a player representative, the Major League Baseball Players Association approached Rogers in 1987 to consult on pension issues, and he began researching collusion cases. He is currently a special assistant to executive director Michael Weiner.

Rogers was inducted into the University of Tulsa Athletics Hall of Fame in 1985, the Montreal Expos Hall of Fame in 1994, and the Canadian Baseball Hall of Fame in 2005. He resides in Princeton Junction, Mercer County, New Jersey with his wife Robin.

BILLY RUSSELL

LOS ANGELES DODGERS
SHORTSTOP

1972-1990

Billy Russell was one of the finest shortstops in National League history. He anchored the infield for four pennant winners and a World Series champion. Three times an All-Star during his long career, Russell played more games than any other Los Angeles Dodger and trails only Hall of Famer Zack Wheat for most games played in behalf of the Dodgers franchise.

The quiet, hardworking Russell combined with second baseman Davey Lopes, third baseman Ron Cey, and first baseman Steve Garvey to form Major League Baseball's longest-lasting intact infield. The foursome played together for eight and a half campaigns.

The consistent Russell hit a career .263 which mirrored his average in 23 Fall Classic games. As his high-water mark, he batted .423 (11-for-26) in the 1978 "Reggie Jackson World Series." The 6' 175-pound right-handed hitter also hit .337 in five NL Championship Series.

* * * * *

William Ellis Russell was born on October 21, 1948 in Pittsburg, Crawford County, Kansas to Fern and Warren Russell. He was raised the third of five children in the Ozark Highlands region of southeastern Kansas, famous for its history of coal mining.

Russell was a basketball star at Pittsburg High, a school then too small to field a baseball squad. Upon graduation, the Dodgers drafted him in the ninth round of the 1966 amateur draft, signed him to a $14,000 bonus contract, and sent him to Ogden in the Pioneer League.

Fearful that he would be released before given a chance to prove himself, he sought assurance from manager Tommy Lasorda. Relieved and newly confident, he went on to hit .356 in 39 games. After struggling with the Class-A Dubuque (IA) Packers of the Midwest League in 1967, he rebounded to hit .280 in

1968 for Bakersfield in the California League.

Following a strong spring training, the 20-year-old Russell earned his major league debut on April 7, 1969 as an outfielder. Manager Walter Alston considered him to be an even better defensive outfielder than veteran Willie Davis. Dodger icon Maury Wills was still the shortstop.

Russell split time between the Triple-A Spokane (WA) Indians and the Dodgers in 1970. Converted to the infield with the aid of coach Marty Basgall in the 1970 Arizona Instructional League, he made the big club to stay in 1971 and replaced the aging Wills in 1972 at shortstop.

After a difficult year leading Senior Circuit shortstops in errors that year, Russell worked hard to polish his defense to become the Dodgers' steady everyday shortstop for the next dozen years. Starting in 1972 when he led the NL with 162 games played, Russell averaged 609 plate appearances through 1980 (excluding 1975), to earn his reputation as an ironman.

He scuffled through perhaps his worst campaign in 1975 with calcium deposits and a bone chip in his throwing shoulder. However, after surgery in the winter before the 1976 season, he resurrected his career by hitting .274 in 149 games and was honored as a NL All-Star.

Lasorda lauded him in 1977 for playing the greatest shortstop he had ever witnessed. Involved in a NL-high 102 double plays, he hit .278 in 153 games, batting in the #2 slot in the lineup and helping to protect base-stealing leadoff hitter Lopes. He struck out a mere 43 times.

Russell was hit in the hand with a pitch in 1980, shattering his thumb. Never quite the same shortstop afterward, his throws became more erratic. He played his last game on October 1, 1986 at the age of 38 as the last member of the famous Garvey- Lopes- Russell- Cey infield.

He announced his retirement on October 24 and soon went to work as a Dodger coach. Offered the Triple-A Al-

> *"I'll tell you this much. The only way you'll get released is if I get released as the manager. As long as I'm the manager here, you'll be here, because I believe you have major league ability."*
>
> *~ Ogden manager Tommy Lasorda to Russell in rookie league 1966*

G	AB	R	H	2B	3B	HR	RBI	SB	BB	SO	BA	OBP	SLG	TB
2181	7318	796	1926	293	57	46	627	167	483	667	.263	.310	.338	2471

buquerque (NM) Dukes managing job again in 1991, he accepted. After a two-year apprenticeship, he returned to coach the Dodgers as Lasorda's heir apparent.

It became evident that Lasorda had no plans to retire, but Russell was patient. In June of 1996, the 68-year-old skipper suffered a mild heart attack. By the time Lasorda recovered, the Dodgers front office had decided to make Russell's appointment permanent on July 29.

Accustomed to Lasorda's histrionics when things went wrong, the players soon embraced Russell's quiet, assured style. The team relaxed and started playing its best baseball of the season. The team finished with a 35-21 flourish and won the 1996 National League wild card berth. During 1997, Russell constructed 101 different lineups as the Dodgers finished 88-74, just behind the Giants in a tight National League West race that came down to the last series.

With Rupert Murdoch's Fox Group News Corporation poised to purchase the franchise in 1998, the new ownership forced a trade of Mike Piazza and Todd Zeile to the Marlins without Russell's or general manager Fred Claire's knowledge. When the club stumbled to a 36–38 start, Russell was dismissed on June 21 along with Claire in a general housecleaning. His final managerial record was 173–149 (.537) and his 30-year association with the Dodgers was over.

Stung by the firing, Russell didn't return to the major leagues until 2000, when he joined the Tampa Bay Devil Rays as manager Larry Rothschild's bench coach. He also managed the 1999 Double-A Orlando (FL) Rays and the 2001 Double-A Shreveport (LA) Captains.

Billy Russell currently works for Major League Baseball's umpiring division as an umpire observer. He can be seen frequently at Angel Stadium in Anaheim seated in the Diamond Club Section observing the umpiring crew.

MIKE SCHMIDT

PHILADELPHIA PHILLIES
THIRD BASE

1972-1989

"Schmidt gave us 110 percent every single night in every single at-bat. He set the standard for profession-alism around here."

~ *Phillies Chairman of the Board Bill Giles*

Mike Schmidt is the greatest third baseman of all-time, displaying an unmatched combination of power and defense. He led the National League in home runs eight times, trailing only Babe Ruth's 12 league titles. A three-time Most Valuable Player and 12-time All-Star, Schmidt holds nearly every all-time Phillies franchise hitting record.

The 6'2" 203-pound Schmidt was the most prolific slugger of the 1980s, clouting 313 home runs. He slammed at least 30 circuit clouts 13 times (second only to Aaron's 15) and launched 35 or more homers 11 times. Only Ruth topped him at 12. Schmidt hit more home runs (509) and drove in more runs (1,595) than any third baseman in history.

An offensive juggernaut, Schmidt led the NL in slugging, extra base hits, on-base percentage and OPS five times each; and walks and RBI four times respectively. He drove in over 100 runs nine seasons while drawing over 100 free passes seven seasons.

Schmidt's stellar glove work earned him a National League record ten *Rawlings* Gold Gloves. With a rifle arm and sure hands, he registered the most assists in the league seven times and turned the most twin killings six times despite Veterans Stadium's hard, fast artificial turf. His 404 assists in 1974 remain a record for third basemen.

The acerbic Philly crowds were slow to warm to Schmidt's undemonstrative style in his early years. But over time, he won them over with his brilliant play, work ethic and durability (he played 145+ games in 13 seasons). In 1983, in celebration of the Phillies' 100th anniversary, these same fans voted Schmidt the greatest player in franchise annals.

★   ★   ★   ★   ★

Michael Jack Schmidt was born September 27, 1949 in Dayton, Montgomery County, Ohio to Lois and Jack Schmidt. His parents managed Jack's Drive In restaurant, adjoining the Phillips Aquatic Club. At Fairview High, he starred in basketball and baseball but two knee surgeries put his focus exclusively on baseball before he graduated.

Schmidt enrolled at Ohio University as an unheralded walk on in 1967, but went on to establish all-time Bobcat season records with ten home runs, 45 runs scored and 38 walks. Schmidt was an NCAA All-American shortstop as both a junior and a senior.

The Phillies drafted him in the second round, the 30th pick overall of the 1971 free agent draft. Signed by scout Tony Lucadello, he was sent to Double-A Reading (PA) and quickly promoted to the Triple-A Eugene (OR) Emeralds. In 1972, he hit 26 home runs.

After the Pacific Coast League season, the Phillies gave him his debut on September 12. In his first full season in 1973, Schmidt didn't even hit his weight, batting an anemic .196 with 136 strikeouts, but heralded his upside by launching 18 home runs.

In 1976, swinging his big 36" K75 *Louisville Slugger* lumber, he pumped out 12 homers in his first 15 games. On April 17, he hit four straight bombs to tie a big-league mark. His all around play carried the Phillies to three straight divisional titles (1976-78).

Schmidt came up as a dead pull-hitter and led the NL in strikeouts three years in a row (1974-76). Seeking more consistency, he set up in the far corner of the batter's box to avoid being jammed, shortened his stroke and started hitting the ball to all fields.

Schmidt enjoyed his dream season in 1980. He broke the Phillies home run record of 43 set by Chuck Klein in 1929 and led the Senior Circuit with 48 round trippers, 121 RBI, a 1.004 OPS, 342 total bases and a .624 slugging percentage. Schmidt was the unanimous 1980 National League Most Valuable Player.

G	AB	R	H	2B	3B	HR	RBI	SB	BB	SO	BA	OBP	SLG	TB
2404	8352	1506	2234	408	59	548	1595	174	1507	1883	.267	.380	.527	4404

The Phillies went on to win their only World Series in the 20th century, besting the Royals in their first Fall Classic appearance since the 1950 Whiz Kids. Schmidt hit .381 (8-for-21) with two home runs and seven RBI to become the World Series Most Valuable Player as well.

In 1981, Philadelphia again reached the postseason and Schmidt won his second NL Most Valuable Player award with personal-bests in on-base, batting and slugging averages. He was voted his third MVP award in 1986, a record for third basemen.

After a stellar 1987, he played injured in 1988 and began slowly in 1989. Without warning, he decided to retire on May 29. Often called "Captain Cool," the normally collected Schmidt gave a tearful farewell. The fans voted him a National League All-Star afterward a final time.

Schmidt was given the 1983 Lou Gehrig Memorial Award, presented to the player best exemplifying the character of its namesake. The Phillies retired his uniform #20 in 1990, and he was elected a first-ballot National Baseball Hall of Famer in 1995. Schmidt placed 28th on *The Sporting News* 1999 list of the "100 Greatest Baseball Players."

He was elected to Major League Baseball's All-Century Team with the highest vote count of any third baseman. The Phillies paid Schmidt tribute with a large dramatic statue just outside the third base gate at the Phillies' new Citizens Bank Ballpark.

Schmidt continues to opine on a variety of baseball issues including his support for the reinstatement of Pete Rose. His golf tournament, the Mike Schmidt Bahamas Winners Circle Invitational, has raised over $1 million for charities. He resides in Jupiter, Florida with his wife Donna. They have raised two children- Jessica and Jonathan.

MIKE SCIOSCIA

Los Angeles Dodgers
Catcher

1980-1992

M ike Scioscia played more games back of the plate (1,395) than any other Dodger. The undisputed Dodgers team leader, he played a critical role on the 1981 and 1988 World Series championship clubs. Scioscia ranks on the Dodgers all-time lists in games played, hits, doubles, total bases and walks. He never played any defensive position other than catcher.

The burly 6' 2" 230-pound Scioscia showed off a cannon arm and was renowned for his plate-blocking ability. In 1985, he was steamrolled by the Cardinals' Jack Clark and knocked unconscious, but still held onto the ball. In another collision in 1986, the Giants' Chili Davis hit him so hard at home plate that he and Davis were both knocked out cold.

The durable Scioscia missed most of 1983 with a torn rotator cuff, but played 100 or more games each year for the rest of his career, earning a .988 fielding percentage and leading National League catchers in total chances three times and assists twice. On the all-time catcher lists, he ranks high with 8,335 putouts (13th) and 9,186 total chances (14th).

Scioscia was especially respected by his pitching staff for his uncanny knowledge of NL hitters. After a game, he could recall the location and velocity of every offering thrown by his pitchers. He caught great hurlers such as Orel Hershiser, Don Sutton and Fernando Valenzuela and was the backstop for no-hitters tossed by Valenzuela (1990) and Kevin Gross (1992).

Scioscia was a solid contact hitter, striking out fewer than once every 14 at-bats over his career. He led the National League in 1987, striking out only once every 20 at-bats and was sometimes used in the #2 slot, most unusual for a big man with below average foot speed. In his best year in 1985, he hit .296 and finished second in the NL with a .407 on-base percentage.

★ ★ ★ ★ ★

Michael Lorri Scioscia was born on Thanksgiving Day, November 27, 1958 to Florence and Fred Scioscia, Sr. in Upper Darby Township, Delaware County, Pennsylvania. He grew up with an older brother and sister in a Sicilian Catholic family and was raised in the same neighborhood where his future Dodger manager Tommy Lasorda grew up.

Scioscia's father was a local beer distributor and his mother was a first grade teacher. A three-sport star before graduating from Delaware County's Springfield High in 1976, he hit .532 as a sophomore and was the 1975 and 1976 Delaware County Baseball Player of Year.

Scioscia was drafted by the Dodgers in the first round with the 19th pick overall in the 1976 amateur draft. Three weeks later, the Dodgers were in Philadelphia to play the Phillies and then third-base coach Lasorda invited him to Veterans Stadium to work out and talk. Afterward, he turned down a full-ride scholarship to Clemson University and signed with scout John O'Neil.

Scioscia climbed steadily through the Dodgers farm system with stops at Class-A Short Season Bellingham (1976); Class-A Clinton (1977); and Double-A San Antonio (1978). He hit .336 in 1979 for the Triple-A Albuquerque (NM) Dukes in the Pacific Coast League and made his major league debut on April 20, 1980, going 1-for-3 with a double against the Astros.

Scioscia took over full time catching duties in 1981 when Fernando Valenzuela arrived. To communicate better with the rookie phenom, he learned Spanish. He hit a homer in the 1981 NLCS Game 1 versus the Expos and contributed to his team's first World Series title since 1965.

In the 1988 NLCS Game 4, the Mets were one strike away from going up three games to one on the Dodgers when Scioscia pumped out a dramatic, game-tying two-run homer off Doc Gooden. The Dodgers went on to win in extra innings and ultimately prevailed in the Series.

"When you evaluate him, you can really only describe Mike one way. Irreplaceable."

~ battery mate Orel Hershiser

G	AB	R	H	2B	3B	HR	RBI	SB	BB	SO	BA	OBP	SLG	TB
1441	4373	398	1131	198	12	68	446	29	567	307	.259	.344	.356	1557

Scioscia's final game was on October 2, 1992, at age 33. Still convinced he had another year in him, he went to the Padres in 1993, only to sustain another torn rotator cuff during spring training. He made another failed comeback attempt with the Rangers in 1994 and then retired.

After his active career, Scioscia was hired back by the Dodgers as a minor league catching coordinator for 1995 and 1996 and then as the bench coach for former team-mate Billy Russell in 1997 and 1998. He skippered the Dodgers' affiliate Albuquerque Dukes in 1999.

New general manager Bill Stoneman took him on to manage the Angels for the 2000 season. In only his third year, he led the Angels to their first world title. His Halos dispensed with the Yankees in the ALDS, the Twins in the ALCS, and the Giants in the Fall Classic. He was *Baseball America's* 2002 Major League Manager of the Year.

Scioscia's 2002 title team broke the franchise season win mark with 99, and his 2008 club eclipsed that total with 100 wins. He is the Angels' all-time leader in games-managed and wins. In 2009, Scioscia was honored a second time as the Major League Manager of the Year.

After his Angels defeated the Indians on May 8, 2011, he became the 56th manager to win 1,000 games and the 23rd to have all 1,000 victories with a single team. He is the first man to reach the playoffs in six of his first ten seasons and the longest tenured major league manager.

Scioscia and his wife, the former Anne Mellqueham, have been married since January 26, 1985. Anne famous-ly met her husband by bringing him cookies at Dodger Stadium. They have two children, Matthew and Taylor, and live in Westlake Village, California.

Scioscia's charitable and civic contributions include his involvement with the American Heart Association, the American Red Cross, the Make a Wish Foundation and an outreach program for United States military per-sonnel serving overseas.

MARIO SOTO

CINCINNATI REDS
RIGHT-HANDED PITCHER

1977-1988

"When Soto gets on the mound, he also has the best combination of fastball and change-up in the game today. He is no bully who pushes people around but an artist who uses the baseball as deftly as if he had a paintbrush in his right hand."

~ writer Murray Chass

Mario Soto was one of baseball's most accomplished pitchers of the 1980s. He struck out 1,248 National League hitters from 1980 to 1985, the most by any pitcher. A three-time All-Star, Soto finished his career ranked only behind Jim Maloney on the Reds' All-Time Strikeout List.

The durable 6' 180-pound Soto hurled four years with 200+ innings and three years with over 200 strikeouts. He led the NL in complete games twice while topping the league in home runs allowed three times. Soto was the Reds Opening Day starter five straight years (1982-86).

In his prime following the Big Red Machine era, he never received the kind of acclaim he deserved due to the second-rate teams behind him. The 1982 and 1983 Reds Most Valuable Player, Soto relied on a mid-90s rising fastball that seemed to explode through the hitting zone.

He also developed three different changeups. Holding them in his three end fingers, Soto threw one that broke away like a circle curve; another that broke in like a screwball; and one that dropped down off the table. Over half of his strikeouts came off his changeups.

Soto was essentially a two-pitch performer, throwing his fastball and his lethal changeup repertoire with the same arm speed and from exactly the same three-quarters release point. His changeup was probably the best and most deceiving changeup in Major League Baseball.

★　★　★　★　★

Mario Melvin Soto was born on July 12, 1956 in Bani, Peravia Province in The Dominican Republic of Chilean ancestry. His parents separated when he was eight, causing his mother to take work doing laundry from the Dominican Air Force to make meager ends meet.

Soto dropped out of school when he was 14 years old to go to work as a mason. He didn't even start pitching until local baseball godfather Juan Melo persuaded him

to try. Reds bird-dog Johnny Sierra watched him for a few months and scout George Zuraw signed him as a project on December 3, 1973 for a $1,000 bonus. He was only 17.

Soto was sent to the Billings (MT) Mustangs (Pioneer League) in 1974, but hurt his arm trying to learn a slider. After his 1975 season with the Eugene (OR) Emeralds (Northwest League), his 13-7 line and 1.86 ERA in 1976 with the Tampa Tarpons (Florida State League) earned him a promotion to the Triple-A Indianapolis (IN) Indians of the American Association.

Soto was the AA strikeout leader when he made his major league debut on July 21, 1977 at age 21. He had pitched for just four years and was still raw. At Indy in 1977 and 1978, Soto refined the devastating changeup he picked up from Reds roving instructor Scott Breeden.

In his first three seasons, Soto pitched just 116 innings, not including the two innings he threw in relief versus the Pirates in the 1979 NLCS. The league began to take notice of him in 1980. He worked in short and long relief and as a starter, yet still was #3 in the NL with 182 Ks.

Soto paced the NL with 25 starts in 1981 and was third with 151 strikeouts. He was a 1982 All-Star and became the Reds' single-season leader with 274 strikeouts, leading the league with 9.57 Ks per nine innings. He also equaled a Reds mark by fanning four Cubs in one inning.

Soto was 17-13 in 1983 with a 2.70 ERA and 242 strikeouts, hurling for a last place club. The Cy Young runner up behind the Phillies' John Denny, he won the 1983 Buck Canel Award as baseball's most outstanding Latin American and started the All-Star game at Comiskey Park.

As the Reds' #1 ace in 1983 and 1984, he was 35-20 with a 2.92 ERA despite hurling for mediocre teams. On May 12, 1984, he came within a strike of throwing a no-hitter. With two out in the top of the ninth, the Cards' George Hendrick hit a homer before the Reds got the win, 2-1.

G	IP	W	L	PCT	SHO	GS	CG	H	ER	SO	BB	ERA
297	1730.1	100	92	.521	13	224	72	1395	667	1449	657	3.47

However, later in the summer, Soto showed his fiery temperamental side on the mound. He was suspended on two separate occasions for on-field altercations. Notwithstanding, he was chosen a National League All-Star again, and won a career-high 18 games.

The hiring of Pete Rose as the Reds manager in August of 1984 caused almost immediate adverse consequences for Soto. Up until Rose, he had gone seven seasons starting games on only three days' rest back-to-back seven times. His first start under Rose was on three days' rest.

In his next start, Soto was pulled after giving up six earned runs in three innings. Instead of going to the DL with biceps tendinitis, Soto rested for 11 days and took the mound again. The 1984 Reds were 22 games out of first in the final game, but Rose again started Soto on three days' rest. He pitched a complete game victory, 7-6, faced 39 hitters, and threw over 150 pitches.

Rose started Soto on three days' rest 19 times in his 36 starts in 1985. Despite his 12-15 record, he finished second in the National League in strikeouts. Soto was never quite right after that season. By 1986, it became evident that he had developed chronic shoulder problems.

Soto was given the ball at Riverfront Stadium on Opening Day 1988, but his arm was shredded. He pitched his last big-league game on June 16. After the Reds released him, Soto attempted a brief one-game comeback with the Bakersfield (CA) Dodgers but he was finished.

Soto is as quiet and self-effacing off the mound as he was intense and emotional on it. He has worked as a Reds pitching instructor, teaching several young hurlers the changeup, including Edinson Vólquez and Johnny Cueto. It is now a strikeout pitch for each.

He and his wife Jacqueline Arias raised a daughter, Stephaneli Mariel Soto Arias. Mario Soto was inducted into the Cincinnati Reds Hall of Fame in 2001 and currently works in the Reds front office.

PAUL SPLITTORFF

KANSAS CITY ROYALS
LEFT-HANDED PITCHER

1970-1984

"Paul didn't have that electric slider or that devastating curveball. But he was always steady and he was always studied, always worked hard to do his very best. That's why he was so successful both on and off the field."

~ teammate Frank White

Paul Splittorff became a key member of the Royals' glory years teams, helping Kansas City to four post-season appearances and its first World Series in 1980. The Royals' most reliable pitcher from 1972 to 1980, he averaged almost 15 victories and 220 innings per year and finished his career as the franchise's all-time leader with 166 wins, 2,554²/₃ innings pitched and 392 starts.

Despite his impressive success on the mound, Splittorff was never an American League All-Star. Underpublicized compared to more high profile Royals hurlers such as Steve Busby, David Cone, Dennis Leonard and Bret Saberhagen, he won more games than any of them. A fierce competitor, Splittorff was particularly effective in the Royals' memorable playoff confrontations with the New York Yankees in the 1970s and 1980s. In seven postseason appearances, he was 2-0 with a 2.79 ERA.

What Splittorff lacked in natural ability he made up for in an uncompromising work ethic. The big, blonde 6'3" 205-pound left-hander did not throw hard, but had superior command of several pitches, and was meticulously prepared for each start. Not the most outgoing Royal in the clubhouse, he was content to go about his business and let his pitching do the talking.

The high-kicking, bespectacled "Splitt" often appeared to squint into his catcher as if he was having trouble seeing the signs. This proved disconcerting to some hitters who weren't quite certain if the tall left-hander could really pick out where he was throwing the horsehide.

★ ★ ★ ★ ★

Paul William Splittorff, Jr. was born in Evansville, Indiana on October 8, 1946 to Bettye Reckner and Paul William Splittorff, Sr. He grew up mostly in Arlington Heights, Illinois, where he graduated from Arlington High School after excelling in both basketball and baseball.

Splittorff continued as a two-sport star at Morning-side College, an NAIA school in Sioux City, Iowa and was a star on the 1967 USA Gold Medalist Team in the Pan American Games. He was taken by the expansion Royals in the 25th round of their first draft class of 1968 before the franchise ever had played a single game, making him a true original Royal.

Hurling for the 1968 Corning (NY) Royals in the low Class-A New York-Penn League before the parent club even existed, Splittorff tossed the first pitch in Royals organization history. He went 28–27 with a 4.01 ERA in three seasons in the Royals farm system before receiving his major league debut call on September 23, 1970. He pitched seven strong innings and gave up only three earned runs, but took the loss against the Chicago White Sox.

Splittorff began the 1971 season with the Omaha (NE) Royals of the Triple-A International League, but after going 5–2 with a 1.48 ERA in eight starts, he soon earned his way back to the bigs. The rest of the season, he produced an 8–9 line with a 2.68 ERA and became a fixture in the rotation. He and his wife Lynn Litterick moved into their permanent home in Blue Springs, Missouri that year where they raised their daughter Jennifer and son Jamie.

Splittorff started the inaugural game at Royals Stadium on April 10, 1973 and earned the victory in a 12–1 trouncing of the Rangers. He was the Kansas City Royals 1973 Pitcher of the Year after becoming the franchise's first 20-game winner, going 20–11 with a 3.98 ERA.

After finishing second to the Oakland Athletics three out of Splittorff's first five major league campaigns, the Royals finally broke through to be the AL Western Division champions in 1976. Kansas City faced the Yankees in each ALCS from 1976 to 1978, but the Bombers won all three years. It was not Splittorff's fault. He went 2–0

G	IP	W	L	PCT	SHO	GS	CG	H	ER	SO	BB	ERA
429	2554.2	166	143	.537	17	392	88	2644	1082	1057	780	3.81

with a 2.84 ERA in five appearances.

The Royals and Yanks resumed their postseason rivalry in 1980. Splittorff started the Game 3 finale as the Royals swept. In the Fall Classic, Kansas City just could not get past the Phillies, losing in six games. Splittorff's only appearance was $1^2/_3$ innings in the Game 6 finale.

In 1984, with the Royals on the cusp of developing a number of young quality pitchers out of their farm system, Splittorff saw his effectiveness decline significantly. After going 1-3 with a 7.71 ERA in 28 innings pitched, he retired. His final game was on June 26, 1984.

Splittorff embarked on a 24-year run as the Royals' popular Fox Sports Kansas City TV color commentator. Well prepared as always, he infused keen insight and humor into each telecast. He also worked as an analyst for Big Eight and Big 12 college basketball.

Splittorff was enshrined in the Kansas City Royals Hall of Fame in 1987. He was also inducted into the Morningside College Hall of Fame; the NAIA Hall of Fame; the Greater Siouxland Athletic Association Hall of Fame; and the Missouri Sports Hall of Fame.

On Opening Day 2009, Kansas Citians noted that his speech was slurred and wondered if he had had a stroke. Splittorff had chosen to keep his mortal battle with melanoma and oral cancer private. Though he did pregame and postgame shows, he was never again able to regain the clear, distinct voice that fans had grown to appreciate for more than two decades.

On May 16, 2011, Splittorff finally decided to make his health struggles public. Only nine days later on May 25, he passed away at his home at age 64. The Royals wore a memorial patch on their uniform jersey sleeves for the rest of 2011 out of respect for one of the most beloved and greatest Royals hurlers ever.

MIKE SQUIRES

CHICAGO WHITE SOX
FIRST BASE

1975 • 1977-1985

"I've seen, played with, and played against some of the finest first basemen in the game, but I've never seen one as nifty with the mitt as Mike Squires."

~ coach Hugh Mulcahy

Versatile Mike Squires was best known as a gifted defensive player, manning every major league position on the field except shortstop and second base. In a genuinely unique baseball career, he played a left-handed third base, catcher, outfield, and even pitcher.

The 1981 American League *Rawlings* Gold Glove award winner at first base, he was known as a Super Sub and defensive specialist. He could really pick it, saving many an errant throw in the dirt and showing cat-like agility on bunts and hot grounders scalded in his direction.

The 5'11" 185-pound Squires didn't have the power numbers of a model corner infielder, but he was a valuable member of manager Tony LaRussa's clubs. He led all 1983 Junior Circuit first basemen in fielding at .992, helping the White Sox grab the AL Western Division title.

The left-handed Squires had his best offensive season in 1980, batting .283. When playing regularly, he hit second in the lineup as a line-drive hitter with a good eye. He stroked the ball to the opposite field often, walked more than he struck out, and was an adept bunter.

★　★　★　★　★

Michael Lynn Squires was born to Donna Jean Teal and Lynn Duane Squires on March 5, 1952 in Kalamazoo, Michigan. His father was a semi-pro catcher and had his young left-handed son catching in Little League using a first baseman's glove. Squires also played ice hockey as a goalie which helped him to develop his hand-eye coordination and quick hands attempting to stop the fast-moving puck.

Growing up halfway between Detroit and Chicago, he was a Tigers fan with Norm Cash his favorite player. Squires excelled at Kalamazoo Central High mostly as a pitcher but also as an outfielder and first baseman. He was not chosen in the 1969 June free agent amateur draft.

After two years at Kalamazoo Valley Community College in 1970 and 1971, Squires went on to star at Western Michigan University. He paced the 1972 Broncos with a

.300 average and was selected an All-Mid-American Conference outfielder the next year. The White Sox drafted him in the 18th round, and he signed with scouts Pete Milito and George Sobek.

Squires' professional career started with the 1973 Appleton (WI) Foxes of the Class-A Midwest League. In 1974 and 1975 with the Knoxville (TN) White Sox of the Double-A Southern League, he batted .287 and .304 respectively. Squires set new standards for SL first basemen in 1974 with 76 straight errorless games, as well as lowest number of errors (5) while fielding .995. He was honored as the 1975 Southern League Most Valuable Player.

The 23-year-old Squires earned his major league debut on Labor Day, September 1, 1975, in the second game of a doubleheader against the Royals at White Sox Park. He grounded into a double play in his first at-bat, but then went 2-for-3 with a walk in the 3-1 loss.

He spent portions of the 1976, 1977 and 1978 campaigns with the Triple-A Iowa Oaks, hitting .253, .323 and .312 in that order. He topped all 1976 American Association first basemen in fielding (.995) and did it again in 1978. He got into only three ChiSox games in 1977.

On May 4, 1980, Squires became the first left-handed catcher to appear in a big-league game since the Phillies' Chris Short in 1961. He caught the final frame of an 11-1 route by the Brewers and caught an errorless ninth again three days later, replacing Bruce Kimm each time.

Only a few lefties, usually slick-fielding first basemen, have played third base in the big leagues. In the 1980s, only two did … the Yankees' Don Mattingly once in 1986 and Squires.

At Kansas City on August 23, 1983, he became the first left-handed third baseman in almost 50 years, dating back to the Nationals' Joe Kuhel in 1936. Squires entered for Vance Law in the bottom of the eighth and made 13 more appearances at third base in 1984, including four starts.

G	AB	R	H	2B	3B	HR	RBI	SB	BB	SO	BA	OBP	SLG	TB
779	1580	211	411	53	10	6	141	45	143	108	.260	.321	.318	502

He also played the outfield and even took the mound once to retire the only man he faced. On April 22, 1984, he threw three pitches to the Tigers' Tom Brookens, inducing him to hit a fly ball to center field to end the inning. They would be the only three pitches of Squires' career.

From 1982 through 1984, LaRussa regularly employed him as a late-inning defensive replacement. Squires had only 153 at-bats in 143 games in 1983. When the White Sox clinched their first Western Division title that year, his teammates chose Squires, an 11-year veteran of the Sox organization, to hoist the American League pennant flag.

Squires played his final major league game on September 24, 1985, at age 33. He served as an advance scout with the Athletics in 1986, coached for the Toronto Blue Jays from 1989 to 1991, and returned to the White Sox in 1993 as a coach. He then spent 14 years as a major-league scout with the Cardinals before taking his current scouting job with the Reds in 2008.

Squires is an inductee of the Kalamazoo Central High Athletics Hall of Fame and the Western Michigan University Athletics Hall of Fame. He currently works as a scout and special assistant to Reds general manager Walt Jocketty. He has been scouting games for over a quarter of a century, still traveling regularly to Detroit, Chicago, Cleveland, Minneapolis or Seattle.

Squires lives in Oshtemo Township (MI) with his wife, the former Maureen Mentor. He and Maureen went to high school and college together and have raised two daughters and a son.

The basement in his home is adorned with wall-to-wall baseball memorabilia. Framed White Sox jerseys line one of the walls and game-used *Louisville Sluggers* hang from bat racks below shelves housing dozens of encased autographed baseballs. Under the glass top on his bar are old photographs and ticket stubs. Squires' 1981 *Rawlings* Gold Glove award sits behind the bar flanked by his two *Rawlings* Silver Glove awards from the minor leagues.

BOB STANLEY

BOSTON RED SOX
RIGHT-HANDED PITCHER

1977-1989

*"I can't recall ever
managing anybody
I could use either long
or short as much
as I use him."*

*~ Red Sox manager
Ralph Houk*

Bob Stanley pitched in more games for the Red Sox than any man in history but may be more remembered as the hurler who threw the wild pitch that tied Game 6 of the 1986 World Series. Stanley was a key factor for the club that came within a strike of winning the Fall Classic.

"The Steamer" to Red Sox fans, he established the all-time Red Sox saves record with 132, surpassed by Jonathan Papelbon in 2009. The 6'4" 220-pound Stanley is the winningest pitcher native to the state of Maine. He ranked eighth in career victories for the Sox as of 2015.

★ ★ ★ ★ ★

Robert William Stanley was born on November 10, 1954 to Agnes and William Stanley in Portland, Cumberland County, Maine. His family moved to his mother's hometown of Kearney, New Jersey when he was two years old so his father could obtain better work. He was held back in second grade, which turned out to be fortuitous for him, especially athletically.

At Kearney High, Stanley bided his time for three years as a position player, watching a class of exceptional prep pitchers eat up all of the mound innings. After all of these stalwarts graduated a year ahead of him, he stepped forward as a senior, going 10-1 on the mound in 1973.

The Dodgers saw his upside, drafted him in the ninth round of the June amateur draft, and offered him a contract but he declined the Dodgers' low proposal. The Red Sox signed him as the seventh pick in the first round of the January 1974 regular phase draft.

After his rookie pro year with the Elmira Pioneers of the New York-Penn League, he pitched for Winter Haven in the Class-A Florida State League in 1975. Stanley was 0-6 before a run was scored behind him, eventually losing 17 games, but the Red Sox noted his 2.93 ERA.

His sinking fastball was already resulting in ground ball outs. Stanley was promoted to Double-A Bristol (CT)

in the Eastern League where he went 15-9 with a 2.66 ERA in 1976. After his spring showing in 1977, Red Sox skipper Don Zimmer kept him on the big club.

Stanley debuted against the Indians in Cleveland on April 16, 1977 in long relief. Allowing one run in four innings pitched, he earned the save. Stanley became "Mr. Versatility," starting 13 games and making 28 more appearances as both a long and short reliever.

He came of age in 1978, getting work in 52 games, almost all in relief. He went 15-2 for a .882 winning percentage which was second only to the Yankees' Ron Guidry with his 25-3 at .883. He had ten saves and was tops in the American League with 12 relief victories, allowing just five home runs in $141^2/_3$ innings with a 2.60 ERA.

His season culminated on September 28 with only his third start of the year. At Fenway Park, Stanley gave up only one hit to the Toronto Blue Jays until handing the ball to Dick Drago in the seventh inning. The two pitchers combined to hurl a three-hit shutout.

Based on that performance, Zimmer gave him 30 starts in 1979. Stanley won a career-best 16 games, four of them shutouts. He also hurled two scoreless innings in his first All-Star performance, shutting down a heavy-duty lineup of National League sluggers at the Kingdome.

New manager Ralph Houk rotated Stanley back into an exclusive relief role in the 1981 campaign. He led the major leagues in relief innings pitched each year from 1981 to 1983. Stanley set an American League record with $168^2/_3$ relief innings in 1982 and finished with a 12-7 mark and 14 saves.

Stanley arguably had his best season in 1983, finishing second in the AL to the Royals' Dan Quisenberry with a Red Sox record 33 saves and a 2.85 ERA. But in the process he tied the big-league mark of 14 blown saves held by two Hall of Famers, Rollie Fingers and Bruce Sutter.

In 1984, his losing mark of 9-10, his high salary and

G	IP	W	L	PCT	SHO	SV	GS	CG	H	ER	SO	BB	ERA
637	1707	115	97	.524	7	132	85	21	1858	690	693	471	3.64

his heavyset frame all contributed to the Fenway Faithful beginning to get on him. Red Sox Nation had not experienced a World Series title since 1918 and their angst was palpable as the Red Sox entered the 1986 postseason.

The Steamer pitched $6\frac{1}{3}$ innings in the Fall Classic, closing out four games versus the Mets with a zero ERA. However in Game 6, he entered in the bottom of the tenth with two out. The Sox needed to retire just one Met to celebrate their first Series title in almost seven decades.

With Mookie Wilson up, Stanley unleashed a wild pitch that got by catcher Rich Gedman, permitting Kevin Mitchell to score from third base. Wilson then hit the slow roller to hobbled first baseman Bill Buckner that skipped under his glove, allowing Ray Knight to score the winning run. The Red Sox has snatched defeat from the jaws of victory once again.

With frustration running rampant and the need for scapegoats, the Hub City fans saw fit to ride Stanley even more severely in 1987. He courageously pressed on, but experienced his worst year. Back as a starter again, he delivered a second rate 4-15 mark with a high 5.01 ERA.

Stanley fashioned a 6-4 line in relief in 1988, helping the Red Sox to another trip to the postseason. After a year squabbling with skipper Joe Morgan, he announced his retirement on September 25, 1989. His career postseason ERA was 2.77, but he never recorded a decision.

Stanley and his wife Joan made their home and raised their three children in Wenham, Massachusetts where he owned a landscaping company and enjoyed playing semi-pro baseball. He was honored as a member of the 2000 class of the prestigious Boston Red Sox Hall of Fame.

Stanley and his wife now live in New Hampshire's Seacoast region. He has coached for the 2012 Las Vegas 51s (Pacific Coast League); the 2013 Buffalo Bisons (International League); the 2014 Toronto Blue Jays; and the 2015 New Hampshire Fisher Cats (Eastern League).

ALAN TRAMMELL

DETROIT TIGERS
SHORTSTOP

1977-1996

"When you're talking about today's great players, Alan has to be included ... There isn't anything he doesn't do well."

~ double play partner Lou Whitaker

Alan Trammell joined Al Kaline and Ty Cobb as the only three men to play 20 or more seasons in Detroit. A six-time All-Star, four-time *Rawlings* Gold Glove winner and three-time Silver Slugger recipient, he was one of the greatest all-around players of the 1980s, batting .300 seven times, and ranked in the Tigers Top 10 in games played, hits, doubles, RBI and steals.

The 6' 165-pound Trammell had a quick release and made the routine plays as well as the spectacular ones. He partnered for 19 campaigns with Lou Whitaker to form the longest continuous double-play combination. The duo turned the most double plays in baseball history.

★　★　★　★　★

Alan Stuart Trammell was born on February 21, 1958 to Anne and Forest Trammell in Garden Grove, Orange County, California. He stood out in both basketball and baseball for San Diego's Kearny High Komets, earning All-CIF San Diego Section recognition in both sports. Trammell graduated in June of 1976 and was selected in the second round of the annual June free agent draft by the Tigers.

His minor league apprenticeship was brief. Performing for the Bristol (VA) Tigers, he was a 1976 Rookie Appalachian League South All-Star. With the Double-A Montgomery (AL) Rebels, Trammell was chosen the 1977 Southern League MVP, hitting .291 with 19 triples.

He and Whitaker were promoted in tandem, making their major league debut at Fenway Park together during the nightcap of a doubleheader on September 9, 1977. The 19-year-old Trammel singled in his first at-bat and quickly became the Tigers' everyday 1978 shortstop.

He hit an even .300 in 1980 and was a first-time All-Star. In 1983, "Tramm" was the AL Comeback Player of the Year, raising his average 61 points from 1982 to .319 with 14 home runs, 66 RBI and 30 steals, the most by a Detroit player since Cobb swiped 34 in 1917.

The Tigers leapt out to a 35-5 start in 1984, won 104 games, and cruised to the AL pennant by 15 games. Trammell produced a 20-game hitting streak during the summer, despite battling season-long shoulder tendinitis, and finished fifth in the AL batting derby at .314.

He had an inspired postseason, starting with his .363 (4-for-11) showing in the ALCS sweep of the Royals. Then Trammell batted an imposing .450 (9-for-20) as the Tigers mauled the Padres in the Fall Classic in five games. His pair of two-run homers in Game 4 accounted for all the scoring in a 4-2 victory. Trammell was an easy choice as World Series Most Valuable Player.

In 1985, hamstrung by injuries, he batted just .258, and opted for postseason surgery on his left knee and right shoulder. Fully healed in 1986, Trammell became only the second Tiger after his friend Kirk Gibson to hit 20 home runs and steal 20 bases. He also knocked in 75 runs.

Manager Sparky Anderson asked him to hit cleanup in 1987. Trammell responded with career-highs of .343 and 28 homers as the first Tiger to register 200 hits and 100 RBI in a season since Kaline in 1955. He hit .416 in September to help grab the AL East title on the last day.

Tramm was among the '87 AL leaders in almost every offensive category including 109 runs scored, 205 hits, 329 total bases, 105 RBI, .402 OBA, .551 slugging percentage, .953 OPS and 16 game-winning RBI. He was just edged out by Toronto's George Bell in the MVP voting.

Trammell followed with another All-Star year in 1988, hitting .311, but nagging injuries curtailed his playing time in 1989 to just 121 games. He hit only .243. After getting back his health in 1990, he batted .304 with 170 hits and 89 RBI to again make the AL All-Star squad.

Trammell performed mainly as a backup in his last three seasons starting in 1994, averaging just 72 games a year. He saw action at second base, third base, shortstop, left field, center field, and as a designated

G	AB	R	H	2B	3B	HR	RBI	SB	BB	SO	BA	OBP	SLG	TB
2293	8288	1231	2365	412	55	185	1003	236	850	874	.285	.352	.415	3442

hitter. He singled in his last at-bat on September 29, 1996.

After two years in the Detroit front office, Trammell was the 1999 Tigers hitting coach. He moved on to be the Padres first base coach until being named the Tigers manager on October 9, 2002. The team sustained 119 losses in Trammell's first year, an AL record, barely avoiding the stigma of being the team with the most losses in history. The 1962 Mets went 42-120.

Trammell piloted Detroit to a 72–90 record in 2004, a 29-victory improvement. It was the second-largest jump in franchise history behind the 1961 Tigers' 30-win increase. With his close friend and Tiger teammate Kirk Gibson as his bench coach for three years, he went 186-300.

After being replaced by Jim Leyland, Trammell sat out the entire 2006 season before being hired on by the Cubs to be manager Lou Piniella's bench coach. In 2007 and 2008, the Cubbies won the NL Central Division back-to-back for the first time in franchise history.

Although Trammell has not yet been enshrined in the National Baseball Hall of Fame, he has been inducted into the National Polish American Sports Hall of Fame in 1998, the San Diego Breitbard Hall of Fame in 1998 and the Michigan Sports Hall of Fame in 2000.

In 1999, Detroit fans voted Trammell as the shortstop on the All-Time Tigers Team. He was rated as the ninth best shortstop ever by *The New Bill James Historical Baseball Abstract* in 2001. Sabermetrician James ranked him high-

er than 14 Hall of Fame shortstops.

Trammell was the Diamondbacks bench coach for manager Kirk Gibson in a reversal of roles from 2011 to 2013. He and his wife, Barbara Jean Leverett, live in Pa-

cific Beach, California and have raised two sons (Lance and Kyle) and a daughter (Jade). He currently serves as a Tigers special assistant. In the offseason Trammell is a keynote platform speaker.

JOHN WATHAN

KANSAS CITY ROYALS
CATCHER • FIRST BASE

1976-1985

"When you talk about John Wathan, you're not talking about catchers, you're talking about athletes."

~ Gene Mauch

John Wathan's major league career corresponded exactly with the best ten-year stretch in Royals franchise history. During those glory years, he was the extraordinary big catcher that not only had the brawn to put on the tools of ignorance but also had the foot speed to steal bases.

The 6'2" 205-pound Wathan was an agile receiver with a strong accurate arm. Although he never displayed consistent power, Wathan hit .300 or more three seasons. He consistently put his *Louisville Slugger* on the ball, striking out a mere 265 times in 2,764 plate appearances.

Later a successful Royals manager, Wathan led his team to runner up finishes in the American League West Division in 1988 and 1989. His .515 percentage (287-270) remains fourth on the Royals' all-time list behind only Whitey Herzog, Jim Frey and Dick Howser.

★ ★ ★ ★ ★

John David Wathan was born on October 4, 1949 to Mary and James Wathan in Cedar Rapids, Linn County, Iowa. His parents divorced when he was two years old and his mother took him to live in San Diego where he came up through the youth leagues and American Legion.

Wathan attended small private Saint Augustine High School in San Diego, starring in football, basketball and baseball. In his senior year in 1967, he was chosen All-Eastern League, but was only recruited by his hometown NCAA College Division University of San Diego.

Under coach John Cunningham, he was All-Southern California Athletic Conference at first base as a freshman and repeated in 1969 as a catcher. As the Toreros MVP in 1970, Wathan hit .430, led the College Division with 61 hits, and stole 30 bases as an NCAA All-American.

Competing in the summer California Collegiate League, he led the USA team to a second place finish in the 1970 World Amateur Baseball Tournament. Royals Scouts Spider Jorgensen and Ross Gilhousen took him

fourth overall in the first round of the January 1971 draft.

During spring training Wathan married his college sweetheart, Nancy Brown, and shortly the Royals sent him to Waterloo (IA) in the Class-A Midwest League. With only 43 games under his belt, he earned a promotion to the California League's High-A San Jose Bees.

In 1972, Wathan jumped from Single-A San Jose to Double-A Jacksonville all the way up to finish out the season at Triple-A Omaha (NE). He lost 1973 to a dislocated shoulder in May, but hit .319 in 120 games in 1974 at Jacksonville, prompting a recall back up to Omaha.

In 1975, Wathan hit .303 for Omaha in 360 at-bats as the American Association's All-Star catcher. After a brief stay at Omaha again, Wathan got his debut on May 26, 1976. He capped his year by catching Larry Gura's AL West-clinching shutout in late September.

Wathan batted .329 in 1977 and saw action in four ALCS games. He hit an even .300 in 1978 while catching and filling in at first base. In his first three years, the Royals won the American League West but were frustrated by the Yankees, losing each year in the playoffs.

The 1979 year turned tragic when his 65-year-old mother was stabbed to death on June 10 in San Diego. Grief-stricken, he had a difficult season, hitting only .206. Even so, he broke John Mayberry's Royals first base errorless games mark of 57 and went on to record 90 straight.

Wathan hit .305 in 453 at-bats as a major contributor to the 1980 American League Champion Royals, demonstrating remarkable versatility. He played in 77 games at catcher, 19 in left field, 17 in right field and 12 at first base to receive mention in the American League Most Valuable Player voting.

Now in his prime, Wathan had become valuable for his defensive skills, veteran knowledge and base stealing. He swiped 36 bases in 1982 in 121 games to break Hall-

G	AB	R	H	2B	3B	HR	RBI	SB	BB	SO	BA	OBP	SLG	TB
860	2505	305	656	90	35	21	261	105	199	265	.262	.318	.343	859

of-Famer Ray Schalk's 1916 mark of 30 steals by a catcher, despite being out a month with a broken ankle.

His final role was in the All-Missouri 1985 Fall Classic against the Cardinals in Game 6. Dick Howser put him in to pinch-run for Hal McRae in the bottom of the ninth with the bases full and the Royals trailing, 1-0. Dane Iorg knocked in the two ahead of Wathan for the walk-off win and the Royals got their world championship when they romped in the Game 7 finale.

Wathan retired on top that winter. He went from Royals coach in 1986 to Omaha Royals skipper in early 1987 to Royals manager on August 28, 1987, replacing Billy Gardner. After a solid run, the front office replaced him after his 1991 club came out of the starting gate at 15-22.

He moved over to the California Angels as the third base coach for 1992. That May, the Angels' team bus crashed on the Jersey Turnpike and manager Buck Rodgers was seriously injured. Wathan took over as interim manager, going 39-50 the rest of the way.

He was the Angels' bench coach in 1993 but was only tendered a minor league coaching position for 1994. Wathan put in time as the Red Sox bullpen coach for a season and, after taking a hiatus in 1995, was chosen to be the Royals television color commentator for two years.

For the next decade he worked as a scout and a minor league instructor for a number of organizations. Wathan returned to the Royals in 2006 as a roving base running and bunting instructor and was named special assistant to the director of player development in 2008.

Wathan's sons both played professional baseball- Derek was in the minors from 1998 to 2008 and Dusty made it all the way to the Royals briefly in 2002. Dusty is the manager of the Clearwater Threshers, the Phillies entry in the Florida State League. John Wathan and his wife still live locally in Blue Springs, Missouri, just outside of Kansas City.

BILL WEGMAN

MILWAUKEE BREWERS
RIGHT-HANDED PITCHER

1985-1995

"I think baseball is the greatest sport in the world to celebrate its history. I think [the Brewers Wall of Honor] is the kind of thing that strengthens a franchise, that gives fans a link to the past and allows generations to connect."

~ fellow Brewer inductee
Craig Counsell

Bill Wegman was a workhorse for Brewers teams that could have given him much more run support. His won/lost percentage did not accurately reflect the quality of his work. Toiling over 190 innings in five seasons, Wegman is on the Brewers' all-time top ten lists for innings pitched, appearances, games started, complete games and victories. He ranks #3 all-time for the Brewers in career wins-above-replacement behind only Ben Sheets and Teddy Higuera at 16.2.

The 6'6" 220-pounder was a control pitcher who spotted his live fastball well and also had an effective, hard-breaking slider. Extremely athletic, he had the best range factor of any major league pitcher in both 1991 and 1992. When pitching well, the superstitious right-hander insisted on wearing the same cap even though it was crusty with sweat, pine tar and dirt.

★　★　★　★　★

William Edward Wegman, Jr. was born on December 19, 1962 to Sandra Lee Huston and William Edward Wegman, Sr. in Cincinnati, Hamilton County, Ohio. His grandfather and father both owned taverns, purveying liquor to a hard-drinking clientele. Growing up in the same Cincy neighborhood as hit king Pete Rose, his father played ball with "Charlie Hustle" growing up.

Wegman's father coached him through Little League. He starred at Oak Hills High School where he was a 1981 All-Ohio State honorable mention shortstop, third baseman and pitcher. The first team All-Ohio shortstop was future Hall of Famer Barry Larkin of the Reds.

Wegman was taken by Milwaukee in the fifth round of the 1981 amateur draft. Picked as an infielder, the Brewers brass liked his rangy frame and arm strength, projecting him as a pitcher. He helped the rookie Pioneer League Butte (MT) Copper Kings to a title that summer.

After a successful turn with Class-A Beloit (WI) of the Midwest League in 1982 (12-6, 2.81 ERA), Wegman hurled for the 1982 Stockton (CA) Ports and paced the California League with 15 complete games, 16 wins and a 1.30 ERA to win the Ray Scarborough Award as the Brewers' Minor League Player of the Year. That year he married Kimberly Fay Santa in July.

Wegman had stints in 1984 with the Double-A El Paso Diablos of the Texas League and the Vancouver (BC) Canadians of the Triple-A Pacific Coast League. He returned to the Canadians for the 1985 season to gobble up 188 innings, win ten games and post a 4.01 ERA.

Wegman made his major league debut at age 22 on September 14, 1985 against Boston at Milwaukee's County Stadium. With his family looking on, he faced 26 Red Sox and gave up only two earned runs in seven innings with no decision. By 1986, Wegman had secured a place in the Brewers' starting rotation, finishing that year at 5-12, and improved to 12-11 in 1987.

In November of 1988, Wegman experienced a Christian conversion and entered the Brewers clubhouse in the spring of 1989 reformed. He was no longer interested in drinking with many of his Brew Crew teammates and they initially mocked him for his transformation.

In late May of 1989, Wegman had surgery on his shoulder to repair his labrum and remove calcium deposits, shutting him down for the year. In 1990, surgery on his elbow for ulnar collateral ligament repair, bone spurs and bone chips put him out for all but $29^2/_3$ innings pitched.

Wegman came all the way back to be the ace of the Brewers staff in 1991. He won a career-high 15 games with a 2.84 ERA and a 1.12 WHIP. After the season, he won the 1991 Hutch Award as the best exemplification of the fighting spirit of the late Fred Hutchinson.

Wegman and Jaime Navarro were the best pitchers on the 1992 Brewers 90-72 team that finished four games behind the eventual world titlist Blue Jays. He absorbed a number of hard luck losses, going only 13-15 despite a solid

G	IP	W	L	PCT	SHO	GS	CG	H	ER	SO	BB	ERA
262	1482.1	81	90	.474	4	216	33	1567	685	696	352	4.16

3.20 ERA in a career- high 261²/₃ innings pitched.

Emblematic of that year on September 11, Wegman took a hard fought complete-game loss opposite Orioles ace Mike Mussina, 3-2. He came back to pitch a ten-inning four-hitter on October 1, retiring the last 13 Mariners he faced in a row to pull his club within two of Toronto.

Entering the 1993 season, Wegman had already thrown over 2,000 professional innings and his effectiveness began to erode. In one of his last complete games on May 7, he tossed a four-hit masterpiece on only 94 pitches but lost 1-0 to the Red Sox. The only run was unearned.

Wegman transitioned to a bullpen role in his final year, making just four starts out of 37 appearances. In his last action in a Brewers uniform on October 1, 1995, manager Phil Garner inserted him in right field for the ninth inning. In his last major league at-bat, Boston's Chris Donnels hit a home run directly over his head in an 8-1 shellacking by Milwaukee.

Wegman decided to retire at age 32 to spend more time with his wife and two daughters, Tricia and Hannah, and begin a Christian ministry at Cincinnati's Faith Fellowship Church. A pastor and an influential speaker, he also had speaking engagements outside his home church.

Along with his speaking and pastoral duties which he performed without taking a salary, Wegman coached at Cincinnati's Taylor High School and hosted baseball clinics on Cincy's west side. He and his wife now reside in New Berlin, Wisconsin.

Wegman was named a starting pitcher for the *Milwaukee Journal Sentinel's* All-Decade Brewers Team of the 1990s. He was also honored as a starting pitcher on the All-Time Brewers All-Star Team along with Chris Bosio, Mike Caldwell, Teddy Higuera and Ben Sheets.

Bill Wegman was feted in the 2014 inaugural class of the Milwaukee Brewers Wall of Honor, celebrating retired Brewers who have made significant contributions to the franchise. Wegman's plaque is on the exterior facade of Miller Park adjacent to the hot corner entrance.

LOU WHITAKER

DETROIT TIGERS
SECOND BASE

1977-1995

"Those two kids [Whitaker and Trammell], they just play good every day. They're the best I've ever seen for their age. On the double plays, knowing where the ball is going to be, that's something you can't teach."

~ manager Ralph Houk, 1978

"Sweet Lou" Whitaker was one of the finest second basemen in history and a Motor City legend. He is still ninth all-time among second basemen in runs scored and RBI. Roberto Alomar, Rogers Hornsby, Joe Morgan, Ryne Sandburg and Whitaker are the only second basemen ever to score 1,000 runs, amass 2,000 hits, drive in 1,000 runs, and hit 200 home runs.

The 5'11" 160-pound Whitaker showed surprising power from the left side, launching 20 or more home runs four seasons. The winner of four *Louisville Slugger* Silver Slugger awards, he is high on the Tigers' lists for games played, at-bats, runs, hits, walks, doubles and home runs.

A five-time All-Star and three-time *Rawlings* Gold Glove award winner, Whitaker made difficult chances look easy, posting a .984 career fielding average. He topped the AL in fielding twice and is the Tigers' all-time leader in double plays (1,527) and runner up in assists (6,653).

Whitaker forever will be linked with his double play partner Alan Trammell. The two played in 1,915 games together, more than any other duo in AL history. They are among only a handful of middle infielder twosomes that earned *Rawlings* Gold Glove awards in the same year.

★ ★ ★ ★ ★

Louis Rodman Whitaker, Jr. was born on May 12, 1957 to Marion Arlene Williams and Louis Rodman Whitaker, Sr. in Brooklyn, Kings County, New York. His father was involved in criminal dealings, so his mother took her infant son to the small town of Martinsville, Virginia.

Whitaker never knew his father. His mother had limited means, but she provided a positive upbringing within a close-knit family. At Martinsville High, he excelled as a pitcher and third baseman and was taken by Detroit in the fifth round of the June 1975 amateur draft.

After scuffling at Bristol (VA) in the rookie Appalachian League, he came back to earn the 1976 Florida State League MVP award at third base with Class-A Lakeland. After-

ward, the Tigers put him at second base and paired him with another young prospect, Alan Trammell.

Whitaker and Trammell were both promoted to play for the Double-A Montgomery (AL) Rebels in 1977, and became immediate friends. Whitaker batted .280 and helped the Rebels to the Southern League title. Both youngsters were rewarded with tickets to the major leagues.

On September 9, 1977, Whitaker and Trammell made their major league debuts together in the second game of a doubleheader at Boston's Fenway Park. When the 20-year-old Whitaker stepped into the box in front of 52,528 hometown fans on Opening Day in 1978, the Motown faithful had already picked up the chant of "Loooooooou!!"

He hit .285 and paced the league with 95 double plays as the 1978 American League Rookie of the Year. However, Whitaker experienced a two-year stretch in 1980 and 1981 when he had to reinvent himself at the plate, hitting a composite .245 while learning to hit big-league pitching. He spent hours working with hitting coach Gates Brown on being more aggressive.

Whitaker returned with newfound punch for 1982. Hitting leadoff, he batted .286 and ripped 15 home runs, developing the ability to park pitches into Tiger Stadium's short right field porch. He also led AL second basemen with 470 assists, 120 twin killings and fielding (.988).

His pinnacle campaign was 1983. As the Tiger of the Year, he batted .320 to finish third in the American League batting race. With 206 hits, he was the first Tigers second baseman to collect more than 200 hits since Hall of Famer Charlie Gehringer did it in 1937.

The 1984 Tigers started the season 35-5 and finished with 104 wins, taking the AL East Division by 15 games. Whitaker hit .289 with 161 hits, 90 runs scored and 13 home runs. After sweeping the Royals in the ALCS, Detroit upended the Padres in the Fall Classic in five games.

Whitaker came out white hot in 1985 and was still #1 in

G	AB	R	H	2B	3B	HR	RBI	SB	BB	SO	BA	OBP	SLG	TB
2390	8570	1386	2369	420	65	244	1084	143	1197	1099	.276	.363	.426	3651

the AL in hitting with a .368 batting average in mid-May. He scored 102 runs with 73 RBI and 21 round trippers, including a missile that cleared the Tiger Stadium right field roof and sailed completely out of the ballpark.

In the 1986 Midsummer Classic at the Astrodome, Whitaker's two-run blast off the Mets' Doc Gooden in the second inning proved to be the margin of victory in a 3-2 AL win. He finished off another exceptional year with 95 runs scored, 20 home runs and 73 runs batted in.

In his final All-Star and Silver Slugger year of 1987, Whitaker scored 110 runs, hit 16 home runs and had 59 RBI. The 98-win Tigers faced the Twins in the ALCS only to lose in five games. Whitaker crushed his only career postseason home run off Bert Blyleven in Game 2.

He was asked to hit in the #3 spot in 1989 and responded by setting the franchise mark for a second baseman with 28 homers and knocked in a career-high 85 runs. He slammed 60 more homers from 1990 to 1992 while Detroit was going into decline. In his final three seasons, Whitaker hit a strong combined .295 and played his last game at age 38 on October 1, 1995.

Whitaker became eligible for the National Baseball Hall of Fame in 2001. He compares favorably with Hall of Fame second basemen Johnny Evers, Nellie Fox, Joe Gordon, Tony Lazzeri, Morgan, Sandburg and Red Schoendienst, but only received 2.9 percent of the votes.

Whitaker is already a 2000 inductee of the Michigan Sports Hall of Fame. In 2003, Whitaker's friend Trammell became the Tigers field manager and immediately asked him to be an instructor in spring training. He coached the Detroit infielders for nine years through 2009.

Whitaker married the former Crystal McCreary in 1979. He and his wife have raised four daughters in Lakeland, Florida. He continues to be deeply committed to his Jehovah's Witness faith, spending as many as five months a year in Christian missionary work.

FRANK WHITE

KANSAS CITY ROYALS
SECOND BASE

1973-1990

"You watch Frank at second base every day and you realize how good he is. He's got super range. He's very quick. He has sure hands, and he can throw and make the double play. I don't think anybody, anywhere, is his equal on the artificial turf."

~ *manager Whitey Herzog*

Five-time All-Star Frank White may have been the best defensive second baseman in American League history. He was the first second baseman to win six consecutive *Rawlings* Gold Gloves, eventually matched by Roberto Alomar. White won a franchise-record eight Gold Gloves as a foundational player in the Royals' glory years.

In White's first 11 years as a regular, Kansas City advanced to the postseason seven times. White and Hall of Fame teammate George Brett set a major league record by appearing in 1,914 games together over 18 campaigns.

★ ★ ★ ★ ★

Frank White, Jr. was born on September 4, 1950 to Daisie Vestula Mitchell and Frank White, Sr. in Greenville, Washington County, Mississippi. His family moved to Kansas City when he was five. Playing daily at Spring Valley and Parade Parks, White would sneak into nearby Municipal Stadium on Sundays to watch the Kansas City A's.

He attended Lincoln High, a school with no baseball team. Without a place to showcase his skills at age 20 and already married with an infant son, his last chance was to try out for owner Ewing Kaufman's new experiment, the Royals Baseball Academy.

Mr. Kaufman's inspiration was to sign great athletes with little baseball experience and train them up to be big-leaguers. White maximized his opportunity by becoming the 1971 co-captain of the charter academy class in Sarasota, Florida and the first and best to graduate to the majors. White and ex-Rangers manager Ron Washington were the most prominent graduates in the academy's four-year existence. His long career by itself made it a great investment, a model employed all over Latin America today.

White made his American League debut on June 12,

1973 in Baltimore. In his first start in Cleveland the next day, he slashed a double and a triple off crafty future Hall of Famer Gaylord Perry. His next time up, the wily Perry promptly knocked him down.

White got his first Royals Stadium start several days later in front of 40 proud friends and relatives. Getting his first look at artificial turf, he played both ends of a doubleheader in 95-degree heat on a muggy day. White could hardly walk afterward.

Complaints were legion about the early artificial turf because it was so rigid and so oppressively hot, but White turned it to his advantage. He trained year around to keep his legs and core strong, giving him endurance to thrive on the "carpet."

White quickly impressed the Royals. When popular second baseman Cookie Rojas retired, White had to overcome initial fan resentment for taking over Rojas' job. But in short order, the silky-smooth fielding White won over the Kansas City faithful with his defensive gems, a strong work ethic and his modest demeanor.

By 1977 his brilliance was apparent to all as he went 62 consecutive games without an error. In 2,323 career games played, White registered 4,942 putouts, 6,626 assists, only 205 errors, and a remarkable 1,459 double plays. His career .983 fielding average helped him lead the American League three times. He displayed unrivaled range on artificial turf and a strong throwing arm in a class by itself.

Although the 5' 11" 170-pound White came to the big-leagues without consistent power, he steadily adjusted to major league pitching. In time he became productive and used his running speed to transform many singles into sliding doubles.

White posted career-bests in 1982, hitting .298, and slugged .469 including 45 doubles, six triples and 11

G	AB	R	H	2B	3B	HR	RBI	SB	BB	SO	BA	OBP	SLG	TB
2324	7859	912	2006	407	58	160	886	178	412	1035	.255	.293	.383	3009

four-baggers. The streaky right-handed hitter demonstrated genuine power late in his career, belting 22 homers in both 1985 and 1986, and garnered the 1986 American League *Louisville Slugger* Silver Slugger award for second basemen.

Leading Kansas City to its first ever World Series appearance, White was named the 1980 AL Championship Series Most Valuable Player. He hit a stalwart .545 with six hits and three runs batted in as the Royals finally subdued the rival Yankees in a sweep.

White was also clutch in the 1985 World Series against the cross-state St. Louis Cardinals, driving in six runs with three doubles and a home run while batting cleanup. His two-run shot in Game 3 gave his Royals a 4-0 lead. It would be the Royals' first victory in their only World Series championship run of the 20th century.

White retired as a player at 39 after the 1990 season. He served as the first base coach for the Royals for four years and for the Red Sox for three. He also managed the Wichita (KS) Wranglers, the Royals' Double-A Texas League affiliate, for three years.

The popular and respected White was inducted into the Kansas City Royals Hall of Fame in 1995 and his uniform #20 was retired on May 2 of that year. A dramatic bronze statue depicting Frank White completing a double play was dedicated at Kauffman Stadium in 2004 and can be viewed on the center field mezzanine.

White worked in the Royals front office for many years and served as a part-time color commentator on Royals telecasts on FSN Kansas City. The two local baseball parks he grew up playing on have both been named in his honor. White remains a hometown hero-true Kansas City royalty. He lives in suburban Lee's Summit with his wife Teresa.

ROBIN YOUNT

MILWAUKEE BREWERS
SHORTSTOP • CENTER FIELD
1974-1993

"Someday you're going to Cooperstown, and what a wonderful thing it would be to say you played your entire career with one team, like Joe DiMaggio of the Yankees, Ted Williams of the Red Sox and Stan Musial of the Cardinals. Sign this contract and you'll go in as Yount of the Brewers."

~ Brewers owner Bud Selig to Yount in 1989

Robin Yount earned MVP awards manning two of baseball's most challenging positions while amassing more hits than any other player in the Decade of the 1980s (1,731). The only man ever to play in 1,000+ games at shortstop and 1,000+ games in the outfield, he is respected as "Mr. Brewer," the greatest player in franchise history.

As one of the first prototypal power-hitting shortstops, the 6' 185-pound Yount hit over .300 six times, scored over 100 runs five times, and knocked in over 100 runs three times. He holds almost every significant Brewers offensive record.

There are only three players who have collected more than 3,000 hits, 250 homers, 200 stolen bases and 100 triples in their careers- Willie Mays, George Brett and Yount. He was just the seventh player ever to hit 250 home runs and also steal 250 bases.

⋆　⋆　⋆　⋆　⋆

Robin Rachel Yount was born on September 16, 1955 to Marion King and Philip Arthur Yount in Danville, Vermilion County, Illinois. When he was one, his father took an aerospace engineering job and moved the family to Woodland Hills, California.

Always having to catch up to his older brother Larry's skill levels and as a late bloomer physically, Yount became resourceful early. As a 165-pound senior shortstop for the William Howard Taft High Toreadors, he hit .455 as the 1973 Los Angeles City Section Player of the Year. He was chosen third overall in the June amateur draft.

After a 64-game apprenticeship with the Newark (NJ) Co-Pilots in the New York-Penn League, the 18-year-old Yount debuted on April 5, 1974 at shortstop. By late 1975, he had broken Mel Ott's 47-year-old mark for most games played by a teenager (243).

Yount tore ligaments in his foot in a motorcycle mishap during spring training in 1978. While rehabbing, he mentioned retiring to become a professional golfer rather than being underpaid by the Brewers. The team reacted by signing him to a five-year contract.

He was an early proponent of weight training during an era when the conventional wisdom asserted a player would become muscle bound. All of the winter work on the *Nautilus* machines paid off for him in 1979 when he led the AL with 45 doubles.

The Brewers and the Orioles were in a dead heat for the 1982 AL East pennant before locking horns in the final contest. Yount finished off a dream campaign by hitting home runs in each of his first two at-bats against ace Jim Palmer to lead a romp, 10-2.

As the first unanimous Most Valuable Player in 1982, he posted career-highs, hitting .331 with 29 home runs and 114 RBI. He paced the AL with 210 hits, tied for most doubles (46), and became the first shortstop to lead the AL in slugging (.578). He received the most All-Star votes, led AL shortstops with 489 assists, and won his only *Rawlings* Gold Glove.

The Brewers made their lone 20th century Fall Classic appearance after downing the Angels for the pennant. Yount hit .414 (12-for-29) with six RBI, but couldn't quite carry his team to the Promised Land. Milwaukee succumbed to the Cardinals in seven.

In 1985, a chronic shoulder injury required his move to center field and later surgery. Embracing the move, he hit above .300 four years in a row starting in 1986, culminating in another MVP year in 1989, batting .318 with 21 homers and 103 RBI.

Yount joined Hank Greenberg and Stan Musial as the only players to win an MVP at two positions. He

G	AB	R	H	2B	3B	HR	RBI	SB	BB	SO	BA	OBP	SLG	TB
2856	11008	1632	3142	583	136	251	1406	271	996	1350	.285	.342	.430	4730

filed for free agency after the season and fans and media applied huge pressure to retain him. The club signed Yount to a new five-year pact, but he batted a composite .257 in his last four years and saw his career average drop from .299 to .285.

On September 9, 1992 against the Indians' Jose Mesa at County Stadium, Yount became the 17th man to register 3,000 hits. He reached the milestone just a week shy of his 37th birthday. Only Ty Cobb at 34 and Hank Aaron at 36 were ahead of his timetable.

Despite his aggressive approach, the durable Yount was only shelved on the disabled list twice- in 1978 and then again in 1991 with kidney stones. He retired after the 1993 season to pursue two of his other passions- pro motorcycle and auto racing.

Yount's uniform #19 was retired in 1994 and he was inducted into the Wisconsin Athletic Hall of Fame in 1995. He was elected as a first ballot National Baseball Hall of Famer with a 77.5 percent vote in 1999 as the first homegrown Brewer so honored.

Yount threw out one of the ceremonial pitches before the 2002 All-Star Game at Milwaukee's new Miller Park and a bronze statue of Yount was dedicated at the entrance. Fans can see him depicted wielding his *Louisville Slugger*, lashing out another line drive.

Yount served as first base and bench coach for the Diamondbacks from 2002 to 2004 and as bench coach for Brewers manager Ned Yost in 2006. He stepped away in 2007 but resumed in the same capacity in 2008 for new Brewers manager Dale Sveum.

Yount married his high school sweetheart Michele Edelstein after the 1977 season. The Younts raised three sons and a daughter and currently reside in Paradise Valley, Arizona outside Scottsdale. He is a frequent and popular visitor to Milwaukee.

CHAPTER SEVEN

THE STEROIDS ERA

1991-2000

Oriole Park at Camden Yards –
Baltimore, Maryland

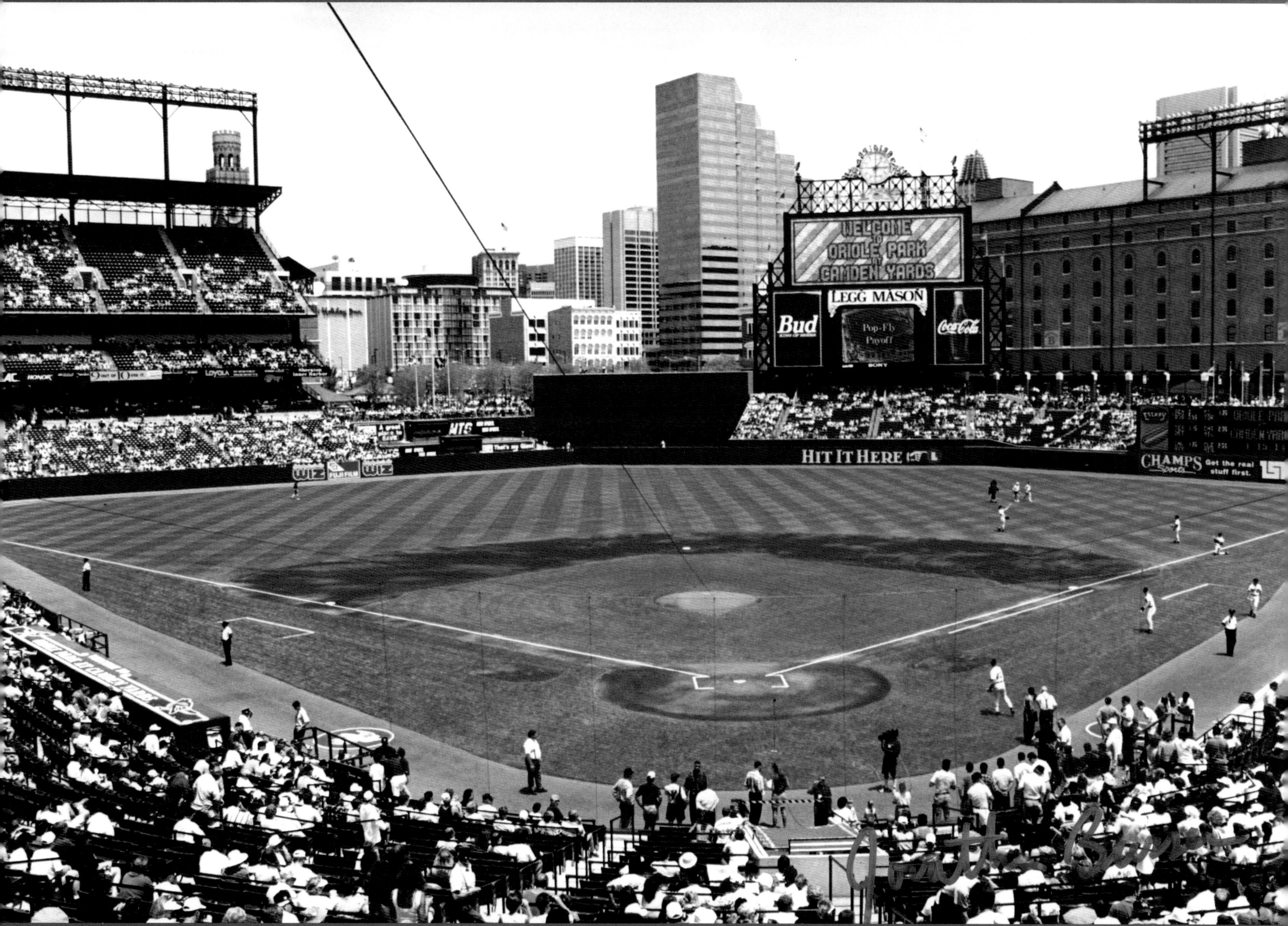

JEFF BAGWELL

HOUSTON ASTROS
FIRST BASE

1991-2005

"Something you don't see as fans, but something that we see as teammates, is the type of person he is. He was the quintessential teammate. He was a superstar who always put the team before himself. [He] always shouldered the blame when we struggled and tried to deflect the credit when we won."

~ teammate Brad Ausmus

Jeff Bagwell was the greatest slugger in Astros history. A four-time All-Star, he was the 1991 National League Rookie of the Year and 1994 Major League Player of the Year. He is the only first baseman to blast 400 home runs and steal 200 bases.

The 5'10" 195-pound Bagwell hit at least 30 home runs and scored 100 runs nine times, drove in 100+ runs eight times, and attained all three milestones for six straight years. He walked over 100 times seven years in a row and hit over .300 six times.

A three-time *Louisville Slugger* Silver Slugger winner, he walloped pitches prodigious distances but still maintained he was not a "home run hitter." The soft-spoken Bagwell was a leader in the Astros clubhouse and one of the game's most respected players. Admired for his old school durability, he played in 156+ games in ten seasons.

With his unique wide-open, crouched stance, Bagwell started in an exaggerated low position with his knees bent, looking like he was sitting on a bench. Sliding his front foot backward, he would rise from his stance to begin his swing, actually stepping back.

The 1994 *Rawlings* Gold Glove winner, Bagwell was an exceptional defensive first baseman, fielding a career .993. An adept base runner with speed and savvy, he swiped 202 bases and became the first full-time "30-30" first baseman in 1997.

* * * * *

Jeffrey Robert Bagwell was born on May 27, 1968 in Boston, Massachusetts to Janice and Robert Bagwell. He grew up in Killingworth, Connecticut as a Red Sox fan. At Xavier High in Middleton, Connecticut, he was even better at soccer than baseball.

Bagwell starred for the University of Hartford Hawks as a two-time NCAA All-American third baseman from 1987 to 1989. He set career university records of 31 home runs, 126 RBI, 293 total bases, a .413 average and a .713 slugging percentage.

Bagwell was selected in the fourth round of the 1989 amateur free agent draft by his hometown Red Sox and spent his first pro summer with the Florida Gulf Coast League Red Sox (.316) and Winter Haven in the Single-A Florida State League (.310).

He was blocked at third base by Red Sox great Wade Boggs. After hitting .333 with Double-A New Britain as the 1990 Eastern League Most Valuable Player, Bagwell was traded to the Astros for aging reliever Larry Anderson... perhaps the most one-sided swap in history.

With Ken Caminiti entrenched at third, the Astros moved him over to first base. He debuted at 22 on April 8, 1991 and went on to bat .294 with 15 homers and 82 RBI. As Houston's MVP, he was the first Astro to be the National League Rookie of the Year.

Bags had his finest year in the strike-reduced 1994 season. In only 400 at-bats, he established franchise records with 39 homers, 116 RBI, 300 total bases, and an NL-best 104 runs scored. He also posted a .750 slugging percentage which still ranks 11th all-time.

Bagwell was the obvious National League Most Valuable Player, only the fourth player to be chosen unanimously. It was the first time any National Leaguer had finished either first or second in home runs, runs batted in, runs scored, and batting average since Willie Mays did it in 1955.

Bagwell led the NL with 48 doubles in 1996 and registered 43 home runs, 135 RBI and 31 steals in 1997. He paced the league with 143 runs scored and 149 walks

G	AB	R	H	2B	3B	HR	RBI	SB	BB	SO	BA	OBP	SLG	TB
2150	7797	1517	2314	488	32	449	1529	202	1401	1558	.297	.408	.540	4213

in 1999. In 2000, Bags topped the league with 152 runs and walloped 47 homers with 132 RBI. In the following four years, he averaged 34 home runs and over 100 runs batted in.

From 2001, he contended with a gradually worsening arthritic shoulder. By 2005, it had sidelined him for all but 39 games. Bagwell was unable to throw or swing his *Louisville Slugger* with his old thunderbolt authority, but was still activated in September.

His role in the successful pennant drive was as a pinch hitter, but it was largely symbolic. He was the Astros' designated hitter in the first two World Series games versus the White Sox and pinch hit in the two games played in Houston's Minute Maid Park.

The Astros filed an insurance claim on his health to recoup some $15.6 million of the $17 million in salary owed to him for the 2006 season. Houston could not release him without losing their settlement, but neither could they allow him to take the field.

The insurance claim was settled the day Bagwell announced his retirement. He was hired on as an assistant to the GM in player development by owner Drayton McLane. He has since served the Astros in several capacities, including the 2010 hitting coach.

Bagwell has been inducted into the University of Hartford Athletics Hall of Fame in 1997 and the Texas Sports Hall of Fame in 2004. On August 25, 2007, his Astros uniform #5 was retired permanently during a pregame ceremony at Minute Maid Park.

Although Bagwell never tested positive for any performance enhancing drug and his name appeared nowhere in the Mitchell Report, he still awaits his National Baseball Hall of Fame induction because of the general cloud of suspicion enveloping his era.

CRAIG BIGGIO

Houston Astros
Catcher • Second Base • Outfield
1988-2007

"The thing that impressed me the most with Craig was he didn't want to be just OK. He told me right away, if we're going to do this transition, I want to be good enough to win Gold Gloves — and he won four of them."

~ *Astros infield coach*
Matt Galante

Craig Biggio is still the only major leaguer with 3,000 hits, 600 doubles, 400 stolen bases and 250 home runs. One of the great versatile players in baseball history, he began his career as an All-Star catcher and then converted to second base, earning four *Rawlings* Gold Gloves. He later moved to the outfield and finished back at second base.

Despite his all-out style, Biggio was incredibly durable. He played in 1,800 games before going to the disabled list. In each of his 18 full seasons, he played 100 games and lined out 100 hits. He is the Astros leader in games played, at-bats, runs, hits and doubles.

Biggio won five *Louisville Slugger* Silver Sluggers as the leadoff catalyst for Astro teams that went to the playoffs six times in nine years. He had power, hitting 20 or more home runs eight times, and holds the NL mark of 50 home runs leading off a game.

The 5'11" 185-pound Biggio took every edge as the consummate competitor. He always hustled to stretch singles into doubles, collecting more two-baggers than any right-handed hitter in history. And he was plunked by an all-time record 282 pitches.

Gritty and scrappy, Biggio was a fleet runner and savvy base stealer, running intelligently and often. He learned how to read pitchers to get a quick jump, even pacing the NL in steals with 39 in 1994. He pilfered a career-high 50 bases in 1998.

★ ★ ★ ★ ★

Craig Alan Biggio was born on December 14, 1965 to Johnna Rae Oie and Lee Biggio in Smithtown, Suffolk County, New York. He graduated from Kings Park High where he earned the 1983 Carl A. Hansen Award, distinguishing him as the best prep football player in Suffolk County as a running back.

Biggio narrowed his focus to baseball at Seton Hall University in South Orange, New Jersey. As a 1987 NCAA All-American catcher, he hit .407 with 14 homers and 68 RBI, leading the SHU Pirates to 45 wins and the 1987 Big East Conference title.

Biggio was taken 22nd overall in the 1987 draft and signed by Astros scout Clary Anderson. After stints with the 1987 Class-A Asheville (NC) Tourists of the South Atlantic League and the 1988 Triple-A Tucson (AZ) Toros of the Pacific Coast League, Biggio got his debut on June 8, 1988.

In his first full season, Biggio garnered the 1989 NL Silver Slugger award. By 1991, he was an All-Star catcher. However, the Astros wanted their young star removed from home plate collisions, foul tips and the career-shortening effects of receiving. The team convinced Biggio to move to second base in spring training of 1992.

No All-Star backstop had ever made the successful conversion to major league middle infielder, but Biggio worked tirelessly and made the transition. In 1992, he was the first player in baseball history to be an All-Star at both catcher and second base.

Biggio, Jeff Bagwell and Derek Bell, later joined by Lance Berkman and Sean Berry, became known as the "Killer Bs." Their explosive offensive production led Houston to National League Central Division championships in 1997, 1998 and 1999.

Biggio was severely injured on a play at second base on August 1, 2000 when Preston Wilson of the Florida Marlins barreled into him trying to disrupt a double play. Wilson hit his planted left leg, tearing Biggio's left knee anterior cruciate and medial collateral ligaments.

He made a complete recovery. When Jeff Kent was acquired to play second base in 2003, Biggio volun-

G	AB	R	H	2B	3B	HR	RBI	SB	BB	SO	BA	OBP	SLG	TB
2850	10876	1844	3060	668	55	291	1175	414	1160	1753	.281	.363	.433	4711

teered to move to center field to help the team. In 2004, he again showed his versatility, moving to left field to accommodate Carlos Beltrán's arrival.

After Kent left in 2005, he moved back to second and set a career-high by belting 26 home runs. He hit .316 in the NLDS against the Braves and .333 in the NLCS versus the Cardinals before the Astros were swept by the White Sox in their first Fall Classic.

Biggio won the 2005 Hutch Award for his fighting spirit and competitive desire. He was given the MLB Players Alumni Association's Heart & Hustle Award in 2006 and 2007 given for his embodiment of the values, spirit and traditions of baseball.

On June 28, 2007 at Minute Maid Park, Biggio went 5-for-6. With his third hit off the Rockies' Aaron Cook, he became the 27th man to reach 3,000 hits. He was out trying to stretch it to a double, but the attempt was emblematic of his hustling style of play.

On September 30, the 41-year old Biggio played the final game of his record 20th Astros season before an overflow crowd of 43,823 at Minute Maid Park. His final career hit, a double in the first inning, placed him 20th on baseball's all-time career hits list.

After the season, Biggio was honored with the prestigious Roberto Clemente Award, bestowed annually to a major league player for his community service and on-field excellence. His uniform #7 was retired forever in 2008 and Craig Biggio became the first Houston Astro to be inducted into the National Baseball Hall of Fame in 2015.

Biggio is revered in Houston where he resides with his wife, the former Patty Egan. They have raised two sons and a daughter. He currently serves as the head baseball coach at Houston's St. Thomas High School.

GARY DiSARCINA

CALIFORNIA & ANAHEIM ANGELS
SHORTSTOP

1989-2000

G ary DiSarcina was an American League All-Star shortstop, an Angels Most Valuable Player, and a leader in the clubhouse. A steadying influence in the middle of the Angels infield in the 1990s, his 1,069 games played at shortstop for the Angels rank third most in franchise history. DiSarcina's 1,086 games played overall ties him for seventh most in Halo annals.

★　★　★　★　★

Gary Thomas DiSarcina was born on November 19, 1967 to Rita and Gennaro DiSarcina in Malden, Middlesex County, Massachusetts. He was raised in nearby Billerica with his brother Glenn and sister Jean Marie. DiSarcina and future Hall of Famer Tommy Glavine were teammates on the 1983 Billerica Memorial High School state championship team.

The 6'1" 180-pound DiSarcina starred for three years with the University of Massachusetts Amherst Minutemen. After he batted .336 with 144 hits, 11 home runs and 74 RBI, the California Angels took him in the sixth round of the 1988 amateur draft. Angels scout Jon Niederer signed him on June 8 and sent him to the Short Season Class-A Northwest League to play for the Bend (OR) Bucks. The 20-year-old DiSarcina hit .305 in 71 games.

After a stint with Midland in the Double-A Texas League in 1989, hitting .286 in 126 games, he was rewarded with his major league debut on September 23, 1989. However, DiSarcina only earned brief trials with the big club from 1989 to 1991, spending most of his time with the Triple-A Edmonton (AL) Trappers. In 1990, DiSarcina batted just .212, but figured out Pacific Coast League pitching in 1991, hitting .310 in 119 games.

"DiSar" replaced Dick Schofield as the Angels regular shortstop in 1992 and began wearing uniform #33 in honor of his boyhood idol Larry Bird. He held the job for seven years. Always a scrappy tough out, DiSarcina's

sixth inning single on April 27, 1993 against Yankees ace Jimmy Key was emblematic. It was the only hit off Key in his masterful one-hit 5-0 shutout.

In the strike-shortened 1995 season, he was an AL All-Star. DiSarcina batted .307 in 99 games with 61 runs scored, 111 hits, 28 doubles, six triples, five home runs and 41 RBI, despite missing six weeks after tearing the ulnar ligament in his left thumb sliding into second base.

DiSarcina's finest season was 1998. He batted .287 in 157 games played with 158 hits, 73 runs scored, 39 doubles, three triples, and 56 RBI- all career-highs. His doubles total set a new franchise mark by a Halo shortstop, since surpassed by Orlando Cabrera in 2006 with 45.

DiSarcina culminated his season leading Anaheim to a victory over the Athletics on September 24. Hitting second in the order, he went 5-for-5 including two doubles and two runs batted in. In his best overall campaign, he was voted the Angels Most Valuable Player.

It would be his last full season unhampered by major injuries. In late April 1999 during infield practice near the batting cage, first base coach George Hendrick accidently hit DiSarcina in the left wrist with his fungo bat, breaking his ulna bone. It cost him half a season and his career would wind down the next two years, with DiSarcina playing just 12 games in 2000.

After appearing in his last major league action on May 8, 2000, DiSarcina spent 2001 out of baseball healing and rehabbing. He attempted a 35-game comeback with Triple-A Pawtucket (RI) Red Sox in 2002, but hit just .243 and retired for good as an active player.

DiSarcina returned to professional baseball in 2006, working for the Red Sox organization for several seasons through 2010. After serving as the third base coach for Italy's 2006 World Baseball Classic team, he was a baseball operations consultant, a New England Sports Net-

> *"Gary DiSarcina was the heartbeat of the Angels teams in my early years. A natural leader, everyone looked to him for insight, direction, and when things needed firing up."*
>
> ~ teammate Tim Salmon

G	AB	R	H	2B	3B	HR	RBI	SB	BB	SO	BA	OBP	SLG	TB
1086	3744	444	996	186	20	28	355	47	154	306	.258	.292	.341	1276

work in-studio analyst, an infield coordinator, and the manager of the Lowell (MS) Spinners of the short season Class-A New York-Pennsylvania League.

As the Spinners skipper during the 2007, 2008 and 2009 seasons, Disarcina led the club to back-to-back division titles in 2008 and 2009, setting a franchise record with 45 victories during 2009. He worked as the Red Sox's minor league infield instruction coordinator in 2010.

DiSarcina returned to the newly christened Los Angeles Angels of Anaheim in 2011 as a special assistant to two general managers, Tony Reagins and Jerry Dipoto, and was the field coordinator of player instruction in the Angels minor league system in 2012.

DiSarcina then was recruited back to the Red Sox organization for the 2013 season as manager of Triple-A Pawtucket. He led the PawSox to a first-place finish in the International League North Division with an 80–63 record. The team made it into the finals of the 2013 Governors' Cup championship, before being stopped by the Durham (NC) Bulls. After the season, DiSarcina was named *Baseball America's* 2013 Minor League Manager of the Year. His four-year minor league managerial record through 2013 is 205–162.

Angels manager Mike Scioscia tapped DiSarcina as his new third base coach before the 2014 season. It was his 15th year with the Angels organization, his first as an Angels coach, and his fifth season overall in a coaching capacity. It is expected that someday the savvy and knowledgeable DiSarcina will get the chance to manage at the major league level.

DiSarcina and his younger brother and former minor leaguer Glenn established the DiSarcina Baseball Academy in Billerica in June of 2003 with the goal of teaching baseball to the children of Massachusetts. Currently, DiSarcina resides in Plymouth, Massachusetts. He and his wife Janee have raised a daughter, Carlee.

TONY GWYNN

SAN DIEGO PADRES
RIGHT FIELD

1982-2001

"The only way to pitch to Tony Gwynn is throw the ball down the middle and hope he hits it to someone."

~ pitcher Al Leiter

Tony Gwynn was baseball's greatest hitting artist in the last half of the 20th century. He parlayed his consistency into a lifetime batting average of .338, the highest of any major league hitter who began his career after World War II. Gwynn is without question the finest player ever to wear a San Diego uniform, forever "Mr. Padre."

His career accomplishments are extraordinary. Gwynn's eight National League batting titles equal the great Honus Wagner's record. Gwynn and hit king Pete Rose are the only two players ever to lead the National League in hits as many as seven times.

He had 14 consecutive years with at least 150 hits and registered five seasons with over 200 hits. Gwynn produced over 900 multiple-hit games, including nine games with five or more hits. He hit safely in more than 75 percent of the games he played and struck out only 434 times in over 10,000 career plate appearances- just once in every 21 at-bats.

Earning his reputation through relentless hard work and video analysis, Gwynn never batted less than .309 in any full campaign and hit over .300 for a National League record 19 straight years. He was the 17th man in major league history to play his entire career of 20 or more seasons for one team.

The 5'11" 220-pound Gwynn was chosen to start in 11 All-Star Games and was honored to play in the Midsummer Baseball Classic a total of 15 years. He led the Padres to two National League pennants and hit a robust .371 in two World Series against the 1984 Detroit Tigers and 1998 New York Yankees.

The left-handed hitting Gwynn was a self-described contact hitter that never hit more than 17 home runs in a season. His trademark became driving laser shot singles through his fabled "5½ hole" between shortstop and third base. Even so, Gwynn's tape measure home run into the upper deck at Yankee Stadium in Game 1 of the 1998 World Series proved he could hit them long if he wanted. He also took special pride in his right field defense, earning five *Rawlings* Gold Glove awards for fielding excellence.

★   ★   ★   ★

Anthony Keith Gwynn was born in Los Angeles on May 9, 1960 to Vendella and Charles Gwynn. With his older brother Charles and younger brother Chris (later a major league player), his family moved to Long Beach when he was nine. He graduated in 1977 from Long Beach Polytechnic High after starring in football, basketball and baseball.

Gwynn attended San Diego State University on a basketball scholarship, but was persuaded to continue with baseball by SDSU head coach Jim Dietz. His .398 collegiate average remains the highest of any Aztec in the Division I era. He is the only athlete in Western Athletic Conference history to earn all-conference honors in two sports.

Gwynn was taken in the third round of the 1981 free agent draft by the Padres the same day the San Diego Clippers took him in the tenth round of the NBA draft. After short 1981 tours in the Northwest and Texas Leagues, he starred for the 1982 Hawaii Islanders of Triple-A Pacific Coast League and made his big-league debut on July 19.

The Padres won the National League pennant in Gwynn's first full year in San Diego in 1984. He was selected to start in his first All-Star Game, and hit .351 to capture his initial batting title. The Padres were overtaken by the Tigers in the Fall Classic.

Gwynn won three straight NL batting crowns from 1987 to 1989, hitting .370, 313 and .336 respectively. A strike in August of 1994 ended the NL campaign and

G	AB	R	H	2B	3B	HR	RBI	SB	BB	SO	BA	OBP	SLG	TB
2440	9288	1383	3141	543	85	135	1138	319	790	434	.338	.388	.459	4259

Gwynn finished at a remarkable .394, just three hits shy of .400. The strike deprived him of a shot at becoming the first man to hit .400 since Ted Williams' .406 in 1941. No major league hitter has recorded a higher average since. The last National Leaguer to post a higher average was the Giants' Bill Terry in 1930 at .401. Every one of Gwynn's major league-leading 165 hits in 1994 was lined out with a single 33" *Louisville Slugger.*

Gwynn was the 22nd man to enter the 3,000 Hit Club on August 6, 1999 off Montreal's Dan Smith. He was inducted into the San Diego Padres Hall of Fame in 2002 and his uniform #19 was retired in 2004. In honor of all of his contributions to the Padres and the San Diego community, the address of the Padres' new PETCO Park is "19 Tony Gwynn Way." A statue of Gwynn has been erected in a park behind right field.

He was voted into the National Baseball Hall of Fame in his first year of eligibility in 2007, the first National Leaguer born in the 1960s to go to Cooperstown. He garnered 97.6 percent of the ballots- only 13 votes shy of the first unanimous selection.

The genial Gwynn was the recipient of Major League Baseball's prestigious Roberto Clemente Man of the Year Award in 1999 for combining sportsmanship and community service with excellence on the field. He succeeded Jim Dietz in 2003 as head baseball coach at his alma mater where his Aztec teams played at Tony Gwynn Stadium.

Gwynn stayed in San Diego to become a true community icon, residing in the north San Diego County town of Poway with his wife Alisha. His son, Tony Gwynn, Jr., is currently playing Major League Baseball. Tony Gwynn passed away in a hospital near his home on June 16, 2014 after a long battle with salivary gland cancer, a disease he attributed to years of chewing tobacco. He was 54.

TODD HELTON

COLORADO ROCKIES
FIRST BASE

1997-2013

> "Todd Helton leads by example — not just on the field, but off it. He works hard, treats teammates with respect and consistently sets a good example of how to deal with success and failure."
>
> ~ writer Troy Renck

The greatest player in Rockies history, Todd Helton is the franchise leader in games played, at-bats, runs scored, hits, doubles, home runs, RBI, walks, intentional walks and total bases. A beloved figure in Colorado sports, he will always be regarded as "Mr. Rockie."

Helton joined Lou Gehrig, Stan Musial, Babe Ruth and Ted Williams as the only 20th century sluggers with 500 doubles, 350 home runs and a .315 average. He hit at least .315 eight straight years as a five-time All-Star and a four-time *Louisville Slugger* Silver Slugger honoree.

The sweet-swinging, left-handed 6'2" 225-pound Helton was a complete player. He used the entire field, drove the ball to the gaps in clutch situations, and had the pop to hit it out of the ballpark. He walked more than he struck out and was issued 184 free passes (22nd most all time).

The durable Helton was among the best fielding first basemen of his generation with a career .996 fielding average (sixth best all-time) and earned three *Rawlings* Gold Gloves. With his legendary work ethic, he took more grounders than anyone else to hone his defensive skills.

★　★　★　★　★

Todd Lynn Helton was born on August 20, 1973 to Martha Ferguson and Jerry Helton in Knoxville, Tennessee. His father had been a power-hitting catcher in the Minnesota Twins chain and passed on a love of sports to him, his older brother Rodney and younger sister Melissa.

As a quarterback, defensive back, pitcher and hitter for Knoxville's Central High, Helton was the 1992 Regional Player of the Year in both sports. He racked up 2,458 total offense yards, scored 33 TDs, intercepted seven passes, hit .655 (51-for-78) and belted ten home runs. A prep All-American, Helton was the National Football Foundation's Scholar-Athlete of the Year.

The Padres took him in the second round of the 1992 amateur draft, but Helton accepted a scholarship to the University of Tennessee. He was the UT starting quarterback in the early part of the 1994 season, but was injured and future NFL star Peyton Manning took his place under center.

Helton hit .407 in 1995 with 20 home runs and 92 RBI, missing the SEC Triple Crown by only a hit, and contributed a record 12 saves and 1.66 ERA to lead the Vols to 52 wins and the College World Series. He was awarded the Dick Howser Trophy as the National Collegiate Baseball Player of the Year. Helton's three-year UT average was .370 with 180 hits, 38 homers and 238 RBI; and he threw 193 innings with 172 strikeouts, 19 wins, 23 saves and a 2.24 ERA.

He was chosen by Colorado eighth overall in round one of the 1995 amateur draft and signed with scout Ty Coslow. Helton quickly jumped from the Class-A Asheville (NC) Tourists to the Double-A New Haven (CT) Ravens to the PCL's Colorado Springs Sky Sox (1996-97).

He made his debut in left field on August 2, 1997 and went on to play 35 games. Back at first in 1998, Helton led all rookies with a .315 line, 25 home runs, 97 RBI, 281 total bases and a .530 slugging average as *The Sporting News* National League Rookie of the Year.

He hit .372 to win the 2000 NL batting title by 17 points and paced the NL with 216 hits and a .463 OBA. Helton hit 42 home runs, walked 103 times and led all baseball with a .698 slugging percentage, 59 doubles, 103 extra-base hits, 147 RBI, 405 total bases and a 1.162 OPS.

In his best year, he earned the 2000 NL "Percentage Triple Crown" to become the first NL player to have 100 runs scored, 200 hits, 40 home runs, 100 RBI, 100 extra-base hits and 100 walks in a season, joining American Leaguers Jimmie Foxx, Hank Greenberg, Gehrig and Ruth.

Helton was the *AP* and *Baseball Digest* Major League Player of the Year, *The Sporting News* NL Player of the Year, and the NL Hank Aaron Award winner as the circuit's best hitter. He also led NL first sackers with 1,326 putouts, 149 assists, 1,482 chances and 143 double plays.

Helton played his entire career at mile-high Coors

G	AB	R	H	2B	3B	HR	RBI	SB	BB	SO	BA	OBP	SLG	TB
2247	7962	1401	2519	592	37	369	1406	94	1335	1175	.316	.414	.539	4292

Field. It has been a hitter-friendly park, even after baseball required that game balls be placed in a humidor in 2002 to negate the effects of Denver's dry climate. Since then, the home run count there compares with the other parks.

In 2002, Helton clouted a career-high 49 home runs (22 on the road). His total equaled Larry Walker's for most by a Rockie in a season. His 105 extra-base hits were the second most in NL history and made him the first ever to have at least 100 extra-base hits back-to-back.

Helton was a protagonist in the closest batting race in NL history in 2003, placing second at .35849 to Albert Pujols' .35871. In his first seven full years, he was one of the most elite hitters ever, *averaging* .340 with 117 runs scored, 192 hits, 47 doubles, 36 homers and 116 RBI.

Helton hit .320 for the 2007 NL pennant-winners. The team overcame the Padres in extra innings in the wild card tiebreaker game and swept the Phillies in the NLDS. After sweeping Arizona in the NLCS, Colorado met the Red Sox in the Fall Classic. Helton led all Rockies hitters at .333, but the Cinderella season ended with no glass slipper with a Boston sweep.

Helton battled a degenerative back condition his last four seasons and retired at age 40 after the 2013 season. The Rockies honored him in a pre-game ceremony on September 25 before his last game at Coors Field. He ripped a home run that day versus the Red Sox.

Helton was recognized twice with the Rockies' Roberto Clemente Man of Year Award for his community contributions to Eastern Tennessee. He and his wife, the former Christy Bollman, reside in Brighton, Colorado with their daughters- Gentry Grace and Tierney Faith.

The Rockies retired Helton's #17 on August 17, 2014, the first number to be retired in franchise history. The team unveiled a large plaque on the façade of Coors Field's second-deck railing bearing his #17. Helton is eligible for the National Baseball Hall of Fame in 2018. If he is denied entry because he competed at Coors Field, no Rockies hitter will ever be inducted.

BOBBY HIGGINSON

DETROIT TIGERS
LEFT FIELD • RIGHT FIELD

1995-2005

Bobby Higginson was the best Tigers player during a decade of Detroit losing years. He ended his career never having played a winning season on a Motor City team. In fact, despite the skills he brought as an outstanding hitter and fielder, Higginson never played on a team with a winning record from his freshman year in college through his 11 years in the major leagues.

The popular Higginson was never named to an All-Star team despite twice being awarded "Tiger of the Year" by the Detroit Chapter of the Baseball Writers Association of America (1997 & 2000). Since the award was established in 1965, Higginson is one of only ten Tigers to have won the honor more than once along with Miguel Cabrera, Cecil Fielder, Travis Fryman, Kirk Gibson, Ron LeFlore, Denny McLain, Alan Trammell, Lou Whitaker and Justin Verlander.

The left-handed hitting 5'11" 180-pound Higginson was a tenacious, hustling, intense throwback player who played the game hard and played it right. His powerful compact swing was ready-made for launching high drives into the short right field porch in Tiger Stadium. He slugged over 25 homers three straight years, and twice hit over .300 and drove in over 100 runs. A free swinger, "Higgy" struck out more than one out of every seven times he came to the plate.

In the outfield he showed off a powerful right arm, one of the strongest in the American League. Playing an almost equal amount in left field and right field, Higginson led the major leagues in outfield assists twice, led the AL four times, and finished runner up twice with a career-high of 20 assists in 1997. He also led all Junior Circuit leftfielders in putouts twice.

* * * * *

Robert Leigh Higginson, Jr. was born on August 18, 1970 to Candy and Robert Leigh Higginson, Sr. in Philadelphia, Pennsylvania. The only son of a German father and an Italian mother, he grew up on Anchor Street as a Phil-

lies fan. Higginson lived around the corner from Frankford High where he was a skinny 1988 *Philadelphia Daily News* All-City second baseman.

With no offers, he walked on to Philly's Temple University. Higginson made coach Skip Wilson's Owls squad and hit a grand slam in his first at-bat, but got no scholarship help until his second year. Drafted by the Phillies in 1991 after his junior year, he resisted signing. Higginson hit .377 and a Temple record 20 home runs but none of his four teams had a winning record.

He was drafted by Detroit in the 12th round of the 1992 amateur draft and climbed up the Tigers ladder steadily. With the Niagara Falls (NY) Rapids (Class-A New York-Penn League); Lakeland (Class-A Florida State League) and London (ON) (Double-A Eastern League) his first two years, he jumped to the Triple-A Toledo (OH) Mud Hens (International League) in 1994. In his three years in the minors, Higginson again didn't play on a winning team.

Tigers manager Sparky Anderson gave him his debut on April 26, 1995. Soon Higgy saw 1980s Detroit mainstays Buddy Bell, Phil Garner, Kirk Gibson, Larry Parrish, Alan Trammell, and Lou Whitaker all reach the end of their careers. He was a top young player, but the farm system was devoid of other prospects. The result was the worst stretch in Tigers history.

After struggling as a rookie, Higginson broke out in 1996, hitting .320 with 45 doubles, 26 home runs and 81 RBI. On June 30 and July 1, 1997, he equaled a big-league mark by mashing four homers in four straight official at-bats. He launched three the first day, followed with the fourth in the first inning of day two, and finished the year with 27 homers and 101 RBI.

On September 27, 1998, Blue Jays rookie pitcher Roy Halladay was making his second appearance in the bigs. With two out in the top of the ninth, Higginson broke up Halladay's no-hitter with a pinch-hit bomb. Halladay fin-

> *"He's a pressure player, and when you get the crowd behind him, that gets him going even more. He feeds off the crowd, and he feeds off the competition and the battle between the pitcher and hitter. He's just a great clutch player."*
>
> ~ teammate Brandon Inge

G	AB	R	H	2B	3B	HR	RBI	SB	BB	SO	BA	OBP	SLG	TB
1362	4910	736	1336	270	33	187	709	91	649	796	.272	.358	.455	2233

ished off the next batter for a one-hitter, his first career victory, 2-1. He enjoyed another excellent year in 1998, batting .284 with 25 homers and 85 RBI.

When the Tigers moved to fabulous new Comerica Park in 2000, Higginson enjoyed his finest year. He became only the 13th man in baseball annals to hit .300, score over 100 runs, pole 30 home runs, bang 44 doubles, drive in 100 runs, and steal 25 bags in a year. But again, the Tigers couldn't follow his lead and came in at 79-83 – his sixth straight losing year in Detroit.

Higgy signed a contract after the 2000 season that would eventually pay him over $40 million. Before his 30th birthday in 2000, his slugging average was .489. Afterward, he could only manage to slug .402. A blue collar player in a blue collar town, Higginson still took heat for his big contract and his diminishing production because of injury and age. The worst part of the stretch for the Tigers was 2003 when the club narrowly averted being the losingest team in baseball history with 119 losses. Higginson hit just .235 with only 14 home runs and 52 RBI.

After a knee injury forced him into his second surgery in less than 14 months, Higginson played just ten games in 2005. His last action was on May 5. Showing real class, he took out a two-page ad in both of the Detroit newspapers to thank the fans for their support over his career.

Higginson was granted free agency on October 31, and he retired at the age of 35. Ironically, the year after Higginson hung up his spikes, the Tigers won the American League pennant under new manager Jim Leyland and met the St. Louis Cardinals in the World Series.

Higginson has remained busy with real estate ventures. Higginson formed the Bobby Higginson Foundation in 1997 with the goal of providing grants to charities connected with critically ill children in the Detroit area. He still owns homes in Lakeland, Florida and in the Detroit suburb of Bloomfield Hills.

CHRIS HOILES

BALTIMORE ORIOLES
CATCHER

1989-1998

*"It was the single toughest thing
I've ever had to do in my life.
I'm not saying it's not the right
thing, but the toughest thing —
because he's such a quality kid.
Your number one catcher is like the
captain of the team. He's been dealt
a horrific setback with his hip, and
it's not going to get any better."*

~ Orioles manager Ray Miller
referring to Hoiles' release

Chris Hoiles was one of the best all-around catchers in Major League Baseball during the Decade of the 1990s, a quality hitter and defender. He led all American League catchers in fielding four times, finishing with a .994 percentage to rank ninth all-time among receivers.

The hardworking 6' 210-pound Hoiles was affectionately known as "The Tractor Mechanic" by his Orioles teammates. His career .837 OPS (on-base + slugging percentage) is seventh highest among catchers and his .467 slugging percentage is 11th best all-time.

His compact, uppercut swing lifted the baseball into the air much of the time. Frequently going deep into the count looking for a low fastball, Hoiles went with the outside pitch to right field well, showing power to all fields. He clubbed 151 homers to rank 12th in Orioles history.

★ ★ ★ ★ ★

Christopher Allen Hoiles was born on March 20, 1965 to Mary Anderson and Roger Hoiles in Bowling Green, Wood County, Ohio. He and a brother and sister grew up just south in rural Bloomdale, attending Elmwood High School. There he starred in three sports as a Royals All-Suburban Lakes League running back, shooting guard and catcher.

At Eastern Michigan University, Hoiles set the career home run mark of 34 while hitting .352 with 130 RBI. He put up new season records of 19 home runs and 70 RBI as the 1986 All-Mid-American Conference catcher and was later inducted into the EMU Athletics Hall of Fame.

Hoiles was taken by the Tigers in the 19th round of the June 1986 free agent draft. After spending three years in the Detroit farm system, climbing to Triple-A with the Toledo (OH) Mud Hens of the International League, Hoiles was traded to the Orioles for Fred Lynn in late 1988.

He made his big-league debut with the Orioles at age 24 on April 25, 1989, and got a start in the October 1 season finale, picking up his first big-league hit, an RBI double, but appeared in only six Orioles games, spending most of the year with the Rochester (NY) Red Wings.

When Hoiles was not on the Baltimore roster during 1990 (he saw action in just 23 Orioles games that year), Hoiles was terrorizing American Association pitching at Rochester. He hit .348 in 74 games with 18 round trippers and a gaudy .656 slugging percentage.

Hoiles began sharing Orioles catching duties with Bob Melvin in 1991. His first home run was a walk off, three-run blast in the last of the tenth on June 27 against the Indians. Hoiles was only the fifth rookie catcher to win a fielding title, committing just one error in 89 games.

A *UPI* 1993 AL All-Star, he led AL backstops with a .310 line, 80 runs scored, 82 RBI, 29 home runs, and a .416 OBA. He just missed being the first AL catcher to bat .300 and hit 30 bombs. His 1.001 OPS was the best for a receiver since Roy Campanella's 1.006 in 1953.

Hoiles' .585 slugging percentage was the highest for any receiver since Johnny Bench's .587 in 1970. The Orioles Most Valuable Player, he was only the fifth AL catcher ever to hit .300 with 25 or more home runs, joining Yogi Berra, Bill Dickey, Carlton Fisk and Mike Stanley.

In 1995, Hoiles caught 838 2/3 innings to lead the Junior Circuit, including the historic game on September 6 when his teammate, Cal Ripken, Jr., broke Lou Gehrig's legendary record for most consecutive games played. He hit a clutch .556 that year with the bases loaded.

Against the Mariners at Camden Yards on May 17, 1996, Hoiles joined an elite list of 23 major leaguers who have hit an "Ultimate Grand Slam." With the Orioles down by three runs in the bottom of the ninth inning with two outs and a full count, he launched a line-drive missile into the left field seats for a 14-13 walk-off win. It sent the crowd of 47,259 into a wild frenzy.

Hoiles ended the 1996 year with 25 homers and 73 RBI to help the Orioles earn a wild card berth. The

G	AB	R	H	2B	3B	HR	RBI	SB	BB	SO	BA	OBP	SLG	TB
894	2820	119	415	122	2	151	449	5	435	616	.262	.366	.467	1318

team defeated the Indians in the ALDS, but lost to the Yankees in the ALCS. He played the entire 1997 schedule without a single miscue, contributing to a club that won the 1997 AL East, then beat the Mariners in the ALDS, but eventually lost out to the Indians in the ALCS.

Hoiles set an all-time record for catchers on April 9, 1998. He was involved in four double plays in a game versus the Royals. He became the first catcher in history to hit two grand slams in one game on August 14. His twin "grand salamis" came in a 15-3 rout of the Indians.

The wear and tear of his position resulted in a degenerative hip, requiring four *ACE* bandage wraps before each game. He eventually needed a hip replacement. The Orioles released him on April 2, 1999 at age 34, but made him a roving catching instructor that day.

Hoiles returned to his alma mater, Eastern Michigan University, where he served as a baseball coach for the Eagles. Later he coached at Bowling Green State University while residing in the village of Wayne, Ohio where he and his wife Dana raised their three sons.

Hoiles was chosen the inaugural manager of the 2006 York (PA) Revolution of the independent Atlantic League, holding down that position for three seasons. He was introduced as the co-host of "Bird Talk" with Adam Gladstone in early 2010. The radio talk show on Baltimore's Fox Sports 1370 AM focuses on the Orioles and their minor league affiliates.

Hoiles also owns the Gold Glove Baseball Academy in the Baltimore metropolitan area, teaching his students the mechanics of hitting. He continues to work Orioles autograph signings, public relations and baseball camps. Chris Hoiles was inducted into the Baltimore Orioles Hall of Fame in 2006.

DEREK JETER

"There's no question his presence in the dugout is important. He's never any different, whether 4-for-4 or 0-for-4. He's still that focused, leader-type of guy."

~ manager Joe Torre

Derek Jeter was the most influential and charismatic player in the game's peak era of growth. The 11th Yankee captain and leader of the last great 20th century Yankee dynasty, his lasting legacy is as a winner. Only Pete Rose, Henry Aaron and Carl Yastrzemski have played on a team winning more than Jeter's 1,722 victories.

In 16 postseasons and 158 games, Jeter hit .308 with 200 hits, 111 runs scored, 20 home runs, 61 runs batted in, and a .465 slugging percentage. In seven World Series, he accumulated five championship rings and batted .321 to earn the title "Captain Clutch."

The all-time runs scored and hits leader for a shortstop, Jeter has five *Louisville Slugger* Silver Slugger Awards and two Hank Aaron Awards as the AL's top hitter. His hit total is surpassed only by Rose, Ty Cobb, Tris Speaker, Aaron and Stan Musial.

Jeter batted .481 as a 14-time All-Star. Amassing over 200 hits eight times, he leads all Yankees in games played, at-bats, doubles, hits and steals. Jeter refined his signature inside-out swing, regularly carving out hits and even home runs to right field.

Respected for his consummate professionalism, he was never ejected from any game. The rangy 6'3" 195-pound Jeter was a shortstop his entire career, winning five *Rawlings* Gold Gloves. His jump throw from the hole became a famous trademark move.

★　★　★　★　★

Derek Sanderson Jeter was born on June 26, 1974 to Dorothy Connors and Sanderson Charles Jeter in Pequannock, New Jersey. His African American father played shortstop at Fisk University. His mother was German Irish, one of 14 brothers and sisters.

Jeter's family lived in New Jersey until he was four years old before moving to Kalamazoo, Michigan. He and his sister spent summers with grandparents in New Jersey and the young Jeter became a Yankee fan, choos-

ing Dave Winfield as his favorite player.

He competed in basketball and baseball at Kalamazoo Central High. In his senior season, he hit .508 with a .637 OBA while slugging .831 and striking out just once the entire year. Jeter was the 1992 National High School Player of the Year. Yankee scout Dick Groch advocated him and he was picked sixth overall in the 1992 free agent draft.

After a slow start in the rookie Gulf Coast League, he started to progress. In 1994, Jeter swiftly moved up from Single-A Tampa to Double-A Albany-Colonie to Triple-A Columbus and was chosen the consensus 1994 Minor League Player of the Year.

Yankees manager Buck Showalter gave him his debut on May 29, 1995, but he spent most of the summer with the Columbus Clippers. New Yankee skipper Joe Torre named Jeter his shortstop in 1996. He quickly became a key player, helping the club to its first World Series triumph since 1978 as the American League Rookie of the Year.

Jeter scored over 100 runs each of his first seven seasons, including during the Yankee World Series trifecta of 1998, 1999 and 2000. He hit .349 in 1999, pacing the Junior Circuit with 217 hits, and was the All-Star Game and World Series MVP in 2000.

In the 2001 ALDS elimination Game 3, on an A's' hit into the right field corner, the relay was wide of the cutoff. Jeter ran to foul ground off first, then caught and tossed the ball backhanded to nip the runner at the plate. "The Flip" is forever in baseball lore.

The team won the ALDS and advanced to a dramatic World Series against the Arizona Diamondbacks. In Game 4, Jeter earned the title "Mr. November" by launching a walk-off home run in the tenth inning just after the stroke of midnight on November 1.

Against the rival Red Sox in the 12th inning at home

G	AB	R	H	2B	3B	HR	RBI	SB	BB	SO	BA	OBP	SLG	TB
2747	11195	1923	3465	544	66	260	1311	358	1082	1840	.310	.377	.440	4921

on July 1, 2004, Jeter snared a foul pop up down the left field line in full sprint. His momentum carried him over the short wall and into the first rows of seats. He emerged bruised and bleeding and had to leave the game, but "The Dive" became symbolic of his iron determination to win.

Jeter's best overall campaign may have been 2009 at age 35. He hit .334 with 212 hits and 107 runs scored, won a Silver Slugger and a Gold Glove, and led the Bronx Bombers to a World Series championship as the *Sports Illustrated's* Sportsman of the Year.

On July 9, 2011, Jeter was the first Yankee and 28th man to achieve 3,000 hits on a home run hit deep into Yankee Stadium's left-field seats off Rays ace David Price. He tied a career-best by going 5-for-5 on the day which also included two doubles.

Jeter broke his left ankle during the 2012 ALCS Game 1. While rehabbing after surgery, he suffered a crack near his previous fracture. He played in only 17 games in 2013 with trips to the disabled list for quadriceps and calf strains and more ankle issues.

Before the 2014 season, the Captain announced that it would be his last. In Jeter's final game at Yankee Stadium in the bottom of the ninth, he capped his legendary career with a classic "Jeterian" opposite field, walk-off single for a perfect storybook ending.

Jeter created his charitable Turn 2 Foundation in 1996 to assist young people to avoid drug and alcohol addiction. Major League Baseball honored him with the prestigious Roberto Clemente Award in 2009 for his play and his work in the community.

One of the greatest Yankees of all time, Jeter is universally respected for his character on and off the field. His uniform #2 was retired forever in 2015. Derek Jeter may be the first unanimous selection to the National Baseball Hall of Fame in 2020.

CHIPPER JONES

ATLANTA BRAVES
THIRD BASE

1993 • 1995-2012

"Chipper Jones is the complete embodiment of loyalty, honor, determination and baseball perfection."

~ country music star
Luke Bryan

Chipper Jones delivered more runs batted in than any other third baseman ever and ranks second only to Eddie Murray on the all-time switch hitters RBI list. Batting a career .300 from both sides of the plate, he is the lone switch hitter to bat .300 and hit 400 homers. He and Mickey Mantle are the only switch-hitters with 400 home runs, a .400 OBA, and a .500 slugging average.

A National League All-Star eight times, the powerful 6'4" 215-pound Jones is the Atlanta Braves leader in hits, home runs, on-base percentage and RBI. He is behind just Henry Aaron and Eddie Mathews on the Braves franchise all-time lists for home runs and RBI.

Lou Gehrig, Stan Musial, Babe Ruth, Ted Williams and Chipper Jones are the only hitters to collect 2,500 hits, 1,500 runs scored, 1,500 RBI, 1,500 walks, 500 doubles and 450 home runs while carrying a .300 batting average, .400 OBA and .500 slugging percentage.

He played the first 17 of his 19 major league seasons for Hall of Fame Manager Bobby Cox. With Jones as the Braves' leading position player in the middle of the batting order, the team won 11 straight NL East pennants (1995-2005) and qualified for the postseason 14 times.

* * * * *

Larry Wayne Jones, Jr. was born in DeLand, Volusia County, Florida on April 24, 1972, the only child of Lynne and Larry Wayne Jones, Sr. His professional equestrienne mother and math teacher/baseball coach father raised him on a ten-acre fern farm in tiny Pierson, Florida.

His father admired the switch-hitting Mickey Mantle and taught his son to hit from both sides, starting at age three. The boy's first bat was a cut down PVC pipe but he soon was hitting with a *Louisville Slugger*. A "chip off the old block" as his father's clone, he became "Chipper."

Jones played for his father in ninth grade at T. DeWitt Taylor High, and then attended Jacksonville's Bolles High

as a three-time Florida Prep Player of the Year. He led the Bulldogs to a 65-19 mark and a state title as a junior, pitching all five of the playoff game victories.

The Braves selected Jones as a shortstop with their first pick overall in the 1990 amateur draft. After a stint at Bradenton in the Gulf Coast League in 1990, he tore up the Class-A South Atlantic League with Macon (GA), hitting .326 with 24 doubles as the 1991 Sally League MVP.

Jones was assigned to the 1992 Durham (NC) Bulls of the Class-A Carolina League before being promoted to Double-A Greenville (NC) of the Southern League. He took a turn playing third base in 1993 at Richmond (VA) in the Triple-A International League and hit .325.

Jones made his major league debut on September 11, 1993 at age 21 as the youngest player in the National League. He carried great expectations into the 1994 spring training, but suffered a ruptured left knee anterior cruciate ligament and spent the year on the disabled list.

In 1995, Jones came back to top all rookies with 145 games, 87 runs scored and 86 RBI as *The Sporting News* NL Rookie of the Year. In the postseason, he hit .364 (20-for-55) with ten runs scored, three home runs and eight RBI in winning his first and only World Series title ring.

Jones connected for a record 20+ home runs in each of his first 14 campaigns. Starting in 1996, he had eight straight seasons with at least 100 RBI. In 1996 he hit .309 with 30 homers and 110 RBI, leading his team to the World Series, albeit losing to the Yankees in six games.

Jones was the 1999 National League Most Valuable Player and *Louisville Slugger* Silver Slugger winner on the strength of a .319 batting average, a .633 slugging percentage, 116 runs scored, 41 doubles, 45 home runs, 126 walks (18 intentional), 25 steals and 110 RBI.

In the heat of the pennant race, the Braves were holding on to a one-game NL East lead before a three-game series with the rival Mets. Jones proceeded to light up Turner

G	AB	R	H	2B	3B	HR	RBI	SB	BB	SO	BA	OBP	SLG	TB
2499	8984	1619	2726	549	38	468	1623	150	1512	1409	.303	.401	.529	4755

Field in a Braves sweep with four homers and seven RBI. Against the Mets, he hit .319 with a .510 OBA, a 1.000 slugging percentage, and seven home runs. Mets pitchers gave Jones nine free passes in the NLCS in a losing effort. The Braves were swept by the Yankees in the World Series.

Starting on June 26, 2006 at Yankee Stadium, Jones slugged extra-base hits in 14 straight games against the Yankees, Orioles, Cardinals, Reds and Padres. It is a major league record that he shares with Hall of Fame Pirate Paul Waner, who achieved the same feat back in 1927.

In 2008, Jones was the NL's starting third baseman in the All-Star game and won his first batting crown at age 36. The oldest switch-hitter to win a batting championship, Jones hit .364, a point shy of the highest batting average for a switch-hitter (.365) set by Mickey Mantle in 1956.

Jones got off to a slow start in 2010 but salvaged 95 games before injuring his left ACL again on August 10. He was lost for the year to surgery. After strenuous rehab, Jones was in the 2011 Opening Day lineup, but suffered from a right knee torn meniscus most of the year.

On March 22, 2012, Jones announced he would retire at the end of the season. He fought through two trips to the disabled list before being named to his final NL All-Star game on July 3. He finished the year hitting .287 on his aching knees, playing the game hard to the end at age 40.

He was inducted into the Atlanta Braves Hall of Fame and his Braves uniform jersey #10 was retired forever on June 28, 2013. Chipper Jones is a presumptive first ballot inductee into the National Baseball Hall of Fame in Cooperstown when he becomes eligible in 2017.

Jones hosts the TV show *Major League Bowhunter* on The Sportsman Channel. He currently is working his 9,000-acre Double Dime Ranch in southwest Texas, named for the #10 jersey both he and his father wore. The ranch is dedicated to raising native wildlife and books guided hunts for trophy whitetail deer, javelina, bobcat, badger and native birds.

RON KARKOVICE

CHICAGO WHITE SOX
CATCHER

1986-1997

Ron Karkovice was one of the best fielding catchers of his era. A Windy City favorite, the popular backstop was nicknamed "Officer Ron Karkovice" by the White Sox television announcers for "arresting" 41 percent of would be base stealers with his bazooka arm.

He was one of the most adept receivers ever at blocking balls in the dirt and committed only 42 errors in almost 7,000 big-league innings behind the plate. Accepting 5,203 total chances, "Karko" recorded 404 assists and 49 double plays for a fine .992 fielding percentage.

Amazingly nimble for his size, the burly 6' 1" 225-pound receiver was called "Cobra" by his teammates. A right-handed hitter, Karkovice was timed out of the batters' box at 4.1 seconds to first and used often as a pinch runner. He also had power, slugging five grand-slam home runs.

Taking over full-time starting duties from the 44-year-old future Hall of Famer Carlton Fisk in 1992, he was a key ingredient for the 1993 club, skillfully handling a pitching staff paced by a young Black Jack McDowell that won the AL Western Division pennant.

★ ★ ★ ★ ★

Ronald Joseph Karkovice was born on August 8, 1963 to Florence and Robert John Karkovice in Union Township, Union County, New Jersey. When he was seven, his father was transferred to Florida by United Airlines, prompting the family to relocate to Orlando, Florida.

Karkovice later attended Orlando's William R. Boone High where he helped lead the Braves to the 1981 Florida State baseball championship in his junior year. He also sported a 9-5 pitching record as a senior. One of his teammates was Joe Oliver, later a major league catcher.

Karkovice was taken in the first round by the White Sox as the 14th pick overall in the June 1982 amateur free agent draft. He spent 60 games with the rookie 1982 Gulf Coast League White Sox, and 96 games with the 1983 Ap-

pleton (WI) Foxes of the Class-A Midwest League.

Karkovice split 1984 between Double-A Glen Falls of the Eastern League and the Triple-A Denver (CO) Zephyrs of the American Association. Back with Glen Falls in 1985, he led all Eastern League catchers with 104 assists. Karkovice hit to a higher level in 1986 with the Birmingham (AL) Barons of the Double-A Southern League, batting .282 with 20 home runs.

He earned his debut on August 17, 1986, going 1-for-4, singling in a run, and scoring a run. Karkovice hit his first circuit clout on August 27. His three-run blast at Comiskey Park against the Royals' Danny Jackson was responsible for all of the White Sox runs in a 3-1 victory.

The 23-year-old Karkovice was the White Sox's Opening Day catcher in 1987, but fanned five times against the Mariners' Randy Johnson. He was sent out for further seasoning with the Triple-A Hawaii Islanders of the Pacific Coast League that year. Karkovice also shuttled back and forth between Comiskey Park and the Vancouver (BC) Canadians in 1988, but stuck for good with the big club in 1989 after working with White Sox hitting guru Walter Hriniak.

Karkovice hit a rare inside-the-park grand slam against the Twins' David West on August 30, 1990 at the Metrodome. He drove a pitch into the gap and the two outfielders, centerfielder John Moses and leftfielder Dan Gladden, went through an *Alphonse and Gaston* routine where both paused expecting the other to move toward the baseball resting at the base of the wall. They then both lurched toward it at the same time, flinching and stopping when they saw the other. As Moses finally grabbed the ball, he fell over and tried tossing it to Gladden, who ducked and moved out of the way when the ball came at him. By that time, Karkovice had rumbled across home plate to account for all of the scoring that Jack McDowell and the White Sox required, 4-3.

"Karko, 31, in his eighth season with the White Sox, is the prototype catcher. He even looks like a catcher. Strong and with a sturdy physique, he has the weathered, rugged features of a New England sea captain."

~ writer Jerome Holtzman, 1995

G	AB	R	H	2B	3B	HR	RBI	SB	BB	SO	BA	OBP	SLG	TB
939	2597	336	574	120	6	96	335	24	233	749	.221	.289	.383	994

SOX
CHICAGO
WHITE SOX

One of Karkovice's career highlights was catching battery mate Wilson Alvarez's no-hitter against the Orioles at Memorial Stadium on August 11, 1991. He supplanted Fisk in 1992, catching 123 games. Although he hit only .237, he slammed 12 home runs and drove in 50 runs.

In 1993, Karkovice cut down 54 percent of would be base stealers, drilled 20 home runs and drove in 54 runs. In 453 plate appearances, he accumulated 171 total bases for a slugging percentage of .417 in the Sox's run for the AL Western Division pennant. The Southsiders were dispatched in six games in the ALCS by the eventual World Series champion Toronto Blue Jays.

Karkovice tore knee cartilage in July of 1994 which ended his year. On May 28, 1995, he hit two home runs against the Tigers and watched Cecil Fielder, Chad Curtis and Kirk Gibson also each hit a pair to set the American League record of four players with two home runs in a game. The clubs also set a big-league record of 12 homers in the 14-12 Sox victory. He caught 113 games in 1995 and then 111 more in 1996, but his body began to break down. Karko got into only 51 games in 1997 and hit only .181. His last game in the bigs was on September 26, 1997.

Karkovice went home to Kissimmee, Florida at age 34 to be with his wife Maureen and two sons, Patrick and Stephen. He has devoted himself to teaching baseball to local youth, serving as an assistant to Orlando's First Academy Baseball Team for two seasons, and coaching baseball at Pine Castle Christian High School for three years. He has also helped with the Triple Threat Baseball Academy, a youth baseball organization started by Terry Abbott and his friend Joe Oliver.

In 2001, Karkovice managed the rookie Gulf Coast League Royals. He was the hitting coach of the independent Newark (NJ) Bears in 2009; the bench coach of the independent Camden (NJ) Riversharks in 2012; and the Riversharks field manager in 2013 and 2014.

BARRY LARKIN

CINCINNATI REDS
SHORTSTOP

1986-2004

"I've had some great players, yet when people ask who was the best and who did I most enjoy managing, it always came down to Larkin with me."

~ Reds manager
Davey Johnson

Native Cincinnatian Barry Larkin revolutionized the shortstop position in the National League by combining high-average hitting, power, speed and exceptional defense. The 1995 NL Most Valuable Player, he was the first "30-30" shortstop and one of the best at his position ever.

The 6' 185-pound right-handed hitting Larkin was a 12-time All-Star, winning nine *Louisville Slugger* Silver Slugger Awards and three *Rawlings* Gold Gloves. He was one of the key players on the 1990 Reds World Series championship team.

Larkin's career was marked by consistency and longevity. He batted over .300 in nine seasons. Three other years he hit .293 or better. He hit .293 against right-handed pitching and .299 against lefties. He hit .297 at home and .293 on the road. He batted .293 in the first half of the season and .297 in the second half. He stole bases at an 83 percent rate. He came to the plate 78 times in postseason play and hit .338 with a .397 OBA and a .465 slugging percentage.

Larkin possessed incredible range and a strong throwing arm at shortstop. Making both routine and amazing plays, he led the NL in range factor three times, games played and putouts twice, and assists and double plays once. His fielding was especially noteworthy because he played home games on the relentlessly hot, unforgiving artificial turf at Riverfront Stadium.

★ ★ ★ ★ ★

Barry Louis Larkin was born on April 28, 1964 to Shirley and Robert Larkin in Cincinnati, Ohio. An athletic family, his oldest brother Mike was a 1985 captain of the University of Notre Dame football team. His brother Stephen reached the majors with the Reds for one game and his brother Byron was an All-American basketball guard at Xavier University.

Larkin attended Cincinnati's Archbishop Moeller High, starring in football, basketball and baseball. He was drafted in the second round of the June 1982 amateur draft by the Reds, but accepted a scholarship to play football and baseball for the University of Michigan.

Performing at shortstop and defensive back for the Wolverines, Larkin was also the starting shortstop for the USA team in the 1984 Olympic Games in Los Angeles. He played with such excellence at Ann Arbor that the Wolverines retired his baseball uniform #16 in 2010.

Reds scout Gene Bennett inked Larkin to a contract after he was taken fourth overall in the 1985 draft and assigned him to the Double-A Vermont Reds of the Eastern League. In 1986 he was the Rookie of the Year and Triple-A Player of the Year with the Denver (CO) Zephyrs of the American Association. He played only 177 minor league games to prepare for The Show.

Larkin was given his major league debut at age 22 on August 12, 1986, hit .283 in 41 games, and soon established himself as the Reds starting shortstop. In 1988 he paced all major league hitters by striking out just 24 times in 588 at-bats (a strikeout rate of only 3.7 percent).

Larkin hit .301 in 1990, the second year of five straight that he topped .300, and batted .353 in the Fall Classic sweep of the A's. He launched 20 home runs in 1991 with five of them coming on June 27 and 28, making him the first shortstop to hit that many in a two-day span.

In leading the Reds to a 1995 NL Central title, Larkin hit .319 with 98 runs scored, 15 home runs and 51 steals. For his efforts he was voted the 1995 National League Most Valuable Player, the first shortstop so honored since Maury Wills in 1962. In the 1995 NLDS, he hit .385 in the sweep of the Dodgers and followed in the NLCS by hitting .389 opposite the Braves.

Larkin enjoyed arguably his best major league campaign in 1996, hitting a career-high 33 round trippers and stealing 36 bases. He became the first shortstop in Major League Baseball annals to join the 30-30 club and was designated the Reds captain before the 1997 season.

G	AB	R	H	2B	3B	HR	RBI	SB	BB	SO	BA	OBP	SLG	TB
2180	7937	1329	2340	441	76	198	960	379	939	817	.295	.371	.444	3527

On September 27, 1998, Larkin, his brother Stephen (first base), Bret Boone (second base), and Aaron Boone (third base) comprised the Reds infield for the last game of the season. It was the first time two sets of siblings were on a major league playing field at the same time.

Larkin's last game was at age 40 on October 3, 2004. After his retirement, he was hired as a special assistant to the Washington Nationals GM. In 2008, he began work with the MLB Network as a studio analyst and moved to ESPN in 2011 to serve as a *Baseball Tonight* analyst.

Larkin was the bench coach for the USA team at the 2009 World Baseball Classic and managed USA's second-round game against the Puerto Rico National Team when manager Davey Johnson left to attend a family wedding. In 2012, he managed the Brazilian National Team in the qualifiers for the World Baseball classic.

During his playing career, Larkin won the 1993 Roberto Clemente Award and the 1994 Lou Gehrig Memorial Award and was elected to the Cincinnati Reds Hall of Fame in 2008. He was among ten players and coaches inducted by the College Baseball Foundation into the National College Baseball Hall of Fame charter class in 2009.

Larkin was voted into the National Baseball Hall of Fame on July 22, 2012 in his third year of eligibility as the eighth Red and 24th shortstop to be enshrined at Cooperstown. On August 25, 2012, his uniform #11 was retired in a ceremony at Cincinnati's Great American Ballpark.

Larkin built the Champions Sports Complex to use sports in the social, emotional and educational development of Cincinnati youth. Larkin and his wife Lisa live in Orlando, Florida where they have raised their son Shane and two daughters, Cymber and Brielle D'Shea, who was named in honor of Shea Stadium, Larkin's favorite away park. Shane played two seasons at the University of Miami before going to the NBA with the Dallas Mavericks and New York Knicks.

EDGAR MARTINEZ

SEATTLE MARINERS
THIRD BASE • DESIGNATED HITTER
1987-2004

"Edgar Martinez leads by incredible work ethic, by example. When he has to say something he pulls you aside. He's very good with young guys, and he's always a team player, unselfish to the utmost."

~ teammate Alex Rodriquez

Edgar Martinez became one of baseball's elite hitting masters and the leading designated hitter of all-time. His endearing humanity and awe-inspiring ability to handle a *Louisville Slugger* bat made him the most popular professional athlete ever in Seattle. In his 18 seasons with the Mariners, Martinez produced seven All-Star appearances, two batting titles and five *Louisville Slugger* Silver Slugger awards. He batted .300 or more in 11 seasons, drove in 100+ runs six times and registered at least 35 doubles eight times.

Of all retired ballplayers that have had at least 8,000 plate appearances, only 15 men boast a .300 batting average, a .400 on-base percentage and a .500 slugging average- ten of those hitters are in the National Baseball Hall of Fame. Only Todd Helton, Chipper Jones, Manny Ramirez, Larry Walker and Martinez are not as yet enshrined.

★ ★ ★ ★ ★

Edgar Martinez was born to Christina Salgado and Jose Martinez on January 2, 1963 in New York City, but was raised in the Maguayo neighborhood of Dorado, Puerto Rico. His major league debut came on September 12, 1987, but Seattle did not give him regular playing time until he was 27 in 1990, despite consistently strong performances.

Martinez earned his first American League batting title in 1992, hitting .343 as a third baseman, but tore his hamstring just before the 1993 season and his legs were never the same. As a result, he spent two-thirds of his career as a designated hitter.

Martinez enjoyed some of his best offensive years despite having to overcome the effects of strabismus, a rare eye condition, which was diagnosed in 1999. Over the seven-year span from 1995 to 2001, Martinez was the most dominant right-handed hitter in baseball, hitting .329 with a .445 on-base percentage and a .574 slugging average. He is the Mariners' career leader in games played, hits, doubles, walks and batting average.

Martinez will always be remembered in Seattle baseball lore for his performance in the 1995 American League divisional series against the Yankees. He hit .571 and was on base a staggering 18 times in five games. In Game 4 of that series, Martinez hit a three-run homer, and then a grand slam home run that gave the Mariners an 11-8 victory. His seven runs batted in set a single game all-time postseason record. The victory tied the series at two games apiece and forced a winner-take-all finale.

With the Mariners down 5-4 in the 11th inning of that crucial game, Martinez hit the famous game-winning, two-run double off Black Jack McDowell. Known forever more in Seattle as 'The Double," it is said to have saved baseball in the Pacific Northwest. The playoff victory over the Bronx Bombers changed public sentiment toward the Mariners and paved the way for the public financing of Safeco Field, the marvelous, state-of-the-art retro ballpark that replaced the antiquated Seattle Kingdome.

Martinez was not a free-swinging slugger, but the consummate hitting craftsman. Playing with a composed, almost regal air, he exercised the plate discipline, patience and acumen of a hitting master. Since World War II, only Mickey Mantle and Ted Williams have finished with a higher on-base average than Martinez.

In an era of statistics-conscious, selfish players, Martinez was the epitome of the team player. He regularly moved the runner to third base with less than two outs by hitting to the right side of the infield and worked the count so the runner could steal- valuable intangibles

G	AB	R	H	2B	3B	HR	RBI	SB	BB	SO	BA	OBP	SLG	TB
2055	7213	1219	2247	514	15	309	1261	49	1283	1202	.312	.418	.515	3718

that don't translate in the box scores. He banged out 514 career doubles (36th all-time) and is ranked 69th all-time in times-on-base (3,619).

His OPS (on-base average + slugging percentage) of .933 ranks him sixth all-time among right-handed hitters behind only Jimmie Foxx, Hank Greenberg, Rogers Hornsby, Mark McGuire and Joe DiMaggio. Martinez has by far the highest OPS of any DH all-time and ranks third in designated hitter plate appearances.

Major League Baseball's designated hitter award is named the "Edgar Martinez Award." He won his second batting crown in 1995 with a .356 average, the only designated hitter to have done so to date. As a designated hitter, Martinez ranks third all-time in home runs and second in runs batted in.

On October 2, 2004, Martinez retired in a grand ceremony at Safeco Field. That month, South Atlantic Street between First and Fourth Avenues just south of Safeco Field, was renamed "Edgar Martinez Drive South" in his honor. Out of respect and affection for him, Martinez's #11 has not been worn by another Mariner since he retired.

Major League Baseball recognized the quality of his character with the 2004 Roberto Clemente "Man of the Year" Award for his humanitarianism and sportsmanship. He was the first Puerto Rican to be so recognized. Martinez was named the third baseman on Major League Baseball's 2005 Latino Legends Team and was inducted into the Seattle Mariners Hall of Fame in 2007.

A beloved figure in Seattle, he has worked countless hours in behalf of local charities and is an inductee of the World Sports Humanitarian Hall of Fame. Martinez currently lives in Bellevue, Washington with his wife Holli and three children.

TOM PAGNOZZI

St. Louis Cardinals
Catcher • Third Base
1987-1998

*"The neat thing for me was to play
in the same place for 12 years.
I got to play for four Hall-of-Famers
[Whitey Herzog, Joe Torre,
Tony LaRussa & Red Schoendienst]
with one organization which, in my
opinion, does things probably the
best out of any organization."*

~ Tom Pagnozzi

In his prime Tom Pagnozzi was the premier defensive catcher in the National League with a highly regarded throwing arm and the ability to lead his pitchers. A NL All-Star, he won three *Rawlings* Gold Glove awards, committing only 38 errors in 874 games behind the plate.

The 6'1" 190-pound Pagnozzi never caught a pitcher better than John Tudor or Bob Tewksbury, but many Cardinals hurlers overachieved simply because of his ability to call a game, handle his pitcher, and control the base paths.

Pagnozzi performed in an era when a catcher's defensive abilities were valued much more than his offensive production. All the runs that he couldn't produce with his *Louisville Slugger,* he saved with his defensive savvy. "Pags" was a team leader who did his job and was such a consummate teammate that he was voted the Cardinals player representative.

* * * * *

Thomas Alan Pagnozzi was born on July 30, 1962 to Priscilla Huhn and Donald Pagnozzi in Tucson, Pima County, Arizona. He was raised with three brothers and a sister in a sports-minded family, participating in Little League and American Legion baseball as a youngster.

At Tucson's Rincon High, Pagnozzi hit .328 in 1978 and .382 in 1979 as an underclassman. As a 1980 senior, he set a school record, hitting .548 to earn All-Tucson City and Arizona Super Team honors, and was one of five selected for Arizona Prep Player of the Year.

While attending Central Arizona Junior College in Coolidge, Pagnozzi batted .423 in 1981 and established Vaqueros school records of 58 runs scored, 80 hits and 115 total bases. He was an All-Arizona Community College Athletic Conference third baseman and JUCO All-American Honorable Mention. He followed with a monster slugging percentage of .660 in 1982.

Pagnozzi came to the University of Arkansas Razorbacks for a single season in 1983. He was shifted to play catcher by head coach Norm DeBriyn and took to the tools of ignorance quickly. He led the Razorbacks with a .362 average, 88 hits, 16 doubles and 50 RBI. Pagnozzi was an All-Southwest Conference selection, won the Bill Dickey Award, and helped Arkansas earn an NCAA regional playoff appearance. He was selected by the Cardinals in the eighth round of the June 1983 free agent amateur draft.

With the Class-A Erie (OH) Cardinals that summer, Pagnozzi made the 1983 New York-Penn League All-Star team. Elevated to the Class-A Springfield (IL) Cardinals in 1984, he was selected to the postseason Midwest League All-Star squad. After playing for the Double-A Arkansas Travelers early in 1985, he advanced to the Triple-A Louisville (KY) Redbirds in the American Association. To hone his game, Pagnozzi also played in the Puerto Rico Winter League for the Mayaguez Indians from 1985 to 1990.

Although he got his major league debut on April 12, 1987, he was sent back to Louisville where he hit .313 with 17 home runs and 71 RBI before being recalled. As a backup to starter Tony Pena, he was part of the 1987 Cardinals club that won the National League pennant but were ousted by the Minnesota Twins in the World Series.

In 1990 Pagnozzi so impressed Cardinals skipper Joe Torre that he moved top prospect Todd Zeile to third base to make room for him. From there Pagnozzi rapidly improved to become the premier NL backstop. In 1991, he was awarded his first *Rawlings* Gold Glove award.

In 1992, he was selected as the top defensive catcher in the National League by *Baseball America*, as well as the best throwing catcher in a *Baseball Digest* manag-

G	AB	R	H	2B	3B	HR	RBI	SB	BB	SO	BA	OBP	SLG	TB
927	2896	247	733	153	11	44	320	18	189	450	.253	.299	.359	1040

ers' poll. That year, he was an NL All-Star and a Gold Glover, committing only one error in 138 games to tie a major league mark with a .999 fielding percentage. He followed with another Gold Glove in 1994.

Pagnozzi remained the Cardinals starting catcher through 1996, the year St. Louis won the National League Central Division pennant under new manager Tony LaRussa. That year Pagnozzi had single-season career-highs with 13 home runs, 48 runs scored and a .423 slugging percentage. He was especially clutch with runners on base, hitting .311 (56-for-180). LaRussa came to trust Pagnozzi as a skillful pitch caller and handler of the Cardinals staff. The Cardinals were eventually upended in the Fall Classic by the World Series champion Atlanta Braves.

Pagnozzi began to wear down physically after 1996, appearing in only 35 games in 1997 and 51 in 1998. His final major league appearance was on August 15, 1998 and decided to retire at age 36 after being released by the Cardinals.

Pagnozzi returned to Fayetteville to make his home with his wife, the former Colleen Marie Duffy, two sons and a daughter. He soon became one of the University of Arkansas baseball program's foremost supporters, serving as a volunteer assistant coach for 2003 and 2004. Under his tutelage, Arkansas catchers threw out 43 would-be base stealers in 2003. The 2004 Razorbacks shared the Southeast Conference title with the University of Georgia Bulldogs

and advanced to the College World Series in Omaha, Nebraska.

Pagnozzi also is a stalwart supporter of the youth of the northwestern Arkansas community. He founded Pagnozzi Charities in 1999 with his motto of "leveling the playing field" for hundreds of disadvantaged youngsters. His foundation gave more than 900 sports scholarships in 2006 for children from kindergarten through eighth grade. His nephew Matt, also a catcher, made his debut with the Cardinals on September 29, 2009.

JORGE POSADA

New York Yankees
Catcher

1995-2011

"People don't appreciate his consistency. To me, it's not about gaudy numbers. I just go by my eyes. He is consistent. It's very difficult to have one good year, or even two. But year in and year out, he is able to come through."

~ teammate Derek Jeter

A switch-hitting five-time All-Star, Jorge Posada won five *Louisville Slugger* Silver Slugger awards. Only seven catchers have hit more home runs- Mike Piazza, Johnny Bench, Carlton Fisk, Yogi Berra, Gary Carter, Lance Parrish and Ivan Rodriguez. He helped his team to win five World Series titles with 103 hits, 23 doubles, 11 homers and 42 RBI in postseason play.

Among catchers since 1901, the gritty 6'2" 215-pound Posada ranks high in numerous categories, including walks (third), OPS (sixth), doubles (seventh) and home runs. He is only the fifth catcher with 1,500 hits, 350 doubles, 275 home runs, and 1,000 RBI in a career. His .474 slugging percentage places him in the middle of backstops already inducted at Cooperstown.

Part of the "Core Four" with Derek Jeter, Andy Pettitte and Mariano Rivera, Posada was strictly old school, wearing no batting gloves. He posted five straight seasons with 20+ home runs and 80+ RBI and amassed more homers and RBI than any other receiver from 2000 to 2011.

Durable and reliable, he worked behind the plate for 133+ games seven straight seasons. Posada caught David Wells' 1998 perfect game and converted Jeter's back-handed toss into a pivotal out to finish off the 2001 ALDS Game 3 "flip play," tagging out the A's Jeremy Giambi.

* * * * *

Jorge Rafael Posada Villeta, Jr. was born on August 17, 1971 to Tamara and Jorge Posada, Sr. in the Santurce district of San Juan, Puerto Rico. His father was a Rockies scout who fled his native Cuba to escape Fidel Castro's repressive regime. His mother was Dominican. An uncle, Leo Posada, played outfield for the Kansas City Athletics from 1960 to 1962.

When Posada was nine years old, his father insisted that from that moment forward he would bat left-handed any time he faced a right-hander. He worked hard but struck out often before he hit his first home run. He was never the best player on any of his youth teams.

Attending the Colegio Alejandrino High School in Guaynabo San Juan, Posada participated in basketball, track, volleyball and baseball. In 1989, he was an All-Star shortstop for his high school squad and went on to Calhoun Community College in Decatur, Alabama.

CCC head baseball coach Fred Frickie recruited him without scouting him and he accepted his scholarship offer without visiting the campus. Posada was voted the top hitter, the Warhawks team co-captain, and the All-Alabama Community College Conference shortstop.

The Yankees took him in the 24th round of the 1990 free agent draft. After his first pro season with Oneonta (NY) in the New York-Penn League, Posada was converted to catcher. He excelled as a 1993 Carolina League All-Star for the Class-A Prince William (VA) Cannons.

Posada matured with the Triple-A Columbus (OH) Clippers in 1994, was the 1995 International League All-Star catcher, and repeated in 1996. Posada made his major league debut on September 4, 1995 at age 24 as a pinch runner, his only appearance that year. He did not receive any major Yankee playing time until 1997, when he became Joe Girardi's backup.

Yankee manager Joe Torre gave Posada the starting nod in 1998 with Girardi assuming the backup role. Posada responded with 17 home runs in only 358 at-bats, and then hit another 12 bombs in 379 at-bats in 1999. Both years the Yankees won World Series championships.

After the Yankees traded Girardi to the Cubs before the 2000 season, Posada became the Yankees' primary catcher. At age 28, he entered his prime, hitting .287 with 28 home runs, 86 RBI and 107 walks with the Yankees winning a third straight title. Posada won the *Louisville Slugger* Silver Slugger for American League catchers four years straight from 2000 to 2003.

The 2002 *Baseball America* Major League All-Star

G	AB	R	H	2B	3B	HR	RBI	SB	BB	SO	BA	OBP	SLG	TB
1829	6092	900	1664	379	10	275	1065	20	936	1453	.273	.374	.474	2888

catcher, Posada blasted a career-best 30 home runs in 2003, tying Yogi Berra's record for most home runs by a Yankee catcher. He also produced a career-high 101 RBI and was third in the AL Most Valuable Player balloting.

Posada's last great campaign was 2007 when he hit a stellar .338 to finish fourth in the AL at age 35. His .426 on-base percentage was third. He is the only major league catcher in history to hit .330 or better with 40 doubles, 20 home runs, and at least 90 RBI in a season.

In 2011, his last season in pinstripes, Posada was used almost exclusively as a designated hitter. He fought through an early slump, but still finished with 14 home runs in 344 at-bats. The veteran also knocked in two runs to help clinch the AL East pennant with a late clutch hit against the Rays at Yankee Stadium on September 21. He hit a torrid .429 (6-for-14) in the loss to the Tigers in the American League divisional series. The 40-year-old Posada announced his retirement in January, 2012.

Posada had married the former Laura Mendez in 1991 with his good friend Derek Jeter serving as his best man. The couple has two children- Jorge Luis and Paulina. His son was diagnosed with craniosynostosis, a birth defect causing the premature closure of the cranial bones, and endured nine surgeries to correct the condition. The family formed The Jorge Posada Foundation in 2000 to promote awareness about craniosynostosis and to provide emotional and financial assistance to families with children affected by it.

In 2000, Posada was honored with the Thurman Munson Award for his baseball achievements and philanthropic work. He won the Yankees' version of the Roberto Clemente Award in 2005 and 2007. Posada was inducted into the Latin American International Sports Hall of Fame in 2012. He will become eligible for the National Baseball Hall of Fame in 2016.

KIRBY PUCKETT

MINNESOTA TWINS
CENTER FIELD

1984-1995

"When things aren't going well, sometimes it's tough to go to the ballpark. But when you'd walk into the park and Puck was there, you'd have to smile. When he was in a room, he brightened it."

~ teammate Kent Hrbek

One of the most popular players ever, Kirby Puckett was the driving force behind both of the Twins' 20th century World Series championship teams. With his infectious smile and generous spirit, he was applauded on the road as loudly as any home star.

Puckett's .318 average is the best of any right-handed hitter since World War II. He was honored with six *Louisville Slugger* Silver Sluggers and *Rawlings* Gold Gloves. A ten-time All-Star, he is the Twins leader in runs scored, hits, doubles and total bases.

★ ★ ★ ★ ★

Kirby Puckett was born on March 14, 1960 to Catherine and William Puckett in Chicago, Illinois. The youngest of nine, he grew up in the South Side's Robert Taylor housing project, playing with broomstick bats and balls made from rolled-up socks.

Puckett earned All-American honors at Calumet High, but was discounted by baseball scouts because of his 5'8" 178-pound build. He worked in the Ford plant, played for the semi-pro Chicago Pirates, and finally gained a scholarship to Bradley University.

After his father died of a heart attack, he transferred back to nearby Triton Community College. There Twins scout Jim Rantz noted his live bat and the joy with which he played the game. He was taken in the first round of the 1982 January Draft.

At Elizabethton (TN), Puckett was the 1982 Appalachian League Player of the Year, pacing the circuit in seven categories, and *Baseball America's* Minor League Player of the Year. He was the 1983 California League Rookie of the Year for the Visalia Oaks.

Puckett debuted on May 8, 1984, going 4-for-5. He went on to lead all AL outfielders with 16 assists, but did not hit a home run in his first 557 at-bats. He finally poled his first homer on April 22, 1985. His all-around play made him the Twins MVP.

In early 1986, coach Tony Oliva suggested that he employ the exaggerated front leg kick which would become his trademark. Emerging as a star, he launched 31 home runs among his 223 hits, batted .328, and started in center field in his first All-Star game.

Puckett carried the Twins to the 1987 World Series title, hitting .332 with 28 home runs. In one weekend in late August, he went 10-for-11 with two bombs and seven RBI. He was brilliant in the seven-game Fall Classic win over the Cardinals, hitting .357.

Puckett averaged a career-high .356 in 1988 with 234 hits, 24 circuit clouts and 121 RBI. By this time, he had become a notorious "bad ball" hitter, swinging freely and drawing just 23 walks. Puckett added a batting title in 1989 with a .339 mark, leading the AL in hits for the third straight year with 215, and was runner up in doubles with 45.

With Puckett leading the way, the Twins won the 1991 divisional title. He was the ALCS MVP, hitting .429, as Minnesota overcame the Blue Jays. The Twins would face the Braves in one of the best Fall Classics ever with four games decided in the final at-bat.

With his team's back to the wall in Game 6, Puckett slammed a triple in the first and made an acrobatic catch off the Metrodome's Plexiglas wall in the third. He singled and stole a base in the eighth. Leading off the 11th inning, Puckett launched an historic walk-off home run to electrify the nation. The Twins finished off the Braves the next day.

He hit .329 with a league-leading 210 hits in 1992 and then filed for free agency. Owner Carl Pohlad took a hard line, angering Puck's legions of loyal fans, but finally signed him to a generous contract only hours before the Red Sox made their play.

G	AB	R	H	2B	3B	HR	RBI	SB	BB	SO	AVG	OBP	SLG	TB
1783	7244	1071	2304	414	57	207	1085	134	450	965	.318	.360	.477	3453

By 1993, he had amassed more hits than any other ten-year player in the century (2,040). He garnered his first AL RBI title in strike-shortened 1994. With only a few games left in 1995, he was hit by a Dennis Martinez fastball that shattered his jaw.

As spring training was coming to a close, he awoke on March 28, 1996 unable to see out of his right eye. Puckett was diagnosed with glaucoma. After several surgeries failed to restore his vision, he retired on July 12, never again to play the game he loved.

During his active career and in retirement, Puckett worked with numerous charities. He received the 1993 Branch Rickey Award given to baseball's top community volunteer and the prestigious 1996 Roberto Clemente Award for his humanitarian efforts.

The franchise retired Puckett's #34 forever in 1997 and named him a charter member of the Minnesota Twins Hall of Fame in 2000. Puckett was swept into the National Baseball Hall of Fame in 2001, the third youngest still living to be enshrined. Twelve busloads of Twins fans traveled to support him at his induction.

Puckett remained in Minneapolis with his wife Tonya, son and daughter to serve as the Twins vice president in charge of the community fund, but never adjusted to life after baseball. After a difficult divorce in 2002, he moved to Scottsdale, Arizona.

Puckett suffered a massive stroke at his home and passed away the next day on March 6, 2006. Minneapolis proclaimed March 12 as "Kirby Puckett Day" where a public memorial service at the Metrodome was attended by over 15,000 people.

His Game 6 heroics became symbolic of his entire career. A bronze statue was unveiled on April 12, 2010 in the plaza off Gate 34 at Target Field, depicting Puckett pumping his right fist high in triumph while rounding the bases after his dramatic blast.

BRAD RADKE

MINNESOTA TWINS
RIGHT-HANDED PITCHER

1995-2006

"He's your professional player. He went about his business, did his job and always did his work. He was under the radar screen, for the most part, but solid in everything he did, the way he handled himself, teammates — the whole package. He's a package deal as a pitcher."

~ *Twins manager Ron Gardenshire*

Brad Radke was one of the finest control artists of the modern era and one of the most consistent pitchers in Twins history. He ranks second in Twins annals in starts, third in wins, strikeouts and innings pitched, and is the only Twins hurler to win 20 games for a losing team.

The unassuming Radke always handled himself with class on the mound, in the clubhouse, and in the community. A composed professional, the 6'2" 180-pound All-Star hurler possessed sharp command and a devastating change-of-pace outpitch.

While averaging 34 games pitched per season, Radke issued bases-on-balls to a pace of only 41 batters per year. He currently ranks 32nd all-time in walks-to-nine-innings-pitched ratio, even ahead of such other famous control pitchers as Greg Maddux and Roy Halladay.

However, he also had a proclivity to give up first inning extra base hits, making his ERA numbers deceptively high. His first-inning ERAs were at times more than a full run higher than for the rest of his games. He served up a career 326 home runs, ranking him 35th all-time.

* * * * *

Brad William Radke was born on October 27, 1972 to Joy Louise Ferch and Leonard William Radke in Eau Claire, Wisconsin. His family moved to Tampa, Florida where he graduated from Jesuit High School after gaining recognition as an exceptional student-athlete.

Radke was not originally touted as a blue chip prospect, though Twins scout Jeff Schugel was a strong advocate. Minnesota drafted him in the eighth round of the 1991 free agent draft, but once they evaluated him, the Twins rejected every trade that would have involved their young prospect.

After steadily making his way through the Twins chain with stops in the Gulf Coast, Midwest, Florida State and Southern Leagues, Radke made the difficult leap from the Double-A Nashville (TN) Xpress in 1994 to a major league debut on April 29, 1995. He was just 22.

During his first two major league campaigns, Radke took his lumps while learning his craft, leading the American League in home runs allowed each year. On the other hand, he established himself as a workhorse, never missed a start, and averaged over 200 innings pitched in his first seven major league campaigns.

In 1997 pitching for a mediocre 68-94 club, Radke paced the American League with 35 starts and went 20-10. He won 12 straight starts, only the third man to do so since 1950. For his 20th victory, a win over the Milwaukee Brewers in ten innings, 93 of his 123 pitches were strikes.

The lone Twin on the 1998 American League All-Star squad, Radke went on to win 12 games in each of the 1998, 1999 and 2000 seasons. He led the Junior Circuit in strikeouts-to-walks ratio (5.27-to-1) in 2001 and was runner up in complete games with six, tying Mark Mulder behind Steve Sparks.

In 2002, Commissioner Bud Selig speculated openly about contracting the Twins. Under new skipper Ron Gardenshire, Minnesota put the AL's youngest team on the field, yet won its first division title in more than a decade. Radke won 15 games. Talk of contraction subsided.

Against the Oakland Athletics in the American League divisional series, he started two of the five games and won them both with a 1.54 ERA. Radke only gave up a single run in Game 5 before the 5-1 lead was all but squandered in the ninth. Nonetheless, the Twins won 5-4 and advanced to the 2002 American League Championship Series against the Angels.

Radke lost his only start against the Halos despite shutting them out for the first six innings. The bullpen could not contain the eventual world champions and the

G	IP	W	L	PCT	SHO	GS	CG	H	ER	SO	BB	ERA
378	2451	148	139	.516	10	377	37	2643	1150	1467	445	4.22

Twins lost the ALCS, four games to one. In the entire postseason, Radke threw 31 innings with a 3.10 ERA.

He had the chance to leave Minnesota in 2002 to chase bigger money in a larger market. He was pursued heavily, but signed an extension to become a major part of the Twins transformation. Minnesota won four division titles in the last five years of his Twins tenure.

In 2006, Radke pitched with a torn labrum and later with a stress fracture in his right shoulder. He still was 8-3 with a 2.68 ERA in 17 starts. Beginning in June, he labored in so much pain that he used his left arm to brush his teeth and eventually stopped throwing between starts.

Radke sustained a stress fracture in his pitching shoulder in late August which landed him on the disabled list. Back on September 28, he worked five innings, yielded one unearned run with no decision, and the Twins beat the Royals, 2-1. His gallant effort helped win the division.

Radke pitched in the American League Divisional Series Game 3 in his last major league appearance, giving up four runs on a pair of two-run circuit clouts in four innings to absorb the loss. He officially announced his retirement from baseball on December 19, 2006.

On July 11, 2009, Radke was inducted into the Minnesota Twins Hall of Fame. He was chosen to raise one of the Twins' two World Series championship flags in left field on April 12, 2010 at the dedication of Target Field, the team's beautiful new downtown outdoor stadium.

Radke lives in the Tampa, Florida area with his wife Heather and two sons, Kacey and Ryan. They have created The Brad & Heather Radke Family Foundation with the goal to help families and children including the Hennepin County Medical Center's Neonatal Intensive Care Unit in downtown Minneapolis.

CAL RIPKEN, JR.

BALTIMORE ORIOLES
SHORTSTOP

1981-2001

"He loves to play.
He loves to compete.
And you can't compete
from the dugout."

~ Oriole pitching coach
Mike Flanagan

After the cancellation of the 1994 World Series, Cal Ripken, Jr. brought back disillusioned fans and helped restore America's faith in the national pastime. His dedication and hard work earned him the remarkable record of 2,632 consecutive games.

The Iron Man's durability is legendary as one of only eight players to have played 3,000 games. He toiled through muscle pulls, twisted knees, back problems, sprained ankles, hyperextended elbows, dislocated fingers and head injuries. He crashed into catchers and was involved in on-field brawls, but he never came out of a game.

Ripken changed his batting stance regularly, but his power and production made him just one of only eight men to reach 400 homers and 3,000 hits. He stockpiled eight *Louisville Slugger* Silver Slugger awards and set the mark for home runs by a shortstop at 345. A .336 postseason hitter (37-for-110), Ripken owns a 1983 World Series title ring.

At 6' 4" and 225 pounds, Ripken broke the stereotypical shortstop mold. With his agility, reflexes, flexibility and anticipation, he proved that a big and tall man could play *Rawlings* Gold Glove-quality shortstop, the most demanding of all infield positions.

Ripken ranks at or near the top in nearly every career shortstop category. He set the big-league record for the highest fielding average by a shortstop (.996) in 1990 and led the AL in double plays eight times, assists seven, putouts six, and fielding four years.

★   ★   ★   ★   ★

Calvin Edwin Ripken, Jr. was born on August 24, 1960 to Violet Gross and Calvin Edwin Ripken, Sr. in Havre de Grace, Harford County, Maryland. His father was a player, coach, manager or scout within the Orioles system for 38 years. Ripken grew up in Aberdeen, 26 miles from Baltimore, with an older sister and two younger brothers.

His father let him travel with his minor league teams at an early age. The access undoubtedly enhanced his development. As a 185-pound senior at Aberdeen High, he pitched (0.79 ERA) and hit (.496 average) the Eagles to a Maryland state baseball title.

After the Orioles took him in the second round of the 1978 draft, Ripken started with Bluefield (WV) in the Appalachian League. He was a 1979 Florida State League All-Star at Single-A Miami and a 1980 Southern League All-Star at Double-A Charlotte.

Starting on April 18, 1981 with the Rochester (NY) Red Wings, he played all 33 innings over three days against Pawtucket in the longest game in professional baseball history (the PawSox won, 3-2). The 1981 International League Rookie of the Year, Ripken made his major league debut on August 10.

"The Iron Man" quietly began his consecutive game streak on May 30, 1982 and would not miss another game until late 1998. As a 22-year-old third baseman, he hit 28 home runs with 93 runs batted in as the 1982 American League Rookie of the Year.

Ripken was the 1983 Major League Player of the Year and the AL Most Valuable Player, batting .318 with 121 runs scored, 211 hits, 27 home runs and 102 RBI. He capped his first year as the Birds' shortstop by snagging the last out of the Fall Classic.

His father replaced Earl Weaver as Orioles manager in 1987 and became the first skipper to write two of his sons onto the same lineup card. Ripken and his brother Billy played as a keystone combo in that July 11 game and teamed up for six years altogether.

Ripken reached his pinnacle in 1991 when he hit .323 and slugged .566 in 717 trips to the plate. He ripped

G	AB	R	H	2B	3B	HR	RBI	SB	BB	SO	BA	OBP	SLG	TB
3001	11551	1647	3184	603	44	431	1695	36	1129	1305	.276	.340	.447	5168

46 doubles and 34 homers with 114 RBI, fanning only 46 times. Ripken was both *The Sporting News* and *AP* Player of the Year; won his second MVP; a Gold Glove; a Silver Slugger; an All-Star MVP; and a Home Run Derby crown.

On September 6, 1995 versus the Angels, Ripken passed Gehrig's hallowed 56-year-old mark of 2,130 consecutive games at Oriole Park at Camden Yards. The sellout Baltimore crowd stood and clapped in homage to their native son for over 22 minutes.

Before the Orioles' final home game against the Yankees on September 19, 1998, Ripken voluntarily took himself out of the lineup to end his streak at 2,632 games. It had extended over 14 seasons and 502 games beyond Gehrig's hallmark achievement.

Ripken was elected to his AL record 19th straight All-Star game in 2001, his final season, and started at shortstop after Alex Rodriguez insisted that they switch and he take third base. The change gave him the All-Star record for most games at shortstop (15).

Ripken then proceeded to win All-Star MVP honors by hitting a dramatic home run. Previously, he had announced that he would retire at the end of the year. Before his last game on October 6 at Camden Yards, his Orioles #8 jersey was retired forever.

Ripken was voted to Major League Baseball's All-Century Team in 1999. In his first year of eligibility in 2007, he garnered 98.53 percent of the National Baseball Hall of Fame votes (third highest ever) as the 21st shortstop to enter Cooperstown.

Ripken and his wife Kelly Geer reside in Aberdeen and have raised two children. He owns three minor league teams and works as a TBS Sports TV analyst. His Ripken Baseball, Inc. has the goal of growing the love of the game from a grassroots level.

MARIANO RIVERA

NEW YORK YANKEES
RIGHT-HANDED PITCHER

1995-2013

"The most amazing thing is Mo's demeanor; not too many people have what he has. He's never intimidated, he'll challenge anyone, and you can't tell from his expression whether he was successful the night before or if he failed the night before."

~ teammate Derek Jeter

Mariano Rivera is the greatest closer in history with his 652 saves and 952 games finished. A key component of the last great Yankee dynasty of the 20th century, he earned five World Series title rings and is the only pitcher to close out three Fall Classics.

"Mo" Rivera was a 13-time All-Star; a five-time *The Sporting News* Reliever of the Year; and a four-time *Rolaids* Relief Man of the Year. Unflappable, the 6'2" 195-pounder went 8–1 in 76 postseason games, setting records with 34 saves, 23 straight saves, $34\frac{1}{3}$ consecutive scoreless innings, and a 0.77 ERA. He had no ERA in 17 series.

Rivera's signature pitch, a sharp-breaking cut fastball, may have been the finest single pitch ever. He threw it almost every time, but was still unhittable. He shattered left-handed hitters' bats especially, as the pitch darted in on the hands at up to 95 miles per hour.

* * * * *

Mariano Rivera was born on November 29, 1969 in Panamá City, Panamá to Delia Jiron and Mariano Rivera Palacios. He grew up in Puerto Caimito, a poor fishing village, playing pickup games with milk carton mitts, tree branch bats and taped up balls.

Rivera dropped out of ninth grade to work on his father's commercial sardine boat. Normally a shortstop, he pitched in a game for his Panamá Oeste team in 1990. Scout Herb Raybourn saw his effortless 87 mph delivery and signed him for $2,500.

Rivera spoke no English coming to America, but thrived at every minor league stop until he underwent Tommy John surgery in 1992. The Yankees left him unprotected in the 1992 Expansion Draft, but the Marlins and Rockies both passed on the future star.

After his Yankee debut on May 23, 1995, Rivera was sent down to the Triple-A Columbus (OH) Clippers that summer. There he suddenly started throwing his fastball at 96 mph and ended the campaign with $5\frac{1}{3}$ innings of scoreless relief in the 1995 ALDS.

Rivera stepped into the set up role for 1996 Yankees closer John Wetteland, hurling the seventh and eighth innings. He threw $107\frac{2}{3}$ frames (26 straight scoreless) and set a club relief mark with 130 Ks. The team was 70–3 when ahead after the sixth inning.

Rivera took over as the Yankees closer in 1997. After finishing 1998 with 36 saves, he was the World Series MVP for perhaps the best Yankees team ever (125 overall victories). The 2000 Yankees again won the Big Trophy for the third consecutive year.

Rivera experienced a most epic defeat in the 2001 World Series Game 7. After tossing a shutdown eighth, he was within two outs of a fourth straight world title when Arizona's Luis Gonzalez flared a soft liner over shortstop to drive in the winning run.

In the 2003 ALCS against the Red Sox, Rivera saved both Games 3 and 5 with two-inning stints in each. In Game 7, he pitched three scoreless innings until Aaron Boone's 11th inning walk-off homer clinched the pennant. He was voted the ALCS MVP.

After the 2004 ALDS, Rivera learned of the deaths of two relatives in Panamá and flew home. After the funeral on ALCS Game 1 day, he flew back in time to save the game against Boston. Rivera came on in the ninth of Game 4 with a 4–3 lead and up 3–0 in the Series. The Red Sox tied the score, mounting an historic comeback, and went on to win four straight. Still he only allowed one run in $12\frac{2}{3}$ innings in that postseason.

Rivera's greatest campaign was 2005. He converted 31 straight saves on his way to 43 of 47. Allowing just one run in all road games, his ERA was a career-low 1.38, as was his 0.87 WHIP. American League hitters averaged only an anemic .177 against him.

G	IP	W	L	PCT	SHO	SV	GS	GP	GF	H	ER	SO	BB	ERA
1115	1283.2	82	60	.577	0	652	10	0	952	998	315	1173	286	2.21

"Super Mariano" set a record by saving his fourth Midsummer Classic in 2009, the year he established a new career-best with 36 consecutive saves. He threw 16 playoff innings, allowed one earned run with five saves, and clinched the Fall Classic finale versus the Phillies. He was *The Sporting News* Professional Athlete of the Year.

While shagging balls during batting practice on Kauffman Stadium's warning track on May 3, 2012, Rivera ruptured his right anterior cruciate ligament. Fully rehabbed in March of 2013, he stated he would retire on his own terms after the season.

"The Sandman" was sent in to pitch in the eighth inning of his last All-Star game. As he trotted on to the field, both teams' players hung back and joined the fans to give him a standing ovation as he stood alone on the mound. Rivera retired the side, preserving his 0.00 ERA in nine All-Star games. As the game's MVP, he was the first to win the honor for a League Championship Series, an All-Star Game and a Fall Classic.

Rivera was the last man to wear #42, Jackie Robinson's number. On September 13, 2013, his #42 was retired forever- the first time for an active Yankee. In his last game on September 26, Derek Jeter and Andy Pettitte came out to get him in a tearful farewell. At age 43, he retired on top as the 2013 American League Comeback Player of the Year.

Outside Yankee Stadium, River Avenue has been renamed Rivera Avenue in his honor. The relief pitcher on the prestigious 12-member 2005 Latino Legends All-Time All-Star Team, Mariano Rivera is treasured as a national hero in his native Panamá.

The gracious and humble Rivera is a committed Christian. His Mariano Rivera Foundation has built schools and churches and given out scholarships. He and his pastor wife Clara reside with their three sons in New Rochelle, New York and Puerto Caimito.

TIM SALMON

CALIFORNIA & ANAHEIM & LOS ANGELES ANGELS
RIGHT FIELD • DESIGNATED HITTER

1992-2004 • 2006

*"He was like Clark Kent.
He could step into that phone booth
and come out Tim Salmon. He went
into that phone booth many, many
times during his career, whether it
was overcoming an injury or helping
take the Angels organization to its
first World Series championship ..."*

~ Joe Maddon

Tim Salmon will always be remembered as "Mr. Angel"—one of the greatest players in Angels history. He is one of only two single-franchise ten-year players in over a half-century of Angels baseball and a foundational high-impact leader of the 2002 World Series champion team.

The 6'3" 235-pound Salmon was one of the Junior Circuit's elite power-hitting outfielders throughout the 1990s. From 1993 to 2000 he averaged over 28 home runs and .927 OPS while free of any performance-enhancing drugs in a steroids-dominated era.

Celebrated by Angels fans and teammates as the "King Fish," he is the Angels all-time leader in home runs, walks and strikeouts. Salmon also ranks second in games played, at-bats, runs scored, doubles, runs batted in, total bases, on-base percentage and slugging percentage.

He holds the dubious distinction of having the most career home runs of any player never selected to an All-Star game. However, for a full season's body of work Salmon was named an outfielder on *The Sporting News* American League All-Star teams in both 1995 and 1997.

Along with Garret Anderson and Jim Edmonds, Salmon was a member of one of the finest outfields ever. Displaying great range and a rocket arm, he topped all AL rightfielders in putouts five times, double-plays and range-factor-per-game four times, and assists once.

* * * * *

Timothy James Salmon was born on August 24, 1968 to Billie Sue and James Salmon in Long Beach, Los Angeles County, California. His parents divorced when he was six. He and his brother Mike challenged each other competitively. Mike became a USC Trojans defensive back.

As a senior at Greenway High in Phoenix, Salmon hit .381 and slugged .905 as an All-Arizona pick and the 1986 Phoenix Prep Player of the Year. He starred three collegiate seasons at Grand Canyon College in Phoenix,

leading the Antelopes to the 1988 NAIA title game.

Scouted by the Angels' Joe Maddon and Tim Kelly, Salmon was taken in the third round of the 1989 amateur draft. With the Bend (OR) Bucks of the Class-A Northwest League, he played 55 games before a pitch shattered his jaw and nearly 30 teeth and broke his nose. He was beaned again playing for the 1990 Palm Springs (CA) Angels of the Class-A California League.

In 1991 Salmon belted 23 circuit clouts and knocked in 98 runs with the Double-A Midland (TX) Angels of the Texas League. Up for a quick look-see with the 1992 Triple-A Edmonton (AB) Trappers, he started off hot and was in a zone all season to lead the PCL with 29 homers and 105 RBI while hitting .347 as *The Sporting News* Minor League Player of the Year.

Salmon was summoned to the major leagues for his debut on August 21, 1992 and manager John Wathan inserted him at cleanup versus the Yankees at Yankee Stadium. He went 0-for-4 in a 9-5 win and saw action in another 22 big-league games as the season closed.

In his first full season of 1992, Salmon hit 31 bombs with a .918 OPS and was the 1993 American League Rookie of the Year- one of only two Angels to ever win the honor (Mike Trout was the other). He had already become one of the most popular Angels and a true fan favorite.

Salmon finished seventh in the MVP balloting in 1995 and earned a *Louisville Slugger* Silver Slugger award. His .330 average placed him third in the AL and he sported a stout 1.094 OPS. He finished seventh again in the 1997 MVP vote with 33 homers and a career-high 129 RBI.

Salmon matched his career-best with 34 home runs in 2000. When he hit his 30th round-tripper on August 27, he joined teammates Garret Anderson, Troy Glaus and Mo Vaughn to qualify the Angels as the first in AL history to have four players reach the 30-home run plateau.

Salmon's 2001 season was substandard, but redemp-

G	AB	R	H	2B	3B	HR	RBI	SB	BB	SO	BA	OBP	SLG	TB
1672	5934	986	1674	339	24	299	1016	48	970	1360	.299	.385	.499	2958

tion was at hand. He was the 2002 American League Comeback Player of the Year, as well as baseball's Hutch Award winner for his desire and fighting spirit. But it was in his first World Series where he stamped his mark on franchise history.

Salmon brought his hot M253 *Louisville Slugger* into the Fall Classic. He went 4-for-4 in Game 2 with two home runs and four RBI including his eighth inning game-winner in the 11-10 victory over the Giants. He hit .346 (9-for-26) in the World Series with a mammoth 1.067 OPS.

The 2002 season was his high water mark. After a solid 2003, his body wore down. Salmon appeared in only 60 games in 2004, and missed all of 2005 with left knee and right rotator cuff surgery. Against ending on those terms, Salmon worked to play one final season.

The Angels invited him to the team's spring camp at Tempe Diablo Stadium and he earned his way onto the roster with a strong performance. Salmon spent the year as a designated hitter and finished with a .811 OPS, passed the 1,000 RBI milestone, and hit his 299th home run.

In his final game on "Tim Salmon Day" at Angel Stadium on October 1, his name and jersey number were cut into the infield and outfield grass. He failed to hit home run #300 in his last at-bat, but 44,000+ fans gave him a lengthy standing ovation in appreciation of his career.

Salmon's Angels uniform #15 has been unofficially retired since he took it off. He is a member of the Angels, Arizona Sports and Grand Canyon University Halls of Fame. Salmon is a pre-game and post-game analyst for Angels' games on Fox Sports West television.

He and his wife, the former Marci Hustead, co-founded the Tim Salmon Foundation, which supports the missions of Concept 7 Foster Family Agency and Laurel House, working to end domestic violence. Salmon and his wife live in Scottsdale, Arizona with their four children.

ROBBY THOMPSON

R obby Thompson was a key leader of the resurgent Giants of the late 1980s. He was the Opening Day second baseman for 11 straight years and retired as the Giants second base leader in at-bats, runs scored, hits, doubles, triples, homers, RBI and steals.

The sure-handed 5'11" 173-pound Thompson led Senior Circuit second basemen in double plays three times and assists once. He retired atop the Giants all-time lists for his position with 1,304 games played, a .983 fielding average and 873 double plays.

* * * * *

Robert Randall Thompson was born on May 10, 1962 to Marion Alberta Schjeveland and Robert Kenneth Thompson in West Palm Beach, Florida. He excelled for the Forest Hill High Falcons in basketball and baseball before graduating in 1980.

At Palm Beach Community College, Thompson was a standout shortstop for two years. During 1982, he was the Athletics' second round pick in the January regular phase and then the Mariners' sixth round choice in the June secondary phase.

Instead he accepted a scholarship to the University of Florida and shined for coach Jack Rhine's 1983 SEC East titlist Gators. Scouted by the Giants' Tom Zimmer, he was their second pick overall in the first round of the June 1983 secondary phase draft.

Thompson signed a bonus contract with the Giants and was assigned to Fresno in the Class-A California League to train two years under manager Wendell Kim. While only hitting a combined .253, he was already demonstrating major league fielding ability.

In 1985, Thompson was promoted to play for the Double-A Shreveport (LA) Captains. As a Texas League All-Star, he showed he might be ready to skip the Triple-A rung altogether, pounding out 20 doubles and swiping 28 bases.

Giants manager Roger Craig settled on Thompson as his 1986 Opening Day second baseman, along with rookie first baseman Will Clark and rookie shortstop Jose Uribe. Thompson proceeded to lead his 1986 club with 149 hits and 73 runs scored as *The Sporting News* National League Rookie of the Year.

In his second year, he helped the Giants win their first NL West title since 1971, combining with Uribe to form baseball's most prolific double play combo with 183 twin killings. In the NLCS, he sparkled defensively, getting a playoff record ten double plays.

At 1988 mid-season, Thompson was hitting above .300. He was voted an NL Al-Star but missed the Midsummer Classic with a pinched nerve in his leg. When he came back, Craig had decided to drop him to #2 in the order and have Brett Butler lead off.

After initially struggling, Thompson flourished in 1989 hitting behind Butler and ahead of Clark and Kevin Mitchell in the Giants order. He topped the National League with 11 triples, scored a career-high 91 runs, launched 13 home runs and drove home 50.

The Giants emerged as NL Western Division champs and faced the Cubs in the NLCS. In front of a record Candlestick Park crowd of 62,065 in Game 3, Thompson hit a game-winning, two-run seventh inning long ball off of Les Lancaster in a dramatic come-from-behind victory that sparked the Giants to the National League pennant.

As the emotional leader of the 1993 Giants, Thompson was raking at a .325 clip by mid-season and got his second All-Star nod. Later in the campaign, he caught fire to carry the Giants on his back in August, blasting round trippers in five successive games.

With ten games left, Thompson was hit in the face by a fastball thrown by Trevor Hoffman and sustained a

"Robby Thompson authored the most courageous feat I've ever witnessed on the diamond during my 25 years covering baseball."

~ writer Larry Stone on Thompson's return to the lineup for the 1993 finale less than two weeks after his cheekbone was shattered by a pitch

G	AB	R	H	2B	3B	HR	RBI	SB	BB	SO	BA	OBP	SLG	TB
1304	4612	671	1187	238	39	119	458	103	439	987	.257	.329	.403	1860

broken cheekbone. The Giants and Braves were all tied in an epic pennant race at 103 wins each before the final 162nd game. He courageously played with a bloodshot eye, wearing a clear plastic protective mask in the season-ending defeat.

With career bests of 30 doubles, 19 home runs, 65 RBI, a .312 average, and .870 OPS, Thompson collected the 1993 *Louisville Slugger* Silver Slugger award as the top hitting NL second baseman. Committing only eight errors and fielding .988, he also earned the prestigious *Rawlings* Gold Glove award for his stellar glove work.

In a 1994 spring exhibition, Thompson was hit on the left ear flap of his batting helmet by 6'5" Rockies fireballer Mike Harkey. His season went south from there as he played in only 35 games with a turn on the disabled list and then surgery on his shoulder.

Thompson averaged a meager 64 games per year from 1994 to 1996, dealing with an array of injuries and ailments. He tied a Giants record with three doubles against the Braves on June 21, 1996, but played his last big-league game at age 34 on September 22.

After his active career, Thompson was a Giants' roving minor league instructor in 1999 and then their first base coach for two years. He then spent a decade with the Indians- first as a coach and then as special assistant to the general manager. Thompson was the Mariners bench coach from 2011 through 2013, assisting skipper Eric Wedge.

He currently resides in Tequesta, Florida with his wife, the former Brenda Cardona. They raised a daughter Kristeena and three sons- Andrew and twins Logan and Tyler. All three sons have played pro baseball. Thompson's career is celebrated with a plaque on the Giants Wall of Honor outside of AT & T Park on The Embarcadero.

JASON VARITEK

BOSTON RED SOX
CATCHER

1997-2011

Jason Varitek epitomized the fiercely competitive style of play that reversed the Curse of the Bambino with Boston World Series triumphs in 2004 and 2007. No Red Sox catcher worked more regular season games (1,488), postseason games (63), or Opening Day starts (ten in a row).

The Red Sox's respected captain, Varitek is the fourth longest-tenured single-franchise player in Boston history. He is the only man ever to play in a Little League World Series, College World Series, the Olympic Games, World Baseball Classic and Major League World Series.

Varitek led Sox staffs by spending hours in preparation with his pitchers and calling on his encyclopedic knowledge of opposing hitters' tendencies. He caught a record four no-hitters with Hideo Nomo (2001), Derek Lowe (2002), Clay Buchholz (2007) and Jon Lester (2008).

The rugged 6'2" 235-pound Varitek was a powerful switch-hitter. He is Boston's all-time leader for catchers in almost every major offensive category including at-bats, runs scored, hits, doubles, home runs and RBI. His 11 homers in the postseason are the most by *any* catcher.

★　★　★　★　★

Jason Andrew Varitek was born on April 11, 1972 to Donna Morosini and Joseph Edward Varitek in Rochester, Oakland County, Michigan. When he was seven, his family moved to Longwood, Florida outside of Orlando where he grew up the second oldest of four brothers.

At age 12, Varitek competed in the 1984 Little League World Series in Williamsport (PA), playing shortstop, third base and catcher. His Altamonte Springs squad won the United States title over Southport, Indiana, but lost in the world championship game to South Korea.

Varitek excelled in baseball for the Lake Brantley High Patriots in Altamonte Springs. In his senior year, he played third base for the Florida state titlists, knocking in

the winning run in the championship game. LBHS was named the top team in the nation by USA Today in 1990.

Varitek was a three-time NCAA consensus All-American catcher for Georgia Tech University. After his sophomore year, he starred for the 1992 U. S. Olympic team. In 1993, he joined the Cape Cod League's Hyannis (MA) Mets and hit .371 as the batting champ and MVP.

Varitek set Georgia Tech career records with 253 games played, 261 runs scored, 351 hits and 82 doubles. He helped lead GTU to the 1994 College World Series final before losing to the Oklahoma Sooners. "Tek" is the only Yellow Jacket player to have his number retired (#33).

Varitek won all the 1994 awards — *Baseball America's* College Player of the Year; the Dick Howser Trophy (National College Player of the Year); and the Golden Spikes Award (best amateur USA player). He was chosen for *Baseball America's* All-Time College All-Star Team.

Varitek was picked 14th overall in the first round of the 1994 amateur draft by the Mariners, but talks broke down and he played for the independent Saint Paul Saints. After signing him in 1995, the Mariners sent him to the Double-A Port City (NC) Roosters of the Southern League.

During 1997, Varitek and Derek Lowe were traded to the Red Sox for reliever Heathcliff Slocumb in a windfall for Boston. On September 24, 1997, Varitek made his cameo debut, singling in his lone at-bat. He became the starter in 1999 by hitting 20 home runs with 76 RBI.

Varitek started off white hot in 2001, launching three home runs in a single game on May 20. In early June, he dove and stretched for a foul ball, catching it on a stellar web gem play. However, he fractured his left elbow and was on the disabled list for the remainder of the year.

By 2003, Varitek was a leader in the clubhouse and on the field. An AL All-Star, he finished at .273 with 25 home runs and 85 RBI. Boston won a wild card spot, but the

---

"In my 23 years of professional baseball I never played with or against a more selfless and prepared player than Jason Varitek."

~ *battery mate Curt Schilling*

G	AB	R	H	2B	3B	HR	RBI	SB	BB	SO	BA	OBP	SLG	TB
1546	5099	664	1307	306	14	193	757	25	614	1216	.256	.341	.435	2220

Yankees' Aaron Boone hit a walk-off homer in the ALCS Game 7, ending the Sox's year on a sour note.

In the magical 2004 season, Varitek hit a career-best .296 with 18 bombs and 73 RBI. On July 24, Sox pitcher Bronson Arroyo plunked Yankee hitter Alex Rodriguez. When A-Rod gestured toward Arroyo and spouted off, Varitek shoved his mitt into Rodriquez's face, igniting a bench-clearing brawl. Both were ejected but the Sox now had their blood up and won, 11-10.

Varitek's reprisal was the season's turning point. From that day forward, the Red Sox posted the best record in the majors. After losing the first three ALCS games to the Yankees, the self-described "Idiots" came back to win four straight. When Boston swept the Cardinals in the Fall Classic, New England celebrated a world championship for the first time in 86 years.

Varitek batted .281 in 2005 with 22 homers. That year he won his first *Rawlings* Gold Glove; his first *Louisville Slugger* Silver Slugger; and got his first nod as the AL's starting All-Star catcher, but the Red Sox bowed to the eventual World Champion White Sox in the ALDS.

The Red Sox won the AL pennant in 2007, helped by Varitek's 17 home runs, his .994 fielding average and his AL-leading 937 putouts. Boston hoisted its second Big Trophy in four seasons with a four-game sweep of the Rockies in the World Series with Varitek hitting .333.

Despite all of his conditioning work, by 2008 Varitek saw his skills slowly decline. He played his last game on September 24, 2011 at age 39. Varitek has represented the Red Sox in numerous charitable activities around the Hub City. Since 2012, he has been a special assistant to general manager Ben Cherington. Only the fourth Red Sox captain since 1923, he is certain to be inducted into the Boston Red Sox Hall of Fame and have the uniform #33 that he wore for the last dozen years of his career retired as a true Boston legend.

BERNIE WILLIAMS

NEW YORK YANKEES
CENTER FIELD

1991-2006

"... the pressure of the game never bothered him. I think good players go on the field knowing there is a danger of being embarrassed and it doesn't bother them at all. Bernie never thought anything negative was going to happen until it happened."

~ Yankees manager Joe Torre

Switch-hitting Bernie Williams patrolled center field for the New York Yankees, one of the marquee positions in American sports. The owner of four World Series title rings, he places high on the Yankee all-time charts in doubles, walks, hits, extra base hits, home runs and RBI.

During the Yankees' dynastic run when the team won six American League pennants in seven years from 1996 to 2002, Williams hit mostly cleanup. As an All-Star five consecutive years, he hit a combined .323, averaging more than 106 runs scored, 25 home runs and 104 RBI.

The lithe 6'2" 180-pound Williams competed in the postseason every year of his career. With 121 games played, he has the most wins-against-replacement (WAR); holds the record of 80 RBI; and ranks #2 with 128 hits, 83 runs scored, 29 doubles, 22 homers and 223 total bases.

The Bronx Bombers' top outfielder during Joe Torre's reign, Williams could outrun drives into the power alleys with his burner foot speed. His range more than made up for his average throwing arm as he earned four *Rawlings* Gold Glove awards for fielding excellence.

★   ★   ★   ★   ★

Bernabé Williams Figueroa, Jr. was born on September 13, 1968 to Rufina and Bernabé Williams Figueroa, Sr. in San Juan, Puerto Rico. His merchant marine father and college professor mother lived in The Bronx until he was a year old, then moved back to Puerto Rico.

Williams was mesmerized by the flamenco guitar music his father brought back from Spain and was also drawn to baseball early. He attended the performance arts school Escuela Libre de Musica and also won international junior track gold medals in the sprints in 1984.

Yankee scout Roberto Rivera sent back glowing reports of Williams when he was not yet 17. The Yankees put him in a Connecticut training camp close to Yankee scouting director Doug Melvin's home. The move made it easier to sign him on his 17th birthday in 1985.

By his third year in pro baseball, he began to show his potential with Prince William (VA) in the Class-A Carolina League, hitting .335. It got him promoted to Double-A Albany (NY), where he spent most of 1989 and 1990 improving from both sides of the batters' box.

With the Triple-A Columbus (OH) Clippers in 1991 and 1992, Williams hit a combined .300 (201-for-669). On July 7, 1991, he made his debut replacing the injured Roberto Kelly. In 1992 when Danny Tartabull went down on the DL, he was recalled from Triple-A and hit .280.

The 24-year-old Williams became the regular Yankee centerfielder in 1993, hitting .268 in his first full campaign. Perceptive manager Buck Showalter understood the value of his reserved, thoughtful, bespectacled rookie before bombastic owner George Steinbrenner did.

In 1995, Williams had a breakout season with 18 home runs and paced the Yankees in runs scored, stolen bases, hits and total bases. He continued his hot hitting in the playoffs, leading New York with a .429 average in the 1995 ALDS defeat at the hands of the Mariners.

In the 1996 ALDS, he hit .467 against the Rangers, smashing a Game 1 walk-off 11th inning home run versus the Orioles. His .474 line and two bombs earned him the ALCS MVP. In World Series Game 3, he hit a clutch homer in the eighth and led the champions with four RBI.

One of the greatest teams of all time, the 1998 Yankees broke the regular season AL record with 114 wins. Hitting cleanup, Williams posted a .339 mark and became the first man to secure a batting crown, a Gold Glove, and a World Series championship ring all in a single year.

With Williams in his prime, the Yankees won three-straight Fall Classics from 1998 to 2000, the first three-peat since the 1972 to 1974 Athletics. Less than a month after the September 11, 2001 World Trade Center Attacks, the Yankees delivered three come-from-behind wins in a

G	AB	R	H	2B	3B	HR	RBI	SB	BB	SO	BA	OBP	SLG	TB
2076	7869	1366	2336	449	55	287	1257	147	1069	1212	.297	.381	.477	3756

row at home. Still, the club lost one of the most dramatic Fall Classics in history against Arizona.

Williams' last great year was 2002. He was rewarded with a *Louisville Slugger* Silver Slugger that season for his 102 runs scored, 204 hits, 102 RBI and .333 average, but the Yankees were upended by the eventual World Series Champion Anaheim Angels in the ALDS.

From 2003 on, his skills steadily eroded. Williams started only 99 games in center field in 2005, but came back to achieve several milestones during 2006. On July 26, he registered his 2,300th hit. On August 16, he hammered his 443rd double to pass Don Mattingly for the #2 spot on the Yankees all-time list. Williams played his last game in pinstripes on October 1 at age 37.

Torre wanted him to return in 2007, but general manager Brian Cashman overrode his field manager and offered him only a non-roster spring training invitation. The proud Williams declined. Pursued by other teams, he chose to remain a Yankee for life and unofficially retired.

Williams made his first return to old Yankee Stadium for the ceremonies preceding the final game at the park on September 21, 2008. He was the last Yankee alumnus to be introduced and received a prolonged standing ovation that continued for a minute and 42 seconds.

In his second career, Williams plays and composes music with jazz, classical, Latin and Brazilian influences. His second major album, *Moving Forward*, was released in 2009. Later nominated for a Latin Grammy, the album features collaborative tracks with Dave Koz, Patti Scialfa, Jon Secada and Bruce Springsteen. He also tours, playing guitar with his All-Star Band.

Bernie Williams' uniform #51 was permanently retired on May 24, 2015 during a special ceremony at Yankee Stadium. Williams and his wife Waleska Ortega have been married since 1990 and reside in Westchester County, New York with their three children.

Allen, Maury. *Baseball's 100: A Personal Ranking of the Best Players in Baseball History.* (New York: Galahad Books, 1981).

----------------. *Jim Rice: Power Hitter.* (New York: Harvey House, Publishers, 1980).

----------------. *Ron Guidry: Louisiana Lightning.* (New York: Harvey House, Publishers, 1979).

Appel, Marty. *Baseball Legends: Joe DiMaggio.* (New York: Chelsea House Publishers, 1990).

----------------. *Munson: The Life and Death of a Yankee Captain.* (New York: Random House, 2008).

Barthell, Thomas. *Pepper Martin: A Baseball Biography.* (Jefferson, North Carolina: McFarland & Company, Inc, Publishers, 2003).

Belth, Alex. *STEPPING UP: The Story of CURT FLOOD and His Fight for Baseball Players' Rights.* (New York: Persea Books, 2006).

Bjarkman, Peter C. *Baseball Legends: Ernie Banks.* (New York: Chelsea House Publishers, 1994).

Bjarkman, Peter C. *Baseball Legends: Roberto Clemente.* (New York: Chelsea House Publishers, 1991).

Blass, Steve, with Erik Sherman. *A Pirate for Life.* (Chicago: Triumph Books, 2010).

Bucek, Jeanine (Editor). *The Baseball Encyclopedia, 10th Edition.* (New York: Maxmillan, 1996).

Butler, Hal. *The Bob Allison Story.* (New York: Julian Messner, 1967).

Cahan, Richard, and Mark Jacob. *The Game That Was: The George Brace Baseball Photo Collection.* (Chicago: NTC/Contemporary Publishing Company, 1996).

Clemente Family, The. *Clemente: The True Legacy of an Undying Hero.* (New York: Penguin Book Group USA, Inc., 2013).

Cohen, Joel H. *Jim Palmer: Great Comeback Competitor.* (New York: G. P. Putnam's Sons, 1978).

Coleman, Jerry. *An American Journey: My Life on the Field, in the Air, and on the Air.* (Chicago: Triumph Books, 2008).

Cramer, Richard Ben. *Joe DiMaggio: The Hero's Life.* (New York: Simon & Schuster, Inc., 2000).

Creamer, Robert W. *Sports Illustrated Presents Mantle Remembered.* (New York: Warner Books, Inc., 1995).

Crehan, Herb. *Red Sox Heroes of Yesteryear.* (Cambridge, Massachusetts: Rounder Books, 2005).

Dean, Bill. *Baseball Legends: Bob Gibson.* (New York: Chelsea House Publishers, 1994).

Dewey, Donald, and Nicholas Acocella. *The Biographical History of Baseball.* (New York: Carroll & Graf Publishers, Inc., 1995).

Dickson, Paul. *Baseball's Greatest Quotations: An Illustrated Treasury of Baseball Quotations and Historical Lore.* (New York: HarperCollins Publishers, 2008).

Drysdale, Don, with Bob Verdi. *Once a Bum, Always a Dodger: My Life in Baseball from Brooklyn to Los Angeles.* (New York: St. Martin's Press, 1990).

Durso, Joseph. *Amazing: The Miracle of the Mets.* (Boston: Houghton Mifflin Company, 1970).

Eckhouse, Morris. *Baseball Legends: Bob Feller.* (New York: Chelsea House Publishers, 1990).

Einstein, Charles (Editor). *The Fireside Book of Baseball, 4th Edition.* (New York: Simon & Schuster, 1987).

Enders, Eric. *100 Years of the World Series: 1903-2003.* (New York: Barnes & Noble Publishing, Inc., 2004).

Eig, Jonathan. *Luckiest Man: The Life and Death of Lou Gehrig.* (New York: Simon & Schuster, Inc., 2005).

----------------. *Opening Day: The Story of Jackie Robinson's First Season.* (New York: Simon & Schuster, Inc., 2007).

Erskine, Carl, with Burton Rocks. *What I Learned from Jackie Robinson: A Teammate's Reflections On and Off the Field.* (New York: McGraw-Hill Company, Inc., 2005).

----------------. *Carl Erskine's Tales from the Dodger Dugout Extra Innings.* (New York: Sports Publishing L.L.C., 2003).

Faulkner, David. *The Last Hero: The Life of Mickey Mantle.* (New York: Simon & Schuster, Inc., 1995).

Forsch, Bob, with Tom Wheatley. *Bob Forsch's Tales from the Cardinals Dugout: A collection of the Greatest Cardinals Stories Ever Told.* (New York: Sports Publishing, L.L.C., 2003).

Frost, Mark. *Game Six: Cincinnati, Boston, and the 1975 World Series: The Triumph of America's Pastime.* (New York: Hyperion, 2009).

Gallagher, Mark, and Gallagher, Neil. *Baseball Legends: Mickey Mantle.* (New York: Chelsea House Publishers, 1991).

Gentile, Derek. *Baseball's Best 1,000: Rankings of the Skills, the Achievements and the Performance of the Greatest Players of All Time.* (New York: Black Dog & Leventhal Publishers, Inc., 2004).

Gibson, Bob, with Lonnie Wheeler. *Stranger to the Game.* (New York: Penguin Books USA Inc., 1994).

Goodwin, Doris Kearns. *Wait Till Next Year: A Memoir.* (New York: Simon & Schuster, 1997.).

Grabowski, John. *Baseball Legends: Jackie Robinson.* (New York: Chelsea House Publishers, 1991).

----------------. *Baseball Legends: Sandy Koufax.* (New York: Chelsea House Publishers, 1992).

----------------. *Baseball Legends: Stan Musial.* (New York: Chelsea House Publishers, 1993).

Guidry, Ron, and Golenbock, Peter. *Guidry.* (Englewood Cliffs, New Jersey: Prentice-Hall, Inc., 1980).

Grant, Jim "Mudcat". *The Black Aces: Baseball's Only African-American Twenty-Game Winners.* (New York: Aventine Press, the Black Aces LLC, 2007).

Halberstam, David. *October 1964.* (New York: Villard Books, 1994).

----------------. *The Summer of '49.* (New York: The Easton Press, 1996).

----------------. *The Teammates: A Portrait of a Friendship.* (New York: Hyperion, 2003).

Hrbek, Kent. *Kent Hrbek's Tales from the Minnesota Twins Dugout.* (Champaign, Illinois: Sports Publishing L.L.C., 2007).

James, Bill. *The Bill James Historical Baseball Abstract.* (New York: Villard Books, 1986).

Jeter, Derek. *The Life You Imagine: Life Lessons for Achieving Your Dreams.* (New York: Random House, Inc., 2000).

Jones, David (Editor). *Deadball Stars of the American League.* (Dulles, Virginia: Potomac Books, Inc., 2006).

Kahn, Roger. *The Boys of Summer.* (New York: HarperCollins Publishers, 1972).

Kavanagh, Jack. *Baseball Legends: Honus Wagner.* (New York: Chelsea House Publishers, 1994).

----------------. *Baseball Legends: Walter Johnson.* (New York: Chelsea House Publishers, 1992).

Leavy, Jane. *Sandy Koufax: A Lefty's Legacy.* (New York: HarperCollins Publishers, 2002).

----------------. *The Last Boy: Mickey Mantle and the End of America's Childhood.* (New York: HarperCollins Publishers, 2010).

Leventhal, Josh. *The World Series: An Illustrated Encyclopedia of the Fall Classic.* (New York: Black Dog and Leventhal Publishers, Inc., 2004).

Lieb, Frederick G. *The St. Louis Cardinals: The Story of a Great Baseball Club.* (New York: G.P. Putnam's Sons, 1947).

Linn, Ed. *Hitter: The Life and Turmoils of Ted Williams.* (Orlando, Florida: Harcourt, Brace and Company, 1993).

Long, Shepard. *Baseball Legends: Carl Yastrzemski.* (New York: Chelsea House Publishers, 1993).

Macht, Norman L. *Baseball Legends: Lou Gehrig.* (New York: Chelsea House Publishers, 1993).

Malta, Vince. *A Complete Reference Guide: Louisville Slugger Professional Player Bats.* (Concord, California: Black Diamond Publications, LLC, 2007).

Mantle, Mickey, and Phil Pepe. *My Favorite Summer 1956.* (New York: Doubleday, a division of Bantam Doubleday Dell Publishing Group. Inc., 1991).

Maraniss, David. *Clemente: The Passion and Grace of Baseball's Last Hero.* (New York: Simon & Schuster, Inc., 2006).

Markusen, Bruce. *Roberto Clemente: The Great One.* (Champaign, Illinois: Sports Publishing Inc., 1998).

Metaxas, Eric. *Seven Men and the Secret of Their Greatness.* (Nashville, Tennessee: Thomas Nelson, Inc., 2013).

McCabe, Neal, and Constantine McCabe. *Baseball's Golden Age: The Photographs of Charles M. Conlon.* (New York: Harry N. Abrams Incorporated, 2003).

McMane, Fred, and Stuart Shea. *The 3,000 Hit Club: Stories of Baseball's Greatest Hitters.* (New York: Skyhorse Publishing, 2012).

Montville, Leigh. *Ted Williams: The Biography of an American Hero.* (New York: Random House, Inc., 2004).

O'Connor, Alan. *Gold on the Diamond: Sacramento's Great Baseball Players 1886 to 1976.* (Sacramento: Big Tomato Press, 2008).

Peters, Nick. *Tales from the Giants Dugout: A Collection of the Greatest Stories Ever Told.* (New York: Sports Publishing, L.L.C., 2003)

Porter, David L. (Editor) *Biographical Dictionary of American Sports: Baseball.* (Connecticut: Greenwood Press, Inc., 1987).

Richardson, Bobby. *The Bobby Richardson Story.* (Westwood, New Jersey: Fleming H. Revell Company, 1967).

Ripken, Jr., Cal, and Mike Bryan. *The Only Way I Know.* (New York: Penguin Books USA, 1997).

Ripken, Sr., Cal, with Larry Burke. *The Ripken Way: A Manual for Baseball and Life.* (New York: Simon & Shuster, 1999).

Ritter, Lawrence S. *The Glory of Their Times: The Story Of The Early Days Of Baseball Told By The Men Who Played It.* (New York: The Macmillan Company, 1966).

Rolfe, Red. *The View from the Dugout: The Journals of Red Rolfe: An Unparalleled Look Inside the Mind of a Major League Baseball Manager.* (Ann Arbor, Michigan: The University of Michigan Press, 2006).

Ross, Allan. *White Sox Glory.* (Nashville, Tennessee: Cumberland House Publishing, Inc., 2006)

Rucker, Mark. *Detroit Aces: The First 75 Years.* (Charleston, South Carolina: Arcadia Publishing, 2005).

Salmon, Tim, with Rob Goldman. *Always an Angel: Playing the Game with Fire and Faith.* (Chicago: Triumph Books, 2010).

Schmidt, Mike, with Glen Waggoner. *Clearing the Bases: Juiced Players, Monster Salaries, Sham Records, and a Hall of Famer's Search for the Soul of Baseball.* (HarperCollins Publishers, 2006).

Schell, Michael J. *Baseball's All-Time Best Hitters: How Statistics Can Level the Playing Field.* (Princeton, New Jersey: Princeton University Press, 1999).

Schoor, Gene. *The Stan Musial Story.* (New York: Julina Messner, Inc., 1955).

Shouler, Ken. *The Real 100 Best Baseball Players of All Time ... and Why!* Lenexa, Kansas: (Addax Publishing Group, 1998).

Skipper, John C. *Charlie Gehringer: A Biography of the Hall of Fame Tigers Second Baseman.* (Jefferson, North Carolina: McFarland & Company, Inc, Publishers, 2008).

Shannon, Mike. *Baseball Legends: Johnny Bench.* (New York: Chelsea House Publishers, 1990).

------------------. *Baseball Legends: Willie Stargell.* (New York: Chelsea House Publishers, 1992).

Simon, Tom (Editor). *Deadball Stars of the National League.* (Washington, D.C.: Brassey's, Inc., 2004).

Smith, Ron. *Sporting News Selects Baseball's 100 Greatest Players. Second Edition.* (St. Louis, Missouri: Vulcan Sports Media, 2005).

Stang, Mark, and Wood, Phil. *Nationals on Parade: 70 Years of Washington Nationals Photos.* (Wilmington, Ohio: ORANGE FRAZER Press, 2005)

Stottlemyre, Mel, with John Harper. *Pride and Pinstripes: the Yankees, Mets, and Surviving Life's Challenges.* (New York: HarperCollins Publishers, 2007).

Syken, Bill (Editor). *Sports Illustrated Baseball's Greatest.* (New York: Sports Illustrated Publishing, 2014).

Tackach, James. *Baseball Legends: Roy Campanella.* (New York: Chelsea House Publishers, 1991).

Taylor, Ted. *The Ultimate Philadelphia Athletics Reference Book 1901-1954.* (Breinigsville, Pennsylvania: XLibris Corporation, 2010).

Thorn, John, and Pete Palmer, Michael Gershman, David Pietrusza, (Editors). *Total Baseball: The Official Encyclopedia of Major League Baseball.* (New York: Penguin Books USA, Inc., 1997).

Torre, Joe, and Tom Verducci. *The Yankee Years.* (New York: Random House, Inc., 2009).

Tygiel, Jules. *Baseball's Great Experiment: Jackie Robinson and His Legacy.* (Oxford; New York: Oxford University Press, 1997).

Van Blair, Rick. *Dugout to Foxhole: Interviews with Baseball Players Whose Careers Were Affected by World War II.* (Jefferson, South Carolina: McFarland & Company, Inc., Publishers, 1994).

Vecsey, George. *Stan Musial: An American Life.* (New York: Ballantine Books, 2011).

Wagenheim, Kal. *Clemente!* (Maplewood, New Jersey: Waterfront Press, 1984).

Ward, Geoffrey and Ken Burns. *Baseball — An Illustrated History.* (New York: Alfred C. Knopof: New York, 1994).

Westcott, Rich. *Baseball Legends: Mike Schmidt.* (New York: Chelsea House Publishers, 1995).

Whittingham, Richard. *The Los Angeles Dodgers: An Illustrated History.* (New York: Harper & Row, Publishers, 1982).

Williams, Peter. *When the Giants Were Giants: Bill Terry and The Golden Age of New York Baseball.* (Chapel Hill, North Carolina: Algonquin Books of Chapel Hill, 1994).

Williams, Ted. *My Turn at Bat: The Story of My Life.* (New York: Simon & Schuster, 1969).

Willis, C. Norman. *Washington Senators' All-Time Greats.* (Breinigsville, Pennsylvania: Xlibris Corporation, 2003).

Wolff, Rick. *Baseball Legends: Brooks Robinson.* (New York: Chelsea House Publishers, 1991).

--------------. *Baseball Legends: Ted Williams.* (New York: Chelsea House Publishers, 1993).

Yastrzemski, Carl, and Gerald Eskenazi. *Yaz: Baseball, the Wall, and Me.* (New York: Doubleday Dell Publishing Group, Inc., 1990).

Zack, Bill. *Baseball Legends: Chipper Jones.* (New York: Chelsea House Publishers, 2001).

www.Ancestry.com

www.Baseball-Almanac.com

www.Baseball-Reference.com

www.SABR.org/BioProject

en.Wikipedia.org/wiki

HOMETOWN HEROES by TEAM

Montreal Expos

Steve Rogers	Montreal Expos	1973-1985	13

New York Mets

Ron Hodges	New York Mets	1973-1984	12
Ed Kranepool	New York Mets	1962-1979	18

New York/San Francisco Giants

Harry Danning	New York Giants	1933-1942	10
Jim Davenport	San Francisco Giants	1958-1970	13
Scott Garrelts	San Francisco Giants	1982-1991	10
Carl Hubbell	New York Giants	1928-1943	16
Travis Jackson	New York Giants	1922-1936	15
Jo-Jo Moore	New York Giants	1930-1941	12
Mel Ott	New York Giants	1926-1947	22
Hal Schumacher	New York Giants	1931-1946	13
Bill Terry	New York Giants	1923-1936	14
Robby Thompson	San Francisco Giants	1986-1996	11
Wes Westrum	New York Giants	1947-1957	11
Hooks Wiltse	New York Giants	1904-1914	11
Ross "Pep" Youngs	New York Giants	1917-1926	10

New York Yankees

Spud Chandler	New York Yankees	1937-1947	11
Jerry Coleman	New York Yankees	1949-1957	9
Joe Collins	New York Yankees	1948-1957	10
Earle Combs	New York Yankees	1924-1935	12
Frankie Crosetti	New York Yankees	1932-1948	17
Bill Dickey	New York Yankees	1928-43 • 1946	17
Joe DiMaggio	New York Yankees	1936-42 • 1946-51	13
Whitey Ford	New York Yankees	1950 • 1953-67	16
Lou Gehrig	New York Yankees	1923-1939	17
Jake Gibbs	New York Yankees	1962-1971	10
Ron Guidry	New York Yankees	1975-1988	14
Tommy Henrich	New York Yankees	1937-1950	11
Derek Jeter	New York Yankees	1995-2014	20
Arndt Jorgens	New York Yankees	1929-1939	11
Mickey Mantle	New York Yankees	1951-1968	18
Don Mattingly	New York Yankees	1982-1995	14
Gil McDougald	New York Yankees	1951-1960	10
Thurman Munson	New York Yankees	1969-1979	11
Jorge Posada	New York Yankees	1995-2011	17
Bobby Richardson	New York Yankees	1955-1966	12
Mariano Rivera	New York Yankees	1995-2013	19
Phil Rizzuto	New York Yankees	1941-1956	13
Red Rolfe	New York Yankees	1931-1942	10
George Selkirk	New York Yankees	1934-1942	9
Mel Stottlemyre	New York Yankees	1964-1974	11
Roy White	New York Yankees	1965-1979	15
Bernie Williams	New York Yankees	1991-2006	16

Philadelphia/Kansas City/Oakland Athletics

Joe Astroth	Phila./K. C. Athletics	1945-1956	12
Dick Fowler	Philadelphia Athletics	1941-42 • 1945-52	10
Dick Green	K.C./Oakland Athletics	1963-1974	12
Mike Norris	Oakland Athletics	1975-1990	10
Eddie Rommel	Philadelphia Athletics	1920-1932	13
Pete Suder	Phila./K. C. Athletics	1941-43 • 1946-54	12

Philadelphia Phillies

Larry Christenson	Philadelphia Phillies	1973-1983	11
Terry Harmon	Philadelphia Phillies	1967 • 1969-77	10
Bob Miller	Philadelphia Phillies	1949-1958	10
Mike Schmidt	Philadelphia Phillies	1972-1989	18

Louisville Colonels • Pittsburgh Pirates

Gene Alley	Pittsburgh Pirates	1963-1973	11
Carson Bigbee	Pittsburgh Pirates	1916-1926	11
Steve Blass	Pittsburgh Pirates	1964-1974	11
Fred Clarke	Louis./Pittsburgh Pirates	1894-1915	21
Roberto Clemente	Pittsburgh Pirates	1955-1972	18
Ray Kremer	Pittsburgh Pirates	1924-1933	10
Vernon Law	Pittsburgh Pirates	1950 • 1954-67	16
Sam Leever	Louis./Pittsburgh Pirates	1898-1910	13
Bill Mazeroski	Pittsburgh Pirates	1956-1972	17
Bob Moose	Pittsburgh Pirates	1967-1976	10
Deacon Phillippe	Louis./Pittsburgh Pirates	1899-1911	13
Willie Stargell	Pittsburgh Pirates	1962-1982	21
Pie Traynor	Pittsburgh Pirates	1920-1937	17
Honus Wagner	Louis./Pittsburgh Pirates	1897-1917	21

San Diego Padres

Tim Flannery	San Diego Padres	1979-1989	11
Tony Gwynn	San Diego Padres	1982-2001	20

St. Louis Cardinals

Ray Blades	St. Louis Cardinals	1922-1932	11
Al Brazle	St. Louis Cardinals	1943-1954	10
Bob Gibson	St. Louis Cardinals	1959-1975	17
Pepper Martin	St. Louis Cardinals	1928-1944	13
Terry Moore	St. Louis Cardinals	1935-41 • 1946-49	11
Stan Musial	St. Louis Cardinals	1941-1963	23
Tom Pagnozzi	St. Louis Cardinals	1987-1998	12

Seattle Mariners

Edgar Martinez	Seattle Mariners	1987-2004	18

Washington Nationals/Senators • Minnesota Twins

Bob Allison	W. Senators/Minn. Twins	1958-1970	13
Ossie Bluege	Washington Nationals	1922-1939	18
Randy Bush	Minnesota Twins	1982-1993	11
Patsy Gharrity	Washington Nationals	1916-23 • 1929-30	10
Kent Hrbek	Minnesota Twins	1981-1994	14
Walter Johnson	Washington Nationals	1907-1927	21
Buddy Lewis	Washington Nationals	1935-41 • 1945-47 • 49	11
Clyde Milan	Washington Nationals	1907-1922	16
Tony Oliva	Minnesota Twins	1962-1976	15
Kirby Puckett	Minnesota Twins	1984-1995	12
Brad Radke	Minnesota Twins	1995-2006	12
Cecil Travis	Washington Nationals	1933-41 • 1945-47	12

HOMETOWN HEROES by POSITION

LEFT-HANDED PITCHERS
Jerry Augustine
Al Brazle
Whitey Ford
Ron Guidry
Carl Hubbell
Sandy Koufax
Scott McGregor
Mel Parnell
Nap Rucker
Paul Splittorff
Hooks Wiltse

RIGHT-HANDED PITCHERS
Steve Blass
Tommy Bridges
Spud Chandler
Larry Christenson
Hooks Dauss
Don Drysdale
Carl Erskine
Red Faber
Bob Feller
Dick Fowler
Scott Garrelts
Bob Gibson
Orval Grove
Walter Johnson
Addie Joss
Mel Harder
John Hiller
Fred Hutchinson
Ray Kremer
Vernon Law
Sam Leever
Bob Lemon
Dennis Leonard
Ted Lyons
Bob Miller
Bob Moose
Guy Morton
Mike Norris
Jim Palmer
Deacon Phillippe
Brad Radke
J.R. Richard
Mariano Rivera
Steve Rogers
Eddie Rommel
Hal Schumacher

Vic Sorrell
Mario Soto
Bob Stanley
Mel Stottlemyre
Bill Wegman
Don Wilson

CATCHERS
Joe Astroth
Johnny Bench
Bruce Benedict
Roy Campanella
Billy Carrigan
Harry Danning
Bill Dickey
Bill Freehan
Patsy Gharrity
Jake Gibbs
Ron Hodges
Chris Hoiles
Arndt Jorgens
Ron Karkovice
Otto Miller
Bob Montgomery
Thurman Munson
Tom Pagnozzi
Biff Pocoroba
Jorge Posada
Mike Scioscia
Jason Varitek
John Wathan
Wes Westrum
Larry Woodall

FIRST BASEMEN
Bob Allison
Jeff Bagwell
Joe Collins
Lou Gehrig
Kent Hrbek
Todd Helton
Ed Kranepool
Don Mattingly
Mike Squires
Bill Terry

SECOND BASEMEN
Jerry Coleman
Rich Dauer
Bobby Doerr

Tim Flannery
Jim Gantner
Charlie Gehringer
Dick Green
Bill Mazeroski
Ron Oester
Bobby Richardson
Robby Thompson
Lou Whitaker
Frank White

THIRD BASEMEN
Ossie Bluege
George Brett
Jim Davenport
Stan Hack
Chipper Jones
Buddy Lewis
Pepper Martin
Brooks Robinson
Red Rolfe
Al Rosen
Mike Schmidt
Pie Traynor

SHORTSTOPS
Gene Alley
Luke Appling
Ernie Banks
Ray Chapman
Davey Concepcion
Frankie Crosetti
Gary DiSarcina
Travis Jackson
Derek Jeter
Barry Larkin
Rico Petrocelli
Pee Wee Reese
Cal Ripken, Jr.
Phil Rizzuto
Billy Russell
Lee Tannehill
Alan Trammell
Cecil Travis
Honus Wagner
Robin Yount

UTILITYMEN
Craig Biggio
Junior Gilliam

Terry Harmon
Gil McDougald
Jackie Robinson
Sibby Sisti
Pete Suder

LEFTFIELDERS
Carson Bigbee
Ray Blades
Gates Brown
Randy Bush
Fred Clarke
Jack Graney
Mike Greenwell
Bobby Higginson
Jo-Jo Moore
Pat Mullin
Stan Musial
Jim Rice
Willie Stargell
Roy White
Ted Williams
Carl Yastrzemski

CENTERFIELDERS
Earle Combs
Dominic DiMaggio
Joe DiMaggio
Mickey Mantle
Clyde Milan
Terry Moore
Johnny Mostil
Kirby Puckett
Mickey Stanley
Bernie Williams

RIGHTFIELDERS
Roberto Clemente
Carl Furillo
Tony Gwynn
Tommy Henrich
Al Kaline
Tony Oliva
Mel Ott
Tim Salmon
George Selkirk
Ross Youngs

DESIGNATED HITTERS
Edgar Martinez

Four Single Franchise Stars dominate the 1937 American League All-Star lineup at Griffith Stadium, Washington, D.C. Left to right: Lou Gehrig, Joe Cronin, Bill Dickey, Joe DiMaggio, Charlie Gehringer, Jimmie Foxx and Hank Greenberg.

Luke Appling	Chicago White Sox 78	
Ernie Banks	Chicago Cubs 196	
Johnny Bench	Cincinnati Reds. 198	
Craig Biggio	Houston Astros 340	
George Brett	Kansas City Royals. 266	
Roy Campanella	Brooklyn Dodgers 132	
Fred Clarke	Pittsburgh Pirates 18	
Roberto Clemente	Pittsburgh Pirates 204	
Earle Combs	New York Yankees 54	
Bill Dickey	New York Yankees 86	
Joe DiMaggio	New York Yankees 88	
Bobby Doerr	Boston Red Sox 142	
Don Drysdale	Brooklyn/L.A. Dodgers 208	
Red Faber	Chicago White Sox 56	
Bob Feller	Cleveland Indians 90	
Whitey Ford	New York Yankees 146	
Lou Gehrig	New York Yankees 92	

Charlie Gehringer	Detroit Tigers 94	
Bob Gibson	St. Louis Cardinals 214	
Tony Gwynn	San Diego Padres 344	
Carl Hubbell	New York Giants 100	
Travis Jackson	New York Giants 58	
Walter Johnson	Washington Nationals 60	
Addie Joss	Cleveland Indians 26	
Al Kaline	Detroit Tigers 224	
Sandy Koufax	Brooklyn/L.A. Dodgers 226	
Barry Larkin	Cincinnati Reds. 358	
Bob Lemon	Cleveland Indians 158	
Ted Lyons	Chicago White Sox 64	
Mickey Mantle	New York Yankees 160	
Bill Mazeroski	Pittsburgh Pirates 232	
Stan Musial	St. Louis Cardinals 168	
Mel Ott	New York Giants 112	
Jim Palmer	Baltimore Orioles. 240	

Kirby Puckett	Minnesota Twins 366	
Pee Wee Reese	Brooklyn/L.A. Dodgers 172	
Jim Rice	Boston Red Sox 304	
Cal Ripken, Jr.	Baltimore Orioles 370	
Phil Rizzuto	New York Yankees 174	
Brooks Robinson	Baltimore Orioles. 246	
Jackie Robinson	Brooklyn Dodgers 176	
Mike Schmidt	Philadelphia Phillies 312	
Willie Stargell	Pittsburgh Pirates 250	
Bill Terry	New York Giants 122	
Pie Traynor	Pittsburgh Pirates 70	
Honus Wagner	Pittsburgh Pirates 42	
Ted Williams	Boston Red Sox 186	
Carl Yastrzemski	Boston Red Sox 258	
Ross "Pep" Youngs	New York Giants 74	
Robin Yount	Milwaukee Brewers 334	

PHOTOGRAPH & LOGO CREDITS

Major League Baseball trademarks and copyrights are used with permission of Major League Baseball Properties, Inc.

The *Rawlings* Gold Glove Award Trophy logo is used with the permission of the Rawlings Sporting Goods Company.

The majority of photographs appear in this book with permission and photographic credit to the National Baseball Hall of Fame.

The following photographs carry a different photographic credit or additional attribution to the photographer:

THE SINGLE FRANCHISE BASEBALL HALL OF FAME FRATERNITY
by Bill Purdom . . . . pages 188-189

Front Row: Barry Larkin, Travis Jackson, Honus Wagner, Don Drysdale, Carl Hubbell, Craig Biggio, Jim Rice, Roy Campanella, Roberto Clemente, Brooks Robinson, Ernie Banks, Johnny Bench, Mickey Mantle, Sandy Koufax, Al Kaline, Joe DiMaggio.

Middle Row: Bill Mazeroski, Bobby Doerr, Red Faber, Pie Traynor, Luke Appling, Whitey Ford, Willie Stargell, Robin Yount, Mike Schmidt, Mel Ott, Addie Joss, Kirby Puckett, Bob Feller, Derek Jeter, Jim Palmer, Tony Gwynn, George Brett.

Back Row: Charlie Gehringer, Ted Lyons, Earle Combs, Ross Youngs, Bill Dickey, Bill Terry, Fred Clarke, Phil Rizzuto, Bob Lemon, Mariano Rivera, Carl Yastrzemski, Bob Gibson, Lou Gehrig, Cal Ripken, Jr., Ted Williams, Jackie Robinson, Pee Wee Reese, Walter Johnson, Stan Musial.

ABOUT THE AUTHOR

Clay Sigg is a national pastime historian. A member of the Society for American Baseball Research (SABR) and the American Baseball Coaches Association (ABCA), he is a ballpark aficionado, having viewed games in all 30 current major league ballparks and 11 past major league stadiums. Sigg is a member of the University of California at Davis Baseball Hall of Fame. He lives in Granite Bay, California with his wife Sandra.

ACKNOWLEDGEMENTS

Many thanks to a number of people who have been a part of this 12-year project:

To authors Jay Feldman, Lucy Sanna, Clifton Blue Parker, Greg King and Dr. Larry McNiesh who have provided important information and insights. To coaches Phil Swimley, the late Elert Boe, and the late Dr. Jim Sochor for their inspiration and guidance. To my friend Matt Walbeck, a teammate of a number of the featured heroes, for his support of the project. To Kim Ross-Polito in Crestline, Ohio for her assistance with the Gates Brown feature. To Bill Francis of the National Baseball Hall of Fame Archives who has been extremely generous and accommodating in providing research information. To John Horne in the NBHOF Archives for his assistance in the photograph department. To Laurel Mathe of Mystic Design for her superlative and meticulous design work. To Kristieanne Karlson of Major League Baseball Properties for her kindness and patience. To artist Bill Purdom for his spectacular cover art. Special thanks to my brother, Dr. Eric Whitman Sigg, as an invaluable editor. And to my wife Sandi for her love, support and faith in me.